BEYOND
FORMAL OPERATIONS

BEYOND FORMAL OPERATIONS

Late Adolescent and Adult Cognitive Development

edited by

Michael L. Commons
Francis A. Richards
Cheryl Armon

PRAEGER SPECIAL STUDIES • PRAEGER SCIENTIFIC

New York • Philadelphia • Eastbourne, UK
Toronto • Hong Kong • Tokyo • Sydney

Library of Congress Cataloging in Publication Data
Beyond formal operations.
    Bibliography: p.
    Includes indexes.
    1. Cognition. I. Commons, Michael L. II. Richards,
Francis A., 1946-   . III. Armon, Cheryl.
BF311.B4964 1983   155.5   83-21142
ISBN 0-03-062559-9

Published in 1984 by Praeger Publishers
CBS Educational and Professional Publishing
a Division of CBS Inc.
521 Fifth Avenue, New York, NY 10175 USA

456789 052 987654321

Printed in the United States of America
on acid-free paper

PREFACE

This is the first book whose subject is cognitive development beyond Piaget's formal-operational period of adolescence. It is a collection of diverse research in this new area. Within this diversity, however, there are strong currents of commonality, perhaps the strongest of which is that the sequence of cognitive development extends beyond adolescence into adulthood.

There are four major reasons for a book on postformal thought. First, a growing interest in adult development has generated a body of data unsupportive of Piaget's assertion concerning formal operations that, " . . . this general form of equilibrium can be conceived of as final in the sense that it is not modified during the life span of the individual . . . " (Piaget, 1958, p. 332). Second, there are commonalities in the ways that these data are being analysed and understood. Despite diverse starting points in postformal research, many developmental theories reinterpret the Piagetian framework, often synthesizing it with other perspectives on development in order to transcend its perceived shortcomings. Presenting these theories in one volume makes more visible their strong theoretical and empirical similarities in identifying postformal thought. Third, the theoretical adequacy of a fixed developmental endpoint has been increasingly called into question. Most writing on adult development gives the impression that cognitive faculties are either at a plateau or in decline in adulthood. However, increased cognitive power in adulthood is reported in most chapters here. Finally, this volume contains a central assumption that competencies identified in higher stages are characteristic of profound and innovative thought in the arts, humanities, and sciences. Researching the nature of these higher stages may lead to a better understanding of real-world functioning of individuals.

The chapters are of different sorts: case histories that trace the development of postformal thought, inductively derived models of postformal cognition, approaches that synthesize formerly discrete traditions, and studies identifying postformal thought in specific content domains. Directly or indirectly, all the chapters derive from Piaget's work. Many chapters can be understood as natural extensions of Piagetian theory or critiques of the structuralist approach to the study of cognitive development. These extensions and critiques expand the possibilities inherent in characterizing the nature of development itself.

Early drafts of the chapters were first presented at the Symposium on Postformal Operations: Reasoning in Late Adolescence and Adulthood, held at Harvard University on March 31 and April 1 of 1981. At that time, the research on postformal thought was so new that most of it had not been circulated. As a result of the exchange at the symposium and review of the chapters, the authors revised their manuscripts. As is always the case, some deserving authors were regrettably overlooked in the invitation process.

This volume is intended for research and professional psychologists, including developmentalists and clinicians, and educators. Their interests could include cognitive science, cognitive, social, and personality development—especially from adolescence through adulthood. It can serve as a text for graduate and advanced undergraduate students in seminars on adolescent and adult cognitive development. It can also serve as a secondary text for courses on cognition, as well as adolescent, adult, human, and life-span development.

An undertaking of this kind depends on the contributions of many. We thank the authors whose research comprises this volume. In addition to contributing their work and knowledge, their prompt response to revision deadlines is acknowledged. Michael L. Commons, Suzanne Benack, and Francis A. Richards organized the symposium that initiated this volume. The symposium was supported in part by the Department of Psychology and Social Relations, Harvard University and by the Dare Association, Inc. Local arrangements were provided by Patrice M. Miller, Terrence A. Youk, David R. Marion, Martin N. Davidson, Eloise Coupey, and Joel R. Peck. We thank Fredrick Ruf, Ashok N. Nimgade, Michael Armstrong-Roche, Ilena Dunlap, Mark Tappan, and Dawn Poley for helping to review chapters. Finally, we wish to thank George P. Zimmar at Praeger Publishers with whom it has been a pleasure to work.

Cambridge, Massachusetts Michael L. Commons
December 1982 Francis A. Richards
  Cheryl Armon

CONTENTS

List of Figures and Tables

Figures

Tables

PERSPECTIVES ON THE DEVELOPMENT OF THOUGHT IN LATE ADOLESCENCE AND ADULTHOOD: AN INTRODUCTION

Francis A. Richards, Cheryl Armon, and Michael L. Commons

In this volume, authors discuss the development of thinking in late adolescence and adulthood. The title, *Beyond Formal Operations* acknowledges a common intellectual debt to Piaget's study of cognitive development. Simultaneously, it expresses some dissatisfaction with that work. Many of the chapters are efforts to expand, improve, or transcend Piaget's endeavor, particularly his model of formal operations as the pinnacle of intellectual development (1950, 1953, 1969, 1971, 1973, among others). Most of the authors share the conviction that by ending the stages of cognitive development in adolescence Piaget truncated developmental conceptions of both adulthood and cognition.

PIAGET'S MODEL OF FORMAL OPERATIONS

Piaget (Inhelder & Piaget, 1958) argued that during adolescence, thinking begins to use propositions and becomes "formal, transformationally related, and equilibrated." By "propositions," Piaget meant a particular kind of declarative statement. Propositions are instances of the possible assignment of truth values (true or false) to the combination of two declarative statements and their negations. These statements may be symbolized by p, q, and their negations by $-p$, $-q$. Any proposition involving these statements derives from assigning a truth value to the terms of the generating proposition, "p & $-p$ & q & $-q$." For example, the simple proposition p results from assigning the truth value T to p in the proposition, p & $-p$ & q & $-q$, and the truth value F to the remaining three terms, $-p$, q, $-q$ (see Inhelder & Piaget, 1958 for the rest of the table of the sixteen possible propositions). Heuristically this is the same as multiplying p by 1, where 1 stands for true; and the remainder of the terms, $-p$, q, and $-q$, by 0, where 0 stands for false. Hence:

$$p = 1(p) \ \& \ 0(-p) \ \& \ 0(q) \ \& \ 0(-q) = 1(p)$$

Note that "&" acts as "+" so that p & 0 =p in this heuristic.

By "formal" Piaget meant the competence to distinguish the logical meaning of propositions from their content. Hence, people with this competence can reason about hypothetical situations. They also can reason about matters of fact without referring to concrete situations.

By "transformationally related," Piaget meant that the 16 possible propositions can be related to one another in a way that makes logical sense. Piaget proposed four kinds of transformations that relate propositions. Propositions are related to themselves by any transformation that preserves their identity. Any proposition p is related to its negation (contradiction) −p by an inversion trans-formation relates a proposition to what is called its "converse" (see tions in adolescent thinking. A reciprocal transformation relates a proposition to what is called its "obverse" and a correlative trans-formation relates a proposition to what is called "converse" (see Barker, 1965 for a discussion of these terms). The result of these transformational relations is that every proposition can be immedi-ately related to three other propositions (four if the relation of a proposition to itself is counted). The importance of this trans-formational organization is that propositions begin to function as elements in an integrated system. Furthermore, through these immediate relations, each proposition is ultimately related to each of the 16 propositions. Piaget proposed that this integration accounts for the new level of power and flexibility in the adolescent's logic.

By "equilibrated," Piaget meant that the new logical organization of propositions forms a cognitive balance. In an equilibrium, the whole, which is the organized system of propositional transforma-tions, preserves the parts. The parts are the individual propositions. The whole preserves the parts by keeping the sense of the proposi-tions intact as they are transformed during the reasoning process. In return, the parts support the whole. Propositions allow the trans-formational organization of reasoning to remain unchanged when the content of the propositions changes. As long as phenomena can be thought about in propositions, reasoning about them can be organ-ized by the transformational system of formal operations. Piaget posited that the final stage of cognitive development, achieved in adolescence, is the organization of the representational elements of cognition and mental actions into the equilibrium of formal opera-tions.

Piaget constructed his model of adolescent thought over an extended period of time. Subsequently, that model has been sub-jected to two principle types of criticism (see Chapter 19 for others). First, it has been argued that the model lacks parsimony (cf. Brainerd,

1978) and empirical fit (cf. Bynum, Thomas, & Weitz, 1972). The general thrust of this type of criticism is that the extensive logical competency made possible by Piaget's model of formal operations cannot be detected in the performance of adolescent subjects. Consequently, a less elaborate model is sufficient to explain adolescent thought.

Secondly, it has been argued that the model of formal operations is too limited to capture the richness of adolescent and adult thought. Kinds of thinking exist that do not show the logical structure of formal operations or of lower stages. These kinds of thinking might develop parallel to formal operations and supplement them, being used in areas not amenable to the logic of propositions. They might also develop after formal operations and replace them, being used in the same areas as formal operations. In either case, the argument is that an adequate understanding of the psychological development of thought cannot be based solely on Piaget's model of formal operations.

Most of the chapters in this volume represent a second phase in the latter kind of criticism. In this phase, the bases of criticism have become the bases of revision. Authors critically evaluate Piaget's model of formal operations, paying special attention to the potential development of thought during adulthood, beyond adolescent formal operations.

The overriding conclusion of these examinations is that there is a great deal of developmental potential beyond formal operations. More sophisticated thinking can be found and described in models collectively labeled "postformal." These models aim at extending conceptions of cognitive development into adulthood.

The most common method of extension is to locate limitations in formal operations, then to describe a kind of thinking that enables the individual to transcend those limitations. Authors use examples of thinking already developed in other contexts, such as the dialectical tradition (Basseches, Chapter 10), philosophy of science (Linn & Siegel, Chapter 11), General Systems Theory and Buddhism (Koplowitz, Chapter 13), relativity theory (Sinnott, Chapter 14), or moral philosophy (Armon, Chapter 17), as models for postformal thinking. This approach predominates in Part III, which contains models that synthesize perspectives in an attempt to identify and describe postformal development. By locating examples of multisystem frameworks in adult thinking, these chapters question the null hypothesis that formal operations are sufficient to solve all problems.

Another method of extension bases statements about cognitive development on analyses of the nature of the developmental process, rather than on the limitations inherent in formal operations. Instead of concentrating on a demonstration that change does occur, this approach attempts to show *how* it occurs. Piaget (1970) had proposed a general process of "equilibrium" and a somewhat more specific process of "reflective abstraction" to account for cognitive development. Fischer, Hand, and Russell (Chapter 3), Sternberg (Chapter 4), Commons and Richards (Chapters 6 and 7), and Pascual-Leone (Chapter 9), all focus explicitly on the mechanism of intellectual development. Here, the attempt is made not only to clarify proposed mechanisms of cognitive development, but also to show that the continued operation of these mechanisms results in postformal thinking.

Either of these two general approaches leads to the general claim that adult thinking contains the formal-operational framework, but encompasses other frameworks as well. This kind of development results in multiple-system frameworks. Thinkers develop alternatives to, and perspectives on, formal operations. They are then able to use formal operations within a higher stage system of operations and transcend the limitations of formal operations.

SOME HISTORICAL ANTECEDENTS OF POSTFORMAL COGNITIVE-DEVELOPMENTAL THEORY

Interest in transforming and, in some cases, revolutionizing the Piagetian developmental framework is the source of internal consistency in this volume. Yet, there is a diversity of approach and perspective, reflecting the interests of the authors in varied disciplines, that counterbalances this consistency. These disciplines have had different objects and objectives of study and have produced different models of phenomena and development. Nevertheless, they have in common a focus on the process of change in complex phenomena.

The historical antecedents of this focus can be found in a variety of nineteenth-century European intellectual contexts. During that century, explanations based on the unchanging nature of things were eclipsed and replaced by explanations based on the concept of change (Schoenwald, 1965). This reorientation brought to the fore a related set of problems that, in contemporary formulation, are the problems of structure, function, and transformation. Set in a cognitive context, these problems are at the heart of this volume.

In order to grapple seriously with the idea that change is an essential feature of natural and social phenomena, nineteenth-century scientists and thinkers developed a mode of explanation that strove to be simultaneously historical and scientific (Coleman, 1971). This involved viewing the present state of phenomena as the result of a connected series of changes across time. This mode of explanation also involved the assumption that change in phenomena is caused by natural, lawful processes. Historical science emerged in the attempt to integrate these historical and scientific modes of explanation.

Historical science is pertinent to the work in this volume in two major ways. First, as mentioned above, its general emphasis on explanation integrates the notions of structure, function, and transformation. These notions form a general model for cognitive-developmental psychology. Second, historical science is specifically pertinent to the concept of postformal stages. Formal operations can be used to formulate and analyze logical and causal relations. The latter are particularly useful for reasoning about situations in which dependent and independent variables are postulated to exist. This has been called functional analysis. But developmental conceptions of phenomena require the representation of states of the phenomona as systems. At this level of complexity, formal operations are not sufficient (for a detailed discussion of this point, see Richards and Commons, Chapter 5, and Commons and Richards, Chapter 6). Postformal operations can formulate developmental conceptions of phenomena. Because these conceptions rest on an integration of structural, functional, and transformational modes of analysis, and because formal operations primarily focus on functional analysis, postformal thinking is likely to resemble some variant of historical science.

Both the novelty of historical science, and the necessity to integrate historical and scientific explanation, can be made more visible by contrasting it with the explanatory framework it replaced. The pre-nineteenth-century framework postulated that nature, society, and human beings were static. It held that the nature of things had been fixed in a hierarchical, unilinear scale at the time of creation.

In the realm of nature, this scale could be seen in the great chain of being (Lovejoy, 1942). This chain organized all natural entities, social groups, and parts of the human mind into unilinear hierarchies. In the realm of natural entities, the hierarchy began in inorganic substance and rose upwards through the plant and animal kingdoms to man. From man it proceeded through the spiritual hierarchy to God. In the realm of social groups, this scale organized society (Tuchman, 1978), in which four classes, or estates, were linked in ascending relations of rights and responsibilities. In the realm of the human mind, the scale organized cognitive faculties. Borrowing from Aristotle (Ross, 1977), prevailing doctrine held that humans possessed nutritive and sensitive souls in common with animals. In addition, they possessed rational, intellective souls, which set them at the apex of material beings, just below spiritual beings. A general pattern, the unilinear hierarchy, pervaded the organizational schemes of this worldview. This pattern can be called structural because it distinguished parts by their relation to one another and set the parts into an overall organization.

Because it was fixed, this all-pervasive hierarchical arrangement could be neither historical nor scientific. Phenomena could have neither antecedent nor natural causes. In this world view, there could be no transformation in structure. When change did occur in the natural order, as when volcanoes erupted, it was not regarded as natural. It was perceived as resulting from the reintervention of the creator, an effective suspension of natural law. Although the world-view contained a comprehensive structure, that structure was not transformed in response to causal, functional relations.

Laplace's (1809) "nebular hypothesis" is an early example of the emerging attempt to integrate change into explanatory schemes. His hypothesis began with the argument that the orbits of the planets could not be on the same plane and in the same direction by chance, based on a probability calculation. In order to explain this situation, Laplace hypothesized a series of historical events, based on the dynamics of a simultaneously cooling and revolving nebular cloud. He hypothesized that solar systems began as diffuse clouds of slowly rotating gas. As these nebular clouds cooled, they condensed and began to revolve more rapidly. The centripetal force of revolution would overcome the force of gravity at certain points in this process. Then the cloud would leave rings of matter along the plane of its equator. These rings would break up and form planets.

Laplace's scheme explained transformations in terms of the functional relations of natural forces but it was not a structural explanation. Structure did not play an essential role in the trans-formational process; it merely emerged as a result of those processes. The internal structure of the nebular cloud was nebulous, any cloud would do as well as any other.

In other developing areas of inquiry, such as paleontology and history, the idea of the inner structure of phenomena was taken more seriously. In part, this was because structures such as those studied by anatomy were more obviously properties of the phenomena under study. When sequences of development began to be discovered in these phenomena, the assumption that the structures themselves affected these transformations was more readily made. However, this assumption made the process of scientific explanation more com-plex.

Given that structure is important in transformational processes, then two types of causal logic may apply to it. First, structure and its transformations may be caused by external forces. Second, the interior structural components may themselves be active agents in transformational processes. For this reason, the problem of estab-lishing natural causation in these areas was twofold. One aspect entailed establishing a logic for observable sequences of structures.

The other was to formulate causal laws that could account for the structures.

An explanation of structure as externally caused appeared in Lyell's (1830–33) geology. Lyell sought to account for disturbances in the sequences of mineral strata observable on the earth's surface. To do so, he hypothesized a molten, pressurized earth-core. This core continually pushed against the crust and occasionally broke through it, erupting and piling up strata. Strata structures would then be further transformed by erosion. Although geological structures were explained, they were assigned epiphenomenal status. In fact, as long as the contrary forces of eruption and erosion remained in balance, there was no reason why geological structures could not repeat themselves in the future. A previous structure played no essential role in the formation of a structure; structures themselves had no active function.

In biology, theories appeared that attempted to give a more active role to structures and their functions in transformational processes. When the fossil record first began to be uncovered, its most salient lesson was that some organisms once existed that no longer did. The coming to be and passing away of entire species made evident the fact of organismic change in the natural order.

One attempt to explain this fact appeared in Lamarck's (1873) zoological philosophy. Lamarck explained that the great chain of being was a temporal plan, an ideal temporal scale in which the uninterrupted ascent of life evidenced the creator's plan for his creation. Uninterrupted ascent meant that each lower organism changed into the next higher organism. Here, the structure of an organism was important because the elements of structure were modified in evolution. Each instance of biological structure in a sequence was at least the necessary predecessor of the next evolutionary step. In addition, structure was analytically necessary for providing the criteria of evolution. Each successive structure could be shown to be an elaboration and improvement upon its ancestor.

Lamarck left the causal logic of these transformations unsatisfactorily explained. In his theory, organisms changed to fulfill a preordained, divine plan. By temporally unfolding, the great chain of being would come into existence. What organisms did, how they functioned, was unrelated to the direction of their transformation.

However, there was evidence in the fossil record of disturbing departures from the uninterrupted ascent of organisms. Some organisms became extinct while others, not obviously higher forms than their ancestors, did not. Departures of this nature contradicted the notion that a divine plan is constantly guiding the evolutionary process. Lamarck explained these as the result of changes in environmental conditions, placing the locus of change outside the structure, as Lyell had done. The function of organisms was to respond to environmental change.

The result was a hybrid theory in which external and internal causality existed unrelated to each other. Organisms were changing, but in both planned and random ways. The two kinds of change were in fundamental conflict. Chance change interfered with progressive change; progressive change overrode temporal change.

This conflict was resolved in Darwin's (1855) account of evolution (see Gruber, Chapter 1, for a discussion of the development of Darwin's theory). Darwin asserted that change by chance, which he called variation, played an essential role in evolution. Evolution, however, was a progressive process. In it, life "radiated" to fill every possible niche, under the constant pressure of expanding populations. As life forms varied to fill these niches, they became more numerous and complex. The principle behind evolution, Darwin stated, is that "the greatest amount of life can be supported by great diversification of structure." This principle can also be seen as the goal of the evolutionary process.

In Darwin's theory, structure is vitally important. It is not the reflection of an external plan, nor is it solely the result of responses to the environment—life is the activity of organic structure. The physiological and behavioral structures of organisms are active and interactive. They can produce some specific actions but are incapable of producing others. In a given organism, these structures function in ways that preserve the organism. Through generations, these structures actively diversify. They function in ways that change themselves with the general consequence of bringing into being "the greatest amount of life."

Thus, structures perform two different functions: they preserve and change, both equally necessary. In contrast to Lamarck's external teleology, Darwin posited an interaction between biological and environmental structure. The internal physiological structure of organisms shapes and constrains the organization of their behavior. For example, vision is coordinated with muscular movements in hunting strategies. Environmental structure determines which hunting strategies are successful. The interaction between internal and environmental structures determines the survival, extinction, or transformation of species. Both these types of causality are compatible with Darwin's notion of structure because what structure does is to maintain and change itself.

Darwin had a marked impact on other prominent thinkers such as Marx (Marx & Engels, 1942), Freud (Sulloway, 1979), Baldwin (1895), and Hall (1904). By coordinating the opposing forces of internal structure and external environment, Darwin eliminated the need to appeal to supernatural forces in scientific explanation. He created the first powerful model of a natural, self-contained system that changed progressively. This dynamic, historical model served as a general model for a subsequent intellectual era that includes Piaget.

These nineteenth-century theories gave scientific explanation a new and distinctly modern cast. What were the goals that motivated the development of historical science? On one level, theorists were striving for more adequately empirical knowledge. They strove to spell out in formal terms the causal relations that were discovered by the careful variation and strict control dictated by the experimental method. The functional relation between independent and dependent variables, found with the experimental method, could predict and be used to control dependent variables. Laplace and Lyell showed how functionally relating causal forces to outcomes can result in scientific theories that are predictive. By reviewing the past, the nature of causal relations could be described and these would predict the future.

The predictive purpose does not necessarily entail a structural explanation, as is shown by Laplace's work. Predictive laws can be stated as correlational relations between postulated independent and observed dependent variables. Thus formulated, these predictive laws tend to be unsatisfying for the very reason that they leave the organization of elements of the phenomena they describe unexplained.

By contrast, nineteenth-century theorists whose purpose was to find the progressive nature of development tended to characterize major developmental movements in terms of the nature and sequence of their stages. They described stages structurally, emphasizing the relations between, and overall organization of, their parts. In sequences, anterior stages brought into being, or caused, posterior stages. In Darwin's theory, one species caused another because the former's rate of reproduction eliminated its own food supply.

However, causing a posterior stage is not equivalent to predicting the nature of that stage. Nineteenth-century progressive theorists could describe functional dynamics that necessitated the transformation of structure. The specific form that this transformation took, however, was indeterminate.

This is because these theorists began to use the idea of inner structure to represent the "true" nature of observable phenomena. Observable phenomena were thought of as possible states that the internal structure could assume. Since there was a plurality of possible states that were randomly produced, future states could not be deterministically predicted. Precisely because the progressive theorists represent reality as active structures, their models go beyond the bounds of simple determinate prediction.

Finally, historical science attempted to interpret the nature of human existence, particularly the nature of what was referred to as the mind. Here, the purpose of historical science is self-interpretation. In the nineteenth century, there was a shift from thinking about mind as an autonomous subject, free will, to a rule-governed producer of thought and mental activity. Towards the end of the nineteenth century, the psycho-physiological tradition (e.g., Fechner, 1966,

Helmholtz, 1882–95, Wundt, 1874, and others) had placed the notion of mind in a physical context. In their approach, mind became physical brain activity that followed natural law. Darwin (1877, 1897) had placed mind in the context of evolutionary biology, and Marx (1967) had placed it within the context of social structure. In these different efforts at self-interpretation, the old distinction between whether structures are internally or externally caused reappears.

Durkheim's theory (1972) provides an analogy to Lyell's; he viewed individual acts as regulated by the norms and values of society. In such a view, the internal structure of the human mind becomes less important than the causal relation between the institutions of society and the individual.

Levi-Strauss' theory of the mind provides a rough analogy to Darwin's insofar as he took seriously the idea that thinking is regulated by an inner structure. Levi-Strauss (1963a, 1963b) advanced the idea that the regulating institutions of society, notably kinship systems, displayed a structure that could also be found in most societal products such as myths and totemic systems. Levi-Strauss (1967) concluded that the commonality of these structures, both within and across societies, was evidence that they had a common source in structures of thought. Mind became an internal set of rules for relating experience. The idea that a set of related rules governs the possible ways in which meaning can be generated has obvious similarities to Piaget's concept of formal operations. The major difference is that Piaget integrated the idea of evolution with the idea that there is structure to thought.

PIAGET AND POSTFORMAL THEORY

Piaget neither began nor ended with the idea that it is the organization of thought, that is, the structure of the mind, that produces the structures of society. A preoccupation with evolutionary concepts led to an early struggle with the general issue of the relation between parts and wholes. As Piaget (1952) saw the situation:

> in all fields of life (organic, mental, social) there exist 'totalities' qualitatively distinct from their parts and imposing on them an organization (p. 242).

The general problem of parts and wholes lies in their possible actions on one another. These are:

> the action of the whole on itself (preservation), the action of all the parts on themselves (alteration or preservation), the actions of the parts on the whole (alteration or preservation) (p. 242).

The relations between parts and wholes allow for three kinds of equilibrium: a first in which the whole imposes order on the parts, possibly altering them to maintain equilibrium; a second in which the parts play the same role with respect to the whole; and a third in which the parts and the whole are engaged in reciprocal preservation.

Piaget regarded this final type of equilibrium as more stable than the other two. He saw clearly that this form of equilibrium was to be found in "states of conscience of a normative nature: logical necessity or moral obligation."

As stated earlier, historical science influences the work in this volume in that its features provide portions of a general model for cognitive-developmental psychology. Historical science strongly influenced Piaget. In his work, development is conceptualized as proceeding in an unbroken sequence from earlier to later organizations of thought, that is, the cognitive structures. Just as the physiological structure of organisms coordinates their physiological activities, cognitive structures coordinate cognitive activities so that they relate to one another, forming a whole. As a whole, a cognitive structure functions to make the world coherent and comprehensible, just as physiological structure makes it possible for the organism to adapt to its environment. Moreover, a present organization of thought provides the basis on which a new organization of thought develops. Finally, the transformations of cognitive organization can be represented as a sequence of stages. These features of cognitive developmental theory are similar to features of historical science.

Recall that historical science influences postformal theory because it offers a general model for postformal stages. Piaget's construal of formal operations makes them logical, mathematical, and scientific, but not historical. They are eminently useful for determining causal relations and generating predictive knowledge, but they do not place these in historical context. The operations, without some mechanism for making them apply to entities more complex than propositions, do not seem to be capable of creating notions of structure and structural transformation. Without these notions of structure, formal operations are unlikely to formulate developmental interpretations of phenomena. Because the interpretations that seem to work (see descriptions thoughout this volume) rest on the integration of the ideas of structure, function, and transformation, and because formal operations can deal with only functions, postformal thinking is likely to resemble some variant of historical science.

This thesis occurs in many different forms in the chapters that follow. Gruber (Chapter 1) and Vidal (Chapter 2) concentrate on tracing the development of thinking and theories as they occur in specific instances. These authors are less concerned with finding a general pattern, or transformational law, that might account for this pattern, than they are with detailing the events that such a law would have to explain. They conceptualize change as a phenomenon involving a complex web of interrelationships between the individual and the intellectual, social, and natural environment. This web is so rich and complex that it cannot be systematically captured in any limited set of generalizations. Since an individual is particularized in historical, social, and intellectual contexts, the idea of a general structure in postformal thinking is deemphasized in these chapters.

Basseches (Chapter 10) attempts to balance the idea of historical particularity with the idea of general structures in postformal cognitive development. He begins with the assumption that change is the basic feature of cognitive, social, and natural phenomena. In order to comprehend change, postformal thinkers use the idea of "form" rather than the idea of "thing." Forms are structures whose fundamental function is to change. Things are structures whose fundamental function is to maintain their stability or identity. In Basseches' formulation, structure is modelled as the momentary, epiphenomenal manifestation of change. As such, structure can never be temporally crystallized, but it can still be used to interpret society, nature, and the self as organization in constant transformation.

Arlin's concept of postformal operations (Chapter 12) is based on the hypothesis that a radical change occurs in the way formal operations are used. While accepting the idea of formal-operational structure, she posits that the whole function of that structure changes. Her argument is that a replacement process takes place whereby problem-solving operations disappear, and problem-finding operations appear.

Other chapters maintain that postformal cognition attempts to accomplish the same functions as formal cognition, but that the complexity of the patterns of thought, and the complexity posited in the objects of thought, is at a new level. One approach, found in Sternberg (Chapter 4) and Fischer, Hand, and Russell (Chapter 3), to describing this new level of complexity is to use the analogy of "unfolding dimensionality."

Unfolding dimensionality uses dimensions in space to convey the idea of the new size and complexity of postformal cognition. Although size may be thought of as quantitative, dimensional increase in size has complexities that must be thought of as qualitative. Importantly, different arithmetics, geometries, and algebras are variously possible and impossible in different dimensions. As an instance, adding a dimension to two-dimensional space makes it possible for the angles of a triangle to sum to more than 180 degrees and for parallel lines to intersect. Intuitively, the complexity of geometric systems increases as the size of the space containing them increases.

Another approach, found in Richards and Commons (Chapter 5), Commons and Richards (Chapters 6 and 7), Labouvie-vief (Chapter 8), Sinnott (Chapter 14), Koplowitz (Chapter 13), and Powell (Chapter 15), uses sets of axioms, or other system properties, to describe the increased complexity of postformal reasoning. Labouvie-vief, for instance, uses the properties of different systems of logics. She describes the limitations of different logics and asserts that these limitations are due to their "strength." A "strong" logical system is one that has several limiting assumptions. When a logic contains many restricting assumptions, it seems clear but causes confusion when applied in areas that do not conform to those assumptions. Postformal reasoning arrives at an understanding of the inflexibility involved in thinking overlogically. It locates the limitations of excessive assumptions and formulates a more flexible, "weaker" logic containing fewer assumptions. Although this logic is weaker than the logics it replaces, it contains these logics because, with further restrictions, it can bring about their use in appropriate situations. By releasing formal thinking from overly restrictive strong logics, a weaker logic allows the development of new kinds of thinking.

Sinnott (Chapter 14) uses the concept of relativity (Einstein, 1954) in a similar way. As weaker logics contain and coordinate stronger logics, so relativistic frameworks contain and coordinate more particular frameworks. Each framework can be thought of as a system of relations among elements. A relativistic framework would then be a more general system for relating systems. A system need not be physical. It could be a system of relations that coordinates people. While a person who thinks in a formal-operational manner could reason within these systems, postformal reasoning deals with the problem of integrating local systems into a framework that deals successfully with the relativity of the systems. Benack (Chapter 16) uses Perry's (1970) stages to test a similar argument and finds that postformal reasoning may be a necessary condition for the empathetic skills required of a clinical practitioner.

A variant of this argument appears in Koplowitz's description of unitary operations (Chapter 13). He argues that, as thinking becomes more developed, the perceived boundaries between people become less useful. A child, for example, cannot be understood outside of its family. In a real sense, a child is part of a larger whole that cannot be disassociated. Unitary operations are used to comprehend wholes that have internal parts. Consequently, they attempt to organize and bring into relation those parts.

Richards and Commons (Chapter 5) likewise describe the new complexity of postformal thinking in terms of systems but attempt to describe systems formally. Their argument for the qualitative nature of change is consequently less tied to the particular nature of either logic or physics. This argument is based on the notion that higher-stage thinking is irreducible to lower-stage thinking. This means that, in the process of stage transformation, new objects of thought appear that cannot be successfully thought about at a lower stage. Considerable attention is devoted to defining irreducibility in Commons and Richards (Chapter 6).

A different perspective on this argument appears in Powell's description of category operations (Chapter 17). Category operations have been developed in mathematics, partly in response to the Bourbaki (1939) program. One of the concerns of the Bourbaki program has been to put the various areas of mathematics into relation. Their approach has been to locate mathematical "mother structures" that can be transformed and combined to produce the various mathematical disciplines (discussed in Piaget, 1970b). Category operations were invented to reach the same goal, but do so by examining the nature of mathematical operations rather than mathematical structures. Since category operations characterize the nature of mathematical activity, they model postformal thinking as an understanding of the ways cognitive activity can be related.

The relation of biological and cognitive development influences the concept of postformal development. Piaget (1971a) acknowledged the biological factor in cognitive development, although he argued that it is not the critical factor. Nevertheless, there is a strong parallel between his sequence of cognitive development and the sequences of biological maturation. In biological maturation, adolescence is the last great period of growth. In parallel, great intellectual disequilibrium also occurs during adolescence. Piaget argued that the subsequent equilibration, formal operations, persists throughout the remainder of the lifespan. Pascual-Leone (Chapter 9) creates an interesting twist to this argument, claiming that postadolescent cognitive development results from the degeneration of this equilibrium. Fisher, Hand, and Russell (Chapter 3) straightforwardly argue that there are physiological limitations to cognitive growth.

Biologically defined stages have recourse to physical evidence in a way cognitively defined stages do not. Consequently, cognitively defined stages present methodological problems when they are defined. Baldwin (1902) was the first to face the problem of defining cognitive stages.

Baldwin specified that stages should be defined by "reconstruction." By reconstruction, he meant that stage theorists should capture all the essential characteristics of thinking at a stage rather than list the various cognitive novelties that appeared. Baldwin specified that a stage should be "a new mode of presence in what is called reality." He also specified that, to be "truly genetic," development through the stage sequence should be irreversible, but neither predetermined nor teleological. Thus the difference between one stage and another rested on abstract description and formal representation.

The problem of specifying what is meant by a stage, and by a stage sequence, remains a critical issue in cognitive-developmental theory. Elsewhere, Piaget (1963, 1972) and Kohlberg (1969, 1981) have devoted it considerable attention. In this volume, such specifications are of central importance in the chapters by Kohlberg and Armon (Chapter 18), and Commons and Richards (Chapters 6 and 7). Kohlberg and Armon's concern is to distinguish "functional," "soft," and "hard" stages. Functional stages refer to the Eriksonian model in which each stage develops in order to perform a new task or function. Soft stages refer to development that is conditioned by particular experiences. These experiences could arise from differences in personality characteristics, education, class, age, and so on. Hard stages refer to development that occurs in a universal sequence, arising out of the overall reorganization of an underlying intellectual framework. They argue that the idea of a hard stage of adult development may be neither theoretically useful nor empirically justifiable. Their argument can be seen as reiterated insistence that a postformal stage be demonstrably "a new mode of presence in what is called reality."

Commons and Richards' (Chapters 6 and 7) concerns lie more with the general specification of any empirical task that could possibly be used to demonstrate either the presence of, or the development into, a postformal stage. They de-emphasize the reconstruction of the "reality" of a person "at a stage," and attempt to develop a general way to specify the structure of tasks in any domain that a person "at a stage" can do. Other attempts to specify what it means to be at a postformal stage can be found throughout the volume.

Reviewing his career, Piaget (1952) remarked:

> My one idea . . . has been that intellectual operations proceed in terms of structures-of-the-whole. These structures denote the kinds of equilibrium toward which evolution in its entirety is striving; at once organic, psychological and social (p. 256).

In part, every chapter in this volume is a response to this one idea. They are attempts to grow out of the form Piaget gave to a wide variety of nineteenth-century thought. The question remains whether the growth of postformal theories is itself proceeding in terms of some sort of structure-of-the-whole. Broughton (Chapter 19) argues that this is not the case and suggests abandonment rather than revision. Another approach to this question is to assume that postformal research does not talk about many different stages, but about many different manifestations of the same stage.

At the rear of the book, a chart presents how the stage sequences discussed here can be aligned across a common developmental "space." The harmony in the alignment shown in the chart suggests a possible reconciliation of Kohlberg and Armon's "hard" and "soft" stage distinction. While each of these stages may be soft stages individually, taken as a whole, they indicate the development of some hard stages.

The true extent and nature of these postformal stages cannot be determined from the chart. Their extent may range beyond the developmental areas so far described. Their nature will only emerge with a clearer understanding of the similarities and differences of the various stage conceptions (cf. Broughton, Chapter 19). Part of what this suggests for the future is that the constructs and language of these various theories of postformal development must be clarified. Similarly, theories of how stages arise must be formalized. For this to happen, the nature of elements and operations must be communicated across the various developmental sequences that appear in the chart.

In order to decide which formulations will ultimately be useful for understanding postformal cognitive development, more ways of assessing development at the proposed stages must be generated and tested. The adequacy of these theories depends on at least two major criteria: accountability and predictability. The extent to which each theory accounts for developmental phenomena in many areas must be examined. In other words, how does each formulation, along with other information, account for adolescent and adult development? Similarities and differences in the predictions made by each theory have to be clarified. Which of these predictions are supported by empirical evidence and which are not? At this point, there have been preliminary efforts in these directions, as the chapters attest. Yet, they are by no means complete. With 13 developmental sequences, there are 72 different possible pairwise comparisons between these theories. The task is huge, but it is an activity that should result in the differentiation and integration that characterizes all developmental movement.

Juan Pascual-Leone   Herb Koplowitz   Gisela Labouvie-vief   Kurt W. Fischer   Michael A. Basseches   Sheryl L. Russell
Philip M. Powell   Patricia K. Arlin   Charles Alexander   Steven Pulos   Helen H. Hand   Howard E. Gruber
Michael L. Commons   David Moshman   Suzanne Benack   Jan D. Sinnott   Marcia C. Linn   Francis A. Richards

PART I

CASE STUDIES OF THE DEVELOPMENT OF POSTFORMAL THINKING

1

THE EMERGENCE OF
A SENSE OF PURPOSE:
A COGNITIVE CASE STUDY OF
YOUNG DARWIN
Howard E. Gruber

It should be said at the outset that by discussing how one may go beyond formal operations we are also striving together to go beyond Piaget. This is our tribute to a great man. We should take some cognizance of his passing. We should also take some pride in the fact that this vigorous group of writers has sprung up not only in criticism of, but also in continuation of, the work that Piaget began.

This chapter will be somewhat different from most of the others in that it will center around a case study of a single person, Charles Darwin. That focus may require some justification. The authors of this volume are embarking in a new adventure in understanding the growth of mind. Some view of the thinking person as a system, as a whole, is needed. Another way of putting the matter is to say that the more advanced and precise the stage of scientific work, the more a grounding in the natural history of the subject of inquiry is required.

A detailed case study provides one of the best ways of obtaining such a view. For some years I have devoted much of my efforts to developing an approach to cognitive case studies of creative work. The purpose of this book provides an opportunity to link those efforts with more general studies of cognitive development and to clarify, maybe even to answer, some questions about adolescence and early adulthood. But first a few caveats.

FIRST CAVEAT: ON THE NECESSITY AND SUFFICIENCY OF FORMAL OPERATIONS

It is not at all clear that everyone attains the stage of formal operations (Gruber & Voneche, 1976). Even among those who do

This paper was completed during a stay at the Institute for Advanced Study, Princeton University. I thank Magali Bovet, Nancy Ferrara, Kurt W. Fischer, and Fernando Vidal for their help.

complete this magnificient human accomplishment, it is certainly clear that not everyone goes on to harness these skills (as I prefer to think of them) to a point of view and a set of tasks that will permit the conduct of creative work and the organization of a creative life.

If it is supposed that somewhere between 25 and 100 percent of adolescents do attain formal operations, it is immediately clear that this attainment is not *sufficient* to guarantee the emergence of a creative life. On the other hand, there is not enough known as to whether formal operations are *necessary* for creative work. At a different operational level, there is at least some evidence to suggest that progress toward concrete operational thought is associated with a *reduction* in artistic, creative expression (Gardner, 1980).

SECOND CAVEAT: ON THE RELATION BETWEEN NOVELTY AND NEW OPERATIONS

It may very well be the case, one as yet largely unexamined, that not everything valuable in the human intellectual economy is an operation. And, certainly, not everything new that happens need result from the emergence of a new operation. Clarifying the concept of intellectual operation is a task that confronts everyone in this volume. An operation must be something like a tool that can be applied to many things. In addition to this breadth of application, a tool remains distinct from the matter to which it is applied and which it transforms. This opens up the possibility that the iteration of this process of application of tools to contents or domains may be what produces novelty. So in studying creative work, one need not assume that if something dramatically new appears, it must mean that a new *operation* has emerged.

THIRD CAVEAT: ON COGNITIVE UNIVERSALS AND UNIQUE ACHIEVEMENTS

Most work on intellectual development has focused exclusively on cognitive universals, that is, species-wide cognitive characteristics. Piaget set the tone by reinventing Baldwin's term *genetic epistemology* and making it his emblem. This was probably a good strategy for making a first sketch of important features of development in infancy and childhood. But we have as yet no strong reason to believe either that development stops in adulthood or that it continues to follow even an approximate standard course. And, certainly, when turning to the study of creative work, the domain of cognitive universals that Piaget and others have centered upon has been left. In a creative person like Darwin certain potentialities are maximized. It may well be that the most interesting properties of the system under study are not merely not universal, but unique. The important book by David Feldman, *Beyond Universals*, discusses this issue in extenso (1980).

Since science aspires to generality and universality, any proposal for a scientific study of unique configurations or systems seems to be almost a contradiction in terms. But not necessarily. In some branches of science, the study of unique configurations is recognized as a central task. A biologist describing a new species is not only interested in showing how it is just like some other species, but also in precisely how its morphology, physiology, and functioning distinguish it from others. These give it its special character. Organic chemists devote much of their energy to deciphering the *unique* character of various complex molecules. What is *general* is the style of analysis. What is *universal* is the conformity to a small number of laws forming a coherent group. Without lively movement between interest in the unique and in the universal, these fields would be much the poorer. The same applies to our work in intellectual development. Those accustomed to measuring, manipulating, and correlating variables across a number of subjects are usually quite happy to agree that the case-study approach provides a sort of natural history setting and prologue for more rigorous research. This makes sense, and it is further argued, with Kurt Lewin (1935) and others, that the demands of the individual case study also provide the acid testing ground for rigorous theory.

This point may become particularly important in connection with the topic of this book. As the developmental tasks of childhood are completed, especially in modern society, the person must search for and construct his or her special place in the scheme of things. If there is no way of dealing with this maturing and heightening of individuality, researchers may be incapable of understanding fundamental development phenomena.

All such issues connected with individuality arise with redoubled force when one considers the life and thought of a person who, often quite unknowingly, organizes his or her energies around the complex ensemble of tasks entailed in creating something new.

THE EVOLVING SYSTEMS APPROACH

I turn now to a sketch of the work my students and I have come to call the evolving systems approach to cognitive case studies of creative work.[1] Each general idea presented will be illustrated with material from the life of young Charles Darwin, mainly between the ages of 20 and 30.[2] Since case studies do not fit nicely into 30-page chapters, the material will have to be compressed severely in order to cover the ground.

It is useful to conceive of the person as being comprised of three organizational subsystems: (1) an organization of knowledge; (2) an organization of purpose; and (3) an organization of affect. All of these interact with and overlap each other. Nonetheless, they each maintain a certain degree of independence, including their partially independent evolution within the thinking person.

Organization of Knowledge

The more it is studied, the more it is realized how complex and densely packed is this first subsystem. It is quite helpful to consider creative scientists as maintaining belief systems that orient them in their work and into which they assimilate new experiences. The belief system is not constructed *de novo* by each creative person, but he or she must reconstruct it in order to assimilate it. In so doing, changes are introduced into the cultural heritage thus being transmitted, and these changes constitute openings for further change. At the same time, experiences arise from the person's intercourse with the world. But this world is not an environment standing outside the person, static and alien, waiting only to impose itself. It is a world chosen by the purposeful play of attention. It is also a world constructed in a personal way by the interpretations the individual incessantly makes of it.

Viewed in this way, it almost seems a wonder that, once it gets started, cognitive change does not become a runaway process. There must be robust control mechanisms that keep it within limits, making it possible for the person to remain in contact with contemporaries, and to develop effective innovations that can be successfully communicated to others. Such controls may in fact be quite similar to those exercised by individuals with *no* desire to innovate, those who devote their efforts to keeping things as they are. A small difference in organization and emphasis can accumulate to large consequences.

As discussed elsewhere (Gruber, 1981), the creative person must develop and bring to bear on his or her emerging subject a novel point of view. There is no need to think of the individual as solving problems in a mysterious way called "genius." Given a novel point of view, and operating within it, the consequences seem natural. Indeed, they might be the same for a number of other thinkers if only they could share that perspective. But the development of a new point of view takes place in a series of phases. It may be quite a protracted process, involving problem solving (among other activities) as one of the tools used to help develop the point of view. So, it may be said that, rather than thinking in order to solve problems, the person striving to develop a new point of view solves problems in order to explore different aspects of it and of those problems and of the domaine to which those problems apply.

Darwin constructed such a new point of view. Soon after he set out on the voyage, he found himself confronted with the contradiction between the Catastrophist and biblically oriented geology he had studied at Cambridge University on the one hand, and the Uniformitarian geology of Charles Lyell, whose new *Principles of Geology* (1830–33) he received as a gift upon embarkation on the other. His thinking through this contradiction took place in an unprecedented and everchanging setting, the circumnavigation of the globe in a five-year voyage by a trained field naturalist.

There was another contradiction to be confronted, one that concerned organic evolution itself. None of Darwin's teachers at Cambridge were evolutionists, and insofar as they discussed the question, they opposed it. Lyell, who, through his *Principles* became Darwin's mentor, wrote a vitriolic and scornful critique of evolutionary theory as exemplified by Lamarck. In contrast, Darwin's grandfather, Dr. Erasmus Darwin, had been a famous eighteenth-century evolutionist. In his adolescence, Charles had read *Zoonomia,* the evolutionary essay, and was apparently quite favorably impressed by it. This is reflected in his account of his later disappointment on rereading it. Moreover, one of Darwin's teachers at Edinburgh University, which Darwin attended before Cambridge, was an enthusiastic Lamarckian. This was Professor Robert Grant who was very important to Darwin. They took walks together and young Darwin's field research provided the material for a paper that Grant published (Barrett, 1977).

But evolution was distinctly not the order of the day for Darwin during the five-year *Beagle* voyage around the world. His empirical work included field work in geology and much collecting, describing, and preliminary classification in botany and especially in zoology. His theoretical work, following increasingly Lyellian lines, was restricted to geology. In the thousands of pages of scientific notebooks that he kept during the voyage, there are few if any hints of evolutionary thought (Gruber & Gruber, 1962). In the Galapagos archipelago and elsewhere, he failed to exploit certain biogeographical opportunities that would have excited his attention had he been concerned with evolutionary questions. Thus, as late as October 1835, when he visited those islands, the collections he made were woefully incomplete. These had to be supplemented years later when their significance was understood (Sulloway, 1982).

Nevertheless, Darwin's knowledge of his grandfather's work, of Grant's, and even of Lamarck's, as presented and trampled on by Lyell, may have left him with an *arrière pensée* or a directive tendency. This tendency may have helped him to move as rapidly as he did toward evolutionary thinking. This took place on the last leg of the voyage and soon after his return to England.

At every point in the story, then, Darwin is seen constructing and reconstructing his belief system and controlling the play of attention in ways determined by it. The growth and changes in his belief system during this period can be presented in a series of diagrams.[3] Figure 1.1 shows six phases. The first three represent the development of Darwin's point of view up to the point where he began to think seriously about the possibility of a scientifically defensible theory of evolution. In these diagrams, an arrow represents a "causal" relationship such as the Creator making organisms. A line represents a noncausal relationship, such as adaptation. One might complicate the diagram with causal arrows emanating from the Creator, showing Him or Her as providing such noncausal relationships (for example, from C to the line OP in Figure 1.1A), to show that the belief system includes the idea that the Creator designed such adaptations.

At some point early in the voyage, Darwin believed that the Creator had created the organisms of the earth and their physical environment, the earth itself. Following this, he converted himself, over a period of some two or three years, to Lyell's Uniformitarian geology. He came to believe that the physical universe evolves according to natural laws, operating uniformly throughout time, today exactly as they had done untold millions of years before. These first two phases are shown in Figure 1.1A and 1.1B.

But Figure 1.1B contains an obvious asymmetry: the physical world to which the ensemble of organisms, O was so beautifully adapted, has changed, but the organisms have not: species are fixed and immutable. Figure 1.1B can also be taken as representing a phase in Lyell's thinking: a dilemma that emerged from the rapid increase in fossil evidences of extinction, in biogeological evidences of repeated changes in habitat, and in geological evidences of a physical world perpetually changing over long periods of time during the first three decades of the nineteenth century. Taken together, these new ideas undermined the belief in perfect adaptation of immutable organisms to an unchanging world ordained for them.

Lyell responded to this theoretical situation in three main moves. First, he allowed a limited amount of adaptive change in organisms in response to changes in their physical milieu—but only within strict limits that did not violate species boundaries. Second, he stressed the accumulation, over untold centuries, of extinctions of organisms no longer suited to their world. Third, to fill the void thus created, he adopted the hypothesis of multiple creations; from time to time, by an unspecified process (but one violating the principle of uniformitarian change), the Creator replenished the natural order by making new, well-adapted species. For a time, probably in late 1835 and early 1836, Darwin entertained this hypothesis of mutiple creations, which is represented in of Figure 1.1D.

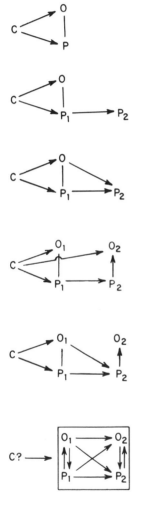

A. 1832 and before: The Creator has made an organic world (O) and a physical world (P); O is perfectly adapted to P.

B. 1832–1834: The physical world undergoes continuous change, governed by natural laws as summarized in Lyell's *Principles of Geology*. In other respects, B resembles A.

C. 1835: The activities of living organisms contribute to the evolution of the physical world, as exemplified by the action of the coral organism in making coral reefs. In other respects, C resembles B.

D. Late 1835. The Creator replenishes the earth's stock of organisms with new species from time to time: the arrow CO_2 represents this hypothesis of multiple creation. Organisms also change to adapt to changing circumstances (P_2O_2), but such adaptive changes never produce new species.

E. 1836–1837: Changes in the physical world imply changes in the organic world, if adaptation is to be maintained: the direct action of the physical milieu induces the appropriate biological adaptations. In other respects, D resembles C.

F. 1838 and after: The physical and organic worlds are both continuously evolving and interacting with each other. The Creator, if one exists, may have set the natural system in being, but He does not interfere with its operation, standing *outside* the system.

Figure 1.1. Six Phases of Darwin's Changing World View

It is striking, however, that this was a delayed reaction on Darwin's part. In 1835, he was more concerned with the special idea sketched in Figure 1.1C: organisms *contribute* to the changes in their physical milieu. He worked out a brilliant and successful theory of the formation of coral reefs through the interactions of the growth characteristics of the coral organism and protracted geological changes in the level of the ocean floor. Darwin was only 24 years old, but he drew a long theoretical bow. The theory was an original synthesis of geological, geographical, and zoological knowledge. It employed thought forms about population limits and about equilibration processes that reappeared in his theory of evolution through natural selection some three years later. It should also be noted that this theory was *opposed* to Lyell's own theory of coral reef formation. Thus, although Darwin was enthusiastic in adopting various mentors, he was able to maintain sufficient freedom of thought to go his own way when necessary.

Figure 1.1D illustrates the hypothesis of multiple creation. Elsewhere (Gruber, 1981), insufficient attention was given to this transitional phase. The subsequent publication of Darwin's *Red Notebook* has made it possible to rectify this neglect.[4] In that notebook, Darwin recorded his ideas at the end of the voyage and shortly after, during the months just before beginning his more celebrated *Transmutation Notebooks*.[5] In the *Red Notebook*, the occurrence of this additional phase becomes much clearer than in other documents. It should be noted that Figure 1.1D shows a system that is symmetrical at the level of substance but not at the level of process. Under this system, new creations replenish the natural order of living things, but the physical world changes through the operation of uniform, knowable, natural laws. The organic world is replenished by some mysterious intervention quite different from ordinary reproduction.

In Figure 1.1E Darwin is going his own way. In a sense, the causal relationship, P_2- - - -O_2 is only an extension of Lyell's ideas. But as representing Darwin's thinking, P_2- - - - -O_2 means the production of new *species* by natural processes, of "breaking the species barrier," an idea that Lyell vigorously opposed. This was not a decision Darwin reached quickly. It took the postvoyage processing of the Beagle collections by a number of zoologists to produce Darwin's full "conversion" to the idea of evolution. This probably took place in late 1836 and early 1837. Only then was Darwin free to begin exploring the domain of possible evolutionary theories indicated very roughly in Figure 1.1D and E.

The empirical evidence was by no means sufficient to effect the conversion. Indeed, the team of experts on whom Darwin relied for the clearest formulation of the evidence was not all disposed to think as evolutionists. It took all the other factors mentioned previously to create in Darwin the special point of view and schematization of nature into which these new facts were assimilated.

The development just described, in very shorthand fashion, takes Darwin from about the end of 1831 to the end of 1836, the five years from the ages of 22 to 27. Some time early in 1837, he began to commit himself seriously to the task of developing a workable theory of evolution. He made some notes on this in the *Red Notebook* mentioned previously and began the celebrated *First* (of four) *Transmutation Notebook*, also known as the *B Notebook*, in July 1837. For the 15 months that followed, we have been able to trace the phases of his evolutionary theorizing. It is not possible to give an exact count of the number of phases. Embryonic theories are often ephemeral, and competing ideas can be entertained simultaneously. Moreover, different scholars dissect and reconstruct the protocol somewhat differently. In spite of these difficulties, it is safe to say that there were about five major theoretical phases during the 15 months preceding his reading of Malthus' *Essay on Population* on September 28, 1838. He then achieved a reasonably clear insight into the idea of evolution through natural selection.

This was not a fallow period. Darwin was not lying in wait for the one great insight. Rather, there were many insights, possibly as many as one or two each day (Gruber, 1981a). Nor can it be said that the supposedly great insight was recognized by Darwin as qualitatively different from all the others. His behavior belies that notion since he simply went on with various preoccupations much as before. Thus, the point at which he had arrived on September 28th was by no means a terminus. He had still to see the pertinence of the model of artificial selection as a sort of microcosm of natural selection. He had still to extend the idea of natural selection to mental evolution (Richards, 1981). He had still to solve the baffling problem of evolutionary divergence (Browne, 1980). He had to come to terms with the unsolved problems of hereditary change and transmission and to construct a theory that detoured this whole intractable subject. These and other problems occupied him during the rest of his life. There were no perfectly satisfactory answers to most of these questions. He had to learn to live with considerably more theoretical uncertainty than his Newtonian aspirations prescribed.

Each of these developments would require considerable time and space to elaborate. Indeed, the list of problems to be faced has been much shortened and simplified. Perhaps enough has been said on the subject to establish the idea that growth of a belief system is extraordinarily complex, which probably helps to explain why it is often such a protracted process (see, for example, Westfall, 1980, on Newton; Wertheimer, 1959, on Einstein).

Before turning to the next major section of this chapter, there are three remarks on methodology to be made. First, Darwin's intellectual development is extraordinarily well documented by the literally thousands of pages of private notes he kept, often in dated sequences. In spite of some differences in interpretation, there is a remarkable degree of agreement among Darwin scholars looking at the same material. Second, a developmental approach, watching the process of thought as it moves through time and seeing it in its historical context (both in the sense of social history and in the sense of the more internal history of science), is often extremely helpful in understanding the material. This is particularly true where interpretation does not spring immediately to the eye.

Third, the abandoned theories were neither useless mistakes for Darwin, nor were they merely way stations on the road to the definitive theory. It is more plausible to suppose that they all served, while they were active beliefs, as tools for organizing what might be called "units" of knowlege and thought. And since they all belong to the same general family of theories, a unit developed in one context often turns out to remain serviceable as theoretical work moves on. Up to this point, researchers have been so absorbed in the difficult task of reconstructing the theoretical steps as distinct and describable structures of belief, that the elaboration of the constructive *functions* of theories while they last has often been neglected.

Organization of Affect

The second great subsystem of the creative mind at work is the organization of affect. Psychologists have relatively little to say of consequence about the affective lives of creative people at work. Far too much attention has been given to negative affects—anxiety, guilt, rage, fear, and so on. Psychological inquiry seldom asks about such things as courage or the joy of discovery. Such positive emotions are the ones most relevant to the understanding of creativity at work.

Moreover, psychologists have paid little attention to the way the affective side of experience is patterned and orchestrated over time. Almost everything written about affect treats the person as though he or she has one affect at a time, or perhaps a conflict of two. But an *affective experience* can be seen as something like a musical experience, such as a sonata or a symphony. When such an event is experienced, it has phases in which different emotions are evoked and the patterned relations among these phases makes the whole what it is. The joyful surprise ending of the Beethoven violin concerto would not be same without the suspenseful, quasi-repetitious buildup.

Such feelings are prominently exhibited in a passage Darwin wrote when he was 23 years old. Not only does he describe a complex, on-going experience, he also consciously anticipates a different affective pattern for a later time. From various autobiographical allusions in his later writings, such as the *Origin of Species*,[6] we can see that this anticipation of a future affective life was paralleled by recollections of the past. An emotional experience, then, can be both extended in time and rich in a given moment.

During the voyage of the *Beagle* (1831–1836; ages 22–27), Darwin kept a diary that was posthumously published (Barlow, 1934). Early in the *Diary*, he wrote one of a number of ecstatic passages about the beauty of nature and the lushness of tropical forests. This love of, and dwelling on, sensuous experience was richly represented in Darwin's life. It was in a sense overdetermined since it combined elements drawn from his grandfather's poetry, from the nature prose and poetry of the day, from his formal education by naturalists, and from his own years of boyhood and adolescence spent in field work. When thinking of someone like Darwin, who was doing all of the more abstract things that entered directly into his theoretical efforts later on, the affective sensuous components must also be remembered.

Early in the voyage, Darwin wrote in his *Diary*:

> About 9 o'clock we were near to the coast of Brazil; we saw a considerable extent of it, the whole line is rather low & irregular, & from the profusion of wood & verdure of a bright green colour. About 11 o'clock we entered the bay of All Saints, on the Northern side of which is situated the town of Bahia or San Salvador. It would be difficult [to] imagine, before seeing the view, anything so magnificent. It requires, however, the reality of nature to make it so. If faithfully represented in a picture, a feeling of distrust would be raised in the mind, as I think is the case in some of Martins' views. The town is fairly embosomed in a luxuriant wood & situated on a steep bank overlooks the calm waters of the great bay of All Saints. The houses are white & lofty & from the windows being narrow & long have a very light & elegant appearance. Convents, Porticos & public buildings vary the uniformity of the houses: the bay is scattered over with large ships; in short the view is one of the finest in the Brazils. But these beauties are as nothing compared to the Vegetation; I believe from what I have seen Humboldt's glorious descriptions are & will for ever be unparalleled: but even he with his dark blue skies & the rare union of poetry with science which he so strongly displays when writing on tropical scenery, with all this falls far short of the truth. The delight one experiences in such times bewilders the mind; if the eye attempts to follow the flight of a gaudy butter-fly, it is arrested by some strange tree or fruit; if watching an insect one forgets it in the stranger flower it is crawling over; if turning to admire the splendour of the scenery, the individual character of the foreground fixes the attention. The mind is a chaos of delight, out of which a world of future & more quiet pleasure will arise. I am at present fit only to read Humboldt; he like another sun illumines everything I behold (Barlow, 1934).

Notice Darwin's (literally) glowing reference to Alexander von Humboldt, who had been his hero for about two years but was soon to be replaced by Charles Lyell. The relationship between Lyell and Darwin later grew into a mature and abiding friendship, and I do not think that Darwin found or sought another hero.

Charles Darwin was not very close to his father, Dr. Robert Darwin, an imposing and eminent physician. Instead, he found a sucession of "father figures": the zoologist, Professor Robert Grant at Edinburgh University, the botanist, Professor John Henslow at Cambridge University, the entomologist, Professor Hope in London whom Darwin once addressed as "my father in entomology," and of course, Humboldt and Lyell. But it should be noted that none of these was the kind of father figure whose influence pervades and dominates the whole of life. Rather, each was an intellectual and scientific collaborator appropriate to one or another of Darwin's scientific purposes. Even his own father would eventually play this role. In the *M* and *N* Notebooks on man, mind, and materialism (1838–1839),[7] Darwin drew greatly on his father's store of medical and psychological knowledge. In the opening passage of the *M Notebook*, Darwin records certain observations his father had made about the intercorrelations among both physical and mental hereditary traits, beginning the notebook with the words, "July 15, 1838. My father says..."

Notice also in the *Diary* passage reproduced previously Darwin's sense of futurity, "I am at present fit only to read Humboldt..." but he was to develop as a person. "The mind is a chaos of delight, out of which a world of future and more quiet pleasure will arise."

At this early point in the voyage, he had not gained much momentum in developing a clear-cut set of purposes to guide him in his work. However, he already had some sense of the relation between the voyage experiences to come and his emerging sense of self.

The uniformly positive tone of this passage characterizes the early part of his *Diary* and his other writings. Then the tone changes. Another note is introduced. Darwin had a lot of experience with death during the voyage. There was the death of a shipmate. There was his direct observation of the wars of extermination conducted by the Spaniards against the Indians of South America. There was his intuitive sense of a changing balance of life and death in different regions he visited. After his first enthusiastic encounter with the luxuriant tropical scenery of Brazil, he visited that bleak southernmost tip of South America, Tierra del Fuego. There he wrote, "... here things are different because death predominates, as compared with life." Figuratively, this expression captures the bleakness of the place. Theoretically, it could not be true in a stable, living ecology where life and death must always more or less balance out. Later, Darwin came to make this very point a premise of his mature theory.

The *balance* between life and death is sometimes forgotten by social scientists exploiting Darwin's theory. There is a kind of differential uptake of ideas, overemphasizing the selective, decimating aspect of the theory—winners survive, losers die off. But there is also a positive aspect that is equally important. Darwin expressed this duality in the famous closing passage of the *Origin*, in his image of the tangled bank. This pictures the same "chaos of delight" that he wrote about in 1832, but in 1859 explosive growth and differentiation and wonderful variation and diversity vie in importance with the war of nature.

Perhaps the first really trenchant summary of the affective sense of ideas occurs in Darwin's *Fourth Transmutation Notebook*. It can be found in the entry for March 12, 1839, an early evocation of the image of the tangled bank. He wrote: "It is difficult to believe in the dreadful but quiet war going on (in) the peaceful woods and smiling fields—we must recollect the multitude of plants introduced into our gardens . . . we see how full nature, how finely each holds its place" (*E Notebook*, p. 114). It is noteworthy that this imagistic coming into affective awareness occurs almost six months after his first clear insight into the principle of natural selection. At that time, September 28, 1838, the pairing of struggle and change, death and innovation was expressed, but in a triumphant vein—Darwin was solving an intellectual problem and feeling good about it. In the March 1839 entry something is added—the note of sadness at this aspect of nature.

Over long periods of time, there is in Darwin a repeated pattern of affective change. An idea expressed first in a positive problem-solving spirit is reiterated with a note of chastening and sadness added. I have come to think that it would be hard for someone to develop mature, disciplined thought without contending at some point(s) with the finitude of life and the realization that problems are only solved in a definitive way inside finite contexts. This brings the thinker up against the idea of personal death. Understanding that there are such limits, and yet, that in some sense they can and must be transcended by the whole cycle of birth and death and reproduction—this is an important part of the story of one's growth as a thinking person. Another example is Piaget's prose poem, *La Mission de l'Idée*, written in 1915 when he was nineteen, in which the young man struggles with the issue of transcending personal finitude (Piaget, 1916, 1977).

When Darwin began his *Transmutation Notebooks* in July 1837, a question that preoccupied him in the first five pages was just that. He asks, "Why is life short, why such high object generation?" (*B Notebook*, p. 2). In other words, what is the function in the entire system of living things of the death and reproduction of individuals? And his answer is: to make way for the possibility of adaptive change. The living system must be kept open and plastic; changes that cannot occur in a mature individual can, through one means or another, occur in an infant creature or during conception. The details of the theory that he was then elaborating are complex and interesting. But at present I want only to draw attention to the fact that there is a connection between this affective change of coming to terms with birth, life, and death and the actual theoretical system he was constructing. The same connection is poignantly expressed in his very personal notes of *Marriage*, written in 1838, just before his marriage to Emma Wedgwood (see Darwin's *Autobiography*, also Keegan & Gruber, in press).

It is reasonable to speak of a set of affective transformations in Darwin that correspond to his intellectual development. The youth is willing to lend his services as a field naturalist and collector to a superior breed of scientific specialists. He then becomes both a specialist himself and a wide-ranging, powerful theoretician, directing and exploiting the work of others—keeping them in the dark about his ultimate purposes. The hopeful lad, with an exalted view of nature as God's handiwork, comes first to see it as the product of natural law and then to temper the unalloyed positive tone of his earlier reactions with thoughts of finitude, war, and death. The open, cheerful student ready to share his thoughts with all comers, begins to realize that he must keep some of them to himself. First, in his long encounter with the *Beagle's* captain, Robert Fitzroy, and later, as he pursued a theory of evolution, he saw that the public world of science would exact a price for revolutionary violation of its norms. To contend with these dangers, purposeful, strategic planning would be necessary. "Mention persecution of early astronomers," he instructs himself in the spring of 1838 (*C Notebook*, p. 123).

At this point Darwin seems still to have intended an open avowal of his beliefs. He wrote, "Love of the deity effect of organization, oh, you materialist! . . . Why is thought being a secretion of the brain, more wonderful than gravity a property of matter? It is our arrogance, it (is) our admiration of ourselves" (*C Notebook*, p. 166, written about May 1838). But only a little later the prudential plan of more limited expression of his ideas begins to emerge: "To avoid stating how far I believe in Materialism, say only that emotions, instincts, degrees of talent, which are hereditary, are so because brain of child resembles parent stock" (*M Notebook*, p. 57, written about August 1838). He hoped to steer between the Scylla of theology and the Charybdis of blasphemy. As he came closer to the moment of insight of September 28, 1838, he had a dream of being executed for his wit. But as in the later reality of his life, so in the dream. The martyr does not flinch; he keeps his thinking mind intact until the very moment that he loses his head. And he does come back to life. Just so, Darwin's ideas lay dormant and concealed; then they were brilliantly expounded in the *Origin* and twelve years later in the *Descent of Man*. They survived bitter attacks and prevailed.

I have been criticized (Richards, 1981) for arguing that Darwin's double delay (first in publishing the *Origin* and second in revealing his views on man in *Descent*) was due to his fear of persecution and ridicule. Exclusively "cognitive" historians of science have insisted that the intellectual difficulties Darwin faced were great enough to account for his hesitancy in publishing. In a sense, I agree. Of course, if he had had a complete and unassailable theory, he could have forged ahead without fear of criticism. But great new syntheses are rarely, if ever, complete and invulnerable. And they are rarely, if ever, advanced in an open, welcoming, and friendly forum where no Establishment stands guard over its vested interest, defending the ideology that justifies its existence. Imperial Britain was then probably an even more repressive society than has yet been brought to light. Darwin's delays were a joint function of his fears of ridicule and his hopes that he would master the unsolved problems of his theory. Directed, purposeful thinking goes on in a feeling person, and Darwin certainly was that.

It was mentioned earlier that Darwin's case is extraordinarily well documented. This cannot be said about his affective development with as much force as about his theoretical work. In his scientific notes, even when he drew on his personal experience, he was not writing in a confessional spirit. Nonetheless, as we begin to look at his letters, notes, and autobiography with his affective development in mind, we see that the record is by no means scanty.

Organization of Purpose

As the third subsystem, the organization of purpose is a general motivational system of a goal-directed person that can be thought of in at least two ways. On the one hand, there is a set of purposes: the tasks, problems, projects, and enterprises that he or she intends to carry out. On the other hand, there may be some underlying motives, conscious or unconscious, that govern the construction and reconstruction of this set of purposes.

A description of the purposes of creative workers requires (1) some scheme broad enough to encompass a varying number of purposes in different sorts of relationships with one another and (2) some scheme that shows the variation over time of the pattern of activities connected with these purposes. I refer to this pattern as a *network of enterprise*. "Network" because the activities expressing the purposes are complexly interrelated; "enterprise"—rather than task, problem, or project—in order to capture the idea that each activity in question may have no fixed end point. It often includes a scheme for replenishing itself with new tasks if ever the original stock nears completion.

The diverse activities comprising the strands of a person's network of enterprise have all sorts of dynamic relations with each other. The concept, network of enterprise, allows for an enlarged view of what psychologists have previously considered under the heading of "intrinsic motivation" or of "task-oriented behavior" (Lewin, 1935). What is new in the present discussion is the life-history approach that assumes that the creative person generally *chooses* his or her goals and *constructs* his or her network of enterprise. Furthermore, it is my intention to describe neither one such intrinsic motivation at a time, nor a conflict between two, but rather, the operation of an entire, complex, long-lasting network.

The dynamic properties of this network of conscious, task-oriented purposes are not offered as a substitute for the dynamics of the unconscious and ego-oriented motives. Nevertheless, it will be seen that the network of enterprise offers an alternative to the notion that the rich dynamics of behavior lie solely below the surface of consciousness.

In speaking of the long-range goals of a person engaged in creative work, some such concept as general direction is needed. Since the goal cannot be specified exactly, and is rarely attainable in a single step, we must either adopt Koestler's (1959) image of the "sleepwalker" or assume that the creative person evolves some strategies for knowing when he or she is moving in the intended general direction.

Some facets of Darwin's network of enterprise will now be discussed. No one will contest the general idea that by the time Darwin began his *Transmutation Notebooks* in July of 1837 he fully intended to elaborate and defend some theory of evolution. But what can be said of his earlier development? To what extent can his early work and growth be considered "purposeful"? It is not, of course, suggested that Darwin knew his end point, or his intellectual destination, when he began the voyage. Nevertheless, the events that shaped his life did not just happen to him. He participated in the making of his own milieu. His prevoyage and early-voyage scientific literary hero was Alexander von Humboldt. This was Darwin's choice. Even his coming to rely on Lyellian theory must be seen as involving a large element of independent choice. He had an extensive geological library on board the *Beagle* and other theoretical approaches were available that harmonized better with his university training. In going beyond Lyell, in his work on the theory of coral-reef formation, Darwin was independently breaking new ground. As I have shown, elsewhere, he was developing the thought forms of an equilibration model that would later reappear in the theory of evolution (Gruber & Gruber, 1962; Gruber, in preparation; see also, Ghiselin, 1966). So, although we cannot speak of a fixed goal, it is not implausible to speak of intentional movements in a direction even in Darwin's early period.

Here a commonplace but false picture must be corrected. It is the idea that Darwin, when he went to Cambridge, or when he began the *Beagle* voyage, was a rather purposeless, flighty young man, and that it took the luck of bumping into Henslow, his teacher, or the luck of being (the last to be) chosen as the naturalist for the voyage, to start him on his career. That would mean, for our developmental picture, that by the age of 18 or 21, depending on which version of that story you believe, Darwin was a kind of nobody, and not even a very bright nobody in most versions of the story. This legend is a little implausible. It is akin to the mythology of sudden great insights, rather than slow growth processes, as the major characteristic of creative lives.

As a matter of fact, the story is entirely wrong. It appears that Darwin had a long and rich history of being very purposeful. The purposes in question were not precise, long-range, theoretical goals, but rather the more general kind—to work at a series of projects all contributing to the making of a scientist. When his older brother, Erasmus, went to Edinburgh University, he wrote detailed letters to Charles, carefully outlining the steps necessary for the completion and operation of their mineralogy laboratory. When Charles went to Edinburgh, he immediately joined a student scientific group, the Plinian Society. Material from papers that he read there on invertebrate organisms was included in papers published by his teacher, the zoologist (and Lamarckian), Professor Robert Grant.

At Cambridge, before he met Henslow, Darwin quickly became engrossed in collaborative work on entomology, especially the collection of beetles, together with his cousin, William Darwin Fox. Although they later went separate ways—Darwin Fox to marriage and the ministry, Charles to sea and science—they kept up a lifelong correspondence, often referring nostalgically to their youthful entomologizing. This relationship is a good example of the kind of brotherly cooperation that is often a part of scientific work. There was a great deal of collaboration among peers in the whole Darwin story. Let these few examples stand for the many in his life.

Darwin met Professor Frederick W. Hope, a distinguished London entomologist, at a dinner party. This began a relationship of mutual admiration of collections, exchanging specimens, and field trips together. Young Darwin was a serious, nearly professional entomologist. He could learn from and work with peers and older friends. Then he met a botanist, the Reverend Professor John Henslow, and became known at Cambridge as "the man who walks with Henslow." Like other English worthies, the latter was a clergyman, a professor, and a working naturalist. For a time, Darwin entertained the plan of emulating his mentor's career.

So, Darwin was a very purposeful young man. Of course, his purposes were changing and evolving. To say that he was considering the ministry bears some explanation. A country parson functioned, among other things, as something like an agricultural county agent in our country. As the educated man in the community, the parson brought new knowledge to the farmers around. Darwin had some excellent models to follow, like the celebrated Reverend Gilbert White of Selbourne, or his own friend, Leonard Jenyns, who later became the parson at Swaffham Bulbeck, not far from Cambridge. These men and others like them were virtually professional naturalists as well as productive writers whom Darwin could hope to emulate in thinking of himself as a parson cum natural historian in that "world of future and more quiet pleasure." Although I do not think that Darwin was a deeply religious man, there was no conflict between being religious and having an evolving sense of purpose as natural historian and scientist. Nor was the *Beagle* opening quite as accidental as it is usually painted. Before the *Beagle* opportunity came along, Darwin was himself organizing a voyage of scientific discovery. It was to be a voyage to Teneriffe, an island of special interest to naturalists and also of special symbolic value. In earlier times, the peak of Teneriffe had been thought the highest in the world, a meeting place of heaven and earth. Milton had written of it in *Paradise Lost* (Darwin's constant companion during the *Beagle* voyage). In 1831, Darwin had been recruiting people to go with him on his voyage. He had been down to the docks in London, investigating the price of chartering a ship. He had been studying Spanish. Professor Henslow was one of his recruits, somewhat reluctantly because he had been recently married. Henslow was relieved when the *Beagle* opening came along, so he could send Darwin off on that adventure instead.

A sense of purpose has a long slow growth, which in Darwin's case probably began in quite early adolescence. There are two early moments when we can see Darwin working out his personal agenda. Written six years apart, the notes in question have one pleasant human feature—a clear-cut division between intellectual interests and concern for creature comforts, with some attention given to each. On board the *Beagle*, but before it weighed anchor and sailed away from Plymouth, Darwin drew up a plan of work:

> *December* 13*th.* An idle day; dined for the first time in Captain's cabin & felt quite at home. Of all the luxuries the Captain has given me, none will be so essential as that of having my meals with him. I am often afraid I shall be quite overwhelmed with the number of subjects which I ought to take into hand. It is difficult to mark out any plan & without method on shipboard I am sure little will be done. The principle objects are 1st, collecting, observing & reading in all branches of Natural history that I possibly can manage. Observations in Meteorology, French & Spanish, Mathematics, & a little Classics, perhaps not more than Greek Testament on Sundays. I hope generally to have some one English book in hand for my

amusement, exclusive of the above mentioned branches. If I have not energy enough to make myself steadily industrious during the voyage, how great & uncommon an opportunity of improving myself shall I throw away. May this never for one moment escape my mind & then perhaps I may have the same opportunity of drilling my mind that I threw away whilst at Cambridge (Barlow, 1934).

These are the resolutions of a young man who has not yet found a very clear sense of direction other than the very broad ones of being an educated man and a naturalist. This impression is borne out by the scientific notes of the first year or so of the voyage.

Six years later in London, contemplating marriage, we see him in full stride, knowing where he is going intellectually. In quick succession, he writes two notes to himself about the pros and cons of marriage. In the first, the varied strands of his network of enterprise are remarkably visible. Marriage will interfere with travel, that is, with field geology. But staying put will permit work on "transmutation of species," on "simplest forms of life," on "physiological observations on lower animals," and speculations on geographical distribution of organisms. Marriage will necessitate earning a living: "Cambridge Professorship, and make the best of it . . . " He is planning not just his work, but his life and work. *And he knows what he wants to do* (Barlow, 1958).

In the second set of notes, he outlines the desirable emotional and social conditions of life: "Only picture yourself a nice soft wife on a sofa and a good fire, and books and music perhaps . . . " *He knows what he wants to feel.*

The problem he confronts in writing these marriage notes is to organize a life that will be physically and emotionally comfortable enough, without deflecting from his chosen course. The solution he was nearing was his marriage to his cousin, Emma Wedgwood. The notes conclude . . . "Marry—Marry—Marry Q.E.D." The conclusion of this passage, "Q.E.D.", means Quod Erat Demonstrandum," the traditional closing of a successful mathematical proof. Darwin's choice of terms underlines the explicit problem-solving spirit in which he approached the organization of his life. These notes have not been dated exactly, but were probably written in the summer of 1838. On November 11, 1838, Darwin proposed to Emma Wedgwood. They were married in January 1839, and their first child, William, was born before the year was out.

Meanwhile, his scientific agenda were also rapidly developing a new shape. On July 15, 1838, he began his notebooks on man, mind, and materialism. The reasons for this major branching in his network of enterprise have been thoroughly discussed elsewhere (Gruber, 1981). Here, two simple points can be made. First, between the decision to begin these notebooks and the decision to write the

Descent of Man, 36 years elapsed. Moreover, after William was born, Darwin kept a diary of observations on the growth of intelligence and of the emotional life of his baby. The material from this diary was published in his paper, "A Biographical Sketch of an Infant" 37 years later. *Enterprises endure.*

Second, as mentioned earlier, Darwin was particularly cautious about revealing his views on human evolution. Between the publication of the *Origin* in 1859, in which he said almost nothing about *homo sapiens,* and the publication of the *Descent* in 1871, 12 years elapsed. *Enterprises need not be public.*

Darwin functioned over long periods of time as though he had a conscious but private agenda. He brought different parts of his work to the public in a highly controlled, strategically regulated way (see Gruber, 1981 and Rudwick, 1982 for further discussions of this point). The geological material surfaced first, the evolutionary material next, and the material on man and mind last.

THE MOVEMENT OF THOUGHT

In this last section, the general movement of Darwin's thought in the period from 1831 to 1839, the voyage of the young naturalist and the few years after, will be characterized. His scope was expanding, moving from being a collector and a describer to being an original theoretician. The scope of his theoretical work expands from rather narrow-gauge hypotheses, for example, about the geology of a region, to far-reaching and well-grounded ideas about the geology of the earth as a whole. Over a period of about two years, he studied the elevation of the mountains of South America. He then saw that a conservation principle must apply: If the figure of the earth is to remain approximately spherical, then there must be a compensatory relation between elevations and subsidences. This hypothesized pattern characterized not only the continents, but also the whole sea bottom of the Pacific Ocean. If such a pattern continues over many years, then there must be corresponding changes in another set of possibilities: the forms of life that can exist in particular places, depending on the depth of the ocean. His whole theory of the formation of coral reefs is based on this notion of cycles of elevation and subsidences. In other words, it is grounded in a conservation principle applied on an enormous scale in a very deliberate way. Part of the originality of this scheme is its breaking down of the distinction between continents and oceans.

The question of scale must be examined carefully. If elevation represented a really big bulge, the figure of the earth would not be conserved. But even the difference, in distance from the center of the earth, between the highest mountain and the lowest sea bottom is only some ten miles or about two-hundredths of a percent of the radius. Compensation rules, then, can apply, keeping the earth approximately round.

This change in scale and its consequences for the very shape of theory are reflected in one striking autobiographical passage in the *Origin*. Beginning with the personal marker, "When a young naturalist..." Darwin goes on to describe the series of dilemmas confronting the young scientist who starts out with a system of classification based on a restricted region (for example, England) and encounters seeming anomalies as his exploration expands to larger and larger regions (for example, the world circumnavigated in the *Beagle* voyage). [His "difficulties... rise to a climax" (*Origin*, p. 50).] The solution must be something beyond mere tinkering with the system of classification: "community of descent is the hidden bond which naturalists have been unconsciously seeking, and not some unknown plan of creation or the enunciation of general propositions and the mere putting together and separating objects more or less alike" (*Origin*, p. 420). Thus, theory moves from classificatory to causal models and theorizing pushes out to wider and wider domains, reaching for the limits of space and time.

Although this growth in scale, scope, and depth in Darwin's thinking during the voyage can be seen, no great degree of reflectivity about the way in which the work of science is to be done is apparent. At the very end of the voyage, there are but a few pages of notes on this subject. During the voyage, and also in the *First Transmutation Notebook*, there is a kind of work that might be characterized as *direct scientific thinking*. There are problems, and those problems are thought about. In the *First Transmutation Notebook*, there is a certain amount of what may be called metascientific thinking, but only a sentence or a phrase here and there, almost tossed off. By the *Second Notebook*, however, some six months into the process of thinking about theories of evolution, there is a rather sharp rise in the amount of meta-scientific thinking. It is not so much that the frequency of his references to various types of problem rises, but each allusion, when it does occur, tends to be longer—a paragraph or even a page in length, rather than a phrase or a sentence.

The end of the *First Notebook* and the whole of the *Second Notebook* are studded with such remarks. There are strategic thoughts; for example, specific genealogies of species are not traceable in fine and continuous detail (*C Notebook*, p. 64)—but enough can be seen to support ideas about the laws of change. Thus, Darwin remarks "... the one end of classification [is] to express relationship & by so doing discover the laws of change in organization" (*C Notebook*, p. 158).

He is expansive and hopeful about finding such laws: "The grand question which every naturalist ought to have before him when dissecting a whale or classifying a mite, a fungus, or an infusorian, is What are the Laws of Life?" (*B Notebook*, p. 229). He welcomes the speculative attitude in a kindred spirit: "Lamarck . . . had so few clear facts, but so bold . . . was endowed with what may be called the prophetic spirit in science. The highest endowment of lofty genius" (*C Notebook*, p. 119). He is frequently critical of anthropocentrism and—perhaps contradictorily—cautiously receptive to the idea of evolutionary progress, a topic which he recognizes as belonging in the domain of "metaphysical speculations" (*C Notebook*, p. 104). He waxes metaphorical on numerous occasions, and he reflects more analytically on the role of analogy in science (*C Notebook*, pp. 138–40).

Explicit metaphysical ideas sprout up here and there: "Love of the deity effect of organization, oh you materialist!" (*C Notebook*, p. 166). "There is one living spirit prevalent over this world . . . which assume a multitude of forms . . . according to subordinate laws. There is one thinking sensible principle intimately allied to one kind of organic matter . . . " (*C Notebook*, pp. 210–11).

Why this rise in metascientific reflectivity? Three reasons are now suggested. First, Darwin was living in London, bombarded with the new findings and controversies of a vigorous scientific community, stimulated by many personal contacts with other scientists (Rudwick, 1982). He had had several years of practice and received a good share of recognition for theoretical work in a related field, geology. Second, he had by then explored a domain of possible ideas fairly thoroughly, reached both a sort of intellectual plateau and a reasonably successful integration of a wide variety of facts and restricted laws, under the general premise of evolution. He was looking for a still higher level of theoretical integration. Third, and most important, he was baffled. This is difficult to document, but it seems to me that when he began the *First Notebook*, he felt he was on the track of (if not in possession of) a viable theory and that this feeling persisted for some time through a number of theoretical changes. But the *Second Notebook* seems more exploratory, and there is no clear sense of direction or specifiable theory that he is working out. One possible objection to this hypothesis of bafflement leading to reflectivity is the very positive upbeat tone of his writing. But bafflement need not be accompanied by depression. Life was going well for him and, on the theoretical front, he was certainly not defeated.

In the *Third Notebook*, a few clear expressions of this sense of being "stuck" come through. On August 27, 1838, he writes, somewhat ineffectually, "There must be some law that whatever organization an animal has, it tends to multiply & *improve* on it. Articulate animals must articulate, & in vertebrate tendency to improve in intellect. . . . " But he goes on to cite a counter example, "Yet fish same as, or lower than in old days . . . ???" (*D Notebook*, p. 49). On September 7, he writes, "Seeing what Von Buch, Humboldt, G. St. Hilaire, & Lamarck have written, I pretend to no originality of idea—(though I arrived at them quite independently . . .) the line of proof & reducing facts to law [the] only merit if merit there be in following work" (*D Notebook*, p. 69).

It took Darwin some time to assimilate the importance of his insight of September 28, 1838. For several months, he seems to have treated it as just one more promising idea and gone on with his earlier preoccupations and problems. His dream of October 30 suggests that he did not, even then, feel that he had put the whole puzzle together in a satisfying way. He dreamed that he had read a page of a French book, pronouncing each word distinctly, "but could not gather general sense of this page" (*N Notebook*, p. 33). In a waking state, he read French often and fluently, so it is reasonable to speculate about the symbolic meaning of this dream of comprehension and to suggest its analogy to the state of his still inchoate emerging theory of evolution.

The idea that Darwin moved *toward* the principle of natural selection almost from the beginning of his *First Notebook* can be demonstrated. His early branching model of evolution, which assumed differentiation and extinction with the number of species constant, strongly implied a formal (but not a causal) principle of selection. In the 15 months that followed, he wrote a number of times of phenomena like natural selection but in very restrictive contexts. Even after September 28, 1838, it appears that he was still moving toward the principle, for he had not yet seized and wielded it with consistent vigor. It took a few years for Darwin to extend the idea to the evolution of mind (Richards, 1981).

I know that the suggestion that Darwin, or anyone, moved toward an as yet unexpressed idea smacks of teleology, as does any idea of "progress." But I believe that a view of the history and development of human thought without the idea of progress is a doctrine of despair. To be sure, contemporary ideas in developmental psychology are confusing. In Piaget's theory, for example, the stage theory of individual development is modeled on the general idea of progress. But since it is a quasi-embryological theory of universally recurring stages, it entails no progress from generation to generation. On the other hand, Piaget's early romantic writings, especially *La Mission de l'Idée*, and his work in the history of science are imbued with evolutionary thought and a firm belief in the idea of progress. This concatenation of embryological and evolutionary ideas is not necessarily contradictory, but the work necessary to make it coherent has only begun (Gould, 1977).

It was mentioned near the beginning of this chapter that intellectual progress does not require the emergence of new operations. However, Darwin's progress suggests that the consolidation of new contents of thought sets up new criteria for next steps. Thus, contents become tools. Moreover, the establishment of new contents sets the scene and opens the way for new undertakings.

Therefore, although Darwin always implicated man in his early evolutionary musings, it was not until he had made sufficient progress on various other fronts that he began the *M* and *N Notebooks* (in July 1838). There he made the explorations of the domains of man, mind, and materialism an explicit set of tasks, a new enterprise. This early, very private sequence in his notebooks was repeated in public much later (*Origin*, 1859; *Descent* 1871).

To understand the movement of thought, a concept such as *sense of direction* is needed. Movement in a direction is one version of the idea of progress. Darwin's life exemplifies movement in the direction of making the implicit explicit and in the direction of demystifying the past. It is our turn to demystify the future.

NOTES

1. The evolving systems approach to creative work is described at length in Gruber, H.E. "And the bush was not consumed" the evolving systems approach to creativity. In Modgil, S. and Modgil C., editors, *Toward a Theory of Psychological Development*. Windsor: NFER, 1980, 269–99.

It is illustrated in Gruber, H.E. *Darwin on Man: A Psychological Study of Scientific Creativity* (second edition). Chicago: University of Chicago Press, 1981.

2. Darwin's manuscript notebooks and scientific notes have all been consulted by the present author in the original at Cambridge University Library. These include the scientific notebooks of the voyage of the *Beagle*. These thousands of pages of manuscript have never been published. The fullest account of them is probably Gruber, H.E., and Gruber, M.V. The eye of reason: Darwin's development during the *Beagle* voyage. *Isis*, 1962, 53, 186–200.

3. This way of presenting the main outlines and internal relationships of a belief system bears some resemblance to the work of Woodger (1952).

4. *The Red Notebook*. A miscellany of notes, mostly on geological subjects, but containing some of Darwin's earliest postvoyage thoughts on evolution. Published as Herbert, S., editor. *The Red Notebook of Charles Darwin*. Ithaca and London: British Museum (Natural History) and Cornell University Press, 1980.

5. *The Transmutation Notebooks*. Darwin labeled *The First Transmutation Notebook B*, the Second *C*, the Third *D*, and the Fourth *E*. Published as de Beer, G., Rowlands, M.J., and Skramovsky, B.M., editors. *Darwin's Notebooks on Transmutation of Species*, Parts I–IV, *Bulletin of the British Museum (Natural History Series)*, vol. 2, nos. 1–6, 1960–1961; Part VI, same journal, vol. 3, no. 5, 1967.

6. *The Origin of Species* and *The Descent of Man* are referred to by their short titles, *Origin* and *Descent*, with page references to the first editions, in 1859 and 1871, respectively. For example, (*Origin*, p. 50).

7. *The Notebooks on Man, Mind, and Materialism*. Darwin labeled these two *M* and *N*. Chronologically, they overlap *The Transmutation Notebooks*. The latter span the period from July 1837 to some time in 1839. The *M* and *N* Notebooks were begun on July 15, 1838, and continue until some time in 1839. Published in Gruber, H.E. and Barrett, P.H. *Darwin on Man: A Psychological Study of Scientific Creativity Together with*

Darwin's Early and Unpublished Notebooks, New York: Dutton, 1974. Reprinted separately as Barrett, P.H., editor. *Metaphysics, Materialism, and the Evolution of Mind: Early Writings of Charles Darwin with a commentary by Howard E. Gruber*. Chicago: University of Chicago Press, 1980.

2

THE DEVELOPMENT OF
THE YOUNG PIAGET:
CASE MATERIALS AGAINST
UTOPIAN PSYCHOLOGY

Fernando Vidal

"It is right," wrote Henri Bergson in *Creative Evolution* (1907), "to say that what we do depends on what we are; but it should be added that, to a certain extent, we are what we do, and that we create ourselves continually" (p. 7). Bergson was right to emphasize the movement between being and doing that constitutes the constant creation of the self. Moreover, what we do depends on what we can think. It is also true that what we can think depends, to a certain extent, on what we do, and that our thoughts do not develop independently from the rest of our lives.

The periods of life that probably illustrate, and perhaps inspire, belief in the interdependence among action, thought, and culture are those times of youth and adolescence. Usually, both periods are seen as not only enabling the individual to clarify the relationship of self and society, but also as ending with his or her integration into conventional structures of social roles. Yet, there is often a tendency to reduce the psychological changes of adolescence and youth to mental or maturational events.

Take, for example, Gruber and Vonèche's (1976, p. 52) "indexes" of the transition from formal to postformal thought: the adoption of a personal viewpoint on things, the working out of possibilities to delay acting directly on the world, and the formation of a personal honor code. Models in psychology often seem to suggest that such indexes are the manifestations of new thought capacities developed spontaneously in a person's mind. It is as if the mind consisted purely of adaptive forethought, similar to T. S. Eliot's "timekept city." However, the case-study approach pioneered by Howard Gruber in his *Darwin on Man* (1974) leads one to see that the indexes are expressions of the interplay between doing, thinking, and being; as manifold objects constructed with the hands of both purpose and chance; and as deeply personal works made possible by a history, a culture, and a society.

Each "index" embodies a different aspect of the way in which an individual's life becomes organized. The adoption of a point of view embodies the organization of knowledge; the working out of a moratorium, the organization of purpose; and the formation of an honor code, the organization of affect. These three organizations (Gruber, 1980, this volume) may be interwoven, coordinated, and integrated in different ways at different moments. They may be mutually supportive, or they may interfere with each other. In any event, the organizations are orchestrated by the person whose growth, in turn, they regulate. In order to constitute an open system, this mutual governing necessitates the kind of reflection implied both by the "systematic operations" that form systems and by the "meta-systematic" ones that compare them (Richards & Commons, Chapter 5, this volume). Operations and indexes involve each other as reciprocally determined conditions and results.

These considerations are illustrated in this chapter with materials drawn from this author's case study of the young Piaget. While tracing the growth of Piaget's thought between ages 13 to 21 (1909–1917), the focus is on the process by which he gradually integrated his scientific, metaphysical, and moral concerns. This occurred first in his concrete doing of scientific work. Later, it occurred in his predominantly affective assertion of convictions. Finally, it occurred in his systematic construction of a point of view.

Through the reconstruction of this part of Piaget's development (see Figure 2.1), this author argues against a monistic view that says that the changes and diversity of development are dependent on the progress of cognitive structures, as reflections inside a rotating kaleidoscope of brightly colored pieces of intelligence. The unity of doing, being, and thinking described does not imply the organicist sort of functionalism that has been criticized in anthropology and sociology. On the contrary, the specificity of such unity requires the decomposition of developmental time into a variety of rates of change; the strict localization of development itself; and the abandonment of the laws of history that moralize all life as an increasingly adaptive equilibration.

Thus, the purpose here is to urge the avoidance of what Jacques Vonèche (1979) calls "utopisation" of the cultural practices and images of development. Utopisation is "the operation that consists of detaching, in the name of the highest ideals and of the noblest values, the human subject from his historical-material context, in order to project him in the abstract homogeneity of a place that is nowhere, and of a time that always is pure thought, at least in appearance" (p. 219). This "utopian" reduction of the person, typical of the ration-

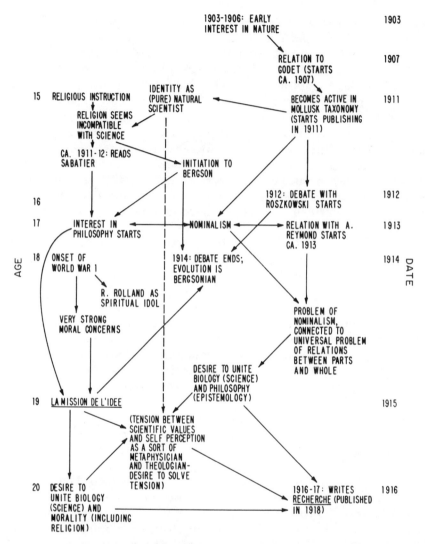

Figure 2.1. Piaget's Development from 1907 to 1917

alistic discourse of present-day developmental psychology, tends to take one away from humanity bring one closer to the central figure of the cognitive mythology: Athena, goddess of Wisdom and Reason, born fully armed from the head of Zeus, omniscient and omnipotent.

PIAGET, YOUNG NATURALIST

Piaget's early scientific socialization into natural history played a fundamental role in the period of development traced here. That socialization helped determine the theoretical and practical discourse that would delimit the possible directions of his intellectual growth. Paul Godet, the main agent of that socialization, was director of the Museum of Natural History of Neuchâtel and a humble naturalist whose main interest was mollusk classification. As a ten-year-old deeply interested in nature, Piaget wished to study the collections of the Museum (for example, see Piaget, 1952). To prove to Godet that he was serious young Piaget wrote an observation of an albino sparrow and sent it to the magazine of a local young naturalist club. After the article's publication, Piaget obtained permission to study at the Museum, and he started helping Godet label the latter's shell collections. In exchange, Godet gave the boy rare specimens and identified them for him. From 1907 until his death in 1911, Godet initiated Piaget into the problems, methods, and values of a predominantly observational and descriptive natural history that was concerned, above all else, with classification. This relationship between Godet and Piaget became close and important. Early on, Godet encouraged and helped his young assistant to prepare his first small publications, and he supported Piaget's candidacy for admission to the Club des Amis de la Nature. According to the traditions of this club of young naturalists, candidates for admission had to present a work of their own. Godet personally talked in favor of Piaget's work, which had been criticized for its "dictionary and catalogue character," although it was typical of the scientific tradition to which Godet belonged.[1] Later, Piaget, who kept his teacher's manuscript notes, was often considered Godet's direct professional successor.

Piaget published his first papers on mollusks when he was 13 and 14 (see, for example, Piaget, 1910). They consisted of short observations of rare snails; the young naturalist identified specimens, described their external features, and sometimes tried to localize their geographical origins. In their style and contents, those early short papers not only reflect Godet's teachings, but they also characterize Piaget's cognitive activity during his early adolescence. Their focus on the concrete suggests that they represent a continuation of Piaget's childhood cognition. Nevertheless, the fact that Piaget was interested in systematics indicates the development of those logical operations indispensable for classification.

From the concreteness of Piaget's early intellectual activity, one cannot merely conclude that he was not yet ready to engage in more formal thinking. Rather, one might take into account that such concreteness was instilled by Godet's teachings; it also fulfilled a central function within the paradigm of mollusk taxonomy. Young Piaget's spontaneous understanding when initiated into a discipline that valued close attention to the concrete and the visible, helps to explain partially how he could quickly become an acknowledged expert in the field. But Piaget's supposedly "spontaneous" intellectual attained level, and his intellectual training, cannot be separated.

Later, Piaget's mastery of observation and specimen identification, as well as his great knowledge of the malacological fauna of French Switzerland, opened the doors of the local scientific community for him, and thus strengthened his adherence to natural-historical ways of thinking.

After Godet's death in 1911, the 15-year-old Piaget began publishing in specialized journals. At a time when mollusk taxonomy was in a very chaotic state, he tackled the challenging task of reorganizing a classification scheme. His method, aimed at reducing the number of species within the scheme, was the usual one. Basically, it consisted of the following: if, on the basis of shell characters, it was possible to join by a continuous gradation, or "series," the type-specimens of two allegedly distinct species A and B, then A and B were considered varieties of a single species.

Apart from the required series, Piaget did not use in his arguments any of the empirical data he had already collected on the snails in question: geographical origins, migratory history, different kinds of adaptation, and fossil species. Instead, he kept this material separate from taxonomic decisions; he justified this procedure by claiming, for example, that "the handling of varieties is more flexible than that of species" (1911, p. 320). Psychologically, the difference between simply identifying specimens and altering classification schemes is that the latter activity presupposes the capacity to both manipulate categories abstractly and to imagine possible alternative schemes.

The kind of implicative propositional reasoning that Piaget used represents formal operations. Thus, his rather abstract justification, and his exclusion of potentially useful empirical material, may indicate that the 15-year-old's power to think independently of concrete objects was being overexerted, as often happens at the onset of the formal-operational stage. However, Piaget's approach must also be seen as an expression of the nominalism then prevalent among naturalists. Nominalism, the belief that species (and, in general, taxonomic categories) are merely useful constructs having no corresponding reality in nature, was a basic way of understanding nature within the school of thought of natural history. Piaget's case is a good example of Pierre Bourdieu's observations in his studies of schooling: "words, and especially the figures of speech and figures of thought that are characteristic of a school of thought, mould thought as much as they express it" (1976, p. 196).

Piaget's 1912 articles show that as a 16-year-old, he had started to classify mollusks on the basis of inferences drawn between previously unconnected sets of information. Phylogenetic considerations, as well as geological and geographical materials, sometimes even provide the decisive elements of the 16-year-old naturalist's classifications. This increased integration within Piaget's work was not only the result of his entering a new cognitive stage by maturation, but also a product of his first efforts to integrate scientific and extra-scientific concerns—efforts related to the events that made 1912 a turning point in Piaget's development.

PIAGET, YOUNG BIOLOGIST

In his autobiography, Piaget relates that his first adolescent crisis had to do with religion. When he was about 15, his mother, a devout Protestant, sent him to religion classes. Piaget writes that, following his father's critical attitude, he attended the classes "in the spirit of free thinking," and was struck "by the difficulty of reconciling a number of dogmas with biology" (1952, p. 239). At that time, he "had the good luck" of finding the Protestant theologian Auguste Sabatier's *Philosophy of Religion* (1897). Sabatier's concept of dogmas as subjective symbols in constant evolution temporarily satisfied Piaget's need to reconcile science and religion and, furthermore, aroused his interest in philosophy. In understanding and paternal tones, Sabatier addressed his work to young people who were depicted as seeking, with all of youth's sincerity and idealism, a solution to the conflict between faith and science. He affirmed a deep faith, examined through calm introspection, and defended through critical history. Sabatier's exhortations to spiritual freedom, and his arguments, subtly oscillating between mysticism and science, strengthened and oriented the young Piaget's religious feelings. According to the recollection of Piaget's sister, the young scientist even thought of becoming a pastor at the time (interview with Mme. André Burger, *née* Piaget, in Geneva, during the summer of 1981).

Some time later, in the summer of 1912, the 16-year-old Piaget visited his godfather, the writer Samuel Cornut (1861–1918). Cornut was a "sweet and quiet man," a melancholic but enthusiastic dreamer who was always running after ideas and chimeras (Brenner, 1929, p. 11). He found the young naturalist too specialized and decided to teach him philosophy. "Between the gatherings of mollusks," Piaget remembered 40 years later, "he would teach me the 'creative evolution' of Bergson. . . . The shock was terrific, I must admit." He continues:

> First of all, it was an emotional shock. I recall one evening of profound revelation. The identification of God with life itself was an idea that stirred me almost to ecstasy because it now enabled me to see in biology the explanation of all things and of the mind itself. (1952, p. 240).

Piaget described the same experience as "a moment of enthusiasm close to ecstatic joy," after which he saw his zoological interests as providing him "with a small sector of study" of the universal process of creative evolution (1971, p. 5).

Between ages 16 to 18 (1912–1914), partly as a result of that experience, Piaget's identity changed. The naturalist turned into what can be described as a "Bergsonian biologist." He was a "biologist," because he was no longer concerned with classification in the naturalist tradition, but with life, evolution, and their mechanisms. He was "Bergsonian" for two reasons: First, because he adopted the French philosopher's critique of science. Bergson opposed life, which he identified with duration, evolution, and constant creation, to matter, which he considered an inert obstacle to the *élan vital*. Life can be known by intuition, the method of metaphysics that can apprehend movement, duration, and evolution as totalities, without segmenting them. Matter can be known by analysis, the method of science that must break the continuous flux of reality to represent and conceptualize it. Both Lamarckian and Darwinian biologies were examples of "mechanistic" science. As such, they were incapable of capturing the evolving and creative nature of life. Secondly, Piaget was Bergsonian because he also took up Bergson's view that the problem of life includes not only those of adaptation and evolution, but also those of matter, spirit, consciousness, intelligence, emotions, instinct, and knowledge.

Piaget worked his religious feelings into the affective and intellectual exaltation that derived from his relation to Bergson's philosophy. In high school, at about the age of 17, he met the philosopher Arnold Reymond—an admirable man, Piaget later remembered, for his unsurpassed quality to awaken consciences and vocations (1959, p. 44). Reymond became Piaget's guide. With his encouragement, the young scientist was able to publish an article that integrated Bergson and Sabatier into a view where religious and moral life belonged in creative evolution (1914a). Piaget's transformation into a Bergsonian biologist, however, was precipitated by an event that was harder for him to work into the new emotional and cognitive experiences than the newly discovered realm of philosophy.

In 1912, disagreements over the classification of certain species gave rise to a debate between Piaget and Waclaw Roszkowski, a Polish doctoral student at Lausanne. (For detailed reconstructions of the debate, see Vidal, 1981a and note 1. The relevant articles are: Roszkowski, 1912; Piaget, 1912a, 1913a, 1913b, 1913c; Roszkowski, 1913; Piaget, 1914b, 1914c; and Roszkowski, 1914). Unlike Piaget and most of his colleagues, Roszkowski was not a nominalist. He adopted the "mutation theory" of speciation (set forth in 1901–1903), according to which new species arise by the occurrence of a large-scale discontinuous variation, or "mutation," rather than by the prolonged natural selection of small continuous variations. Species are then defined by strictly hereditary traits of mutational origin.

Thus, Roszkowski countered the nominalist position by showing the possibility of determining such traits. He did so through the use of experimental methods alien to the naturalist tradition, and through the testing of Mendel's laws of heredity (rediscovered in 1900), which, at the time, were interpreted as laws of discontinuous variation.

To counter Roszkowski's empirical arguments, Piaget skillfully integrated much of the material that had remained uncoordinated in his earlier papers. Yet, in addition to representing adequate problem solving, Piaget's use of material expressed an emerging point of view that determined the way in which he formulated the problem and the strategy he chose to look for a solution. Piaget adopted a Bergsonian perspective to formulate the problem of the species; his theoretical alternative to Roszkowski's mutationism made direct use of Bergsonian concepts. In so doing, Piaget gave scientific content to philosophical ideas, and philosophical relevance to scientific issues. Such integration was catalyzed by the need to solve a concrete scientific problem, and by the crisis of encountering a technical and theoretical framework new to him, and one apparently incompatible with natural history. (The "knowledge crisis" that the overspecialized young naturalist began to experience during the debate, still echoed in his 1918 doctoral thesis; cf. 1921, *avant-propos*.) Nevertheless, Piaget could have chosen to respond to Roszkowski with a purely scientific discourse. Had he done so, he probably would have remained a naturalist. But the fact that his argument belonged essentially to philosophical biology manifests both a change in his interests and an effort to construct a personal point of view on the scientific and metaphysical problems that concerned him.

Indeed, Piaget's first attempt to relate Bergson's philosophy to the problems of natural history dates from shortly after his first exposure to *Creative Evolution*. In a lecture, given at the Club des Amis de la Nature on September 26, 1912, Piaget had already used Bergson's critique of science and view of life to argue for a radically nominalistic conception of systematics (note 2). By the end of the debate in 1914, he was defending not just a conception of the species, but a point of view on evolution and life that he was constructing independently from the problems raised by the debate (cf., for example, 1913d). By that time he had become a Bergsonian biologist and had rejected the possibility that a science of life could be either classificatory natural history or "mechanistic" biology.

The papers Piaget published between 1911 and 1914 reflect developments of his thought consistent with those he would describe years later in his own work on cognitive development. Thought is initially rather concrete, then overly abstract, before becoming increasingly adapted to its own objects by means of formal operations. Finally, through conscious integration, it starts creating systems, and becomes capable of examining them critically. But, as

Piaget's case suggests, these developments are dependent on many factors: the historical and discursive fields that determine their possible forms; creative efforts that make them go along branching paths of exploration and discovery; education, training, and guidance; and random and purposeful human contact. Moreover, their function is not merely problem solving. For example, the young Piaget's organization of knowledge bred a point of view that contributed to define his problems and his solutions and to regulate his life at large.

In 1914, Piaget's growing sense of purpose in constructing a point of view became temporarily dominated by his organization of affect. Testimony of the intricate union of knowledge, purpose, and affect in the development of his thought, is the 18-year-old's letter of resignation to the Club des Amis de la Nature. On September 25, 1915, he regretted not having contributed enough to friendship, which he called the "only objective" of the Club; and he added: "Do not cry 'blasphemous,' I do not scorn your science, our science (for I am still one of yours), I say that this science results from friendship, and not the other way around."

PIAGET, YOUNG METAPHYSICIAN AND THEOLOGIAN

It has been illustrated how Piaget changed from being a naturalist whose activity could be entirely defined within a scientific discourse focused on description and classification, to being a biologist whose activity, in contrast, could be defined only by reference to a nascent point of view including the great questions of life, philosophy, and religion. His assertion that science results from friendship implied that he felt he could be a scientist only insofar as he belonged in a moral and intellectual world somehow defined by friendship. By 1915, the object itself of the young Piaget's science started to acquire moral qualities. In turn, science itself, as a possible mode of knowledge, became superseded by metaphysics and theology as possible modes of affect.

Consider just some aspects of these transformations. The world in which Piaget began to elaborate his point of view on life was seemingly peaceful. People in Europe generally thought that the twentieth century was going to be a continuation of the good things of the nineteenth. With great innocence, they affirmed the inevitability of progress and the consequent unlikelihood of war. Yet a few days before Piaget's eighteenth birthday, World War broke out.

The convulsions generated in European culture by an unjustifiable struggle that ravaged a civilization, catalyzed the development of strong moral, social, and political concerns in Piaget. In 1916, at about age 20, he published a long prose poem, *The Mission of the Idea*.

In it, he expressed his indignation against what he saw as the causes of the ongoing war—conservative forces, nationalism, egoism, the bourgeois spirit—and affirmed his belief in justice, equality, people, Jesus, and socialism. In *Mission*, evolution appears as the progressive tendency of life to form increasingly larger units according to natural, primitive instincts of solidarity and altruism. Evolution is identical to morality, and opposite to the "struggle for life." Piaget's rejection of the Darwinian metaphor of "struggle," and of Darwinian evolutionary theory in general, had already taken place. Thus, the new moral significance of evolution came to reinforce a basic scientific and philosophical conviction of his Bergsonian biology.

Piaget's "moralized" conception of evolution not only contributed to unify his scientific and philosophical concerns but also expressed his emerging commitments concerning the self and its relation to the social and political world; his growing point of view on the great questions of science, philosophy, and life began to include a conception of, and a mission for, the self. Jean-Christophe, the hero created by the French writer Romain Rolland, became for Piaget the model of a young person and probably inspired the representation of youth elaborated in *Mission*. This elaboration of an image of the self was accompanied by commitments: Piaget was not afraid of choosing and affirming an unpopular "Rollandism" that later, in 1918, would give rise to bitter criticism from his teacher Reymond. As for many other young people, Rolland, a foremost pacifist and internationalist in a divided Europe, became for Piaget a sort of spiritual, moral, religious, and political guide. The 19-year-old Piaget sent Rolland a copy of *The Mission of the Idea*, and received from him, as he later wrote to Rolland, "a letter whose value I understood in many days of struggle when it supported me, when it was a precious link, because personal between your work and me" (Piaget, 1917). At the same time, he felt that the adoption of a political and moral faith demanded concrete action.

In *Mission*, Piaget affirmed that human beings must combine faith in progressive and moral evolution with efforts to realize it. But he did not think that faith could be blind. On the contrary, faith should be enlightened by a conscientious search for truth, which, for the author of *Mission*, could be carried out by means of metaphysics and speculation. Thus, Piaget's formation of commitments, related to his reflection on the self, was worked into concrete intellectual projects. The organizations of knowledge and affect came to join the organization of purpose. In 1916, for example, the Société Académique of Neuchâtel awarded Piaget a prize for a never published paper in which he presented the first version of his theory of equilibration. According to Arnold Reymond's recollection (1950, p. 153), its motto was "the ideal is nothing other than the law of reality." Reymond also recalled that the Société jury, to which he belonged, praised the 20-

year-old Piaget for his knowledge, his maturity of thought, his power of synthesis despite the diversity of subjects approached (zoology, morality, aesthetics, religion), and also congratulated him for the boldness of his attempt.

That work was still centered around the problem of nominalism versus realism that had worried the young naturalist and was carried out in the speculative mode accepted in *Mission*. It is not surprising, however, that someone socialized very early into a positivistic view of science would feel that doing and thinking must be in some sense scientific if they are to lead to concrete, effective, and firmly grounded action. In *Mission*, Piaget set forth his belief, for the first time, in the possibility of the unity of evolution, life, and morality. When he first tackled the question in his 1916 prize-winning paper, he seems to have done so according to modes of thinking and feeling in which he felt trapped against his will. Thus, in the letter to Rolland previously cited, Piaget (who was about to turn 21) wrote:

> Everyone is a metaphysician at eighteen and, in addition, a theologian if one is French Swiss. But I believe I have gotten rid of all that, I have been trying for two years. . . . [T]he great problem is to base morality on science, because faith is independent from metaphysics, and because metaphysics is vain, and it is the problem that makes up my life.

Clearly, Piaget's cognitive decision to reject metaphysics and theology as modes of knowledge was not separate from the elaboration of an image of youth and of science. These images helped Piaget orient his purpose toward formulating methods and goals for basing morality on science.

What was the form of his cognitive decision? On the one hand, it seems to reflect the emergence of metasystematic operations. Piaget had compared the "speculative" system elaborated by 1916 both to *Mission* and to an ideal "scientific" system. Then, under the light of the comparison, he reformulated it. These cognitive events may indicate an increased capacity to decenter and delineate the approaching end of adolescent thought. Piaget's formulation of a project represents the onset of "youth," similar to Tolstoi's character Nikolas Irteniev, whose youth started the day he had the "moral revelation" that he should not waste any more time speculating, but apply to his concrete life the great ideas that filled his mind.

On the other hand, these representations, like the ones of today's psychologists and sociologists, both reflected and inspired Piaget. In addition, the normative character of his self-image was particularly strong at a time and place in which his professional, religious, and political commitments were often united in a single passion for or against a particular cause. What may appear as a decision made possible by the spontaneous development of cognitive structures was not independent of the expression of historical events in Piaget's immediate environment. Nor was it separate from the development of his personality as a whole. It included the choice of commitments, principles, and models. As Piaget told Rolland, "faith is the decision to live in spite of the mystery that is at the bottom of everything." But Piaget's faith is not the competence needed to perform the act of living. This faith and living are a unity constitutive of the interplay between Piaget's changing organizations of knowledge, purpose, and affect. This interplay is usually split into competence and performance, into the spontaneous and the nonspontaneous. Yet, as Vygostsky (1962, ch. 6) has illustrated, the barrier between development and action must collapse when the specificity of experiences is taken into account. It also must collapse when the subject is defined only within a context. It also must be in relation to a subject's zone of proximal development.

CONCLUSION

In his 1917 letter to Rolland, Piaget said that he thought he solved the problem of basing morality on science and that he was working at supporting his solution. Indeed, he had already finished *Recherche* (1918a), the 210-page volume that opens the realization of his enterprise. *Recherche*, meaning both "search" and "research," is a spiritual self-portrait in the form of a novel. Its subject matter is the development of a young man, Sébastien. After being contented for a while with a more or less vague evolutionary philosophy, Sébastien enters a crisis that coincides with that of the world around him. He emerges from the crisis disappointed with metaphysics, but with a renewed faith in science. He is a biologist, and the laws of biology provide him with the starting point from which to build the system relating evolution, knowledge, and morality that is set forth in his *Bildungsroman*.

Recherche is the most patent example of the materialization of a personality in the fulfillment of a task found in Piaget's writings. For example, Sébastien affirmed that science would, by describing evolution in detail, discover that "the good is life itself" (p. 173) and thus provide the foundations for "a morality of altriusm corresponding to the highest aspirations of human conscience" (p. 174). Although, in his opinion, a scientific morality had not yet been established (p. 193), Sébastien believed that its results could only confirm the Christian morality that, by itself, individual conscience would have adopted (p. 182). The laws of equilibration that regulate all vital, social, and moral phenomena were determined by an ideal equilibrium that implied an altruistic morality. Since *Recherche,* a large part of Piaget's work was regulated by a mode of inquiry whereby an ideal equilibrium that was postulated on the basis of moral and philosophical convictions would determine the real disequilibria that science can discover. With the last article that Piaget wrote before turning to psychology, "Biology and War" (1918b), the organizations of knowledge, purpose, and affect attained maximal consistency. It was only later that they started to acquire the specificity that has led readers and commentators to believe that Piaget turned to psychology only to verify a theory about the relations between biology and knowledge (cf. Vidal, note 3).

It is clear that Piaget's development as traced here confirms the idea that there is much growth beyond formal operations. Yet, the syntheses and integrations that in part characterize such growth are neither purely maturational events nor problem-solving adaptations. They emerge from a unity of doing, being, and thinking, and from the interplay between a person's organizations of knowledge, purpose, and affect. Moreover, these processes take place, as Erikson says, when an individual "intersects with history" through activities in an immediate environment made up of, for example, family, friends, teachers, school, and place of residence. The milieu establishes the field of possibilities and conditions where a purposeful person may open diversified and nonlinear paths. An attitude toward the self should be added to the need for circumstance and intention. From the individual, in turn, one must go back to the world. Each person's image of the developing self is partially inspired by those representations of the self that are an integral part of the individual's culture. Emblematic of this is the way in which Piaget described himself in his 1917 letter to Rolland: "I am just a good young man who takes himself seriously."

NOTE

1. In *Procès-verbaux* of the Club, June 9, 1910. I take the opportunity to thank Mr. Gaston Rod, first Secretary of Public Works of Neuchâtel, who helped me trace the Club des Amis de la Nature in that city, and Dr. Paul Ducommun, guardian of the Club's papers, who kindly facilitated my access to all of the unpublished Club documents cited here.

PART II
INDUCTIVELY DERIVED MODELS

3

THE DEVELOPMENT OF ABSTRACTIONS IN ADOLESCENCE AND ADULTHOOD

Kurt W. Fischer, Helen H. Hand, Sheryl Russell

Twelve-year-old thought is not yet fully formed. Dramatic developmental reorganizations continue beyond the age when Piagetian formal operations are said to have emerged (Inhelder & Piaget, 1955/1958). The change at 10 to 12 years that has been termed "formal operations" is not an end but a beginning. It marks the start of the development of abstract thinking (Fischer, 1980).

At around ten years of age, children become able to understand single abstractions, an ability that brings with it enormous cognitive advances but that still has important limitations. Adolescents and young adults gradually overcome these limitations as they progress through three additional developmental levels involving the progressive coordination of abstractions in more and more complex relations. At the final level, which first appears at approximately 25 years of age, clusters of abstract relations can be integrated into general principles, such as the principle of evolution by natural selection, or a principle for making moral judgments within diverse contexts and cultures.

Preparation of this chapter was supported by a grant from the Spencer Foundation and the Carnegie corporation of New York. The statements made and views expressed are solely the responsibility of the authors. The authors would like to thank Michael Bender, Daniel Bullock, Howard E. Gruber, Susan Harter, Sybillyn Jennings, Arlyne Lazerson, Marilyn Pelot, Sandra Pipp, and David G. Thomas for their contributions to various phases of this work. We would also like to thank Dr. Ingemar Petersen for sending us EEG data collected in his laboratory and allowing us to present some of it here (Figure 3-2). Finally we would like to express our appreciation to James VanderMeulen, Eldon Dyk, and the teachers and students of the Denver Christian Schools for their participation in some of the research reported here.

The manner in which these four successive reorganizations occur differs sharply from the classical conception of stage (Fischer & Bullock, 1981). Only the individual's best performances, his or her optimal level, show consistently stagelike change. Across task domains, development progresses unevenly. The detection of the emergence of each new optimal level requires a special set of methods that take account of this unevenness. With these methods each new level can be shown to produce a cluster of developmental spurts in optimal performance across many domains.

Although optimal performance may demonstrate developmental levels, most behavior is not optimal and does not clearly demonstrate levels. In everyday life adults typically function below their optimal level. Careful task analyses are necessary to detect this lower-level functioning because people are adept at simplifying complex tasks so as to produce a superficially adequate solution with a lower-level skill.

A THEORY OF THE DEVELOPMENT OF ABSTRACT SKILLS

According to the approach presented here, called skill theory, the organization of behavior undergoes massive restructuring during adolescence and early adulthood: The individual gradually moves from being limited to the concrete toward an ability to organize concrete experiences into abstract categories and relations. The implications of that change are at least as important for social behavior and emotions as they are for cognitions about the physical world.

This restructuring of behavior into abstractions is only one of several massive restructurings, called *tiers*, predicted by skill theory. For each tier, an individual's skills develop through four successive levels, as in the geometric metaphor shown in Figure 3.1. The first level involves a single set of some sort, such as an abstraction, represented by the single dot at the top of the figure. The second level relates two or more such sets into what is called a mapping. At the third level, several mappings are coordinated to form a system. And, finally, the fourth level requires the combination of two or more systems to form a new type of set, which like the cube in Figure 3.1 provides a building block that can begin the cycle again. Several converging lines of evidence support the existence of these hypothesized tiers and levels (Fischer, 1980; Fischer & Pipp, in press, in preparation; Hand, 1981a).

In addition to this general outline of the large changes in development, skill theory is designed to deal with three of the important specifics of development. First, it provides a set of transformation rules for predicting particular developmental se-

LEVEL

I

II

III

IV

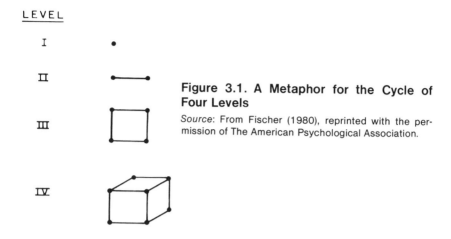

Figure 3.1. A Metaphor for the Cycle of Four Levels

Source: From Fischer (1980), reprinted with the permission of The American Psychological Association.

quences in detail (Fischer, 1980). Second, it supplies procedures for dealing with the effects of environmental factors and for analyzing the influences of the tasks posed to the individual (Fischer, 1980; Fischer & Corrigan, 1981). And finally, it suggests methods and techniques of measurement for analyzing both the particulars and the generalities of psychological development (Fischer & Bullock, 1981; Fischer, Pipp, & Bullock, in press). Together, these several components of skill theory characterize the properties of the developing human information-processing system.

With these rules, procedures, and methods, skill theory provides a general tool for making detailed predictions of not only developmental sequences within domains but also developmental synchronies across domains. Thus far a number of predictions about both macrodevelopment (large-scale changes) and microdevelopment (small-scale changes) have been tested and strongly supported (Bertenthal & Fischer, 1978; Bertenthal & Fisher, in press; Fischer & Bullock, 1981; Fischer & Corrigan, 1981; Fischer, Hand, Watson, Van Parys, & Tucker, in press; Fischer & Pipp, in press; note 4; Fischer & Roberts, 1982; Hand, 1981a, 1981b; Hand & Fischer, note 5; Van Parys, note 6; Watson, 1981).[1]

In the remainder of this chapter, the main emphasis will be on the developmental levels of abstractions, and so a point about skill theory's general portrait of development needs to be stressed. The levels are not stages in the classical sense. As such, they do not imply that development proceeds uniformly across all or most behavioral domains or contexts. On the contrary, décalage or unevenness across domains is the rule in development (Biggs & Collis, 1982; Fischer, 1980; Kuhn & Phelps, 1982). Only under special circumstances do individuals show synchronous emergence of a new developmental level in many domains. Because people always acquire specific skills tied to particular environmental circumstances, context always plays an enormous role in developing behavior. Cognitive-developmental researchers need to go beyond acknowledging the importance of the environment and to begin to analyze the interaction of organism and environment in development. Skill theory is designed to facilitate such analysis.

PSYCHOLOGICAL DEVELOPMENTAL LEVELS

The focus of this chapter is on the understanding and use of abstractions. To provide a full portrait of the development of abstractions, Levels 6 through 10 will be described (see Table 3.1). For those levels, continuing examples will be used from two studies done at the Cognitive Development Laboratory at the University of Denver, as outlined in Table 3.2. The first is a study of the development of concepts of intention and responsibility (Hand & Fischer, 1981, note 5). The second is a study of the development of the arithmetic operations of addition, subtraction, multiplication, and division for positive whole numbers (Russell & Fischer, 1982, note 7).

Analysis of the level of a task requires careful consideration of the structure of the behavior elicited by that task. Many tasks evoke diverse behaviors, and so they cannot be said to assess one specific skill. Tasks first need to be designed so that they elicit one predominant type of behavior. Then task analysis can be used to determine the structure of that behavior.

In skill theory, all skill structures are defined in terms of sources of variation, termed "sets," and relations between those sets. A task analysis must therefore specify which sets and relations the person must control in order to perform the task. For example, in a task that requires relating the operations of addition and subtraction, the person must control the concept of addition, the concept of subtraction, and the relation between those two concepts. This meaning of skill is similar to the behaviorist notion of an operant, in which the organism controls a set of behaviors within a specific operant class (Skinner, 1969). It is also similar to the information-processing concept of a production system, in which a person or a computer controls a set of program statements relating to input and output (Klahr & Wallace, 1976).

The tasks outlined in Table 3.2 were all subjected to task analysis within the skill-theory framework, and all involve relatively pure tests of the levels for which they were designed. More detailed descriptions of the tasks are available from the authors (Hand & Fischer, 1981; Russell & Fischer, 1982).

Table 3.1. Seven Cognitive Levels of Representations and Abstractions

Level	Name of Structure	Representational Sets[a]	Abstract Sets
4	Single representations	[R] or [T]	
5	Representational mappings	[R———T]	
6	Representational systems	$[R_{j,k} \leftrightarrow T_{j,f}]$	
7	Systems of representational systems, which are single abstractions	$\begin{bmatrix} R \leftrightarrow T \\ \updownarrow \\ V \leftrightarrow X \end{bmatrix} \equiv$	$[\mathscr{E}]$
8	Abstract mappings		$[\mathscr{E}———\mathscr{F}]$
9	Abstract systems		$[\mathscr{E}_{A,B} \leftrightarrow \mathscr{F}_{A,B}]$
10	Systems of abstract systems, which are single principles		$\begin{bmatrix} \mathscr{E} \leftrightarrow \mathscr{F} \\ \updownarrow \\ \mathscr{G} \leftrightarrow \mathscr{H} \end{bmatrix}$

[a]The structures of representational sets for Levels 8 to 10 have been omitted because the formulas become complex and bulky, but the representational sets can be filled in by substituting the representational structure of Level 7 for each of the abstract sets at Levels 8, 9, and 10.

Note: Plain capital letters designate representational sets. Script capital letters designate abstract sets. Subscripts designate differentiated components of the respective set. Long straight lines and arrows designate a relation between sets or systems. Brackets designate a single skill.

According to skill theory, individuals develop through at least three tiers. These tiers are sensorimotor actions, representations, and abstractions. Each tier involves four successive developmental levels, as shown in Figure 3.1 and Table 3.1. The levels of sensorimotor actions first develop in infancy. The levels of representations develop throughout most of childhood. Abstractions first emerge shortly before adolescence and continue to develop into adolescence and adulthood. Although they are built upon representations, they are a new, more powerful type of skill structure. Representations designate concrete characteristics of particular objects, people, or events, whereas abstractions designate general, intangible characteristics of broad categories of objects, people, or events. One representation for subtraction, for example, is a specific arithmetic problem, such as $16 - 9 = 7$. One abstraction for subtraction involves a general definition of the operation and application of that definition to a specific arithmetic problem, as illustrated in Table 3.2.

Level 6 representational systems first emerge at about age 6 in most middle-class children, and they are extended and consolidated during

Sounds like they use "abstraction"
the way some people use "concept",
or even "symbol".

Table 3.2. Examples of Each Cognitive Level

Level	Characteristic Structure	Examples from Arithmetic Study	Examples from Study of Intention and Responsibility
6	Representational systems: coordinations of several aspects of two or more representations	Calculation and explanation of concrete arithmetic problems $9 + 7 = 16$ $3 \times 8 = 24$	Concrete instances of intention or responsibility In a concrete story involving two characters, the specific mean actions and nice intentions of one individual toward a second are compared to the specific nice actions and mean intentions of the second individual toward the first.[b] Compounded concrete instance of intention and responsibility In a concrete story involving three characters, the specific nice actions and mean intentions of one individual toward the other two are compared to the specific mean actions and nice intentions of the other two characters toward the first.[b]
7	Single abstractions (which are systems of representational systems): coordinations of two or more systems to form an intangible category.	General definitions of arithmetic operations "Subtraction is when you take one number away from another number, and you end up with a smaller number called the difference."[a]	General definitions of intention or responsibility The concrete actions and intentions of two individuals are not merely compared but are integrated under a single abstraction, such as "Intentions matter more than actions."[b] Shift of focus from a general definition of intention to a general definition of responsibility The concrete actions and intentions of two individuals are not merely compared but are integrated under a single abstraction, such as "Taking responsibility means a person shows she really cares about the effects her actions have on other people." The abstractions of intention and responsibility are not integrated in any way, but are simply linked together temporally.

| 8 | Abstract mappings: coordinations of two or more abstractions in a simple relation | General relations of two similar arithmetic operations

"Addition and multiplication are similar operations. Both combine numbers to produce a larger number, but the numbers are combined in different ways—by single units in addition and by groups of numbers in multiplication. Multiplication is really addition repeated a specific number of times."[a] | General relations of intention and responsibility

The individual relates the concept of intention to the concept of responsibility to explain what it is about taking responsibility that absolves one of having shown a negative intention towards another person.

Compounded general relations between intention and responsibility

In the context of harm inflicted upon someone, harmful intention is related to two types of responsibility (dealing with the flaw in one's character and being concerned for the person harmed). |
| 9 | Abstract systems: coordinations of several aspects of two or more abstractions in a complex relation | General relations of two dissimilar arithmetic operations

"Addition and division are opposite operations in two ways. Addition increases by single units, while division decreases by groups of units. The fact that one increases and the other decreases is one way addition and division differ, and the manner in which they increase or decrease by units or groups is the other way they differ. Repeated addition might be used to express a division problem like $32 \div 8 = 4$. Eight added four times yields 32, so we know there are four eights in 32."[a] | General relations of several types of intention and responsibility

In the context of harm inflicted upon someone, two types of intention (deceit and unintentional harm) are related to two types of responsibility (dealing with the flaw in one's character and being concerned for the person harmed). The two types of intention require that one take different types of responsibility. |

(continued on page 50)

49

Table 3.2 *(cont.)*

Level	Characteristic Structure	Examples from Arithmetic Study	Examples from Study of Intention and Responsibility
10	Single principles (which are systems of abstract systems): coordinations of two or more systems to form an overarching framework or theory	Principle unifying the four arithmetic operations "Addition, subtraction, multiplication, and division are all operations, which means that they all transform by either combining or separating numbers and doing so either in groups or one number at a time. There are relationships between all possible pairs of operations. Some pairs are closely related, and others are more distantly related . . . (Elaboration explaining the pairs, as diagramed in the table below)."[a]	Principle unifying various types of intention and responsibility (This level has not yet been investigated for intention and responsibility.)

	Unit	Group
Increase	Addition	Multiplication
Decrease	Subtraction	Division

[a] In each of these cases, the person can not only give the definition but also apply it appropriately to specific arithmetic problems, as illustrated for Level 9.

[b] The example is for intention only, not for responsibility.

Note: The table is based on studies by Russell and Fischer (note 7) and Hand and Fischer (note 5). The arithmetic concepts deal with positive whole numbers only.

(6)

the grade-school years. At this level, children can relate two differentiated aspects of at least two representations, as shown in Table 3.1. For example, they can represent two people interacting in terms of two intersecting concrete social categories, such as nice and mean. Two children playing together can show both nice and mean behavior simultaneously, as when one child says he wants to be the other's friend but simultaneously pushes him, and the other child responds with appropriate nice and mean behaviors. With a Level 6 skill, the individual can understand two people interacting with each other in such complex combinations of concrete categories (Fischer, Hand, et al., in press; Hand, 1981a; Harter, in press(a)). The intersection of the categories of nice and mean gives rise to a precursor of an abstraction, such as differentiation between nice intention and mean action in a real social interaction (Hand & Fischer, note 5). While these interactions can become complex, they are always founded on tangible social categories and relations.

As early as 10 or 11 years of age, preadolescents can begin to control their first *Level 7 single abstractions*, such as the arithmetic concepts of addition or subtraction or the interactional concepts of intention or responsibility. These types of abstractions are described in Table 3.2. Other single abstractions include personality descriptions such as conformity or hypocrisy (Rosenberg, 1979) and sociomoral concepts such as law, society, or justice (e.g., Adelson, 1975; Broughton, 1978; Lee, 1971; Selman, 1980). With this new ability, preadolescents can start to understand abstract concepts as they are used by adults.

Single abstractions overcome important limitations of Level 6 representational systems by coordinating several systems around a single general concept or relation. Thus, they constitute the culmination of development in the representational tier. At the same time, they initiate the development of abstract skills, and, consequently, they are only the most primitive form of abstraction. One reflection of this primitiveness is that with single abstractions, individuals have difficulty differentiating two similar abstract concepts, such as liberal and radical in politics, or addition and multiplication in arithmetic. For example, at Level 7 many people say, "Addition and multiplication are the same thing. Both combine numbers to make a bigger number."

Early abstractions tend therefore to be confused and poorly articulated. One adolescent described them as being "like a fog." To differentiate two abstractions, a person must have the capacity to compare them, which requires later developmental levels. It is important to note, however, that with Level 7 skills the person is able to compare two concrete instances of concepts, as explained later in the section on simplifications.

Not until approximately age 14 or 15 can adolescents first

coordinate two or more abstractions in a single skill, a *Level 8 abstract mapping*. Consequently, they can compare and relate abstractions, and the early fog of concepts from Level 7 begins to lift. Individuals can understand, for example, how multiplication is similar to addition without confusing the two operations. Instead of saying that addition and multiplication are the same, as is common at Level 7, they explain how the operations are similar but different, as shown in the example in Table 3.2. Level 8 mappings produce not only new cognitive clarifications, but also new social capacities. These new capacities include the ability to coordinate parts of one's own identity with parts of someone else's in an intimate relationship (Fischer, 1980, p. 496; Harter, in press (b); Selman, 1980), the ability to differentiate and relate intention and responsibility (Table 3.2), and an initial, primitive understanding of the relativity of knowledge (Broughton, 1978; Jaques, Gibson, & Isaac, 1978; Kitchener & King, 1981; Perry, 1970). Although comparatively little research has focused on this developmental change, several studies do suggest that such a change may be occurring in performance on cognitive tasks at this age period (see, for example, Biggs & Collis, 1982; Inhelder & Piaget, 1955, 1958; Martarano, 1977; McCall, Applebaum, & Hogarty, 1973; Neimark, 1975; Tomlinson-Keasey, 1982).

A few years later, probably at age 18 or 19 on the average, people start to be able to coordinate several aspects of two or more abstractions in *Level 9 abstract systems*. Thus, they are able to understand the subtleties and complexities of relations between abstractions. With such skills, the social-cognitive fog dissipates completely. Individuals can understand the relations between dissimilar or distant arithmetic operations, such as division and addition (see Table 3.2). Similarly, they can understand the relations between several types of intention and several types of responsibility as required, for example, in the U.S. legal system. Many other major changes in thinking that have been suggested for this age period also involve systematic, complex relations among abstractions. These include understanding the relativity of knowledge (Broughton, 1978; Jacques et al., 1978; Kitchener & King, 1981; Perry, 1970), the dialectical nature of particular social or epistemological domains (Basseches, 1980, Chapter 10, this volume), the social contract (Broughton, 1978; Kohlberg, 1969; Rest, 1976; Selman, 1980), and the systematic nature of logical and arithmetic analyses (Commons, Richards & Kuhn, 1982; Richards & Commons, Chapter 5, this volume; Jacques et al., 1978; O'Brien & Overton, 1982). Indeed, most of the empirical work in this volume deals in part with this developmental level.

One final reorganization is predicted, as shown in Table 3.1. Starting at approximately 25 years of age, individuals can begin to integrate abstract systems to form *Level 10 general principles*, such as those involved in many general ideologies (Broughton, 1978;

Kitchener & King, 1981), and in scientific theories such as Darwin's analysis of evolution by natural selection (Gruber, 1981, Chapter 1, this volume). With this attainment, and with the requisite environmental support or stimulation, individuals can presumably construct a fully mature organization of identity, morality, or political ideology. Most of the highest levels posited by various theorists in this volume seem to require Level 10 skills.

It is possible that there are additional cognitive-developmental levels after Level 10 principles, as posited by Commons, et al., 1982 and Richards and Commons (Chapter 5, this volume). Following the geometric metaphor in Figure 3.1, for instance, another tier could be predicted using Level 10 principles as a new building block and moving through three more levels. As such, there could be mappings of principles, systems of principles, and systems of systems of principles. The hypothesis presented here, however, is that the emergence of Level 10 principles marks the end of cognitive-develomental change involving new developmental levels. Later developmental changes may be substantial, but they probably involve the application, elaboration, and extension of abstract skills to new domains, with no new developmental levels emerging. It is important not to underemphasize the importance of such elaborations and extensions, however. One of the characteristics of skills at the higher levels of abstractions seems to be that people need large amounts of time to consolidate and generalize them. This will be described more fully in the subsequent section entitled "Levels of abstractions in spontaneous behavior."

Abstractions are already so far removed from actions in the real world that further developmental levels might well be not merely useless but maladaptive. This removal from actions in the world is one of the most serious potential limitations of abstractions. High-level abstractions clearly can have enormous power in integrating and interpreting widely divergent observations and behaviors. But when not securely anchored to observations and other actions, they can be readily abused, or they can turn into relatively arbitrary, untestable categories and relations. Individuals can easily generalize them from the situations in which they were constructed to other, dissimilar situations, where they can be loosely and carelessly applied. This problem may be especially serious when the abstractions are shared by a social group that supports overgeneralization, as in various cultures and ideologies. One of the reasons that science has proved to be so powerful may be that it requires the careful, methodical anchoring of abstractions to specific sensory-motor actions (observations and experiments), which must be repeatable by other scientists. In this way, science can keep the power of abstractions while reducing or eliminating their looseness, specifically their distance from feedback based on actions in the world. *one heavy paragraph*

Two Kinds of Developmental Processes

Skill theory defines two types of processes that account for structural-developmental change. These are optimal-level processes and skill-acquisition processes.

Optimal Level

Processes based on optimal level account for most *macro*-development, the big changes in development. There is an upper limit on the complexity of skill that an individual can control, called the optimal level, and that limit shifts systematically upward with development.[2]

Increases in optimal level with age are not linear or monotonic, however. As a new developmental level emerges, the individual's optimal level shows a spurt. The individual goes through rapid change in many behaviors and also apparently in certain brain functions, such as the electroencephalogram, or EEG (Epstein, 1980; Fischer & Pipp, in preparation, note 4; Matousek & Petersen, 1973). Global measures of EEG demonstrate age-related spurts for Levels 6, 7, 8, and 9, as shown in Figure 3.2. Data have not yet been obtained to test for an EEG spurt at Level 10.

Skill Acquisition

Shifts in optimal level do not produce automatic changes in all of an individual's skills, however. The optimal level is merely the person's highest capacity, the most complex type of skill that he or she is capable of constructing and controlling. Actual developmental changes in particular skills require processes of skill acquisition, in which the person combines and differentiates more elementary skills to produce more advanced skills. Thus, each individual skill must be constructed separately, and optimal level merely limits the most complex type of skill that a person can construct.

The processes of skill acquisition are described by a set of transformation rules that specify how simpler skills can be combined to form more complex ones. These transformations can be thought of as rewrite rules, indicating how a structural description of the simpler skills must be rewritten to form the more complex ones. Most of the transformation rules describe *micro*development, how skills at one level can recombine to form more complex skills at the same level.[3]

Consider a hypothetical 11-year-old girl who is in the midst of the emergence of optimal Level 7 single abstractions. Her new optimal level allows her to coordinate two specific, concrete arithmetic

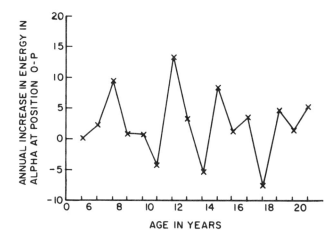

Figure 3.2. Increase in Percentage of Energy in Alpha Waves as a Function of Age

Note: The EEG was measured in the occipital-parietal area, and the percentage of energy was calculated by dividing the amount of energy in alpha waves by the total amount of energy in all waves.

Source: Data from Matousek & Petersen, 1973.

problems, such as $9 - 7 = 2$ and $15 - 5 = 10$, to form an abstract skill for subtraction. At first, her abstraction will be limited to those two particular problems, but typically she will work to extend it to additional problems (see Lawler, 1981; MacWhinney, 1978, for instances of this process at other levels).

Two of several possible types of extension are described by the transformation rules (a) shift of focus, and (b) compounding. In shift of focus, the girl can shift from coordinating $9 - 7 = 2$ and $15 - 5 = 10$ to coordinating a pair involving one of the original problems plus a new one, such as $9 - 7 = 2$ and $17 - 6 = 11$. With this transformation, she has extended her concept to one additional subtraction problem, but she still cannnot coordinate all three problems at the same time.

The transformation rule of compounding allows her to coordinate all three problems, $9 - 7 = 2$, $15 - 5 = 10$, and $17 - 6 = 11$, into a single abstraction based on three instances. Now she can treat all three specific problems as instances of the same concept of subtraction without being limited to dealing only with two problems at a time. Gradually she uses various skill-acquisition processes to extend her concept to a large number of specific problems. In this way she constructs a generalized, differentiated concept of subtraction, which she can apply to most simple subtraction problems.

She cannot relate two abstractions, however. Such a relation requires an optimal level of at least Level 8 abstract mappings. So long as she is limited to Level 7, the best that she can do with the relation of subtraction to addition, for example, is to simplify the coordination into a relation of a specific subtraction problem with a specific addition problem, such as $9 - 7 = 2$ and $7 + 2 = 9$. If she has abstractions for both subtraction and addition, she might also use the transformation rule for shift of focus. As such she may first define subtraction and then shift to defining addition, but never actually relate the two concepts. For a further discussion of this phenomenon see the discussion of types of simplifications that follows.

As implied in this analysis of the girl's behavior, the results of the microdevelopmental transformations produce an ordering that predicts a detailed developmental sequence. With the 11-year-old, the sequence implied in the previous description includes the following steps:

Isn't she already exhibiting the skill by working problems—ie, has the skill but not yet able to articulate it? Concept vs. skill? no, more like abstracting a definition of the skill being one step beyond having the skill itself.

1. calculation of several concrete arithmetic problems (Level 6 representational systems);
2. intercoordination of two specific problems to form the first abstract skill for subtraction (a beginning level 7 single abstraction) or to relate a specific subtraction problem to a specific addition problem;
3. shift of focus from one pair of subtraction problems to a second pair, both involving the concept of subtraction;
4. compounding of three subtraction problems involving the concept of subtraction; and
5. shift of focus from defining subtraction to defining addition.

Skill theory provides tools for predicting many such sequences in detail.

A Mind Both Unified and Fractionated

In the study of development, theories seem typically to embody a pair of correlated dichotomies, such as "Does develement occur in stages, or does it show unevenness (décalage)?," or "Is intelligence fractionated or unified?" Many theorists, especially in behaviorism (for example, Skinner, 1969) and information processing (for example, Klahr & Wallace, 1976), argue both that unevenness or décalage is the rule in development and that intelligence is a conglomeration of a million distinct operants or production systems or conscious and unconscious impulses. At the other pole, many theorists, predominantly within the cognitive-developmental and rationalist perspectives, argue both that developmental change is stagelike, with the person showing consistent performance at the same stage across many domains and that intelligence is unified or integrated. The best known example of this latter view is Piaget's (1957) position that development shows *structures d'ensemble* (structures of the whole, or structured wholes), in which the individual's many schemes form a single coherent logical system (see also Broughton, 1981).

The problem with these polar oppositions is that nature does not honor such human dichotomies (Newell, 1973). Intelligence is both fractionated and unified, and its development is both uneven and stagelike, as shown by enormous numbers of studies supporting both sides of the argument (see reviews by Fischer, 1980; Fischer & Pipp, in press; Favell, 1982). What is needed is a framework that explains and predicts the various ways that intelligence can be both uneven and stagelike, both fractionated and unified.

Skill theory attempts to do exactly that. It specifies, for instance, that skill acquisition begins with separate skills limited to specific contexts, which produces fractionation. It then explains how the person generalizes and differentiates those skills through micro-developmental processes so that they become much more general and integrated. The example of the 11-year-old girl constructing a concept of subtraction illustrates how skill acquisition can move from fractionation toward unification. Also, skill theory specifies how psychological development is both uneven and stagelike. To elaborate this second point, it is important first to discuss how developmental sequences and levels can be predicted and detected.

THE DETECTION OF DEVELOPMENTAL SEQUENCES AND LEVELS

Together, the levels and transformation rules in skill theory provide a basis for predicting developmental sequences and synchronies in psychological development. Note, however, that the nature of the predicted sequences and synchronies is different in important ways from those predicted by traditional theories of cognitive development. According to skill theory, all psychological development involves systematic changes in the organization of skills, which are defined transactionally (Sameroff, 1975) in terms of both the specific activities of the child and the particular objects or events to which the activities are applied. That is, all skills are defined jointly in terms of both organism and environment.

Developmental Unevenness

One major implication of the transactional approach is that skill acquisition (microdevelopment) is relatively context-specific. Consequently, skills in different domains will normally not develop in close synchrony. As such, they will not show the sort of stagelike change required by Piaget's (1957) structure of the whole. Adolescents and adults will perform at different levels for different skills because of variations in both their prior experience and the task's difficulty. For example, English majors' experience with literature will typically lead them to show advanced performance in criticism, or in other analyses of literature, but not in physics (DeLisi & Staudt, 1980). And adolescents' "ability" to do algebra will depend fundamentally on the complexity of the tasks they are faced with, such as as whether the problems include complex fractions (Karplus, Pulos, & Stage, 1982). Developmental unevenness is therefore the rule, as demonstrated by many studies (see Biggs & Collis, 1982; Fischer & Bullock, 1981; Flavell, 1971, 1977; Jackson et al., 1978).

Experiences during adolescence and adulthood may encourage uneven development even more than experiences during infancy and childhood (Flavell, 1970; Neimark, 1975; Piaget, 1972; Rest, note 8). In industrial cultures, for example, all grade-school children are exposed to arithmetic concepts in school. However, the diversity of schooling experiences increases in adolescence and adulthood, depending on the particular aspirations, abilities, and social situations of each individual. Consequently, there should be even less synchrony across skills for adolescents and adults than for children.

Stagelike Properties

The prevalence of unevenness does not preclude the existence of stagelike change, however. Under certain conditions, a developmental level will produce both developmental synchronies and stagelike spurts, according to skill theory.

Synchronies

A global type of synchrony can occur in a wide sample of skills, such as those assessed on the most comprehensive intelligence tests. Across such a large sample, individuals show variations in the degree of synchrony as a function of the time of emergence of a new optimal level. When first developing an optimal level, they demonstrate a period of relatively low synchrony because they have had the time to construct skills at the new level in only a few domains. Once they have consolidated a number of skills at that level, they will show relatively high synchrony across many skills. The synchrony will be of only moderate magnitude, however.

For the sensory-motor levels of infancy, research clearly supports this prediction of systematic variations in synchrony (Fischer, 1982; McCall, Eichorn, & Hogarty, 1977). There are also several studies that suggest such changes in synchrony for Levels 6, 7, and 8 in childhood and adolescence (Epstein, 1974; Kuhn, 1976; McCall, Applebaum, & Hogarty, 1973). It appears as though no analyses have been published that provide tests of the hypothesis for other levels.

A second type of synchrony depends upon practice. For skills in two domains to show a high degree of developmental synchrony, the person must be performing at his or her optimal level in both domains. One way to increase the likelihood of optimal performance is to provide extensive practice in both domains. Then a high degree of synchrony can be expected across domains, as has been found in a few studies (for example, Corrigan, in press; Jackson et al., 1978).

Of course these are only two types of synchrony. Many other types can be predicted from skill theory, but in most cases they will involve local relations between domains (Fischer & Bullock, 1981). For example, the acquisition of a new concept of subtraction may facilitate performance in algebra, geometry, and basic science classes.

Developmental Spurts

Every time a new optimal level emerges, the individual shows spurts in developmental change in each of a wide range of domains, but these spurts are distributed across an age region. Most spurts for Level 7 single abstractions, for instance, seem to occupy the region from 10 to 13 years of age for middle-class children.

There are at least two senses in which spurts for a new optimal level occupy a region. First the spurt in each single domain does not occur instantaneously but unfolds over a period of time. In other words, it is sudden only relative to the person's life span. The spurt for EEGs at each level of abstractions, for instance, seems to cover a period of at least a year and sometimes more, as shown in Figure 3.2. Second, in psychological development, the person shows not a single spurt but a whole family of spurts. This means that there is a separate spurt for each domain, as illustrated for three domains in Figure 3.3. The family of spurts is predicted to cluster in the first few years after the initial appearance of skills at each new optimal level of abstractions.

Sequences

The specificity of skill development means that precise synchronies are rare in the child's development, and that strong psychological spurts are mostly limited to single domains. Its implications for developmental sequences are very different, however. The individual routinely and frequently moves through developmental sequences, which can be predicted with great precision so long as the task domain remains constant from step to step. Ideally, all components in step 2 should be identical to those in step 1 except for the elements that make step 2 more complex. That is, the procedure and content of the task for each step should remain nearly constant while the complexity of the task varies. Thus, task specificity is controlled,

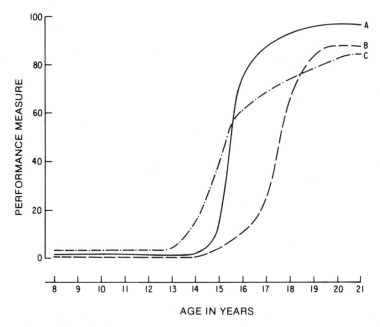

Figure 3.3. Spurts in Three Hypothetical Behavioral Domains as a Result of the Emergence of a New Developmental Level

Note: A, B, and C are different behavioral domains. The spurts were chosen to represent the emergence of Level 8 abstract mappings.

and the transformation rules of skill theory can be used to predict a person's developmental sequence within the task domain.

At times researchers have treated developmental sequences as sufficient evidence for stagelike change. By themselves, sequences constitute weak evidence for stages, because alone a sequence demonstrates no developmental synchrony and no developmental spurt. What a sequence can demonstrate is that behavior shows qualitative change, which is one criterion for a stage (for example, see Kohlberg, 1969). But many approaches that deny the existence of stages nevertheless accept the existence of developmental sequences that show qualitative change within a domain (for example, Flavell, 1982; Klahr & Wallace, 1976). Consequently, sequences show developmental change, but by themselves they do not demonstrate the existence of stages in any strong sense.

Better Methods for Analyzing Development

Testing these predictions of synchronies, spurts, and sequences requires methods of some power. How can investigators determine if skills in two different domains in fact emerge in synchrony? How can they detect whether a developmental change is fast enough to be

Table 3.3. Strong Scalogram Method: Profiles for an 8-Step Developmental Sequence

Developmental Step	Tasks							
	A	B	C	D	E	F	G	H
0	–	–	–	–	–	–	–	–
1	+	–	–	–	–	–	–	–
2	+	+	–	–	–	–	–	–
3	+	+	+	–	–	–	–	–
4	+	+	+	+	–	–	–	–
5	+	+	+	+	+	–	–	–
6	+	+	+	+	+	+	–	–
7	+	+	+	+	+	+	+	–
8	+	+	+	+	+	+	+	+

Note: Correct performance of a task is indicated by a +.

called a spurt? The methods used in most developmental research do not allow one to answer such questions because they provide little precision or detail of measurement. Indeed, the standard cross-sectional design assessing children of different ages on one task cannot provide rigorous evidence for a developmental sequence (Fischer & Bullock, 1981; Wohlwill, 1973).

More precise and powerful methods are available for assessing developmental changes of various sorts, including sequences, synchronies, and spurts (Fischer, Pipp, & Bullock, in press).

Strong Scalogram Analysis

One of the most useful general methods is called strong scalogram analysis. A sequence of steps in the development of some particular skill is predicted, and then a separate task is designed to assess each step. Individuals varying across an appropriate age range are selected, and every individual performs every task. Each individual's performance should fit a Guttman scale. That is, all performance profiles should follow the pattern shown in Table 3.3. Also, predictions can be tested about tasks that do not form separate steps, as illustrated in Table 3.4. Note that this method provides a direct test of a developmental sequence with either cross-sectional or longitudinal data.

Although this strong scalogram method has been known for a long time (Wohlwil, 1973), it has been neglected, perhaps because of the difficulty of designing a priori a different task for every predicted step. This difficulty does not apply, however, to any approach that predicts a developmental sequence in a particular domain, including many of the models in this volume. Also, skill theory is designed to facilitate the invention of such tasks, and so makes the method much

Table 3.4. Profiles for a Measure with Two Tasks at Step 3

Developmental Step	Tasks					
	J	K	L	M	N	O
0	−	−	−	−	−	−
1	+	−	−	−	−	−
2	+	+	−	−	−	−
3 {	+	+	+	−	−	−
	+	+	−	+	−	−
	+	+	+	+	−	−
4	+	+	+	+	+	−
5	+	+	+	+	+	+

Note: Correct performance of a task is indicated by a +.

easier to use even without a specific model for a domain. Indeed, a number of sequences predicted by skill theory have been tested with this method, and approximately 95 percent of the subjects have fit the predicted scalogram profiles in each test (Bertenthal & Fischer, 1978; Fischer & Roberts, 1982; Hand, 1981a; Hand & Fischer, note 5; Russell & Fischer, note 7; Watson & Fischer, 1977, 1980).

In addition, this method eliminates the need for a troublesome assumption that is commonly made in developmental research, where the investigator assumes that a task will naturally differentiate all developmental steps without any independent assessment of these steps. A moral dilemma, for example, is assumed to be sufficient for discriminating all stages of moral judgment, even though the normal ages for those stages vary by 20 years or more (Kohlberg, 1969, 1976). When every developmental stage or step is assessed independently, this assumption is no longer troublesome since it becomes a hypothesis to be tested (Roberts, 1981).

Using Practice Effects to Find Synchronies

Most developmental research has paid little attention to the implications of the effects of experience for developmental assessments. According to skill theory, experience is a major determinant of the specific skills that a person develops. The effect of one type of experience, practice, is especially simple. In almost all cases, it leads the individual to perform at a higher developmental step (for example, see Jackson et al., 1978; O'Brien & Overton, 1982). Such practice effects substantially reduce the normal unevenness of psychological development and thus increase the degree of synchrony across skill domains. This is because they tend to make the individual move to his or her optimal level in all the practiced skills.

A practice manipulation can therefore be used to produce high synchrony across tasks at a given developmental level. If the skills for all or most of the tasks move to the individual's optimal level, then they will necessarily show a high degree of synchrony. In a study of arithmetic concepts, this hypothesis was tested by comparing performance before and after practice (Russell & Fischer, note 7). Participants aged nine to 20 performed a large number of arithmetic problems for each of three developmental levels (6, 7, and 8, as shown in Table 3.2). The first session instituted a practice manipulation in which the participants performed each problem and were then given a good answer to it. They were told that they would be tested on all the same problems again in two weeks and that during that interval they were free to work on any of the problems. The second session thus assessed the effects of practice and instruction.

The results confirmed the predicted relation between practice and degree of synchrony. With Level 7 single abstractions, for example, students produced a wide range of performances in the first session. In the second session, however, the distribution of performances became bimodal, with almost every student either failing virtually all problems or passing two-thirds or more. The same general pattern of high developmental unevenness in the first session and high synchrony in the second obtained for Level 8 abstract mappings, and pretest data suggest that it will also hold for Level 9 abstract systems. Because the sample tested did not include ages before the emergence of Level 6, however, the hypothesis for that level could not be fully tested. A similar pattern of results also obtained in two studies of infant development that used the strong scalogram method. Practice reduced developmental unevenness (décalage) and produced high synchrony across domains (Corrigan, in press; Jackson et al., 1978).

Tests for Developmental Spurts

Strangely, there have been few attempts to test for spurts in developmental change, even though one classic criterion for stages is sudden change or discontinuity. With powerful methods such as strong scalogram analysis or the use of multiple tasks assessing a given level, the spurt hypothesis can be tested in a straightforward manner (Fischer, Pipp, & Bullock, in press). In well-practiced skills, individuals will show relatively sudden developmental change upon the emergence of a new optimal level.

With the strong scalogram method, testing this hypothesis requires a developmental sequence with multiple microdevelopmental steps for each level. After practice, individuals will tend to move quickly through the microdevelopmental steps at their new optimal levels. However, they will fail to pass even the simplest step at the following level. With the method of multiple tasks, which was used in the arithmetic study, a developmental spurt will be evident in a similar rapid change in performance. In other words, as a result of practice, individuals will show a sudden movement from failing all

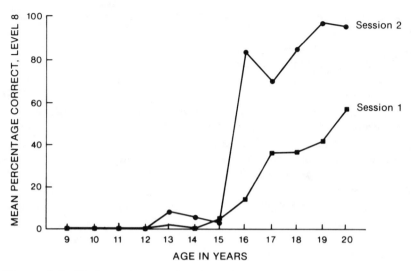

Figure 3.4. Performance on Level 8 Arithmetic Problems before and after Practice as a Function of Age

Note: Every subject performed sixteen Level 8 problems in each session. Session 1 involved no practice except for the effects of doing multiple Level 8 problems during the session. In Session 2 (two weeks later) students performed the same problems again.

problems for a given level to passing most or all of them. In a homogeneous population, the spurt may also be restricted to a narrow age range across individuals.

The spurt hypothesis was tested for Levels 7 and 8, and it was strongly supported for both levels. For Level 7 single abstractions (generalized definitions of single arithmetic operations), performance in Session 1 showed slow improvement over a long period, from 9 to 20 years of age. In Session 2 (after practice), performance spurted between 9 and 11 years from zero to almost 50 percent correct. For Level 8 abstract mappings (relations of two similar arithmetic operations), performance in Session 1 demonstrated a gradual improvement between 15 and 20 years, as shown in Figure 3.4. Performance in Session 2, on the other hand, spurted between 15 and 16 years from near zero to over 70 percent correct. Pretest data suggest that the same pattern will hold for Level 9 abstract systems, with the spurt occurring at approximately 20 years.

FINDING ORDER AMIDST THE AMBIGUITY OF BEHAVIOR

With so much emphasis on developmental levels and the methods for detecting them, one might infer that the levels are blatantly obvious in behavior. That is not the case. Most behavior is naturally ambiguous, so that without intervention in the form of assessment one cannot easily tell which particular level or micro-developmental transformation a behavior involves (Fischer & Corrigan, 1981). Only with careful method and measurement does it become a straightforward matter to analyze the skill structure of a behavior. And even then, some behaviors may have a structure that is intrinsically ambiguous, so that it cannot be assigned to a single level (for example, see Hand 1981a).

In much research, the ambiguity of behavior obstructs the formulation of an accurate portrait of development, because the researcher cannot assume that the "same" behavior in several individuals or in one individual at different ages reflects the same cognitive ability. Take, for example, a group of students who all gave a good definition of "noun": "a person, place, thing, or idea." Based on this behavior alone, all the students seemed to understand what a noun was. The picture changed, however, when they were given a sorting task in which they had to pick the nouns from a set of words printed on cards. In this new task, some students picked out all the nouns correctly, but others picked cards randomly. Performance on the sorting task was strongly related to age. At 9 and 10 years students could define the term "noun," but they could not sort out words that were nouns. By 16 and 17 years most students could sort nouns correctly (Anglin, 1970).

The minimal levels of the skills required by the definition task and the sorting task seem to differ. The definition task requires memorization of a definition for a concept (Level 6 representational systems), but the sorting task requires the application of that concept to a set of real words (Level 7 single abstractions). The use of either task alone may misrepresent a child's understanding of "noun."

Just the opposite of the math problem, where it was "do" before "say".

Interpreting Errors

Extension of this example leads naturally to strong scalogram analysis, in which a separate task is used to assess each step or skill. Strong scalogram analysis and other multiple-task methods (Fischer, Pipp, & Bullock, in press; Siegler, 1981) eliminate a problem that plagues most cognitive-developmental research, namely the use of types of errors on a single task to infer the normal developmental sequence in some domain. With this method, one task is presented to individuals varying in age, and their performance on the task is recorded and analyzed into types. Most of the types normally involve less-than-ideal responses to the task. These responses are called errors. If the types are in some way correlated with age, they are inferred to demonstrate a developmental sequence for the domain in question.

Such a method does not, of course, provide a convincing test of sequence, as discussed previously (Fischer & Bullock, 1981). In a critique of this kind of research, Roberts (1981) points out three additional problems with this method. It tends to produce (1) a biased picture of the individual's skills, with emphasis on failures and inadequacies, (2) vague results, where the reason for a failing response cannot be pinpointed, and (3) uncertainty about whether performance on a task that is far beyond a person's ability level reflects that person's actual ability. Use of such a method, he concludes, yields a portrait of development that is at best incomplete and at worst inaccurate.

In contrast, by testing people on a series of tasks assessing a range of developmental steps, the researcher can observe the best performance of each individual and relate it to his or her errors on tasks that are more complex. In this way, the significance of the errors can be assessed instead of merely being assumed. Also, with an analysis of the structure of each task, such as that provided by skill theory or some information-processing theories (see, for example, Case, 1978; Halford & Wilson, 1980; Siegler, 1981), the investigator can begin to explain the relations between best performance and errors.

Types of Simplifications of Complex Tasks

In the research presented here on the development of abstractions, errors on more difficult tasks tend to show systematic relations with an individual's best performance on less difficult tasks. In particular, with tasks that require a higher level of performance than people are capable of in a particular domain, they commonly simplify the tasks to some form that they can handle. This suggests that this type of simplification typically appears when the task requires no more than one level beyond the person's highest capacity in that domain. When the task is more than one level beyond a person's capability, she or he is more likely to use a fallback strategy, which does not represent her or his best capability.

According to skill theory, one way that people prepare for the next level of development in a domain is by using a process called *mimicking*. They build a skill that remains at the lower level but includes most or all the component sets that will be required for the next level (Fischer, 1980). In this way the mimicked skill comes close to the skill required at the next level, but it lacks the specific organization required for the next level, including the higher-level relations between sets.

The most common types of task simplifications detected in the research reported here thus far seem to involve mimicking. Three types of mimicking simplifications have been common in the problem-solving efforts of individuals in these studies. These three types are shift of focus, globbing, and reduction to the concrete. Examples of each of these types are given in Table 3.5, one from the arithmetic study and one from the study of intention and responsibility. In every example in the table, the task required a Level 8 mapping skill, and the person simplified it to a Level 7 single abstraction. Mimicking simplifications are not limited to Level 8 tasks, of course, but the examples were restricted to Level 8 so that they would be easier to follow and compare.

Shift of Focus

In a task that requires the *coordination* of two components, simplification by shift of focus occurs when an individual deals with one component and then shifts to the second component. For example, on a Level 8 task involving the coordination of addition and subtraction, participants often simplified the task by using a shift of focus between the two Level 7 abstractions of addition and subtraction. They defined addition and showed how it applied to a concrete problem, and then they defined subtraction and showed how it applied to a concrete problem, but they never related addition and subtraction. An ability to talk clearly about each of the two operations does not demonstrate that the person understands the relation between them. A true coordination of addition and subtraction into a Level 8 mapping produces both an understanding of the relation between the two operations (opposition or negation), including an explicit statement of the difference between the operations specified by that relation, and an understanding of the similarities between the two operations (Russell & Fischer, 1982, note 9).

Globbing

The second type of mimicking simplification is globbing, in which the person confuses and intermingles two components of the task. That is, the person fails to differentiate the two components. In the study of intention and responsibility, for example, components of the two concepts were globbed together. The person would combine one aspect of intention, such as the negative intention of deceit, with one aspect of responsibility, such as its negation—irresponsibility. The result was a Level 7 abstraction for deceitful irresponsibility, not a Level 8 relation of intention and responsibility (see Table 3.5).

Similarly, in the arithmetic study, people failed to differentiate addition and multiplication. Instead of recognizing that the two operations are similar yet different, they asserted that the two were identical, just different ways of doing the same thing.

Table 3.5. Types of Simplifications of Tasks by Mimicking (Examples of Level 8 Tasks Performed at Level 7)

Types of Mimicking	Relations of Two Similar Arithmetic Operations	Relations of Intention and Responsibility
Shift of focus: shift from one component to another component without relating the components	Addition and subtraction: "Addition combines two numbers to produce a larger number. Subtraction takes one number away from another number to produce a smaller number."	The person defines or discusses intention and then defines or discusses responsibility, but the two abstractions are never related.
Globbing: mixing together of two components with no differentiation between them	Addition and multiplication: "They're the same thing. Both of them involve combining numbers to get a bigger number."	The individual attempts to discuss both concepts but actually mixes one feature of intention with one feature of responsibility to form a mixed concept. For example, the negative intention involved in deceit is mixed with a notion of irresponsibility resulting in the conclusion that a deceitful person is irresponsible. No general relation of intention and responsibility is specified.
Reduction to the concrete: Treatment of higher-level components in terms of concrete instances or simpler, lower-level features involved in those components	Addition and subtraction: "Addition and subtraction are opposites, because they use the same three numbers in these problems $[12 + 9 = 21$ and $21 - 12 = 9]$. You can add 12 and 9 to get 21, and then you do the opposite when you subtract 12 from 21, and you get 9 again."	The relation between intention and responsibility is discussed only in terms of the concrete behaviors involved. For example, "Ed doesn't think that Joe was that bad for lying because he said he was sorry. Beth didn't even say she was sorry, and she lied too. So Ed forgives Joe but not Beth."

Reduction to the Concrete

The third type of mimicking simplification, reduction to the concrete, preserves the relation of the components but does so by reducing that relation to lower-level concrete instances or features. Nine-year-olds, who were not yet capable of constructing the Level 7 abstraction for addition, for example, said things such as "Addition is like taking 4 and putting it with 6 to get 10." They turned the abstract concept into a concrete instance. Similarly for a Level 8 mapping of addition and subtraction, students commonly reduced the mapping to a relation of two concrete arithmetic problems, such as $12 + 9 = 21$ and $21 - 12 = 9$. As shown in Table 3.5, this concrete relation can be understood with a Level 7 single abstraction such as "opposite." It is important to note, however, that the abstraction may not be obvious in behavior unless the individual is asked follow-up questions about the relation.

Although these three types of mimicking simplifications seem to represent distinct strategies, people can use several of them in one task. In attempting to relate addition and subtraction, for example, an individual can first use shift of focus, defining each concept separately, and then use reduction to the concrete, presenting two concrete arithmetic problems to show that an addition problem can be changed into a subtraction problem.

The types of simplifications should not be thought of simply as errors. They may well be signs of intelligence. In other words, they may be the sorts of strategies that good students use when they encounter concepts or tasks that are beyond their present capabilities. Indeed, facility in using these types of simplifications might well turn out to be one of the best predictors of school success, especially for fields where instruction is often at a level beyond the students' optimal level, as with mathematics and science in high school and college.

Fallback Strategies

When people cannot cope with a task by mimicking, they commonly use a fallback strategy, in which they resort to a low-level skill that gets them through the task (Roberts, 1981; Shatz, 1977; Siegler, 1981). The most common fallback strategies in the studies of abstractions seemed to be an extreme version of reduction to the concrete. As such, instead of simplifying a task to the highest level that they could handle, students reduced the task to something much simpler, a concrete recitation of facts or numbers.

This type of fallback strategy is probably most common when the task requires a skill that is more than one level greater than the person's highest level in that domain. The difficulty of the task seems to "blow" the person's mind, leading him or her to function far below capacity.

A person who can handle Level 7 single abstractions, such as division or addition, for example, may use a fallback strategy when asked to explain the relation between division and addition, which requires a Level 9 abstract system. He or she will simply explain concretely how relevant arithmetic problems are calculated, by stating that "You take 24 and divide it by 3, and you get 8. And you add 8 plus 8 plus 8 to get 24." Similarly, a person faced with a Level 9 story relating several forms of intention to several forms of responsibility will revert to merely describing concrete interactions that went on between the characters in the story. In such fallback strategies, the behavior does not accomplish what mimicking simplifications do. It neither demonstrates the best the person can do nor preserves most of the key components of the task. Methods that evoke fallback strategies should not be used to assess a person's best capabilities.

Levels of Abstractions in Spontaneous Behavior

Fallback strategies are more than curiosities of assessment. In fact, they seem to be common in adolescent and adult behavior, especially in unstructured or "spontaneous" settings. Adults are not likely to do their best in most situations. To the contrary, they seem to commonly function below their optimal level. Although this hypothesis is based mostly on informal observations, there are some research results showing surprisingly poor performance in adolescents and adults (Flavell, 1970; Martarano, 1977; Neimark, 1975). One of the reasons for this poor performance may be the adult tendency to rely on fallback strategies when there is no strong incentive to do the hard work necessary for a high level of abstraction (Siegal, 1975).

There may be a system in this apparent laziness. Within the abstract tier, people may be progressively more likely to show this effect as they move to higher optimal levels. That is, as their optimal level moves up, they may become less and less likely to demonstrate that optimal level in their spontaneous behavior (Hand, 1981b). They will still function at their optimal level in settings that are structured to support such performance and in domains in which they are highly motivated (see, for example, Rest, note 8), but otherwise they will tend to fall back onto lower-level skills. Thus the discrepancy between their optimal level and their modal spontaneous performance will increase as they progress to higher levels of abstraction. Perhaps optimal level and spontaneous level routinely match at only one point, when the person's optimal level is at the beginning of the abstract tier, Level 7 single abstractions.

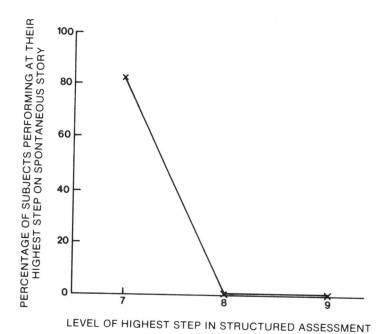

Figure 3.5. Percentage of Students at Each Level in Structured Assessment Who Performed at Their Highest Step in Spontaneous Story

Data collected thus far in the study of intention and responsibility support this hypothesis (Hand & Fischer, 1981 note 5). Participants were assessed in two conditions, a structured strong scalogram condition and a less structured "spontaneous" condition. For both conditions, assessment involved the same developmental sequence and the same situation and task material. Despite these similarities, virtually every person whose highest step in the structured assessment was at Level 7 also showed a similar step in the spontaneous assessment. But no one whose highest step in the structured assessment was beyond Level 7 showed so high a step in the spontaneous assessment (see Figure 3.5). No wonder researchers have had such difficulty with developmental unevenness. What seems at first blush to be a minor change in testing condition can produce an enormous difference in assessed developmental step.

SUMMARY AND CONCLUSIONS

In this chapter the following claims and arguments have been made:

A human being does not have a unified mind, nor does he or she have a mind made up of unrelated pieces. Instead, according to skill theory, people acquire specific skills in particular contexts, and they have to work to generalize and differentiate those skills to produce more integrated, powerful ways of thinking.

The acquisition and generalization of skills operates in accordance with certain general properties of the human information-processing system. Some of these general system properties are described by a series of cognitive-developmental levels that place upper limits on the structure of a skill, and a set of transformation rules that specify how specific skills are generalized and made more complex.

By the postulate of structural imperialism, cognitive levels are defined by skill structure. They cannot be equated with any psychological or logical categories because such categories always prove to cut across cognitive levels.

Development in adolescence and adulthood involves the emergence and elaboration of abstractions, proceeding through four cognitive levels and culminating in the appearance of general principles. Each level emerges at an age region in which the individual shows both spurts in well-practiced skills and spurts in brain changes.

To test for these levels and the developmental steps predicted by the transformation rules, one should ideally use a methodology in which each predicted step is assessed by at least one independent task. With such a methodology, developmental synchronies and spurts in cognitive growth can be detected relatively easily as an individual moves to a new optimal level.

Behavior is normally ambiguous with respect to developmental level and process, especially when it is observed under "spontaneous" conditions. Careful skill analysis and sampling of tasks can lead to the extraction of order from the obscurity, however. One kind of order involves the discovery that people seem to deal with tasks that are slightly beyond their higest capacity by simplifying the tasks in several systematic ways. These include shift of focus, globbing, and reduction to the concrete.

Without support from structured situations, most adults seem normally to function far below their optimal level of abstraction.

Most of the existing models of adult cognitive development can be interpreted in terms of skill theory. When important methodological differences are considered, the stages or levels described in other models seem in most cases to involve realizations of the levels of skill theory in particular domains. Most models also share skill theory's emphases on the active construction of skills and on the fundamental contribution of context to development. One process highlighted in skill theory but specified in only a few other models is the joint occurrence of simplification and complication in development.

NOTES

1. In these first few pages, the attempt has been made to indicate which articles present various aspects and implications of skill theory. For the rest of the chapter, these citations will be generally assumed so that it will not be necessary to refer to them repeatedly. The single most complete presentation of skill theory is Fischer (1980).

2. The optimal level is the highest level of skill that individuals can control by themselves. In situations where social support is provided, as when parents scaffold their children's behavior (Ratner & Bruner, 1978; Vygotsky, 1978), individuals can effectively function at higher levels, which are termed "maximal."

3. Note that when skills in different domains share the same general type of formula or the same microdevelopmental transformation rule, that does not mean they constitute the same specific skill.

4

HIGHER-ORDER REASONING IN
POSTFORMAL OPERATIONAL THOUGHT
Robert J. Sternberg

Theorists disagree as to whether intellectual development is best characterized in terms of discrete stages (for example, Piaget, 1976), or in terms of continuous accretions (for example, Brainerd, 1978). There seems to be widespread agreement, however, that the ability to perceive and understand abstract relations is central to intelligence and that increases—either discrete or continuous—occur with age. This agreement cuts across theoretical paradigms and proclivities. Consider, for example, the learning-theory, psycho-metric information-processing, and Piagetian literatures.

Within the learning-theory literature, Gagné's (1968) hierarchy of learning processes assumes that the ability to form and use higher-order relations, such as concepts and principles, develops with the age and experience of the child. Concept-learning studies also support the claim that the ability to comprehend abstract relations develops with age. For example, Odom (1966) and Osler and Kofsky (1966), using subjects ranging in age from 5 to 14, have found that younger subjects tend to form concepts by rote learning of individual stimulus-response relations for the various instances of a concept. Older subjects, however, tend to employ higher-order categories as a basis for their reasoning.

Within the psychometric literature, Terman (1921) defined intelligence, in part, as the ability to carry on abstract thinking. Cattell (1971) viewed abstraction, or the "building up of relations among relations" (p. 186), as an essential part of what he called fluid intelligence. Two of Spearman's (1923) three principles of cognition—the education of relations and the education of correlates—involve the understanding and application of abstract relations. In

Preparation of this chapter was supported by Office of Naval Research Contract N0001478C0025 to Robert J. Sternberg. I am grateful to Michael Commons for comments on an earlier draft of the chapter.

Guilford's (1967) structure-of-intellect model, relations form one of six possible products of cognitive processing.

Within the information-processing literature, the ability to form and understand abstract relations has provided a central focus in much research on intellectual development. For example, Siegler (1976, 1978) has shown that increased sophistication in understanding the balance-scale task depends largely upon more complete encoding of successively wider ranges of relevant relations between weights on the scale. Siegler (1981) has shown that this trend in intellectual development applies to a fairly wide range of Piagetian types of intellectual tasks. Lunzer (1965), Sternberg and Rifkin (1979), Gallagher and Wright (1979), and others have shown that improvement in analogical reasoning depends in large part upon improvement in the understanding of the various kinds of relations that constitute an analogy.

Finally, the ability to understand transitive relations has been used as an indicant of the transition from preoperational to concrete-operational thinking within the Piagetian literature (Piaget, 1970a). Moreover, the ability to understand relations between relations, or "second-degree operations" (Piaget, 1976), serves as an indicant of the transition from concrete-operational to formal-operational thinking. Piaget, Montangero, and Billeter's (1977) studies of analogical reasoning arrived at results similar to those of the information-processing researchers. These results suggest that the ability to comprehend relations, and especially second-order relations, that is, relations between relations, seems to be the single critical skill in the development of analogical reasoning ability.

Implicit in this brief review is the assumption that improvements in relational thinking derive not only from improvements in the ability to carry on thinking with relations of a given order, but also from improvements in the ability to carry on thinking with relations of successively higher orders. "Orders" of relations are defined in terms of what is related: First-order relations are relations between primitive terms, second-order relations are relations between relations, and so on. Thus, the transition from preoperational to concrete-operational thinking seems to be marked by an increase in the ability to carry out first-order relational thinking of the kind required by classification, seriation, causation, and similar reasoning tasks. The transition from concrete-operational to formal-operational thinking seems to be marked by an increase in the ability to carry out second-order relational thinking of the kind required by analogical and similar reasoning tasks. If one were to consider the possibility of a postformal-operational period of thought, one might extrapolate this "sequence" and look for an increase in the ability to carry out thinking with third-order relations. Indeed, Case (1978) has proposed that "the search for 'development beyond formal operations' should . . . concentrate on clarifying the nature of second-order

intellectual operations and on searching for third-order operations"
(p. 63).

The main thesis of this chapter is that progress beyond formal-
operational thinking can be understood, at least in part, in terms of
the development of third-order relational thinking, as suggested by
Case (1978), and as pursued further by Commons, Richards, and
Kuhn (1982), Sternberg & Downing (1982), and others. The remainder of this chapter is divided into three parts. First, a theory of
higher-order relational thinking is proposed in one domain that seems
particularly well suited to the study of such thinking—analogical
reasoning; some data are presented that bear on the theory and
support it. Second, suggestions are made regarding how the theory
could be extended beyond the domain of analogical reasoning to
serial and classificational reasoning, and potential tests of the
augmented theory are described. Finally, it is suggested that the
theory applies beyond the domain of laboratory and testlike tasks to
the kinds of complex reasoning one must actually do in the real
world.

HIGHER-ORDER REASONING BY ANALOGY[1]

Theory

Analogies of the Second Order

In order to understand the proposed theory of higher-order
analogical reasoning, it is necessary first to understand the theory of
analogical reasoning as it applies to standard second-order analogies.
Two kinds of issues need to be considered: issues of representation
and issues of processing.

It is proposed, following Rumelhart and Abrahamson (1973; see
also Sternberg & Gardner, in press) that the terms of a standard
second-order analogy can be represented as a parallelogram in a
semantic (or other conceptual) space. Figure 4.1 depicts a second-
order analogy in a three-dimensional semantic space in which the
various words of our language might be placed. In a "perfect" second-
order analogy, the vector distance from A to B is exactly equal to the
vector distance from C to D. Equivalently, the vector distance from A
to C is exactly equal to the vector distance from B to D. This equality
implies that the magnitude (length) of the vector linking A to B is the
same as that of the vector linking C to D and that these two vectors
are parallel to each other. Imprecision in the analogy could result
from mismatches in either lengths or directions of the vectors.

It is further proposed that processing of a standard second-order
analogy of the form A : B :: C : D (such as Bench : Judge :: Pulpit :

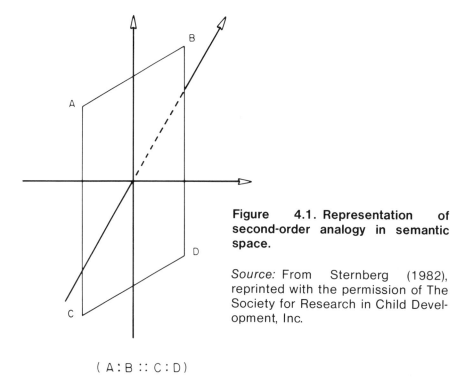

Figure 4.1. Representation of second-order analogy in semantic space.

Source: From Sternberg (1982), reprinted with the permission of The Society for Research in Child Development, Inc.

(A : B :: C : D)

Minister), can be understood in terms of seven basic components of information processing.[2] These components include:

1. *Encoding.* The individual perceives each analogy term and retrieves potentially relevant semantic (or other) attributes from long-term memory. These attributes are temporarily placed in working memory.

2. *First-order inference.* The individual discovers the relation(s) between the first two terms (A and B) of the analogy. This operation corresponds to what Spearman (1923) referred to as education of relations and also to discovery of first-order relations in Piaget's (1976) theory. In the example, the individual might recognize that a judge sits on a bench.

3. *Second-order mapping.* The individual discovers the second-order relation between the two halves of the analogy, establishing the vector that connects C—Bench (and all points on the vector emanating from Bench and terminating at Judge)—to D—Pulpit (and all points on the vector emanating from Pulpit and terminating at Minister). Note that the processing component is "second-order" because it relates two relations (vectors) rather than two primitive terms (points). The component corresponds to the discovery of second-order relations in Piaget's (1976) theory, and is also similar in conception to Fischer's (1980) concept of mapping.

4. *First-order application.* The individual carries over the relation inferred from A to B as mapped to C and applies it from C to an ideal. In the example, the subject applies the inferred relation from C to some ideal completion for the analogy. It is not necessarily the case that there will be any word in the language that precisely corresponds to the correct concept. In terms of the spatial representation, the fourth point completing a parallelogram does not necessarily correspond to a real word. This component corresponds to what Spearman (1923) has referred to as eduction of correlates.

5. *First-order justification.* The individual decides how distant the given D term is from the ideal completion. In the example, the individual must decide how close Minister is to the ideal completion for the given analogy. The greater the distance, the poorer the analogy, that is, the less well the analogy approaches a parallelogram in semantic space.

6. *Response.* The individual provides some kind of response indicating his or her evaluation of the goodness of the analogy.

Although the theory holds that the components listed above are sufficient to solve any given second-order, four-term analogy, research evidence indicates that some individuals, and especially younger children, use an additional component instead of, or in addition to, the components listed above (see, for example, Achenbach, 1970; Gentile, Tedesco-Stratton, Davis, Lund, & Agunanne, 1977; Sternberg & Nigro, 1980):

7. *First-order association.* The individual decides how semantically associated (spatially proximal, in terms of our representational metaphor) the C and D terms of the analogy are, independent of their relation to the A and B terms, and evaluates the goodness of the analogy in whole or in part on the basis of this associative relatedness. Thus, the associative relatedness of Pulpit and Minister becomes a basis for evaluating the goodness of the analogy.

Analogies of the Third Order

Consider now a higher-order analogy of the third order of the form $(A_1 : B_1 :: C_1 : D_1) :: (A_2 : B_2 :: C_2 : D_2)$, such as (Bench : Judge :: Pulpit : Minister) :: (Head : Hair :: Lawn : Grass). The subject's task is to evaluate the degree of (third-order) analogy between the two (second-order) analogies. In other words, the subject must rate how analogous the two analogies are. In this task, as in the standard second-order analogy task, there are no "right" or "wrong" answers: There are never right or wrong answers, strictly speaking, in inductive tasks. But whereas there is a set of generally accepted procedures for evaluating the goodness of a second-order analogy, there is no set of generally accepted procedures for evaluating the goodness of a third-order analogy. Hence, in proposing a set of procedures that subjects might use in making such an evaluation, one must start from intuitions, which can then be tested empirically. As was the case for second-order analogies, two kinds of issues need to be considered, issues of representation and issues of processing.

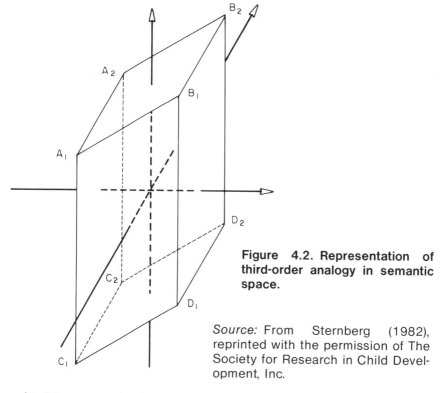

Figure 4.2. Representation of third-order analogy in semantic space.

Source: From Sternberg (1982), reprinted with the permission of The Society for Research in Child Development, Inc.

$$(A_1 : B_1 :: C_1 : D_1) :: (A_2 : B_2 :: C_2 : D_2)$$

With respect to representation, it is proposed that third-order analogies, like those of the second order, can be represented in a multidimensional semantic (or other conceptual) space. But whereas the representation of a second-order analogy is via a parallelogram, the representation of a third-order analogy is via a parallelepiped—a parallelogram extended to a third dimension (see Figure 4.2). Each planar surface of the parallelepiped represents an embedded analogy, with the $(A_1 B_1 C_1 D_1)$ and $(A_2 B_2 C_2 D_2)$ surfaces forming the main analogies of interest.

With respect to processing, it is proposed that each of the two main analogies constituting the third-order analogy is solved in essentially the same way as individual second-order analogies that occur in isolation. However, the evaluation of a third-order analogy requires the consideration of additional relations that are not considered and, indeed, are not relevant in the evaluation of a second-order analogy. Four relations are proposed to form "valid" bases for evaluation. A fifth is proposed to form an "invalid" additional basis that is nevertheless sometimes used:

1. *Second-order relatedness of corresponding* inferences *across second-order analogies*. This relation is a function of the closeness of the second-order relations between A_1-B_1 and A_2-B_2. To the extent that these relations do not correspond, the three-dimensional object representing the third-order analogy will depart from being a parallelepiped. Either one of the $\overline{AB}$ bases will be longer than the other, or the two $\overline{AB}$ bases will depart from parallelism with each other. In the sample third-order analogy, Bench : Judge is compared with Head : Hair much as these relations would be compared if they formed the two halves of a regular analogy. The more correspondent the two relations are, in terms of lengths and directions of their correspondent vectors in semantic space, the more they contribute toward the formation of an acceptable higher-order analogy.

2. *Second-order relatedness of corresponding* mappings *across second-order analogies*. This relation is a function of the closeness of the second-order relations between A_1-C_1 and A_2-C_2. To the extent that these relations do not correspond, the three-dimensional object representing the third-order analogy will depart from being a parallelepiped. Either one of the $\overline{AC}$ bases will be longer than the other, or the two $\overline{AC}$ bases will depart from parallelism with each other. In the sample higher-order analogy, Bench : Pulpit is compared with Head : Lawn. The more correspondent the two relations are, in terms of lengths and directions of their correspondent vectors in semantic space, the more they contribute toward the formation of an acceptable higher-order analogy.

3. *Second-order relatedness of corresponding* applications *across second-order analogies*. This relation is a function of the closeness of the second-order relations between C_1-D_1 and C_2-D_2. To the extent that these relations do not correspond, the three-dimensional object representing the third-order analogy will depart from being a parallelepiped. Either one of the $\overline{CD}$ bases will be longer than the other, or the two $\overline{CD}$ bases will depart from parallelism with each other. In the sample higher-order analogy, Pulpit : Minister is compared with Lawn : Grass much as these relations would be compared if they formed the two halves of a second-order analogy. The more correspondent the two relations are, in terms of lengths and directions of their correspondent vectors in semantic space, the more they contribute toward the formation of an acceptable higher-order analogy.

4. *Second-order relatedness of corresponding* inferences and applications *across second-order analogies*. This relation is a function of the closeness of the second-order relations between A_1-B_1 and C_2-D_2 and between A_2-B_2 and C_1-D_1. To the extent that these relations do not correspond, the three-dimensional object representing the third-order analogy will depart from being a parallelepiped. There will be a discrepancy in the lengths or directions of the two corresponding sets of $\overline{AB}$ and $\overline{CD}$ vectors. In the sample third-order analogy, Bench : Judge is compared with Lawn : Grass, and Head : Hair is compared with Pulpit : Minister. The more correspondent the two relations are, in terms of lengths and directions of their correspondent vectors in semantic space, the more

they contribute toward the formation of an acceptable higher-order analogy.

The last relation that is sometimes used but that is irrelevant to the goodness of the parallelepiped's structure is associative in nature.

5. *First-order* associative relatedness *of corresponding terms across second-order analogies.* This relation is a function of the closeness of associations between A_1 and A_2, B_1 and B_2, C_1 and C_2, and D_1 and D_2. Reference to these relations as "associative" underscores the belief that use of this variable in evaluation is essentially "regressive." The closeness of corresponding terms across second-order analogies affects the volume of the parallelepiped but does not affect the goodness of the figure as a parallelepiped. Use of this criterion could possibly lead to a rather unfavorable evaluation of the sample higher-order analogy since none of the pairs of Bench and Head, Judge and Hair, Pulpit and Law, or Minister and Grass are highly related. On this associative criterion, a better higher-order analogy than the sample one would be (Bench : Judge :: Pulpit : Minister) :: (Chair : Courtroom :: Pew : Church). Its superiority stems from the fact that Bench and Chair, Judge and Courtroom, Pulpit and Pew, and Minister and Church are all highly related pairs of words. Yet, almost anyone would agree that the third-order analogy between these two second-order analogies is not as good as that between the two second-order analogies constituting the higher-order analogy, (Bench : Judge :: Pulpit : Minister) :: (Head : Hair :: Lawn : Grass). The terms of the newly introduced third-order analogy are more highly associatively related across the two second-order analogies; but the degree of analogical correspondence between the two second-order analogies is lower.

There are certain parallels in the evaluation of second- and third-order analogies that are instructive to note. First, the third-order analogy requires a second-order inference (Relation 1 for third-order analogies) in addition to the first-order inference (Relation 2 for second-order analogies) required for second-order analogies. Second, the third-order analogy requires a second-order mapping (Relation 2 for third-order analogies) in addition to the second-order mapping (Relation 3 for second-order analogies) required for second-order analogies. Third, the third-order analogy requires a second-order application (Relation 3 for third-order analogies) in addition to the first-order application (Relation 4 for second-order analogies) required for second-order analogies. Finally, associative relations can play a role in the solution of third-order analogies (Relation 5 for third-order analogies), just as they can in the solution of second-order analogies (Relation 7 for second-order analogies). The associative relationship is actually irrelevant to the true goodness of the analogy. These various informational inputs are combined to form the basis for the third-order analogical mapping between the two analogies. This mapping is used to rate the goodness of the third-order analogy. This mapping seems to correspond to interrelation of systems as expressed in the theoretical schemes of Fischer (1980) and of Commons et al. (1982). In Piaget's (1976) theory, the mapping represents an extension of relation discovery to the third order of relations between relations.

The representational and process homologies between second-order and third-order analogies suggest at least the possibility that solution of the two kinds of analogies may undergo parallel courses of development, although at different time periods in the cognitive-developmental course. In particular, a parallel is hypothesized here between some of the processing changes in second-order analogical reasoning observed in the transition from concrete- to formal-operational reasoning and processing changes in a possible transition from formal- to postformal-operational reasoning. Consider some of our main developmental findings for the concrete- to formal-operational transition, and possible parallels in a formal- to postformal-operational transition:

1. Children tend to decrease their use of first-order associative relations (Relation 7 for second-order analogies) with increasing age (Sternberg & Nigro, 1980). Therefore, one might expect decreased use of associative relations in third-order analogies (Relation 5 for third-order analogies) with increasing age.
2. Children show a compensating increase in their use of first-order inference (Relation 2 for second-order analogies) with increasing age (Sternberg & Nigro, 1980). One might therefore expect increased use of second-order inference in third-order analogies (Relation 1 for third-order analogies) with increasing age.
3. Children seem to acquire the ability to map second-order analogies (Relation 3 for second-order analogies) with the onset of formal operations. One might therefore expect adolescents to acquire the ability to map third-order analogies (Relation 2 for third-order analogies) with the onset of postformal operations. This result would be a reasonable extension not only of our own work (Sternberg & Rifkin, 1979), but of both the Piagetian and information-processing work mentioned earlier (for example, Lunzer, 1965; Piaget with Montangero & Billeter, 1977).

In essence, then, the thrust of the predictions is that there will be, in the onset of postformal operations, a recapitulation of developmental trends that appeared in the onset of formal operations. The recapitulation, however, will be at an order of analysis one level higher than was made possible at the onset of formal operations.

Results

The higher-order analogies that formed the basis for the experiment comprised 72 different items that subjects were asked to rate on a 1 to 9 (low to high) scale indicating how related the two analogies were to each other, how "analogous" they were. Examples of higher-order analogies are: (1) (Sun : Day :: Moon : Night) :: (Sunny : Summer :: Snowy : Winter); (2) (Sand : Beach :: Star : Galaxy) :: (Water : Ocean :: Air : Sky); (3) (Bench : Judge :: Pulpit : Minister) :: (Hair : Head :: Grass : Lawn); and (4) (Letter : Mailman :: Newspaper : Paperboy) :: (Empty Bottles : Milkman :: Garbage : Garbageman). Among these analogies, the first (1) was rated as relatively poor, whereas the third (3) was rated as relatively good.

Subjects solving these higher-order analogies were 20 eighth graders, 20 eleventh graders, and 20 college freshmen. An additional 140 subjects (in grades 8 through 11) supplied ratings of various kinds (to be described). Subjects in this second group were nonoverlapping with subjects who solved the third-order analogies.

Performance on the higher-order analogies was modeled by using ratings of the goodness of higher-order analogies as the dependent variable and ratings of distances between terms and relations as independent variables. The ratings were chosen so as to provide appropriate measures of the psychological constructs of interest. These ratings were on a 1 to 9 scale, with 1 indicating low distance and 9 indicating high distance. For example, the independent variable for estimating the effect of second-order inference (Relation 1 for third-order analogies) was the distance between the (A,B) relation for the first analogy in the third-order pair and the (A,B) relation for the second analogy in the third-order pair. The independent variable for estimating the effect of first-order associative relatedness (Relation 5 for third-order analogies) was (X_1, X_2), where X_1 is a term of the first analogy in the third-order pair and X_2 a term of the second analogy in the third-order pair. In the first example in the preceding paragraph, "Sun" would be paired with "Sunny" and would be rated for its degree of semantic relatedness.

The model of third-order analogical reasoning accounted well for the goodness ratings. It accounted for 78 percent of the variance in the eighth-grade data, 81 percent of the variance in the eleventh-grade data, and 90 percent of the variance in the college data. All of these percentages were statistically highly significant in comparison to the null model accounting for 0 percent of the variance in the data. Thus, the model predicted the data at better than a chance level. In contrast, a model based simply upon the basic model for *second*-order analogical reasoning as described earlier in the chapter (without augmentation by the higher-order variables) accounted for only trivial and nonsignificant percentages of variance in the data.

All three hypotheses were confirmed:

1. *Associative relatedness*: First-order associative relatedness showed decreasing standardized regression (β) weights across the three grade levels: .23, .10, and .09 for grade 8, grade 11, and college, respectively. Only the weight for grade 8 was statistically significant. Thus,

adolescents did appear to show a declining use of associative related-ness with increasing age.

2. *Inference*: In contrast, second-order inference showed increasing stan-dardized regression weights across the three grade levels: .68, .81, and .82 for grade 8, grade 11, and college, respectively. All three weights were statistically significant, indicating that second-order inference played at least some role in reasoning at each age level, although a diminished role at the grade 8 level relative to the grade 11 and college levels.

3. *Mapping*: The standardized weights for second-order mapping across third-order analogies did not show a monotonic trend over age levels: .13, .09, and .16 for grade 8, grade 11, and college, respectively. However, only the weight at the college level was significant (at the 1 percent level). Thus, there is at least some evidence of increased use of mapping at the highest grade level.

In sum, there is at least some support for each of the develop-mental predictions. The results suggest that patterns of development for third-order analogical reasoning recapitulate earlier patterns of development for second-order analogical reasoning. Are individual differences in third-order reasoning related to such differences in second-order reasoning, thereby suggesting that third-order reason-ing is truly a higher-order extension of second-order reasoning? A preliminary index of quality of performance on the higher-order analogies correlated at the level of .52 with scores on Miller Analogies items for the college students. Unfortunately, comparable Miller item scores were not available for the younger students. This correlation suggests the likelihood that there are, indeed, significant parallels—ontogenetic, structural, or otherwise—between the third-order anal-ogies used in this study and the second-order analogies used in many previous studies and on ability tests. The results of our experiment, although not conclusive, suggest the fruitfulness of further investi-gation of third-order reasoning involving analogies and possibly other types of problems as well.

HIGHER-ORDER INDUCTIVE REASONING

It has been argued that third-order relational reasoning repre-sents a significant cognitive advance beyond the second-order rela-tional reasoning characteristic of formal-operational thinking. In order for this case to be convincing, it is necessary to show that third-order reasoning is not a phenomenon limited to analogy problems. Indeed, it is claimed that third-order reasoning can be applied to kinds of inductive situations other than the analogical one and, hence, that third-order reasoning is a generalizable cognitive construct. In particular, third-order reasoning can be shown to be potentially applicable to the two kinds of problems other than analogies that are most frequently found on tests of inductive reasoning ability (usually as parts of intelligence tests): series completions and classifications.

Theory

Series Completions

The stems of series-completion problems often take the form A, B, C, D, . . . , where each letter represents an item in a continuing series. In an evaluation task, the subject might be presented with a final E, and be asked whether the final E provides a satisfactory completion. When presented in this form, the series completion does not require a second-order "mapping" because the items in the series completion are from a homogeneous domain. For example, the series stem "rarely, sometimes, often, almost always" does not require one to map the second-order relation between any first-order relations because all of the first-order relations are from a homogeneous domain.

Mapping can be introduced into a series-completion problem by first presenting a single series with a certain unifying relation, then presenting the beginning of a related series, and finally asking for an evaluation of the series as a whole in terms of the relation from the first series as mapped to the related series. For example, the dual series, "rarely, sometimes, often, almost always : some, *most*," introduces a mapping. The subject's task is to evaluate the appropriateness of *most* as a series completion. In this problem, the first four items constitute the first part of the series, and the last two items constitute the second part. *Most* continues the increment in quantity mapped from the increment in frequency of the first part of the series. Thus, the incrementing relation continues, albeit in the domain of quantity rather than in the domain of frequency of occurrence. Presumably, this dual series would be evaluated favorably.

Sternberg and Gardner (note 10) have shown that the information-processing components that apply to second-order analogies apply as well to second-order series. In particular, a person must (1) *encode* each term of the series; (2) *infer* the relation between each successive pair of terms within the first part of the series (rarely-sometimes, sometimes-often, often-almost always); (3) *map* the second-order relation from the first part of the series to the second part (the rarely . . . almost always part to the some-most part); (4) *apply* the relation as inferred from the first part of the series and mapped to the second part of the series from the first to the second term of the second part of the series (some-most); (5) *justify* whether the completion (most) is good enough, even if not ideal; and (6) *respond*. Geometrically, the second-order series forms a quadrilateral in two-dimensional space. Each of the two parts of the full second-order series represents a line segment in semantic space (rarely, sometimes, often, almost always is one line segment; some, most is the other). When the two line segments are connected, they form the quadrilateral.

Third-order mapping can be applied to series completions, as to analogies, by requiring an evaluation of the degree of higher-order relation between two second-order series problems. Consider, for example, these two second-order series completions: (rarely, sometimes, often, almost always : some, most :: once, twice, thrice, four times : one-quarter, three-quarters). The subject's task is to evaluate the degree of higher-order relation between the two halves of the third-order series problem. Presumably, the evaluation would be quite favorable: The first half of each part of the series represents increments in frequency of occurrence and the second half of each represents increments in quantity. Obviously, the quality of the third-order mapping could be impaired by destroying some or all of the parallelisms of relations.

The augmented theory of third-order analogical reasoning can be carried over in full to third-order series completions. Consider the abstract form of the third-order series presented earlier:

$$A_1, B_1, C_1, D_1: \qquad\qquad\qquad A_2, B_2, C_2, D_2:$$
$$::$$
$$E_1, F_1 \qquad\qquad\qquad\qquad E_2, F_2$$

How do each of the relations for third-order analogies apply to third-order series problems?

Second-order relatedness of corresponding inferences *across second-order series completions* is a function of the closeness of the inferred relations in each of the two halves, that is, of A_1-B_1 to A_2-B_2, of B_1-C_1 to B_2-C_2, and of C_1-D_1 to C_2-D_2. *Second-order relatedness of corresponding* mappings *across second-order series completions* is a function of the closeness of the mapped relations in each of the two halves, that is, of A_1-E_1 to A_2-E_2. *Second-order relatedness of corresponding* applications *across second-order series completions* is a function of the closeness of the applied relations in each of the two halves, that is, of E_1-F_1 to E_2-F_2. *Second-order relatedness of corresponding* inferences and applications *across second-order series completions* is a function of the closeness of the juxtaposed inferred and applied relations between the two halves, that is, of each of A_1-B_1, B_1-C_1, and C_1-D_1 to E_2-F_2, and of each of A_2-B_2, B_2-C_2, and C_2-D_2 to E_1-F_1. Finally, *first-order* associative relatedness *of corresponding terms across second-order series completions* refers to associative relations between corresponding terms of the two halves of the higher order series completion, that is, A_1-A_2, B_1-B_2, C_1-C_2, D_1-D_2, E_1-E_2, and F_1-F_2. Geometrically, the third-order series completion is represented by a closed three-dimensional figure. This figure connects the two two-dimensional quadrilaterals representing each of the second-order series completions that together constitute the third-order problem.

Classifications

The stems of classification problems can take the form A_1, B_1, C_1 : A_2, B_2, C_2, where each letter represents an item in a group. In an evaluation task, the subject might be asked to rate the conceptual relation between the first three terms and the second three terms.

Sternberg and Gardner (note 10) have shown that processing components that apply to second-order analogies apply as well to second-order classifications. In particular, one must (1) *encode* each term of the item; (2) *infer* the relation between each pair of terms within each triple of terms (or among the three terms of each triple simultaneously) in order to discover what the terms within a triple have in common; (3) *map* the second-order relation between each of the two inferred relations to discover similarities and differences; and (4) *respond* with an evaluation of how similar the two higher-order relations are. Application and justification are not relevant to this form of problem because there is no extrapolation to form an ideal point for the problem. It is possible, however, to add components by expanding the problem. Consider, for example, the case in which a D term is added and in which the subject's task is to decide whether D fits better with the first group of elements (A_1, B_1, C_1) or with the second group of elements (A_2, B_2, C_2). Here, the subject must apply the inferred relations as mapped between domains to decide whether the target item fits better with the first or the second group of terms.

Third-order mapping can be applied to classifications, as well as to analogies and series completions, by requiring an evaluation of the degree of higher-order relation between two second-order classification problems. Consider, for example, these two second-order classification problems: (daisy, tulip, rose : poodle, boxer, collie :: pine, maple, oak : jersey, guernsey, holstein). The subject's task is to evaluate the degree of higher-order relation between the two halves of the third-order classification problem. Presumably, this problem would be favorably evaluated: The first half of each classification deals with related elements—flowers or trees—in the plant kingdom; the second half of each classification deals with related elements—dogs or cows—in the animal kingdom. For each part of the third-order classification, then, plants are paired with animals.

The augmented theory of third-order reasoning can be carried over to third-order classification problems. Consider the abstract form of the third-order classification problem presented above:

A_1, B_1, C_1 : A_3, B_3, C_3 :

                                    : :

A_2, B_2, C_2 A_4, B_4, C_4

Again, a subset of the relations used to evaluate third-order analogies can be applied to third-order classifications.

Second-order relatedness of corresponding inferences *across second-order classifications* is a function of the closeness of the inferred relations in each of the two halves, that is, of (A_1, B_1, C_1) to (A_3, B_3, C_3) and of (A_2, B_2, C_2) to (A_4, B_4, C_4).[3] *Third-order relatedness of corresponding* mappings *across second-order classifications* is a function of the closeness of the mapped relations in each of the two halves of the item, that is, of $(A_1, B_1, C_1) - (A_2, B_2, C_2)$ to $(A_3, B_3, C_3) - (A_4, B_4, C_4)$.[4] Finally, *first-order* associative relatedness *of corresponding terms across second-order classifications* refers to associative relatedness between corresponding terms of the two halves of the higher-order classification, that is, A_1-A_3, B_1-B_3, C_1-C_3, A_2-A_4, B_2-B_4, and C_2-C_4.[5] Geometrically, a third-order classification is represented by a closed three-dimensional figure connecting the two halves of the problem. The exact form of the figure will depend upon the number of items in each n-tuple forming the two halves of the third-order problem.

Relations Between Analogies, Series Completions, and Classifications

Given the close relationship between the components of information processing theorized to apply to all three inductive-reasoning tasks, it should not be surprising that the three tasks are closely related both structurally and psychologically. The most general form of problem is the classification, which, in its second-order form, asks for an evaluation of the degree of relationship between two unordered triples (or n-tuples) of terms. The analogy is a bit more restricted than the classification in that the terms on each side of the second-order item are specified to be ordered proportionally. In other words, the relation between the third and fourth terms (on one side of the item) is specified to be parallel to the relation between the first and second terms (on the other side of the item). The series completion is more restricted yet, requiring that the terms in the stem of the item be related specifically in terms of a linear ordering. Each term represents an increment or decrement over the last term on some linear dimension.

Generalization of Item Formats

The illustrations provided above for the three types of inductive reasoning problems are all based on a relation-evaluation format. This format proved conducive to theory testing in the third-order analogies study cited earlier (Sternberg & Downing, 1982). It seems to be suitable for theory testing with series completions and classifications as well. It should be noted, however, that the theory is indifferent with respect to item format. The theory of second-order inductive reasoning has been applied to true-false and multiple-choice item formats as well as to the evaluation format (see Sternberg, 1977; Sternberg & Gardner, note 10; Sternberg & Rifkin, 1979). The theory of third-order reasoning could be applied to these other formats as well.

Testing of the Theory

The *augmented* theory of third-order reasoning—as extended to series completions and classifications—has not yet been empirically tested. The theory is directly testable, however, and a test of it is planned. Testing will involve administration of third-order analogies, series completions, and classifications to subjects ranging in age from early to late adolescence. Each subject will receive items of all three types, and data analysis will follow that of Sternberg and Downing (1982). In particular, it is predicted that:

1. The theory of third-order inductive reasoning can be applied to series completions and classifications as well as to analogies.
2. The weight of associative relatedness in evaluating the induction items will decrease with increasing age through adolescence.
3. The weight of inferential relatedness in evaluating the inductive items will increase with increasing age through adolescence.
4. The weight of mapping relatedness will be trivial in early adolescence and will become statistically significant in later adolescence.
5. Weights of corresponding relations (as estimated parameters) across tasks—for example, relatedness of corresponding inferences for the analogies, series completions, and classifications—will be significantly correlated across subjects. This would indicate consistent patterns of individual differences over tasks for the corresponding relations.

BEYOND TESTLIKE PROBLEMS

The third-order analogies, series completions, and classifications discussed above are obviously testlike in form and content. Whether the proposed augmented theory of third-order reasoning applies beyond testlike items remains an important question. I believe the theory does apply beyond such items. Consider, for example, the third-order analogy, (Machine Language : Hardware :: Programming Language : Software) :: (Language of the Brain : Neural Connections :: Ordinary Language : Cognitive Structures). This implicit analogy seems to underlie much of the current debate regarding the usefulness of computer programs as bases for understanding linguistic and other forms of human information processing. Making the implicit analogy explicit facilitates understanding of the tacit assumptions underlying the debate, at least as put forward by researchers in artificial intelligence. Or consider the third-order analogy, (U.S. Advisors : El Salvadoran Government Forces :: Communist Advisors : El Salvadoran Rebel Forces) :: (U.S. Advisors : South Vietnamese Rebel Forces). The validity of this third-order analogy may be seen as a point of contention underlying recent debates regarding the advisability of the U.S. intervention in the El Salvadoran conflict.

Those who accept the third-order analogy as valid are unlikely to support U.S. intervention through military advisors. Again, clarifying the implicit analogy underlying the conflict helps one understand just what the conflict—in this case, over intervention in El Salvador—is about.

Less testlike higher-order reasoning problems have also been examined under experimental conditions by Commons et al. (1982). These investigators asked subjects to find higher-order relations between elements of four fairly long and involved stories concerning topics as diverse as preferences among Indian foods and gambling styles. Their results suggested systematic developmental differences in people's ability to discern higher-order relations, at least at the level of undergraduate and graduate students.

To conclude, it appears that third-order reasoning is a genuine psychological phenomenon in the real world and one that can be studied in a laboratory setting. It is debatable whether the ability to perform third-order reasoning represents a genuine incremental stage beyond those postulated by Piaget (1976). Indeed, the whole notion of stages is debatable. But there seems to be little doubt that the ability to perform third-order reasoning increases during the years that in the past have been associated with formal operations. The combined data from the Commons et al. (1982) study and the Sternberg and Downing (1982) study suggest that individuals early in the formal-operational period are able to perform third-order reasoning only at a minimal level, if at all.

Is third-order reasoning a worthwhile construct to pursue in future research? I believe that it is. Consider several reasons.

First, from the standpoint of the theory of inductive reasoning, the augmented theory presented in this chapter shows that the theory of inductive reasoning can be extrapolated at least to the third order, and probably to higher orders as well. Work such as that proposed here suggests that theories of inductive reasoning cannot only be extended horizontally across tasks (as we and others have done for analogies, series completions, and classifications), but also vertically across orders of tasks.

Second, from the standpoint of theories of development, research on third-order reasoning suggests one way of understanding postformal-operational development (Case, 1978). Certainly, other kinds of research could be, and have been, advanced for the same purpose. An example is Arlin's (1975) proposals regarding a postformal-operational period of problem finding. The data accumulated to date suggest that third-order reasoning does, indeed, represent one valid way of understanding adolescent and possibly later development.

Third, from the standpoint of the measurement of intellectual functioning, and especially the measurement of reasoning skills, third-order reasoning problems provide a means for assessing advanced intellectual functioning. Too often, reasoning problems attain their difficulty from either the advanced level of vocabulary required for problem solution, as on the Miller Analogies Test (see Sternberg, 1977), or from the high level of spatial visualization or working-memory capacity required for problem solution (see, for example, Case, 1978; Guyote & Sternberg, 1981). Third-order reasoning problems seem to provide a basis for measurement of advanced reasoning processes that is uncontaminated by vocabulary and visualization skills.

Finally, third-order reasoning seems to underlie very complex real-world decisions of several types (for example, the computer and foreign-policy analogies described earlier). Because of the complexity of the underlying relations, these relations seem most often to remain implicit and unarticulated. However, rendering them explicit and articulated may clarify the kinds of thinking required to arrive at solutions to complex problems.

NOTES

1. My work on higher-order reasoning by analogy was conducted in collaboration with Cathryn J. Downing (Sternberg & Downing, 1982).

2. The exact components that apply depend upon the exact format of the task. For example, a comparison component would also be needed in multiple-choice format (Sternberg & Gardner, note 10).

3. If the two halves of the second-order classification are assumed to be order free, then $(A_1, B_1, C_1) - (A_4, B_4, C_4)$ and $(A_2, B_2, C_2) - (A_3, B_3, C_3)$ might also be compared.

4. Note that the mapping in the classification problem is at the third order.

5. If the two halves of the second-order classification are assumed to be order-free, then $A_1\text{-}A_4$, $B_1\text{-}B_4$, $C_1\text{-}C_4$, $A_2\text{-}A_3$, $B_2\text{-}B_3$, $C_2\text{-}C_3$ might also be compared.

5

SYSTEMATIC, METASYSTEMATIC, AND CROSS-PARADIGMATIC REASONING: A CASE FOR STAGES OF REASONING BEYOND FORMAL OPERATIONS

Francis A. Richards and Michael L. Commons

The purpose of this chapter is to revise and expand the framework that guided the research reported by Commons, Richards, and Kuhn (1982). That research found evidence supporting the proposition that forms of reasoning exist that are qualitatively distinct from and more complex than the form of reasoning characterized by Inhelder and Piaget (1958) as "formal operational." Here, the framework for conceptualizing and measuring the development of postformal reasoning is more rigorously defined in terms of a hierarchy of task demands. Attention is given to (1) defining tasks in the context of cognitive developmental research; (2) specifying how tasks relate to the notions of stage and stage sequence; and (3) describing the tasks used in this research.

Three postformal stages are discussed in this chapter. The systematic and metasystematic stages were introduced earlier (Commons and Richards, note 11, abstracted in Stevens-Long, 1979; Commons, Richards, and Kuhn, 1982).[1] A third postformal stage, the cross-paradigmatic, is introduced. Each of these stages will be shown to be "higher than" its predecessor stage. It is argued that the systematic stage is hierarchically constructed out of the elements and actions of Piaget's formal operations, the metasystematic stage is hierarchically constructed out of the elements and actions of the

This research was supported in part by a Dare Association Grant No. 10032 to the second author. Portions of this study were presented at the Western Psychological Association, San Francisco, 1978, and at the Jean Piaget Society, Philadelphia, 1979. The extract portions appeared in Michael L. Commons, Francis A. Richards, and Deanna Kuhn, Systematic and Metasystematic Reasoning: A Case for Levels of Reasoning beyond Piaget's Stage of Formal Operations, *Child Development,* 1982, 53, 1058–69. We thank Deanna Kuhn, Joan Richards, Patrice M. Miller, Joel R. Peck, Barbara Mahon, Eloise Coupey, David K. Pickard, and Cheryl Armon for their work on various portions of the study.

systematic stage, and the cross-paradigmatic stage is similarly constructed out of the elements and actions of the metasystematic stage.

In this framework, it is assumed that any task measuring cognitive development can be represented as actions coordinating elements. For example, conserving the volume of a plasticine cylinder as it is rolled out into a longer cylinder is accomplished by an action that coordinates the elements of the cylinder's length and diameter. Length and diameter are properties of plasticine in that form, and the action of reciprocal inversion is applied to these properties. In reciprocal inversion, when the volume is conserved the product of length and diameter remains constant while either the length or the diameter changes. Since one action, reciprocal inversion, is applied to a set of elements, the task demands are of first-order complexity. It then follows that an intuitive notion of stage is that it is an underlying construct detectable by a set of diverse tasks with the same order of complexity.

An action of second-order complexity would be the coordination of the conservation of volume, as an element with another element. The order of complexity of tasks used to detect stages causes them to be sequenced. In the example above, the second order of complexity is created by the application of an action to an element that itself constitutes the application of an action to an element. This is called hierarchical construction. Hierarchical construction is an action upon, including the coordination of, the products of previous coordinations, as long as the new action does not belong to the stage being acted upon (Commons and Richards, Chapter 6, this volume). Thus, a person must have previous stage coordinations, or schemata, to develop actions sufficient to deal with tasks at the next order of task complexity.

An example of hierarchical construction (referred to as hierarchical composition in the next chapter) can be found in the coordinations of the actions (operations) of addition or multiplication that result in the discovery (the stage product) of associativity. The associative act is the recognition that the order in which a set of numbers is added or multiplied is irrelevant: the combination $a + (b + c)$ is equal to the combination $(a + b) + c$, and the combination $a \times (b \times c)$ is equal to $(a \times b) \times c$. The act involves recognizing that the order of applying addition or multiplication is irrelevant, regardless of (1) the specific numbers (elements) involved and (2) the number of such numbers. In other words, the general equivalency between patterns is recognized. Such equivalency does not directly depend on specific numbers or on any given instance of addition or multiplication. The product, associativity, cannot be defined in terms of the application of predecessor-stage actions to predecessor-stage elements. An analogous example of postformal reasoning is given further on, showing how the structure of higher-stage reasoning cannot be described within the limits of a formal-operational framework.

In sum, it is only tasks that have complexity and that can be arranged hierarchically. Domains and stages are generalizations of sets of tasks. They are abstracted properties of sets of tasks. For instance, various coordinations of length and diameter might define the domain of solid polar geometry. Similar degrees of task complexity across extremely diverse elements define a stage.

In our stage sequence, Piaget's system of successive stages is made use of only in its most general form. Thus, sensory-motor operations are defined as actions on material objects; symbolic operations as actions or operations on collections of symbolically represented material objects; and formal operations as operations on organized sets of symbolically represented sets of objects. These general features show the repetitive structuralization of Piaget's developmental sequence. Piaget's stages are regarded as successive stages of cognitive representation and constitute a conceptual description of forms of cognition. In the construction and evaluation of such a conceptual description, analytic, not empirical, criteria are applied (Bickhard, 1979). Empirical evidence may indicate that a particular sequencing of tasks is misordered. Also, empirical evidence may indicate that some tasks do not belong to a domain or stage, but only structural analysis of the tasks can confirm these indications.

When our definition of hierarchy is applied to Piaget's sequence, it gives the status of true stages to both A and B substages of concrete and formal operations. In order to emphasize this new status of Piaget's substages, stage names have been given to them. The argument that these are true stages rests on demonstrating analytically that at each stage an irreducibly higher-order coordination of stage elements and actions takes place. These arguments appear in a later section of the chapter and in the Appendix.

Although more stages are added as a consequence of our analysis, it is not our intent to argue that there are indefinitely many stages. Since each higher order of task complexity results from the application of one action upon a new element, there can be no intermediate stages in a correctly specified stage sequence. Table 5.1 shows these stages and their order of complexity, that is, the number of times actions are applied to elements that are themselves actions applied to elements. Traditionally, formal operations have been referred to as "operations on operations," or second-order operations (Piaget, 1976; Case, 1978). Here, formal operations are called fourth-order operations. See Fischer, Hand, & Russell (Chapter 3, this volume) for a parallel argument. In Table 1, stages are described as action structures that are either domain operations or relation operations. Domain operations collect elements into a whole,

Table 5.1. Schematized Representation of Piaget's Concrete and Formal-Operations Stages and of the Postformal Stages

Stage Name	No.	Order of Operations	Action Structure — Relation Operation	Action Structure — Domain Operation
Primary operations	3a	First order; operations on objects $e(a,b,c)$	Relations $(<,+,=,\text{etc})$ applied to pairs, triples	Objects unified (U) into a set $\{a,b,c\}$
Concrete operations	3b	Second order; operations on organized set of objects $f(e(a,b,c))$		Relation applied across a set of objects (summed number sequences, transitively ordered sets, etc)
Concrete (extended)	3b	Multiple second; $f(e_i(a,b,c))$		Relations applied across two or more sets: multiple seriation, one-to-one correspondence
Abstract operations	4a	Third order; operations applied to organized sets $g(f(e(a,b,c)))$	Relations applied across discrete cases of variables	Discrete cases of variables are unified into variables
Formal operations	4b	Fourth order; operations applied to sets of variables $h(g(f(e(a,b,c))))$	Relations are applied to isolated variables	
Formal (extended)	4b	Multiple fourth; $h(g_i(f(e(a,b,c))))$	Relations are applied to combinations of variables including interactions	
Systematic operations	5a	Fifth order; operations on systems $q(h(g(f(e(a,b,c)))))$	Test for properties of relations within systems; comparison of properties across systems	Combines all possible combinations of elements and relations into system
Metasystematic operations	5b	Sixth order; relations on operations in systems $r(q(h(g(f(e(a,b,c))))))$	Test for properties of relations within entire systems and compare all properties of relations across sets of systems	
Cross-Paradigmatic operations	6a	Seventh order; operations on fields $s(r(q(h(g(f(e(a,b,c)))))))$	Test for properties of fields and relate properties across fields	Combines systems to form fields

95

surely interactions happen before formal operations

whereas relation operations establish or test for conditions within this whole.

From an analysis of Piaget's tasks, his stages may be grouped into pairs. In the first stage of a pair (a), a domain operation can be executed without a relation operation, or a relation operation can be incompletely carried out because a domain has not been operationally established. At the second stage of the pair (b), these operations are integrated, and relation operations can be applied to domains completely and systematically. This integration marks the completion of a Piagetian stage structure and is the necessary antecedent for further structural development. An "extended" form of this structure also appears in Table 5.1. This represents the increasing equilibration of the second member of the pair of stages as it is applied more diversely and versatilely. This most likely is accounted for by experience resulting in overlearning (Pascual-Leone, Chapter 9, this volume) and may be the sufficient antecedent for further structural development.

The bottom portion of Table 5.1 shows the general features of systematic and metasystematic reasoning. These types of reasoning are jointly referred to as reasoning at the first postformal stage. All the general features of Piaget's description of operational reasoning have been inductively extended. Analysis of the action structure and order of operations of the postformal stages shows that they are qualitatively distinct from, but hierarchically related to, formal operations. The a and b stages show that the manner of stage construction is parallel to that found in primary and concrete operations and in abstract and formal operations.

If forms of advanced cognition are to be identified that make reference to, and build on, Piaget's sequence of stages of cognition, they must take the general form of the higher fifth- or sixth-order operations (and beyond) referred to above. To make this claim is not to assert that all forms of adult cognition necessarily fall within such categories. Indeed, current research and theory in adult cognitive development run strongly counter to such a claim (Kuhn, Pennington, and Leadbeater, 1983; Labouvie-Vief 1980, 1982). Rather, our claim is that if one postulates more advanced and developed forms of reasoning of the type studied by Piaget—specifically, forms that build in the forms of reasoning that constitute his existing stage sequence—then this more advanced reasoning must take the general form indicated above.

What might such higher-order operations look like in the cognition of an individual? Formal operations can be characterized as "interrelational thinking," that is, thinking based on ordered relations of classes and relations (Stage 4b). The individual executes operations on these classes and relations. For example, the individual may formulate and test hypotheses about the relations that obtain among two classes of objects. (See the Appendix for a formal example.) In these operations, cognitive ability is limited to pairs of variables, or larger subsets of variables, which are lesser in amount than the total set of possible relations among the two classes of objects. In executing these formal operations, however, the individual does not deal with, act or operate on the system as a whole. The postformal stages would then appear as follows.

Systematic, or fifth-order operations, consist of exhaustive operations on the classes and relations between the members of these classes, which in their totality form systems. Systematic operations apply to the entire set of constituents of a system. For example, they might be the use of iterative operations (such as summation, S_i, or multiplication, M_i) to create properties of systems, or they might be the use of abstract properties (such as $a * 0 = 0$ and $a + 0 = a$) to represent features of a system. Systematic operations represent the properties of operations at the formal-operational stage and coordinate these representations.

Metasystematic, or sixth-order operations, consist of operations across systems. Given that systems are operations on the classes and relations between the members of these classes, metasystematic operations start at the level of relating systems to systems. Metasystematic operations end when a complete class of relations between a class of systems (a system of systems) can be constructed. They are cognitions about multiple (two or more) systems and are required in the formation of a framework (or "metasystem") for comparing and contrasting systems with one another. The relationship of one system to another is expressed with metatheoretical acts such as comparing properties of systems, which in some domains are expressed by axioms, theorems, or other limiting conditions of systems. The relationships are expressed within the framework of a "supersystem" that contains all the variant systems. Metasystematic reasoning is defined as the set of operations necessary to construct the supersystem and to execute the analysis of the systems contained therein. These operations guide everyday actions in areas where reasoning about interrelations of systems is called for.

Cross-paradigmatic, or seventh-order operations, relate families of systems. These families, or systems of systems, constitute fields. The beginning substage of cross-paradigmatic operations appears with the ability to generate collections of systems of systems. This substage ends when an initial understanding is reached concerning why a field is a field. At this substage, fields can be systematized but not operated on further. Initially, the subject appreciates that fields have some relationship but cannot find it.

The next substage consists of the basic cross-paradigmatic operations that are constructed to relate fields that appear to be independent of one another. Fields are compared by detecting and describing relations between systems of systems. These are the operations of inter-field unification. At the highest substage, field relations are systematized and formed into a new unit. At this time there are only rare cases exhibiting this stage of thought. No tasks exist to test for it, but comparing epistemologies for different fields would suffice.

While people whose thought is scored at this stage should appear wise, it is not clear that all wisdom reflects this stage of thought. There has also been discussion as to whether mystical thinking characterizes this stage (Baldwin, 1895; Koplowitz, Chapter 13, this volume). Again, while some mystical thinking might be scored at this stage, not all mystical thought reflects the use of cross-paradigmatic operations. For either wisdom or mysticism to be at this stage, they must have subjects as complex as fields. If a field represents the most complex element of epistemology for which there is any evidence of instantiation, then cross-paradigmatic operations represent the present terminus of genetic epistemology.

An example of metasystematic reasoning is found in that aspect of Einstein's general theory of relativity that deals with the coordination of inertial and gravitational mass. Prior to Einstein's formulation, there was one system for describing inertial mass and a separate one for describing gravitational mass. Each separate system included *systematic* representations of properties of *formally* defined relations between variables. Inertial mass was the property of the system that described a body's resistance to acceleration. Gravitational mass was a property of another system that described the weight of a body in a given gravitational field. In fact, since the same constant for mass represents both the inertia and the weight of a body, it follows that it is impossible to discover by experiment which of the following is true: The motion of a given system of coordinates is straight and uniform and the observed effects within the system are due to a gravitational field, or the system of coordinates is uniformly accelerated and the observed effects within the system are due to inertia. Recognition of an equivalence between the two cases constitutes the equivalence principle of general relativity theory. This principle states that the inertial system is isomorphic (contains the same structure and elements) to the gravitational system; that is, any relationship that is true in one is true in the other. Whether the same property appears as weight or as inertia depends on which description of the coordinate systems is employed; that is, motion in a gravitational field appears in relation to an inertial system of coordinates, while motion in the absence of a gravitational field appears in a coordinate system that is accelerated. This principle requires a coordination of two distinct systems, each generated by systematic operations: the inertial system and the gravitational system. The cognitive operations that effect this coordination are at a "metasystematic" level, distinct from that of the operations applied within either of the individual systems.

The above example serves to illustrate the irreducibility of the higher-order operations to operations of the next lower order. Operations at the metasystematic level must be expressed in the language of metalogic, or its psychological equivalent, because statements about the relation between systems cannot be reduced to statements about the properties of the relations within any single system. Similarly, statements about systems properties cannot be contained within any of the individual systems. Hence, systematic operations cannot be reduced to formal operations because the formal operational systems themselves do not contain descriptions of the system. These formal operations are not rich enough to describe their own properties. If this were possible, Russell's paradox (the sentence, "This sentence is false") would not exist. In other words, a property of a system cannot be described by a proposition within a system.

Method

Task

In the problem we developed to assess systematic and meta-systematic reasoning, the subject was asked to compare and contrast four systems, each comprised of a set of asymmetric relations. Two similar forms of the problems were constructed. One form of the problem and the instructions given to the subject are shown below.

Here are four stories. After you read them, you will answer questions on which are most similar and which most different. Use the "greater than" symbol ">" to indicate the order of things. For example, indicate "Brown prefers Oregon over Texas," by $O > T$. Only attend to order.

1) On counter earth, Richard Reagan has been elected President of the United States. As a gesture of gratitude to the people of his home state, California, Reagan has convinced them to leave California and either wander around with no state, or take a combination of one, two, or three of the following states: Oregon, Washington, and Indiana. Reagan thinks that the economic value of Oregon and Washington are equal, and that the value of either is less than that of Indiana. The boundary and passport bill which he submitted to Congress, requiring the barbed wiring and mining of the boundaries at considerable expense, did not pass. Instead, Congress specified that the funds asked for in that bill were to go to the states selected to be used as the states saw fit. Only Washington and Oregon have common boundaries and, therefore, a union of these two states would receive a smaller amount of the fortification funds. Therefore, even with the value of their combined economies, Reagan thinks that the pair Oregon and

Washington is less valuable than the pairs Oregon and Indiana or Washington and Indiana. Since Indiana makes boats which can be used on the Columbia River, Reagan thinks that the economic benefits of pairing Washington and Indiana are slightly greater than the benefits of pairing Oregon and Indiana. Reagan thinks that three states are worth more than any combination of 0, 1, or 2 states, and any 2 states are worth more than 0 or 1 states, except he cannot decide which is worth more, Indiana or the pair Oregon and Washington. Reagan also thinks that any state is worth more than no state at all.

2) Bad Bart ambles into the local casino and converts his gold watch into chips of the following colors: silver, bronze, and gold. Bart likes to play the one-chip candy machines. He likes the chips in the following order: gold better than silver, silver better than bronze, and gold better than bronze, and any chip over none. Bart also likes to play the one-armed bandit machines which use combinations of two chips. He likes the two-chip combinations in the following order: golds and silvers first, golds and bronzes second, and silvers and bronzes third. With one exception, Bart knows he likes to play with any two chips over one or none; he is not sure about a gold versus a silver and a bronze. Because Bad Bart likes to play with three chips best, there is one machine that he likes better than any other: the washing machine, and it takes a silver, a bronze, and a gold chip.

3) In Madras, India, V. P. Vanktesh, a man of habit and variable income, has a favorite restaurant. Although his tastes never vary, the food he can afford does. Of the three foods the restaurant serves he prefers curry, birani, and alu paratha, in that order. Also, he likes curry better than alu paratha, and anything better than nothing. When V. P. has more money he buys two dishes, except it is not known whether he would choose the curry over both the birani and the alu paratha. He likes the combination of curry and birani better than curry and alu paratha, and he also likes curry and alu paratha better than birani and alu paratha, and birani and alu paratha better than curry and birani. Although a temperate man, at festivals, given the means, he has all three dishes instead of any single dish or pair.

4) A jeweler has three boxes, the first containing different kinds of broken 18-carat gold necklaces, the second various scratched earrings, and the third different kinds of 18-carat gold pins that are broken. He keeps the old jewelry because he occasionally uses the gold. To get the approximate amount of gold he needs, he weighs and then melts down a combination of objects. To do the weighing he uses a simple, somewhat variable balance-beam scale. It consists of a beam that pivots in the middle and two pans hanging from each end of the beam, equidistant from the pivot. The beam is almost level when the pans are empty. The jeweler can place combinations of from 0

to 3 object types into one pan, but never more than one of each object type in a pan. Beginning with empty pans, he notices that whenever he puts any combinations containing at least one object into a pan, that pan sinks down, indicating that it is heavier that the empty pan. Using this same method, he finds that any pin is heavier than any earring. Necklaces are always heavier than pins. He has discovered two rules that reduce how many combinations he needs to try to find out how the weights of the combinations are ordered. First, he notices that if the combination in the right pan is heavier than the combination in the left pan, and a single object type not already in either of the pans is added to both pans, the right pan remains heavier than the left. Secondly, if he weighs three combinations of objects, he finds that the following is always true: If the first combination is heavier that the second, and the second heavier than the third, then the first is heavier than the third.

Space was left after each story for subjects to make notations. On a separate page, the following instructions were presented.

Now that you have read the stories and are familiar with them, answer the questions below. Make your comparisons on the basis of properties of the orderings found in each story, in the best and most complete way that you can. Write out all the comparisons that you can in a systematic way. Use symbols to represent the order of things, and explain what the symbols stand for. Also include an explanation in English. You may want to use a chain, for example, Oregon → Texas, in addition to an ordering, Oregon > Texas. Then explain what are the most important similarities and differences in the stories, and explain how you arrived at deciding the relative importance of these similarities and differences. You may refer to more than one framework. Make sure to give the strongest, most thorough, broad, inclusive, and complete explanations possible for the similarities and differences. It is necessary that you show all of your work in forming the orders and making the comparisons, as well as your commentary in English.

The following form was used for subjects to provide their answers.

1. Which of the stories are the most similar?
1 and 2_____ 2 and 3_____ 1,2, and 3_____ 1,3, and 4_____
1 and 3_____ 2 and 4_____ 1,2, and 4_____ 1,2,3, and 4_____
1 and 4_____ 3 and 4_____ 2,3, and 4_____

2. Which of the stories differ the most from the ones you listed as similar (1), even though they may have many characteristics in common?

1___	4___	1 and 2___	2 and 3___
2___		1 and 3___	2 and 4___
3___		1 and 4___	3 and 4___

3. Explain why the stories you listed above as similar are similar.
4. Explain why the stories you listed as different from these are different.

Space was provided for subject's answer. (This problem is used with the permission of the Dare Association, Inc.)

Each of the four systems within the problem consists of a finite, partially ordered, commutative semigroup, with a binary operation for combining objects and a partial order relation defined among all possible combinations of elements. The systems were presented as stories about which combinations of three objects, $a, b, c,$ were greater than others. The combinations could include no item, single items, or two or three items. In the first three stories, for the most part, the orderings of combinations of objects were explicitly stated. One object is preferred over another, or over none at all, for example, a over none, c over b, b over a, and so forth; some pairs are preferred over others, for example, $b + c$ over $a + b$; or the complete group is preferred over a pair, for example, $a + b + c$ over $b + c$. In the fourth story, the structure of the order was stated in propositional form which did not provide direct access to the orderings of the elements; these had to be derived by the subject.

An alternate form B was presented to a portion of the sample. Forms A and B were identical except for the structure reflected in story 1 (see fig. 1) and the names of the elements in each of the stories, for example, the names of the states in story 1 and the foods in story 3.

The subject was allowed an unlimited amount of time. The average amount of time spent was 1 hour, with an approximate range from 30 min to 2 hours.

Two additional problems were presented to a portion of the subjects (73 of the 110): a simple transitivity problem (requiring concrete operations) and a version of Inhelder and Piaget's (1958) pendulum problem (requiring formal operations).

At all stages of operations (first, second, and so on) the problems used here tested reasoning in the very specific domain of operations on order relations. These problems and their task structures are described below. A more rigorous description of task structure appears in the Appendix. Although intermediate levels of responses may appear in performances, only the discrete, ideal stages of structure are defined.

PRIMARY AND CONCRETE: FIRST- AND SECOND-ORDER OPERATIONS (3a THROUGH 3b)

The transitivity problem consists of a set of statements about orders of pairs, "Chris is taller than Bill, Abe is shorter than Bill" and asks "Who is tallest?". The primary-operational or first-order task is to construct a "task subset" from a larger set of elements. Creating a task subset simply means defining the task domain. In this problem, this means determining that the solution involves only the elements Abe, Bill, and Chris, and does not include elements from outside this set (extraneous information).

The concrete-operational or second-order task consists of constructing the height relation between the third pair of people. This task can be thought of as coordinating the first coordinated pair of people (Chris > Bill) with the second coordinated pair of people (Abe < Bill) to produce a third coordination between people (Abe < Chris). The operation creates an ordered set out of ordered pairs, and, consequently, it operates on the operations that create the ordered pairs. This structure defines the task as a second-level operation.

ABSTRACT AND FORMAL: THIRD- AND FOURTH-ORDER OPERATIONS (4a THROUGH 4b)

The written pendulum problem consists of six informational episodes that are followed by one test episode. In each episode there are four independent variables, pendulum weight (W), string length (L), height of pendulum release (H), strength of push (S), that are the possible causes of one dependent variable, pendulum periodicity (P). Periodicity is how often the pendulum weight crosses the center line. In this problem only one independent variable, string length, is causally related to pendulum periodicity.

Each variable displays one of two possible values. For example, string length may be long ($L = 2$) or short ($L = 1$). Informational episodes have the form:

$$W_i + L_i + H_i + S_i \rightarrow P_i$$

Each variable subscript, i, has the value 1 or 2 and $\rightarrow$ indicates "causes". Test episodes have the form:

$$W_i + L_i + H_i + S_i \rightarrow ?$$

The "?" asks for a prediction of the value of P. In their entirety, episodes can be represented:

	variable				outcome
	W_i	$+ L_i$	$+ H_i$	$+ S_i \longrightarrow$	P_i

episode

1	2	2	1	1	$\longrightarrow$	2
2	1	2	1	2	$\longrightarrow$	2
3	1	1	2	2	$\longrightarrow$	1
4	1	2	2	1	$\longrightarrow$	2
5	2	1	2	1	$\longrightarrow$	1
6	2	1	1	2	$\longrightarrow$	1
Test	2	2	2	2	$\longrightarrow$	?

As this set of episodes shows, the column values for string length, L, perfectly predict the column values for periodicity, P. The ideal formal-operational performance on this task predicts short periodicity in the test episode on the basis of this relation between the columns. All other independent variables can be rejected because they do not perfectly predict P.

The format of the pendulum task already embodies first- and second-order operations. First, episodes are laid out so that, when read from left to right, episodes can be perceived as a whole. If they are perceived as a whole, a primary operation has been performed (Stage 3a). Second, the order of the variables in an episode can be seen as constant across episodes. If they are seen as constant, a concrete order operation has been performed (Stage 3b). Combining these two operations creates an ordered set, or matrix, M, which contains the elements (variables) of formal operations.

The abstract-operational (4a) task is performed on the ordered set M. One abstract-operational task is to isolate five variables, W, L, H, S, and P from the episodes. The isolation-of-variables act consists of classifying the information into variables. This is done by looking down columns of values one at a time. This act is an operation performed on an ordered set. Each application creates a class of values called a variable.

The formal-operational (4b) task consists of locating one causal variable and of eliminating all noncausal variables by operating on these variables. To see which variable is causal requires the application of a logical relation to these variables. A variable is possibly causal if it is never the case that the value of the variable is not correlated with the value of the outcome it is supposed to cause. A typical abstract-operational performance is to apply the logical relation to the ordered set rather than to the variables. This results in incorrect predictions.

Succeeding at one of these tasks, but not both, is a performance at the abstract-operational stage (4a). Coordinating these two tasks is a fourth-order operation (4b)—an operation on an operation on an ordered set—where the ordered set is an operation on an operation. It meets the general structural criteria outlined in Table 5.1 for a fourth-order task at the consolidated level of formal operations (4b). Note that in the problem cause has the formal properties of an order relation such as transitivity: if $a \rightarrow b$ and $b \rightarrow c$, then $a \rightarrow c$.

SYSTEMATIC & METASYSTEMATIC: FIFTH- AND SIXTH-ORDER OPERATIONS (5a THROUGH 5b)

The stories in the metasystematic problem are the elements of operations that require two higher-stage competencies, the systematic and metasystematic. At the systematic stage, these operations completely and parsimoniously coordinate all relations across the objects described in each of the four stories. In each story, the objects and their combinations can be represented as the set of all subsets of elements that can be generated from three elements. Finding this set requires combinatorially generating the full set of possible subsets of three elements. This is the power operation, 2^n. Representing all relations among these subsets requires generating the full set of possible relations across these subsets (2^n things taken two at a time). These two steps create a set of elements and relations for each story that can be represented as the lattice structures that appear below in Figure 5.1. The first step, counting combinatorially, is a fourth-order formal operation on an ordered set. The second step, establishing an order relation, is a fifth-order, systematic operation on the fourth-order operation.

At the metasystematic stage the stories are compared on the basis of properties of the relations between the sets of elements. For example, this could involve representing that addition or any operation with the formal properties of addition can be performed across the elements of story 2. It could also involve representing the fact that addition cannot be performed across the elements of stories 1 and 3.

Addition can be performed in story 2. Consequently, this story contains a transitive order relation. For this reason, the story structure conforms to the INRC group structure of formal operations, and a performance that represents the structure of story 2 is at the highest level (extended) of formal operations and the lowest substage of systematic operations. It is quite possible to detect a performance that has the properties of both extended 4b and 5a. However, the task structures do not overlap. In a formal sense, task structure at different stages is assumed to reflect a strictly hierarchical generating process in which predecessor-stage products become successor-stage elements (Commons and Richards, Chapter 6, this volume).

Representing the structure in stories 1 and 3 is an operation at the systematic stage (5a) since these structures do not contain simple addition. They conform to directed graph structure, but are non-standard and possibly extra-formal. These stories are not counter-factual; the situations they portray could in fact exist. Nevertheless, the structures of stories 1 and 3 do fail to meet simple formal-operational notions of what is logical. In story 4, elements and order relations are not given directly. Instead, a set of rules (axioms) describes the outcomes of a weighing process. In this story, the task is to use this set of rules to generate and represent a structure that is comparable to the other three stories.

Metasystematic operations (5b) determine how similar stories are to each other. The similarity of one system to another is a morphism. For example, story 2 and story 4 are structurally the same, and their relation to one another can be described as an isomorphism. This means that each system contains operations with the same formal properties and that the elements and relations of the systems can be put in one-to-one correspondence. One-to-one correspondence means that every element in one story has a corresponding element in the other story. With respect to order, applying the relations in one story will have the same effect as applying the relations in the other.

In order for there to be an isomorphism between two systems, A and B, the following two conditions must hold:

$$A = T(B) \text{ and } T^{-1}(A) = B.$$

These conditions specify that there must be a transformation (T) that can be performed on B that will make it the same as A. Furthermore, this transformation must be reversible (T^{-1}) in the sense that applying the inverse to system A produces system B. As an illustration of transformation, take the following two parts of the lattice structure of stories 1 and 2:

Story 1. $(O = W) < (I = O + W) < O + I < W + I$
Story 2. $B < S < (G = S + B) < B + G < S + G$

The problem in going from story 1 to story 2 is that in story 1, $O = W$ does not imply that $O + I < W + I$. The relation between O and W does not remain constant under addition, while the analogous relation does remain constant in story 2: $B < S$ implies $B + G < S + G$.

There is a transformation that will preserve the structure of story 1 and make it possible to map its structure onto story 2. If the relation "equal to" is transformed to "equal to or less than," then story 1 becomes isomorphic with story 2; the relation between O and W remains consistent when I is added:

$O \leq W$ implies that $O + I \leq W + L$

Thus there is a transformation, T, such that:

$T(A) = B.$ *the transformation is not reversible.*

However, the inverse of this transformation does not exist. The transformed relation "equal to or less than" in story 2 cannot be used to recover the original structure of story 1 because there is no easy way to decide whether the relation between O and W in story 1 is < or =. For this reason the inverse transformation fails and an isomorphism cannot be constructed between the two stories.   *no way? or no easy way?*

    Problem order was counterbalanced. It was hypothesized that performance on the three problems would show a hierarchical pattern, that is, no subject would master the pendulum problem who did not master the transitivity problem, and no subject would master the multisystem problem who did not master the pendulum problem.

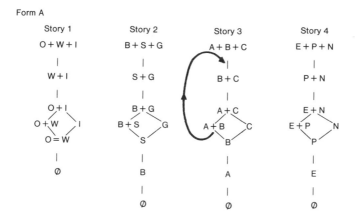

Figure 5.1. Representation of the system of order relations reflected in the four stories

Subjects

The 110 subjects were 39 undergraduates and 71 graduate students attending one of several private universities in the Northeast. The mean ages for the groups are 20.6 and 26.1 years, respectively. All participated on a volunteer basis. The multisystem problem was administered a second time to 41 of the 71 graduate students, directly following the initial administration for 22 of them, and 8 months following the initial administration for 19 of them. (Half of the students received form A first, the other half form B first.)

Results

Analysis of subjects' protocols suggested six distinct levels of response. The scoring system was developed based on an intensive analysis of 25 of the protocols, guided by the theoretical perspective set forth in the introduction. It was then applied to the remaining 85. Fifty-five of the 85 protocols were evaluated independently by raters 1 (first author) and 2 (research assistant); 61 of the 85 protocols by raters 1 and 3 (research assistant). There was 76% and 62% agreement, respectively. Differences were resolved by discussion and a final level assigned to each protocol. Detailed examples of scoring performances on the post-formal problem appear in Commons, Richards, and Kuhn (1982).

Concrete Operations (3b)

The initial stage, labeled C, resembles the mode of thinking termed concrete-operational in Piaget's system. Subjects categorized in this level base their judgments of similarity/dissimilarity on superficial features of the stories rather than on the order relations (either within or across stories) that the task instructions direct. If order relations are attended to at all, this attention is limited to a representation of the discrete order relations explicitly given in the story. The subject does not perform any operations on these elements, to derive additional order relations or more general properties of the system (story).

Abstract and Formal Operations (4a-4b)

These stages are postulated to be equivalent to the level of formal operations in Piaget's sequence (Piaget's levels IIIA & B; see Inhelder & Piaget [1958]). Order relations within stories are operated on in a systematic manner, but the entire system is not regarded (operated on) as a single entity having characteristic properties that may be compared with the properties of other systems. Thus, the subject's attempt to relate the stories with respect to their similarity/dissimilarity is limited to establishing the fact that single elements or two-element order relations map to some degree from one of the first three stories to another.

Systematic Operations (5a)

Responses at this stage reflect the application of what we have termed systematic reasoning. At this level, subjects clearly show that they understand that the logical structure of each story must be examined as an integral whole or structure. In representing the structure of each story, the subject may choose one of two possible courses. A schematic representation of each of the systems can be generated and these representations compared with respect to their deviations from one another. Alternatively, the subject can represent the systems on the basis of the axioms that do or do not characterize each of the systems. The two methods yield equivalent results. Use of these representations is taken as evidence that the subject perceives the story as a system, that is, a coherent whole that determines the internal pattern of relations across its elements. When systematic operations are fully consolidated, full representations are constructed. There is no evidence for the presence of a framework for intersystem comparison; cognition is focused on intrasystem analysis.

Metasystematic Operations (5b.1)

At this substage, the first evidence of metasystematic operations appears. Comparisons across stories are based on variations of the structural properties, implicitly indicating the possibility of conceptualizing one story as the transformation of another story. The subject generates a much more complete set of lattices and/or axioms to represent or characterize the stories. However, some axioms or orderings necessary to complete the analysis are clearly missing.

Metasystematic Operations (5b.2)

This is the second substage in the emergence of truly metasystematic operations. This level, and the two that follow it, are progressive steps in the consolidation and organization into a whole, the operations of which are involved in comparisons across systems. Subjects at this level have, either explicitly or implicitly, full and integrated representations of the systems of ordered relations reflected in each of the four stories. (Systematic thinking is now fully consolidated.) These representations are used to check (again either explicitly or implicitly) their assertions about the systems in a systematic and complete fashion. These subjects choose a single property that is appropriate for comparing the integrated structures of the stories, as opposed to one that would enable comparisons of parts only. For example, the subject might compare the stories on the basis of either additivity or transitivity properties. Such properties are used to construct comparison frameworks. For a subject who represents the systems underlying the stories graphically, the comparison framework may consist simply of a set of dimensions along which the physical drawings of the systems are tested for resemblance. A subject may imply that he or she has generated complete orderings in all four stories without actually showing the work. Thus, the simple assertion that "stories 2 and 4 follow the law of additivity while 1 and 3 do not" is enough to classify a subject at substage (5b.2). (In protocols classified at substages (5b.1) or (5a), in contrast, there exists clear evidence that certain combinations, i.e., relations between elements, were not considered in generating the representation.)

Metasystematic Operations (5b.3)

At substage (5b.3), the subject understands the ambiguity of the questions requiring judgments of similarity and dissimilarity. Individuals understand that there exists a multiplicity of dimensions which could provide the basis for such judgments, that is, a multiplicity of comparison frameworks. The substage (5b.3) subject deals with this ambiguity by experimenting with a number of comparison frameworks and comparing and integrating the results of each.

This reasoning can still be of a nontechnical sort, because the properties in terms of which the systems vary are not complicated ones. The lattices of stories 2 and 4 are isomorphic (see Fig. 5.1); the same set of axioms applies to both. Story 1 violates irreflexibility, since two states are equally preferred. Story 3 violates transitivity, a more serious violation. The substage (5b.3) subject understands that lack of transitivity means that one no longer has an order, whereas the inclusion of an equality rather than an inequality with some indeterminacy on addition still means that one has an order, although partial. Therefore, the former constitutes a more serious deviation. Another way to see the seriousness of the deviation is to examine what happens in the transformation from one system, A, to another system, B. Such a transformation causes a loss in information to the extent that the two systems are not isomorphic. This is seen when the reverse transformation is performed. Thus, the result of transforming system A into system B and then back into A (by another transformation) must be judged from a multiplicity of frameworks. Subject HC provides an example of substage (5b.3) and supplies the analyses that appears below:

Under story 1, HC wrote:

$$\text{Illinois} > \begin{cases} \text{Utah} \\ \quad \parallel \quad > 0 \\ \text{Colorado} \end{cases} \tag{1}$$

Law 1 violated; law 2 does not apply,

$$\text{Utah} + \text{Colorado} > \text{Colorado} + \text{Illinois} > \text{Utah} + \text{Illinois}, \tag{2}$$

$$\text{Utah} + \text{Colorado} + \text{Illinois} > ? - \left[\begin{array}{l} U + C > C + I > U + I > I > \quad \begin{array}{l} U \\ \| \\ C \end{array} > 0 \\[3em] I > U + C > C + I > U + I \quad \begin{array}{l} U \\ \| \\ C \end{array} > 0. \end{array} \right. \qquad (3)$$

Under story 2, HC wrote:

$B > R \; O \; R > W \; O \; B > W,$ any, none.

$1 > 2 \; O \; 2 > 3 \; O \; 1 > 3$ Law 2: Is this the ordering pair to   (1)
pair also?

Transitive property 2: Does it exist here? Yes.

$B + R > B + W > R + W$ What about the other 2 chip combinations?
$\quad R > W \quad | \quad B > R$ bracelet; ring + watch. Story 4 is limited
$\quad + B \; + B \quad | \quad + W \; + W$ in that only one of each type can be used.   (2)

$R + B \; W + B \; | \; B + W \; R + W$

(2 and 4 are similar.)

$R + W + B > B + R > B + W > ?$ $\left[\begin{array}{l} B > R + W > R \quad W > 0. \\[1em] R + W > B > R > W > 0. \end{array} \right. \qquad (3)$

Uncertainty happens at the last two-item combination—same as story 4—
ring + watch bracelet.

Under story 3, HC wrote:

$C > B > Y,$ also $C > Y,$ any $> 0.$ (1)

$C + B > C + Y, \; C + Y > B + Y, \; B + Y > C + B, \; Y \not> C,$ therefore,
law 1 OK,   law 1 OK,   law 1 does not apply;   (2)

$? \rightarrow C > B + Y$ or $B + Y > C$ $\left[\begin{array}{l} C > B + Y > C + B > B > Y > 0. \\[1em] B + Y > C + B > C > B > Y > 0 \text{ already} \\ \hspace{8em} \text{used} \end{array} \right.$

$C + B + Y > C + B > C + Y > ?$ (3)

Or is it $2C$—when has money, always 2 dishes. Illogical unless does not
care for baklava at all—may not—creature of habit, saves money, just C.
Transitive property—or whatever the proper name for it is—is not
working here.

Under story 4, HC wrote:
broken gold watches (without works); scratched gold rings: broken
bracelets; any $> 0.$ $W > B > R,$ uncertainty here, too, cannot rank exactly
unless you know whether $W > B + R$ or $B + R > W.$ Laws:

$$\left. \begin{array}{c} \text{If right} \quad > \quad \text{left} \\[1em] + \text{ equal weight} + \text{equal weight} \end{array} \right\} \text{additive property.} \qquad (1)$$

$$\left. \begin{array}{c} \text{Right still} > \text{left} \\[1em] 1 > 2, \; 2 > 3, \quad \text{then} \quad 1 > 3 \end{array} \right\} \text{transitive property.} \qquad (2)$$

$$W + B + R > ? - \begin{cases} W + B > W + R > W > B + R > B > R. \\ W + B > W + R > B + R > W > B > R. \end{cases}$$

HC then wrote:

Stories 2 and 4 are the most similar because in each the same laws are established for ranking. Each allows only two possible rankings (outcomes) which arise because of uncertainty as to whether one item carries a higher ranking than the sum of the two others, or vice versa. If the uncertainties were settled the same way in both problems (i.e., the one item sum of the other two, or vice versa) the same ranking would have been established for each. A possible difference between stories 2 and 4— the fact that (not stated) in story 2, one-armed bandit machines might use two of the same color chip, whereas in story 4 it was specified that only one item of each type could be used—was eliminated by assuming that the hierarchy of preferences for each combination of two chips in story 2 represented the complete possible choice of performance. Therefore, two chips of the same color were not a possible choice. . . . Refer to my above diagram where it is shown that the laws developed in story 4 are the same as those that govern story 2. Notations within the section for story 2 prove this in the diagrams of story 2.

Story 3 is the most different because it violates both laws by which 2 and 4 are bound and because the information does not limit you to only two possible rankings. Story 1 is similar to stories 2 and 4 in that the laws given are adequate for determining that there are only two possible rankings. However, one of the laws used in 2 and 4 is violated and the other does not apply to 1. Story 3 is most different from stories 2 and 4 because: (1) It does not set forth the same laws as those governing stories 2 and 4, in fact violating both of them; and (2) the laws governing the preference for combinations of two items are circular, i.e.,

$$C + B \quad \overset{\displaystyle B + Y}{\underset{\displaystyle C + Y}{}}$$

such that more than two possible rankings exist, even after the uncertainty of preference for chicken over baklava and yogurt, or vice-versa, is removed.

Metasystematic Operations (5b.4)

Though no examples of substage (5b.4) have occurred in our research, so far, one can postulate this level as comprised of an idealized, maximally formalized solution to the task and as an example of metasystematic reasoning.

At substage (5b.4) explicit use is made of the transformational notion. Here, for instance, it may be used to show how many changes of order there are in 28 pairs of combinations that are necessary to go from one story to another and then back to the original. There are other ways to assess the effects of the transformations back and forth. The degree to which the information in a story may be recovered in a transformational process is a measure of its similarity. The notion of an inverse transformation is used, and whether or not it can be performed without losing information is shown. The properties of the system are represented in a language that is not particular to any one system. Just as fully formal operational subjects in Piaget's system no longer need concrete values to be assigned to the elements to which their formal operations are applied, at the level of idealized metasystematic reasoning, the subject can operate on systems independent of their specific representations. The idealized substage (5b.4) performance, then, would consist of a general theory of systems of order relations, within which any particular order system is evaluated. Properties of the axiom systems which are used to generate these systems, such as completeness, consistency, decidability, and so on, would be considered.

Performance of Subjects in the Present Sample

The levels at which subjects in the present sample were categorized are shown in Table 5.2. The relation between performance on the formal operational problem and performance on the multisystem problem is shown in Table 5.3. All subjects passed the concrete operational (transitivity) problem, which indicates that they functioned at least at the level of simple concrete operations. The relations reflected in Table 5.2 are in accordance with expectation: With only one exception, only those subjects who showed

Table 5.2. Performance Levels on the Postformal Task

		Sample			
		Undergraduate		Graduate	
Stage		N	%	N	%
3b	C	9	23	4	5
4a–4b	F	23	59	19	27
5a	S	5	13	21	30
5b.1	M1	0	0	10	14
5b.2	M2	2	5	8	11
5b.3	M3	0	0	9	13
	Total	39		71	

C stands for Concrete Stage (3b). F stands for Abstract Operations and Formal Operations Stages (4a) and (4b)—here no distinction was drawn between Abstract Operations Stage (4a) and Formal Operations Stage (4b) in scoring. S indicates Systematic Operations Stage (5a). M1, M2, and M3 stand for Metasystematic Operations Substages (5b.1), (5b.2), (5b.3), respectively.

Table 5.3. Relation between Performance on Formal and Postformal Tasks

Formal Task	Postformal Task						
	C	F	S	M1	M2	M3	Total
Concrete	1	0	0	0	0	0	1
Abstract	5	2	1	0	0	0	8
Formal	4	30	15	2	7	6	64
Total	10	32	16	2	7	6	73

attainment of formal operations showed any level of proficiency in systematic or metasystematic reasoning.

Among the 41 graduate students who received multiple administrations of the multisystem problem, most subjects showed no change or a slight advance from first to second administration. Twenty of the 41 showed no change, 14 advanced one stage, one advanced two stages, one advanced four stages, and five declined one stage. This change pattern did not differ appreciably according to time that elapsed between administrations, which suggests that change was largely attributable to effects of repeated testing.

Discussion

The present results support our postulation of discrete modes of cognition composed of third-order and fourth-order operations. Empirical support for the validity of the proposed constructs, labeled systematic and metasystematic reasoning, is of two sorts. First, performance levels of the two samples (undergraduates and graduates) are in accordance with expectation. Few undergraduates show evidence of systematic or metasystematic reasoning; its incidence is considerably greater, however, among graduate students. Second, performance on the problem designed to assess systematic and metasystematic reasoning shows the appropriate relation to performance on a task designed to assess formal operational reasoning: Only one of 31 subjects who did not show fully formal operational reasoning exhibited any proficiency in the use of systematic or metasystematic reasoning, but not all subjects who were proficient in formal operational reasoning exhibited proficiency in systematic or metasystematic reasoning.

The purpose of the present report has been to present the instrument we have developed to assess this higher-order reasoning and to describe the performance of the initial samples of subjects to whom the instrument has been administered. It is, therefore, not appropriate in this report to embark on an extended discussion of the factors or conditions that may govern the development of such higher-order reasoning. To some extent, fruitful speculation in this regard awaits fuller understanding of mechanisms of cognitive development (Kuhn, in press). We should comment, however, that the performance differences between the undergraduate and graduate samples in the present study almost certainly reflect a combined contribution of self-selection and differential experience.

While the "general experience" that comes with increasing chronological age appears to be a sufficient condition for attainment of the earlier stages in Piaget's system, we would not expect it to be a sufficient condition for mastery of the thought operations assessed in the present work. Exposure to and experience with problems that require abstract representational modes of analysis are undoubtedly necessary factors, but just how native ability, education, and experience interact in this regard is a difficult issue to address.

The caveat introduced earlier bears reiteration. It is not necessarily the case, and indeed is most unlikely, that all adult thought is of the form proposed here. One of the pressing issues in the study of adult cognitive development, in fact, is to discover the analytic role that formalistic, systematic reasoning plays in the real-world thought that occurs in adulthood (Gilligan & Murphy, 1979; Kuhn, Pennington, & Leadbeater, 1983; Labouvie-Vief, 1982). Nevertheless, within the realm of the organized, systematic thought studied by Piaget, stages of reasoning beyond Piaget's formal operations, in our view, must be of the general form of fifth- and sixth-stage operations that we have outlined. It is too restrictive to say that systematic and metasystematic operations are limited to the domains of mathematics and science. Numerous other disciplines, such as literature, history, philosophy, anthropology, and music entail the evaluation of entire systems and of systems within multisystem frameworks.

Unlike our example in which reasoning refers to coordinations based on the relations of physical objects (Einstein's physics), reasoning in other areas may be based on relations between objects with different kinds of properties. For example, moral reasoning involves relations between people, or elements with the property of subjectivity. But these relations can display the same order of complexity that appears in physical thought. In music, reasoning involves the esthetic, or expressive, relation of a person to aurally perceived objects. It can be argued that many existing compositions display high stages of the sort described here. But even in these extra-scientific modes of reasoning, where operations in the Piagetian sense may not play a dominant cognitive role, levels of complexity, based on the repetitive structuralization of relations to elements, may be discerned that are analogous to the sequence described here.

APPENDIX

This appendix details the task structure of the problems used to test concrete, formal, and metasystematic performances in this research. The symbols and conventions used here are the same as those used in Commons and Richards (Chapter 6, this volume). Structure is written in Table 5.1 as:

e_i (a, b, c) where e is an operation that is applied to elements a and b, and results in the outcome c. This is written more explicitly as: e_i (element$_1$, element$_2$, outcome).

This expression can be written in the equivalent form:

e_i (element$_1$, element$_2$, outcome) → element$_1$ o element$_2$ = outcome.

In this expression two elements are coordinated (symbolized by "o") and this coordination is the outcome. This leads to the further equivalence:

outcome = element$_1$ coordinated with element$_2$.

In this nomenclature, a cognitive act is always the act of establishing a relation between two or more cognitive elements. In Piaget's sequence, these acts are generally operations, or relations characterized by reversibility.

Primary-Operations Task Structure

There are two primary-operational tasks. The first establishes the domain within which further operations will occur. The second coordinates elements without establishing this domain.

The first task requires a coordination of sets of names with uncollected names. It produces a subset within which further operations can be performed. With the nomenclature from the next chapter, the operation can be represented:

$e_i(a_{nj}, a_{nk}, a_{nl})$ → e_i(set of names A_j, names$_k$ in story, subset of names$_l$)

→ set of names A_j o names$_k$ in story = subset of names$_l$.

In this expression e_i represents a broad class of coordinating actions at the primary-operational stage. These actions relate at least two elements, symbolized here as a_{nj} and a_{nk}. These elements are respectively a set of names (a_{nj}) and the names in the story (a_{nk}). These two elements are coordinated in an operation similar to intersection. The intersection of the names in the story with a set of names creates a task subset (a_{nl}).

The second stage task requires relating elements (names) in ordered pairs. In the problem, these relations are two element comparisons. Names are coordinated by operations, e_i. Each outcome, or ordered pair, is represented as an operational act that coordinates an ordered pair of elements:

$$e_i \, (c, \, b, \, (c < b)) \rightarrow c \text{ coordinated with } b \rightarrow c < b.$$

In this expression the elements c (Chris) and b (Bill) are coordinated by e_i into an ordered pair (c < b), the product of the coordination.

Concrete-Operations Task Structure

Formally, the concrete task involves establishing a complete set of ordered pairs within a defined task subset. It can be represented as:

$$f_i(a_{pj}, \, a_{pk}, \, a_{pl}) \rightarrow f_i(e_i(c, \, b, \, (c < b)), \, e_i(a, \, b, \, (a < b)), \, (a < c))$$
$$\rightarrow f_i \, (\text{ordered pair}_j, \, \text{ordered pair}_k, \, \text{ordered pair}_l)$$
$$\rightarrow \text{ordered pair}_j \, o \, \text{ordered pair}_k = \text{ordered pair}_l$$

This expression has the same form as the expression of primary operations given above; a coordination f_i relates two elements a_{pj} to a_{pk} and forms an output a_{pl}. This more complicated expression shows why the coordinating operation f_i is a second-order operation.

Abstract-Operations Task Structure

The representation of the isolation-of-variables act is:

1) $g_i(a_{cj}, \, a_{vk}, \, a_{vl}) \rightarrow g_i(\text{column}_j, \, \text{values}_k, \, \text{variable}_l)$
$\rightarrow \text{column}_j \, o \, \text{values}_k = \text{variable}_l.$

The small g_i represents the operation that creates a variable by coordinating the column arrangement with specific column values. It decomposes the matrix M into the scalars (variables) X_{jk} and the outcome variable Y_{jk} as defined on page 104.

Formal-Operations Task Structure

The formal representation of detecting causal relations between variables is:

2) $h_i(a_{vj}, a_{vk}, a_{rl}) \rightarrow h_i(X_{j1} \& Y_{52}, -(X_{j1} \& -Y_{52}), X_{j1} \rightarrow Y_{52})$

$\quad\quad\quad\quad \rightarrow h_i(\text{independent variable}_j, \text{dependent variable}_k,$
$\quad\quad\quad\quad\quad \text{causal relation}_l)$

$\quad\quad\quad\quad \rightarrow \text{independent variable}_j \text{ o dependent variable}_k =$
$\quad\quad\quad\quad\quad \text{causal relation}_l$

Here the subscript j indicates the identity of the independent variable and "$\rightarrow$" indicates cause. Note that cause has the formal properties of an order relation such as transitivity: if $a \rightarrow b$ and $b \rightarrow c$, then $a \rightarrow c$. The first expression represents the isolation-of-variables operation, h, that decomposes the matrix M into scalars (variables) X_{j1} and Y_{52}. Expression 2 represents the coordinated application of concatenation (&) and complementation (−) operations to the variables. Complementation means that a value is in one of two states, A or −A. For example, the string is either long (A) or short (−A). This action tests variables one at a time to see whether a causal order relation holds between any independent variable and the dependent variable. The order relation formalized in expression 2 is (1) every high value of the independent variable is paired with a high value of the dependent variable, and (2) no high value of a causal independent variable is paired with a low value of the dependent variable. The coordination of these two operations can be generally represented:

$$h_i\left(g_i\left(f_i\left(e_i\left(a_1, a_2, \ldots, a_n\right)\right)\right)\right).$$

Here h_i is a relational operation (#2 above), g_i is a classificatory operation (#1 above), and the remainder of the expression represents concrete operations that order task information.

Systematic Task Structure

In the systematic task, the full set of possible relations across the possible group of things (2^n things taken two at a time) is constructed. This is an operation on a combinatorial operation, or a fifth-order operation:

$q_i(a_{ej}, a_{rk}, a_{ll}) \rightarrow q_i(\text{elements}_j, \text{relations}_k, \text{lattice structure}_l)$

$\quad\quad\quad\quad \rightarrow \text{elements}_j \text{ o relations}_k = \text{lattice structure}_j.$

In this expression, sets of elements are coordinated with sets of relations to produce lattice structures. The more general expression of this process is:

$$q_i\left(h_i\left(g_i\left(f_i\left(e_i\left(a_1, a_2, \ldots, a_n\right)\right)\right)\right)\right).$$

At the next stage, the metasystematic, the coordination of systems produces morphisms:

$$r_i(a_{sj}, a_{sk}, a_{ml}) \rightarrow r_i \text{ (system}_j, \text{ system}_k, \text{ morphism}_l)$$

$$\rightarrow \text{ system}_j \text{ o system}_k = \text{ morphism}_l.$$

In this expression, systems are coordinated by a transforming act (r_i) and produce morphisms. The general level of operative complexity is:

$$r_i \ (q_i \ (h_i \ (g_i \ (f_i \ (e_i \ (a_1, a_2, \ldots, a_n))))))).$$

NOTES

1. The method of generation of postformal stages appeared in Michael L. Commons, 1977. "The Coordination of Concrete Actions and Elements and Formal Operations and Elements". Unpublished Research Fellowship Application submitted to the National Institute of Mental Health.

6

A GENERAL MODEL OF STAGE THEORY

Michael L. Commons and Francis A. Richards
with Frederick J. Ruf, Michael Armstrong-Roche,
and Stephen Bretzius

In Chapter 5, Richards and Commons suggested that the cognitive-developmental model presented there could be generalized to a number of fields. This chapter introduces such a general developmental stage model. It gives formal requirements for any stage model, including our version with its generating process for stage development. The next chapter shows that applying the general model in different domains guides the production of problems with different stage demands and surface features. By adding decision theory, the general model offers a universally applicable, domain-independent scoring paradigm.

LIMITATIONS OF PREVIOUS STAGE MODELS

A general stage model transcends several stage-model limitations, especially Piaget's. First, it adds stages beyond formal operations absent in Inhelder and Piaget's (1958) model of development but found by Commons, Richards, and Kuhn (1982) and Sternberg and Downing (1982). Second, it makes a minimal number of assumptions and unifies most current models of development. Third, it is consistent and compatible with a systematic paradigm for scoring performances across a wide variety of domains.

Current limitations originate in the common methodology used to understand development. This begins with tasks that require a given level of competence. Subjects of different ages do the tasks. Their performances are analyzed and differentiated into discrete levels, in order of increasing sophistication. These performances are then explained by hypothesized competencies that may be inferred in

The acknowledgment on page 141 for Chapter 7 applies to this chapter as well.

other task performances. The repeated application of this approach builds up a set of tasks, performance levels, and hypothesized competencies. These competencies are then analyzed to reveal the development of an underlying set of cognitive actions, usually called a stage. These stages are then ordered so as to lead to a definite endpoint. Finally, stage theorists specify more formalized criteria for what constitutes a stage sequence (see Piaget, 1963, 1972; Kohlberg, 1969, 1981; Wohlwill, 1973).

Three major problems limit the systematicity and generality of these approaches. Most basic is borrowing stage and task structure from nondevelopmental fields without establishing clearly why each stage is more highly developed than its predecessor. Establishing possibly arbitrary developmental endpoints is related to this. Other problems stem from the imprecise formalization of assumptions that order tasks adapted from other fields. This results in extra assumptions about the requirements for a given stage of performance. Imprecisely formalized stage schemes cannot produce a connected, steplike scoring metric.

Borrowing categories from other fields helps generate testable models, but compromises validity. The order imposed on nondevelopmental categories may be arbitrary. For example, in fields such as moral philosophy, theories have not been neatly ordered by level of cognitive sophistication (but see Armon, 1982). Various fields offer competing arrays of assumptions. For instance, there are many kinds of logic, each with different strengths and weaknesses. Each works best under certain assumptions, but there is no all-purpose or "best" logic. Fields such as logic or moral philosophy do not supply sufficient reasons for ordering these sets of assumptions developmentally. That task is left to developmental psychologists. It entails constructing explicit criteria for ordering cognitive categories into coherent stage sequences.

The criteria that order the categories should be internally consistent. Each successive level of development should be higher than the previous level for specific reasons that are consistent across the entire developmental sequence. This will eliminate aspects of arbitrariness when developmental courses and goals are proposed.

As cognitive-developmental categories become more rigorously ordered, their relation to thought will become clearer. Detailing this relation is a two-directional process. On the one hand, there are the analytic specifications of idealized cognition, operationalized as task demands. On the other, there are performances, or responses, to task demands. Since the performances are cognitive in nature, it is possible to think of the task as creating cognitive demands isomorphic with task demands. For developmental categories, borrowed or otherwise, to play a valid role in cognitive psychology, the correspondence of task demands and cognitive performance must be empirically specified. This cannot be done until task demands are clearly specified.

FORMAL REQUIREMENTS OF STAGE MODELS

In this section, the formal requirements for three types of cognitive theories are introduced. First, having some minimal requirements for any psychological theory produces *models* consistent with traditional cognitive theory. Second, adding requirements for hierarchy produces *stage models* consistent with traditional cognitive-developmental theory. Third, specifying a generator produces a *general stage system* consistent with systematic developmental theory.

To develop the notion of stage, it is necessary to have some term that stands for something that might or might not have stage properties. Here that "something" is called an entity. The term specifies collections of task demands that can be met by corresponding collections of cognitive sets. Some overall requirements of tasks in a given domain operationally define an entity. For example, Inhelder and Piaget's (1958) colorless liquid, pendulum, bending rods tasks, and so on, together exemplify experimental thinking in a physics domain. For each of these tasks, there is a set of task demands, detailed by Inhelder and Piaget. The entity in that domain is formed by the collection of such sets of task requirements. The common task demands of isolating variables form part of an entity. Apparatus-specific demands are not common and do not belong to the entity. Thus, some (but not all) task demands may belong to an entity.

Not all demands common across tasks belong to the same entity. Tasks can require different amounts of working memory. However, demands such as memory are common to many entities. They occur in higher- and lower-level entities. Only those demands common within an entity and distinct across entities can form stage sequences. The relationship between entities is determined by comparing the task demands of one entity to another. To form a stage sequence, there must be at least three entities in linear order. For any single entity to be called a stage, it must belong to such a sequence. Entities that do not meet all such requirements are extrastructural or nonstructural entities. They do not have what will be later defined as structural properties.

For a cognitive theory to be a model, it must meet at least the following metalogical requirements: (1) its postulates must be consistent with each other; (2) its postulates must be independent of each other; (3) its postulates and their derivable properties must be both operationalizable and falsifiable; and (4) distinct entities derivable from the model must be sufficiently defined to decide whether a form, action, or element belongs to the entity.

For any cognitive theory to be developmental, it must meet the following stage model requirements. The set of entities defined by the theory must use a "higher than" relation to form its stage sequence. Here "higher than" means "higher than or at the same level as." To form a stage sequence, entities must be in a discrete, irreflexive, inclusive order. To be so ordered, a set of entities, A, B, C . . . N−1, N, N+1, . . . , and the corresponding cognitive demands of their tasks must have order properties 1 through 4 below:

1. Internal integrity: No entity, N, is empty. Each contains collections of task demands met by sets of elements and nontrivial actions. This insures that stages will refer to actions and elements in some real domain.

2. Connectedness: Each entity's cognitive demands must be at a higher, lower, or equivalent level with respect to every other cognitive demand. This simply means that the stages will be comparable and that every action on an element will belong to some stage.

3. Transitivity: If entity A's cognitive demands are higher than entity B's cognitive demands, and entity B's cognitive demands are higher than entity C's, then entity A's cognitive demands are higher than entity C's. This means that the stages will be sequenced.

4. Antisymmetry: If some of entity A's cognitive demands are higher than some of entity B's, but some of entity B's demands are higher than entity A's, then the two entities are at equivalent levels. This means that cognitive demands in different domains can be at the same stage.

These four properties mean that entity N+1 will be higher than entity N, which in turn will be higher than the predecessor, entity N−1. For sets of entities to form a stage model, three other conditions must be met:

5. Inclusivity: If some cognitive demands of entity N do not belong to entity N−1 but all cognitive demands of N belong to entity N+1, then the cognitive demands can be arranged in an inclusive order. Inclusivity means that higher-stage actions will be more powerful than lower-stage actions because they can do all of what the lower ones can do and more.

6. Discreteness: If for every entity, N, there exists a successor entity, N+1, such that no intermediate entity exists between entity N and entity N+1, then the entities are discrete. This makes the sequence of entities discontinuous and stagelike.

7. Irreflexitivity: If no task can be found in entity N with demands that exceed the highest demands of another task in entity N, then the order relation on entities is irreflexive. This means that no entity N task is higher in stage than another entity N task although one task can be "harder" than another because of extra-stage demands. Note that this holds for tasks across domains within an entity. Hence, no entity can be higher in stage than itself, ensuring that an entity represents only one stage.

Stage models meeting the above conditions are hierarchical in the traditional sense that elements and demanded actions of successor stages will be qualitatively more complex. Relations between elements of successor stages will be more integrated. The applications of actions will be more differentiated than those of the predecessor stage.[1]

DEFINITION OF GENERATORS

A generator is defined as a process by which stage models are generated. Extra-cognitive generators can be biological, as in sexual maturation (Freud, 1961) or in the maturation of working-memory and information-processing capacity (Pascual-Leone, 1970). Societal forces are the generator in psychosocial theories of development (Erikson, 1963, 1969). Diverse examples of cognitive generators include learning mechanisms (Gagné, 1968, 1977), skill learning (Fischer, 1980; Fischer, Hand and Russell, Chapter 3, this volume), thought mechanisms (Guilford, 1967), and equilibration mechanisms (Piaget, 1954).

A generator functions at any stage to move to the next stage. By repeated application a generator produces the entire stage sequence. Here, the proposed generator is the composition of actions. The output of one stage's actions are formed into new elements that serve as the input for the next stage's actions. Output is defined as a coordination of stage elements. When an action is performed on these coordinations, a new level of action has been generated. The generator is implicitly reflective because actions are applied back onto previous stage products. It is not explicitly reflective in the sense that stage change involves conscious reflection on previous thinking. While it is possible for the generator to become explicitly reflective, it does not necessarily become so.

HOW THE PROPOSED FORMAL MODEL OF THE GENERATOR AND OF STAGE DIFFERS FROM TRADITIONAL MODELS

The approach taken here is to model a process for generating stages formally and then describe how this process might be accomplished psychologically. The stages are formally thought of as ideal sets of task demands rather than as actual psychological processes. This differs from using stages to model psychological processes and their changes over time. Current theories have made a number of assumptions about the psychological basis of stagelike development. For example, Piaget (1963) has proposed that equilibration is the basis for stage change. In his view, the perceived contradiction between the predictions and observed outcomes is resolved by constructing a new "structure."

The model of the generator presented here makes only one formal assumption. It embodies fewer psychological assumptions about processes than most, yet accounts for most of the formal properties of stage phenomena. The formal model is divided into two parts.

The first is a formalization of Piaget's notion of "operations on operations." The formal model of the generator assumes that the output of one stage's processes serves as the input for the next stage's processes. Output, or a stage product, is always a coordination of the elements of the stage, or more broadly, the construction of a relation between two or more elements. The input–output model is at a level of generality that makes it a theory of the structure of information-processing requirements, rather than a theory of development in any particular domain. That is, it delineates formal principles that may account for all domain-specific stage theories.

The second is a description of how this generating process might work psychologically. It examines how output might become input and specifies a set of processes that generate stages as their products. These psychological processes reflect the qualitative difference and hierarchical organization of task requirements. Psychological processes that meet task requirements underlie the observable sequences in development.

THE FORMAL MODEL OF THE GENERATOR AND OF THE NOTION OF STAGE

The generator portion of the general model begins by assuming that elements and actions can be the products of an earlier stage. Subsequent stages are generated out of the products of actions on elements. The term "actions" is general. Actions are always relations, where a relation R_{ab} is a set of ordered pairs, $\{(a_i, b_i)\}$. There are two possible ordered pairs, $(a, b) = \{a, \{b\}\}$ and $(b, a) = \{b, \{a\}\}$, that can be formed from the elements a and b. The ordered pair (a, b) does not equal (b, a) since:

$$(a, b) = \{a, \{b\}\}$$
$$= \{\{b\}, a\}$$
$$\neq \{b, \{a\}\} \text{ (because } a \neq \{a\} \text{ and } \{b\} \neq b), \text{ hence}$$
$$(a, b) \neq (b, a).$$

Ordered n-tuples can be formed in a similar manner:

$$(a, b, c, \ldots n) = \{a, \{b\}, \{\{c\}\}, \ldots \{\{..\{n\}..\}\}\}.$$

Relations can be sets of ordered n-tuples also. The relationship most often referred to in this chapter is the trinary relation, built out of 3-tuples: ordered triplets $= (a, b, c)$.

There are many ways to organize elements at the same stage level. These organizations are all relations, the application of actions to elements. They are the stage products or the output. This shows that there are two distinct products defined on the same elements:

$R_{a_i, b_i} \neq R_{b_i, a_i}$ since $\{(a_i, b_i)\} \neq \{(b_i, a_i)\}$.

To illustrate this more concretely, to divide 4 by 2 is not the same as to divide 2 by 4, but both are products, or relations:

$R_{4, 2, 2} \neq R_{2, 4, \frac{1}{2}}$ since $\{(4, 2, 2)\} \neq \{(2, 4, \frac{1}{2})\}$.

For the elements 2 and 4 and the relation division, there are two possible stage products, or coordinations of the elements by division. More examples of relations are the expressions $a = b$ and $a > b$.

According to Piaget, relations are operations when they have:

1. Closure: The relation R yields closure if when R is applied to any members of a set A, then the outcome also belongs to A. Stage change relations do not yield closure but operations within a stage do.
2. Associativity: Suppose the trinary relation $R_{a,b,c}$ can be written $R(a,b) = c$. Then the relation is associative if $R(R(x, y), z) = R(x,R(y,z))$ holds generally. This means that the order in which relations are applied does not matter. This also does not hold for stage change relations.
3. Identity: Suppose the binary relation $R_{a,b}$ can be written $R(a) = b$. The relation has the identity property if there is a relation $R_{b,a}^{-1}$ that can be written $R^{-1}(b) = a$ and such that $RoR^{-1}(x) = x$ holds generally. This means the relation is in a sense reversible.

Addition is an arithmetic operation. Flips, spins, and rotations are geometric operations. Transposing key signatures is a musical operation. Whether actions are relations or operations, they can potentially be applied to one or more elements. All elements must potentially have at least one action applied to them.

The following symbols are used to model stages and a proposed generator:

1. Double brackets { } represent boundaries defining the limits of a stage. Stages as sets both include and exclude actions and elements.
2. The subscripted letter a_i represents elements of a stage.
3. Small roman letters b, c, d, e, f, g, h, l, p and their subscripted forms represent the actions of a stage.
4. The specified relation $f_i(a_1, \ldots, a_n)$ represents the application of an action to an element or elements. For example, $f_1(4, 2, 6)$ can be thought of as either a trinary relation or as a binary operation that coordinates the elements 4, 2, 6, as follows, $4 + 2 = 6$. In the expression $f_2(a_1, a_2)$, for example, the action can be liking and the elements

people: person a_1 likes person a_2. If the outcome is a friendship, a_3, then it is the trinary relation $f_2(a_1, a_2, a_3)$.

5. The set $\{a_1, \ldots, a_n, f_i, f_i(a_1, \ldots, a_n)\}$ represents the set of possible inputs, actions, and outputs in a cognitive stage. It also represents the set of task demands at a given stage, referred to here as the structural set for the stage task. Elements and actions are included in the set of task requirements because they specify the domain and the context for task requirements.

6. The composition of actions $f_k \circ f_j(a_i)$ represents the application of an action to an action performed on elements. This is a general expression for the composition of actions. In the composition of actions, the action on an element $f_j(a_i)$, becomes an element itself. Another action, f_k, is then applied to it. This composition of actions is also symbolized as $f_k(f_j(a_i)) \rightarrow f_k(a_1, f_j(a_2, a_3, a_4), a_5)$ where a_5 is the product of the action. The following section explains when the composition of actions results in successor stage actions and when it does not. The hierarchical composition of actions, a special case of composition, is the stage-generating mechanism proposed here.

To summarize points 1 through 6, stage activities occur within boundaries containing and excluding elements and actions. New elements may be incorporated at the same stage as actions at that stage are applied to them, resembling what Piaget calls assimilation. At a given stage, actions, which include operations, may be extended to new domains, and new actions may be developed because elements in different domains afford opportunities for their discovery. Adding actions and elements by the simple application of actions to elements constitutes quantitative increase. It can yield no more than quantitative change. New stage products are added but are contained in the same stage boundary. Without the hierarchical application of actions, stage is not abandoned.

The Generator is the Hierarchical Composition of Actions

What is crucial for qualitative change is that there be a hierarchical composition of actions. In hierarchical composition, an action generates a product that is at a higher stage. To be at the successor stage, the action cannot be fully definable on the elements of the preceding stage. This means that a successor stage action cannot be performed on the elements of a previous stage. Piaget usually says that these actions coordinate actions from the previous stage. The coordination action does not belong to the same stage as the actions that it coordinates.

What follows is a detailed example of what is meant by hierarchical composition. The example deals with the case of simple distribution of multiplication across addition applied to numbers, a task at the concrete-operational stage. Readers not interested in an extended discussion of the nature of hierarchical, qualitative change should go on to the next section.

For this example, assume that beginning concrete-operational thinking children learn their addition and multiplication tables. It will be shown that the distributive act coordinates these additive and multiplicative acts. Each instance of multiplication or addition in the tables can be represented by a trinary relation of the form:

action e_j (element a_1, element a_2, outcome a_3) =

$e_j(a_1, a_2, a_3) \rightarrow a_1 \; o \; a_2 = a_3$.

In this expression, "o" stands for one instance of either of the two classes of actions, addition or multiplication. The subscripted "a's" stand for the elements (numbers) to which one of these actions is applied. In this expression it is critical to distinguish between a_3 and the entire expression:

$a_1 \; o \; a_2 = a_3$.

There is a strong tendency to think of a_3 as the stage product. While 3 is the outcome of applying addition to the elements, 1 and 2, and is therefore the third term of the additive relation, it is not the stage product. The additive relation $1 + 2 = 3$ is the stage product. This product is the coordination of preoperational stage products, namely numbers. A stage product is the entire scheme of coordination from beginning to end. It is this product that becomes an element for an action at the next stage.

Instances of the trinary relation that occur in an addition and multiplication table respectively are:

$e_{1+} (1, 2, 3) \rightarrow 1 + 2 = 3$
$e_{1\times} (1, 2, 2) \rightarrow 1 \times 2 = 2$.

These are but two instances of a large number of additive and multiplicative primary stage actions, or e_{ij}'s, each of which is a trinary relation. Start with the set of elements, $E = \{a_i\} = \{1, 2, 3, 5, 6, 9\}$ and two actions, addition and multiplication, e_+ and $e_\times$. Let the actions be applied to any pair of the elements $\{1, 2, 3, 6\}$. The application of stage actions to stage elements, $e_{ij} (a_i)$, yields the following products:

1. $e_+(a_i) \rightarrow$	$e_{1+}(1, 2, 3) \rightarrow$	$1 + 2 = 3$
	$e_{2+}(1, 3, 4) \rightarrow$	$1 + 3 = 4$
	$e_{3+}(2, 3, 5) \rightarrow$	$2 + 3 = 5$
	$e_{4+}(3, 6, 9) \rightarrow$	$3 + 6 = 9$
2. $e_\times(a_i) \rightarrow$	$e_{1\times}(1, 2, 2) \rightarrow$	$1 \times 2 = 2$
	$e_{2\times}(1, 3, 3) \rightarrow$	$1 \times 3 = 3$

$$e_{3\times}(2, 3, 6) \rightarrow \qquad\qquad 2 \times 3 = 6$$
$$e_{4\times}(3, 3, 9) \rightarrow \qquad\qquad 3 \times 3 = 9.$$

This is a subset of possible stage products for the simple application of actions to elements. Other stage products are possible if actions are applied iteratively to elements. For example, if addition is composed twice, more stage products become possible:

3. $e_+(e_+(a_i)) \rightarrow e_{2+}(1, (e_{1+}(1, 2, 3)), 4) \rightarrow 1 + (1 + 2)$
$$= 1 + (3)$$
$$= 4$$
$$\rightarrow e_{3+}(2, (e_{1+}(1, 2, 3)), 5), \text{ etc.}$$

This is an example of nonhierarchical composition because any e_+ could be directly applied to the numbers. The order of application does not matter. There is no coordination of operations or relations, other than doing the e_+ again. These compositions are not at the concrete-operational stage because any of the actions within the composition are at the primary-operational stage and could be applied directly to the numbers.

For a composition of actions to be at the next stage, an action must directly apply only to the actions of the previous stage and not directly to elements. An example of a hierarchical composition of the actions defined above (e_{1+} through $e_{4\times}$) would be an action, $f_{1\times}$, that organizes multiplication and addition distributively. Distribution poses the problem of how to interpret multiplication on addition on numbers. The person does not know whether to multiply or add first. If addition is done first, then the problem is to know what to multiply. If multiplication is done first, the problem is to know what number(s) need(s) to be multiplied. This can be shown with the example of multiplying 3 times the sum of 1 and 2. While it may seem obvious what the correct procedure is, it is not obvious to the beginning concrete-operational thinker. The concatenation of two actions, multiply and add,

$$f_{1\times}(e_\times, e_+(a_i), e_+(e_\times(a_j))),$$

must be worked out in terms of actual cases. In the following, the more general expression of distribution is given, and then converted into the specific terms in which it would be worked out at the concrete-operational stage;

4. $f_{1\times}(e_\times, e_+(a_i), e_+(e_\times(a_j))) \rightarrow$
$f_{1\times}(3, (e_{1+}(1, 2, 3)), [e_{4P}(e_{2\times}(1, 3, 3), e_{3\times}(2, 3, 6), 9)])$

This complex expression is just a form of a trinary relation, $f_\times(a, b, c)$, where $f_\times$ is multiplication (on sums). This relation can be thought of as the conventional expression $a \times b = c$. Each letter is equal to the following:

$f_{1\times}(a, b, c) \rightarrow a \times b = c$. This is the operation of multiplication over the three elements:

$a = 3$. The number 3 is a primary-operational stage element.

$b =$ the trinary relation $e_{1+}(1, 2, 3) \rightarrow 1 + 2 = 3$,

$c =$ the complex trinary relation, $[e_{4+}(e_{2\times}(1, 3, 3), e_{3\times}(2, 3, 6), 9)]$,

which has the form $e_{4+}(r, s, t) \rightarrow r + s = t$ where:

$r = e_{2\times}(1, 3, 3) \rightarrow 1 \times 3 = 3$

$s = e_{3\times}(2, 3, 6) \rightarrow 2 \times 3 = 6$

$t = 9$.

Thus, $r + s = t$, or in numbers, 9 is the sum of 1 times 3 and 2 times 3. Expression 4 may have r, s, and t substituted into it:

4a. $f_{1\times}(3, e_{1+}(1, 2, 3), [e_{4+}(e_{2\times}(1, 3, 3), e_{3\times}(2, 3, 6), 9)]) \rightarrow$

4b. $f_{1\times}(a, b, c) = f_{1\times}(a, b, e_{4+}(r, s, t)) \rightarrow$
$3 \times (1 + 2) = (1 \times 3) + (2 \times 3) = 9.$

The most critical aspect of this discussion has been to show that $f_{1\times}$ is at the successor stage. Acting on and organizing elements and products from the previous stage is our definition of how hierarchical composition generates an act at a successor stage.

For $f_{1\times}$ to be an action at a successor stage:

1. It cannot be directly defined exclusively on the elements a_i of the predecessor stage. This implies:
   a. It must directly act on some products, $e_j(a_i)$, of the predecessor stage.
   b. There must be some predecessor stage elements, a_i, to which $f_{1\times}$ cannot be directly applied.
2. It must relate (organize) the acts and elements from the predecessor stage.

First, from the expression $f_{1\times}(a, b, c)$, it will be shown that $f_{1\times}$ is not directly defined on the elements of the predecessor stage. Of the three elements organized by the trinary relation $f_{1\times}$, only $a = 3$ is an a_i element of e_+ from the predecessor stage. The relation $f_{1\times}$ acts on element b, which is a previous stage product defined by $e_{1+}(1, 2, 3)$. The $f_{1\times}$ act cannot organize the predecessor stage elements 1 and 2 directly. The same is true for element c, which is the product of the organization of two previous stage products, $c = e_{4+}(e_{2\times}(a_i), e_{3\times}(a_j), a_k)$. The $f_{1\times}$ act cannot apply directly to some elements of the predecessor stage. It is also clear that it does act on some successor stage products. More specifically, $f_{1\times}$ acts on $e_{1+}, e_{4+}, e_{2\times}$, and $e_{3\times}$.

Second, the distribution act organizes specific acts of addition and multiplication. It establishes an order relation across these acts and elements, as is specifically shown in 4a. Actions must be performed from the innermost parentheses to the outermost. The relation $f_{1\times}$ therefore organizes the products and elements from the previous stage. The stage action $f_{1\times}$ is consequently an action on, or organization of, the products of a predecessor stage.

This complex example shows what the concrete-operational thinker is faced with. It illustrates why the introduction of variables, at the next stage, called here abstract operations (see below), will simplify matters so that the distribution act becomes:

$$f_\times (a, e_+(b, c, d), e_+(e_\times(a, b, r), e_\times(a, c, s), t)) \rightarrow$$
$$a_i \times (b_j + c_k) = (a_i \times b_j) + (a_i \times c_k).$$

In this expression, simple operational (see below) elements, numbers, have been replaced by beginning formal elements, variables.

Composition of actions is not unique to this specific example of arithmetic operations composed by arithmetic operations. Arithmetic operations can be composed within other systems that have some of the formal properties of arithmetic such as propositional logic. As an example, the action of adding numbers, when logically composed, becomes at the next stage an element in an "if . . . then . . . " statement such as, "If two dollars and three dollars are repaid, then the loan of five dollars is canceled." Addition is treated as an element and is itself compared to subtraction. Subtraction is another action treated as an element in this statement.

Categorizing activity also shows composition. A collection of elements that have both shape and color affords the opportunity for classification by both properties separately. Once these classifying actions have been performed, the objects could be placed in an array, rather than along a line, so that both properties are simultaneously represented. Constructing arrays is a new action discovered by hierarchically composing classifying actions on color and form.

Hierarchical Composition Generates Stage Sequences

The stage of cognitive task structure depends on the number of hierarchical compositions in a task defined as being at a given stage. The stage of a task is synonymous with the number of layers of actions hierarchically applied to earlier compositions. For example, in the composition $g(f(x))$, g is the second action, $f(x)$ is its element, and two actions, g and f, are composed. This action composition is at the second stage of a stage sequence the initial stage of which contains the actions f_i and elements x_i. A second stage would consist of a collection of tasks with second-stage structure.

A successor stage is formed by the generation of composed actions, that is, actions applied to predecessor stage products. These actions are not fully definable on the elements of the preceding stage but require products of actions on elements of that stage. For hierarchy to hold in a stage sequence generated this way, no g can belong to, or be embedded in, an f whereas each f must belong to some g. That is to say, an action of a given stage cannot be part of a previous set of actions, whereas every action of a given stage will become an element in a successor stage.

It will now be shown how the general model and the generator, as developed so far, can produce the Piagetian stage sequence as well as postformal stages. Since Piaget developed examples for his sequence in many different areas, this illustration will be confined to an area already discussed, the distributive action. Here, each of Piaget's major stages have been split into two stages. The earlier of the two stages has been given a new name (see Richards and Commons, Chapter 5, this volume).

Circular Sensory-Motor Actions

This sequence starts with the circular sensory-motor stage when sensory acts, a_{si}, and motoric acts, a_{mj}, are coordinated with each other (Piaget, 1954). The coordinating act, a_o, is a n-ary relation. The order of the relation n depends on the number of sensory-motor acts that are related. The output is a set of coordinated sensory-motor acts, that set, a_{rk}, is called a scheme. This is diagrammed:

$$a_o(a_{si}, a_{mj}, a_{rk}) \quad \rightarrow \quad a_o \text{ (sensory act}_i, \text{ motor act}_j, \text{ scheme}_k)$$
$$\rightarrow \quad \text{sensory act}_i \text{ o motor act}_j = \text{scheme}_k.$$

In this expression, sensory-motor acts a_{si} and a_{mj} are coordinated by the relation a_o; "o" is the general symbol for a coordinating act. Coordination, in this expression, is the relation that acts on the elements, sensory acts and motor acts. The stage products, a_{rk}, are relationships called schemes.

Sensory-Motor Actions

At the sensory-motor stage schemes are organized into objects:

$$b_o(a_{ri}, a_{rj}, a_{ok}) \rightarrow b_o \text{ (scheme}_i, \text{ scheme}_j, \text{ object}_k)$$
$$\rightarrow \text{scheme}_1 \text{ o scheme}_2 = \text{object}_1.$$

In this expression, sensory-motor schemes a_{ri} and a_{rj} are coordinated ("o") to form an object, a_{ok}.

Nominal Actions

Nominal acts are at least binary relations that assign names to objects. Such acts can also be higher relations if more than one object is related to a name:

$$c_o (a_{oi}, a_{nj}, a_{dk}) \rightarrow c_o (object_i, name_j, designated\ object_k)$$
$$\rightarrow object_1\ o\ name_2 = designated\ object_1.$$

Assigning names to objects produces a set of successor stage elements. Names may be applied to all types of properties: role (Mother, Father), physical (size, shape, weight), evaluative (good, bad, ugly), numerical (counting), and so on.

These names are an important step in the differentiation of cognition into what subsequently become more defined domains. For example, role properties become some of the elements of actions that develop into moral thought. It is not assumed here that the process of assigning names is well understood. In particular, the processes that result in the designation and nondesignation of names is not understood. Consequently, the current domains of cognition are not assumed to be well demarcated.

Preoperations

At this stage, names are assigned to the names of things. For example, apples, oranges, and bananas can be named "three" fruits. This naming act d_o is applied to the stage product of the designated objects (apples, oranges, and bananas). Numbers are not a property of individual elements but of the set as a whole. One has to have the designated elements of a set in order to count them. To count two objects, one may do the following: name with the number 1 designated object$_1$ and name with the number 2 designated object$_2$.

$$d_o (a_{di}, a_{dj}, a_{nk}) \rightarrow (d_o (designated\ object_i, designated\ object_j, number_k)$$
$$\rightarrow designated\ object_1\ to\ designated\ object_2 = number\ 2.$$

Primary Operations

At the primary stage, simple operations begin to be performed on elements such as numbers, sizes, colors, and so on, as Piaget and Inhelder (1969) point out. Hence, these operations are carried out over names of names. Numbers are names of names. Three oranges, three apples, and three bananas can all be called three. The example below shows how addition of numbers, $1 + 2 = 3$, can be performed. This is the additive act $e_o (1, 2, 3)$. This additive act creates a stage product at the next stage level:

$$e_o (a_{ni}, a_{nj}, a_{sk}) \rightarrow e_o (1, 2, (1 + 2 = 3))$$
$$\rightarrow 1\ o\ 2 = 3.$$

Concrete Operations

In concrete operations, relations can be related. For instance, the long example above shows how the distributive relation comes into

existence. Two kinds of composed, or concatenated, operations are of
interest here. Distribution f_{x+}, or simply f_x as before, has been
discussed previously in the section on hierarchical composition. A
second operation is naming an abstract subset formed by using
primary operations. Named abstract subsets, such as numbers, differ
from sets formed at the primary level. This is because they depend on
a previous operation that produced the original set. Forming an
original set and operating on it are the necessary conditions for
forming such subsets.

For example, given the set of numbers $\{1, 2, 3, 4 \ldots\} = A$, a
subset B of even numbers is formed and named by the act f_o. Numbers
that are evenly divisible by 2 are "even." The act f_o forms B by turning
the uncollected even numbers into a named abstract subset. Forming
the subset depends on previously carrying out primary operations.

$f_o\,(a_{si}, a_{mj}, a_{bk}) \rightarrow f_o\,((\text{set A})_i, (\text{members of A})_j, (\text{members of subset B})_k)$
$\rightarrow (\text{set A})_i \;\; o \;\; (\text{members of set A})_j = (\text{members of subset B})_k$
$\rightarrow a_i$ belongs to A and 2 divides a_j; $\rightarrow a_i$ belongs to the
class A_1. This class is named by B, the set of even
numbers.

The stage product, B, is a set of numbers and not one of the members
of A. The set is abstract because its name, B, does not refer to any
member of A. That is, B is not itself a member of the set A, which
consists solely of numbers.

This allows sets that have a special property, such as the set of
even numbers (shown previously), to be formed. Another example is
the set of instances in life when working hard achieved a goal. Notice
that these sets contain concrete instances, not the propositions and
not the variables that represent them. They are defined by what their
members are and do not contain the general rules, or operations, that
create membership. For example, the set containing 2, 4, 6, and so on,
is defined by some finite collection of instances of even numbers. The
set does not contain the operation of dividing all numbers by two.

Abstract Operations

There are two kinds of relations carried out in the stage of
abstract operations: one relation forms variables; the other relation
coordinates relations applied to concrete-operational elements.

In abstract operations the members of the subsets, B_k, are
abstracted into a variable, $x = a, b, c, d. \ldots$ Thus the subset $B_k = \{x\}$.
This is done by applying action g_o to B_k, the set formed in preopera-
tions by f_o described above. In terms of the above example, the set of
even numbers becomes a set containing the operation of division by

2; [a is a member of B iff a is divisible by 2]. At this stage, even numbers can be represented by 2x, where x is a variable that can stand for any number. Subset B with the rule "include any number divisible by 2," produces the variable 2x.

$$g_o \, (a_{mi}, a_{bj}, a_{vk}) \to g_o \, ((\text{members of A})_i, (\text{operation forming B})_j,$$
$$\text{variable}_k)$$
$$\to \text{members of A o divisible by 2} = 2x.$$

Abstract-operational thinkers do not have to learn each particular instance of long division, they can apply the rules to any member of a set. These rules cannot be applied generally, as happens in elementary algebra. What they cannot do is use variables and coordinate relations defined on those variables.

At this stage, formulae can be applied as long as they are stated as rules rather than as formulae containing variables. Using the example of distribution, abstract-operational thinkers know whether distribution has been carried out properly for any set of three numbers. That is, given three numbers, they know the rule, "adding the 2nd and 3rd number and multiplying the sum by the 1st number will be equal to multiplying the 1st and 2nd number and adding the product to the product of the 1st and the 3rd number."

Formal Operations

With formal operations, the usual statement of the distributive law can be applied to variables defined on sets, such as the positive integers, fractions, and so on:

Distributive Laws
1. $x(y + z) = xy + xz$
2. $x \cup (y \cap z) = (x \cup y) \cap (x \cup z)$
3. $x \cap (y \cup z) = (x \cap y) \cup (x \cap z)$
The coordination of variables into laws is symbolized:
$$h_o \, (e_i \, (a_{vi}), e_j \, (a_{vj}), a_{lk}) \to h_o \, (\text{operation on variables}_i, \text{operation on}$$
$$\text{variables}_j, \text{law}_k)$$
$$\to \text{multiplication of variable}_1 \text{ o addition of}$$
$$\text{variable}_2 = \text{law}_1.$$

For an example of extended formal operations, let $\Sigma \, j$ be the iterative sum of the values of a variable. This is an extended formal operation because $\Sigma \, j$ is a new coordinating act built upon the formal-operational law of associativity applied to variables:

$$\Sigma \, j = a_1 + a_2 + a_3 \ldots \ldots a_n.$$

In this expression, $\Sigma \, j$ is the sum of all values assumed by a variable. Using associativity, the sum of three variable values can be defined as:

$\Sigma j = a_1 + a_2 + a_3$ since $a_1 + (a_2 + a_3) = (a_1 + a_2) + a_3$.

When the two alternative expressions of the variable, $a_1 + (a_2 + a_3)$ and $(a_1 + a_2) + a_3$ are coordinated (in an equivalence relation), the coordination produces a general law (of associativity): when one has associativity, the parentheses do not matter as long as a single operation is used.

Systematic Operations

The first postformal stage of complexity occurs in the development of distribution when expressions with addition are multiplied. In this case, addition itself, Σj, is treated as a variable in stating the distributive principle. At this stage, addition, represented by + and Σ is generalized to any binary relation with the properties of addition. This is represented by replacing "+" by the general symbol "o". Likewise, the multiplicative act "$\times$" is replaced by the general relation "$*$". Then, by the definition of the general distributive property given above, the systematic stage act is:

$q_o (a_{oi}, a_{oj}, a_{sk}) \rightarrow q_o$ (operation$_i$, iterative operation$_j$, system$_k$) $\rightarrow$
$q_o (m (a), s(j), h(a, j)) = q_o (a*, \Sigma j, a * \Sigma j = \Sigma a *j) \rightarrow (a * \Sigma j = \Sigma a * j) \rightarrow$
$a * (j_1 \text{ o } j_2 \text{ o } j_3 \ldots \text{ o } j_n) = (a * j_1) \text{ o } (a * j_2) \ldots \text{ o } (a * j_n)$.

For numerical multiplication and addition this is:

$a \times (j_1 + j_2 + j_3 \ldots + j_n) = (a \times j_1) + (a \times j_2) \ldots + (a \times j_n)$.

Sigma (Σ) is the general, iterative concatenation of the elements of variable j. Not only are the values that j assumes variable, but j itself is a variable since it stands for a broad class of entities. The elements of j may be numbers, matrices, propositions, tone frequencies, and so on. But all these are instances of the variable j because the higher-stage expression of the distribution property holds for all these sets of elements. The act:

$a * (j_i \text{ o } j_2 \text{ o } j_3 \ldots \text{ o } j_n) = (a * j_1) \text{ o } (a * j_2) \ldots \text{ o } (a * j_n)$

is at the systematic stage because it is a generalization of the act:

$a \times (b + c) = (a \times b) + (a \times c)$

of the formal-operational stage. The act no longer coordinates single numbers, it now coordinates coordinated subsets of numbers.

The operation "Σ" has become a variable in two ways. First, it is general and applies to more than addition of numbers. Second, "Σ"

stands for a series of actions and can be treated as a single operator in an equation. In particular, it can be factored. This means that "Σ" can be moved outside of "a *":

$$h(a, j) = (a * \Sigma j = \Sigma a * j).$$
$$= (a * k(j) = k(a * j)).$$

In this equation, k has been substituted for "Σ" to show the factoring process more clearly. This equation shows the coordination of the formal-operational stage products, "Σ" and "*". The coordination is the factoring act.

This coordination is qualitatively different in nature from the coordinations at the formal-operational stage. This is because it is performed on previous stage products that were not elements of that previous stage. Those products were the generalized operations such as iterative addition.

Metasystematic Operations

At the second postformal stage, systems that may or may not contain a property are themselves coordinated. In our example, a property of a system is the distributive property. Remember that the distributive property means that "*" and "o" can be coordinated. This coordination of systems in terms of their properties cannot be done at previous stages because the systems that are the previous stage products are not elements of that previous stage.

As an example of turning systems into variables, take two systems that contain addition and multiplication. The elements of one system are the positive integers (natural numbers). The elements of the other system are the negative integers. What is the relation between these two systems? One way to coordinate systems is to see what maps from one system to another and what maps back from the second system to the first:

$$r_o(a_{si}, a_{sj}, a_{mk}) \rightarrow r_o (\text{system}_i, \text{system}_j, \text{morphism}_k)$$
$$\rightarrow \text{system}_1 \text{ o system}_2 = \text{morphism}_1.$$

The two systems will have an isomorphic relation if the properties of the systems are the same. For the positive and negative numbers, the elements of each are coordinated by addition. But for multiplication, the situation is different. In the positive numbers, a number times a number always yields a positive number. In the negative numbers, a negative number times a negative number yields a positive number, which is not a negative number. Hence, multiplication is not defined. The systems cannot be the same. One has a property that the other does not. One can transform the positive numbers into the negative numbers by multiplying each by -1. But one less operation is possible in the negatives.

Cross-Paradigmatic Operations

At the third postformal stage, families of systems are themselves coordinated. These families constitute fields. Fields are compared by detecting and describing relations between systems of systems. Cross-paradigmatic operations relate fields by constructing unifying theories between them;

$$s_0 (a_{fi}, a_{fj}, a_{uk}) \rightarrow s_0 (\text{field}_i, \text{field}_j, \text{unificatory theory}_k)$$
$$\rightarrow \text{field}_1 \text{ o field}_2 = \text{unificatory theory}_1.$$

If a field of endeavor represents the most complex element of epistemology for which there is any empirical evidence, then cross-paradigmatic operations represent the present terminus of genetic epistemology. The first substage of cross-paradigmatic operations appears with the ability to generate collections of systems of systems, or fields. This substage ends when an initial understanding is reached about why a field is a field. At this substage, fields can be systematized but not operated on further. Initially, the subject appreciates that fields have some relationship but cannot find it.

The second and third substages consist of the basic cross-paradigmatic operations that are constructed to relate fields that appear to be independent of one another. These are the works of unification. One might speculate that certain sciences have certain operations that are distributive while others do not. In order to explore this relation, the algebra of distributive systems would be formalized, and its relation to nondistributive systems would be elucidated. This is a way the theory of groups and the theory of rings in Abstract Algebra can be distinguished and related. For instance, within economics, psychology, and ethology, utility, U, could be defined as the sum of the products of the probability of obtaining an outcome multiplied by the value of an outcome:

$$U = \text{sum}[p(\text{Outcome}_i \text{ for a behavior})v(\text{Outcome}_i)].$$

Motivational variables could be multiplicatively related to U:

$$m(U) = m[\text{sum } p(O)v(O)] = \text{sum}[mp(O)v(O)].$$

Hence, there is distributivity if and only if it can be shown that m multiplies each $p(\text{outcome})v(\text{outcome})$ as well as U. If utility were the

Stage	Name	Elements	Actions	Products	Example
3a	Primary Operations	Single set of concrete particulars	Simple counting, showing comparability on basis of surface features	Single surface particulars, simple set size, multiple dual classifications	Cardinal numbers 1,2,3...
3b	Concrete Operations	Mappings of surface particulars; objects, numbers	Ordering or classifying particulars relative to each other	Relations of particulars; classes, relations, operations	Simple argument with numbers, letters, percepts.
4a	Abstract Operations	Single set of variable values; only one operation applied to a variable	Abstractly representing elements; simple combining and permuting	Variables or single abstractions, repeated operations or relations	x, a variable, is defined; transitivity is found: $a > b$, $b > c$, then $a > c$
4b	Formal Operations	Mappings (relating abstractions); iterative functions, relations, or operations	Coordinating two operations and a relation	Two coordinated relations on variables or abstractions yielding a value; iterative operations	Doing algebra, solving equations such as $a + bx = c$
5a	Systematic Operations	Two subdivided sets and the iterative relations or operations performed; properties of systems	Operate on sets of operations. Abstractly represent the set of relations and operations within each system	Systems and frameworks	Propositional calculus, simple theory of equations
5b	Metasystematic Operations	Representations of systems	Axiomatization of relations; transforming systems, determining relations between systems	System of systems: (supersystems or theoretical structures across frameworks); new theories	Comparing group structures; theory of groups, rings, and fields from arithmetic
6a	Cross-Paradigmatic Operations	Super-systems representing knowledge in a given field	Relate and transform paradigms; show how paradigms from one field can transform another	New paradigms	Discovery of evolutionary theory of Darwin; invention of analytic geometry

key relationship between these fields, and, on the face of it, utility were not the same concept in each field, then these fields might be unified by this cross-paradigmatic operation. At the fourth substage, field relations are systematized and formed into a new unit. Gödel's proof (1931) is cross-paradigmatic because it shows that a metasystem of metalogic cannot be reduced to any member of the supersystem of algebras.

THE SEQUENCE OF STAGES

In order to clarify the general stage model and its crucial component, the generator, the upper portion of Table 6.1 formalizes the Piagetian developmental sequence in terms of the model. The lower portion of Table 6.1 summarizes the levels of postformal reasoning and also shows how these levels conform to the specifications of the general stage model.

This concludes the analytic discussion of the general stage model and a possible generator of stages. In this form, no empirical evidence is necessary to validate either formulation since they are analytic in nature. The case of geometry as an analytic system is an instance where the model and generator may describe phenomona in the world. The case of geometry as a descriptive system that has extensive application, is an instance where the model (if it is to be useful in accounting for development) will need empirical validation. The next chapter sets forth a way of seeing how well the general stage model— and therefore stage theory in general—might explain development.

NOTES

1. There are other general stage theories (e.g., Fischer, Hand, and Russell, Chapter 3, this volume; Pascual-Leone, Chapter 9, this volume), but they have not yet generated problems that require postformal reasoning in a variety of domains. They were instrumental in suggesting a differentiation of a and b stages and, along with Kohlberg and Armon, (Chapter 18, this volume), suggested issues to be addressed.

7

APPLYING THE GENERAL STAGE MODEL
Michael L. Commons and Francis A. Richards

Using the general stage model to detect cognitive development in a person's performance requires specifying four crucial relations. First, since the general model applies to developmental theory but not to cognitive development, the relation of the model to cognitive development must be specified. It must be demonstrated that thinking in a specifiable domain is an instance of the requirements of the general model before a case can be made that such cognition develops qualitatively, rather than quantitatively. Hence, it must be demonstrated that cognition can be described in terms of actions performed upon elements and that its development can be described as hierarchical compositions of actions on elements. Second, the relation between cognitive sequences in domains and the tasks that detect that cognition must be specified. It must be shown how general model requirements can be used to construct tasks, and conversely, how tasks can be analyzed using general model requirements. The task requirements have to be expressible as actions upon elements. Third, it must be shown how performance relates to task requirements. Since some tasks are likely to produce performances at lower levels than people are capable of, this involves specifying how tasks

This chapter was prepared under a grant from the Dare Association. A number of people have been instrumental in the development of the chapter. Deanna Kuhn collaborated on much of the research starting in 1976. Her work has been an inspiration. A number of people worked on the Choice and Signal Detection Analysis of the Stages. Michael P. Krupa suggested that choice theory might apply. The others were Rosemary Basile, Pattie Bellinger, Dennis C. Cornwall, Eloise Coupey, Martin N. Davidson, John R. Ducheny, Ping Lee, Lynn Liakos, Barbara Mahon, Joel R. Peck, Annays Sotolongo, Steven Torres, and Joseph J. Vallone. Judith Long-Stevens, Sharon Kantrowitz, and Deanna Kuhn made many useful comments on drafts of the chapter. Our co-editor, Cheryl Armon has read the chapter many times making extensive suggestions. Solomon B. Katz, Patrice M. Miller, and Ashok N. Nimgade made extensive stylistic suggestions.

should be chosen, administered, and scored. Finally, it has to be shown how performances can be related to metrics to produce scales of development. It will be shown that if performances are ordered the same way as the structure of the tasks is ordered, the general stage model begins to do part of the developmental job that psychometric appoaches to the development of intellegence set out to do.

SPECIFYING THE RELATION BETWEEN THE GENERAL MODEL AND A COGNITIVE DOMAIN

Stage theory can be seen as a metaphor for the capacity of organisms to form classes, or products of actions, which they can act upon. A pigeon, for example, can peck the left key in a two-choice situation, differentiating fish from not-fish. It thereby tacitly assigns fish a class name and acts upon that name. Humans act in similar, but increasingly involuted, ways upon such primitive classifications. This happens to the extent that names, or other unifying "gestalts," come to stand for their referents. Humans can say "I want the fresh fish." Here, "fresh" is the name of a property that can apply to classes other than fish, a property twice removed from its objects. In each case, classification orders names of things and subsumes them under another name. Primitive classifications are assumed to be at the base of any sequence of cognitive development, and are referred to as initial, or polymorphous, sets (Dennis, Hampton, and Lea, 1973). No operational definitions exist for members of such sets, such as pattern perceptions, but such definitions may be better approximated in the near future (Cerella, note 12). This ability to form patterns, by their nature vague, serves as the stimulus for successive advances in thought and is central to cognitive development.

The general model is a source of testable hypotheses because it predicts a pattern of development, originating in polymorphous sets, for knowledge in any domain. According to the model, there should be an initial specification of properties in the polymorphous set that creates a defined set of elements contained in the initial set of any stage sequence. While primitive elements have uncountably many cognitive properties, only small groups of these properties, or possibly single properties, are captured in any particular developmental sequence. Elements can be of any sort as long as they are organizable by actions. Elements can be, but are not necessarily, "things." They can be movements (as in a theory of rigid body displacements, Poincare, 1952), changes (as in Basseches' dialectical thinking, Chapter 10, this volume) or relations (as in Gilligan's theory of female conceptions of social relations, 1982). All that the general model specifies is that elements can be thought about. As members are defined, actions that are coordinated set members are also defined. Actions, as stated earlier, can be of any sort as long as they construct relations between elements.

Given that elements and actions can be specified, at least three stages must be specifiable, a predecessor stage, an initial stage, and a successor stage. The initial stage and its predecessor stage must meet the requirement specified in the general stage model. Successive stages must be generated according to a hierarchical pattern of differentiation (by the application of an action to an increased number of elements) and integration (by the generation of higher-level variable elements). Each stage that succeeds the initial stage must contain cognitive products that are not reducible to the actions and elements of any lower stage. This is perhaps the most difficult condition to test in a cognitive sequence.

If a stage sequence conforms to the general model, tasks can be characterized by the stage of their internal structure. Tasks within a sequence will have their structure hierarchically related. Instances of cognition have internal structure parallel to the internal structure of the corresponding task requirements. All same-stage cognitions will have same-stage internal structure. The cognitive structure must be expressible as task demands. Any preceding stage cognition will have an internal structure hierarchically less complex than the structure of any cognition from the initial stage. This relation must also be expressible in terms of task demands.

Development in any domain can be examined to see whether it meets the conditions of the general model. The necessary, but not the sufficient, conditions for higher-stage development can be explained by this model. The formalized general stage model requires empirical work to apply it in any given domain. It assumes that the elements of a set can be defined for a domain of cognition, not that definitions will be necessarily complete or easy to come by. Case (1974, 1978) and Pascual-Leone (1970) have shown that finding the actions and elements in a given domain is difficult. It is nevertheless necessary since qualitative transformations cannot be specified without an initial definition of elements and actions.

SPECIFYING THE RELATION BETWEEN DOMAIN AND TASK

The internal-stage structures mentioned earlier are composed of specified actions and elements. Structure, as commonly used, is a construct, described by the possible application of actions to elements included in the set of tasks used to test for the presence of thinking at a given stage. As defined here, structure is concretized only in task requirements. It refers to the specific requirements an investigator puts together as a task.

The task must explicitly and clearly delineate requirements. To insure this, task requirements are best represented by a formalized model. Such models are related to the general stage model. They are a more concrete instance of it. A formalized task model must specify the arrangement of action(s) and element(s) that make up the ideal performance or answer. It must also specify them in a system (a complete sequence with a specified generating process) and not merely be a description of each in isolation. The formalized model of the task requirements has restrictions. The statements must be consistent, that is, noncontradictory. They must also be falsifiable, that is, nontautological and possible to refute with evidence.

Since a task is only an instance of a structure, several tasks may share the same structural requirements even though they vary in nonstructural dimensions. Also structural requirements can vary while nonstructural dimensions remain constant. When verbal tasks are used, sentence length, word difficulty, and so forth must be equalized. The essential consideration is that the correspondence of each task to the model must be unique and nonambiguous. Different theorists applying the same general model to the same task performance must agree on the number of operations (or concatenations) discerned. Otherwise, the theory needs further specification. Nevertheless, theorists may differ in their definitions of operations and elements.

Since measured stage performance is compared to the products of ideal problem-solving efforts (endpoints), rather than to the processes people use in discovering solutions to problems, this stage theory classifies ideal task solutions. Therefore, it is argued subsequently that cognitive task performances reflect the requirements of that task. According to traditional stage theory, scored stage of performance arises out of the relationship between "cognitive structure" of the subject and the task requirements. Here, structural demands are differentiated from nonstructural information-processing demands even though they both place cognitive-processing demands on subjects. To the degree that nonstructural demands are ignored, this model is not isomorphic to Pascual-Leone's (Chapter 9, this volume). The same task structure performed in two different contexts with different nonstructural demands might elicit significantly different performances. To identify accurately the appearance of the same stage across different domains (synchrony), the relevant structural demands of each stage must be separated from the range of domain-specific nonstructural demands that affect performance.

SPECIFYING THE RELATION BETWEEN TASK AND PERFORMANCE

Structure is located in task requirements because the task creator gives them structure either implicitly or explicitly. The subject performs at one of the ideal stages specified by the task requirements. Structure is detected in performance and only inferred in the subject. The general model addresses only the structure of task requirements and the performance these elicit. When a subject completes a task, the proximity of a performance to a level specified by the task requirements is also the degree to which the subject's performance reflects the task's ideal structure.

Two principal types of tasks are used in current developmental cognitive research, the problem and the interview. The structure of the problem can explicitly require a performance that either does or does not meet the structural demands of the task. The rules for doing an interview include implicit structural demands. Each question is posed as a hypothetical problem. Both the questions and their corresponding ideal answers supply most of the interview's structure. The interviewer merely compares the subject's response to the ideal answer. So the rules by which experimenters interview subjects are part of the task demands and, together with the "dilemmas" (that is, topics or issues) that usually begin such interviews, constitute the entire task.

The first interview rule requires that the subject be faced with a conflict or a dilemma. The second requires that the experimenter always ask for greater clarification. The experimenter continues to probe the subject when responses differ from the ideal response until movement toward the ideal ends. Knowing when to stop probing for higher reasoning, that is, to stop looking for a performance that simulates the ideal responses with greater fidelity, depends on knowing which answers reflect a consistent stage. The set of probes in an interview implies a set of ideal answers because the clarification probes go beyond the initial perceived demands of a dilemma.

An interview does not necessarily reflect a subject's highest possible level of reasoning. Rather, an interview sees whether a performance matches the explicit demands of an ideal level and many undermeasure competence (Erdynast, 1972). This is because some tasks can be performed entirely adequately at a lower stage of reasoning than a person can display. By focusing on scoring responses, not enough attention is given to the effects of task demands on the performance. For instance, Kuhn and Brannock's (1978) plant problem, a mixture of problem and interview, could be solved at a postformal level. However, a person at a postformal stage of development might choose to solve the problem at the formal level because such a solution is perceived as sufficient for the task. Assuming the subject will be motivated to use the highest structure available for any task, rather than a less-advanced but appropriate structure, results in systematic bias. People may be capable of higher-stage solutions, but the task may not require it. The task must clearly demand performance up to the highest level being tested. The subject's best performance can be detected by increasing the demands of the task until the subject's success begins to drop.

Also, tasks that are thought only to require a given stage of thought may be interpreted differently by a person at a higher stage from the way the tester intended. Formal-operational problems sometimes elicit discussions as to whether the logical solution is counter-factual or not. This kind of discussion is postformal since the entire system of logic is compared to the entire system of evidence. The subject has no difficulty doing the task at the formal-operational stage when instructed to ignore the higher-level issue.

Once an adequate set of probes and rules is identified and can be accurately applied, a task with explicit structural demands can be constructed. These structural demands may be presented either more explicitly (in problems) or less explicitly (in interviews). The performances that result from tasks with specific structural demands should manifest structures analogous to those of the tasks. However, any given task may contain several ideal answers corresponding to several levels of structure, so that a performance will match one or more of those levels. If the task requirements can demonstrate hierarchy as specified by the general stage model, then each set of structures of task requirements constitutes a stage. If a subject then reliably performs using structures analogous to those of the task requirements, it is possible to infer that isomorphic structures exist in the subject and that the subject is "at" a particular stage.

SPECIFYING THE RELATION BETWEEN PERFORMANCE AND A METRIC SCALE

The detection of stage level and transition involves determining whether a subject applies an action to a stage element of a given level and whether this performance changes. Whether subjects can or cannot (1) apply the action or (2) reject an inappropriate action, determines their scored stage and level. In principle, stage and level can be scored using these performance categories in any structural-developmental area, including: Inhelder and Piaget's (1958) tasks, Kohlberg's (1963, 1973, 1976) stages of moral reasoning, Basseches' (1980) dialectical schemata, Fischer's (1980) tiers of skills, Kuhn, Pennington, and Leadbeater's (1982) historical intepretation, Selman's (1976) social perspective-taking tasks, and Erdynast, Armon, and Nelson's (1978) stages of the Good, and others that are presented in this volume.

In order to understand this approach to stage detection, previous psychometric attempts at measuring mental development are reviewed. These attempts have had two related interests. The first has been to establish norms of intelligence in populations, which allows testers to place individual test results in population percentiles. This allows the tester to decide whether a particular performance is within the normal bounds of a given age range. This approach has had more to say about the failure to attain normal development than it has had to say about the nature of normal cognitive growth due to the unspecified meaning of test items. Psychometric tests have been able to predict school performance, and more recently to identify particular kinds of deficits such as the Face-Hand test (Bender, 1952) and the Bender Visual-Motor Gestalt Test (Koppitz, 1964), but the tests have not led to a systematic cognitive-developmental theory.

The second interest has been in detecting different components of intelligence and establishing their relations to one another (Spearman, 1927; Thurstone, 1938; Thompson, 1939; Guilford 1967). This results in notions of the structure of mental abilities and in changes in that structure over time, such as the differentiation-integration hypothesis (Baltes et al., 1980).

These interests are reflected in traditional approaches to scoring tests. Both interests can be satisfied simply by knowing the number of questions answered correctly. Since the tests usually use a multiple-choice format, numerous attempts have been made to compensate for guessing without increasing the number of multiple-choice alternatives. Typically, one subtracts a percentage of incorrect answers from the total of correct answers:

Score = correct − (k) incorrect

The constant k is determined by the probability of a correct guess given the number of alternatives in the multiple-choice format. No real interest existed in incorrect answers.

Piaget departed from traditional psychometric testing by assuming that incorrect answers, interpreted from the subject's viewpoint, shed as much light on intelligence as correct answers do. He assumed that incorrect answers, when probed by the clinical method, reveal a coherent logic of their own. According to his analysis, young thinkers do not use faulty versions of adult logic to generate their answers. They use a different kind of logic to generate answers that make sense within the framework of their own logic.

The clinical method proved extremely useful for revealing certain aspects of cognitive performance. But, since Piaget's principal interest in wrong answers was to show how they could be understood as right answers, he neglected to assign a numerical score to either correct or incorrect answers. This has resulted in psychometric disadvantages.

These disadvantages are apparent in Inhelder and Piaget's (1958) analysis of formal operations. By analyzing responses to a wide range of problems, Inhelder and Piaget developed a descriptive set of substages. In one version of their scheme, concrete operations and formal operations each had two substages (A and B). However, as Piaget remarked, these substages tended to become less clearly distinguishable as the number of instances of reasoning increased. Given a large number of protocols, the differences between protocols became more and more difficult to determine. His substages, as he stated, were stereotypical and provided only the typical features of reasoning at a substage. Furthermore, the differences between substages were also only approximate, providing only loose categorical distinctions.

Kuhn and Brannock (1977) improved on this situation by creating a more systematic categorization of subject responses to an isolation-of-variables problem. They had a more fine-grained scheme of four substages between stages. They used two strategies to collapse problematic protocols and establish an ordered sequence of substages. First, they required subjects to give correct predictions and support them logically with evidence. This represented an effort to make the clinical method more specific and standardized. Second, the ages of the subjects at the different substages were checked during the development of the scoring scheme. This insured that substage competencies claimed to be more advanced appeared later than competencies claimed to be less advanced. This was done longitudinally as well as cross-sectionally. But a weaker logical criterion was used for right answers than for correct rejections (saying a variable was not causal when it was not).

Changes in the production of right answers and correct rejections were found to be correlated with age, but that is because two variables, the correctness of the solution and the logic to support it, were used to generate a single scale. Their use of empirical evidence is somewhat circular and confounds substages with age.

The Kuhn and Brannock sequence of substages has other problems. One problem has to do with analyzing the results of a sequence of tests and retests on a subject. The substages can be used for simple categorization of a performance on each administration of the test but are not adequate for computing changes in competency. Unlike test-retest variation, by definition a shift in competency occurs during substage transition, and it presents psychometric difficulties to the researcher. Without a weakly ordered metric, or unidimensional substage scheme, in which additive relations hold, the results of repeated testing are not in principle interpretable. Krantz, Luce, Suppes, and Tversky (1971) show there is no meaningful way to add categories that are not weak or, preferably, linearly ordered.

Additive categories allow meaningful averages and these in turn permit real estimates of stage competencies. As long as a scale of development is categorical, regardless of how finely its categories are distinguished, it cannot detect transition across categories in a linear developmental sequence. To be weakly ordered, substages have to show transitivity. They do not show transitivity if they are multidimensionally scaled. To be linearly ordered, they have to be above, below, or at the same level as every other substage. Changes must occur along one dimension for that required comparability to hold.

The current difficulty with the sequentiality of substages arises because a subject's performance is conceived to be at a single substage. This is a requirement of a categorical scale. Repeated testing, which might show a gradual process of improvement in different areas, can only be recorded as a series of quantum leaps between substages. Since this is a problem for recording development within a single subject, it is also a problem for scoring subjects in a cross-sectional sample. In such a sample, if there are subjects in transition between substages, they will be scored either higher or lower than their true level if no central tendency measure can be used. Categories of cognitive performance must be related to each other in a way that allows the computation of additional measures (that is, average substage measures, standard deviations, and so on) of subject performance that reflect changes of decision-making rules (the tendency to assert that a given relation or set of operations holds) independently of changes in substage competence.

THE APPLICATION OF CHOICE AND SIGNAL DETECTION THEORY TO SCORING STAGE

One way to deal with this set of scale- and measurement-related problems is to make Kuhn and Brannock's isolation-of-variables problem into an explicit-choice problem (Commons, Davidson, Browne, and Burgard, note 13; Davidson and Commons, note 14). In an explicit-choice format, the subject is to predict both negative and positive instances of an outcome. The subject is also to indicate which combinations of variables actually make a difference in affecting the outcome. The actual variable causing the outcome is masked by irrelevant variables that do not affect the outcome. Correctly predicting the outcome presumes that the subject employs an isolation-of-variables scheme to identify the causal variable and chooses this causal variable from an array of noncausal variables. This choice format makes four kinds of answers possible, all of which are summarized in Figure 7.1. These answers are in the form required by choice theory (Coombs, Dawes, and Tversky, 1970).

In principle, choice theory is applicable to the three most common approaches used in detecting cognitive structure. These approaches require the subject to: (1) make explicit choices, as in the multiple-choice test format; (2) describe or assert a position, as in the dialectical interview; (3) explain a choice or position, as in the moral dilemma. In each of these approaches, it is necessary to have at least two states for the subject to choose between, one in which the target signal is present and one in which the target signal is absent. Having the target signal (what a subject detects at each stage) present simply

Subject Assertion

Stimulus		Signal Present	Signal Absent
	Target Present	Hit	Miss
	Target Absent	False Alarm	Correct Rejection

Figure 7.1. Categorization of Task Performances

means that the form of reasoning the researcher is looking for is recognizably present. This approach, coupled with the general stage model, can be applied to the tasks traditionally used by psychometricians concerned with cognitive measurement (for example, see Binet and Simon, 1916; Jensen, 1972; Guilford, 1967; Terman, 1916; Terman and Merrill, 1960; Vernon, 1961; Wechsler, 1944, 1955, 1958) because it has a coherent, theoretically based description of tasks and why they are ordered the way they are.

Choice theory, along with the general stage model, can be used instead of more recent approaches. For example, Rest's (1976) test for moral-judgment preference assumes that there are patterns of moral reasoning in test passages that the subject can recognize. These passages contain signals that the subject either accepts (a hit) or rejects (a miss). For the highest-stage paragraph, a hit would indicate the subject preferred the highest-stage judgment. Given paragraphs that either contain or do not contain a signal and subject responses that assert that a signal is either present or absent, Figure 7.1 shows the four response categories sufficient to represent the entire response range to each paragraph.

These categories of responses can be used to classify the four substages of formal-operational reasoning identified by Kuhn and Brannock as shown in Figure 7.2. Each of the substages can be translated into a cognitive process that represents partial attainment of formal operations. For example, an overinclusive strategy that does not fully separate variables by generating all possible combinations would result in a consistent pattern of hits (asserting a variable is causal when it is) and false alarms (asserting a variable is causal when it is not). Substage III, defined by a pattern of correct rejections and misses, is an advance from substage II (hits and false alarms) because it represents the development of the ability to exclude noncausal relations. The subject must respond to dissimilarity rather than to similarity, a more complex and comprehensive cognitive task.

Task Performance

Substage		
	1	Misses and False Alarms
	2	Hits
	3	Correct Rejections
	4	Hits and Correct Rejections

**Figure 7.2. Kuhn and Brannock Type Substages
Classified by Task Performances**

This approach also solves the problems posed by retesting and by transitional subjects mentioned earlier since it constructs an additive relation across substage levels. This relation is constructed by determining the number of hits and the number of false alarms and by using these numbers to calculate a competency measure. This eliminates the problems caused by scoring subjects solely on the basis of their best performance.

In previous scoring schemes, the dimensions of hits and false alarms have not been used together. Here the values along these different dimensions are added and the levels are extracted from this composite score. This is a critical difference when performance is determined over multiple measures. If, for example, a subject shows a pattern of hits and false alarms on one test of formal operations at substage II and a pattern of misses and correct rejections at substage III on another, a simple average of substages would score the subject as 2.5, or transitional II-III. Scoring the subject at the highest level of performance would result in a score of III, on the basis of hits at that level.

In choice theory, the scoring procedure is different. The number of hits in the two problems is $1 + 0 = 1$ on the first problem and $0 + 1 = 1$ on the second problem. This yields a hit probability of .5 for the two problems. Likewise, the probability of a false alarm is .5 across the two tests. These two probabilities sum to zero, indicating no sensitivity or bias. In other words, there is pure guessing. Sensitivity is the ability to accurately detect whether a representation is correct. Bias is the tendency to make causal judgments on the basis of plausibility. If, on the other hand, the subject makes a hit and a false alarm on one test and a hit and a false alarm on another test, the hit probability is 1 and the false alarm probability is 1. Although the subject exhibits no sensitivity, there is consistent bias, indicating a higher level of cognitive performance.

Detecting the development of the postformal-operational stages described previously involves analogous use of signal detection. For example, the metasystematic reasoning task described in Commons, Richards, and Kuhn (1982) and Richards and Commons (Chapter 5, this volume) contains four stories, two of which have the same structure. The structure contained in these two stories is presented in different forms. In one story the structure is described in terms of elements and relations among elements, and the axiomatic scheme has to be constructed. In the other story, the axiomatic scheme is given, and the elements and relations derivable from this scheme have to be generated.

The systematic operational task is to describe the structures in each of the stories. This task determines whether a person represents story structure in terms of a compact set of properties or axioms that hold in the story. In terms of choice theory, a task equivalent to representing structure on a systematic level is to determine which two stories are structurally equivalent. Given that subjects are able to represent the structure of the stories, no further competence is required to recognize when two structures are equivalent. Thus, if subjects assert the two equivalent stories are equivalent, they perform a task that in choice-theoretic terms is the same as describing a structure.

The metasystematic task is to represent the differences and similarities among the four stories. Subjects are able to create a way of transforming one story into another and thereby to judge similarity, or they are not. Each of these tasks in the story, and their structural level, is summarized in Table 7.1.

STAGE TRANSITION: A CLOSER LOOK AT THE GENERATOR AND ITS EFFECTS

The following section hypothesizes how a person working at a lower stage produces thought at a higher stage. Stage transition is hypothesized to occur by induction, by analogy, and by the application of simplified forms of higher-stage axioms. Transition occurs when the actions and elements of stage N have become overlearned in many domains, while confrontation occurs with problems and tasks from stage N+1 that cannot be solved using N stage reasoning. Stage transition requires three steps:

1. the development of new ways of thinking (nascent);
2. the replacement of the old ways by the new (transitional);
3. the integration of the new ways into other areas.

The first part of the stage change—the process of developing new operations—could involve the use of analogs of operations present at the lower stage to work on problems requiring the higher stage. The material from the problem may be simplified to aid in this. In the second step of the transition, new problem-solving operations are used. However, these new operations do not replace the old operations immediately; rather, they complement them.

How operant reinforcement affects behavior in a choice situation could explain why new operations are not used exclusively after they have been acquired and why old ones persist for so long. Old operations work well on most problems a person encounters. Thus, old operations are used more and are, consequently, rewarded more often than new operations. The ratio of successful use of the old operations to the new determines the ratio of total use (Herrnstein and Vaughan, 1980) as stated in the momentary matching law (Commons, Woodford, Boitano, Peck, and Ducheny, in press).

In the third step of the transition, old operations are no longer used on new problems because the new operations have been learned successfully and are integrated to become the elements of another new stage after they have been overlearned. Logical development is an unceasing process whereby new actions are introduced, struggled with, and finally assimilated to become the elements that later new actions work on.

CONCLUSION

It is beyond the scope of this chapter to show how choice theory can be applied to scoring protocols in different domains. However, the scheme presented in Table 7.1 has been used to score material from the Heinz dilemma of Kohlberg (1973, 1976), the Korean dilemma of Erdynast (1972), and the free-will dilemma of Armstrong-Roche and Commons (note 15). The process is straightforward; the descriptions in Table 7.1 are used to analyze the stage of task demands contained in various idealized solutions.

There are limits to the usefulness of hierarchical stage sequences. At every stage, there are characteristic stage demands, but this does not mean stage theory accounts for all cognitive phenomena. Cognitive stage theory accounts for just one dimension: the cognitive stage demands. To understand phenomena in the various domains, it is necessary to combine any stage theory with a theory of each of the nonstructural demands that occur in the situation. Pascual-Leone (1970) and Case (1974, 1978) have shown how to categorize some of these nonstructural demands in a structural theory. Surely, as processing difficulties due to unfamiliarity or excessive information are introduced into tasks, the stage characteristics of performance will be eclipsed.

Table 7.1. Metasystematic Scoring Sheet

Problem Dimension	Performance Characteristics and Cognitive Level	Ignore	Miss	False Alarm	Hit	Correct Rejection
Representational Scheme	3b (Concrete Operations) Incomparability on basis of elements. Comparability on basis of surface features.					
	4a (Abstract Operations) Abstractly representing elements					
	4b (Formal Operational) Abstractly representing elements and all their combinations produced by the operations within the system.					
Set Size or Cardinality	4a (Abstract Cardinality) Counting of values of a variable.					
	4b (Formal Cardinality) Forming combinations and permutations of values of a variable.					
	5a (Systematic Cardinality: Relations on the Power Set) Reentrant counting: enumerating the results of constructing all combinations.					
Relations and Operations	3b (Concrete) Ordering and classifying.					
	4a (Abstract) Ordering and classifying after operating.					
	4b (Formal) Coordinating at least two operations and a relation.					
	5a (Systematic) Coordinating laws.					

154

	5b	(Metasystematic)
		Exploiting the structure of a system to derive truths or untruths in the same or a related system. Adding or subtracting propositions or properties; transforming systems.
Relational Structure	5a	(Systematic)
		Representing the set of relations and operations within a system across individual elements.
	5b	(Metasystematic)
		Axiomatization of relations. Topological graphing.
Overall Structure	5b	(Metasystematic)
		Representing the set of relations and operations across the set of elements in the systems produced by certain operations.
Transformation	5b	(Metasystematic)
		Transforming in a stepwise manner from one system to another to create a metric for distance between systems.
Morphism	5b	(Metasystematic)
		Structural determination of the morphic relation between systems; equality, inequality, embeddedness, noncomparability between systems. Structuring the relations between systems.

There is one kind of nonstructural thought that could be extremely useful in understanding the relationship between stage of thought and stage of behavior in everyday situations, that is, knowledge of value and the operations used to perceive value. One way of simplifying the account of behavior is to say that organisms understand the relationship between events and the environment, especially causal paths. Traditionally, motivation has been used to explain whether that knowledge is acted upon. To be consistent with the approach offered here, the motivational or economic variables should be reduced to knowledge about value and how it is obtained, as well as the intrapersonal conditions, such as drives, that establish the values themselves. In this approach, economics determines the distribution of behavior at the various stages. If the preponderance of highly preferred outcomes occurs for lower-stage behaviors, the lower-stage behaviors will actually be preferred. Understanding actual behavior cannot occur without understanding how value is embodied in the organism and influenced by the environment. Theories of behavior will have to integrate a number of paradigms without violating what is known about each.

There are also internal limits to stage theory. The universality claims of stage sequences are limited to cultures where tasks belonging to the sequence play a significant role in that culture. Since cognitive development is based on interaction tasks, such as running a non-face-to-face government, or solving scientific problems that require schooling, upper levels of some sequences and some whole sequences may be absent from some cultures (Edwards, 1975). While these competencies are required for some people on a very wide range of problems within Western cultures, not enough is known about the nature of cognitive demands within other cultures to say all cultures (including Western cultures) provide experiences that produce all possible competencies. In fact, the concept of "all possible competencies" is a dubious one. However, it is assumed that, with proper tasks and experiences, stage sequences would become universal.

Within Western cultures, the present empirically detectable developmental termini would seem to be determined by current biological and cultural limitations, not by inherent limitations in the inductive stage generator. The differentiation of knowledge as it is applied and the integration of differentiated schemes into higher-level systems of epistemology imply no endpoint to the genesis of epistemology. While higher stages may not yet be constructed or observed, there is no demonstration that any stage's coordinations are fully equilibrated. The operations of a stage appear to be fully equilibrated only with respect to the elements of that stage. Each stage generates products that do not belong to it and therefore cannot be coordinated from within it. New operations have to be invented to coordinate these products. Hence, the number of stages is theoretically boundless.

Another concern is the notion that higher stages are better. It is one thing to have more developed thought, it is another to claim superiority or ultimate worth for such thought. If thought is developed by the continuous construction of new forms that transform contradictions, no organism's thought adequately deals with problems. This does not rule out improvements in understanding, but it does imply that there will never be final solutions. Errors generated by the inevitable inadequacies of each successive stage, and the zealousness accompanying the acquisition of powerful new mental tools, create ongoing difficulties. With each advancement in stage, more power is acquired. A young adult shifting to systematic thought may think in terms of coherent systems of ideas to forcefully convert whole societies, while the child shifting to concrete thought may merely consider threatening a weaker sibling for not conforming to rules. While increasingly complex thought is a source of great achievement in art and science, its consequences are played out in an arena of greater dimensions than lower-stage thinking. The potential errors of such thinking affect more people, with a proportional growth in the magnitude of their consequences.

8

LOGIC AND SELF-REGULATION FROM YOUTH TO MATURITY: A MODEL
Gisela Labouvie-Vief

Unlike most contributions in this volume, this work began by approaching the question of postadolescent thought from the study of aging. These efforts to understand a number of theoretical ambiguities suggested that developmental regularities in later life are to be sought, in part, in their early-life precursors. Thus, in inching backwards from old age to adolescence, it appeared that certain views of adulthood and aging are easily distorted if examined through concepts of development that focus on growth from birth to adolescence. The goal of establishing a proper theoretical baseline in mature adulthood, therefore, led to a critical examination of Piaget's claim that mature adult cognition reaches its heights in adolescence.

Geropsychological research represents an overwhelming impression not only of biological decline (see, for example, Shock, 1977), but also of regressive movements in memory (see, for example, Craik, 1977), and decline in competence of problem solving (see, for example, Hooper & Sheehan, 1977; Rabbit, 1977). In general, later life adult thought has appeared to display an erosion of formal logical competence and a return to the concrete. At first sight, such findings appear to be readily assimilable to prevalent notions and extensions of youth-centered developmental theorizing that hold that regression proceeds from higher to lower levels of functioning.

If Piaget's assertion that formal thought constitutes the crowning achievement of human ontogeny is accepted, such a pessimistic view of adulthood becomes a logical necessity. Our perspectives on growth and decline are, in a kind of self-fulfilling teleology, oriented from the idealized apogee that serves both as a theoretical observation point and as a conceptual filter (Labouvie-Vief & Chandler, 1978). Thus, from this perspective, adulthood inevitably becomes a period precariously suspended between the rush of early adolescent growth and later predeath deterioration. Yet, a number of phenomena do not readily fit this theoretical mold. If the perfection of formal logic appears to occupy a relatively minor place in the lives of most adults, indeed restricted to the small minority with formal logical training, fairly normative changes are observed in other domains. While Piaget felt that, in adulthood, creative achievements (cf. Furth, 1981) take place almost exclusively in the arena of logic, and, indeed, mathematicians and logicians appear to peak in their early adulthood, creative peaks in other empirically richer areas usually occur much later (Dennis, 1966). Freud and Kant, for example, reached their peaks in their forties and fifties, respectively. Further, as is true of Piaget himself, the thought of creative adults does undergo significant qualitative changes over time, appearing to move to a greater concern with all-encompassing regulative dimensions and often with moral and humanistic issues (see Feuer, 1974; Kohlberg, 1973b). Are the moral concerns of an aging Bertrand Russell or Albert Einstein to be called the rantings of senility?

Such qualitative changes are also observable in typical lives. Many adults first elaborate a structure of preliminary stability that permits them to embark on early adult life with a sense of buoyant optimism. They then feel compelled to reexamine those structures some years later. They reinterpret their early sense of autonomy as a mere living out of social expectations (for example, Cytrynbaum et al., 1980; Dabrowski, 1970; Jung, 1933: Levinson et al., 1978; Vaillant, 1977) and restructure their lives around a new sense of self-conscious choice and search for personal, moral, and ethical integrity.

In researching adult cognition, apparently regressive features in the cognitive performance of older adults appear that also display features profoundly different from the concretism of childhood. For example, there is concern with the concrete constraints of real life or refusal to sever cognition from its affective, social, and pragmatic ties. It is not only a more conscious, reflective awareness of the concrete constraints of real life, it is also an awareness that is closely integrated with action. "Have you ever considered," an elderly woman asked recently, "that there is no point in remembering just anything. Choices are made about what is worth remembering?" This insight can be interpreted as a mere compensatory, defensive adjustment to inevitable biological and logical decline. However, it can also be interpreted as a profound process of structural growth in which a truce is negotiated between the more formal mode of youth and the deeper layers of one's active and affective life.

Adolescence viewed in light of the latter interpretation illuminates the uneasy co-existence of formal brilliance and the disequilibria of affect and action. The adolescent move from the intra- to the interpropositional that accompanies the transition to formal operativity appears to be, contrary to Piaget's claim, content-bound. This quality is readily visible in the formalistic, physicalistic settings studied by Piaget. But when turning to the regulation of one's affect and social action, formal operativity achieves a preliminary and partial integration, at best (Blos 1962a; A. Freud, 1966). Thus, adolescence may be a period in which logic erects all kinds of dualisms and, with them, disequilibria. Broughton (1981) has documented the inability to integrate mind and body, self and nonself. With the new-found ability to move in the possible rather than the real, youth perceives the constraints of socialization, institutions, and ideologies, yet is unable to transcend them (Jung, 1933). Authority, rather than self, regulates one's behavior (Perry, 1970; Loevinger, 1977). The adolescent's life structure is lived out automatically and compulsively, rather than freely and consciously. Complex thought structures run a danger of becoming rigidly directed against individual autonomy (Blos, 1962a; Freud, 1966).

This broad base of data constitutes a foundation for a theoretical account of postformal development, whether progressive or regressive. My approach is to attempt to reconstruct Piaget's account of development so as to permit a more adequate interpretation of the voluminous literature on adulthood.

This chapter presents a preliminary formulation of the resulting model. Specifically, it will attempt two tasks. The first is to show that the development of formal operations, as described by Piaget (for example, Inhelder & Piaget, 1958), only prefigures important adult accomplishments and thus fail to provide a comprehensive model of mature adult adaptation. The second goal is to utilize this discussion in the construction of a theoretical model that has as its aim a description of adulthood development. In this model, structures of formal thought are merely a precursor form of those thought structures that permit the expression of the characteristics often associated with maturity: moral integrity, constructive generativity, social responsibility, and individual agency and autonomy.

A CRITIQUE OF 'PURE LOGIC'

This critique begins by pointing out some of the main reasons why Piaget's model has put such strong emphasis on logic as the main characteristic of mature thought. It is a core assumption of Piaget's developmental-structural position that the study of development must be aimed not at the description of variations in isolated parameters, but at the description of the formal laws inherent in the organization of systems or structure wholes. This emphasis derives from the notion that advance in developmental competence is the increased capacity for self-regulation. In this self-regulation, the action of parts, elements, or contents is integrated by, and subordinated to, the equilibration-maintaining mechanisms of the system as a whole. Systems or structures, then, provide a certain closure in that they constrain the variability of the parts. In this way, they afford a larger measure of stability or relative independence from environmental fluctuations. Ultimately, Piaget's emphasis on logic is motivated out of his interest in outlining parameters of individual adaptation. It is in this same context that the issue of postformal structures is presently placed.

Piaget has offered at least two different, and somewhat incompatible, accounts of what constitutes objective and autonomous self-regulation. The first account is probably the most popular. In this account (for example, Piaget, 1971, 1977), formal logic perfects the process of equilibration by its ability to idealize, to abstract from one's concrete experience, to posit *zero deviations*, and to search for them with deductive certainty. The adolescent, by dissociating form and content, becomes able to envision universal, transcendental conditions for truth and objectivity.

If this view of formal logic is accepted, it is pointless to posit postformal growth in the structure of logic. However, as Piaget has argued at other points (for example, Piaget, 1970), such a view is logically impossible. According to this second account, no logical system can demonstrate its conditions of validity and thus be universal. Rather, logical truth is achieved by relinquishing such claims to certainty, by delegating one's current logical system to the status of content, and by thus relativizing it by embedding it in a new and higher-order form. Structural change, as a consequence, can never be understood by an absolute dissociation of form from content. Rather, as Piaget (1970) states, it is involved in an endless nested regress " . . . there is no 'form as such' or 'content as such' . . . each element, from sensori-motor acts through operations to theories, is always simultaneously form to the content it subsumes and content for some higher form" (p. 35).

This view of objectivity as a process by which universalistic claims are relativized and contextualized is, in fact, one Piaget has emphasized in contexts other than logical development. The spatially egocentric child, for example, commits the fallacy of overgeneralizing a relationship that is in actuality relativized by different spatial and interpersonal perspectives (Piaget & Inhelder, 1969). Similarly, in moral development (Piaget, 1965b), the young child's conception of rules changes. Rules that were seen as eminent, universal, and unalterable become relativized rules that are changeable and validated only by their intersubjective context.

It is argued here that structural development in adulthood proceeds by a similar relativization of formal thought, although occurring at a higher level. Thus, as is true for morality and spatial egocentricity, pure logic must be reunited with content and context. Conversely, it is also claimed that formal thought in adolescence achieves a preliminary equilibrium at best. Like spatial or moral egocentrism, it entails a formal mode of egocentrism. Like earlier structures, it contains the dynamism for further disequilibration and equilibration.

The argument that formal logic is a limited standard for mature thought is based on several lines of reasoning. The first line draws on recent developments in metalogic that strongly support a view of objectivity that relies on intersubjective dimensions. The second relies on recent philosophical discussions that similarly locate objectivity in intersubjectivity. The third is psychological and claims that, unless integrated with self and other dimensions, formal thought may well constitute a model of rigid defense, rather than mature and autonomous self-regulation.

Logic and Certainty

Recent developments in metalogic have demonstrated logical claims to deductive certainty to be logically inconsistent and impossible. Piaget, in attempting to locate a model by which consistency criteria might be settled solely by reason, turned to propositional calculus (Piaget & Inhelder, 1958). This choice, as Piaget may himself have later felt (cf. Furth, 1981), was somewhat unfortunate since the truth claims of propositional calculus are extremely limited from psychological, and even logical, perspectives.

This logic requires a differentiation between two notions of truth (cf. DeLong, 1970; Hofstadter, 1980). The first of these is the notion of *internal* consistency and concerns the structure of interrelating arguments. In the propositional calculus, for example, any set of propositions or premises satisfying truth table criteria is true. On the other hand, an *interpreted* formal system must also satisfy external truth conditions. In propositional calculus, one is concerned merely with the argument structure, not the structure of meaning of the premises.

When judging the interpreted or external truth value of a propositional calculus will state that an argument (for example, "if come to be important. In a conditional argument, for example, propositional calculus will state an argument (for example, "if Socrates is dead, there is no highest prime number") is true if and only if antecedent and consequent premises are both true or both false. However, there is no method to examine the truth or falsity of the premises. If they are accepted, then the argument is true, but if they are rejected, the argument is irrelevant. The choice is not a matter of propositional calculus. Either the premise is asserted to be true, or an attempt to ascertain the truth value of the premise is made by consulting authority or by finding consensual agreement in an interpersonal network (for example, via discussion). Ultimately, propositional calculus starts from an intuitive or socially shared knowledge base that has no logical foundations. Piaget's logic, therefore, is only one element in a broader structure. Its goal or conclusion is dependent on 'extraneous' factors, such as what kind of conclusion the thinker *wants* to reach.

It is exactly this feature of propositional logic that attracted the Sophists and the fury of many a parent of teenagers. Moreover, this feature has been the source of logical paradoxes that led both to a recognition of the limitations of propositional calculus (cf. DeLong, 1970) and to the development of the predicate calculi (a group of more complex methods that attempt to consider the structure of the premises by the formalization of quantifiers, which premises particularize). The claim is made that quantifiers apply over indefinite domains and are therefore universally true, but they have, in turn, produced their own paradoxes. Delong (1970) proposed to circumvent these problems by axiomatizing the propositional and predicate calculi within the theory of recursive functions. This, in essence, is an approach in which definitions are definitions by induction and proofs are proofs by recursion. Skolem's method is extremely powerful and provides a generalization. Yet Skolem's original hope of banishing uncertainty from logical discourse, through the theory of recursive functions, was proven futile. His universalistic claims were laid to rest by the so-called limitative theorems of Skolem, Church, and Godel (DeLong, 1970; Hofstadter, 1980).

Church's thesis is the most relevant in this context. It concerns the hierarchical ordering of logical systems. According to this thesis, which may be closer in status to a natural law, truth claims become successively less certain as a logical system becomes more complex or more differentiated. Thus, the propositional calculus has a set of effective and computable formulas by which (internal) truth and nontruth can be clearly differentiated. It too, however, is extremely limited in its interpretive range.

The predicate calculus does not yield effective formulas to establish its validity. Instead, it allows for a kind of partial truth in which truth is established by not establishing nontruth. It has, in other words, the status of an inductive law. Truth in this system is *constructive* in Piaget's (1970) sense, and also in the sense in which theories are said to be refutable rather than provable (Popper & Eccles, 1978).

On the other hand, if one moves from a purely formal system to one that interprets reality, even inductive certainty disappears. In a system as modest in empirical content as arithmetic, neither true nor false sentences are effectively or constructively possible. That is, some sentences are proven false that are true under other interpretations and vice versa. Individual true-false statements become absorbed in systems. Practical and empirical truth comes to be a stronger notion than logical provability.

In this view, the logical absolutism of the propositional method must be given up in a process of progressive differentiation. First, the focus of analysis is on the internal construction of the system within which truth claims are relativized. Second, logic no longer affords a determinate, deductively certain plan of action. Ultimately, truth claims come to be temporally displaced in the future and must be negotiated by dimensions of subjective communicative dynamics. DeLong (1970) has remarked:

> The analogy of a game is useful in explaining . . . (this notion) . . . It often happens that a game is invented (and the rules are laid down which define that game), but at a later time a circumstance occurs for which the rules give no guidance. At this point a decision has to be made as to what will henceforth be the rule concerning that circumstance. The decision might be made on the basis of fairness, whether it makes it a better spectator sport, whether it increases the danger, and so on. However, it cannot be made on the basis of the rules of the game because they are incompletely defined. Now part of the impact of the limitative theorems is that the rules of which we discover mathematical truths *not only are, but must be, incompletely defined*. We are thus forced to define the notion of arithmetical truth historically; that is, it cannot be explicated once and for all but must be continually redefined (pp. 224–225, emphasis added).

The resulting need to reexamine logic in the contexts of personal and interpersonal praxis shows a parallel with Piaget's (1965) views on the dynamics of developmental progression in infralogical and extralogical domains. Piaget is explicit in stating what constitutes growth in abstractive complexity when he differentiates between two notions of abstraction. The first is usually represented in the tree-structure models of many current information-processing theories. It is a notion of successive reduction of existing logical structures to less and less common dimensions. This abstractive notion results in impoverishment rather than growth in Piaget's view. As the structure closes, it removes the organism more and more from any context of praxis. Structural growth, in contrast, happens as current modes of organization are extended to new contexts of activity, modified by those contexts, and eventually transformed to new structures.

Consequently, postformal structures cannot be posited from within formal models per se. Rather, the process of structural reorganization exposes the limiting conditions to earlier levels of structural organization. A discussion of these limiting conditions follows.

Logic, Self, and Other

By recognizing the need to relocate truth claims in the internal construction of systems, modern metalogic has returned to the old philosophical tension between theoretical and practical reason. Kant's revolutionary formulation of this tension placed the two types of reason in an interactive relation. However, he formulated a static, transcendental idealism in which reality, and the categories by which it is construed, participate in nonconflictive interaction. Ultimately, Piaget returns to such idealism with his model of propositional logic.

Epistemologically, formal operations imply that the subject operates on a reality that, though constructed by abstract principles, is nevertheless concrete and unambiguous. The individual becomes absorbed in the universal. When laws and norms are universal, individuals are homogenized in these universal structures. Individuals become interchangeable, and the epistemic subject interacts monologically with an objectified reality.

This naive realism is embedded in, and undifferentiated from, a further transcendental world. Reality is by no means objective but is prestructured by symbolic meanings located in the intersubjective and is internalized in the subjective. The purely cognitive remains undifferentiated from the intra- and interpersonal.

As Habermas (1971) has argued, reason must return to the task of forming these prior, categorical meaning structures. The logical realist must confront his/her own interpretive schemata and coordinate those schemata with those of others in a attempt to achieve reciprocity. This task causes the epistemic subject to confront the causality of individual interpretive schemata. The idea of causality can transcend the merely physical in this process. It can move to include the dynamics of symbolic contents and individual histories.

Formal logic, by giving up the need for further self-reflective differentiation, runs the risk of subjective and intersubjective distortions in cognitive inquiry. By disavowing the need for self-reflection, the epistemic subject can only turn to positivism, an epistemology presumably uncontaminated by "philosophical" bias. Yet, as Habermas (1971, p. 5) notes, "by making a dogma of the sciences' belief in themselves, positivism assumes the prohibitive function of protecting scientific enquiry from philosophical self-reflection." In positivistic universality, the epistemic individual is ultimately left with a private language, a limited categorical framework. In this framework, truth can be delegated by fiat but not negotiated. The individual is absolved from the responsibility of facing the multiple, polysemic dimensions, both personal and cognitive, that fuse in the process of inquiry.

The transcendence of such monologic epistemology is different from the transcendentalism of Kant or Husserl. Earlier transcendental logic sought a solution to the problem in the reconstitution of prior conditions of possible universal knowledge. In contrast, Habermas (1973) views the solution to be found not in the attributes of a transcendental consciousness, but in the symbolic environments out of which these logical structures materialize.

Logic and Self-Regulation

Piaget's emphasis on formal logic as a tool by which the individual regulates behavior has its roots in the belief that the movement from the real to the possible permits contact with a symbolically structured reality. Thus, it shapes the self-other differentiation and the autonomous individuality necessary for generative participation in culture. Yet the considerations mentioned generate some doubt that formal operationality can adequately model (mature) psychological organization.

The deficiencies of formal operations as a psychological model of self-regulation derive exactly from the structural characteristics of the propositional method outlined so far. By failing to differentiate between universal truth table structures (formal relationships), and the internal construction of systems (content), the propositional method will produce a number of severe distortions in the perception and interpretation of reality. Such distortions are an aspect of the interpretation of reality at any level of development because cognitive structure is focused on the analysis of a segment of reality that exceeds that structure in complexity (Sinclair, 1973). They are particularly severe in adolescence, however, since the move to formal operations equips the individual with a sense of omnipotent autonomy that hides profound symbiotic fusion with the environment.

It is no surprise that logic is applied by adolescents with relative ease when operating on those classes and systems that are familiar and intuitively accepted because they originate in a commonly shared world. Such a modus operandi permits precisely the kind of synchronic, ahistoric, and unidimensional thought characteristic of propositional logic. Yet it results in more or less severe distortions when applied in multidimensional contexts. In these contexts, meaning structures may be diverse, diachronic aspects are important, and the internal organization of systems under consideration is characterized by divergence, change, or interactivity.

> Ironically, enthralled by the underlying psychological realities . . . (the adolescent) . . . often appears to overgeneralize simple or unidimensional (stereotypic) traits as the primary features of the psychological aspects of persons. Another limiting aspect of this stage is that subjectivity within the person still is understood to occur on one plane, the plane of conscious awareness. The powerful idea that the mind, the conscience, or the "little person inside" can

organize the self's inner psychological life leaves no room for psychological phenomena unavailable to this roving eye (Selman, 1980, p. 134).

This exclusionary method of regulating behavior by the brute force of a monodynamic will entails limitations. This will continues to be conditioned by upbringing and runs the danger of becoming no more than an internalized tool for perpetuating the very structures it wishes to reject (Blos, 1962a). Moreover, its very monodynamic quality resists effective integration and thus creates profound swings in equilibrium. In attempting to maintain internal balance, youth may swing back and forth between a physical reductionism and a pan-psychic determinism (Broughton, 1980a), between a sense of omnipotence and a sense of defeat (Elkind, 1974). The subject is like the child who has not yet achieved a multiplicative concept of volume and vascillates in centering from height to length to width. The subject relies on a logical model that is too simplistic and splits reality into fragmented dimensions that resist integration.

In sum, it is argued that Piaget's emphasis on formal logic reveals a conceptual breach with a broader view of development that is much richer and of a higher level of generality. In this broader view, development can never close in on universal structures. To do so prevents steps toward further differentiation. Such steps are initiated when, after a first integration that appears to tie reality into a universal framework, the thinker discovers that this integration is egocentered. This discovery requires engaging in further processes of differentiation, initiated by submitting the conceptual system to an audience of others. Development, then, can be visualized in terms of spirallike swings back and forth between relatively subject-centered, egocentric modes of thought and relatively object-centered or decentered ones. Each movement up the spiral, to be sure, achieves a more mature and less egocentric form of egocentrism. Nevertheless, it is the exposure of that form of egocentrism that constitutes the next level of developmental advancement.

TOWARD ADULT AUTONOMY

Core Assumptions

The present theory assumes an organism is born into a polysemic and symbolic environment. Its task is to master the structure of that environment before it can go on to a more autonomous level of psychological organization. The outcome of the autonomous level is a generative element in evolution. Two elements are contained in this core assumption.

First, by calling the environment polysemic and symbolic, emphasis is placed on a reality that is not 'real' in the naive sense of realism. It is rather a reality that has been co-constructed by biological and cultural processes of evolution. The environment is an ultrastructure in which individual development is embedded and by which it is regulated. Concretely observable objects and events are analyzable at multiple levels of meaning. They can be understood concretely as basic dimensions of reality. They can also be seen as concrete manifestations or material products of human symbolic systems, in the widest sense of the term symbolic. The 'concrete' dimensions of reality, therefore, are themselves dimensionalized by more abstract, symbolically constructed systems.

Second, by speaking of the organism's developmental task, a (somewhat) teleological perspective is adopted. This teleological orientation is not to be understood in its classical idealist and transcendental sense. Rather, it is used in the system-theoretic sense used by Piaget (1971). Thus, to attribute a goal to development is merely to assert that development processes are directed by processes of evolution. These processes, having achieved a characteristic state of complexity at a particular historical time, have a causative role and act back on the regulation of individual development (see Campbell, 1974; Waddington, 1975). This characteristic state of complexity indexes the proper level of analysis for the theoretical and methodological investigation of development. This historical level of complexity is the polysemic, abstract-symbolic nature of reality and the humanly produced ultrastructure.

The organism is born into this environment with an endowment of predominantly biological regulatory mechanisms, such as those described by Piaget. These mechanisms provide preliminary means of equilibrium maintenance. However, these mechanisms are limited and require additional symbiotic interfacing with a cultural environment that provides protective buffering. There is an explicit dialectic, therefore, between individual and cultural development: being biologically programmed for plasticity, the individual is highly dependent on cultural mechanisms of regulation.

As more complex modes of interfacing with the environment are developed, the individual progressively decodes and differentiates the self from both the biological and cultural heritage. But in so doing also encodes, in a stage-appropriate fashion, many dimensions that remain as yet undifferentiated. Thus, at any particular level, the individual not only is able to differentiate previous levels but can also internalize information from more complex levels. That form, however, is structually degraded.

Development, therefore, is bilaterally organized. On the one hand, it is characterized by increasing self-other differentiation and conscious development. On the other hand, this differentiation goes along with the unreflected and automatic carrying over, and taking on, of cultural automatisms (such as described by Shiffrin & Schneider, 1977 and Pascual-Leone, Chapter 9, this volume). Elsewhere (Labouvie-Vief, 1981a), this bilateral organization has been referred to as the co-existence of proactive and reactive processes in developmental organization. Along with Piaget (1971), this work assumes that the conscious part of organization increases throughout development while the automatic part decreases *once* the cultural automatisms have been stably internalized.

It is proposed, then, that individual development is, in essence, a biphasic process. The first phase of this process takes place, roughly, from birth to adolescence. It consists of the decoding of certain biological automatisms and the bilateral encoding of cultural automatisms. Preliminary psychological structures are built that permit the organism to function as a biological individual even though culturally fused. This whole phase of development might be called intrasystemic, even though that term will be used merely for the last level of this phase.

A second phase of development is initiated after adolescence. The individual, having formed the requisite structures, separates from the primary cultural origin. In this second phase is the confrontation of the cultural-symbolic foundations of the cognitive structures. This confrontation initiates a fuller decoding of the cultural environment, and a progressive differentiation from the regulations imposed by culture. It eventually permits active, conscious, and generative participation in cultural progress.

Core Progression

As in Piaget's model of development, this theory views development as a recursively constructed, nested hierarchy. The original building blocks of this hierarchy are biological and behavioral regulations that allow behavior to be structured and adapted, relative to a particular level. Such regulations are always seen to have historical or 'genetic' dimensions. They are the result of incorporating feedback from the outcomes of previous levels of regulation into the present schemata regulating action. The regulation of each level may itself become the object of regulated behavior at a unique level. The next higher level regulates the level below it by decoding the conditions of regulation that have been operative, but opaque, at the lower level. Such shifts are achieved when local regulations are extended and multiplied into diverse-action contexts. They become progressively differentiated and increasingly lead to contradiction and centering. The self eventually transcends this conflict by construing both its original self and the process of centering within multiple ego-centered perspectives.

New regulations thus mediated tend to become more and more explicitly self-referential. Developmental complexity proceeds from simple regulations to regulations of regulations, which represent a relatively autonomous level of self-regulation (Furth, 1981; Piaget, 1977b, 1979). In general, the process of development is a movement from relatively peripheral regulations to more central regulations, 'transcendent' in this sense to more peripheral ones. The self experiences qualitative reorganizations that reflect the progressive development of both inward- and outward-directed regulations. This deepening and temporal-spatial expansion of self is indicated in the diagonal progression from the upper left to the lower right corner of Figure 8.1.

The core diagonal progression of Figure 8.1 is, in essence, Piaget's account of development. Each level of self-centeredness achieves a characteristic reversible subject-object equilibrium ($_iS_i$ <--------> $_iO_i$). In addition, the progression brings another feature of Piaget's model into explicit focus. Development not only moves 'inward' from periphery to core, but also moves outward from the core, restructuring the periphery from the vantage point of each new level. From level to level, the individual not only functions at the new, stage-appropriate mode, but also previous modes (sensori-motor, symbolic, and so on) become structurally reorganized. At the first level, the equilibrated 'self' is defined as sensory-motor ($_1S_1$ <---->$_1O_1$) regulations. At the second level, the 'self' is defined by symbolic regulations ($_2S_2$ <----> $_2O_2$) that superordinate (for example, selectively facilitate and inhibit) reflected sensori-motor ones ($_1S_2$ <----> $_1O_2$). In the same fashion, intrasystemic ($_3S_3$ <----> $_3O_3$), intersystemic ($_4S_4$ <----> $_4O_4$), and autonomous ($_5S_5$ <----> $_5O_5$) regulations come to eventually superordinate previous modes of functioning.

For example, at Piaget's formal-operational level (located at the resolution of the intrasystemic level in the present theory), critical modes of action are not only those of propositional thought. Action also has concrete symbolic and sensori-motor manifestations. However, action is reflected in the stage-appropriate fashion onto the corresponding higher mode. Development is not seen as a cumulative, layer-upon-layer construction of 'advanced' upon 'primitive' modes. Rather, it is augmentative and partially disjunctive. At each level, a new modality is added to the organism's repertoire, and this modality provides the opportunity, though not the necessity (see below), for complete reorganization of all previous modalities. Development by augmentative construction is largely reconstructive, although it remains constructive as well. Through this process, psychological organization achieves a degree of flexible independence from its original, inflexible biological-instinctual precursors. Figure 8.1 represents reorganization by the gradual expansion and reorganization of all modes from level to level.

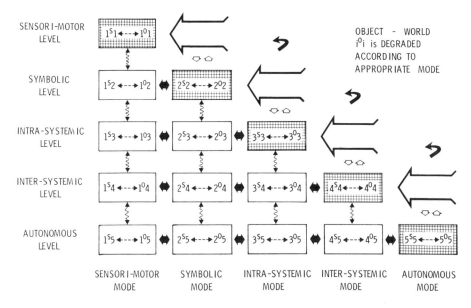

Figure 8.1. Syntonic and Dystonic Modes of Equilibration in Development. Each box represents a specific segment of a reversible subject (S)–object (O) transaction or equilibrium. From level to level, former equilibrium modes may or may not be reflected onto the mode added to the cognitive repertoire by the new level. Syntonic equilibration consists of the complete reflection of former modes to a new level of development ($_1S_1 \longleftrightarrow {}_1O_1$ to $_1S_1 \longleftrightarrow {}_1O_2$, etc.). Dystonic equilibration involves partial reflections, automatisms, and asynchronies resulting from lack of self-reference. Dystonic equilibration can be effectively reequilibrated only with entry of the autonomous mode.

Syntonic and Dystonic Equilibria

In addition to preserving, though extending upward, Piaget's account of the development of progressively broader equilibria, this theory adds another dimension. In Piaget's theory, each level is primarily characterized by a form of equilibrium that is maintained through the conscious operative co-regulation of requisite schemata and that is built primarily by the organism's own conscious effort. In this theory, not all equilibration actions are based on conscious cognition. In contrast, equilibria are elaborated in two somewhat opposing modes that reflect qualitatively different organizations of cognition and affect.

Take as an example the equilibria of the young girl who broke out in tears because a tray of ice cubes had melted (Shantz, personal communication). Her emotional disorganization is a mode of reequilibration, which resulted from her lack of an appropriate conscious equilibrium transformation by which melting and freezing become reversible. Once this reversibility was acquired consciously, the structure of her behavior changed. It became characterized by specific organized action and indicated an ability to plan and to delay gratification.

Note that in this conceptualization, issues of affect are immediate correlatives of issues of the structure of the operatory rule systems available to the individual. At first, the child is in a state of dystonic organization. The reaction is externally induced (that is, external to the operatory rule system), it is automated or nonconscious, it is nonspecific (not related to the goal of reversibly removing distress), and it simply achieves equilibrium by affective and motor discharge. Moreover, as Luria (1960) points out, it follows, rather than precedes, the external events. Not being based on reversible schemata, this automatic mode is largely reactive.

In contrast, after cognitive reorganization, affect shows different features. Action becomes transformed and differentiated. It precedes rather than follows external events (Piaget's notion of the 'precorrection of errors'). It involves a representation that incorporates knowledge about the causal mechanisms involved in the transformation operation. This knowledge is both object- and self-referential. It permits a new level of syntonic organization in which representations and actions are coordinated toward the same goal.

However, representing syntonic organization as the process by which the individual constructs the self through increasing levels of self-reference and reflective abstractions is idealized. Feedback from the social environment is structured independently of the individual. When developing, the individual is vulnerable to obscuring the multiple functions of objects and people. With the addition of more complex representations, for instance, a new relationship with the external world is established, and reality can be constructed *more passively, less self-referentially* by merely, through a kind of symbiosis, feeding on the reflective abstractions of others.

Piaget (for example, Piaget & Inhelder, 1969) has remarked on this process of passive, partial reflection by which behavior is not invented, but rather transmitted in ready-made compulsory and collective external forms. This process, while essential to cultural progress, also constrains the individual's consciousness because objects, signs, and symbols are assimilated at their face or surface value. They are not, as yet, fully differentiated, and exert their regulatory function automatically.

To summarize, the present model conceptualizes each stage more broadly by a particular modality in which reality is elaborated and by which equilibria are maintained. This modality can work in either of two ways: (1) it can differentiate reality consciously; or (2) it can assimilate it in a global, syncretic, and undifferentiated way. The differentiating submode is one of progressive individuation, while the automatic submode is one of symbiotic fusion. Both submodes act together in the progressive development of equilibrium mechanisms. Working in concert, they establish a somewhat oppositional dynamism in the process of development. The differentiating submode functions as a progressive mode by which cognitive-affective schemata are brought under conscious superordination. In contrast, the automatic submode is an inertial model of processing. It records deviations from an unconscious and global equilibrium level and offers affective resistance to excessive changes in that level.

Levels of Adult Development

How does the adolescent move to the level of autonomously participating in the system while maintaining and generating concerns of the collective? It is proposed here that this progression follows exactly the levels of logic outlined earlier. Specifically, three ordered, general levels are distinguished: the intrasystemic, the intersystemic, and the autonomous modes of organization (see Figure 8.2).

Intrasystemic Level

The intrasystemic level corresponds to level 3 of Figure 8.1. It is initiated when the individual is able to operate on abstract quantities and relations. It corresponds chronologically to the period from concrete to formal operations.

The logical structure of intrasystemic thought is akin to the model of logical empiricism in which truth is seen as exhaustible. Reality is viewed as singularly ordered in a unihierarchical framework based on normative and universal laws. As in Piaget's heteronomous morality, these laws are seen to be immanent and immutable. Their tie to the concrete personal context of socialization from which they are derived is not recognized. The basic 'truth' structure is one of formal realism. The inherent duality of logic, deriving from the fact that it is built on subjective premises that may or may not be true, remains opaque. Reality is ordered in terms of logical truths and nontruths, and the latter are rejected or deregulated.

Figure 8.2 represents this structure by reordering the 'boxes' corresponding to level 3 of Figure 8.1. The intrasystemic mode permits reversible relations (represented by continuous lines) between sensori-motor ($_1O_3$), symbolic ($_2O_3$), and relational ($_3O_3$) entities. The role of the self ($_1S_3$) in the construction of this formal system is obscured. This is indicated both by the shading of the self circle and by the interrupted arrows. The latter denote the fact that the self-object relationship is irreversible at this level. The self

INTRA - SYSTEMIC

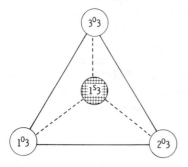

INTER - SYSTEMIC

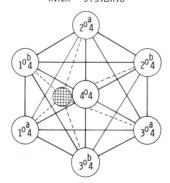

Figure 8.2. Three Hierarchical Levels of Logic Moving from Formal Realism (Intrasystemic) through Contextual Relativism (Intersystemic) to Autonomy.

AUTONOMOUS

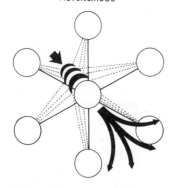

constructs but does not realize its constructions emanate from it.

Psychologically, the intrasystemic structure (at its conclusion) permits the individual to step outside of concrete systems of classes, relations, and people and to consider them *qua* systems. This third-person perspective allows the individual to step outside of him/herself or other systems and to manipulate dimensions of the systems in a coherent fashion (Selman, 1980). At this stage, the individual acquires a notion of 'mind' as a regulatory agency (Mead, 1934). Thus, in a fashion, the individual is truly able to take responsibility for self-regulation.

While the intrasystemic structure permits a representation of single abstract invariant systems, it will split the reality of systems in change or in interaction. This splitting is only partially directed by conscious differentiation. It is also directed by the intuitive base acquired in life. Authority, convention, and conformity regulate large domains of behavior.

Several domains of research depict this aspect of formal realism. Perry (1968) has charted the conflicts college students encounter as they confront the multiplicity of university life. Their search for a single perspective on truth creates a disequilibrium. They become highly concerned with the role of authority in disambiguating truth. The failure to realize that, ultimately, the thinker must accept responsibility for his/her thought, creates an obsession with finding safe techniques to unveil truth, rather than with inquiry into the nature of truth iteself.

As a consequence, the intrasystemic subject may perform well in abstract tasks where the task structure is clearly defined. In information-processing tasks, young adults focus on an analysis of logical and semantic surface relationships of propositions explicitly contained in research problems. Units of information are isolated as if they referred to abstract entities and are not integrated with psychologically complex transformations. Task structures are accepted at face value, and compliance with authority motivates performance, as does the search for correct solutions.

If competent in abstractions, however, intrasystemic thinkers fail in other contexts. For the intrasystemic subject, reality is one-dimensional. Selman (1980) has found that for youths entering formal operations, the behavior of others appears to have clear and unambiguous interpretations. There is no appreciation of the multiple, possibly conflicting, meanings of the words and actions of others. The notion of self and others as systems of multiple, partially coordinated, and often unconsciously motivated layers appears to develop only later to any degree of effectiveness. Such data appear to indicate a failure to differentiate between one's self and one's thought, and others and others' thoughts. Elkind (1974) has remarked on this lack of differentiation and has related it to a propensity toward egocentric and projective distortions that confounds the thought contents of self and others.

Intersystemic Level

At level 4, the intersystemic level, the expansion of context reveals the basic duality of logical truth. This realization initiates a movement away from logical absolutism to logical relativism. In the latter, truth is derived from the system within which it is hierarchicalized. Logical truth is recognized as a necessary but not sufficient criterion for empirical, interpreted truth.

Figure 8.2 symbolizes this structure by expanding the intrasystemic structure so as to permit two formal systems ($_1O_4^a$, $_2O_4^a$, $_3O_4^a$, and $_1O_4^b$, $_2O_4^b$, $_3O_4^b$) to represent the same aspect of reality. This contextual relativism requires the construction of a superordinate system ($_4O_4$) that integrates the two subsystems. In actuality, the number of subsystems can, and will, exceed two.

The present theory assumes that, with the solidification of formal operations in late adolescence, the individual enters the intersystemic structure. Progression through this structure is characterized by the hierarchical steps outlined by Piaget (1977; see also Furth, 1981). First the substructures are applied intuitively and sequentially. Eventually they become intercoordinated to form a super-oriented intersystemic structure.

At this juncture, however, a new element is added. As much as truth is relativized, attention must be particularized. The erosion of logical certainty throws the self explicitly back on its own resources. Perry (1970) describes nascent self-reference and personal commitment:

> Reason reveals relations within any given context; it can also compare one context with another on the basis of metacontexts established for this purpose. But there is a limit. In the end, reason itself remains reflexively relativistic, a property which turns reason back upon reason's own findings. In even its farthest reaches then reason will leave the thinker with several legitimate contexts and no way of choosing among them—no way at least that he can justify through reason alone. If he is still to honor reason he must now also transcend it; he must affirm his own position from within himself in full awareness that reason can never completely justify him or assure him (pp. 135–36).

For Perry, youth eventually accepts the inherent relativity of multiple intellectual perspectives. This realization signals a new integration. The youth needs to discontinue the search for logical certainty, to accept the pragmatic constraints of adulthood, and to give up absolutism and idealism for commitment and specialization.

Autonomous Level

With the explicit reintroduction of the self, the next structure, the *autonomous level*, is initiated. The elaboration of autonomy is characterized by a shift in focus from the logic of formal systems to the logic of self-regulating systems. The latter are understood in the widest sense to encompass the self and the other, as well as their thought and action products. Thus, as argued by Kuhn (1970), formal systems, too, acquire the status of self-regulating systems.

On the formal side, truth becomes differentiated from the personal and social motivation of truth definitions. Formal laws are redefined by their regulative function and become subordinated to social and self systems as equilibrium systems. Within this dialectic of self-regulations and mutual regulations, systems are reexamined from the aspect of their historical construction.

This addition of a temporal dimension has been symbolized in the lower part of Figure 8.2. Systems now are examined from the perspective of their trajectory, and consistency derives, in part, from the inertial properties of trajectories. Similarly, the individual embarks on a historical reconstruction of its own layers of selves vis-à-vis those systems (this explication of the historical self is indicated by a blackening of the self circles in Figure 8.2). This reconstructive process permits a newly differentiated concept of personalized truth to arise. Truth no longer propagates itelf but is created and propagated by individuals. Questions of truth thus acquire dimensions that are unabashedly pragmatic, social, cultural, moral, and personal.

The meaning of the term autonomy in reference to this structure needs further explication. It is to be differentiated from the common connotation of autonomy as the rejection of interpersonal dependency, in which a person fails to confront subjective and intersubjective roots. This connotation is self-protective in Loevinger's (1976) sense rather than autonomous. The autonomous structure here derives from an examination of the relational constraints on one's courses of action and modes of thinking. It entails the ability to accept responsibility for one's course of development, to engage in generative endeavors and interpersonal relations out of a sense of integrity and conscious choice that emanates from an understanding rather than denial of the interactivity of equilibrium systems.

The transition to autonomy appears to be marked by crisislike symptoms as the self explicitly focuses consistency criteria on its own structure (see Cytrynbaum et al., 1980, for an excellent summary) and, finding it lacks the conscious regulation desired, sets out to construct it. The resulting process may be marked by regressive features, such as the reemergence of previously denied fantasy. Yet this process is mislabeled regression. More properly, it reflects the need to reactivate structures before they can be deactivated and then rebuilt (Werner, 1957). Cytrynbaum et al. (1980) refer to this dual sequence as one of destructuring and restructuring. In psychoanalytic writings, the same process is referred to as 'regression in the service of the ego,' and the present position concurs with the connotation that such processes of restructuring are the hallmark of mature cognitive structures. Dabrowski's (1970) concept of 'positive disintegration' is a particularly apt term to refer to the process described here, which consists of a major decoding and refocusing of the dystonic relationships of Figure 8.1. Again, individual variations in the specific resolution of this stage are to be expected.

The organization of the autonomous structure enables the 'criss-crossing of purposes' (Gruber, in press) of past life to be consciously integrated and permits new differentiation and choice in the projection of one's life. The duality between formal reason and its base in the 'older' layers of one's organization is rejected. The transcendence of cultural canalization necessitates reliance on one's multimode organization to break away from motoric and symbolic deposits binding thought and action. The exploitation of one's multimode structure is seen as a precondition for qualitative reorganizations.

The resulting 'dialectical' mode of organization breaks rather than perpetuates paradigms as has been emphasized both in life-span psychology (Riegel, 1973) and in discussions of scientific creativity (Gruber, Chapter 1, this volume; Koestler, 1964). Reliance on the self, interplay of motoric, symbolic, and abstract forms, breaking up well-trodden paths of thought, and conscious utilization of such multimode organization to *reculer pour mieux sauter* (Koestler, 1964) all appear to mark the achievement of autonomy.

The psychological ramifications of this reorganization are wide-ranging. Elsewhere (Labouvie-Vief, 1980a, b; 1981a, b; Labouvie-Vief & Schell, 1981), these ramifications have been discussed in terms of the broad cognitive restructuring of logic, social responsibility, and moral action and thought. Indeed, they may be so broad as to require a reconceptualization of cognitive dimensions in later life. It is possible that there are many deficits in the cognitive characteristics outlined here (Blanchard-Fields, 1981, note 16; Labouvie-Vief & Schell, 1981).

Young adults, as discussed earlier, focus on logical and semantic surface relationships of propositions. They isolate units of information as if they referred to abstract entities and do not explore psychologically complexity latent in these propositions. Tasks are accepted at face value, performance is motivated out of compliance with authority, and the search is for 'correct' solutions. Older adults, in contrast, evaluate task structures within systemic matrices and vis-à-vis social and personal goals. Superficially, older adults resemble children in the latter activity but, unlike children, are aware of the psychological contradictions creating logical ambiguity.

CONCLUSION

The present theory proposes that adulthood is marked by a major reorganization of structures of logic and self-regulation. The structures of self-regulation emerge in abstract precursor forms only in adolescence and are fully elaborated only in adulthood.

Two potential implications of this theory need brief mention. First, the developmental outline may appear somewhat idealistic. However, individual variations in stylistic expression and functional breadth are entirely compatible with the view proposed here. Although levels of logic are used as an organizational principle for adult development, it is not implied that adults are logicians. Rather, the general characteristics of logical structures, such as logical multiplicity, tolerance of uncertainty, and self-reference, serve as broad regulatory schemes.

Second, currently the theory is relatively nonspecific about the mechanisms employed to negotiate movement through levels or failure to do so. It is possible to assume that these structural changes are the concomitant of a gradually expanding information base and are somewhat specific to culture and cohort. However, changes of the type discussed here have been well documented in the analysis of literary and scientific creativity, as well as in the more mundane phenomenon of adult midlife transition, suggesting less context-bound developmental mechanisms.

Wide individual differences in the resolution of the specific levels are nevertheless expected to be the rule. There is some evidence suggesting that qualitative differences exist in the gender-correlated negotiation of pathways to autonomy (Gilligan, 1979; Rossi, 1980).

Finally, pronounced individual differences in rate of progression are expected. Cytrynbaum et al. (1980) located the transition into the autonomy crisis between 35 and 55 years, and its duration may extend from 5 to 20 years. Many individuals appear to retreat from a successful negotiation of the crisis, maintaining a highly defended and rigidified pattern of thought and coping throughout late adulthood (Neugarten, Crotty, & Tobin, 1964). Such variation is entirely compatible with this theory, since the theory locates development in the dialectical interplay between individual and cultural evolution.

PART III

MODELS
THAT SYNTHESIZE
PERSPECTIVES

9

ATTENTIONAL, DIALECTIC, AND MENTAL EFFORT: TOWARD AN ORGANISMIC THEORY OF LIFE STAGES

Juan Pascual-Leone

In this chapter a dialectical constructivist view of the organism is assumed. A descriptive developmental theory that first recognizes the existence of stages from childhood to adolescence, as Piaget and Erikson did, and that then recognizes stages of adulthood, as Jung (1931) and Levinson, Darrow, Klein, Levinson, & McKee (1978), among others, have done, is also assumed. From these assumptions, the chapter describes a functional-structural conception of the organism. Its processes are thought of as decomposable in terms of very active "subjective operators" or schemes (information-carrying functional units—figurative or operative procedures) of various sorts, that, in their interactions, construct the world of outer or inner experience. These are the qualitative-structural aspects of the organism. An organization of these qualitative-structural aspects is suggested and contrasted with other views from cognitive science. At a deeper level, there are universal (situation-free), quantitative-dynamic processes, or "silent operators" that are the causal factors in the emergence of stages. The "silent operators" that cause the emergence of stages can be regarded as constituting, in their interplay, a process model of mental attention (of which mental effort is but a component). The organismic historical course of this mental-attention model is the efficient cause of life stages; the dynamics of its functioning, its inner dialectics, is the origin of the qualitative-structural characteristics of these stages.

In a constructivist conception of an organism, the subject constructs the environment by attributing the content and/or structure of his or her information-carrying processes or schemes to the environment. In that regard, even prior to the emergence of an "I," the organism operates like a gambler, ready to bet on the unwarranted assumption that the schemes' construal of the environment is the environment itself. This gambler, however, learns from its errors:

whenever the expectancies raised by the schemes are violated (new constraints are experienced), the schemes adapt by differentiation, adding to the repertoire other scheme variants that epistemologically reflect (henceforth called *epi-reflect*) the functional form of the new experience. Like in the "symbolic forms" of Cassirer (1957) or in the schemes of Piaget, *the form of a scheme's structure is the structure of its functioning.*

A scheme is a purely functional-relational structure—a blueprint for action or for anticipatory planning. Schemes tend to coordinate into manifold purely functional totalities that constitute the organismic representations of distal objects—the "beings" or things of the world. This tendency of the human organism to spontaneously transform the learned (that is, epi-reflective) structural totalities[1] into ontological entities—to transform them into "beings" or things of the organism's environment—was not explained but, rather, assumed by Piaget. Cassirer has explained it by stressing, as a modern scientist would, that structural totalities of any complexity (Piaget's reflective and constructive abstraction in structural learning) are marvelous ways to condense the relevant information. They creatively epi-reflect the functional essence while abstracting from the unnecessary content or structural details, that is, extracting by disregarding. Further, Cassirer tacitly followed the suggestion put forward by Gestalt psychologists (for example, Koffka, 1935; Goldstein, 1939) that the organism's creative structural-learning ability was, at least in part, due to the information-condensing power of the organismic resource that Gestalt psychologists called internal field (F) forces.

This constructive-rationalist conception of an organism that constructs its own world implies, as Hegel and Marx saw earlier, that the organism will not learn—will not change its own world representation—unless it experiences a mismatch between its structures of the world and the environmental constraints. These mismatches were called "disturbances" by Piaget (1956); they were called "contradictions" by Hegel and Marx (Marx, Engels, & Lenin, 1977). The experience of disturbances/contradictions induces the organism to undergo "creative" structural learning (new constructive abstractions and reorganizations) to avoid further disturbances/contradictions. This constructive process has been variously called adaptation and reequilibration by Piaget, reintegration and plasticity by life-span psychologists such as Baltes, Reese, & Lipsitt (1980), inner, purely organismic dialectics by dialectical psychologists such as Riegel (1973) or Piaget in his later writings.

Piaget contributed (equilibration theory or inner dialectics) to the dynamic theory of organismic change by empirically demonstrating that there are stages in the course of the organism's developmental change. These stages were initially thought to be general (in the sense of relatively invariant across types of situations) and related to some sort of limitation in the constructive, structural-complexity capability of the organism. Biological changes within the organism in the form of new internal constraints would cause internal disequilibrium (disturbances, contradictions) that in turn would bring about general structural growth. Piaget (1967a) thought this biological change was a cause of autochthonous disequilibrium and was in turn the result of a special sort of cognitive-structural learning that he called operative/operational learning (that is, reflective abstraction, constructive abstraction, logico-mathematical learning). Notice the paradoxical or circular character of this explanation of development: contradictions are made both the cause and the result of learning.

This developmental hypothesis of Piaget and of Marxist psychologists like Léontiev (1976) and Vygotsky (1978) may be stated in modern psychological language. The subject's active use of action processes automatically leads to operative reflective abstractions of these action-pattern coordinations. These hypotheses are somewhat similar to Tolman's (1932, 1959) "means-end readinesses" or "sign-gestalten". These abstracted action-pattern coordinations resembled, and subsequently serve as, plans. These plan structures are called here executive schemes. In the late seventies Piaget called them "procedural schemes."

According to Piaget, the active use of executive schemes leads to further operative/operational learning and to the emergence of more and more complex executive structures, although Piaget did not use this language. These complex executive structures can be characterized as resulting from executive automatization (see, for instance, Hasher & Zacks, 1979). As the executive automatization progresses, an increasingly greater mass of executive processes can be effortlessly mobilized in a situation to serve the performance. This "executive mass," reminiscent of Herbart's and Wundt's "apperceptive mass" (Wundt, 1886), Piaget called the field of Centration. This is a construct that classic constructivist psychologists such as James (1961) and Baldwin (1968) have variously adopted. Piaget characterized organismic stages by a given never quantified growth in the size of centration. The stages are measured in a qualitative-structural way by the types of automatized executive and action structures, the operational structures, that they exhibit. Piaget's operational models of Groupments and INRC groups are his stage-measurement tools. (The interesting dialectical reorientation of Piaget's work in the late seventies pointedly did not change this part of the theory.)

Notice that this Piagetian conception, although paradoxical in its explanation of development, is in fact quite congruent with modern views of mental attention and working memory (Schneider & Shiffrin, 1977; Hasher & Zacks, 1979). These views, as much as Piaget's theory, would lead one to expect that stage transitions in developmental growth end as soon as the organism reaches its peak of executive automatization. At that point, no more powerful "executive mass"—no greater Centration field—can be developed. Of course, at this point, learning would still occur, prompting change or coordination of action structures, but new organismic stages should not appear because the operative/operational complexity (the mass of automatically mobilized executive processes) could no longer increase.

In the sixties, the discovery that in middle and old age there is often, under suitable testing conditions, a regression in operative/operational performance that looks like a regression along Piaget's organismic stages actually added credence to the empirical reality of Piaget's stages. At the same time, these data could not, in fact, be accounted for by Piaget's explanatory operative/operational learning theory. For a long time, it has been known from Wechsler subtest performance that automatized conceptual skills (Horn & Cattell's crystallized intelligence; Horn, 1978; in press) do not regress much with age when compared with skills that need nonautomatized or fluid intelligence. Fluid intelligence underlies the sort of cognitive performances that are also described as requiring mental effort, as being effortful (Hasher & Zacks, 1979) or mindful (Labouvie-Vief, 1982; Pascual-Leone, in press). As mentioned earlier, the purpose of this chapter is to present a neoPiagetian explanatory theory that predicts the emergence of adulthood stages and that corrects the theoretical anomaly that is an epistemological contradiction as intimated above.

This theoretical anomaly is as follows. In Piaget's theory, as in Marxist or Hegelian dialectics, cognitive growth is a spontaneous (autochthonous) organismic reaction to correct contradictions, to change from disequilibrium to equilibration. There is no other mechanism of change. The organism only learns if it has to. Piaget's concept of operative/operational learning explains growth in size of centration and therefore the transition from one stage to the next via executive automatization, or the strong coordination of executive structures. However, overlearning and automatization cannot occur unless the schemes and structures involved are infraconsistent and noncontradictory for the set being learned. But the idea that executive automatization results from the equilibration tendency leads to an anomaly. If logical structures must be internally consistent to be overlearned, the existence of contradictions should prevent, rather than permit, the development of more comprehensive executive structures.

This anomaly in the theory of Piaget is solved by admitting two types of organismic change. The first change is the situational information-carrying schemes and structures, the software of the organism. The second change is in the situation-free organismic resources, the hardware of the organism. While learning within organismic stages still may be caused by operative/operational disequilibrium, the development across stages, expressed in a developmental transition rule, must result from an inner (autochthonous) biological change in the amount of hardware available for cognitive processing. This organismic change in the hardware brings about a disequilibration, even without prior structural contradictions. As a result, new operative/operational learning begins (Pascual-Leone & Smith, 1969; Pascual-Leone, 1969, 1970, 1976a, 1976b, 1976c, 1980; Pascual-Leone, Goodman, Ammon, & Subelman, 1978; Pascual-Leone & Goodman, 1979).

Thus, this neoPiagetian theory posits the existence of two kinds of disequilibration: subjective[2] software disequilibration that subjects could experience in their consciousness as caused by violations of expectations, and silent hardware disequilibration that subjects may experience as states of anomalous self-experience without contradictions. Subjective (software) disequilibration causes within-stage learning, while silent (hardware) disequilibration causes the transition from one developmental stage to the next.

This chapter summarizes aspects of the Theory of Constructive Operators (TCO) that may serve to explain subjective disequilibration and silent disequilibration. The theory is then used to explain the nature of changes encountered in childhood and adulthood stages.

A SELECTIVE "COGNITIVE SCIENCE" SUMMARY OF THE THEORY OF CONSTRUCTIVE OPERATORS

The TCO formulates the organismic processes that co-determine performance. These processes are: (1) situation-specific interactive processes or software of the psychological organism, referred to here as schemes[3] and (2) situation-free resource processes or hardware of the psychological organism, referred to as silent operators.[4]

Before discussing in more detail these two sorts of processes, two remarks are pertinent: one about the schemes and another about the silent operators.

As explained previously, schemes are functional structures, and the form of a functional structure is the structure of its function. The structure is the relational patterns of figurative constraints (predicates) and/or of operative constraints (transformations) that are necessary for its praxis. The word *praxis* needs clarification. Praxis is a goal-directed activity addressed to the environment in an immediate or mediated way. The goal is a given outcome and/or the representation of a given distal object (that is, of a "real" object as a manifold of constraints that the subject experiences). The subject's praxis is an experiential totality that is internalized by him or her by means of a multiplicity of schemes, each epi-reflecting a functional aspect or component of this praxis totality. These schemes in turn have a praxis (a praxis component of the praxis totality from which they come). Their praxis (for a scheme, its praxis) is to reproduce, as they generate performance, the functional component of the praxis totality of which they are an internalized epi-reflection (Piaget's "reflective abstraction"). Thus, if the infrastructure of a praxis component is defined as the real, necessary, and sufficient (figurative and operative) constraints that make this praxis component possible in actual performance, then the following can be said: a scheme is the organismic epi-reflective (re-presentational) model of the infrastructure of its praxis component. Thus, praxis (goal-directed activity) is the essential constructive determinant of schemes as forms. Further, schemes are descriptors of neurophysiological processes, but the form of these processes is determined by the form of neuroanatomical structures. Real-life information (the semantics of goals and praxis) is encoded in the brain in a semantically decomposed and topographically coded manner. In other words, schemes must, in neurophysiological terms, appear as molar-distributed patterns of co-activation in the brain, that is, as populations of equifunctional neurons distributed over multiple brain sites. These equifunctional populations of neurons, or the organismic schemes, can be represented "qua" functional structures as subjective operators: a set of (disjunctive or conjunctive) releasing conditions that, when satisfied, necessarily lead to a set of (disjunctive or conjunctive) effects. Thus defined, schemes may serve as the natural unit of neuropsychology because they constitute the interface between the detailed neuronal processes of the brain and experience, the holistic performance of the body.

Silent operators (and silent principles) are referred to as the molar representation "qua" functional structures of the brain's hardware. In computer science, it is often said that the distinction between hardware and software is only relative. That is to say, the hardware (the intrinsic, autonomical, structural constraints of a machine that cannot be changed) and the software (constraints that can be changed because they result from programming) can be varied by building a more general-purpose machine and writing as software the previous hardware constraints. Notice, however, that this change of hardware into software can only be done by an engineer who builds a more general-purpose machine to which a programmer will add software. In the human case, Nature is the engineer; the machine does not change. Thus, the programmers (the human environment and culture) writing the software must always adjust to the same hardware: the innate, functional, general-purpose characteristics of the central nervous system. This hardware is functionally, but globally and holistically, conceptualized in the TCO by the metaconstructs and by the general laws of schemes. Metaconstructs epi-reflect the purely organismic constraints, which are invariant across brain localizations.

The Psychological "Software"

From a phenomenological perspective, there are three modalities of schemes: purely affective schemes, purely cognitive schemes, and personal schemes. Personal or personality schemes are context-specific processes that coordinate within the same structure the purely cognitive and purely affective schemes. Preconscious (potentially conscious) or conscious personal schemes are, by definition, ego schemes. Note that with the ego, the subject's repertoire of ego schemes, all the world schemes are included whether they are schemes of Others (other humans) or contextual schemes.

Affective and Personal Schemes

Affective schemes (purely affective schemes or affects) are constituted, as all schemes are, by two components: a releasing component constituted by conditions that become cues if they are matched by features of the situation (whether the external context or the internal mental state); and an effecting component, constituted by effects that become aspects of the performance when the schemes are applied. In affective schemes, the conditions are global cognitive states of affairs, usually content schemes. The effects are of two kinds: either physiological reactions (for examples, paling with fear, blushing with love) or conative-motivational reactions (for example, escape with fear, attack with anger, hate). The conative effects of affective schemes serve to generate affective goals that boost the activation of their appropriate plans, organismically embodied in executive (procedural) schemes. If this coordination of affective goals with executive (plan-defining) schemes is conscious or preconscious, the logical structures (ultra-executives) doing the coordination, are called ego schemes. Ego schemes are conscious (or preconscious) personal structures. Unconscious personal schemes also exist and can coordinate affective goals with cognitive schemes. Reinterpreting one of Jung's concepts, all unconscious personal schemes are called shadow schemes. Ego schemes and shadow schemes, together, constitute the biases and beliefs of the person. They heavily influence the kind of strategy (operations or operational systems) chosen by the subject in a given context to produce a performance.

Cognitive Schemes

From a process-analytical perspective four kinds of cognitive schemes are distinguished: (1) executives, which either embody plans for tasks and jobs of all sorts or serve to control and administer the organismic resources (silent operators) in the context of tasks (these are the controls). Executives are psychological structures organized in time that are usually developed with the help of mental effort. (2) Action schemes—action used broadly (as Piaget does) to subsume both figurative representations (simple perceptual or complex intellective-knowledge representations) and operative procedures. Monitored by executive schemes, action schemes can implement into a performance (execution of action) the tasks' executive. Action schemes can be concrete, Content schemes, structures (substantive patterns), or generic Logical structures that embody simple or complex (spatial, temporal, semantic, linguistic, and so on) modular knowledge networks. (3) There are structures that coordinate executive and action schemes, which, with Piaget, are called mental operations (cf. Vuyk, 1981). Operations are systems of executive schemes coupled to their corresponding action schemes that allow the subject to operate successively in particular restricted contexts. Thus defined, mental operations include what Piaget calls pre-operations. (4) Finally, there are the operational systems (what cognitive scientists now call schemas or scripts). Operational systems are systems of operations that serve to cope with kinds of situations with contextual realms or domains of experience. These four kinds of cognitive schemes are discussed in the next two sections.

Executive and Action Schemes. Following the constructivist tradition initiated by Kant, four categories of knowing: particulars, generic ideas, becomingnesses, and beings are here accounted for separately. The first set of experienced realities, particulars versus generic ideas, are represented by two all-encompassing categories (repertoires) of structures assumed to be stored in the brain's two hemispheres. Piaget calls these two kinds of structures logical versus infralogical. Kant refers to them by distinguishing between the structures of understanding and structures of sensibility or intuition. Here, the two structures are referred to as logological (generic-conceptual) and mereological (particular-experiential).

Logological structures (*logos* in Greek means *word* or *clear idea*) are the subject's generic structures that embody concepts (for example, my idea of an airplane), relations (for example, my idea of flying, my idea of "bigger-than"), or propositions (for example, a propositional network such as my idea of an airport with all the experiential possibilities it contains). In the inner semantics of logological structures, the relations of logical inclusion (the "is a" link of propositional networks) and/or semantic-pragmatic case-grammar relations (for example, subject, object, recipient, agent, action, and so on) are very important.

Mereological structures are the experiential structures (perceptual, intentional-motor, spatial, temporal, and so on) that embody the constraints experienced in reference to the distal objects or things of the actual environment. They were called mereological (*meros* in Greek means *part*) by the logician Lesniewski (Bunge, 1973) because fundamental in these structures' inner semantics are part-whole relations stipulating how each part is materially interconnected with other parts and with the whole.

A second set of experienced realities is represented in modern cognitive science by two contrasted sets of psychological notions. Namely, both perceptual (data-presentational) and representational structures together called figurative structures by Piaget (Vuyk, 1981), versus ordinary operative and executive-control structures, together called operative structures by Piaget. The former produce psychological states (mental objects) and mental representations of distal objects. The latter produce or plan (anticipate) changes on the figurative states and on the environment.

Table 9.1 summarizes a hierarchy of types of structures that the cross-classifications of logological versus mereological and of figurative versus operative generate. Brief comment on them will convey their relation to other commonly used cognitive constructs.

The simplest mereological figurative structures are predicate schemes (codes for one or more perceptual features that become cues when activated by the features in question). Still simple are the temporally organized structures (Tolman's, 1959, $s_1 r_1 s_2$ units or "sign-gestalten") that underlie figurative expectancies (for example, the "sit-on-ness" of the chair, an example we owe to Tolman, or the "you-better-do-what-I-say" look of an assertive employer)—expectancies that serve to anticipate from appearances future or possible operative consequences. These schemes are relational predicates that characterize figurative states in terms of the transformations that could apply to them and their results. Borrowing the term from McCarthy & Hayes (1969), these schemes are called figurative fluents because in them the flow of time is recorded internally.

More complicated mereological figuratives are the representations of distal objects[5] that, for short, are called *obs*. *Ob* structures are systems of figurative fluents coordinated with relevant executives and transformational fluents. In the recent cognitive literature, obs are called either prototypes or simple schemas (Anderson, 1976). Prototypes are not particular obs, but rather abstractions from them, that is, kinds of obs; and schemas (at times called frames in the cognitive literature) are actually systems of prototypes and obs coupled with procedures.

The simplest mereological operatives are transformations (change-producing schemes) that change a figurative state (or an ob) into another state (or a modified ob). Still simple are the operative

Table 9.1. Hierarchy of Epistemological Levels (Epi-levels) of Cognitive Structures.

Schemes	Executive	Operative	Figurative
		Action	
Logological (conceptual)	(2) Program executive = system of ultra-executives[a] (1) Ultra-executives: = system of executives[b] (0) Executive (LM)	(2) Skill theory[a] (1) Conceptualization script[a] (0) Conceptual pro[b] (−1) Conceptual trans-fluent	(3) Conceptualization theory[a] (2) Propositional schema = proposition—network[a] (1) Proposition=system of conceptual fluents and predicates[a] (0) Conceptual predicative fluent = generic Ob[b] (−1) Conceptual Predicate = property or relation-scheme
Mereological (experiential)	(2) Executive (LM) (1) Pre-executive (LM or LC) (0) Proto-executive (LC)	(3) Skill = system of scripts[a] (2) Script = system of functions, pros, and prototypes[a] Function = kind of pros[a] Pro = procedural blueprints[b] Transformational fluent = operative expectancy Transformation = change-producing scheme	(3) Domain or Cognitive map = system of schemas[a] (2) Schema or Frame = system of prototypes, Obs and functions[a] (1) Prototype = kind of Ob[a] (0) Ob = distal-object representation[b] (−1) Predicative Fluent = figurative expectancy (−2) Predicate = feature-coding scheme

[a] Usually is an operational system or a supersystem (system of systems) or a macrostructure (system of supersystems).
[b] Usually is an operation.

Note: The distinction between operation and operational system (or supersystems or macrostructures) is relative to the psychologist-observer (e.g., sensori-motor, concrete operational, etc.); what appears as a system at a lower level becomes operational at a higher level.

fluents that are similar to the figurative fluents in that they are relational predicates. They connect, in a time-ordered way, sets of transformations that are related in terms of the outcomes (types of ob) they produce or the type of object to which they apply. Operative fluents underlie operative expectancies (for example, the "my-body-will-immediately-fall-down" feeling when jumping in the air, the "I-am-going-to-hear-my-voice" feeling about to speak aloud, the "he-will-look-at-me-angrily" feeling when challenging a police officer). The process-analytical units that underlie Skinner's operants are operative fluents. More complicated mereological operatives are procedural blueprints of various complexities that, for short, are called *pros*. *Pros* are systems of operative fluents coordinated with relevant executives, figurative fluents, and predicates. The functional prototype of a pro (a quasi-generic abstract pro) is often called in psychology, or in education, a function. A function is a generalized kind of pro.

The simplest mereological executives—simple because they are not easy to generalize across kinds of situations and because they easily fall prey to interferences—are the proto-executives. Proto-executives are often locally developed, automatized executives that result more from practice (*LC*-learning) than from the use of mental effort (*LM*-learning). Plans for scanning and for perceptual-exploratory attentional activities are examples of proto-executives often developed in early childhood. Other proto-executives are the usually unconscious plans (strategies) that guide people's coping with emotionally loaded unexpected situations or with tasks for which their life experience does not provide a preparation. These proto-executives are part of the affective defense mechanisms discussed by psychoanalysts and of the games described by Eric Berne (1976).

Proto-executives often function as executive controls regulating and monitoring the use of organismic resources in the synthesis of a performance. They often also function as pre-executives. A pre-executive is an executive scheme that, in a task or situation-specific performance (where it is not the task executive), can be activated in a top-down or bottom-up manner and thus facilitate the activation of a suitable task executive. Examples of pre-executives are common in everyday life as well as in the laboratory. The disposition of some people to spontaneously read the instructions when they unwrap a to-be-assembled toy or machine while other people proceed directly to attempt the assembly work by trial-and-error is caused by pre-executives resulting from their life style and history. Another example of a pre-executive is found in the tendency of people who perform well in the Raven matrices, thoroughly exploring and contrasting (randomly comparing) the figural constituents of an item prior to any serious attempt to find a solution. This is expressive of sophisticated pre-executives. Exploration, bringing to mind differences among figural constituents of the matrix item, generates cues that activate relevant task executives (such as a comparison executive and a "try-the-different-options-successively" executive).

Mereological executives (whether they function as pre-executives or as main-task executives) differ from logological executives in the manner in which they are abstracted. Mereological executives are abstracted using mental effort that is directly applied to the overall patterns of performance in the here-and-now task context, with the mediation of language being relatively secondary (for example, learning to play tennis or squash by means of practice and trial-and-error). Logological executives are abstracted using mental effort that applies to patterns of performance that are already decontextualized and suitably segmented and organized, often by means of language (the teacher's or the learner's). As a result, mereological executives tend to be more closely associated with action schemes, are more situation-bound, and are easily evoked by bottom-up processing. In contrast, logological executives are freer from the context and from action schemes. In fact, they can often be learned (with the aid of tutors or of human-mediated learning) before the learner actually has developed the mereological action schemes necessary for the executive's implementation. The other logological structures listed in Table 9.1, Operative and Figurative logological schemes, differ from their corresponding mereological schemes in similar ways.

The purpose of Table 9.1 is not to provide an inclusive taxonomy of process units. Rather, its purpose is to convey the explicit idea that knowledge is organized, by virtue of the psychogenetic process of construction, in hierarchically ordered epistemological (epi) levels of constructive abstraction. These levels of abstraction will henceforth be referred to as epi-levels. The epi-levels are constructed in the organism while the subject internalizes (learns) functional schemes of any structural complexity that emerge as invariances in the context of his praxis (of his goal-directed activity addressed to the environment). The praxis in question is purposefully seeking certain results. The epistemological level at which these results are found (for example, within or across situations; across minutes or days or years) determines that epistemological level at which the performatory invariances relative to these results are found. This in turn determines the epi-level that corresponds to the organismic schemes that internalize these invariances. In other words, the tolerance level in practical consequences (the error that the organism can afford without hurting its praxis) determines the epi-level of the internalized scheme. The scheme finally learned embodies precisely those functional invariances that insure, without more effort than needed, that the praxis be successful. If, in everyday life, it is unimportant which object one uses, the overlearned (automatized) structure developed by the organism will be generic. Thus the prototype of the object will constitute the habitual epi-level or epi-level (0) that is automatized in the subject's repertoire. Habitual epi-levels usually change with the content area being examined. For instance, in the case of humans, it does matter in praxis who is the person with whom the subject interacts. Therefore, in the content area of humans the habitual epi-level or level (0) should usually be the distal-object representation of particular persons, the sort of structure called an ob in Table 9.1.

These notions of epi-levels and of habitual epi-levels (epi-level (0)) are important. In any content area, the habitual epi-level constitutes the origin (epi-level (0)) from where higher-level structures (epi-level (1), epi-level (2), and so on) are constructed by way of structural learning and from which lower-level structures (epi-level (-1), epi-level (-2), and so on) are synthesized by means of effortful analytical decomposition of the epi-level (0) or of other previously constructed structures. The more a structure departs upwards (in the macro, generic direction) from the epi-level (0) of its content area through epi-level (1), epi-level (2) and so on, the less automatized it will tend to be. Thus, more effortful mental processing is required to both constructively abstract this structure and/or bring this structure into activation to produce performance. Correlatively, the more a structure departs downwards (in the micro, specific-particular direction) from the epi-level (0) of its content area through epi-level (-1), epi-level (-2), and so on, the less automatized it will tend to be and thus the more effortful the mental processing required to both constructively synthesize this structure and/or bring this structure to the point of activation where it influences performance. Adapting the useful terminology introduced by Van Dijk (1980), macrostructures are those structures that are very far removed, upwards, from the subject's epi-level (0); superstructures are those structures above epi-level (0) not so far removed; and microstructures (substructures) are those that are in a similar way placed below the subject's epi-level (0).

Operations and Operational Systems. The notion of operation is central to cognitive development and to cognitive science. Phenomenologically, operations are organized sequences of mental or behavioral acts that intentionally in Husserl's (1970), Piaget's (1967a), or Tolman's (1932) sense, attempt to bring about a given outcome.[6] This definition, with its reference to intentionality, implies that operations are subjective structures (subjective in Kant's or Husserl's sense of real from the perspective of the subject's organism). One such structural operation coordinates the executive schemes and the action (operative or figurative) schemes that partake in the intended sequence of acts. Piaget makes clear (Vuyk, 1981) that these structural operations (henceforth called operations) are more or less detached structurally from the executive and action schemes that they coordinate (this is part of his concept of reflective abstraction). Defined in this manner, the concept of an operation is still weaker than the concept of operational structure (operational operations) that Piaget uses to characterize his developmental stages. An operational operation is a structural operation that is structurally coordinated to other pragmatically related structural operations so as to constitute an operational system, that is, a system of operations capable of organizing praxis across types of situations within a given content area or context. Piaget's own classification of operational operations (of operational systems) as sensori-motor, preoperational, concrete-operational, and formal-operational actually emphasized the psychogenetic constructive complexity of the operational system in question.[7]

Alternative classifications of operational systems could focus on their logological (conceptual) versus mereological (experiential) character, or their operative versus figurative usefulness. These two alternative classifications are most important in adult development. They are suggested in Table 9.1 by marking with * the structures that seem to be operations and marking with ** those that need to be operational systems (operational operations). Readers are likely to be familiar with the notions of procedure, cognitive function, script, schema (or frame), propositional network, skill, and so on. Therefore, their explication is omitted.

The Organismic Hardware and its Relation with Software: Executiveless Processing, the Overdetermination of Performance, and Effortful (LM) Learning

Adequate explanation of human growth must account for logological-to-mereological, that is, declarative to procedural, or top-down performance and learning, as well as mereological-to-logological or bottom-up performance and learning.

Purely mereological and mereological-to-logological performance and/or learning go from the concrete of experience to the abstract. Without presupposing executive guidelines about what to do (and thus presupposing the very kind of generic-logological structures whose origin this learning aims to explain), this sort of learning is possible only if the organism is endowed with at least three kinds of resources that Anderson's (1982, 1981, 1976) cognitive theory (a theory characteristic of current cognitive science) does not properly examine. Namely: (1) an innate repertoire of purely affective schemes or affects that can provide affective goals and instant affective evaluations to performances and learning possibilities; (2) an innate and perfectly situation-free, purely organismic mechanism for mental attention, a complex hardware facility; and (3) an innate ability to learn: to content-learn (henceforth called C-learning), an ability to internalize effortlessly, in the manner of figurative or operative traces, the salient invariances of experience, as well as an innate ability for recursive "logical-structural" learning (henceforth called L-learning), that can internalize relational-functional patterns of coactivation among schemes, in the form of schemes.

Affects serve to cue the subject's executive schemes (or directly cue action schemes) so that the executive schemes in turn can monitor the mental-attention mechanism to boost executive-relevant action schemes while actively inhibiting executive-irrelevant ones. This mental-attentional intervention is often called mental effort (see for example, Hasher & Zacks, 1979; Kahneman, 1973; Pascual-Leone, 1969, 1970). As a result of mental effort (executive-driven performance), or perhaps without it as a result of the direct boosting by affect of action schemes (affect-driven performance), or perhaps due to the strong cue-saliences of the input (input-driven or data-driven performance), a highly activated or dominant cluster of pragmatically compatible schemes may emerge that can in turn generate the actual performance. This performance, whether operative (behavior, mental transformations) or figurative (perception, imagery), is the result of overdetermination (deRibaupierre & Pascual-Leone, in press). That is to say, the pragmatically compatible effects of all the schemes that simultaneously can apply combine, in accordance with the Gestalt and S-R Compatibility laws (both laws together called the F operator in the TCO), to produce a performance. Note that this performance, forced as it is by the assimilation tendency of activated schemes—a tendency manifested in the just summarized principle of Schematic Overdetermination of Performance or SOP principle—does not need to have been planned by an executive. It could be a truly novel or serendipitous, executiveless performance. Once the performance is produced, it can lead to either content learning (C-learning) as perceptual-differentiation learning or simple conditioning, or to executive, operative or figurative, relational-pattern learning, that is, logical-structural learning (L-learning—Pascual-Leone & Goodman, 1979).

First, L-learning can result from structuring (chunking) produced by mental (M) effort, when several compatible schemes are conjointly boosted with mental attention (LM-learning, see Pascual-Leone, 1976a, 1976c, 1980; Pascual-Leone & Goodman, 1979). Second, it can result from the accumulation of C-learning that comes from repeated practice without the help of mental effort (learning by means of overpractice or automatization). LC-learning is slow and leads to structures that are holistic or analogous. They are strongly context-bound in the sense that all schemes concurrently activated when the LC structure is formed tend to retain associative links with the structure. In fact, the LC structure is nothing but the associative net interconnecting all the coactivated schemes. As a consequence, performances driven by *LC* structures are prone to suffer considerable interferences whenever a situation elicits misleading cues previously associated with the *LC* structure in question. Still, in facilitating situations (that do not elicit misleading cues), *LC* structures are very convenient. They are activated quickly, without requiring mental effort, and are thus not subject to the severe mental-capacity constraints (developmental-intelligence constraints) that mental effort usually exhibits (Burtis, 1976; Parkinson, 1975; Pulos, 1979). Finally, *LC* structures may be stored more easily in the right hemisphere of normal right-handed people than in the left hemisphere (Pascual-Leone et al., note 17).

In contrast, *LM*-learning is fast and leads to structures that are analytical-selective or digital and are relatively context-free. This is so because only schemes that were highly activated at the time when the *LM* structure was formed retain associative links with the *LM* structure. Since mental effort in this kind of learning is the usual source of the schemes' high activation, irrelevant contextual schemes not boosted with mental effort rarely become associated with the structure. As a result, *LM* structures tend to be relatively free from interference and thus permit rational (Piaget's operational) thinking. However, since other task-relevant schemes that were not highly activated when the *LM* structure was developed are only weakly associated with the *LM* structure, mental effort is usually needed to produce performances that are driven by *LM* structures. As a result, performance driven by *LM* structures is slow and it is severely restricted by limits imposed by the available reserve of mental effort (*M-reserve*, see below).

Returning to Table 9.1, consider the kinds of learning (*C-*, *LC-* or *LM*-learning) that may be involved in the formation of the various epi-levels (epistemological levels) of structures that are numbered in the table. The more irrelevant schemes activated by the context (the input) and the less affect-driven or input-driven (data-driven) are the to-be-structured relevant schemes, the more the formation of the structure will depend on *LM*-learning. On this account, it is apparent that logological structures, being generic, will tend to necessitate *LM*-learning, while mereological structures, being concrete, may be done with either *LC* or *LM*. Further, the higher the epi-level of the structure in question, the more abstract the structure and therefore the more likely that it requires *LM*-learning. Since automatization (defined as effortless processing—Hasher & Zacks, 1979) has *LC*-learning as its constructive process (Pascual-Leone, 1976a, 1976c; Pascual-Leone & Goodman, 1979), it can be expected that distant epi-level structures, whether logological or mereological, are usually not automatized and often may even not be fully *LM*-learned. Distant is an epi-level that, relative to the habitual epi-level (epi-level (O)) of the content area in question, has a distance number n (epi-level (n), as informally illustrated in Table 9.1) that is far removed from zero (it is separated from the habitual epi-level by n different constructive epi-levels). If these distant epi-level structures (macrostructures and microstructures) were not fully *LM*-learned, they would remain virtual structures (structures not schematized, not stored in the subject's memorial repertoire) and would have to be synthesized anew, effortfully, whenever they are needed.

Note that this status of virtual structure that needs to be synthesized anew every time is likely to be found among complex and time-deep executive schemes, such as complete task executives (executive programs) and ultra-executives (conscious, self-referential executives), unless they are formally taught with human-mediated instruction (Vygotsky, 1978; Feuerstein, 1979). Generally, therefore, many tasks of complexity (professional tasks, life tasks, social tasks) will not only necessitate mental effort to be carried out, but, as totalities, will also have to be synthesized every time by means of a sequence of silent organismic choices. Note that these choices of the organism that take place in it, by virtue of its built-in heuristic silent mechanisms, are made in the absence of a decision maker: an inner choice occurs, but there is no homunculus or executive within who does the choosing. Elsewhere and above, I have called the Principle of Schematic Overdetermination of Performance, SOP, and the *F*-operator the heuristic mechanisms that produce these executiveless choices (Pascual-Leone, 1976c, 1976d, 1980; Pascual-Leone & Goodman, 1979). Each of these choices makes dominant a partial executive that, in its action implementation, advances the task for a brief segment until, exhausted, it is overcome by other organismic processes (whether executives or not) and a new silent choice takes place.

Figure 9.1 summarizes the speculated processing flow that can synthesize a performance for which a complete executive program (or production system) is not available.

This figure suggests important ideas because development and learning usually occur serendipitously, often in an executiveless manner, and in the context of contradictions, in the midst of disequilibrium. As discussed earlier, complete executive programs cannot be *LM*-learned before all the contradictions are overcome, and executiveless syntheses of performance become necessary mediations in human reequilibration and growth. As Gadamer (1976, p. 105) has said: "the power of the spirit lies in synthesis as the mediation of all contradictions."

The TCO Model of Mental Attention

If, as suggested earlier, mental effort, or the application of mental attention, is needed to develop and maintain optimal (mental or

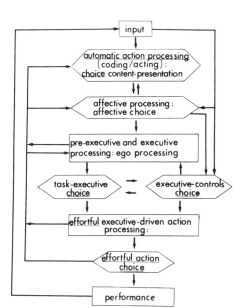

Figure 9.1. Subjective Process Flow Chart of the Synthesis of Performance.

behavioral) performance in humans, an explication of what is mental attention becomes mandatory. In the Theory of Constructive Operators, mental attention is the output of a general-purpose hardware facility controlled by the organism's software. Piaget (1956) called this hardware facility the Centration mechanism and included in it are the software executive controls needed for its use.

Thus, mental attention (or what Luria (1973) and Wundt (1886) called voluntary attention) results from hidden interactions among four kinds of constructive processes. Three of these generating processes are silent operators. The others are task executives, pre-executives, and executive controls. The silent operators are denoted by the letters M, I, and F; the attention-monitoring executive schemes are denoted by the letter E.

Silent operators are internal resources (functional capabilities) of the organism that the dominant executive (the currently active E factor) can mobilize and use to produce the performance. Every performance, regardless of context or dominance, results from interactions among schemes and silent operators. When an input situation arrives (initially coded out by content schemes, automatized structures, and affective schemes), it leads to an affective choice that creates affective goals. The goals in turn activate relevant executive schemes. At the same time, silent operators may have been mobilized by particular patterns of scheme coactivation and of scheme dominance (of activation strength) found in the field of activated schemes (the field of activation, which neuropsychologically corresponds to the collection of distributed patterns of coactivation in neuronal populations of the cortex). An example of a silent operator that is easily mobilized by the initial pattern of coactivation and dominance is the F operator—(F for brain's field of activation). F corresponds to described as *praegnanz* and human-performance psychologists have described as S-R compatibility (Allport, 1980; Attneave, 1972). In described as S-R compatibility (Allport, 1980; Attneave, 1972). In neurophysiological terms, it seems to correspond to central processes of lateral inhibition (Pribram, 1971; Thatcher & John, 1977; Walley & Weiden, 1973). In ordinary language, F corresponds to the salience or good-form qualities that the pattern of performance-to-be-produced whether a percept or a movement, exhibits. It is a salience or good form that can facilitate or, if absent, hinder the production of that performance. In functional abstract terms, the F operator can be described as boosting the relative activation strength of those schemes that can produce the best good-form performance. Alternatively and more realistically, F can be described as inhibiting—lateral inhibition—those schemes that can interfere with a good-form performance. Elsewhere, task-analytical rules for the F factor that serve to predict its effect in tasks are described (Pascual-Leone, 1969, note 17, 1976a, 1978; Pascual-Leone & Goodman, 1979).

Depending upon the kind of task, this F operator can be task-facilitating (by boosting relevant schemes) or task-misleading. Whenever F is misleading, it can be decremented by the interruption function of the I operator discussed below. To insure that the pattern of coactivation and dominance in the field of activation is such that the appropriate performance occurs, the dominant executive mobilizes and applies the M and I operators. Performance results from the conjoint effect of (is co-determined by) the application of the dominant (most active) cluster of compatible active schemes when the performance occurs. M and I can influence the performance-to-be-produced by changing the activation strength of schemes in the field of activation, thus changing the dominant cluster of schemes and therefore the performance. The M (mental-energy) operator and the I (interruption/disinterruption) operator constructs are together the source of mental effort (Kahneman, 1973) or focal attention (Neisser, 1967) of the subject. Neurophysiologically, M seems to correspond to the ability of the dorsal-lateral prefrontal lobe to energize, via the reticular system's connections with the thalamic gate to the cortex (or via cortico-cortical connections), relevant information-carrying processes of neuronal populations (relevant schemes or structures) placed elsewhere in the cortex (Fuster, 1980; Luria 1973; Thatcher & John, 1977; Schiebel, 1981; Steriade, 1981).

A separate inhibitory system seems to exist, mediated by the reticular-hippocampus-septal connections with the medial-orbital cortex of the forebrain. This system may allow the prefrontal lobe to actively inhibit (interruption) or disinhibit (disinterruption) schemes

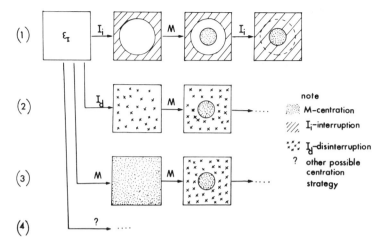

Figure 9.2. The Processing Effects of the Silent Operators *M* and *I* within Different Centration Strategies.

or structures that are irrelevant for the executive (E) plan at hand (Fuster, 1980; Luria, 1973; Pribram, 1973; Schiebel, 1981; Steriade, 1981; Thatcher & John, 1977; Weiskrantz, 1977). This inhibitory system is what, in abstract-functional terms, is referred to as an Interrupt (I) operator.

Figure 9.2 illustrates, in abstract-functional terms, the processing effects of the silent operators M and I within different centration strategies, that is, different operating formulas monitored by E for allocating or for controlling the silent operators of centration (M, I, F) in order to achieve the attentional control needed for different sorts of task situations (misleading situations, facilitating situations, and so on). In this figure, the square must be interpreted as representing the field of activated schemes (or structures) in the subject's repertoire (in the brain). Further, for the sake of this diagram, assume that the field of activation has been rearranged inside the squares around the dominant executive E_I (the executive that carries the instructions for the present task). In this diagram, it is assumed that the closer the activated schemes are topographically to E_I, the more relevant they are to the action process that that dominant executive requires. In the case of misleading task situations (strategy (1) of Figure 9.2), the first thing a dominant executive E_I may do to produce a certain action process is to mobilize the Interruption (I_I) mechanism and actively inhibit schemes that are clearly irrelevant for it. The interruption of irrelevant schemes appears in Figure 9.2 (the hatched area stands for inhibited irrelevant schemes). Thus, the initial effect of the interruption is to reduce the sampling pool from which relevant schemes will be chosen by the executive. This act of interruption requires some interruption criterion (I-criterion) of relevance that the subject's executive E must acquire psychogenetically in the course of action-based learning (cf. Pascual-Leone, Johnson, Goodman, Hameluck, & Theodor, 1981). A key developmental postulate of the I operator model is that this I-criterion of relevance is developed by the organism according to a basic heuristic rule that is innate. Namely, schemes that have in the past been boosted by M (or alternatively that were otherwise highly activated) at the moment when a given performance was produced shall be regarded as relevant for that performance; all other (low-activated) schemes are considered irrelevant by the I criterion. Executive controls for the I operation are psychogenetically developed following this or an equivalent rule. As the I-criterion becomes progressively more refined with experience, more irrelevant schemes come to be interrupted. It becomes easier for the task executive to allocate appropriately M energy to the relevant schemes. Experimental tests of this I-criterion rule have already been conducted (Pascual-Leone et al., 1981).

After the task executive has interrupted irrelevant schemes, mental energy is mobilized and allocated to those noninterrupted schemes that are closer to being optimal for bringing into action (execution) the executive plan. This boosting of schemes with M energy (functional M, that is, M_f) is represented by a densely dotted area. At this point (and this is the last square in strategy (1) of Figure 9.2), the schemes that were not chosen for M boosting are finally interrupted by the I operator, thus ensuring that the M boosted schemes will constitute the dominant activation cluster that determines the performance. Notice that this final I interruption of schemes that were left outside M is automatic. Unless the executive actively disinterrupts (I_d), or inhibits this automatic interruption, the interruption will take place and schemes left outside M will be deactivated. (A test of this theoretical prediction will be presented below under the name of fixation-centration effect.) Notice further that other centration strategies for combining sequences of interruptions, M applications and disinterruptions, are available to the subject. For instance, strategy (2) in Figure 9.2 illustrates an operating formula often found in facilitating situations (when no irrelevant schemes are activated) or in situations offering complete uncertainty about task relevance (ill-defined tasks, such as the participant-observer's situation where the subject maintains an open, receptive mind vis-à-vis events whose importance cannot be evaluated at the time). This centration strategy consists of an initial disinterruption (represented by a starred area) that is followed by one or more M applications without I interruption of the outside schemes. Another centration strategy (line 3 in Figure 9.2) quite similar in results to the previous one is found, for instance, at the initiation of a mental memory search (retrieval from memory) and in a mindful-awareness approach to a free-recall situation where the items-to-be-remembered are not known in advance. Under these conditions, the best strategy would be to spread the M energy over all the schemes in the field of activation (all the items-aspects of the situation) and then, without I interrupting, concentrate the M energy on those that are recognized to be more important.

Now the action choice has taken place, and the actual action processing to produce a performance can begin. Usually, tasks require many cycles of step sequences more or less similar to the one illustrated. Some tasks necessitate more interruption, others less, in order to be handled well; others may require disinterruption. As mentioned earlier, disinterruption (I_d), is the functional reciprocal to interruption (I_i). It is the active elimination by the executive control of the final operation of interruption just described. In summary, if the interruption is very strong, the outer circle in strategy (1) of Figure 9.2 will be small. If the interruption is weak or if the subject disinterrupts, the circle obtained will be very large, maybe as large as the square itself. Thus, the so-called narrow beam of attention needed in expectancies (expectative readiness-to-act, this is an important operating formula of attention) or needed whenever the subject has to cope with misleading tasks (this is another important operating formula), is explained in terms of a high M activation and a high I interruption. The so-called arousal with wide-beam of attention (this is a third formula) necessitates M activation with I disinterruption. These are the three neuropsychological functions of attention described by McGuiness and Pribram (1980) under the names activation, effort, and arousal.

The Operations of Mental Attention: Decentrations, Recentrations and Attentional Strategies

But there are other strategic aspects of mental attention that are more qualitative in the sense that they are not defined (characterized) by the silent-operator allocation formulas, but rather by the functional-structural (semantic-pragmatic) characteristics of the schemes and structures that are being simultaneously and/or successively centrated. That is, in addition to the quantitative silent-allocation strategies just discussed, there are qualitative subjective-centration strategies. Two of these subjective-centration strategies I call decentration and recentration.

If an act of attention, i.e., the mobilization and allocation of M-energy to schemes (and the concomitant possible interruption of some other schemes), is called (explicating a notion of Piaget) a *centration*, then decentration and recentration are two qualitative modalities for changing from one centration to another. In a *decentration operation* the control executive cancels the centration of (i.e., removes allocation of M-energy from) a set of schemes that *epireflect* constraints (i.e., invariant aspects, features, configurations, patterns) corresponding to a given epilevel. Then it places a centration onto (i.e., allocates M-energy to) schemes that epireflect *a different epilevel* but that *correspond* (if this is a pure decentration, see below) *to the same content-area*. An example of mereological decentration is a sequence of mental attending acts such as:

$$M``(nose(X_1) \ eye(X_2) \ eye(X_3))\text{'': } M``(face(X_1,X_2,X_3, \dots))\text{''}.$$

In this symbolization *nose*(X) represents the scheme of a nose successfully applying onto (in Piaget's terms assimilating) X, i.e., that aspect of the content-area corresponding to the real nose; the expression M``(_____)'' indicates that the schemes placed inside the quote-parentheses are being M-boosted; the semicolon (:) indicates immediate succession. Since the face contains the nose and eyes as parts, the scheme of face (that, as a totality unit, is more than the collection of its parts) must be a mereological superordinate of the schemes of nose and eyes. Thus, the scheme of face epireflects a higher epilevel. An example of logological decentration is the sequence:

$$M``(dog \ (X_1))\text{'': } M``(animal \ (X))\text{''}.$$

That is, I look at the object X and see a dog; then, still looking at object X, I see an animal. Since the scheme of animal is logologically superordinate (by means of an inclusion relation) to the scheme of dog, the scheme of animal epireflects a higher epilevel.

Decentration can occur in either one of two directions:(1) In the direction of *macro-decentration*, i.e., towards generic abstraction and idealization (i.e., from dog to animal) or, in the mereological case, towards a holistic encompassing of a content-area as a totality (i.e., from nose to face); (2) In the direction of *micro-decentration*, i.e., towards particularization and concretization (i.e., from animal to dog) or towards executive focussing on a particular aspect of a content-area (i.e., from face to nose).

Notice that the operations of decentration (back-forth, macro-, micro-) allow the subject to *experience* in coordination different epilevels of reality and thus to develop (*LM*-learn) structures that actually epireflect, in a selective way, a given epilevel of experience while relating it to other epilevels and aspects of its content-area. Although the neurophysiological mechanisms of these functions are not well understood, some evidence may be available of their existence (e.g., Creutzfeldt, 1981; Sprague, Hughes & Berlucchi, 1981).

In a *recentration operation* the control executive cancels the centration of a set of schemes that epireflect a *given aspect* of a content-area, (i.e., a *referent*) observed from a given epilevel, and then places a centration onto schemes epireflecting different aspects (different referents) from *the same* epilevel.

An example of logological recentration is the sequence:

$$M\text{"(animal } (X_1))\text{"}: M\text{"(plant}(X_2))\text{"}$$

that is: I think of the concept animal, perhaps looking at an instance of it (any animal), and then of a plant (perhaps looking at an instance). An example of mereological recentration is

$$M\text{"(this cup } (X_1))\text{"}: M\text{"(this telephone } (X_2))\text{"},$$

i.e., I look at the cup that is on my desk and then *I scan* and look at the telephone that is on my desk. Mereological recentration (and perhaps also logological recentration) is often accompanied by eye movements. Scanning is often instrumental in causing the mereological recentration; but it is not always so. Outer change, movement in the world around us, are also causes of recentration. For instance, the referent of our centration can change by itself or move by itself, e.g.

$$M\text{"(serious-face } (X_1))\text{"}: M\text{"(smiling-face } (X_1))\text{"},$$

that is, I look at her (X_1) face and she smiles. As Husserl emphasized using a very different terminology, the recentration operations serve to constitute (construct) the spatio-temporal world that surrounds us, i.e., the life-world. The recentrations relating the immediate past with the immediate future (what Husserl called the "horizon" of the given centration) constitute the psychological present. The recentrations relating the more distant past with the present and the present with the more distant future constitute the structure of time, of the personal or collective history, and of the personal or collective project (Sartre, 1943). The two main recentration operations are in fact distinguishable in relation to time. There is a *retrospective recentration* that changes a centration back to a previously occurring centration (recall, or retrieval from memory, could be an instance of this operation); and a *prospective recentration* that moves from the present centration to a new one, future or possible (imagination, expectancy, anticipatory inference are instances of this).

Decentration and recentration operations can be combined into suitable centration strategies that can generate new structural organizations. An example of this is the perception (or the intuition) of "*becomingnesses*", i.e., of the changing flow of events or of things. This structural intuition is achieved by having a decentration apply on the result of a retrospective recentration that coordinates a sequence of recentrations. The emerging and changing pattern of differences among the centrations from this sequence is abstracted by a macro-decentration. The resulting pattern of emerging and changing differences is precisely the intuition of a *"becomingness"*.

The intuition of an "eternal", unchanging *being* results from another such coordination. If the subject centrates not the differences, but the similarities across centrations in the recentration sequence, then the intuition of an *invariant, unchanging being* will emerge. In fact, attentional strategies for coordinating decentrations and recentrations, so as to obtain certain results, are the key constituents of executive structures. Good examples of this sort of attentional executives strategies are the psychological structures of Piaget, such as the "groupings" and the "group" of four transformations INRC (Inhelder and Piaget 1958) when suitably reinterpreted. Other examples are provided by the set-theoretical, diagrammatic, or production-system models of neoPiagetian (e.g., Case, 1974; Fischer, 1980; Klahr & Wallace, 1976) and of information-processing psychologists (e.g., Anderson, 1981). As an illustration consider Piaget's grouping I of addition of classes.

In this grouping Piaget usually represents the subordinate class as a low-rank letter (such as A relative to B) and its superordinate (general) class as a high-rank letter (B relative to A). A letter with a "prime" mark, i.e., A', B', C', represents the set-theoretical complement of A (or B, or C) over a reference superordinate class (such as B). Thus he writes: $A + A' = B + B' = C + C' = \ldots$. This structure is best understood as the type of attentional strategy of a subject that centrates A, then *decentrates* and centrates B, then *recentrates,* contrasting A and B, and when he notices that there are B-members different from the A-members that together constitute the class A', he then notices also M "$(B-A=A')$". Having thus examined the logical relations holding between centrations M "(A)", M "(B)" and M "(C)", he retrospectively recentrates again and compares B and C, ending on the centration M "$(C-B=B')$" etc. . . . This grouping represents a *generic* sequence of logological macro-decentration and retrospective recentrations.

Every structure of Piaget's psycho-logic is interpretable as a kind of attentional strategy of recentration/decentration sequences.

The fact that Piaget's, as well as some neoPiagetians', psychological structures are *characteristic* of developmental stages (in the sense that they are only found when the subject has attained a certain stage, such as concrete operations) suggests that these models of attentional executive strategies (i.e., of centration strategies) place characteristic demands on the mental resources of the subject.

The Quantitative Aspects of Mental Attention and Task-Characteristic Allocation Strategies

To examine this aspect of the centration model, it is useful to mention three basic aspects of attention, that Wund (1886) already mentions, and Pascual-Leone (1970) explicitly discusses in terms of the present model. I refer to the "content of mental attention", the "span of mental attention," and the "intensity of mental attention." The content of mental attention is precisely the schemes that are M-boosted in the centration. Since the M-reserve is limited, only a number of schemes can be M-boosted. This number, however, depends on the amount of M-energy that is to be allocated to each of them. This "amount of allocated M-energy" corresponds to the concept of "intensity of mental attention", when attention is construed as a construct and not as a performance. In practice, the amount of M-energy that the executive *must* allocate to a scheme depends on whether the input-situation activates irrelevant or misleading schemes, i.e., schemes that interfere with application of the relevant cluster of schemes vis-à-vis the production of performance. If there are misleading schemes, that is, schemes in misleading situations where the relevant schemes are interfered with, I-interruption must be applied to misleading schemes and the M-energy allocated to the relevant schemes must be *maximal*, to insure that they determine the performance (Pascual-Leone, 1969, 1976a, 1980; Pascual-Leone and Bovet, 1966; Pascual-Leone and Goodman, 1979). *These are circumstances that allow the number of relevant schemes required by the task to be a reliable behavioral measure of the M-energy the subject can muster.* This measure I call *M-power*. Multiple experiments have shown that M-power (when measured this way) is a numerical parameter characteristic of Piaget's substages of child development. This numerical parameter exhibits the uncommon property of quantitative invariances across types of subjects (e.g., across social classes, Case, 1974; DeAvila, Havassy, & Pascual-Leone, 1976; Globerson, 1981; Miller, 1980) as well as across types of content-area situations. (The same estimates of M-power have been found to apply in Piaget's tasks, in visual information-processing tasks, in figural problem-solving tasks, in short-term memory centration tasks, in motor tasks, and in language tasks.) In this sort of situation, the empirically measured "space of attention" (or "channel capacity" or "working memory") corresponds to M-power. This is so because misleading situations are M-concentration tasks, since M-power must be maximally allocated to each relevant scheme to insure performance. Note that M-*concentration* tasks (that characteristically occur in misleading situations) are often called *effortful* in the current literature (for example, Hasher and Zacks, 1979). Very different conditions of attention exist in *facilitating situations* where no irrelevant or misleading schemes are elicited by the input. In facilitating situations, *I-disinterruption* (a "wide-beam" of attention) can be used so that other organismic factors such as A(affects), C(content cues), L, or F may help to activate the relevant schemes. Because of this help and because no misleading schemes are activated to interfere, the relevant schemes can control the performance even if M-power is not concentrated on a few schemes but, rather, is spread over all available schemes (*M*-dispersion). *M*-facilitating tasks are *M*-dispersive tasks that in their performance level often yield wrong estimates (overestimates) of the subject's *M*-power.

I-disinterruption and *M*-dispersion constitute the appropriate *mental attitude* (or mental formula) when the task is ill-defined, or during creative imaginal searches ("brainstorming", divergent thinking), or when the subject attempts to abstract analogically from his own cognitive map.

The process of growing into human maturity may increase these kinds of achievements because of the developmental quantitative and qualitative changes that the centration operators (i.e., *M, I, F, E*) undergo. I turn now to examine these changes.

THE INNER DIALECTICS OF HUMAN GROWTH FROM CHILDHOOD TO ADULTHOOD

In general terms, after the work of Hegel, Marx and, their followers (Gadamer, 1976; Hook, 1978; Ilyenkov, 1977; Marx, Engel, and Lenin, 1977) and that of the many dialectical constructivists nurtured by modern physics and mathematics (Bachelard, 1971; Bohm, 1980; Bohr, 1961; Feyerabend, 1970; Gonseth, 1975; Hanson, 1958; Holton, 1975; Krajewsky, 1977; Kuhn, 1962; Lakatos, 1980; Polya, 1957; Piaget, 1967b; ULlmo, 1958), *dialectic* appears as a conceptual method for analyzing and describing the inner process of change and development in nature, in science, and in thought. As Hegel would have it, dialectic is the intrinsic logic of change, the intrinsic logic of becoming. Classic formal or symbolic logic cannot represent change, but some modern logic, operator logic, in some sense, does.

Mathematical calculus and combinatory logic (Curry, 1963) are examples of operator logic. Yet a comparison of mathematical calculus with Hegelian or Marxist or constructivist dialectic shows differences that highlight important peculiarities of the dialectical method: (1) Contrary to calculus, which admits of no contradictions, Hegelian, Marxist, or constructivist dialectic proceeds by way of (*is driven by*) the analysis of so-called *dialectical* contradictions or (what is the same) *scientific anomalies.* (2) Contrary to calculus, which within a simple application must always maintain the same epistemological level (*epilevel*) of description of the content-domain where it applies, dialectic proceeds by a combined mental strategy of decentrations and recentrations so that changes in the epilevel of description within the same analysis of a content-domain are the norm. In fact, that resolution of dialectical contradictions (i.e., the *dialectical synthesis,* what the dictionary calls "sublation") is often accompanied, as Hook (1978, p. 66) has pointed out, by a re-structuring at a higher epilevel (the analysis of the "totality") and a redefinition of terms of reference. (3) In calculus (or in other classic operator logics), where an absolute distinction is made between operators and figurative states, operators are said to apply onto states to change them. In this way the two terms, *operators* and figurative *states*, exist prior to *change* and serve to define it. In contrast, dialectic operators or forces (generic causes of change) and figurative states (state kinds—"beings") are explicitly regarded as secondary to change ("becoming"). That is, they are seen as emerging from the efforts of the human mind to comprehend the experience of intrinsic historical becoming in the subject matter, from the perspective of the subject matter (e.g., Bachelard, 1971; Bohm, 1980; Charon, 1983; Gadamer, 1976; Ilyenkov, 1977; Krantz, Luce, Suppe & Tversky, 1971; Marx, Engels, and Lenin, 1977; Ullmo, 1958).

Developmental psychology, as it becomes process-analytical, must necessarily (explicitly or not) invoke dialectics to refer to the actual processes taking place within the organism, as Vygotsky (1978), Wallon (1945), and the later Piaget (1975, 1980) have emphasized.

In this view, change is primary and can be understood by the scientist's mind as the functional manifestation of an innate (and silent) organization of operators of various kinds to be discovered. In the TCO these operators are hypothesized to be *subjective operators,* i.e., schemes of various kinds (e.g., operative, executive, mereological, logological, etc.), and *silent operators* (distinct sorts of organismic resources). There are also organizational principles (*silent principles*), describable as sorts of silent meta-operators, that help the organism to produce a response (an overt or covert performance) even if no single or no set of operators could actually produce it by itself. The principle of Schematic Overdetermination of Performance described above is an illustration (Pascual-Leone, 1976a, 1976d, 1980, 1983; Pascual-Leone and Goodman, 1979). Silent principles insure that the *generative constructivity* (the ability to produce responses) of the organism is *universal* (i.e., exists in all situations) and that the organism does not "get jammed" as often as computers do. This universal generative constructivity of the organism corresponds to what Hegel and Marx called sublation or *dialectical syntheses.* Freud has called this phenomenon *overdetermination* of performance by all the applying operators, while Piaget has called it *equilibration.* Since a response is often prompted by a "disturbance" of the organism caused by either external or internal determinants, *equilibration* (dialectical synthesis) often leads to a new inner state (or organization) that restores the *equilibrium* (avoids or adapts to the disturbance).

Here I have attempted to provide a brief process-analytical insight into the meaning of the ill-defined concepts "disturbance," "equilibration", "equilibrium", by emphasizing the role of mental centration in generating new epistemological levels and new referents. Elsewhere, other aspects of these notions are discussed in more detail and illustrated with concrete examples.

A Comparison of "Adolescing" with "Aging"

In essence, the model states that the stage transition in Piaget's stages is constituted by growth in silent operators that make up the Centration mechanism, in particular M and I. When measured behaviorally M (and perhaps I as well) grows in a discontinuous fashion as suggested in Table 9.2. This step-function, developmental-growth curve (a sudden growth of M power at about the beginning of the odd-numbered years of age, after and including the third year of age) has considerable empirical support. Recently this quantitative stage growth function has been demonstrated in several careful studies of 5- to 12-year-olds that use different M measure tasks from content domains as diverse as visual information processing, motor performance, and language (Fabian, 1982; Goodman, 1979; Johnson, 1982; Todor, 1979). The assumption is that M and I grow at the physiological level continuously with age (cf. Pascual-Leone, 1970, 1976a). However, this continuous neurophysiological growth appears as discontinuous when measured behaviorally because the unit of measurement used is a scheme or structure (a more or less complex semantic-pragmatic organization of brain processes). This happens because, unless there is enough developmentally accumulated M energy to drive another scheme or structure of the appropriate stage complexity to high activation so as to ensure its manifestation in performance, additional M energy will not be behaviorally manifested. For this reason, the behaviorally measured M stages appear as discontinuous. In this discontinuous scale, the measure of M is called M power (M_p, where $M_p = e + k$) and it grows linearly every other year from $M_p = e + 1$ at the age of 3 to $M_p = e + 7$ at age 15 years. In this scale, e represents the amount of M energy, constant across ages after 2 years of age, that is commonly used in boosting the currently dominant executive schemes. This component e (*the Me-reserve*) has not been empirically quantified, although it could be done. It should be pointed out that the units of the scale e are much smaller than the units of the scale k ($M_k = reserve$) and therefore units from these two scales cannot be directly added. The component k ($M_k = reserve$) has been empirically quantified, using theory-guided task analyses and simple mathematical modeling derived from them. The units in this k scale are the action schemes (or the corresponding task-specific executive prescriptions) that must be simultaneously M boosted by the organism to synthesize the to-be-produced performance.

The inner dialectics of the organism appear here in the manner in which a quantitative change, the growth of M_p, gets converted into a qualitative change: the emergence of new qualitative operational

Table 9.2. Predicted M-capacity Corresponding to the Average Chronological Age of Subjects in Piaget's Developmental Substages.

Predicted Maximum Power of M	Piaget's Substage	Average Chronological Age
$e + 1$	Low preoperations	3–4
$e + 2$	Preoperations	5–6
$e + 3$	Low concrete operations	7–8
$e + 4$	High concrete operations	9–10
$e + 5$	Transition to formal operations	11–12
$e + 6$	Low formal operations	13–14
$e + 7$	High formal operations	15–adult

structures that have a constructive M demand equal to the newly acquired M power. Although a detailed demonstration of this dialectical conversion of quantity into quality is beyond the scope of this chapter, the reader may grasp more easily the idea by considering the following remarks. The qualitatively different structure that can be constructed at different epi-levels of experience (see Table 9.1) usually imposes a psychogenetic constructive M demand that is correlated with the epi-level at which the structure is defined. This is so because the minimal number of different substantive or relational dimensions of experience needed to construct a given structure as an invariant usually increases with its epi-level (cf. Ullmo, 1958; Reuchlin, 1964; Krantz, Luce, Suppes, & Tversky, 1971). The idea that developmental complexity is correlated with the psychological constructive complexity of developmental tasks appears full-blown in Piaget (Beth & Piaget, 1961).

Recent work of Piagetians and neo-Piagetians, using more explicit and logico-mathematically weaker, more general models than Piaget did, makes very explicit this structurally cumulative construction of structures (for example, Case, 1978; Commons & Richards, Chapter 6, this volume; Fischer, Hand, & Russell, 1980, Chapter 3, this volume; Pascual-Leone, 1969, 1976a, 1976b, 1980; Pascual-Leone & Smith, 1969).

Piaget's main stages of development (sensori-motor, preoperational, concrete-operational, formal-operational) appear from this viewpoint to correspond to the minimum M_p values that are needed to solve the Piagetian tasks under the special, partly facilitating conditions of the Piagetian testing methodology.

Thus, the growth of adolescing[8] (the childhood stages) is marked by an incrementation in the content-free organismic resources (silent operators) M and I. As a result, the general characteristic of these stages is a cumulative growth of potentialities: all the qualitative capabilities of earlier stages are usually maintained while some new capabilities are added.

The growth during aging (the adulthood stages) differs in this regard. It is argued here that aging is marked by a decrement of these main silent operators: M, I, and C (Content learning). While in childhood the disequilibration that precipitates the inner dialectics and brings structural growth is an endogenous organismic augmentation in M and I power, in the later years the disequilibration is caused by an endogenous organismic reduction in the functionally available M, I and C power. This quantitative reduction has great qualitative-dynamic consequences because many superstructures (high epi-level structures) and macrostructures (very high epi-level structures that represent functional totalities like knowledge structures or ultra-executives) must often be driven by M power to be applied. This is so because they usually are LM structures (Pascual-Leone & Goodman, 1979). Thus, the general characteristic of growth in adulthood stages is, as Labouvie-Vief (1981, 1982), Baltes (Baltes & Baltes, 1980; Baltes, Reese, & Lipsitt, 1980), and others (for example, Birren, Kinney, Schaie, and Woodruff, 1981; Langer, 1981; Levinson et al., 1978; Woodruff, in press) have emphasized, a selective and non-cumulative (or less cumulative) growth of new functional potentialities. This selective growth is prompted by the change of cultural-historical circumstances (history-normative life-span variables, individual-difference-normative and nonnormative variables—Baltes, Reese & Lipsitt, 1980; Baltes & Willis, 1979; Pascual-Leone, 1983) as well as by the progressively frequent functional breakdown of previously available macrostructures and superstructures—a breakdown caused by reduction and thus unavailability of the M and I power that is needed by the structures to be properly driven. This functional breakdown disturbs adaptation and forces new selective cognitive growth—what Baltes and his associates have called a neointegration (cf. Baltes, Cornelius, Spiro, Nesselroade, & Willis, 1980). As a result, a regression of the previously cumulative functional potentialities occurs in these domains that are not used while much growth and structural coordinations and integration, that is, growth of mediational and scientific-logical or cultural-logical structures, take place in content domains currently in use.

For process-analytical reasons discussed elsewhere (Pascual-Leone, in press) this selective growth of aging generates a number of adulthood stages of development. Levinson (Levinson et al., 1978), following Jung's lead (Jung, 1931), was perhaps the first to describe these stages and to emphasize that, contrary to the adolescing stages that are strongly sequential and obligatory, the aging stages are not obligatory; they are more like seasons or dialectical moments of the human life. They may go unmanifested in performance unless the organismic and environmental/cultural/historical factors suitably interact.

It is not the purpose of this chapter to discuss these stages of adult development. I have discussed my own formulation of them elsewhere (Pascual-Leone, 1983), and various chapters in this book have independently offered similar views and discussed various aspects of them. The purpose of this chapter was to outline the process mechanisms that generate adulthood stages and to exhibit the basic functional-organismic continuities that relate adolescing with aging.

CONCLUDING REMARKS

In this chapter, I have suggested that the process of human growth is driven by an inner dialectic among information-carrying, situation-specific subjective operators, the schemes and structures, and information-free purely organismic universal resources, the silent operators. Two of these silent operators, M and I, together explicate the descriptive notion of mental effort (Hasher & Zacks, 1979; Kahneman, 1973). These mental-effort (in TCO terms, Centration) operators are postulated to be, by virtue of their quantitative change throughout the life span, the efficient causes (that is, transition rule, Pascual-Leone, 1970, 1976a, 1978, 1980) of the neo-Piagetian, purely organismic, stages of development. The power (the measure) of M and I, is said by the theory to increase linearly every other year (when measured behaviorally), after 3 years of age, until the age of 15, when normally an asymptotic plateau is reached. Then, some time around 35 (+3) years of age a decline in M and I power occurs, with an abrupt decline perhaps between 40 and 45 years. This decline, a cause of the so-called mid-life crisis, forces structural reorganizations (Baltes et al., 1980; Baltes, Reese, & Lipsitt 1980), personality maturation, and selective growth (Baltes & Baltes, 1978; Labouvie-Vief, 1981; Pascual-Leone, 1983). Evidence supporting these neo-Piagetian constructs is considerable from childhood to university undergraduate years.

In adulthood, empirical evidence for the decline of these silent operators was until now indirect, but quite revealing. One indirect source is the extensive research on the lawful stagewise regression with aging of a subject's performance in Piagetian tasks. This regression tends to follow the stages of Piaget in inverse order (see Hooper, note 18; Hooper & Sheehan, 1977, for excellent reviews of this literature).

A second indirect source is the empirical evidence accumulated by Cattell (1971) and Horn (for example, 1970, 1978, in press) showing the decline with age of fluid intelligence G_f (Spearman's g factor). This evidence speaks for the decline of M and I because G_f has been shown to be related to developmental intelligence as studied by

Piaget (for example, DeVries & Kohlberg, 1977; Hooper, Fitzgerald, & Papalia, 1971; Humphreys & Parsons, 1979; Kohlberg & DeVries, 1980; Longeot, 1978; Reuchlin, 1964; Vernon, 1969). More specifically, fluid intelligence can be explicated process-analytically as a combination of M, I, and executive controls (Pascual-Leone, 1970; Pascual-Leone & Goodman, 1979).

Strong direct evidence in support of the decline of M and I is provided by the work of Jedrzkiewicz (1983).

These findings of a regression in M and I not only explain the upsurge of the inner dialectics (in good cases, growth and reorganization) characteristic of the transition to middle adulthood, but they have great significance for child development and cognitive science as well. This importance comes from the fact that the majority's view in psychology, with regard to mental attention, is constituted by what could be called the WM-effort-automatization model. According to this model, the increasing capacity for mental effort (the size of working memory) that accrues with age throughout childhood is the result of automatization—executive automatization—(for example, Anderson, 1981; Case, 1978; Chi, 1977; Hasher & Zacks, 1979; Naus, Ornstein, & Hoving, 1978; Rabbitt, 1982; Shiffrin & Schneider, 1977; Trabasso, 1978). However, since older persons tend to perform poorly in effortful tasks where they used to perform well while young; and since so-called automatized (or crystallized) activities are well preserved in old persons (for examples, Horn, 1978, 1982), the logical inference is that effortful tasks are solved by using mental (M) energy and I interruption—attentional mental resources (*M-reserve* and *I-reserve*) that increase up to adolescence and then decrease in the later years.

The concept of purely organismic universal resources, that is, silent operators, that can be quantitatively measured and are limited as reserves was probably pioneered by Pierre Janet (his mental-energy ideas), by Freud (his ego cathesis), and by Spearman (his g-factor energy), but has been rejected by modern cognitive science as it was rejected by Piaget. The neo-Piagetian developmental work that I have initiated as well as our recent work on aging briefly summarized previously, together with recent neurophysiological research (see for review Fuster, 1980; Pompeiano & Marsan, 1981), clearly reopen the need to reconsider the silent-operator approaches.

NOTES

1. Totalities because the structures therein are lawfully coordinated in their use (that is, vis-à-vis praxis).

2. I use here subjective in the manner introduced by Kant and found in Fichte, Hegel, Husserl, Cassirer, and their many descendants. In this sense subjective does not mean private and unreliable, as it does in common sense; rather, contrasted to objective

or behavioral, it means the reliable subjective experiences and subjective actions, more or less accessible to the subject's own consciousness, that in the subject produce, or at least are correlated with, her/his overt performances.

3. Schemes are process structures as defined above. However, I often use structures to refer to superschemes that coordinate a number of simpler schemes. Within this special use, structures are semantically contrasted with (simpler) schemes. In this sense, a structure is a complex superordinate scheme and a scheme is a simple, subordinate structure.

4. An operator is a holistically defined (that is, molar) process or procedure P such that, if a given initial state of affairs s_n exists and P applies on it, a determinate result, the state of affairs s_{n+1}, will occur. This is often symbolized by the expression $P(s_n) = s_{n+1}$. This expression implicitly suggests that a usual condition for the formal definition of an operator is that the application of P on s_n must result in s_{n+1}, irrespective of which are the states $s_{n-1}, s_{n-2}, \ldots$, and so on, that have preceded s_n. This so-called markovian property of operators can, at times, be achieved by defining s_n at a high epi-level as the sequence of states $\ldots s'_{n-3}, s'_{n-2}, s'_{n-1}, s'_n$ such that when P applies, the result is state s_{n+1} (which could also be a sequence). This sequence of states is part of the history of the system or process or subject under study. The operators are so defined that they serve to decompose the holistic historical process of change of the system (or subject) into invariant (history-free or universal) functional components. The Piagetian schemes as well as the computer scientist productions are defined in this manner. So are the silent operators of the TCO.

5. Distal objects are the external objects of the practical life-world. From an epistemological viewpoint they are reliable experimental manifolds, content and structure invariants that emerge in the subject's praxis.

6. Husserl, Tolman, and Piaget have all emphasized that intentionality can be defined empirically by showing that an organism, if in his praxis he intends a given outcome, will change appropriately the concrete sequence of his actions, whenever the context is suitably changed by the experimenter, so as to maintain invariant the attainment of the outcome.

7. One must distinguish two kinds of constructive processes, psychogenetic and generative. Psychogenetic processes are those, like learning and maturational-developmental growth, that cause the schemes of the organism to change so as to be better adapted. Generative processes are those that cause the actual synthesis or assembly of the subject's mental or behavioral performance in a situation. Psychogenetic difficulty (complexity) and generative difficulty (complexity) are defined accordingly. Note that this difficulty presupposes the spontaneous acquisition (unaided by a direct teaching-intervention from the environment) of the operation in question.

8. I thank Dr. J. Johnson for sending her notes of the November 1982 Berkeley Colloquium by Dr. Levinson where this idea was expressed.

10

DIALECTICAL THINKING AS A METASYSTEMATIC FORM OF COGNITIVE ORGANIZATION

Michael A. Basseches

One approach to conceptualizing the nature of cognitive development beyond formal operations takes intellectual history as its starting point. Klaus Riegel (1973) observed that the dialectical philosophical tradition played a significant role in the history of philosophical, scientific, and social scientific inquiry. Within this tradition, the limits of formalistic thinking and formal logic were pointed out and transcended. Based on his observation, Riegel suggested that cognitive ontogenesis might recapitulate this historical process. A dialectical form of thinking may develop in individuals as a means of transcending the limits of formal-operational thought.

The conception of dialectical thinking to be presented in this chapter differs considerably from Riegel's. He described dialectical thinking in a way that did not presuppose formal thought. Dialectical thinking as described here both presupposes formal thinking and integrates formal-operational thinking within a broader framework. Nevertheless, both conceptions of dialectical thinking are rooted in the notion that cognitive psychology ought to look to the dialectical philosophical perspective for an understanding of the limits of formal thought.

DIALECTIC AS A PRINCIPLE OF COGNITIVE ORGANIZATION

To clarify the thinking to be described here, it is important to consider two key features: (1) its level of organization and (2) its form of organization. The level of dialectical thinking as discussed here is metasystematic. The metasystematic level is characterized in general terms and contrasted with previous levels of cognitive organization in the contributions of Commons and Richards (Chapters 6 and 7) and

Fischer et al. (Chapter 3, this volume). Metasystematic thinking includes systems among its objects of analysis and describes relationships among and transformations of entire systems. It is one level of reflection removed from formal-operational thinking that takes propositions as its objects of analysis and organizes relationships among propositions and transformations of propositions into implicit structured wholes or systems.

Riegel's account included sensory-motor dialectic intelligence, preoperational dialectic intelligence, concrete dialectic operations, and formal dialectical operations. Piaget's (1952, 1974, 1980) work on dialectics focused on the dialectical nature of the process of equilibration and the development of thought at all levels of organization. Here, dialectical thinking refers explicitly to a metasystematic level of cognitive organization, as do other forms of thinking described in this volume, for example, Sinnott's relativistic reasoning and Koplowitz' general system reasoning.

What differentiates dialectical thinking from other metasystematic modes of reasoning is its form of organization. Whereas a variety of modes of reasoning discussed in this volume deal with relationships of systems, they differ in how they organize relationships of systems. In the case of dialectical thinking, the organizing principle is the concept of dialectic. Dialectic refers to the process by which structured wholes, forms or systems, evolve and change. Dialectic may be defined as developmental transformation, developmental movement through forms, which occurs via constitutive and interactive relationships.

Movement through forms is distinct from movement within forms. To illustrate this distinction, consider what happens when a road is built from one city to another. The road has a certain form to it that regulates the movement of the vehicles traveling between cities. This movement of the vehicles may be taken as movement within a form. On the other hand, change associated with decay of the road and with the process of building a better road with a different form to replace the old road, can be seen as a movement through forms, a transformation. The definition of dialectic relies upon both the notion of movement and the notion of form and focuses on the developmental relationship between them. Describing movement through forms, or transformation, as developmental implies a certain direction to it associated with increasing inclusiveness, differenatiation, and integration.

Developmental transformational movement occurs via constitutive and interactive relationships. A relationship is a connection. Relationships often are thought of as connections between things, with things taken to exist prior to the relationship. Here, constitutive relationship indicates the opposite; it indicates that the relationship itself has a role in making the parties what they are. Interactive implies that the relationship is not static but is characterized by action of the parties on each other.

The example of the road may be used to illustrate the concepts of constitutive and interactive relationships. Constitutive and inter-active relationships exist among the builders of the road, the road itself, and the users of the road and their vehicles. The road is constituted not only by its interaction with road builders but also by its relationship with the vehicles which travel on it. If no vehicles travel on the road, it is no longer a road. It might be a road that had been converted to a mall. Or if only airplanes traveled on it, it would be a runway. Thus, its being a road depends on (is constituted by) its particular relationship to vehicles. Similarly, it is clearly relationships with roads that make road builders road builders. Perhaps less obviously, relationships with roads make vehicles vehicles. Vehicles are vehicles because they have the capacity to transport one some-place, and the extent to which they have this capacity is dependent on the extent to which suitable thoroughfares exist.

The relationship between vehicles and the road is interactive both because vehicles change the road, such as when they cause road wear, and because the road changes the vehicles, such as when its trouble spots cause accidents. The interaction between road and vehicles leads to transformation when the new road is built. This is the sense in which the transformation occurs by constitutive and inter-active relationships. The movement whereby a new road is built as a result of the relationships among the previous road, vehicles, and road builders may be seen as an instance of dialectic.

Formal-operational thinking can be understood as efforts at comprehension relying on application of an implicit model of an unchanging structured whole, a closed system of lawful relationships among possibilities, to the phenomenal world. Dialectical thinking can be understood as efforts at comprehension relying on application of an implicit model of dialectic, developmental transformation via constitutive and interactive relationships, to the phenomenal world. The latter efforts may be termed dialectical analyses, in contrast to formal analyses. Dialectical analyses entail recognition of constitutive and interactive relationships, of forms, and of fundamental changes, as well as their integration as aspects of dialectics [Hegel (1967), Marx (1967), Engels (1940), Piaget (1952), Ludwig Von Bertalanffy (1968)].

OPERATIONALIZATION OF DIALECTIC THINKING

For the idea of dialectical thinking to be useful in describing subjects' thinking it had to be operationalized: there needed to be some way of recognizing when subjects were thinking in a dialectical way. Dialectical thinking was operationalized by creating an interpretive coding system called the Dialectical Schemata (DS) framework (Basseches, 1980, in press). The framework consists of 24 cognitive schemata, or general types of moves-in-thought, identifiable in discourse. Each of these moves in thought in some way relates to the dilectical philosophical tradition, and each plays a somewhat different role in dialectical thinking.

In defining schemata, the DS framework draws on the work of many writers within the dialectical tradition. These include Hegel (1967), Marx (1967), Engels (1940), Ollman (1971), Kosok (1972), Gould (1978), VonBertalanffy (1968), and Piaget (1952). On the one hand, the DS framework was intended to leave out no important component of dialectical thinking. On the other hand, an effort was made to avoid redundancy by abstracting commonalities of what appeared to the author to be essentially similar ideas. The result is a hybrid set of schema names, some drawn from the terminologies established by different thinkers within the dialectical tradition, and others representing the author's own abstractions. (For detailed explanations of the nature of each schema, and each schema's sources in branches of the dialectical tradition, see Basseches, 1979, in press).

The 24 Dialectical Schemata are listed in Table 10.1, categorized according to whether they function primarily in orienting thought toward motion, forms, or relationships or in integrating these three orientations. Motion-oriented schemata function to direct attention toward processes of change and to recognize dialectical qualities of these change processes. Form-oriented schemata function to direct attention toward wholes or contexts and to conceptualize these wholes as forms or systems. Relationship-oriented schemata function to direct attention to relationships and to grasp the interactive and constitutive nature of these relationships. Finally, a fourth group of meta-formal schemata integrate the orientations toward motion, form, and relationships by describing relationships among forms and transformations through forms, as well as the process of form construction.

The roman numerals in Table 10.1 indicate a more differentiated accounting of the functions of the various schemata within dialectical thinking. These functions typify the cognitive actions of this stage. Since they are not reversible (Basseches, 1978), they are not operations; rather, they are similar to what Piaget (1978) calls regulations.

MOTION-ORIENTED SCHEMATA

Schemata 1 and 4 function to preserve fluidity in thought. For example, Schema 1 involves a thesis-antithesis-synthesis movement

Table 10.1. Analysis of Functions of Dialectical Schemata

A. Motion-Oriented Schemata
    i. Preserve fluidity in thought
       1 Thesis-antithesis-synthesis movement in thought
       4 Recognition of correlativity of a thing and its other
    ii. Direct attention to actual or potential processes of change
       2 Affirmation of the primacy of motion
       6 Affirmation of the practical or active character of knowledge
       7 Avoidance or exposure of objectification, hypostatization, and reification
       8 Understanding events or situations as movements (of development) of a process
    iii. Describe movement as dialectical movement
       3 Recognition and description of thesis-antithesis-synthesis movement
       5 Recognition of ongoing interaction as a source of movement

B. Form-Oriented Schemata
    i. Direct attention to organized or patterned wholes (systems)
       9 Location of an element or phenomenon with the whole(s) of which it is a part
      11 Assumption of contextual relativism
    ii. Recognize and describe systems as systems
      10 Description of a whole (system) in structural, functional, or equilibrational terms
      11 Assumption of contextual relativism

C. Relationship-Oriented Schemata
    i. Direct attention to relationships
      12 Assertion of the existence of relations, the limits of separation and the value of relatedness
      13 Criticism of multiplicity, subjectivism, and pluralism
    ii. Describe relationships as constitutive and interactive, thereby relating them to the idea of dialectic
      14 Description of a two-way reciprocal relationship
      15 Assertion of internal relations

D. Meta-Formal Schemata
    i. Direct attention to and describe the limits of stability (change potential) of forms or systems
      16 Location (or description of the process of emergence) of contradictions or sources of disequilibrium within a system or between a system and external forces or elements which are antithetical to the system's structure
    ii. Direct attention to and describe transformation or movements from one form to another
      17 Understanding the resolution of disequilibrium or contradiction in terms of a notion of transformation in development direction
      21 Description of open self-transforming systems
      22 Description of qualitative change as a result of quantitative change within a form
    iii. Direct attention to and describe relationship among forms or systems
      19 Evaluative comparison of systems
      20 Attention to problems of coordinating systems in relation
      24 Multiplication of perspectives as a concreteness-preserving approach to inclusiveness

(Continued next page)

Table 10.1 *(continued)*

iv. Direct attention to relationship of forms to process of form-construction
  18 Relating value to (a) movement in development direction and/or (b) stability through developmental movement
  23 Criticism of formalism based on the interdependence of form and content

---

within the subject's own thought. Such thought moves from reflection upon one idea to reflection upon something that is apart from, left out of, contrary to, or excluded from the first idea. Then such thought moves on to reflection upon a more inclusive idea that relates the original idea to that which was excluded from it.

Schemata 2, 6, 7, and 8 all function to direct the attention of the thinker to processes of change or to creative processes that allow for the possibility of change. For example, Schema 7 involves the avoidance or exposure of objectification, hypostatization, and reification. These moves counteract tendencies to describe complex processes as if they were static things. If one person were to talk about marriage as if it were a thing, another might use Schema 7 to point out the processes of change characterizing marriage.

In Schemata 3 and 5, and to some extent Schema 8, processes of change are described in ways that appeal to the idea of dialectic. For example, Schema 3 involves recognition and description of thesis-antithesis-synthesis movement. Here, changes outside the thinker's own thought are described as forming a pattern where generation of an alternative to something leads to the formation of a relationship between the thing and its alternative.

FORM-ORIENTED SCHEMATA

Schema 9 locates an element or phenomenon within a whole(s). It functions to direct the thinker's attention from the object of reflection to the larger whole(s) of which that object is a part. Schema 10 describes wholes in structural, functional, or equilibrational terms. Employing Schema 10 involves recognizing wholes as organized forms or systems. Schema 11 articulates the epistemological assumption of contextual relativism (Perry, 1968); it functions to direct attention from ideas and values to the conceptual contexts of ideas and values and to the structural properties of those conceptual contexts.

RELATIONSHIP-ORIENTED SCHEMATA

Schema 12 asserts the existence and value of relationships and of the limits associated with maintaining separations. Schema 13 criticizes epistemological and meta-ethical perspectives founded on principles of separateness, multiplicity, pluralism, and subjectivism. Both turn the thinker's attention to relationships.

In Schema 14, for description of two-way reciprocal relationships, the interactive aspect of relationships is brought out. Schema 15, which asserts the existence of internal relations, brings out the constitutive aspect of the nature of relationships. It does this by asserting that relationships make the parties to the relationships what they are.

META-FORMAL SCHEMATA

The meta-formal schemata of the DS framework most clearly show the metasystematic level of organization attributed here to dialectical thinking. These schemata presuppose the explicit recognition of forms or systems (such as those implicit at formal operations) because they are cognitive actions performed upon forms and systems.

For example, Schema 16 involves locating sources of disequilibrium within a system or between a system and external forces antithetical to the system's structure. Such thought makes salient systems' limits of stability. Schemata 17, 21, and 22 are those most clearly related to the process of transformation. Schema 17 relies on the concept of development to conceptualize the transformations that occur when a system reaches its limits of stability.

Schemata 19, 20, and 24 relate systems or forms to each other. For example, when Schema 19 is employed, systems or forms are evaluatively compared to each other. Finally, Schemata 18 and 23 both function to bring the process of form construction into awareness. Schema 18 asserts the value of facilitating the process of transformation in a direction in which more sophisticated forms are constructed. (A detailed account of each schema's relationship to the other schemata appears in Basseches, 1978, in press).

This framework made it possible to read interview text and note instances of the 24 elements of dialectical thinking. Interview protocols have been reliably coded for use of dialectical schemata. An Index (I) designed to measure the number of schemata employed in a protocol and the clarity with which they were exhibited could be computed with an interrater reliability of $r = .91$ ($p < .005$). The probability of agreement on the presence of any given schema in a protocol was 76 percent ($p < .003$). (Rules for coding and computing index scores appear in Basseches, 1978.) The following illustrates the coding process.

ILLUSTRATION OF SCHEMA 16

Schema 16 is the schema for locating contradictions or sources of disequilibrium either within a system or between a system and external elements or forces that are antithetical to the system's structure. The following excerpt, from the interview of Subject No. 40, a 20-year-old senior philosophy and linguistics major, was identified as an example of Schema 16. In this excerpt, the subject emphasizes sources of potential future disequilibrium in a world-view which she attributes to some premedical students.

Subject: I was just thinking, maybe if you know that that is what you're doing and your theory is 'this is your social structure and you are going to fit into it by putting yourself in this niche and getting along well in that niche,' then you do have a theory and you can just learn Organic Chemistry and Biology II and study all those things, and they have the effect of causing you to be able to do that, fit into that niche. But as long as you don't...

Interviewer: So the structures work, but as long as you don't...

Subject: Yeah, but then you run into a real problem if your view of the kind of niche that was... turns out not to have been a real view or if the niche changes between when you become a premed and when you become a doctor. If the whole... If the whole thing crumbles under you and that is no longer the form that society takes, I guess that's a problem.

Interviewer: What might lead that to happen?

Subject: Well, the fact that social structures evolve and change. I guess that is the problem, OK, social structures evolve and change. If you are not always watching to see how your social structure is evolving and changing, if instead you are just working on a static theory of what the social structure is and deciding how you are going to fit into some niche that you see in the static structure, you are going to be in for a lot of surprises when you find out that other people are developing and changing while you are sitting still.

In the above excerpt the subject first describes the equilibrative effectiveness of the premedical student's world-view when she says that acting on the premed's theory will "have the effect of causing you to be able to do that, fit into that niche." However, the potential sources of disequilibrium for that theory are also located in the possibility that in time the specific social structure on which the theory's equilibrative effectiveness depends may change. She refers to this potential disequilibrium in the expressions: (1) "you run into a real problem," (2) "that's a problem," and (3) "you are going to be in for a lot of surprises."

RESEARCH USING THE DIALECTICAL SCHEMATA FRAMEWORK

Basseches (1980) conducted lengthy interviews with college students and professors about the nature of education and coded them for the spontaneous use of dialectical thinking (Study I).[1] Olsen, Basseches, and Richards (in preparation) developed a comprehension instrument in which subjects read pairs of arguments on a wide range of topics. They were then asked to explain the line of reasoning followed in the arguments. For each pair, one of the arguments contained one of the dialectical schemata while the other was a nondialectical argument. The arguments were matched for linguistic difficulty using the judgment of a reading expert as a criterion. The protocols of these sessions were coded for comprehension of the dialectical and nondialectical arguments (Study II).

Study I

Method

Subjects consisted of six male freshmen and three female freshmen, age range 18–20; three male seniors and six female seniors, age range 20–22; and eight male faculty members and one female faculty member, age range 30–48.

Procedure

Subjects were sent letters explaining that interviews use these seven questions.

1. How would you go about formulating a conception of the nature of education?
2. How would you go about trying to understand, explain, or analyze the way in which Swarthmore education functions?
3. What do you think could be done to improve or to optimize the value of Swarthmore education?
4. To what extent or in what way do you think that the thoughts you have shared with me could or could not be said to form a logically coherent conception of education?

Table 10.2. Comparison of Freshman, Senior, and Faculty Subsample Means for Measures of Dialectical Thinking

Subsample*	Mean Number of Schemata Clearly Present	Mean Number of Schemata Absent	Mean Index
Freshmen	5.22	9.56	29.50
Seniors	8.78	6.56	41.00
Faculty	12.89	3.89	50.50

Note: n = 9 for each subsample

5. To what extent or in what way do you think that the thoughts you have shared with me could or could not be said to form a useful conception of education?
6. What do you see as the relationship between your conception of education and your experience and activities as a member of this community?
7. On the basis of what you know about it, how would you explain the existence of the current concern over the revision of the honors program.

Interviews averaged two hours in length. Subjects' answers to the skeletal questions above were probed by (1) asking them to elaborate upon their initial responses; (2) asking questions that their remarks provoked; and at times (3) presenting them with counter-arguments. Subjects were asked to justify any values asserted, to explain any phenomena described, and to present arguments that might convince others who held contrary positions.

The number of schemata clearly present in the interviews ranged from 2–19. The number of schemata absent in the interviews ranged from 0–16. The index computed for the interviews ranged from 16–62. Table 10.2 gives the mean for these categories by sample subgroup.

Clear differences exist among freshmen, seniors, and faculty on all three scores. In each case, faculty show more evidence of dialectical thinking than seniors, who in turn show more evidence than freshmen. Analyses of the variance of the number of schemata clearly present ($F=7.07$, d.f.$=2$), the number of schemata absent ($F=6.13$, d.f.$=2$), and the index ($F=6.35$, d.f.$=2$) reveal that, in each case, subsample membership accounted for a significant ($p < .01$) portion of the variance. The correlation coefficient for the relationship between subject's age and interview index was 0.67.

A standard item analysis was done on the dialectical schemata. A point-biserial coorelation was computed between the number of clear occurrences of each schema and the index score. The index

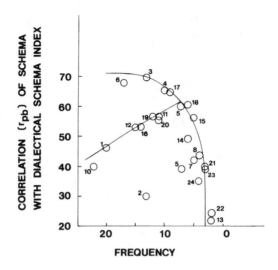

Figure 10.1. Correlation of Schema with Dialectical Schema Index

(Basseches, 1978) is a summary score of the different strengths of the occurrences of all schemata in an interview. The point-biserial correlations were plotted against the frequencies of clear occurrence of each schema, as shown in the Figure 10.1. There seem to be two distinguishable groups of schemata in this figure, indicated by the two functions visually fit to the data points. The first group (A) of schemata behave as normal items. As the items occur less frequently, their correlation with the index score becomes higher. This means that these less frequent items are harder, or at a higher level of dialectical development. It also means that they are central to the normal course of dialectical development since they correlate highly with the total amount of dialectical development evident in an interview.

The second group of schemata (B) are more idiosyncratic. They are all infrequent but vary greatly in their correlation with the index. The group that are the worst predictors (2, 7, 22, 24) are possibly schemata that are learned in specialized academic settings and may be learned without an accompanying organization of a dialectical framework. The remainder of this group may also be of this type; however, they are better indicators of an organized dialectical framework (at least of the index). It may be that the kinds of particular experiences that account for the appearance of these schemata converge with the kinds of experiences that produce the normal course of dialectical development.

To complement these quantitative analyses, the profiles of schemata present and absent were inspected and recurring patterns were noted.

Study II[2]

Method

Subjects were 10 freshmen, 10 seniors, and 10 second-year graduate students recruited from the College of Human Ecology and the College of Arts and Sciences at Cornell University, with mean ages 18, 21.7, and 25.1.

Procedure

Subjects were presented with 12 pairs of arguments on cards, one card at a time. After reading each passage, subjects were asked to reconstuct the argument in their own words. Comprehension was scored after the subject had finished responding to individual passages. Half (6) of the pairs of passages began with dialectical arguments, and half (6) began with nondialectical arguments. All subjects received the passages in the same order to insure comparability of scores across subjects.

When both passages of a pair had been read and responded to, the examiner asked subjects which passage they thought had the highest quality argument and why.

Coding

A response received a score of 0 if it indicated a complete lack of comprehension, 1 indicated partial comprehension, and 2 indicated full comprehension. Given the 0–2 scoring scale, subjects' comprehension scores could range from 0–24 on both dialectical and nondialectical passages.

Results

The comprehension of dialectical passages mean for all subjects in the study was 15.77, with a standard deviation of 4.47. Scores ranged from 7 to 24. The comprehension of nondialectical passages mean for all subjects in the study was 21.97, with a standard deviation of 2.31. Scores ranged from 13 to 24. Means for sample sub-groups appear in Table 10.3.

Table 10.3. Mean Scores on DS Scale

	Freshmen	Seniors	Graduates
Dialectical	13.5	15.1	18.7
Nondialectical	21.6	20.9	23.1

Effects of Academic Level of Comprehension

To reproduce the analysis from Basseches' (1980) study, a one-way analysis of variance was performed. Whether a subject was a freshman, senior, or graduate student was significant in accounting for comprehension of dialectical passages ($F_{2,27}$=4.38, p < .02). No such differences were found to exist among the three groups' comprehension of nondialectical passages ($F_{2,27}$=1.87, nonsignificant).

Preference

A Pearson's Correlation between preference for dialectical passages and comprehension of dialectical schemata indicates a strong positive relation between the two (r=.7, p < .01). An across-subjects comparison of percentage of dialectical passages preferred among those wholly comprehended, partially comprehended, and not comprehended showed a steady decline in preference toward chance level with decreasing comprehension, the percentages being 83, 77, and 58, respectively.

Formal Operations

Seventeen out of the 18 subjects who participated in this part of the study demonstrated formal operational ability on a test by Commons, Miller and Kuhn (1982). One freshman who had demonstrated low comprehension of dialectical schemata (a score of 5.5 out of a possible 24) on the comprehension measure did not demonstrate formal operations.

Discussion

The results from these studies are consistent with the claim that dialectical thinking, as measured by the DS framework, represents a possible direction of cognitive development after formal operations. The studies do not prove the existence of a postformal dialectical thinking stage, since alternative interpretations of the results are possible (see Basseches, 1980), and the Olsen, Basseches, and Richards study II contained too few nonformal-operational subjects. However, converging patterns of results from the studies indicate an increase in dialectical thinking capacities with academic status in a population well past early adolescence. These results provide considerable empirical support for a conception of a postformal operations dialectical thinking stage that is justifiable on conceptual grounds.

DIALECTICAL THINKING FROM THE
EQUILIBRIUM STANDPOINT

Dialectical thinking not only reflects the development of thought beyond formal operations, it also reflects a fundamentally different form of equilibrium from the equilibrium produced by formal thought. This novel form of equilibrium characterizes dialectical thinking and distinguishes it from other aspects of postformal thinking described in this book. Many of the other authors in this book describe aspects of thinking that in fact correspond to specific dialectical schemata. But some authors do not articulate the organizational principle underlying the reasoning they describe. None describes the overall form of equilibrium characteristic of dialectical thinking.

The study of equilibration in genetic epistemology (Piaget, 1952, 1970) is based on the recognition of two properties of human cognition. First, there is a human need to impose stability on the reality that people experience. Cognitive schemata allow one to make sense of, to cognize and re-cognize, what without those structures would be James' "blooming, buzzing, confusion." Second, there is a human process of applying and extending cognitive schemata by putting them into practice in the world (assimilation), which tends to result in changes (accommodation). Structures of equilibrium allow this process of extension and change to occur while keeping something constant.

According to Piaget (1978), a cognitive system in equilibrium is one with the ability to compensate all virtual work that can be carried out by the system. It has the ability to respond to all perturbations of the system in ways that return the system to its original state. A system in equilibrium is one with the capacity to remain the same system, with the same laws of operation, as those laws are applied to a varied environment. Piaget (1970) reserves the term structure for closed systems that have this property. Binary, truth-valued, propositional logic and the INRC group are clearly structures in this sense.[3]

In contrast, a dialectic is a system that changes in fundamental and irreversible ways over time as a result of dynamic relationships within the system and between the system and its context. More becomes incorporated into the system as the system evolves. Thus, a dialectic is not a structure in the traditional Piagetian sense, nor is thought organized by the concept of dialectic a Piagetian structure. Nevertheless, there is a form of equilibrium in dialectical thinking. Dialectical thinking allows the recognition of something as remaining constant amidst a far broader range of changes than formal reasoning can equilibrate. In formal-operational thought, equilibrium is pro-

vided at a second-order (operations on operations) level of organization by an underlying model of a closed-system or structured whole.
In dialectical thinking, equilibrium is provided at a third order of
organization (operation on systems of operations on operations) by
an underlying model of dialectic. The concept of dialectic builds
upon, but is more complex than, the concept of structured whole.

From the perspective of dialectical thinking, what remains
recognizable across a range of changes is the historical process as an
evolving whole. Any change at all, no matter how radical, can be
equilibrated if it can be conceptualized as a moment in a dialectical
process of evolution. New events are integrated within a dialectical
conception of a process as later steps in the evolution of that process.
Old constructions are conserved. Although their historical role is
reconstructed in the light of subsequent transformations, the old
constructions remain part of the process of dialectic.

Consider a dialectical anaylsis of sex roles. Systematic regularities
have existed throughout history in male and female sex roles. In each
era, the description of regularities in male and female sex roles has led
to abstractions about how women's nature and temperament are
different from men's. Now that certain changes in society have
occurred, for example, overpopulation, phenomena occur more
regularly that are discrepant with traditional sex roles. The abstract
models, as well as social norms and laws that are based upon and
support those models, are coming to be viewed as no longer adequate.
Contradictions or tensions emerge in the system of sex-role regulated
behavior, including demands for political, social, and economic
equality of the sexes. These contradictions will be resolved only as
new, more developed, conceptions of maleness and femaleness
emerge that are consistent with a greater range of male and female
activities, and with equality between the sexes.

The bases of equilibrium in the way of thinking illustrated in the
previous paragraph are: (1) the assumption that change is what is most
fundamental; and (2) the ability to conceptualize changes as contradictions within existing systems and as formations of new, more
inclusive systems. The nature of maleness and femaleness is not
viewed as fundamental; it is seen as likely to change through history.
At any point in time, it may be useful to conceptualize the regularities
in male and female roles, but these conceptualizations are meaningful
as part of a historical process in which they will be challenged and
transcended. A closed-system model of sex-role behavior that claims
that it derives from fundamental immutable laws of male and female
temperament must necessarily ignore or attempt to suppress what
begin as anomalies and later become new patterns of behavior by
males and females. This must be done if the equilibrium of the system
is to be maintained[4] or, in this example, if maleness is to continue to
be recognized as maleness. In contrast, a dialectical model can
incorporate such anomalies and new patterns while maintaining

equilibrium by recognizing them as developments in the continuing dialectic of the relations of the sexes.

The example indicates how dialectical thinking provides a novel type of equilibrium. Such thinking makes it possible to recognize and systematically order continuities across a far broader range of potential changes than the equilibrium provided by formal operations. In dialectical thinking, equilibrium is provided by a dialectical model of the nature of radical system transformation over time. Such a model can be used to describe the properties of open systems. Any change, in principle, can be equilibrated if one can create a dialectical analysis in which the process of dialectical change over time is recognized as continuous.

The argument that dialectical thinking describes a postformal cognitive organization is partly based on dialectic, as an organizing principle, building upon the concept of system, the organizing principle of formal operations. Dialectic also has greater complexity since it deals with the changes of systems over time. The argument is also based on the greater equilibrating power of dialectical cognitive organization vis-à-vis formal-operational organization. It is the ability to maintain recognizable continuity in the midst of a broader range of change.

The epistemological importance of dialectical thinking, as a necessary advance in equilibration, rests on a general ontological assumption that people will be confronted with anomalous events that do not conform to prior closed-system laws. In the natural sciences, this amounts to the assumption that scientists will have to deal with scientific revolutions (Kuhn, 1970). In the life sciences and social sciences, it amounts to the assumption that the phenomena dealt with are highly susceptible to rapid and radical change that scientists will need to comprehend. In day-to-day life, it amounts to the assumption that for making practical decisions, closed systems, including moral systems, that are constructed on the basis of limited data and from limited perspectives will be inadequate (see Sinnott, Chapter 14, this volume). Confrontations, in science and in life, with phenomena that demand recognition of multiple interacting systems and radical transformation of systems will point out the limits of formal thinking. When this occurs, reflection on the process of one's own thought, described as a dialectic in Piaget's (1952) assimilation-accommodation theory, may provide initial access to a model of dialectic. On the basis of this model, more dialectical forms of reasoning in all domains of knowledge may be constructed.

THE DEVELOPMENT OF DIALECTICAL THINKING

It is reasonable to equate thinking that uses a coordinated set of dialectical schemata with a metasystematic-dialectical form of equilibrium. Data consistent with, though not demonstrative of, this view have been presented. However, the development of a dialectical form of equilibrium must begin with using some of the dialectical schemata. It may well be the case (1) that some of the individual dialectical schemata do not presuppose formal thinking, (2) that others develop as part and parcel of formal thinking, (3) that others emerge as part of a transition from formal to dialectical levels of equilibrium, and (4) that still others reflect the achievement of dialectical equilibrium. Hypotheses about the developmental roles of various dialectical schemata can be generated by looking separately at the thought of three groups of subjects identified in earlier research using their index scores (Basseches, 1978, 1980). These groups include:

I. Subjects for whom the narrow range, lack of frequency, and lack of clarity of expression of dialectical schemata used made it reasonable to infer the absence of an organized structure of dialectical thinking. This group consisted of 10 subjects (6 freshmen, 3 seniors, and 1 faculty member) whose indexes were less than or equal to 30.
II. Subjects who seemed to manifest a partial but conspicuously incomplete coordination of dialectical schemata (who could be called transitional, partially coordinated thinkers). This group consisted of 9 subjects (2 faculty, 4 seniors, and 3 freshmen) whose index scores were greater than 30 but not greater than 50. For all members of this group, there was some cluster of dialectical schemata that plays an important role in dialectical thinking but seemed relatively undeveloped in the subjects' thinking. The particular cluster that was undeveloped was not the same for all subjects in this group. Consequently, three subgroups were defined (IIA, IIB, and IIC), based on which cluster was missing.
III. Subjects who clearly seemed to employ a well-coordinated, wide range of dialectical schemata in their interviews (who could be called dialectical thinkers). This group consisted of 8 subjects (6 faculty, 2 seniors) whose index scores were greater than 50.

Table 10.4 indicates the percentage of each group that clearly manifested each dialectical schema.

GROUP I SUBJECTS

Table 10.4 indicates that all subjects in the sample employed Schema 9, the form-oriented schema for locating an element in the whole of which it is a part. The schema that appeared next most frequently in Group I was Schema 10, for description of a whole in structural, functional, or equilibrational terms, and was used by 60 percent of this group. Schema 10 is also a form-oriented schema, and both Schemata 9 and 10 are probably related to formal-operational thought since they involve the recognition of systems.

Table 10.4. Proportion of Clear Evidence of Schema by Group

Schema	Group III N = 8	Group II N = 9	Group I N = 10	Group IIA N = 3	Group IIB N = 2	Group IIC N = 4
1	1.00	.78	.20	.67	1.00	.75
2	.63	.67	.30	0	1.00	1.00
3	.88	.67	.10	.67	1.00	.50
4	.88	.22	.10	0	.50	.25
5	.63	.22	0	0	1.00	0
6	.88	.89	.30	.67	1.00	1.00
7	.38	.11	0	0	.50	0
8	.38	.11	0	.33	0	0
9	1.00	1.00	1.00	1.00	1.00	1.00
10	1.00	.89	.60	1.00	.50	1.00
11	.63	.56	.10	.67	1.00	.25
12	.88	.56	.30	.33	1.00	.50
13	.13	.11	0	.33	0	0
14	.50	.22	0	0	.50	.25
15	.50	.11	0	0	.50	0
16	1.00	.44	.30	.67	0	.50
17	.75	.33	0	.67	0	.25
18	.63	.11	0	.33	0	0
19	.88	.56	0	1.00	0	.50
20	.75	.44	.10	.33	0	.75
21	.38	0	0	0	0	0
22	.13	0	0	0	0	0
23	.25	.11	0	0	.50	0
24	.38	.11	0	0	.50	0

No other schema was clearly present in the interviews of more than 30 percent of the Group I subjects. Schemata that appeared in 20-30 percent of the subjects were Schema 1, for the unselfconscious thesis-antithesis-synthesis movement in one's own thought; Schema 2, for the affirmation of the primacy of motion; Schema 6, for the affirmation of the practical or active character of knowledge; and Schema 12, for the assertion of the existence of relations. These four schemata may function as early foundations of dialectical thinking and may develop either prior to, concomitant with, or subsequent to the development of formal thought.

Schema 16, for the recognition of contradictions or sources of disequilibrium within a system or between a system and external forces, also appeared in 20–30 percent of the subjects. This schema prima facie appears related to formal thought since it makes reference to the idea of a system. Contradictions are important in both formal and dialectical thought although they play different roles in each. In formal thought, contradictions function as indicators that a particular formal model contains an error. In dialectical thought, they are indicators of opportunities for growth in cognitive, social, or physical systems. Thus, Schema 16 may play an important role at the stage of formal operations, prior to shifting to a different and more central role within dialectical thinking. Schema 16 has three variants: (1) recognition of sources of disequilibrium internal to a system, (2) recognition of limits of scope of equilibrium of a system, and (3) recognition of temporal limits of equilibrium. The first variant is most likely to play a role within formal thinking, while the latter two are tied more closely to dialectical thinking.

GROUP II SUBJECTS

Among Group II subjects, the transitional dialectical thinkers, nearly all the dialectical schemata are evident in at least one interview. But the transition to dialectical thinking seems to be characterized by three quasi-independent clusters of dialectical schemata that appear in different orders in different subjects. The characteristic that Group II subjects share is that one of these three clusters is much less salient than the other two.

In Group IIA, the absent cluster could be termed the advanced critical dialectical schemata. These schemata are most often employed in pointing out the limitations of formalistic analyses. The cluster includes the following schemata: Schema 7, which points out problems with treating as separate entities things that are parts of large processes; Schema 14 and Schema 5, which together show the problem with treating things as stable when they stand in relationships to other things; and Schema 15 and Schema 4, which together show that the meaning of any assertion or object of reflection depends on all of the things to which the object or assertion is related.[5] The cluster also includes Schema 23 and Schema 24, in which Schema 23 directly attacks the assumption on which all formal analyses depend, that general inclusive formal laws are independent from content and can be derived by abstraction and applied to all particulars. Schema 24, multiplication of perspectives, provides an alternative method to abstraction for overcoming the narrowness of analyses that tie particular situations to particular points of view. The subjects who did not use these schemata were called formalist transitional thinkers.

Schema 2, for assertion of the primacy of motion, is an elementary schema, but one that is related to the critical cluster. While Schema 2 was manifested in most of the transitional subjects as well as in some Group I subjects, it was not clearly present in any of the three interviews classified as formalist transitional.

In Group IIB the critical dialectical schemata were well represented. However, the cluster that seemed underrepresented in these interviews contains the advanced constructive dialectical schemata.

This cluster includes the following schemata: Schema 16 and Schema 17 together allow one to model the evolution of systems; Schema 8 makes possible the integration of specific events in system-evolution models. Schema 20, which provides a basis for creating models that comprehend multiple systems and their interactions; and finally, Schema 19 also involves modeling multiple systems in relation to each other but in a framework for evaluative comparison rather than for modeling interaction.

Schema 10 is the more elementary schema on which the cluster of advanced constructive schemata is based. As mentioned earlier, Schema 10 was clearly manifested in 60 percent of the Group II interviews. Although it was clearly present in all of the Group IIA and Group IIC interviews, it was only clear in half of the Group IIB interviews. The Group IIB subjects in which the advanced constructive schemata were underrepresented were called nonformalist transitional thinkers. It is not clear whether formal-operational thinking had never fully developed in Group IIB subjects or whether they had not yet developed methods of integrating thinking about systems with their awareness of the limits of formal analysis. The former hypothesis is perhaps more likely for the subject who did not clearly manifest the basic Schema 10.

In Group IIC, critical and constructive dialectical schemata were about equally well represented. The more basic schemata related to each of these clusters were frequently present, the more advanced ones not. The most striking characteristic of these subjects' interviews was the unwillingness to make value judgments. They also asserted that such judgments could not be made rationally. The two schemata that play a central role in integrating practical (evaluational) reasoning within dialectical thinking were completely absent in Group IIC interviews. These are Schema 18, for relating value to (1) movement in developmental direction and/or (2) stability through developmental movement and Schema 13, for criticism of multiplicity, pluralism, and subjectivism. The term multiplicity is used here, following Perry (1968), to refer to an assumed sphere of subjectivity where subjectivity can not be transcended. The separate-but-equal status of a plurality of alternatives must be affirmed in this sphere. Schema 13, criticizing the assumptions of multiplicity, subjectivism, and pluralism, can be seen as the opposite side of Schema 18 where a nonformalistic mode of evaluation is affirmed. Those interviews in which the cluster of schemata conspicuously absent comprised these two were called value-relativist interviews.

The relationship of these three subgroups can be hypothesized as follows. The concept of development is the keystone of integration in dialectical thinking. This concept integrates connotations of value (development is progress), of motion (development is change), and of form (development is differentiation and integration). In each subgroup, one aspect of development is incompletely elaborated. For the value-relativist, it is value that remains difficult to assert. For the nonformalist, it is form that is not regularly grasped or created. For the formalist, it is transformational motion that is not regularly given attention. The most salient themes in the interviews of these subgroups were as follows. For the nonformalists, the themes were "all is changing" and "all is one". For the formalists, they were "formalizations are limited but we must accept their limits and work within them because that's all we've got." For the value-relativist, they were, "everything is changing, but one can't say its getting anywhere" and "values are relative and their basis is purely subjective."

GROUP III SUBJECTS

In Group III all three clusters of advanced dialectical schemata were well represented. In addition, two schemata appeared in Group III interviews that were not present in any Group I or Group II interviews. These were Schema 21, for description of open self-transforming systems; and the closely related Schema 22, for description of qualitative change of a form as a result of quantitative change within a form. We hypothesize that these schemata represent the most advanced dialectical schemata and are most likely to be indicative of well-coordinated dialectical thinking.

Table 10.5 summarizes the above hypotheses about the developmental roles of various dialectical schemata and the course of development of dialectical thinking.

SUMMARY

Dialectical thinking as described here represents a particular form of organization of thought at the metasystematic level of cognitive organization. The conception proposed here assumes an implicit model in thinkers' minds of dialectic, a process of developmental transformation via constitutive and interactive relationships through which systems evolve and change. This model presupposes an understanding of abstract systems and serves as the basis for a novel form of equilibrium more powerful than that provided by formal operations.

Dialectical thinking has been operationalized by means of the DS framework that identifies 24 component moves in thought that dialectical thinkers tend to make. This operationalization has been the foundation for two studies, one of reasoning about education, the

Table 10.5. Possible Phases in the Development of Dialectical Thinking

Phase I—Early Foundations

Elementary Dialectical Schemata that don't necessarily presuppose formal thinking (Riegel's "dialectical thinking")	Elementary Dialectical Schemata related to formal thinking
Schema 1	Schema 9
Schema 2	Schema 10
Schema 6	Schema 16 (recognition of internal contradictions)
Schema 12	

Phase 2—Intermediate Dialectical Schemata appear

Schema 3
Schema 11
Schema 16 (limits of scope, limits of durability)

Phase 3—Elements of several clusters of advanced Dialectical Schemata appear but some cluster (and its related elementary schemata) remain underrepresented

Cluster	Cluster II	Cluster III
(Schema 2) elementary	Schema 10 (basic)	Schema 13
Schema 4	Schema 16 (basic)	Schema 18
Schema 5	Schema 8	(absent in value-relativist group)
Schema 7	Schema 17	
Schema 14	Schema 19	
Schema 15	Schema 20	
Schema 23	(absent in non-formalist group)	
Schema 24		
(absent in formalist group)		

Phase 4—Elements of all 3 clusters above well represented

Schema 21
and
Schema 22
appear

other of comprehension of dialectical arguments. These have sup- ported the claim that dialectical thinking represents a postformal stage. Other research using the DS framework is still in progress. The schemata also facilitate understanding the relationships of other descriptions of adult cognitive phenomena in this volume to dia- lectical thinking (see Basseches, in press). While these phenomena may reflect particular schemata, or elements of dialectical thinking, dialectical thinking as a whole is equated with the use of a wide range of schemata, organized into a form of equilibrium by a model of dialectic.

NOTES

1. In addition to the studies reported in 1980, the DS framework is also currently being employed in research by Rettig on dichotic listening, Bopp on conceptions of psychotherapy, Weeks on paradoxical therapy, Richards on dialectical thinking and metasystematic reasoning, and Slepitza on DS and the Perry Scheme.

2. From Olsen, Basseches, and Richards (note 19).

3. For these structures to be successfully applicable to analyzing systems that the formal-operational subject encounters, those systems must also be closed. They must contain a finite number of variables, and must not be susceptible to being fundamentally altered by factors outside the system. As other authors in this volume also point out (Sinnott, Koplowitz), the limits of formal-operational thought derive from the fact that the world does not consist of neatly closed systems. Only in special cases can one successfully analyze phenomena as if they were closed systems because in those cases, over the time span to which the analysis pertains, variables outside the phenomena cognized as a closed system have negligible effects.

4. Note the arguments of the Moral Majority here.

5. This includes that from which the object or assertion is distinguished since the relation of negation is reflected in making distinctions. This is the sense in which the law of noncontradiction (A or not A but not both) is rejected in dialectical thinking since the positing of A implies the positing of not-A and vice versa. In other words the figure is distinguished from the ground and the figure is not the ground, but the recognition of figure is dependent on its relation to the ground.

11

POSTFORMAL REASONING: A PHILOSOPHICAL MODEL

Marcia C. Linn and Harvey Siegel

A central problem in the contemporary philosophy of science is that of understanding the nature of conceptual change in science. Several philosophical models of such change have been proposed (Kuhn, 1970; Toulmin, 1972; Hanson, 1961; Lakatos, 1970). In this chapter, Lakatos' model is utilized in an effort to construct a theoretical model of postformal reasoning. The argument presented in this chapter centers on two main points. First, postformal reasoning is differentiated from other reasoning in terms of context, not logic. Second, Lakatos' model of conceptual change is especially useful in studying the development of postformal reasoning. This is because it allows that special attention be paid to the role of context and expectations. Both of these concepts play a central role in the model developed below.

Two distinctions are borrowed from Lakatos' model. One is the distinction between the "protective belt" of ideas and the "hard core" of ideas. The other is the distinction between a "progressing" and a "degenerating" research program. The hard core consists of unquestioned assumptions that are not challengeable by data. The protective belt is differentiated from the hard core in that it consists of ideas that change as often as necessary, responding to data. A scientific research program is a series of theories with the same hard core of ideas and differing protective belts. A progressing research program is a series of theories that predicts novel facts. A degenerating research program does not predict new facts.

In the theoretical model of postformal reasoning proposed below, postformal reasoning and postformal reasoning research are informed by the notion of a progressing research program in two

This chapter was prepared while Siegel was a visiting scholar at University of California, Berkeley. Research there was conducted as part of the Adolescent Reasoning Project with Steven Pulos and Cathy Clement. This material is based upon research supported by the National Science Foundation under NSF Rise No. SED 79-19494. Any opinions, findings and conclusions or recommendations expressed in this publication are those of the authors and do not necessarily reflect the views of the National Science Foundation.

senses. In the first sense, the role of problem context in postformal reasoning requires explanation. The notion of postformal reasoning as a series of progressing research programs offers such an explanation. Although most would agree that context influences reasoning, models of reasoning generally ignore context. Empirical research, described subsequently, illustrates how context influences reasoning. Moreover, Lakatos' theory describes a possible model for this influence.

In the second sense, researchers, such as those contributing to this volume, are collectively following a progressing research program to understand postformal reasoning. In other words, the theory of postformal reasoning is developing. For example, the focus here on context differs from a focus on content-free strategy acquisition following Piaget. The variety of perspectives on postformal reasoning, if jointly pursued, may lead to better understanding of this important developmental period.

This chapter deals with both senses of postformal reasoning as a progressing research program. In considering the first sense, it discusses context influences on reasoning and considers how Lakatos' views could form a model of these context influences. In considering the second sense, the focus here on context is compared with the views of other researchers studying postformal reasoning.

These points are subdivided into five sections:

1. Definitions and perspectives on context in developmental theory.
2. Research evidence for context influences in postformal reasoning.
3. Lakatos' philosophy of conceptual change.
4. A model of postformal reasoning: a progressing research program.
5. Postscript: some alternative perspectives.

DEFINITIONS AND PERSPECTIVES ON CONTEXT IN DEVELOPMENTAL THEORY

Context influences on reasoning are often neglected by developmental theorists, such as Piaget, but are often considered by philosophers of science. Context influences have, however, recently received more serious attention from developmental theorists (see Fischer, 1980; Mishler, 1979). Defining context influences operationally presents difficulties, as Mishler (1979) illustrates. Although context influences have been considered by some theorists in social psychology (see Bates, 1976), they have been ignored by others. Most researchers acknowledge the influence of context but subordinate context to other concerns.

What is meant by context? Context influences on reasoning are influences from the researchers' beliefs and expectations about a problem (see Linn & Swiney, 1981). It is important to note that what is meant here is the cognitive context, as opposed to the environmental or situational context. Expectations are ideas about which variables influence which phenomena. Expectations are an aspect of context. They are not predictions. One can have expectations without making predictions.

An example of context influence comes from an interview about what makes things float. In this interview, the subject remarked that metal sinks and wood floats. When asked what the local ferry boats were made of, the subject replied that they were made of metal. When asked how the ferries could float if they were made of metal, the subject responded, "Well, actually I think ferries are made of wood, not metal" (Smith, note 21). Thus, the subject denied an accurate recollection, since the ferries really are made of metal, to maintain his expectations about what floats and what sinks. The context of these questions about floating and sinking influenced the reasoner's response.

An example (Linn, 1977) more characteristic of adult reasoning concerns responses to observations of a pendulum. In this experiment subjects were asked how the weight of the bob influenced the rate of oscillation of the pendulum's arm. Frequent responses included "Weight slows things down. A heavier bob will cross the center less frequently." These reasoners applied expectations about weight, which are influential in many situations, to the pendulum, where it is not influential. Linn (1977) found that, when confronted with experiments demonstrating that weight does not influence pendulum oscillation, many reasoners discounted the experimental results. Instead, they maintained their beliefs about weight.

Does experience directly determine conceptual change? It is tempting to imagine that conceptual change reflects an incremental accumulation of information. Research suggests that this is not the case. For example, many subjects in the pendulum experiment persisted in their beliefs despite evidence to the contrary. Discontinuous reorganizations of information appear to be required in order to develop more accurate conceptions of scientific phenomena.

Another example comes from research on Predicting Displaced Volume (Linn & Pulos, note 22). In this task, metal cubes of varying weight and size were presented to seventh- through eleventh-grade students. Subjects knew that all the cubes would sink when immersed in water. Over 50 percent of the eleventh graders expected that the weight of a cube, and not its size, determined how much liquid would be displaced when it was immersed in water. Development, for this particular task, consists of coordinating two separate insights. First, the reasoner must overcome the inaccurate belief that weight is important in predicting displaced volume. Secondly, the reasoner must incorporate an accurate belief that the size of the metal cube, and not its weight, is the critical factor in determining how much liquid will be displaced. Development requires not only increased knowledge about predicting displaced volume, but also change in an inaccurate belief about the role of weight.

Context thus appears to have a systematic influence on reasoning. In addition, context influences appear to persist despite contradictory experiences. In both experiments described above, subjects sometimes discounted experiences that demonstrated weight was unrelated to the problem outcome. This is presumably because weight is frequently influential. Context influences how new information is viewed. New information is incorporated into previous beliefs and expectations. This process needs to be represented in developmental theorizing.

Piagetian View of Context

Piaget focused his theory on context-free strategies acquired during the course of development. He did not focus on context influences on reasoning because he believed context influences were idiosyncratic. For example, Piaget (1971) discussed "resistances" due to context and said that the effects of resistances were easy to explain after they had occurred but hard to predict. Thus, Piaget indicated that context influenced reasoning. He did not, however, include these influences in his theoretical formulations because he supposed them to be unsystematic.

It should be noted that when Piaget was confronted with research evidence (see Lovell, 1961) suggesting greater inconsistency in performance on reasoning tasks than his theory predicted, he responded that individuals with expertise for a problem may perform better than those without expertise. Insofar as those with expertise may have a more accurate understanding of the problem's context, Piaget's statement appears to suggest that he anticipated systematic influences of context on reasoning although he did not pursue them.

By emphasizing the context-free strategies that develop during childhood and adolescence, Piaget drew attention away from issues concerning the role of context. As will be discussed later, systematic influences of context on reasoning have recently been identified and now deserve integration into developmental theory.

Several researchers have posited competence-performance distinctions to deal with context influences on context-free strategy usage (see Flavell & Wohlwill, 1969; Stone & Day, 1980). These distinctions assume that context-free strategy development reflects competence and is necessary but not sufficient for performance at a particular level. These researchers assume that performance does not mirror competence because context interferes. In contrast, it is suggested here that strategy development, and so competence, is not context free, but rather interacts with context to produce performance.

Context as Viewed by Philosophers of Science

Philosophers of science such as Kuhn (1970), Hanson (1961), and Lakatos (1970) have focused on how new knowledge is acquired. They note that context influences how reasoners respond to new information. Reasoners may discount or ignore information, as illustrated in the previous pendulum example. They may also undergo discontinuous changes in their expectations, as illustrated in the previous Predicting Displaced Volume example. Similarly, philosophers of science have noted that major advances in scientific understanding reflect sudden incorporation of previously discounted information. As such, they are frequently discontinuous with previous thought. Kuhn referred to such changes as "revolutions."

In characterizing how scientists think about scientific problems, philosophers of science have generally assumed that the context-free strategies of formal reasoning, as defined by Inhelder & Piaget (1958), are acquired by scientists. They assume that all mature scientists use the logic represented by the strategies of formal reasoning rather than some other more sophisticated logic (see Siegel, in press).

We find the views of many philosophers of science, and especially of Lakatos (1970), very relevant to understanding postformal reasoners because these views focus on context influences on reasoning. (Of course, context influences are relevant to understanding reasoning at all stages.)

RESEARCH EVIDENCE FOR CONTEXT INFLUENCES IN POSTFORMAL REASONING

Two types of research reflect context influences on postformal reasoning. One approach identifies alternative conceptions of scientific phenomena. The other focuses on the role of expectations in reasoning about problems from different content domains.

In this section, research specifically focused on context influences on reasoning of those who have achieved formal operations will be considered. Later, when the proposed model of postformal reasoning is discussed, research describing logical influences on reasoning of those who have achieved formal operations will be considered. In contrast to the other chapters in this book, this chapter analyzes postformal reasoning from the point of view of context influences, rather than from the point of view of logical influences. In particular, the focus here is on alternative conceptions of phenomena that reflect context influences. This approach should be distinguished from that taken by many other researchers, who focus on alternative conceptions of phenomena that reflect logical influences.

Alternative Conceptualizations in Reasoning

What are alternative conceptualizations? Reasoners such as mature scientists, who have achieved formal operations, may still hold "alternative conceptualizations" for certain phenomena. Di Sessa (in press), for example, provides evidence that sophisticated scientists often apply what he calls "naive physics" to everyday nontextbook problems. Physicists often have difficulty explaining the forces on a yo-yo when the yo-yo is laid on a table and the string is pulled horizontally. Similarly, physicists and other mature reasoners frequently display naive physics when asked to indicate what happens to the motor of a vacuum cleaner when its air intake valve is blocked. In short, many adult reasoners who have achieved the logic of formal operations nevertheless often have incomplete understanding of problems from physics. This incomplete understanding is reflected in the development of alternative conceptualizations.

Much evidence (see Table 11.1) suggests that adult reasoners continue to deepen their understanding of complex phenomena, such as predicting displaced volume or understanding planetary motion, by developing their alternative conceptualizations. This development occurs subsequent to the development of formal operations. It is this development that must be explained by a theory of postformal reasoning.

In like fashion, conception of postformal reasoning proposed here is contextual, not logical. Indeed, if stages are conceived, following Piaget, as logical structures, then formal operational reasoning is the zenith of stages. There can be no stage of postformal reasoning, if "stage" is understood as "logical structure." This is because the formal-operational stage is as thoroughly and sophisticatedly logical as a stage can be (see Siegel, in press). Thus, it is argued here that insofar as postformal reasoning constitutes a stage at all, it is not logically superior to formal-operational reasoning. Rather, postformal reasoning is reasoning that is, logically speaking, formal-operational, but it is reasoning that is augmented by considerations of context. While all stages may be augmented by context, procedures of augmentation, or procedures of incorporating context, become standardized when formal-operational logic is standardized. Primarily, reasoning is improved by incorporating context influences that make reasoning about phenomena more faithful to the observation of those phenomena. In this way, postformal reasoning may be seen as reasoning that utilizes both sophisticated logic and considerations of context in a systematic and efficient way.

Table 11.1. Representative Misconceptions about Observable Phenomena that Appear to Persist into Adulthood

Domain/Content Area	Example of Misconception	Source of *Study
Displaced volume	The weight of an immersed object influences the amount of liquid displaced.	Linn & Pulos, note 1
Oscillation of the pendulum	The weight of the bob influences the rate of oscillation of the pendulum.	Linn, 1977
Dynamics	Aristotelian notions of force and motion, e.g.:	
	A coin in mid-air has an upward force on it.	Clement, 1979
	Wheels on a coasting bicycle apply a force.	Gilbert, Watts, & Osborne, note 2
	Forces acting on juggler's balls captured at a single height are related to their motion.	Viennot, 1979
	Objects released from a curved path will continue to follow the same curved path on their own.	McCloskey, Carramazza, & Green, 1980
	A falling eraser has constant velocity during the first meter.	Champagne, Klopfer, Solomon, & Cahn, note 3
	Objects on differently shaped metal ramps have equal velocity when they are equal distances from the end of the ramp.	Trowbridge & McDermott, 1980 1981
Heat and temperature	When water, sand, and sugar are each heated, the water gets hotter, but the sand and sugar remain the same temperature.	Barboux, Chomat, Sere, & Tiberghien, 1981; Erikson, 1979.
Electricity	Electricity is a fluid.	Tiberghien & Delacote, 1976
Gravity	The pull of gravity is greater for objects further from the earth's surface.	Driver, 1980
Concepts of earth	The earth is round like a pancake.	Nussbaum & Novak, 1976
Proportional reasoning	A balance beam will balance if two objects are hung such that the difference between their weights equals the difference between their distances (additive rule).	Linn & Pulos, note 4
	Additive rules for mixing larger batches of lemonade and orange juice.	Karplus, Stage, & Pulos, 1980; Noelting, 1980

(continued next page)

Table 11.1 *(continued)*

Domain/Content Area	Example of Misconception	Source of Study
Pulley systems	Adding weight to one pail connected to another by a pulley system will not change the location of the pails.	Gunstone & White, note 5
Combustion	When things burn, they *always* become lighter. (Actually, steel wool gets heavier when burned.)	Norrby, note 6
Particle theory	When a chamber is half evacuated, remaining air is at the bottom of the chamber.	Nussbaum, note 7
Experimental design	Only the variables that prior experience suggests are "important" should be controlled; others can be confounded.	Linn & Swiney, 1981; Linn, Clement, & Pulos, note 8
Probability	Small samples are just as good as large samples to predict an outcome (lack of awareness of sampling error); extreme scores are just as likely to reoccur as mean scores (lack of awareness of regression towards the mean).	Tversky & Kahneman, 1974
Logic	To test a rule, seek confirming rather than disconfirming instances of the rule.	Wason, 1968
	Evaluate relationships using content not logic, e.g., Question: If all cats swim and this is a cat, can it swim? Answer: No, cats cannot swim.	Scribner, 1977; Wason & Johnson-Laird, 1970; Johnson-Laird, Legrenzi, & Legrenzi, 1972; Wason & Shapiro, 1977; Griggs & Cox, in press
	Inclusive relations hold for collections (pines in forests), but not for classes (pines and trees).	Markman, 1973, 1978
Water level	Water in a tilted jar will be parallel to the bottom of the jar.	Inhelder & Piaget, 1973; Linn & Kyllonen, 1981
Circumference	Adding a yard to a cord stretched tightly around the earth would imperceptibly change the tautness of the cord.	Wittgenstein, as reported by Malcolm, 1958

*Study sources available from authors.

In so far as the evidence has been reviewed, no clear indication of a logical Piagetianlike stage of postformal reasoning has been identified. Moreover, such a stage seems impossible since there is no logic more logical than formal-operational logic. Postformal reasoning should therefore, in the view expressed here, be constructed as a contextual, not a logical, phenomenon. This point of view is elaborated following the presentation of the proposed model.

Research suggests that alternative conceptions of many scientific phenomena are widespread and persistent (see Tversky & Kahneman, 1974; Linn, 1977). A wide range of alternative conceptions about scientific phenomena that researchers have documented is shown in Table 11.1. These alternative conceptions reflect inaccurate expectations about problem variables. A model of postformal reasoning needs to clarify how reasoners change from alternative conceptions to more accurate conceptions of scientific phenomena.

Role of Expectations in Reasoning

A study conducted by Linn, Clement, and Pulos (in press) lays the groundwork for clarification of context effects on reasoning. These researchers focused on expectations about problem variables in laboratory and naturalistic tasks. The tasks all had the same logical structure. Experimentation questions required subjects to set up controlled experiments, that is, experiments where one variable was changed and all the others were kept the same.

Linn, Clement, and Pulos (in press) hypothesized that, for the laboratory tasks, such as those studied by Inhelder and Piaget (1958), subjects would expect most of the specified variables to influence the outcome. In contrast, for naturalistic tasks, such as those encountered in everyday life, they hypothesized that subjects would have less uniform expectations about the variables. For example, individuals would disagree about the variables influencing weight loss, success in jogging, or success in fishing. To investigate the role of expectations in reasoning performance, responses to these two types of tasks were contrasted. Linn et al. (in press) found that expectations account for at least 8–12 percent of the variance in performance between laboratory and naturalistic tasks.

All 90 subjects in this study of seventh, ninth, and eleventh graders were able to employ the context-free strategy for controlling variables. In other words, they correctly set up controlled experiments for at least one of the ten tasks that were used. Therefore, they could be thought of as having attained formal operations. These reasoners have acquired a formal-reasoning strategy, and Linn et al. examined how they employed this strategy in a variety of contexts.

The Linn et al. experimental procedure was as follows. They established expectations for the laboratory and naturalistic tasks and

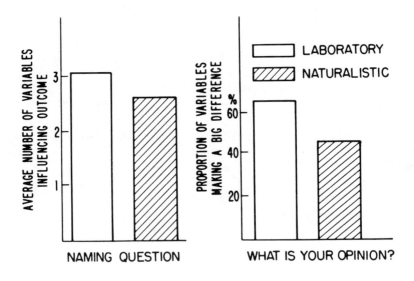

Figure 11.1. Subjects' Expected Variables

then looked at the parallels between differences in expectations and differences in performance on the experimentation questions. Two measures of expectations were used. The first was the Naming Question used by Linn and Swiney (1981). Subjects were asked to name the variables they thought would influence the problem outcome. The second was the "What Is Your Opinion?" survey. In this survey, subjects were asked to indicate how much difference they thought each of the variables in the problem would make.

Results for the two measures of the subjects' expected variables are given in Figure 11.1. For the Naming Question, subjects named more laboratory variables than naturalistic variables. This indicates that they expected more laboratory variables to influence the problem outcomes than naturalistic variables. Similarly, for the "What Is Your Opinion?" survey, subjects indicated that a larger proportion of laboratory variables than naturalistic variables would make a big difference in the problem outcome. Thus, in both cases, subjects expected more laboratory variables than naturalistic variables to influence the problem outcomes.

In the Linn et al. study three experimentation questions were used. These were controlling questions, planning questions, and analyzing questions. Controlling questions, described in Linn and Swiney (1981), requested subjects to set up controlled experiments. For example, subjects were told, "Do an experiment to show that the

thickness of the rod makes a difference in how far the rod bends."
They were then asked, "Why did you do it that way?" Subjects passed
the task if all variables, except the variable under investigation, were
kept constant in two or more trials. Failures were categorized into
two groups based on subjects' explanations. One group consisted of
subjects who declared that the variable was not important and, when
probed, indicated that the uncontrolled variable did not need to be
controlled. The other group consisted of subjects who gave any other
reason, such as pointing out that they had controlled some variables
or had investigated the correct variable.

Planning questions consisted of asking subjects to plan a series of
experiments to investigate all the variables that influenced the
problem outcome. For example, the interviewer said, "Tell me the
experiments that you would do to find out whether each of these
variables on this list make a difference in the problem outcome."
Subjects passed if they conducted one or more controlled experiments.

Analyzing questions measured subjects' ability to criticize an
experiment when shown the result but not told the procedure. For
example, in Bending Rods, two rods painted different colors, made of
different materials, and often of unequal lengths were protruding
from a wooden stand. Hanging equal weights on the rods, the
experimenter demonstrated that the short rod bent more than the
long rod. The experimenter then asked "Is this a good experiment to
prove that short rods bend more than long rods? Why?" and "Do you
have any questions to ask about the experiment?" The length variable
is called the "alleged causal variable" in this problem because the
experimenter alleged that length caused the outcome. Subjects were
not told that the rods differed in material. Subjects passed if they
indicated that the results might reflect some variable that was not
controlled. Responses were categorized into one of two groups. The
first group consisted of statements of a rule for controlling the
variables such as, "Everything else has to be the same." The second
group consisted of indications of a possible confounding element, for
instance, "I don't know if the rods are made of the same material."

The three experimentation questions were analyzed separately.
Context effects were analyzed using a three (age) by three (school) by
two (context) repeated measures ANOVA. In this design, context
(laboratory and natualistic) was the repeated measure. It should be
noted that the schools were from three different socio-economic
areas.

As shown in Figure 11.2, context influenced controlling. Laboratory tasks were solved correctly 85 percent of the time while
naturalistic tasks were solved correctly 65 percent of the time.
Analysis of variance revealed that more than 20 percent of the

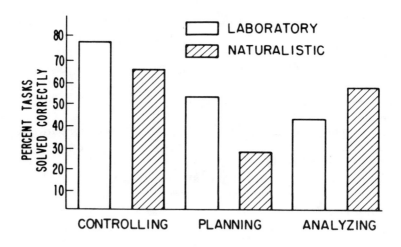

Figure 11.2. Percent Correct on Each Experimentation Question

variance in controlling was accounted for by context. Significant effects for age, which accounted for 2 percent, and school, which accounted for 15 percent of the variance, were also found.

The context effect for controlling can be interpreted in terms of differences in the subjects' expected variables. Since subjects expect more variables to influence laboratory task outcomes than naturalistic ones, they control more variables on laboratory tasks. If subjects controlled their expected variables more often than other variables, they would succeed on laboratory tasks more often than on naturalistic tasks, as found by Linn and Swiney (1981).

Explanations of errors on controlling varied for the two contexts and are consistent with the difference in proportions of expected variables for the two contexts. Unsuccessful subjects were asked why a specific variable in their experiment was not controlled. If this variable was not one of their expected variables, the anticipated explanation would be "I don't think that variable influences the outcome." Consistent with the smaller number of expected variables for naturalistic context, these responses were twice as frequent for naturalistic (10 percent) as for laboratory tasks (5 percent). This difference was statistically significant (t = 2.93, p < .01).

Thus, context effects for controlling reflect differences in subjects' expected variables. That is, subjects controlled more laboratory than naturalistic variables. When they failed naturalistic tasks, they were likely to claim that the variable omitted did not influence the outcome. This is presumably because it was not one of their expected variables.

Planning questions request that the subject plan a series of experiments. As expected, planning is more difficult than controlling, with a 28 percent success rate for naturalistic tasks and 53 percent success rate for laboratory tasks, as shown in Figure 11.2. The analysis of variance verified this finding, demonstrating that 10 percent of the variance was associated with context. There were also significant effects for age, which accounted for 7 percent of the variance, and school, which accounted for 11 percent of the variance. As was the case for the controlling question, the context effects for planning can be interpreted in terms of differences in the number of the subjects' expected variables. If subjects employed their expected variables in responding to the planning question, then they would succeed on laboratory tasks more often than on naturalistic tasks.

As described previously, analyzing questions required subjects to criticize experiments when they were presented an alleged causal variable, but not told whether other variables were controlled. On the average, analyzing is more difficult than controlling, but easier than planning, as shown in Figure 11.2. Analysis of variance showed that context accounted for 8 percent of the variance. Age and school effects were also significant, each accounting for about 5 percent of the variance.

The context effect for analyzing can be interpreted in terms of differences in the subjects' expected variables. Subjects who questioned the alleged causal relationship probably did so because the variable alleged to cause the outcome was not one of their expected variables. The alleged causal relationship is less likely to involve the subjects' expected variables for naturalistic tasks, which have relatively fewer expected variables, than it is for laboratory tasks. In fact, subjects expected alleged causal variables in laboratory tasks to make a "big difference" in the experimental outcome 92 percent of the time, as compared to 49 percent of the time for alleged causal variables in naturalistic tasks. This difference was also statistically significant ($t = 8.68$, $p < .01$).

Thus, the context effects for analyzing questions are consistent with the subjects' expected variables. If subjects expected a variable to influence the experimental outcome, they appeared to be relatively less likely to challenge the result of a possibly uncontrolled experiment than if they did not expect a varible to influence the experimental outcome.

The impact of the subjects' expected variables on questions were verified by examining the reasons given for correct responses to analyzing questions. Two types of correct responses were possible. The first was to question the alleged causal variable by saying, for example, "It may not be the length of the rod like you said, but the material that caused the effect." The second type of response was to cite a rule about controlling, saying "I don't know if all the other possible influences were the same, everything else should be the same." Questioning of the alleged causal variable was almost twice as likely for naturalistic analyzing questions (43 percent) as for laboratory (26 percent) analyzing questions. This difference was statistically significant ($t = 4.3$, $p < .05$). In contrast, for both contexts, citing the rule about controlling was equally likely and infrequent (5 percent of responses). Thus, subjects critically question results more frequently if the alleged causal variable is not one of their expected variables than if it is.

Role of Context in Reasoning

Research demonstrates both the pervasiveness and the systematic nature of context influences on reasoning, which in turn result in alternative conceptions. Numerous alternative conceptions of specific phenomena are held by mature reasoners. Expectations influence reasoning performance in systematic ways.

Philosophers of science, in particular, have grappled with context influences on reasoning. They have suggested that scientists often respond to problems by developing alternative conceptions. Do postformal reasoners respond to problems with their conceptions in the same way? Views from philosophy of science will be considered subsequently, and some possible parallels identified.

LAKATOS' PHILOSOPHY OF CONCEPTUAL CHANGE

Lakatos' (1970) model of conceptual change in the history of science appears especially useful for understanding conceptual change in postformal reasoners. Two concepts from Lakatos' model appear relevant to postformal conceptual change. The first is the distinction between the protective belt and the hard core of ideas. The second is the distinction between a progressing and a degenerating research program.

Hard-core ideas consist of unquestioned assumptions that are not challengeable by data. The protective belt consists of ideas that change as often as necessary in response to data. Scientists, when confronted with data that contradict their viewpoint, change the protective belt so that the hard core can remain unchanged. Thus, Lakatos differentiates the ideas in the hard core, which are immune to data, from ideas in the protective belt, which are responsive to data.

An example of a hard-core idea would be Kepler's idea that the orbit of Mars must be circular. Kepler accepted Aristotle's pronouncement that planets exhibit "perfect motion," which was circular motion. Kepler developed a procedure called the method of area for verifying an orbit. Using this method, Kepler found that his calculations did not conform to observations of the position of Mars. Rather than question the shape of the orbit of Mars, since that was part of his hard core of ideas, Kepler came to doubt his method of area, which was part of his protective belt. In this example, the hard core of ideas influenced how new information was incorporated into a conceptualization.[1]

Applying Lakatos' distinction to postformal reasoners' expectations about scientific phenomena, the hard core of expectations can be distinguished from the protective belt of expectations. Expectations that respond to data and change, when necessary, are part of the protective belt. Expectations that are not challengeable by data form the hard core. When confronted with contradictory data, reasoners alter expectations in their protective belt but not in their hard core.

Simply naming reasoners' expectations in this way, of course, does not lead to a claim to have offered any explanation of reasoning. Nevertheless, it is argued here that the recasting of reasoning behavior in Lakatosian terms will provide a fruitful avenue of inquiry into this area. Ultimately, it is hoped, this will also contribute to an explanation of the phenomenon of postformal reasoning.

Concerning the second distinction mentioned above, Lakatos evaluates "scientific research programs" in terms of whether they are progressing or degenerating. A scientific research program is a series of theories with the same hard core of ideas and differing protective belts. A progressing research program is a series of theories that predicts novel facts while a degenerating research program does not. A progressing research program maintains the hard core by creatively modifying the protective belt. Following a progressing research program requires tenacity in protecting the hard core. When a program fails to predict novel facts, even by creative manipulation of the protective belt, it is degenerating.

Degenerating research programs have inadequate hard cores. They are replaced by new research programs, which are new series of theories attached to new hard cores. When choosing from among competing research programs, according to Lakatos, the rational scientist/person chooses the progressing research program.

If reasoners can be perceived as having research programs, the development of their reasoning can be evaluated by examining the development of their research programs. One can assess how reasoners protect their hard core. One can document the tenacity with which the hard core is defended and the creativity with which the hard core is protected. This kind of protection occurs, we conjecture, when reasoners confronted with anomalies, such as experimental results incompatible with their theories, creatively alter the protective belt. As a result, the anomaly becomes positive evidence for the hard core.

It is hoped that Lakatos' model, borrowed from philosophy of science, will shed light on important questions in postformal reasoning. However, as Siegel (1978, 1979, 1980) has argued, there are important ways in which psychology and philosophy cannot interact. In this regard, the recent work of writers such as Quine (1969) and Toulmin (1977), who argue for the incorporation of psychology into epistemology, is called into question. The point here is not to seek philosophical answers to psychological questions. Rather, the point is that recent work in philosophy of science, especially that of Lakatos, appears to be a useful heuristic device for psychological investigation. It is argued here that Lakatos' characterization of conceptual change in science provides a framework to explore and ultimately to more fully understand postformal reasoning.

Philosophy of science is useful in identifying metaphors that characterize conceptual change. It is especially useful in describing the context-specific research programs characteristic of adulthood. Others have sought guidance from the philosophy of science to identify metaphors for conceptual performance (see Carey, in press; di Sessa, in press). Those seeking a metaphor for performance look to philosophy of science for descriptions of alternative conceptualizations characteristic of those that have occurred in the history of science. Both of these avenues are likely to be as useful in the future as they have been in the past.

It may be useful to reiterate this chapter's appeal to philosophy of science. It is claimed here that the changes that occur during postformal reasoning, from inaccurate conceptions to accurate conceptions, are similar to changes that occur in scientific conceptualizations. Clearly, conceptual change is a crucial part of postformal reasoning. Consequently, models to account for this conceptual change are needed to clarify the postformal period. It has been argued here that Lakatos' model of conceptual change in science, when applied to postformal reasoning, offers the needed clarification.

A MODEL OF POSTFORMAL REASONING: A PROGRESSING RESEARCH PROGRAM

During the postformal-reasoning period some reasoners develop more accurate conceptualizations of scientific phenomena (see Table 11.1). Postformal reasoners overcome inaccurate expectations and context influences and develop more accurate conceptualizations. Those who do not achieve postformal reasoning do not update their conceptualizations.

How do reasoners develop accurate conceptualizations? Lakatos suggests that reasoners whose conceptualizations are developing follow progressing research programs. Those whose conceptualizations are not developing follow degenerating research programs. Ideally, postformal reasoners could be considered to follow progressing research programs within each content domain they conceptualize. Postformal reasoners would protect their hard core tenaciously and creatively. They would respond to anomalies by creatively altering their protective belt and only give up their hard core and adopt a new hard core after exhausting the possible explanations for the anomalies. When a new hard core was adopted, it would be better than the previous hard core at explaining anomalies.

Lakatos' ideas about how context influences reasoning appear relevant to postformal reasoning. So far, empirical results suggest the importance of context. Results also show that context influences decrease with development and that some reasoners overcome inaccurate conceptualizations (see Linn & Pulos, note 23). Research is needed to establish the characteristics of postformal reasoners. Lakatos' ideas offer useful hypotheses for researchers to investigate.

Postformal reasoners are hypothesized to follow progressing research programs for each content domain they conceptualize. Thus, the boundaries among content domains become critical for this discussion. It seems likely that even in the postformal period, reasoners continue to differentiate concepts. For example, just as the differentiation between the concepts of heat and temperature occurs among young children, the differentiation between the concepts of instantaneous and average velocity may occur during the postformal period. Possibly, during postformal reasoning a metaresearch program governs the relationships among content-specific research programs. This question deserves scrutiny, but it has not, as yet, been seriously researched.

By postulating content-specific research programs as characteristic of postformal reasoning, the existence of numerous research programs is assumed. In the view expressed here, each of these research programs is separate in the conceptualizations of the reasoner, and each responds idiosyncratically to environmental influences. As a result, it is postulated that the development of thinking is asynchronous across content domains. This is reminiscent of Piaget's discussion of décalage. Insofar as the reasoner views a particular content domain as having definite limitations, then environmental influences will be limited to that content domain. Thus, asynchronous development among differently perceived content domains is to be expected.

Besides postulating asynchronous development across content-specific research programs, qualitative changes in reasoning during the postformal period are also suggested. These resemble qualitative changes in research programs described by Lakatos. These are changes from degenerating to progressing research programs. But incommensurability among research programs, as suggested by Kuhn (1970), is not postulated here. Rather, it is suggested that new research programs are qualitatively different from the ones they replace, but not incommensurable.

The view of postformal reasoning presented in this chapter focuses on context-specific research programs. This focus accentuates certain questions useful for developmental psychologists. It is suggested that a focus on context-free strategies will also clarify the field's understanding of this stage of reasoning. The context-free strategies of postformal reasoning may be hierarchically more sophisticated than those of formal reasoning, which they also include. For example, postformal reasoning may involve the ability to form third-order relationships. Third-order relationships may be necessary to establish isomorphisms between one context-specific research program and another. Reasoners might construct such isomorphisms in order to develop their research programs but without considering new empirical information.

POSTSCRIPT: SOME ALTERNATIVE PERSPECTIVES

The Role of Context-free Strategies

Piagetian theory focuses on context-free strategies available to formal reasoners. Others extend this notion to postformal reasoning (see Commons, Richards, and Kuhn, 1982; Richards and Commons, Chapter 5, this volume). It is postulated here that the context-free strategies of formal reasoning are related hierarchically to the contextual strategies of postformal reasoning. Postformal reasoning, it is argued here, incorporates the context-free strategies of formal reasoning. As noted previously, even expert reasoners like Albert Einstein use the context-free strategies of formal reasoning, and not a different logic, to solve certain problems (see Siegel, in press, for a discussion of this point). Expert reasoners may also use more complicated strategies than those of formal reasoning. However, it is not necessary for the strategies of formal reasoning to be left behind in order for the more complicated strategies to be employed.

In particular, the more complex strategies indicative of postformal reasoning enable reasoners to consider third-order relationships. Theorists proposing a capacity change between formal and postformal reasoning indicate that postformal reasoners might be able to consider more pieces of information simultaneously (see Pascual-Leone, Chapter 9, this volume; Fischer, Hand, & Russell,

Chapter 3, this volume; Commons & Richards, Chapters 5 and 7, this volume). Several empirical studies support the plausibility of this view. Sternberg (1981; Chapter 4, this volume) demonstrated that sophisticated reasoners could analyze analogies among analogies, an example of third-order relationships. Richards & Commons (Chapter 5, this volume) demonstrated that reasoners could evaluate third-order interactions only after achieving formal operations. Thus, there is some theoretical and empirical justification for the existence of more complex strategies, characteristic of postformal reasoning, which involve the ability to make third-order relationships.

The ability to form third-order relationships would facilitate context-based reasoning by allowing comparison of one view of a particular context with a different view. It would also facilitate identification of isomorphisms between contexts. This ability may be critical to the context-specific research programs characteristic of postformal reasoning. Ultimately, the understanding of postformal reasoning must include comprehension of the interaction between context influences and strategy influences during this period.

NOTES

1. Of course, eventually Kepler gave up this hard-core idea and adopted a new research program with a more accurate hard core. This illustrates how degenerating research programs are replaced, as discussed subsequently.

12

ADOLESCENT AND ADULT THOUGHT: A STRUCTURAL INTERPRETATION
Patricia Kennedy Arlin

About 20 years ago Ann Roe characterized the life of the creative scientist as "a way of life which emerges from a background of absorption in a topic and begins in a state of imaginative, muddled suspense" (1963, p. 177). That state of imaginative, muddled suspense may well characterize the current state of research on structures that differentiate adolescent thought from adult thought. Adolescents and adults appear to reason differently along a number of nontrivial dimensions within the cognitive, social, and moral domains.

The "muddle" has resulted from at least two sources. The first is the conflicting findings that some of these differences between adolescent and adult thought may be better described as regression rather than progression. The second is the difficulties in describing, with precision, the characteristics of adolescent thought that distinguish it from child thought (Keating, 1980; Neimark, 1975a), and from adult thought. The issue of the formal operations controversy illustrates the first point. Neimark (in press) has made an accurate observation in commenting that clarification is needed for a host of relevant questions about how adult cognition copes with the tasks of life. Some of these questions include: "How does one codify experience, assess probabilities, order priorities, or combine these components in planning, problem solving, and decision making?" (p. 13). The answers to these questions are found neither in Inhelder and Piaget's (1958) descriptions of logical thinking, nor are they adequately answered in the judgment and information-processing literatures (Shaklee, 1979; Simon, 1978, 1979).

It is significant that Inhelder and Piaget (1955) titled their work on formal operations *De la logique de l'enfant à la logique de l'Adolescent.* Their purpose was to describe the development of logical thought and to develop a model of that thought up to the point of young adulthood and not beyond. However, there is little reason to believe that no new structures develop in adulthood. There is also little reason to believe that all adult thought represents only a generalization and application of existing strategies, structures, and operations to new categories of problems. There is a need for a work, *De la logique de l'adolescent à la logique de l'adulte*. Current conceptualizations of adult cognition may actually describe forms of intellectual behavior that are a preliminary stage to adult cognitive development (Labouvie-Vief, 1980).

Monnier and Wells (1980) point out that, despite the characterization of formal operations as "the final equilibrium," Inhelder and Piaget (1955, 1958) do not exclude the possibility of the structure of formal operations being included in a larger system. Inhelder and Piaget conclude that:

> ... this general form of equilibrium can be conceived of as final in the sense that it is not modified during the life span of the individual (although it may be integrated into larger systems (polyvalent logics)) ... (p. 332).

This type of integration of a lesser system into a more encompassing system is an example of subsumption. Inhelder (1964) includes the subsumption of less mature, less generalizable structures into new, more generalized forms as one of the major criteria for a stage model of cognitive development. The possibility that there are structural differences between adolescent and adult thought, then, is present within Inhelder and Piaget's original formulation.

Apostel (note 24) speaks directly to the Genevans about the necessity for an extension of their theory to a conceptualization of postformal thought. He believes that after the formal stage has been reached, "the combination of different spaces of possibilities" occurs. It is too costly, according to Apostel, to act on the formal level in the face of most problems presented for solution. The main problem for adult cognition is "how to cut down, how to contract the space of logical possibilities, and how to develop an efficient method for this contraction" (p. 10). Postformal thought makes this contraction occur. The possibility exists that adolescent and adult thought are based on two different logical systems. They represent, in traditional terms, two distinct stages in the development of human intellectual activity. If a hypothetico-deductive logical system defines the structure of adolescent thought, then it is possible that a type of relativistic logical system may best define the structure of adult thought.

The purpose of this chapter is to argue for structural differences between adolescent and adult thought. It is also to suggest that a type of relativistic logical system is required as one possibility for a larger system. It is into that system that Inhelder and Piaget's hypothetico-deductive logic might be integrated. This argument will be developed by showing that the adoption of a relativistic logic as the supporting structure for adult cognition would (1) be consistent with the general Piagetian model; (2) have explanatory power with respect to what appear to be contradictory findings in contrasting adult thinking with adolescent thinking; and (3) provide a framework for research on postformal operations.

CONSISTENCY WITH THE GENERAL PIAGETIAN MODEL

A relativistic logic of the type proposed here would have to parallel, in at least an analogous fashion, the assumptions of the theory of relativity. It would also have to be consistent with the relativistic metatheory of life-span developmental psychology as outlined recently by Sinnott (1981). From this perspective, the strategies and structures associated with postformal thought may interact with each other in what appear to be contradictory ways. From various experimental approaches, they may assume contradictory sets of coordinates depending on one's defined experimental goal. In other words, the assumptions are "in the eye of the beholder," or more aptly, the "observer."

The appearance of logical relativism in the thinking of older adolescents has been identified by a number of researchers. Murphy and Gilligan (1980), for example, emphasized the importance of this logical relativism in Perry's (1968) work. Perry states that the stimulus for cognitive change in young adults is the "recognition of the conceptual relativism of all knowledge which leads to a revolutionary transformation in intellectual and ethical thought" (p. 79). Similarly, Selman and Byrne (1974) emphasize the emergence of logical relativism in the ability to take roles late in adolescence. They identified a stage, occurring late in adolescence or in young adulthood, when a person becomes aware of the relativity of perspectives held by the self and the social group. Moreover, Apostel (note 24), while not specifically using the concept of relativity in his description of postformal thought, nonetheless implies its presence. He speaks of certain cognitive events occurring after the formal stage has been attained. What he thinks occurs is the "combination of different spaces of possibilities." This combination involves two simultaneous movements. He identifies these movements as contractions and expansions. These contractions and expansions "consist in the comparison of different types of universal logical possibilities." These comparisons would involve "the combination, the synthesis of very many INRC groups with each other" (p. 11).

Apostel's conceptualization of the postformal stage implies a type of relativity and flexibility of thought similar to that described by Labouvie-Vief (1980). This type of thought was impossible in earlier stages. In the postformal stage, "contractions" and "expansions" can occur. The postformal thinker can focus on "selected aspects of a problem as the result of applying certain heuristics rather than the universe(s) of possibilities" (Apostel, note 24, p. 10). The postformal thinker can, by this process, "codify experience, assess probabilities, and order priorities" (Neimark, in press) for the sake of efficiency, economy, or sanity.

Postformal thinking, in this view, represents a new freedom in thought. Thought is no longer constrained by adopting a style of problem solving that is characteristic of a particular stage (Blasi and Hoeffel, 1974; Montangero, 1980). Rather, one selects the strategy and style appropriate to the problem, the context(s), and to the problem's assigned priority.

This description is very close to Riegel's (1973) modified model of cognitive development, but there are two notable exceptions. The first is that the present model of postformal thought implies that the requirements of earlier stages be satisfied in a simple, sequential order. Second, it is only at the postformal stage that it becomes a complex sequence model (Riegel, 1973). It is through this model that individuals may not only exhibit competencies and skills in one area that are typical of one set of operations, but also exhibit quite a different set of competencies and skills in another. The choice of competencies and skills is dependent on the person's perception, selection, and/or construction of a particular problem space or spaces and the priority given them. The behaviors observed and the sequences of actions selected are, in this view, the direct result of the choice of the problem solver. By virtue of postformal thought, the problem solver is no longer constrained to choose one course of action or one method of solution.

One can visualize Piaget's stages in the development of hypothetico-deductive logical reasoning as arranged in a simple sequence with the one exception. The exception is that the constraints of a particular problem may require a different approach. One must approach that problem with skills and competencies developed in a previous stage. The stage that one has attained sets limits on maximum performance. It has little to say about minimum performance. At the postformal stage, what changes is the specification of the problem in relative rather than absolute terms. Moreover, a flexibility is introduced with which one can select, from all available operations, competencies, and skills, the subset that best defines the problem. Thus, what appears to be regression on the part of the adult is really progression. The change is from an absolute to relative problem definition. For reasons such as economy, efficiency, or sanity, one finds solutions that are "best fits" (Murphy and Gilligan, 1980). This is to be contrasted to problem definitions that are absolutely determined in the sense of exhausting the universe of possibilities within one system.

It is this type of flexibility and relativism that differentiates the artwork of a Jackson Pollock from that of a young child. Both splash paint on paper. The child does so because he/she is constrained by his/her limited competencies and skills to do so. A Pollock does so because he chooses to out of his universes of possibilities. For him these "splashes" represent a "best fit" with his multivariate perceptions, experiences, and definitions of reality. It is this type of flexibility and relativism that guides the discovery of scientists. Scientists' behavior mimics the first cognitive discoveries of the young child in a manner similar to the artist's mimicking of the young child's art (Gruber, 1973; Karmiloff-Smith & Inhelder, 1974). Sometimes adults choose to use strategies, processes, and techniques that are similar to those used by children. The fact that it is a choice and not a constraint is one way to represent the flexibility of thought that is peculiarly the domain of the adult.

A relativistic logic would make the various descriptions of postformal operations and stages consistent with the Piagetian model. The consolidation and integration of Inhelder and Piaget's (1958) eight formal-operational schemata into the "structure d'ensemble" of formal operations may make the transition to new forms of adult thought possible. One particular scheme, the coordination of two or more systems of reference, may be the pivotal concept that marks the transition between adolescent and adult thought structures. It may represent this transition in the same way that conservation of volume is said to represent the transition between concrete-operational thought and formal thought.

EXPLANATORY POWER IN RESOLVING APPARENTLY CONTRADICTORY FINDINGS

Despite claims to the contrary (Cowan, 1978; Cropper, Meck & Ash, 1977; Fakouri, 1976; Inhelder & Piaget, 1958; Monnier & Wells, 1980), when the hypothetico-deductive model of formal-operational thought is examined closely, it requires that problems be presented to subjects for solution. The model becomes operative in the face of these problems. Possibilities and hypotheses are a part of the Piagetian model, but they are constrained by the nature of the problem presented. Possibilities and hypotheses are initiated in the presence of the classical Piagetian problems, not in their absence. They are constrained within the given system.

How does one break out of that system? How does one coordinate several theoretical viewpoints, several conflicting systems, or several points of reference? How does one formulate, define, frame, or pose new problems that represent radical departures in thought for an individual, for a discipline, or for a society?

The formal-operational scheme by which one coordinates two or more systems of reference represents the simplest requirement for these types of cognitive activity. The coordination of two systems of reference requires distinguishing and combining two types of transformation, cancellation and compensation (Inhelder & Piaget, 1958). Inhelder and Piaget's systems of reference problems involve a direct and an inverse operation. One of the observed systems is always in a relation of compensation or symmetry with respect to the other. The coordination of two systems of reference involves two processes. It involves the decomposition of what is observed into two or more successive systems and the simultaneous reunion of the observed systems into a single whole (Piaget, 1971, ch. 5, 8).

The thought required in the coordination of two systems of reference is relativistic by definition. Compensation always occurs in one system relative to a second system. The Inhelder and Piaget tasks represent the simplest case of coordination of systems or frames of reference. In the Piagetian framework, it appears to be the last formal-operational scheme to appear on the performance level (Arlin, note 25, Neimark, 1975a). These tasks require synthesis and quantification of both the relationships of place, or displacement, and of the intervals in the context of physical, observable objects and events. Advanced forms of these schemata involve the coordination of one plus "n" frames of reference across domains that require increased levels of abstraction.

In summary, the relativity of thought associated with the systems-of-reference scheme appears late in adolescence. A type of relativistic logic is required to think in this way (Murphy & Gilligan, 1980; Perry, 1968; Selman & Byrne, 1974). The adoption of a relativistic logic, in addition to being consistent with the general Piagetian model, can provide a partial explanation of what appear to be contradictory findings in the comparisons of adult thinking with adolescent thinking.

If contractions and expansions are characteristic of relativistic, flexible, postformal thought, two things may result. Various conflicting statements on the nature of adult thought and its application can be reconciled, and the diverse characteristics of that thought can be unified. Many characteristics of adult thought can be categorized as either expansions or contractions. Some of the contractions are in the areas of problem solving, decision making, and the discovery-oriented behaviors of scientists. Each of these "contractions" presents adult performance in less than optimal terms that lead to the inference of regression in adult cognition.

Problem-solving behaviors represent the first contraction. They often require the use of classificatory and serial abilities and skills rather than combinations of all possible values of variables and their relations (Apostel, note 24; Simon, 1978, 1979). This is particularly evident in self-report protocols utilized in the construction of computer program simulations for the solutions of specific problem types (Simon, 1978, 1979). Under these conditions, the problem-solving performance of adults appears less than optimal. However, optimal performance may not be the top priority for the problem-solver relative to other priorities and allocations of time and effort.

Decision making by adults that often is comprised of both faulty logic and simplified representations of reality (Shaklee, 1979; Slovic, Fischoff, & Lichtenstein, 1977) represents a second contraction. Systematic deviations from the principles of formal logic are observed with regularity, but appear to conform to the decisionmaker's own performance criteria. Simon (1957) has termed the pattern of these deviations "bounded rationality." Bounded rationality seems to imply again the notion of "best fit" rather than "perfect fit." This casts the decisionmaker's performance in relative rather than absolute terms. This implies that the decisionmaker's choice of a less than optimal use of formal reasoning is made on the basis of an internal executive program through which priorities have been set and the allocation of mental energy has been predetermined. If such priorities exist, then the nonuse of formal reasoning occurs because of choice rather than inability.

Discovery-oriented behaviors of scientists represent a third contraction. These behaviors often involve overgeneralization in the search for new explanations for phenomena (Karmiloff-Smith and Inhelder, 1974). Overgeneralization can be observed as "the creative simplification of a problem by ignoring some of the complicating factors. . . . Overgeneralization is a means not only to simplify but also to unify" (p. 211). It can represent the themes of both contraction and expansion. While the scientists' behavior mimics that of the children, levels of discovery and levels of meaning may interact. What one brings to the situation may represent the limits of meaning that one can derive from the experience. The child discovers "what is" through overgeneralization. The scientist may discover "what might be."

Some of the expansions that may be associated with the stage of postformal reasoning include problem finding, metasystematic reasoning, dialectic operations and displacement of concepts.

Problem finding, as differentiated from problem solving, represents the ability to raise general questions from many ill-defined problems (Mackworth, 1965). It represents the ability of the adults to ask generative questions of themselves, their life's work, and of the phenomena that surround them. The very nature of these questions requires the coordination of multiple sources and systems of reference. The Piagetian model simply does not account for this type of creative, inventive thought. It is the type of thought alluded to by Wertheimer (1945) when he observes that:

> ... the function of thinking is not just solving an actual problem but discovering, envisaging, going into deeper questions. Often in great discovery the most important thing is that a certain question is found (p. 46).

Mackworth (1965) dismissed simplistic definitions of problem finding that set this process on a continuum with problem solving. He believed that there was "an all-important qualitative difference" between problem finding and problem solving (p. 57).

The argument that elements of problem finding can be found across the various Piagetian stages (Commons, Richards, & Kuhn, 1982) or that they can be derived from formal operations (Fakouri, 1976), and therefore do not require a separate stage, misses an important distinction. Skills, competencies, and concepts associated with particular Piagetian stages are foreshadowed in earlier stages but achieve their most generalized form in the appropriate stage (Inhelder, 1964). In the Piagetian scheme the "whole" of a new stage is always defined as greater than the contributions of the parts of lesser, prerequisite stages.

Pitt (1976) provides a comprehensive model of problem solving that highlights the distinction between problem solving and problem finding in a given problem space. Pitt identifies developmental differences between 15-year-olds and 20-year-olds in their ability to define problems. The 20-year-olds were clearly superior on the processes associated with problem definition in Pitt's model. Developmental differences were not found for the subprocesses of data acquisition or data interpretation.

The subroutines associated with problem definition in Pitt's model relate to the formulation and evaluation of questions and to the generating of hypotheses from these questions. Problem definition seems to require, in the face of uncertain outcomes, that subjects coordinate several possibilities. These possibilities may entail several referential frames. Subjects must then make evaluation judgments with respect to these uncertainties and proceed on the basis of their own judgments toward a solution. In effect, subjects formulate or define the problem themselves before resolving it. Defining problems involves processes akin to Mackworth's definition of problem finding, namely, the raising of many general questions from many ill-defined problems. The argument for a fifth stage is based on this definition of problem finding and on the observations that "general questions" are uncommon in adolescent thought (Arlin, 1975, 1976, 1977, note 25).

Metasystematic reasoning, as opposed to hypothetico-deductive reasoning within one system (Commons, Richards, & Kuhn, 1982, Richards & Commons, Chapter 5, this volume) clearly is an example of expansion. This type of reasoning aptly belongs to any formulation of a postformal stage. It represents a thinker's ability to integrate and coordinate systems or frames of reference within a problem space. It also generates new problem spaces and systems as the result of this coordination and integration.

Dialectic operations are a third type of "expansion" (Basseches, 1979). They are characteristic of the cognitive activity of mature adults (Riegel, 1973). This activity is directed at the creation and tolerant coexistance of inconsistency rather than its removal. Their use in decision making seems to depend on: (1) the type of situation one must decide about; (2) the number of conflicting demands; and (3) the logical ability of the decision-making adult (Sinnott & Guttmann, 1978). These three requirements for the use of dialectic operations assume the coordination of conflicting frames. This is coupled with a willingness to live with a lack of closure that implies a degree of indeterminism. The synthesis that can emerge from the use of dialectic operations is possibly an example of the application of metasystematic reasoning. It is not so much the sense of coexistence of inconsistency, but rather the recognition of the contradictory coordinates that locate the problem within each system of reference.

Displacement of concepts and the use of metaphor as a process of thought are a fourth type of "expansion." Schon (1963) defines the displacement of concepts as the shift of old concepts to new situations. The old concept is taken as a symbol or metaphor for the new situation. The new concept grows out of the process of making, elaborating, and correcting the original metaphor. Displacement serves two functions: the radical function of creating new concepts and the conservative function of retaining the patterns of old concepts. These two functions can be described in terms of contractions (the conservative function) and expansions (the radical function). Displacement involves processes similar to those required for coordinating frames (systems) of reference. Displacement may represent a possible end-product of such coordination.

Boswell (1979) presents some preliminary findings on metaphoric processing in the mature years. Older persons "evidence a synthesizing, integrative perspective when asked to produce explanations of metaphors. High school students' explanations are more analytic" (p. 373).

The apparent contractions and expansions associated with adult cognition are grounded in the possibility that a relativistic logical system can be constructed. Through this system, these various contractions and expansions are coordinated into a "structure d'ensemble" of the postformal stage. This construction awaits development and defines a possible framework for research on post-formal thought.

A FRAMEWORK FOR RESEARCH ON
POSTFORMAL THOUGHT

The postformal or fifth stage in cognitive development can encompass the "contractions" represented in some forms of problem solving, decision making, and discovery-oriented behavior. It can encompass as well the "expansions" represented in problem finding, metasystematic reasoning, dialectic operations, and the displacement of concepts. The next step in defining the postformal stage is to establish its relationship to the fourth or formal-operational stage. The argument of "subsumption" has been made with respect to the need for a relativistic logical system that would include the hypothetico-deductive system as a special case. The task remains to establish that the stage of formal operations is a necessary but not sufficient condition for the emergence of the fifth or postformal stage.

This argument was made (Arlin, 1975, 1976, 1977) with respect to one of the "expansions" that might belong to a postformal stage, problem finding. This work started from the simplest observable behavior, namely, samples of "many general questions from many ill-defined problems." This was what Mackworth (1965) defines as the outcome of problem finding. There are other ways one can approach the study of problem finding. Getzels and Csikszentmihalyi (1965, 1976, note 26) and Csikszentmihalyi and Getzels (1970, 1971) define the artists' formulations of problems, that subsequently the artists solve through works of art, as problem finding in art. Throughout these authors' work, one is struck by the complementarity of their descriptions of young artists with themes that represent, in another framework, formal-operational and postformal thought.

Discovered problems in art can be related to a number of observable behaviors. These behaviors are present in the activity of those artists whose work was judged as "original" by artists and nonartists alike. Getzels and Csikszentmihalyi's (1965, 1976, note 26) experimental situation is one in which the young artists are individually presented with an array of objects. From these objects, they are free to select those objects that they will use for a still-life drawing. They then proceed to complete their drawing. The situation and materials are the same for each artist. While there is no time limit, most complete the task in one hour. Some of the variables in performance that seem to differentiate the artist whose work is judged as "original" (the problem finders) from the one whose work is not are listed in Table 12.1. Opposite each variable are listed types of formal and postformal reasoning that can be associated with the problem formulation behaviors identified by Getzels and Csikszent-mihalyi (1965, 1976, note 26). This table provides an example of how these variables might be represented in terms of their cognitive demands and/or cognitive prerequisites. It also shows the dialectical schemata they might employ. The implication is that reasoning in terms of these schemes might be a necessary but not sufficient condition for the particular behavior to occur. This is simply a restatement of the proposed relationship between problem solving (formal operations) and problem finding, which led to the fifth-stage hypothesis (Arlin, 1975).

The Getzels and Csikszentmihalyi's work was recently replicated with 15 young artists who were completing their fifth and final year of university. The artists were then tested with tasks based on the following six schemata: combinations, proportions, probability, correlations, mechanical equilibrium, and frames of reference.[1] They were also administered the original problem-finding task (Arlin, 1975), a displacement-of-concepts task, and the questionnaire (inter-view) used by Getzels and Csikszentmihalyi (1965, 1976, note 26). This questionnaire includes items that can be analyzed from a dialectical perspective if one wishes to employ this framework (Basseches, 1979). This work with artists (which is part of a larger on-going project) is used as an example of how their problem-formulation behaviors can be interpreted in terms of formal and postformal reasoning abilities. The purpose here is to demonstrate the feasibility of using the "contractions" and "expansions" asso-ciated with postformal thought as a research framework.

Consider the performance of two of the artists, both male, whose works were judged the most and the least original. S1, the subject whose work was judged the most original, gave the following response to the question, "Why do you paint, draw, and so forth?":

> Why do I make art? Because I often am shocked by the results and this reaction is interesting because many times I feel that the medium I am using acts as an extension of myself. This leads me to question what exactly it is that I gather within my own entity and my own environment. I question my knowledge, experiences, actions, thoughts and just basically I gather consciously and subcon-sciously—because my eyes and hands are greedy for texture and images.

This questioning, probing, and exploring as expressed by S1 is precisely the definition of "the concern for discovery" that Getzels and Csikszentmihalyi identify as essential to problem finding in art.

Table 12.1. "Discovery-oriented Behaviors"* of Artists and Their Proposed Formal and Postformal Cognitive Prerequisites

Discovery-oriented Behavior	Formal Prerequisite	Postformal Prerequisite
Problem Formulation		
Number of objects manipulated	Combinations "Possibilities"	
Exploratory behavior and arrangements	Probabilities Combinations	
Openness of Problem Structure		
Change of arrangements and substitutions	Probabilities	Metasystematic reasoning Dialectic operations
Change in problem structure and content, perspective and relative magnitude	Proportions Two or more systems of reference.	Relativistic logic
Quantification of Concern for Problem Finding		
Concern for problem finding in general . . . seeking for meaning		Problem finding Relativistic logic Dialectic operations Relativistic logic
Concern for problem finding at the problem solving stage		Dialectic operations Fischer et al.'s levels 7 to 9

*Based directly on the work of Getzels & Csikszentmihalyi (1976).

Artists formulate problems for themselves that are only partially resolved in doing art. When one uses Basseches' dialectical schemata, one finds an example of the highest-order schemata in S1's response. S1's response is filled with metaphoric expressions. These expressions are consistent with the work of Schon (1963) and Boswell (1979). They provide further evidence of postformal reasoning.

The second subject, the subject whose work was judged as one of the least original, gave this response:

> My art is part of myself—awareness and self-concept. Without it I would not be me. I cannot pin-point when or what first made me want to do art but I always have, one way or another, because it always has been one "purpose" of mine. You do what makes you feel good or what seems right for you.

S2's response provides little evidence of postformal reasoning. No higher-level dialectic scheme can be identified. There are no instances of metaphoric reasoning or the displacement of concepts. The "concern for discovery" is not expressed. Art is doing and being for S2. It is questioning and extending for S1.

A second question that differentiated the problem finders from the non-problem finders in Getzels and Csikszentmihalyi's study was the question, "Could any of the elements in your drawing be eliminated or altered without destroying its character?" To this question the first subject responded: "Sure, there are many ways to arrange a composition, eliminating some elements may destroy the character at present but would create new meaning." The second subject responded, "Once a drawing is finished it is finished and any change will alter the character."

Both subjects gave clear evidence of formal-operational reasoning. The first subject had a more stable performance on the proportional reasoning task and on the coordination of two frames-of-reference tasks. The second subject gave the "correct response" to one of the two frames-of-reference questions. Yet S2 explained his correct response by referring to the experience of "staying in the same spot" on an escalator. He did not correctly respond to the second item. The first subject's problem-finding quality score was 4.66 (the possible range of scores being 0 to 6). He asked a total of six questions. The second subject's score was 2.8. He also asked six questions. The mean score for quality for these 15 art students was 3.5. S1's score was the second highest, and S2's was the second lowest (range = 2.5–5.2). (For a complete discussion of quality scores see Arlin, 1975–1976.) Quality represents the degree to which the subjects' questions approached a "general" or "generic" question (Arlin, 1975, 1975–1976; Mackworth, 1965).

On the displacement-of-concepts task, S1 gave six abstract responses to the first seven questions posed on the task. S2 gave two abstract responses and five concrete. S1's quality score on this task, computed on the basis of item 8 in the same manner as the original problem-finding quality score described above, was 4.75. S2's quality score was 1.7.

One should keep in mind that both did quite well on the formal-operational thinking tasks, but began to diverge along the dimensions associated with postformal thought. In a very descriptive and general way, one can analyze the two subjects' statements as to why they paint in terms of their willingness to "create and tolerate the coexistence of inconsistency." Clearly this is the choice of S1 and is little in evidence in the responses of S2.

These two artists were chosen for the purpose of illustrating the possibility of combining some of the "contractions" and "expansions" of postformal thought in a single exploratory study. They were also used to support the suggestion that the characteristics of postformal thought discussed throughout this book occur together more often than not. They may form a "structure d'ensemble" for the fifth or postformal stage.

There is much work to be done if one is to describe in detail the "structure d'ensemble" of the postformal stage. At present the "state of imaginative, muddled suspense" still prevails. It is possible, however, that the question of the existence of a postformal stage, with its associated logic and operations, is one that will lead to great discovery.

NOTE

1. The complete protocols can be obtained from: Patricia K. Arlin, Department of Educational Psychology, The University of British Columbia, 2075 Wesbrook Place, Vancouver, B.C. V6T 1W5, Canada.

13

A PROJECTION BEYOND
PIAGET'S FORMAL-OPERATIONS STAGE:
A GENERAL SYSTEM STAGE AND
A UNITARY STAGE
Herb Koplowitz

This chapter describes formal operations and two postformal stages, a general system stage and a later unitary stage. The discussion centers on four concepts and how they are structured in formal operations and in each of the postformal stages:

1. Causality: how events are seen as determining aspects of other events.
2. Variables: how objects and forces, and their characteristics, are seen as relating to each other.
3. Boundaries: how the differentiation between two events or two objects is conceived.
4. The permanent object: the conception of self-existing entities in an external world.

I will describe how each of these concepts is structured in formal operations and in each of the postformal stages, and will demonstrate how the structure of concepts affects problem solving in the three stages. The descriptions are illustrated with examples taken from family therapy, physics, and spiritual traditions. I will discuss not only the stages themselves but also the issues of sequence and hierarchy among the stages.

The postformal stages introduced here were primarily derived from writings that exhibit concepts more sophisticated than those of formal operations. The last considerations of this chapter are how these writings are affected by being assimilated into Piagetian theory as well as how Piagetian theory changes by accommodating to their inclusion.

a. Event A as determined by   b. Event A as determined by
the previous event B.   a string of previous events

Figure 13.1. The Linear Concept of Causality

FORMAL OPERATIONS

The Concept of Causality: Linear

The formal-operational concept of causality is a linear one. An event is conceived of as being the result of a previous event as is shown in Figure 13.1(a). The previous event may itself be thought of as resulting from a previous event or string of events, as illustrated in Figure 13.1(b).

This aspect of the formal-operational concept of causality is barely mentioned by Piaget in his classical works on causality (Inhelder & Piaget, 1958; Piaget, 1974), but is of greater interest to students of adult reasoning. Watzlawick, Beavin, and Jackson (1967) refer to the concern of science "with the study of linear, unidirectional, and progressive cause-effect relations" (p. 30). Barry Commoner (quoted in M. Bateson, 1972) and G. Bateson (1972) refer to the inability of adults, scientists, and laymen alike to understand cyclical, patterned phenomena such as interpersonal relationships and a variety of biological processes because they attempt to understand cause-and-effect patterns as linear.

The linearity of the formal-operational concept of causality is also revealed in questions commonly asked about events. "Who started it?" "Whose fault is it?" "How did it begin?" These questions imply a causal chain that has a beginning and while, they are typically not asked by persons in postformal stages of development, they are often asked by formal thinkers. As Watzlawick, Beavin, and Jackson (1967) explain:

> While in linear, progressive chains of causality it is meaningful to speak about the beginning and end of a chain, these terms are meaningless in systems with feedback loops. There is no beginning and no end to a circle. Thinking in terms of such systems forces one to abandon the notion that, say, event *a* comes first and event *b* is determined by *a*'s occurrence, for by the same faulty logic it could be claimed that event *b* precedes *a*, depending on where one arbitrarily chooses to break the continuity of the circle.

Wood   Iron   Brass

Figure 13.2. The Problem of the Flexibility of Rods (after Inhelder and Piaget, 1958). The rods are made of wood, iron, or brass. Some are two feet long and some are three feet long. Some are one inch thick and some are two inches thick. Equipment is provided to determine which of two given rods will bend more when a standard force is applied to each. *Question:* How would you test to see which are more flexible, the long or the short ones?

The Concept of Variables: Independent

Inhelder and Piaget (1958) describe the strategy of "separation of variables" and the schema "all other things being equal" as being important aspects of formal-operational thinking and problem solving. These constructs are demonstrated by formal-operational approaches to solving problems such as the one posed in Figure 13.2.

A preformal thinker might compare the flexibility of a short, thick, wooden rod with that of a long, thin, iron rod; formal thinkers would compare a short, thin, wooden rod only with a long, thin, wooden rod, a short, thick, wooden rod only with a long, thick, wooden rod, and so on for the iron and brass rods. Formal operations are identified by the systematic testing of various rods differing only in length in order to prove that a longer rod is more flexible than a shorter one, "all other things being equal." Implicit here is a view that length operates independently of all other variables and that one can describe the contribution of length to the flexibility of a rod without knowing anything about the other variables that might affect the rod's flexibility.

The concept of variables as independent is also used by formal-operational thinkers in social contexts. Consider, for example, the concept of blame, as when the low income of a family is blamed on one family member. The implications are that the family's income is the sum of the contributions to it by individual family members and that the contributions of all members, except the blamed one, are deemed satisfactory; the family's problem is conceived of as being an inadequate contribution by the blamed member.

The Concept of Boundary: Closed

In formal operations, events, objects, variables, and the systems to which they belong are thought of as having closed boundaries. The term "closed boundary" is used in two interrelated senses, both of which apply to this situation. In the general system theory literature, a system is said to have a closed boundary if it does not exchange energy or information with its environment (Watzlawick et al., 1967). In addition, the term "closed" can be applied to a boundary that clearly and completely separates what is on its inside from what is on its outside. In set theory, for example, sets have closed boundaries; there is no ambiguity as to whether a given element is a member of a given set.

The closed-boundary concept affects problem solving. In formal-operational thinking, attempts to understand what is contained within a boundary are made by examining only what is inside the boundary without regard for what is on the outside, that is, the context in which the event, object, or variable operates. For example, a person's emotional problems may be examined by exploring intrapsychic processes without regard for the family or work situation that might be causing stress for the individual.

Piaget himself does not draw attention to this aspect of formal-operational thought. This may be because the problems he posed for his subjects tended to be ones that could be solved without examining the problem area's context; this is true, for example, of all the experiments in *The Growth of Logical Thinking from Childhood to Adolescence* (Inhelder and Piaget, 1958). He does, however, mention the congruence of his own theory with general system theory, both of which do not consider organisms to have closed boundaries, and the difference between his theory and other biological and psychological theories that do consider organisms to have closed boundaries (see Piaget, 1971). Watzlawick, Beavin, and Jackson (1967), M. Bateson (1972), G. Bateson (1972), and Watts (1961) have noted the tendency for adults to examine systems from the inside while ignoring their contexts and to consider events, objects, variables, and systems to be surrounded by closed boundaries.

The Concept of the Permanent Object: Existing as Known and Independent of the Knower

A permanent object is a physical entity thought of as existing whether or not it is perceived or known. The concept of a permanent object is developed during the sensory-motor stage, and the Piagetian literature on that stage discusses its development in great detail (Piaget, 1952, 1954). Piaget's books on postsensory-motor development make little reference to the concept, most likely because it is stable from the end of the sensory-motor stage to the end of formal operations. Throughout the development of formal operations, one believes that a permanent object, such as chair, closely resembles one's knowledge of it and that the nature and existence of the object are independent of the knower. The permanent object is the major building block of the formal-operational view of reality.

Sequence and Hierarchy: Formal Operations as a Successor Stage to Concrete Operations

Formal operations are considered to succeed concrete operations for several reasons. First, formal-operational thinking appears later in an individual's development than does concrete-operational thought. Second, a person capable of formal-operational thought is also capable of concrete-operational thought. Someone who can systematically prove that longer rods are more flexible than shorter rods, all other things being equal, would also be able to compare flexibility of short and long rods in a less systematic concrete-operational manner and, indeed, would have done so earlier in his or her life.

In addition, the transition to formal operations follows two trends that are apparent throughout development. First, later concepts are more flexible than earlier ones (Piaget, 1971), that is, they can be usefully applied in a greater variety of situations. Second, earlier cognitive structures are special cases or simplified versions of the structures that replace them (Koplowitz, note 27). The concrete-operational method for comparing rods, however, is more flexible, as example, is valid as long as the rods in question are all of the same material, thickness, cross-sectional area, and so on. The formal-operational method for comparing rods, however, is more flexible as it is valid even when there is more than one variable. The concrete-operational method for comparing rods, then, is a special case of the formal-operational method. The formal-operational method entails two steps: finding two rods that are comparable and making the comparison between them. In the special case where all rods are comparable because they differ only in length, the first step would not be required. The formal-operational method would then be reduced to the concrete-operational method.

Since the formal-operational concepts are more flexible than the concrete-operational concepts, and the concrete-operational concepts are special cases of the formal-operational ones, formal operations are considered a successor stage to concrete operations.

GENERAL SYSTEM CONCEPTS

As the transition to formal operations typically begins early in adolescence, most published writers are well beyond concrete operations. One does, however, find writings in which nonformal-operational concepts can be identified. These authors are not preformal-operational; often they have done scientific research and have demonstrated an understanding of separation and control of variables. However, these authors are critical of some of the approaches used in traditional scientific analysis. Moreover, they use conceptual structures not found in Piaget's studies of formal- or preformal-operational thought.

Many of the authors referred to here identify themselves as advocates of general system theory, an approach to the systematic study of phenomena that is more holistic than classical analytical science and that takes into account the interdependence of parts within a system and the interdependence between a system and its environment (von Bertalanffy, 1968). General system theory has affected thought in such disciplines as business and economics (Emery, 1969), family therapy and politics (Watzlawick et al., 1967), education (Koplowitz, 1976), physics, biology, and ecology (M. Bateson, 1972). Ashby's historical view of science illustrates the distinction between the traditional scientific and the general system theory approach:

> The fact that such a dogma as "vary the factors one at a time" could be accepted for a century, shows that scientists were largely concerned in investigating such systems as allowed this method; for this method is often fundamentally impossible in the complex systems. Not until Sir Ronald Fisher's work in the '20's, with experiments conducted on agricultural soils, did it become clearly recognized that there are complex systems that just do not allow the varying of only one factor at a time—they are so dynamic and interconnected that the alteration of one factor immediately acts as cause to evoke alterations in others (in Watzlawick et al., 1967, p. 124).

It is not only science that has been affected by general system theory but also the thinking of scientists. The transition in science from the classical analytic approach to general system theory must have a parallel transition in the scientist (and in other cognitively developed individuals) from the use of formal-operational concepts to the use of general system concepts. Such a transition is described by Haley (1972), who noted several changes that happen to family therapists when they gain experience:

1. The beginning family therapist focuses on the individual patient while the more experienced therapist focuses on the family as a whole.
2. The beginning therapist sees family therapy and individual therapy as being two different kinds of activity. The experienced therapist sees any kind of therapy as a way of intervening into a family.
3. The beginning therapist believes he or she observes the family itself. The experienced therapist believes he or she observes the family in interaction with him or her. The experienced therapist will say that the family is showing him or her how hostile it is rather than saying that the family is hostile.

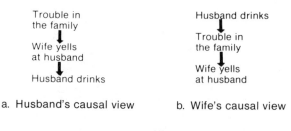

a. Husband's causal view   b. Wife's causal view

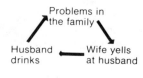

c. Therapist's causal view

Figure 13.3. The Linear and Cyclical Concepts of Causality

Haley's observations can be interpreted in cognitive-developmental terms. The beginning therapist's thinking is formal-operational, treating family members as though they acted independently of each other and the family as though it acted independently of its context. The experienced therapist's thinking, however, uses general system concepts, treating the family as though it acted as a whole in the context of family therapy and in wider contexts. The transition from formal operations to general systems has minor effects on the permanent-object concept and major effects on the other three concepts studied here, as will be shown below.

The Concept of Causality: Cyclical

The general system concept of causality is cyclical. Its differences from the linear formal-operational concept may best be illustrated by means of an example: A formal-operational man may feel that he drinks too much and that the cause of his drinking is his wife's yelling at him; he may feel her yelling is caused by trouble in the family such as the cutting off of the electricity because the bill was not paid or the family's being without transportation because he got into an automobile accident. The husband's view is illustrated in Figure 13.3(a). The wife may feel that she yells at the husband because she is distressed by trouble in the family caused by his drinking, as is shown in Figure 13.3(b). Both husband and wife have linear concepts of causality and both have an answer to the question "How does the problem start?" A family therapist, using general system concepts, will not see the problems as having a starting point, but will see the husband's and wife's problems as being mutually causative in a cyclical manner. The therapist's view is shown in Figure 13.3(c).

This cyclical view of causality is less concrete and more abstract than the linear formal-operational concept. Formal-operational reasoning locates the cause of the difficulties in concrete events: troubles in the family, according to the husband, and the husband's drinking, according to the wife. General system reasoning locates the problem not in any single event but rather in a pattern of interaction in which family members affect each other.

The formal-operational view is contained within the general system view, as is shown in Figure 13.4, and the therapist understands both the husband's and the wife's points of view. Any causal cycle can be broken at any point to produce a linear causal pattern. Any aspect of a system's dynamics is part of a cyclical causal pattern, whether that pattern is a simple pair of mutually causative events (the simplest causal cycle) or a more complex causal network, as shown in Figure 13.5.

The change to cyclical causal patterns is of interest from the point of view of operations, Piaget's term for reversible actions. From a formal-operational point of view, an action is reversed by means of an action in the opposite direction. Thus, the wife yells at the husand because she believes that punishment will get him to stop his irresponsible behavior; the husband drinks alcohol, a pain killer, in order to reduce the pain of his life situation. These attempts to restore order fail, however, as the wife's yelling eventually increases the husband's drinking and his drinking increases the problems in his life which cause him pain. A therapist, on the other hand, may attempt to stop the husband from drinking by instructing him to get drunk every day. This tactic of "prescribing the symptom" (Watzlawick et al., 1967) is especially likely to succeed if the client is rebellious or needs to believe that his problem behavior is under control and that he can decide whether or not to drink. Here, the therapist applies a force in the direction of the problem and away from the desired behavior. By a formal-operational analysis, in-

Figure 13.4. The Linear Concept of Causality Contained in the Cyclical Concept of Causality

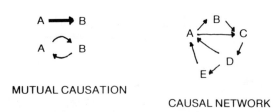

MUTUAL CAUSATION

CAUSAL NETWORK

Figure 13.5. Varieties of General System Concepts of Causality

structing the husband to drink should worsen the problem. This tactic has, however, proved effective when used properly.

The Concept of Variables: Interdependent

The general system thinker conceives of variables as acting interdependently rather than independently as the formal-operational thinker does. This results in a different analysis of any situation in which variables interact. Consider again a family's income, the result of the contributions of the various family members. The formal-operational thinker might analyze the family's income by the following equation:

$I = F + M + D$ where
I is the family's income, say, $31,000,
F is the father's contribution, say, $30,000,
M is the mothers contribution, say, nil, and
D is the daughter's contribution, say $1,000 from a paper route.

According to this analysis, if the mother took a job at a salary of $35,000, the family's income would increase by the same $35,000. A general system thinker, however, would recognize that family members act interdependently, not independently, and that the wife's taking a job may affect the husband's behavior and income. For example, it may spur him on to work harder, thus increasing his contribution, or it may threaten him, leading to decreased self-confidence and contribution. The general system approach would surpass a more sophisticated equation that takes interactions into account, such as

$I = F + M + D + FM + MD + DF + FMD$

(The reader with a background in statistics will recognize this as the model underlying the F-test.) This equation suggests that one can talk of the mother's contribution itself, all other things being equal. When the mother takes a job, a number of aspects of the family change: how much money comes home in the wife's purse, the husband's and daughter's incentives and abilities to work, how much money the family spends, and so on. The whole of this is the mother's contribution to the family's income. One can separate the $35,000 salary from the rest and call it the mother's contribution and call the rest of it contributions to interaction effects. However, there is nothing natural about this separation; the designation of the $35,000 as the mother's contribution is not a fact of nature, but the result of an artificial system of separating the mother's contribution into identified aspects. Also, such a designation is misleading in that it ignores the effects of other family members on the mother's salary; the mother, too, might make more or less if other family members' salaries were different. The only equation to represent the general systems analysis of the family income is:

$$I = FMD$$

That is, the family's income is the result of the interaction of the family members.

The concept of variables as interdependent also sheds a different light on the family in which a member drinks excessively. According to formal-operational reasoning, the husband and wife act independently of each other, so that the husband is seen as causing his behavior and the wife is seen as causing hers, as is shown in Figure 13.6(a). According to the general system concept of interdependence of variables, the husband's drinking is due in part to the wife's yelling and the wife's yelling is due in part to the husband's drinking. Both of them contribute to the action of each, as is shown in Figure 13.6(b), so that one comes to see any action of either as being (husband + wife)'s action being done by (husband and wife), as is shown in Figure 13.6(c). According to general system reasoning, we cannot describe the husband's contribution to the family situation, "all other things being equal," because the husband will make a different contribution depending on how other family members act. The general system concept of variables also excludes the concept of blame; no situation can be seen as the result of any one individual's actions because no action is the result of any single individual.

The concept of interdependence of variables leads to different operations from those resulting from the concept of independence of variables. Piaget and Inhelder consider the operations undertaken by a formal-operational reasoner trying to understand why "a round, thin, steel bar has the same flexibility as a round, thicker, brass bar" of equal length:

> The fact that the first rod is thin compensates for the lesser flexibility of its steel composition. But since these two factors are

a. Formal operational concepts of independence of
variables and closed boundaries

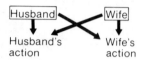

b. Contribution of actors to action

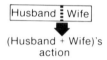

c. General system concepts of interdependence of
variables and open boundaries

Figure 13.6. Formal-operational and General System Concepts of Boundaries and Variables

dissimilar, the subject must first separate out the relevant variables. . . . In both cases the subject must cancel the effect of one of the factors in order to determine the effect of the other. Since the two factors are always present simultaneously, in both cases he must limit himself to holding constant only the factor to be cancelled out (mentally or experimentally). Thus, he actually cancels not the effect itself but rather possible variations in the effect (Inhelder and Piaget, 1958, p. 64).

The effort here, then, is to determine the effect of thinness and the effect of material (steel or brass) on flexibility.[1]

A family therapist using general systems reasoning may vary the behavior of one family member but will not conclude that the changed family situation is the result of just that one variable. If the therapist is successful in changing the behavior of one family member, for example, by getting the husband to stop drinking, the other variables, the behavior of other family members, are changed *ipso facto*. The wife cannot continue her previous behavior by yelling at her husband for drinking too much if he no longer drinks. The therapist will see the intervention as being not a change in one variable (the husband's behavior) but, rather, a change in the entire family system. Operations in general system are made at the level of the system rather than at the level of the variable.

The Concept of Boundaries: Open

The boundaries drawn by general system thinkers are open. The term "open boundary," like "closed boundary," is used in two senses, both of which apply here. An open boundary around a system is one that allows a flow of energy and information between the system and its environment; organisms are said to have open boundaries because they import energy from their environments in the form of food or sunlight (von Bertalanffy, 1968). A boundary is also said to be open if it does not clearly and completely separate what is on its inside from what is on its outside. A general system thinker will not see a clear ending to one event and clear beginning to another; the husband's drinking is seen as an outgrowth of the wife's yelling and both are seen as manifestations of tension within the family. There is no clear boundary between the two people: the husband's drinking is as much as determinant of the wife's behavior as her own history and habits. They are seen to act jointly, as is shown in Figure 13.6(c). No clear boundary separates a system from the environment in which it operates and with which it interchanges energy. A family may consist of a husband, a wife, and two children, but examinations of the family and interventions in it take into account the other relatives, the neighbors, the school, and the work environments that affect the family system. There is no clear distinction between one variable and another. The wife's yelling may be considered part of the husband's behavior if it results directly from his drinking.

Operations, particularly in the area of problem solving, will differ depending on whether one has an open or closed concept of boundaries. With a concept of boundaries as closed, one locates a problem as being inside of an individual and, more particularly, as being inside of the area where the problem is most clearly manifested. Thus, a man's drinking problem would be located inside the man himself. An appropriate treatment, therefore, would be the administration of a drug such as Antabuse, which would prevent him from drinking.

With a concept of boundaries as being open, neither the "problem area" nor the appropriate area for intervention has clear limits. The problem may be solved by changing the man's recreational style, helping him straighten out his finances, helping him set clearer goals for his life, and so on. Or, the problem may be attacked not by intervening directly with the man, but by making an intervention elsewhere in a system of which he is a part. His employer may be convinced to tell him to sober up or look for employment elsewhere. His wife may be shown how to stop taking responsibility for his problems. If the problem area is seen as having an open boundary around it, a range of interventions provides more opportunities to reverse the problem situation.

The Concept of the Permanent Object: Existing Independently of the Knower with Meaning Constructed by the Knower

The general system concept of the permanent object is very like the formal-operational one. The object exists as known independently of the knower and the permanent object is still the major building block of reality. A therapist with a general system concept of the permanent object may not distinguish between a husband's and a wife's actions and may not be clear where the boundary is between the two people, but he or she will be quite sure that the husband and wife exist as objects and will continue existing with or without the therapist's knowing them.

However, the therapist will be aware that the meanings that objects carry are constructed by the knower. For example, although a formal-operational husband and wife may both know a bottle of whiskey as an object, the bottle may signify relief to the husband and disaster to the wife, and each will think of these meanings as being an intrinsic part of the object just as its shape, size, and color are. The wife may wonder how the husband could have the nerve to set on the table such a horrible object as the bottle, and the husband may wonder why the wife objects to the presence of such a beautiful object. An outside observer with a general system concept of an object would understand the feelings of both. Perry (1968) calls this recognition of different frames of reference and different value systems "relativism". He notes that a major aspect of cognitive development is an increase of the areas in which one is able to operate in a relativistic manner.

General System as a Successor Stage to Formal Operations

General system concepts are different enough from formal-operations concepts to locate them in a separate stage. It is appropriate to consider that stage to be a successor to formal operations as it comes later in an individual's development; general system thinkers understand formal-operational concepts while formal-operational thinkers do not understand general system concepts.

I have seen this when teaching general system theory to family therapists who had no previous training in that approach. Before the teaching starts, I give the therapists a case study involving a problem family and ask them to answer questions about the family and also to say how they believe the family members would answer those questions. The therapists' answers have typically been based on a general system conceptualization of the family, while the client's reasoning is typically formal operational. The therapists have reported that they have accurately represented how their clients analyze family problems and that their clients do not initially understand the therapists' (general system) analyses of the problems. A similar set of questions could be used to test whether an individual has developed the general system concepts of cyclical causality, interdependent variables, and open boundaries. One would expect persons who passed the test of general system reasoning to be able also to pass a test of formal-operational reasoning, but not all formal-operational reasoners to be able to pass the general system test.

General system reasoning is more flexible than formal-operational reasoning. General system thinkers are able to solve problems in situations where variables have significant interdependence, where a system's context has impact on the system in a major way, and where one needs to be aware of the effects a recurring event has on the events which cause it. Formal-operational thinkers are unable to solve such problems.

Finally, formal-operational concepts are special cases or simplified versions of general system concepts. As was shown previously, a cyclical causal pattern can be simplified into a linear one by breaking it at any point. Independence is the special case of zero interdependence. Closedness of a boundary is the special case of zero openness; someone who conceives of boundaries as open can reproduce the analysis of someone who conceives of boundaries as closed simply by ignoring the contribution of a system's context.

UNITARY CONCEPTS

Although general system reasoning is more advanced and more flexible than formal-operational reasoning, it has some inherent instabilities in it. As Barry Commoner noted,

> It's hard to explain how to even go about thinking about (holism) without getting caught up in mysticism, yin and yang, the whole oriental business (M. Bateson, 1972, p. 68).

And Hall and Fagen raise

> the natural question of when an object belongs to a system and when it belongs to the environment; for if an object reacts with a system . . . should it not be considered a part of the system? The answer is by no means definite (Watzlawick et al., 1967, p. 121).

If a family is affected by a factory in which one family member works, and that factory is affected by the national economy, and that is affected by the world economy, it becomes impossible to draw a boundary separating the family system from that by which it is not affected. Eventually, it is affected by everything. Thus, the general system reasoner, having dealt with boundaries all throughout life and having made sense of the world using boundaries, is not at all sure of how, where, and, ultimately, whether to draw them.

A similar dilemma arises over the concept of the permanent object. If the actions of the husband cannot be separated from those of the wife, what sense does it make to separate the husband himself from the wife herself? The source of action is not located in something as concrete as a person but in a system, a more abstract entity. And the state of a system results from events that could in some sense be attributed not to individuals' actions but to the system's dynamics, a more abstract notion. Thus, the general system reasoner, having based knowledge and explanations on the concept of the permanent object since the end of the sensory-motor period, comes to dematerialze his or her world view.

The concept of the permanent object becomes even less viable because of developments in physics in this century. The commonsense notion of objects as solids with clean Euclidean shapes was replaced by that of a collection of vibrating molecules with much empty space between them. Molecules are now thought to be made of atoms that were found to be made of subatomic particles that, at first, were conceived of as solid, round, hard matter, the ultimate in permanent objects. But more recent developments in physics, which will be discussed subsequently, lead physicists to think of even the subatomic particles to be more like forcefields or concentrations of energy with ill-defined boundaries whose characteristics, and, perhaps, existence, depend on their being observed and measured.

The difficulties inherent in general system concepts are resolved in the next stage, that of unitary concepts (Koplowitz, note 27). Unitary concepts have advantages over general system concepts as models of thought and for problem solving. Both aspects will be discussed in the following pages. An argument is also presented that a stage of unitary concepts succeeds the general system stage. That argument is primarily a logical one, and no data have been collected to demonstrate that there is a unitary stage that follows a general system stage that follows formal operations. However, it should be possible to devise a test to collect such data.

Thought of a unitary nature is found most often in modern physics, particularly in quantum mechanics, and in the spiritual and mystical traditions. A spiritual tradition is one that holds that the material world in which we live is not the ultimate reality but is derived from something more basic such as consciousness or a universal soul. Mysticism may be defined as "the type of religion which puts the emphasis on immediate awareness of relation with God, on direct and immediate consciousness of the Divine Presence" (Scholem, 1974, p. 4). The writings of and about certain sages and spiritual masters indicate that the shift to unitary thought can affect cognition and problem solving in all areas of one's life.

Quantum mechanics, Pribram and Bohm's holographic model of reality (Bohm, 1980) and Sheldrake's theory of morphogenetic fields (Sheldrake, 1981), offer unitary models of physical reality. Whether scientists who develop unitary models use unitary concepts in all areas of their lives is not clear, but spiritual traditions are probably not the only way of entering the unitary stage completely.

The Concept of Causality: Pervading Space-Time

The unitary concept of causality is radically different from less developed concepts of causality, and this is due to differences between the unitary and preunitary structures of two other concepts: space and time.

In unitary thought, time and space are thought of as part of a four-dimensional space-time continuum rather than as existing independently as one temporal dimension and three spatial dimensions as in general system and previous stages. The division of experience into spatial and temporal dimensions is thought of as an action taken by the knower (like the division of a map into east-west and north-south dimensions) rather than as an intrinsic aspect of reality. This is a fundamental aspect of relativity theory.

Time and space are both seen as constructs, artifacts of the knower's attempt to make sense of his/her experience, rather than as intrinsic aspects of reality. The concept that variables such as space and time are constructs will be explored in more depth later. The most important implication for the concept of causality is that any two events can be considered to be adjacent to each other since any time or space separating them is a construct;[2] therefore, any two events may be considered causally related to each other.

Quite simply, according to Jack Sarfatti (Toben, 1975), "All things are interconnected. Each part of three-dimensional space is connected to every other part."

Sarfatti quotes quantum physicists Bohm and Hiley:

We now find that the relationship between any two particles depends on something going beyond what can be described in terms of these particles alone. Indeed, more generally, this relationship may depend on the quantum states of even larger systems, within which the system in question is contained, ultimately going on to the universe as a whole (pp. 134–35).

The unity and interconnectedness of the universe is a basic tenet not only of quantum mechanics, but also of Taoism:

> Without going outside you may know the whole world. Without looking through the window, you may see the ways of heaven (Lao Tsu, 1972).

One implication for problem solving of this concept of causality is that interventions may be made beyond the limits of what might be considered the system in which the problem occurs. Thus, an incantation in India may produce a change in Switzerland (Rama, 1977), and a ceremony may be performed by a Native American to affect events hundreds of miles away or to bring events from the past into balance (Boyd, 1974). Such causal phenomena have been studied scientifically on a limited scale at the Menninger Foundation (Boyd, 1976) and an excellent discussion of the difficulties inherent in studying them is given by Boyd (1974).

The Concept of Variables: Unity

In preunitary thought, variables such as space, time, and momentum are thought of as existing independently of their being observed. Measurement of a variable is considered akin to noticing: noticing that a particular length is two meters, noticing that a given duration is three minutes, and so on.

According to the unitary view, there is an essential unity among variables. Space, for example, is not considered to exist separate from space-time, and it is only by being measured that a length comes to be two meters and hence comes to exist as a length. Thus, measurement is more a process of construction than one of observation. Variables do not exist separately in reality, but, rather, it is the nature of reality that it allows us the opportunity to construct variables and to separate them from the unity in which they are enmeshed.

In physics one of the strongest statements of this view is the Heisenberg uncertainty principle, which states that:

> The better we know the position, the hazier will its momentum be, and vice versa. We can decide to undertake a precise measurement of either of the two quantities; but then we will have to remain completely ignorant about the other one.... If we decide to measure the particle's position precisely, the particle simply does not have a well-defined momentum, and vice versa (Capra, 1975, p. 158).

That is, the properties that the physicist measures exist only while they are being measured. The velocity of a particle is as much created as it is discovered by the physicist.

In atomic physics, we cannot talk about the properties of an object as such. . . . In the words of Heisenberg, "What we observe is not nature itself, but nature exposed to our method of questioning" (Capra, 1975, p. 140).

The Heisenberg uncertainty principle, therefore, indicates that the physicist is not studying an external world when measuring properties of particles, but, rather, the physicist's interactions with the external world. Relativity theory indicates that measurements of space and time do not yield information about a world external to the observer either. That is, reality is undifferentiated. The process of naming or measuring pulls that which is named out of reality, which itself is not nameable or measurable.

In the Hindu tradition, the concept of variables as constructs appears in the notion of maya, or illusion. According to Tigunit (1981):

"Maya" means "that which makes experience measurable," and from this stage, diversity begins to be created. It draws a veil on consciousness, causing it to forget its real nature, and thus at this stage individuality, limitations, and causations are produced (p. 135).[3]

The concept of variables as constructs leaves day-to-day behavior much the same. The physicist will still make measurements in experiments using instruments constructed by technology rooted in Newtonian physics, and a Swami will still remember his zip code and make use of a spatial address when mailing a letter. The importance of this concept, rather, is that neither the yogi nor the quantum physicist considers the world of space and time to be ultimate reality and both are motivated to achieve better knowledge of that reality, the yogi through meditation and other practices (Rama, 1977) and the physicist through the building and testing of theories in which space, time, and other variables appear as constructs rather than as fundamental aspects of reality (Zukav, 1979).

The Concept of Boundaries: Constructed

The unitary concept of boundaries is that they are constructed by the knower to help in making sense of experience. The universe is conceived of as an undifferentiated mass, and any division of it into one object separated from others, one event separated from others, or one variable separated from others is a division made, not discovered, by the knower. This is a natural extension of the unitary conception of variables as constructs.

This concept of boundaries affects how opposites are conceived of. In the unitary view, goodness and beauty are constructs. They do not exist separated from the rest of the world but are pulled out of the world, separated from it by people who pursue them. They cannot, however, stand on their own. Goodness is good only in contrast to evil, and beauty is beautiful only in contrast to ugliness:

> Under heaven all can see beauty only because there is ugliness. All can know good only because there is evil. Therefore having and not having arise together. Difficult and easy complement each other. (Lao Tsu, 1972).

One cannot draw a boundary around good without at the same time delineating evil. One cannot create a world that is completely good or completely beautiful, because goodness and beauty cannot exist without evil and ugliness.

The Concept of The Permanent Object: Constructed

The unitary concept of the permanent object, like the unitary concept of variables and boundaries, is that objects are constructed by the knower to make sense of perceptual data and that objects are not an aspect of reality waiting, as it were, to be noticed by an observer. This is a difficult notion for most adults to assimilate as they experience objects as existing in a world external to themselves. But Piaget himself noted that the "external world" in which the permanent object exists is itself constructed early in one's development:

> The neonate grasps everything to himself—whereas . . . when language and thought begin, he is for all practical purposes but one element or entity among others in a universe that he has gradually constructed himself, and which, hereafter he will experience as external to himself (Piaget, 1956, p. 9).

In physics, the notion of objects as constructs is apparent in the dual nature of light that in some circumstances behaves as a particle (that is, an object) and in other circumstances behaves as a wave.

> Light behaves like waves or like particles depending on which experiment we perform. . . . The wave-like behavior that we observe . . . is not a property of light, it is a property of our interaction with light. Similarly, the particle-like characteristics that we observe . . . are a property of our *interactions*. . . . Transferring the properties that we usually ascribe to light to our interaction with light deprives light of an independent existence. Without us . . . light does not exist (Zukav, 1979, pp. 94–95).

In unitary thought, unlike in preunitary thought, the permanent object is not the fundamental building block of reality.

Quantum field theory...is premised on the assumption that *physical reality is essentially nonsubstantial.* ... Matter (particles) is simply the momentary manifestations of interacting fields (Zukav, 1979, p. 200).

Matter is also derivative rather than primary in the yogic view of reality:

The material base proposed by the reductionist systems of Western psychology is directly denied in yoga psychology. The causal sequence in yoga psychology *begins* with Consciousness, proceeds through the mind, and then there is the body. The physical structure is the least powerful and the least significant (Nuernberger, note 28, p. 6).

Unitary Concepts as Successors to General System Concepts

The course of development from formal operations to the stage of unitary concepts is charted in Table 13.1. The most radical difference between the unitary stage and previous stages is in the concept of the permanent object.

The separation of the self from its environment and the construction of the accompanying notion that sensory data originated from a world external to the knower constitute the major cognitive work of the sensory-motor period. The bulk of one's cognitive work until the end of the general system stage, including almost all scientific work, is the exploration of the external world one has constructed and of its major building block, the permanent object. The notion of a permanent object in an external world is fundamental to postsensory-motor knowledge; it is only in the stage of unitary concepts that one lives in recognition that that notion is a construct, not an aspect of reality that one has discovered.

Table 13.1. The Structure of Each Concept in Each Stage

Concept	Stage		
	Formal Operations	General System Theory	Unitary
Causation	Linear	Cyclical	Pervades space-time
Relation among variables	Independent	Interdependent	Unity
Boundaries	Closed	Open	Constructed
Permanent objects	Basic	Basic, but meaning is constructed	Constructed

Unitary concepts develop later in one's cognitive growth than do formal operational and general system concepts. Quantum physicists who use unitary concepts are competent in earlier stages of physics structured by formal-operational and general system concepts. Spiritual writers who use unitary concepts may also use formal-operational and general system concepts in their writings. In both cases, those still in the earlier stages do not understand unitary concepts. Studies could be devised to support these assertions.

Unitary concepts are more flexible than general system concepts. This is demonstrated in physics where preunitary concepts proved insufficient to describe quantum phenomena.

Finally, general system concepts are simplified forms of unitary concepts. The causal cycles of general systems are part of the causal networks pervading space-time in the unitary conception of causality. And the interdependent variables of general system are part of the larger unitary picture of "variables + constructor of variables." The interdependent variables with which the general system thinker deals are completely contained within the unitary concept; the general system thinker, unlike the unitary thinker, ignores his or her contribution in constructing the variables. These arguments establish unitary concepts as successors to general system concepts, and, again, testing could support some of them.

IMPLICATIONS

Implications for General System Theory, Quantum Physics, and Spiritual Traditions of Being, Incorporated into Piagetian Theory

General system theory, quantum physics, and spiritual traditions have been used in this chapter to generate models of postformal-operational thought. These disciplines are affected by being assimilated to Piagetian theory, and it is important to examine some of these effects. (For a broader examination of these implications, see Koplowitz, note 27.)

Perhaps the most important implication for the discipline of general system theory is that general system theory becomes not only a guide for building models of phenomena in the natural world but also a way of thinking. The general system theory literature refers to such questions as whether a particular system has a closed or an open boundary and whether a particular element is part of a given system or part of its environment. When general system theory is considered to be a stage in the development of thought, these cease to be questions and become instead points of choice: one chooses to treat a given system as though its boundary were open or closed, and one chooses to consider an element as part of a system or as part of its environment. The formal-operational thinker, on the other hand, will not have this choice, and must consider the boundary closed and will endeavor to discover whether the element is really inside or outside the system.

When general system theory is seen as a model of thought, it is apparent that the advantage of it over the traditional scientific approach is not that it more closely models reality. Rather, the advantage is that general system theory is more flexible and allows one to think about a system in the manner that is most useful for a given purpose.

The extension of Piaget's theory beyond formal operations has implications also for science. If formal operations were the final stage of cognitive development, one might assume that such formal-operational concepts as those that structure traditional scientific thinking also structure reality. By this view, one would also make the common assumption that scientific investigations are essentially explorations about the world yielding information about reality.

But formal operations is not the final stage in cognitive development. Its concepts are not valid in all circumstances, and they are replaced by others that are more flexible. Most important, they do not structure reality. Scientists use statistical tools such as the F-test not because reality has the same underlying structure as the F-test, but because the scientists' thinking does.

Scientists, whatever their stage of cognitive development, are not exploring reality so much as exercising and explicating their concepts. "A theory is primarily a form of insight, that is, a way of looking at the world, and not a form of knowledge of how the world is" (Bohm, 1980, p. 4).

Finally, spiritual tradition and classical science appear different when they are considered as unitary disciplines. They become less mysterious, more understandable, and less in conflict with scientific thought. Spiritual traditions do not reject classical science. Rather, they transcend it as the unitary stage is a transcendence of the formal-operations and general system stages. And classical scientific thought is not a rejection of spiritual approaches, but, rather, their foundation as the formal-operations and general system stages are the foundation of the unitary stage. Putting classical science and spiritual traditions in a cognitive-developmental perspective removes the conflict that is commonly believed to exist between them and highlights, instead, their relatedness.

Implications for Piagetian Theory of Incorporating the General System and Unitary Stages

Piagetian theory also is altered by the addition of two postformal-operational stages. Most obviously, this addition means that the stage of formal operations is not the end point of the development of human cognition. This consideration carries further implications.

Throughout his work, Piaget repeatedly asserted that knowledge is not a copy of reality but, rather, a construction by the knower, and this may be considered the foundation of his epistemology (Koplowitz, note 29). Though Piaget was clear that knowledge is not a copy of reality, he was not explicit about what the relationship is between knowledge and reality, and, in fact, used the formal-operational picture of reality as the standard by which preformal thought was judged. Piaget wrote as though he believed that, whatever reality was, it was something like the formal-operational view of it. But if the concept of knowledge as construct is taken seriously, as it is in unitary thought, then a different relation between reality and knowledge must be assumed:

> We must never say that our knowledge is "true" in the sense that it reflects an ontologically real world. Knowledge neither should nor could have such a function. . . . The fact that some construct has for some time survived experience—or experiments for that matter—means that up to that point it was viable in that it by-passed the constraints that are inherent in the range of experience within which we were operating. But viability does not imply uniqueness, because there may be innumerable other constructs that would have been as viable as the one we created (von Glasserfeld, note 30, pp. 12–14).

And this view carries one final implication. The question to be raised about Piaget's theory and about any extension of it, including the present one, is not whether it is true, but whether it is viable. Any differences among theories described in this volume do not imply that some of the theories must be right and others wrong. Rather, the differences appear because the various authors have operated in different ranges of experience and have chosen different paths through the constraints inherent in those ranges. We are none of us writing about reality, but, rather, about our experiences and the sense we make of it, and our contributions are valuable not for their truth, but for their viability.

NOTES

1. That the variables in the problem posed by Inhelder and Piaget (1958) did operate independently is due to the structure of that problem rather than to properties inherent in the variables themselves. In the situation in Figure 13.7, for example, material and length would operate interdependently. An iron bar long enough to touch the magnet suspended from the ceiling would bend less than a slightly shorter one, but wooden or brass bars would bend more if longer than if short. If this seems a contrived situation, it is no more contrived than the one posed by Inhelder and Piaget. In fact, it is

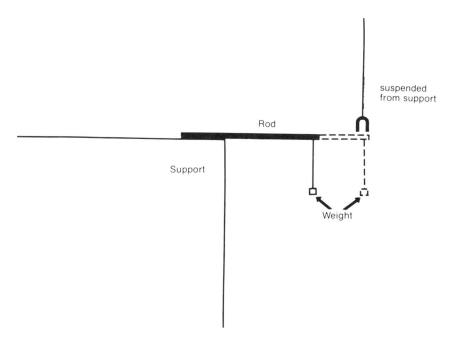

Figure 13.7. A Situation in which Material and Length Interact in Affecting Flexibility

at the heart of the traditional scientific method to devise exactly such situations in which variables can be seen to operate independently of each other.

2. In holographic photography, information about each point of the scene photographed is contained in every point of the negative. There are no spatial relationships within the negative itself, but spatial relationships are constructed by shining laser light through the negative. Bohm (1980) and Pribram suggest that primary reality may be like a holographic negative, with spatial relationships not being inherent in it but constructed by the knower.

3. The mystic does not deny the existence of an external reality. Rather it is the truth of our picture of reality that the mystic denies.

PART IV

MODELS OF
SOCIAL
REASONING

14

POSTFORMAL REASONING:
THE RELATIVISTIC STAGE
Jan Dynda Sinnott

This chapter describes a model of adult postformal cognitive operations that extends the thinking of Piaget and Riegel to describe some intellectual developments that may be unique to adults. Postformal operations as described here permit the adult thinker to operate in a world of relative choices. They also permit the thinker to overcome the fragmentation and isolation inherent in knowing the world through abstract-formal logic. The purposes of this chapter are to:

1. describe the dynamics of understanding or interpreting either relations among people or physical relations that change constantly as a function of being known;
2. discuss how these intellectual operations can be described in terms of relations like those underlying relativity theory in physics (Sinnott, 1981);
3. provide a mechanism to explain how people adapt intellectually to the demands of everyday adult life;
4. describe a postformal cognitive state that relates contradictory systems of formal operations to permit practical choice among systems; and
5. suggest how shared relativistic operations might influence the behavior of individuals in groups.

These goals are not as incompatible as they may initially seem. They all result from asking and attempting to answer simple questions about the nature of knowledge. This chapter explores the nature of adaptive adult intelligence. Like Piaget's work, this chapter suggests that adaptive adult intelligence means assimilating reality in such a way as to survive.

This chapter was completed with the support of a National Institute on Aging (NIH) grant to the author.

How must an adult structure thinking, over and above the operations of the formal-operational adolescent, in order to be in touch with reality and to survive? Two skills seem necessary to an intelligent adult. The first is cognizance of interpersonal and social reality in family, work, and other cultural situations. The second is knowledge of how to apply abstract-formal operations selectively as needed in practical situations (Sinnott, note 31). But is there anything special or complex about the operations that would underlie those interpersonal, social, and practical skills? Are they different from Piaget's concrete or formal operations on physical relations?

There is at least one important difference. It is the concept of necessary subjectivity. Knowledge of physical relations, such as number, volume, conservation, binary relations, and transitivity, are the result of abstractions from action on the physical world. Practically speaking, physical relations are objectively present in reality and are not the creation of the observer. The knower structures physical reality without seriously changing the real physical phenomena. Interpersonal relations, in contrast, are mainly a reflection of how people interact socially and know this interaction. Interpersonal relations seem to change constantly in their reality as a function of their being known or perceived in different ways by different individuals in the relationship.

For example, if a child knows its mother in terms of its own needs, it relates to its mother on those terms. The mother reacts by trying to serve her child's needs. The interpersonal relationship results from both the child's and the mother's understanding. There is a basis in reality here, but cognition of interpersonal relations rests on the ability to make sense of what is being created from moment to moment by two persons. Interpersonal relations and the practical choices that effect them are necessarily partly subjective. Knowledge of interpersonal relations must therefore include operations for understanding necessary subjectivity.

Competent adults must be able to structure various interpersonal realities that they help create. This problem of the influence of "necessary subjectivity" does not intrude into problems like everyday cognition of volume. In order for formal operations and the scientific method to exist, people must eliminate subjectivity. Those analyzing formal operations and logical knowledge of reality through scientific inquiry have traditionally considered subjectivity to be prescientific. However, in contrast to this type of logical knowledge is the adult's knowledge of interpersonal relations. It requires cognitive operations that take necessary subjectivity, and the unavoidable unity of subject and object, into account in structuring knowledge.

Perhaps it is not prescientific to view reality partly as a creation of the knower. There might be both a prescientific form of egocentric knowing and an advanced form of scientific knowing that include necessary subjectivity. This brings one to consider relativity theory and quantum theory physics, both of which underlie the model of postformal operations presented in this chapter. Relativity theory in physics does include some intrinsic operations that incorporate necessary subjectivity and that organize physical relations in a more complex way than do formal operations. Relativity theory reintroduces necessary subjectivity into cognition at a sophisticated level. It accomplishes for physics what Riegel was trying to accomplish for human development. Namely, it closes the subject/object gap in a way that can not only be operationalized, but also be adaptive in allowing a better understanding of reality. The operations unique to relativity theory's structuring of physical reality, going beyond formal operations, suggest the nature of operations that adults might develop. These operations can structure the adult's interpersonal and everyday world efficiently, when concrete or formal operations, which lack a way of explicitly handling necessary subjectivity, prove inadequate for the task (Sinnott, 1981).

In describing postformal operations, then, this chapter addresses initial questions concerning the nature of adaptive adult intelligence. These questions involve the cognition-related demands of adulthood and old age, the operations specific to knowing continuously created reality, and the cognitive operations suggested by modern physics. The argument presented here will suggest that adults must use relativistic operations to organize their complex understanding of interpersonal and everyday reality adaptively.

DEFINITION OF POSTFORMAL OPERATIONS

Postformal operations are defined in this chapter as relativistic operations. They form a stage in a developmental hierarchy of cognitive operations that goes beyond Piagetian formal operations. As such, they construct a system of formal-operational systems, or metatheories. Relativistic operations permit selection of one formal-operational system among many, based on a subjective selection of *a prioris,* or givens. This selection occurs in a situation where several contradictory formal-operational systems could apply. Formal operations presume logical consistency. In contrast, relativistic operations presume subjective selection among logically contradictory formal-operational subsystems, each of which is internally consistent.

FOUR INTELLECTUAL ANCESTORS OF RELATIVISTIC OPERATIONS

The hypothesis of a stage of relativistic operations is influenced by four factors. The first is Piagetian theory, which provides the orderly stage structure for it. Second, Piaget and Riegel describe dynamics of development that are applicable to a relativistic stage. Third, the focus on interpersonal relations content comes from the suggestions of adults themselves. Finally, relativity theory in physics helps provide the basis for the actual operations expected at this advanced stage.

The postformal stage of relativistic operations presupposes Piaget's findings (summarized in Furth, 1969; Piaget and Inhelder, 1969) that the developing child passes through the following stages of cognitive growth at an individual rate in an invariant order: sensorimotor, preoperational, concrete-operational, and formal-operational.

Although both Piaget (1972) and Riegel (1973) describe later stages, those descriptions are fragmentary and not very useful. However, the mechanisms of development that they describe can be applied to adult cognitive development. In Piagetian theory, knowledge is based on the progressive coordination of the individual's own actions on reality (Piaget and Kamii, 1978). The coordinations, or structures, are constructed by the developing individuals themselves during a process in which new experience is assimilated into the present structures. The structures then accommodate themselves to the actuality of the new information (Piaget and Inhelder, 1969). These structures indicate not only what an individual can do with a given situation, either physically or mentally, but also how individuals come to know their world in an adaptive manner. Therefore, Piaget's developmental theory is also a theory of genetic epistemology. That is, it is a theory of ways in which one gradually makes contact with reality. Although Piaget's work focuses mainly on the development of operations for knowing physical reality (Piaget and Kamii, 1978), his theory need not be confined to the understanding of physical relations.

Riegel describes the mechanisms of a dialectical interpretation of human development (1973, 1975a, 1975b, 1976, 1978). His method of analysis applies dialectical logic to behavioral events. Its primary emphasis is on change and activity rather than on stability and permanence. Riegel (1976) emphasizes contradictions and their syntheses in the development either of the individual in society or of society itself. These contradictions are thought to be the impetus behind life-span development, including development in old age (Riegel, 1976).

The dialectical analysis of developmental mechanisms is similar to Piagetian theory in several respects. There is agreement that Piaget's concepts of assimilation and accommodation represent two aspects of a behavioral event that seems to possess dialectical qualities (Youniss, 1974). According to Piagetian theory, a combination or synthesis of these two aspects is present in every act of knowing (Furth, 1969). Both Piagetian and dialectical studies focus on transitions, or dialogues, leading to equilibrations, or syntheses (Piaget and Kamii, 1978; Riegel, 1976; Youniss, 1974). In Piagetian theory, initial noncorrespondence between figurative and operative elements in cognition is the impetus for further cognitive development (Furth, 1969). This is similar to the thesis/antithesis concept in dialectical theory. In the past, Piagetian research focused more on the nature of equilibration, on child development, and on the knowing of physical relationships. In contrast, dialectical theory has focused more on the nature of the transition process, on life-span development, and on development as an historical event. In their separate ways, both Piagetian and dialectical theory seem to have relied on an ongoing history of contradictions and equilibrations to explain the development of the individual's knowledge of the world.

Piaget's and Riegel's dynamic systems can be used to provide a descriptive structure to chart the development of relativistic operations in adults. They can also be used to suggest the dynamics of moving from Piaget's stage 1 to stage 5. However, one must ultimately rely on information processing or skills analysis (see, for example, Fischer, Chapter 3, this volume) to determine how a given individual actually develops to an advanced stage.

Relativity theory is a final intellectual ancestor of relativistic operations. Piaget's analysis of formal-operational thought provides sufficient structure to describe scientific thought up to and including the operations of Newtonian physics. It is insufficient, however, for the description of Einsteinian physics. The intellectual operations used by contemporary physicists can and may be used by other adults in other areas of life. Relativistic operations are a description of how this may be accomplished because they permit sophisticated, necessary subjectivity to be ordered within complex adult thought (see Sinnott, 1981 for an overview of relativity theory and relativistic thought). Table 14.1 outlines some of the characteristics of relativistic operations on the physical world. These characteristics would be difficult to understand within a formal-operational view of physical reality.

Responses of ordinary adults also contribute to the idea of relativistic operations. As part of an ongoing study (Sinnott, note 31), adults are expressing their beliefs concerning both the skills needed at various stages of adulthood and the behaviors that they would consider intelligent at those stages. Most respondents mention interpersonal skills at every stage of adulthood. "Intelligence" in adulthood includes the ability to make relative judgments and to understand and deal with the complexities of interpersonal events. Some of the same themes have also been found in responses solicited by Scheidt and Schaie (1978) and Kramer (note 32).

To summarize, the relativistic stage utilizes the operations of relativity theory to extend the hierarchical stage approach of Piaget.

Table 14.1. Prerelativistic and Relativistic Concepts

Prerelativistic Concept	Relativistic Concept
Space is Euclidean.	Space is non-Euclidean, except in small regions.
Time and space are absolute.	Time and space are relative and are better conceptualized as the space/time interval.
Space is uniform in nature.	Space is composed of lesser and greater resistances.
Events are located topologically on a flat surface.	Events are located topologically on the surface of a sphere.
Undisturbed movement is on a straight line.	Undisturbed movement is on a geodesic, i.e., by the 'laziest' route.
Events are continuous.	Events are discontinuous.
No region of events exists which cannot be known.	Unknowable regions of events exist.
Observed events are stable.	Observed events are in motion, which must be taken into account in the observation.
Formation of scientific postulates proceeds from everyday activity through generalizations based on common sense, to abstractions.	Formation of scientific postulates also includes a stage characterized by resolution of contradictions inherent in the abstractions.
Causality is deterministic.	Causality is probabilistic, except in limited space/time cases.
Cause is antecedent to and contiguous with effect.	Cause is antecedent and contiguous to event only in limiting cases. When events are grouped about a center, that center constitutes a cause.
Egocentrism is replaced by decentration during development of scientific methods.	Egocentrism and decentration are followed by taking the ego into account in all calculations.
Concepts in natural laws conform to verbal conventions.	Concepts in natural laws may appear contradictory in terms of verbal conventions.
Universe is uniform.	Universe is non-uniform—either because it is continually expanding or because it is continually being created and negated.

It also utilizes the dynamics of movement within and between stages that have been described by both Piaget and Riegel. In this stage, the adult develops the complex operations of metasystematic thought, and applies them in an everyday content area. The goal of the present model is to describe this part of what is unique to adaptive adult intelligence and epistemology. Table 14.2 summarizes prerequisites for the development of relativistic thought.

This chapter hypothesizes that postformal operations develop due to demands on the mature knower for dealing effectively with

Table 14.2. Prerequisites for Shift from Formal Thought to Relativistic Thought

---

Ability to structure inherently logical formal systems

Acceptance of validity of more than one logical system pertaining to a given event

Commitment to one set of a *priori* beliefs of many possible sets

Awareness that the same manipulation of the same variable can have varying effects due to temporal and environmental contexts

Awareness that the concept of causal linearity is erroneous when reality is multicausal

Understanding that contradiction, subjectivity, and choice are inherent in all logical, objective observations

Taking into account that contradictory multiple causes and solutions can be equally "correct" in real life within certain limits

Awareness that an outcome state is inseparable from an outcome process-leading-to-state

---

reality. This reality includes interpersonal relations, which have a large component of necessary subjectivity. It is a reality constructed and modified by an individual knower. Adults can use relativistic operations to structure physical, interpersonal, and practical areas of knowing. In short, adults with postformal relativistic operations can act intelligently in complex, everyday situations that require several mutually contradictory systematic logical interpretations. Table 14.3 compares relativistic and formalistic applications for everyday situations.

DEVELOPMENT OF RELATIVISTIC OPERATIONS

Development from sensori-motor operations to relativistic operations in the context of interpersonal relation structures, a knowledge area high in necessary subjectivity, will be discussed briefly below. It may be easier for the layperson to appreciate necessary subjectivity in interpersonal relations than in Einsteinian physics. Understanding interpersonal relations is also a skill salient to successful adult development.

This model is *not* meant to emphasize stable levels. The stages or levels fluctuate and are hierarchical only at acquisition. The dynamics to be described below are as important as the levels, which are merely points frozen in time. Descriptions of hierarchical levels of understanding of interpersonal relations are presented in Table 14.4(a), which will also be explained below. Table 14.4(b) contains examples of levels of understanding for two typical two-person relationships. The thinker is an adult who develops from level to level. New information is first taken in and interpreted, or assimilated, and then joined with other information and structures in a balanced way to reach equilibration.

An interpersonal behavior can be understood only at the knower's level of interpretive complexity, through which it is filtered or assimilated, to use Piagetian terms. As in Piagetian theory (Piaget and Inhelder, 1969), the conflict between aspects of the experience and aspects of the knower's structures would be the impetus for change in the structure and subsequent changes in the mode of future perceptions of the same event. These changes would be described by Piagetian theory as "accommodation" and "structural development," respectively. But changes in the knower's interpersonal structures would have an additional effect not discussed by Piagetian theory. Behavior based on a structure that imperfectly mirrors social reality would appear to lead to changes in the social reality itself. The process would be similar to that of a dialogue, as described by Riegel (1975). Both knower and social reality would change from encounter to encounter.

Stages

What might be the stages of complexity of the interpretive system used by adults to understand interpersonal relations? One hypothesis is that the adult has available five levels of interpretation, the first four of which correspond in very general ways to the Piagetian stages. These five stages are: (I) sensori-motor thought, (II) preoperational thought, (III) concrete-operational thought, (IV) formal-operational thought, and (V) relativistic thought. The fifth stage is added in order to provide a categorization for the type of

Table 14.3. Mundane Applications: Interpersonal Relations

Relativistic

Relations are:
   logical within a set of "givens" that we choose to utilize.
   based on both our past relations to each other and our relations to other significant persons.
   knowing "where you're coming from" and interacting on that level.
   never knowing "YOU" completely, because in knowing you I am necessarily subjectively "creating" you.
   always "in process"; cannot be described as stable until they end.

Formalistic

There is only one way to structure our relationship to reflect reality.
Our relationship exists "out there" in reality.
Our relationship involves only *us*, now.
The relationship has just one "reality"—no need to match levels to understand.
We can know the essence of each other.
Role is more important than process.

Table 14.4(a). Examples of Stages

Interpretive Complexity	Temporarily Equilibrated	
	Parent–child	Peer–Peer
Level I Sensori-motor: Based on need, or gut-level reactions; nonmutual relations.	Parent conceptualizes child as gratifier of needs or as maker of demands.	Peer conceptualizes peer as gratifying needs or giving pain.
Level II Preoperational: Ego-deformed relations; single roles occur; nonmutual relations.	Child seen as extension of parent; his/her actions reflect on the parent's identity.	Peer sees peer as extension of self, and expects total "togetherness" for the relationships to continue.
Level III Concrete operational: Relations are classified; between relations; mutual relations possible.	Child viewed by the parent within a hierarchy of roles.	Peer sees peer as capable of many roles—spouse, friend, worker–in relation to him/her.

306

	Child	Peer
Level IV Formal operational: Logical systems of relations.	Child seen as presently or potentially assuming a complex of interpersonal roles in one given system; parent begins to treat child accordingly; role complex seen as a logically structured whole.	Peer sees peer as embedded in a system of relationships; such system seen as a logically structured whole.
Level V Metatheoretical: Systems of structured systems relativistically applied.	Child seen as presently or potentially embedded in several mutually contradictory systems of roles; child may be attempting to conform to both parents' lifestyle and a contradictory counterculture lifestyle simultaneously, by choice.	Peer seen as presently or potentially embedded in several mutually contradictory interpersonal systems; s/he may be acting on a model of social determinism and rugged individualism simultaneously, by choice, although the two are contradictory in theory.

Table 14.4(b). Strangers Communicating

Person No. 1	Person No. 2
(Actually level 5) "I'm beat! I was up all night with the baby." (*matter-of-fact tone*)	(Hears Person No. 1; focuses on a logical, concrete role. "She looks conservative. She's probably a traditional homemaker type. A mother, not a worker. (I finally met someone here I don't have to impress))")
	"I won't bore you with the details of my project. I envy people like you who can enjoy those tennis courts during the day when they're not crowded." (*patronizing 4*)
(Hears in terms of level 5; can appreciate a lower level; speaks in terms of level 5. "That person thinks women with babies don't work outside the home. I understand the logic, but I have a different approach. Besides being logical, that person is being patronizing. That's a need [level 1]. I need some revenge.")	
"I don't work, I guess, I'm a government research psychologist. Actually, many of my colleagues have children and careers. We sometimes do envy those tennis players, though." (*cool, understanding 5*)	
	("Can this be a dual-career liberal type or is she a crazy housewife who's telling a wild story? [level 4/5, unstable.] I'll say liberal.")
	"You picked a complicated lifestyle. You're for the ERA, right?" (Making logical assumption.) (*tentative, thinking challenged*)
("This person seems to understand that it's possible to be a mother and a worker but wants to put me in a nice consistent liberal box.") Speaks from Level 5 (4).	
"My life does get complicated. I do happen to be for the ERA, but I know a mother with a career who isn't in favor of the amendment because her church disapproves." (*pushing differentiation*)	
	("A liberal mother/scientist and a mother/scientist with some other orientation can differ on this issue due to 'philosophical differences' ".)
	"I guess your view on lots of things depends on your philosophy. So then, let me tell you about my project..."

thought that will result when an adult accommodates logical, formal-operational systems to everyday reality. When this happens, presumably the adult will find that several mutually contradictory realities comfortably co-exist. This stage coincides with the acquisition of concepts of relativity. These five stages are described in more detail below.

Sensori-motor-level interpretation (I) is defined by Piaget as understanding at the level of basic needs and gut-level reactions, without inclusion of a full-fledged symbol system. To extrapolate to social understanding, interpersonal relations at the sensori-motor level might include the relation between the parent as food giver and the child as food taker.

Preoperational-level interpretation (II) is defined by Piaget as understanding at the level at which relationships can be symbolized, yet deformed by the egocentrism inherent in the knower's thought. Egocentrism is used inappropriately, not as a controllable variable. To extrapolate, at this level, a child might perceive a parent as capable of only those relationships that the child currently has with the parent. For example, some of Furth's young respondents comment that a man cannot be both a father and a postman (Furth, Baur, and Smith 1976).

At the concrete-operational level (III), interpersonal relations are defined by Piaget in terms of classes of relations and relations between relations. Types of relations can be subsumed under one another in a hierarchy of relations. To extrapolate, an adult may have several different relationships to a child, for example, parent, physician, friend. However, these are all subsumed under a nurturant relationship that has been further subdivided into nurturant-authoritarian and nurturant-equalitarian types of relationships.

At Piaget's formal-operational level (IV), systems of interpersonal relations are structured in a binary logical system like that employed by persons at the formal-operations level in their understanding of the physical world. To extrapolate, the parent-child relationship might be viewed at this level as part of a set of relationships possible within a nuclear family system.

Finally, at the metatheoretical relativistic level (V), not included in Piagetian theory, an interpersonal relationship might be interpreted as part of any number of equally logical formal systems of relationships, systems that may contradict each other. One might understand a parent-child relationship as a manifestation of several ways of looking at reality, or of two philosophical systems. Although they systematically contradict each other, both may be valid in reality. For example, if the child slaps the parent, the parent may view him/her as a "noble savage" or as a "tabula rasa" who needs the guidance of a concerned adult. The parent's reaction is based on the choice of a formal logical explanation.

Dynamics

One characteristic of the model presented here is that any social or interpersonal behavior can be filtered or encoded in terms of any level of thought. This is similar to the way physical phenomena, in Piagetian theory, can be assimilated to a sensori-motor structure, a concrete-operational structure, or a formal-operational structure. Of course, the information received will be a function of the type of structure receiving it. An interaction can be understood either at, or below, a knower's usual level of interpretive complexity. As Tinbergen (1974) notes, this selective modeling can be adaptive. For example, adults may apply relational structures of a lower level to "match" those of a child with whom they wish to relate.

Incongruity between the knower's interpretation of the relation and the actual complexity of the communicated relation leads gradually to changes in the knower's structures of thought. This is similar to the case in Piagetian theory where the child's interaction with experience leads to changes in the child's simple operations. The next behavior based on the original interpersonal event is different because of the knower's altered thinking about the event. Both the event and the knower's structures determine how the event is interpreted. This will determine the next resulting interpersonal event, which in turn determines the complexity of the next encoded interaction.

It is expected that three dialogues will have taken place. The first will have taken place within the first knower's structures, the second within the second knower's structures, and the third between the structures of the first knower and the second knower. Both participants will have changed, if development goes smoothly, as a function of past organismic states and current experiences. Figure 14.1 includes a dialogue that reflects changes in understanding based on each knower's changing cognitive level, which, in turn, is based on the earlier events in the dialogue.

There are, then, two sources of change in the operations within each adult knower. Both sources of change stem from conflict. First, conflict exists between the potentially applicable structures that the individual brings to an event, and the group or extrinsic consensus of the structure for the social event.

The second possible source of conflict is the high probability that any social relational knowledge is at some point in conflict with some other perceived social relational knowledge. This second source of conflict would come from the necessary subjectivity of social reality, which is in contrast to that of physical reality that only sometimes includes subjectivity. Each interaction would numerically increase the chance for conflict and growth in structures.

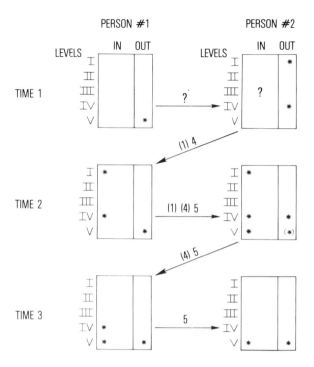

Figure 14.1. Strangers Communicating. Changes in each knower and in the interpersonal event due to conflict generated by the multiple-filter system.

A Preliminary Empirical Test

If interpersonal cognition develops through interpersonal inter-actions and thereby leads to structural growth, two-person dialogues, focusing on interpersonal relations, should contain evidence of this process. For example:

1. Adults should interpret others' statements in light of their prevailing levels of interpretation.
2. Mature adults should demonstrate some high-level elements in their statements.
3. Speakers utilizing different levels of statements should be perceived to be "in conflict" if they do not become more similar in levels over time.
4. Pairs of individuals continuing relationships should be expected to converge at a common level of social-cognitive interpretation.

A preliminary exploration was made to see whether these expecta-tions would hold true (Sinnott, note 33). Content analyses were performed on two-person dialogues recorded from selected dramas. Overall, statements ranged from level I to level V. Of 29 adult speakers, 21 made statements indicating a level V awareness of the relativistic nature of social-relational structures. However, most of their statements indicated lower levels. No conversations were held entirely at only one level of understanding except for some brief exchanges (in three of 25). Seven of the eight persons failing to make a level V statement were young adults in their teens or early twenties. Only two of nine young adults made a level V statement.

In an attempt to see whether each speaker would interpret the statements of the other from his/her own level, the first and second statements of speakers were examined. The result was a bell-shaped distribution with 52 percent of speakers maintaining the same level in their second statement, 15 percent moving up one level, 15 percent moving down one level, and the remaining 18 percent divided at the extremes. From the beginning to the end of the dialogues, on the average, 39 percent of the pairs moved one level closer together in understanding, 39 percent remained at the same comparative distance from one another, and 21 percent moved one level further from one another. These results emerged in the course of the dialogues despite separations of as much as four levels between pairs. Pairs in ongoing relationships in the drama ended their dialogues as close or closer in understanding than when they started. This was not generally true for other pairs.

The data reported above represent only a pretest of the concepts in the proposed model. However, they lead to the preliminary conclusion that complex, relativistic understanding of the structure of social relations may exist and develop through conflict. The preliminary evidence suggests that knowers themselves create the social environment known by others. A long-term association between persons may be related to structure convergence or synthesis.

RELATIVISTIC THOUGHT OF ORDINARY ADULTS

In order to test the assumption that relativistic, postformal operations are present in the thinking of mature adults who are neither physicists nor college students, male and female volunteers in the Baltimore Longitudinal Study of Aging between the ages of 26 and 89 were interviewed (Sinnott, note 24). Table 14.5 gives the age and sex distribution of the participants in this study. A modified clinical method was used in which standard problems were followed by probes to clarify responses.

Table 14.5. Percent of Participants Solving Problem, Age by Sex

Age	Male		Female		Total	
	No.	%	No.	%	No.	%
30–49	14	17.7	12	15.2	26	32.9
50–69	22	27.8	10	12.7	32	40.5
70 or older	15	19.0	6	7.6	21	26.6
Total	51	64.6*	28	35.4*	79	100.0

*Error due to rounding

The focus of the intervews was on problem solving. Six stimulus problems were presented in written form in random order along with the standard probe questions.

The problems were designed to test both formal and relativistic operations. They demanded combinatorial reasoning and proportionality with either two or three variables involved. The problems ranged from totally abstract demands, like making pairs of letters, to fairly realistic scenarios with embedded abstract demands. Respondents were scored on abstract-formal operations, real-life formal operations (as appropriate), and relativistic operations.

SCORING

A subject was considered "abstract-formal operational" on a problem if two conditions were present. The first condition was present if the correct numerical or verbal answer was given to the abstract problem. The second condition was present if a correct description was given of how the answer was obtained. This type of reasoning involved outlining the variables manipulated and the strategy used to maintain proportionality or to make exhaustive combinations. If in doubt concerning whether the subject arrived at the answer without guesswork, the interviewer asked a "distractor" question. This question was one that appeared logical on the surface but that would prompt an incorrect response if formal operations were not present. Doubts about the subject's reasoning would be removed if the distractor question were properly answered.

Since each problem could be read in several ways, a subject might not only pass the abstract-formal demands of a problem, but might also give an alternative formal logical solution. Alternative real-life solutions such as these were scored for formal operations. The subject passed if the variables and strategy were outlined and the correct logical answer in terms of the variables at hand was given.

CRITERIA FOR PRESENCE OF RELATIVISTIC OPERATIONS

In addition to being scored for presence of abstract- or real-life formal operations, the responses were scored for presence of the relativistic operations listed below. The following criteria were used.

1. *Metatheory shift*: There is the production of abstract and practical (real-life) solutions as well as a shift between conflicting abstract and real *a priories*. This shift is stated by the subject. The solution always includes problem definitions. For example, the subject might ask whether we want the hypothetical solution that is logical on paper or the solution that would really be viable. (The respondent may or may not then proceed to give both solutions.)

2. *Problem definition*: There is a statement of the meaning and demands of the problem for the subject. There is also the decision to define problems in a certain, chosen way. The subject indicates a change in the types of parameters from solution to solution. Defining the problem is the first concern, but the subject need not give alternative solutions since these solutions might be precluded by the problem definition. The problem definition may include a metatheory shift. For example, the subject might wonder what the real problem is, whether it is the need to have peace in the family or to use all the space. The subject might then decide to treat it like an algebra problem.

3. *Process/product shift*: There is a description of a process as one answer and an outcome as another answer. Or there may be a description of two processes that achieve the same outcome. Often there is a statement by a subject that there is a solution and that finding the solution is actually a never-ending process. There may be a discussion of process differences in arriving at two different outcomes.

4. *Parameter setting*: The subject names key variables to be combined or made proportional in the problem other than those given in the written demands of the problem. Often the subject explicitly writes out key variables. Alternatively she or he may change the variables that limit the problem from solution 1 to solution 2. Parameter setting differs from problem definition in that it is less inclusive.

5. *Pragmatism*: One can choose a best solution among several, or, one can choose the best variant of a solution that has two processes. For example, the subject might say that if you want the most practical solution, it's number 2, but if you want the quickest, easiest solution, it's number 1. This is the only operation that cannot be given a passing score unless the subject actually gives more than one solution.

6. *Multiple solutions*: There is a direct statement that there are many correct solutions intrinsic to a problem with several causes, or that no problem has only one solution. Also, the subject may create several solutions. For example, the subject might respond that he or she sees four solutions that could be termed correct or there are limitless arrangements that would be correct if you change the constraints.

Table 14.6. Percentage of Respondents Giving Evidence of Postformal Operations, by Problem (N = 79)

Operation Element	Problem Type		
	Bedroom (%)	Work (%)	Alphabet (%)
Metatheory	34.2	21.5	—
Problem definition	92.4	49.4	2.5
Process/product shift	20.2	59.5	26.5
Parameter setting	81.0	45.6	1.3
Pragmatism	73.4	63.3	—
Multiple solutions	38.0	11.4	—
Multiple causality	31.6	49.4	—
Paradox	12.7	—	—

7. *Multiple causality*: There is a statement that multiple causes exist for any event or that some solutions are more probable than others. For example, some subjects state that the solution depends on all past relations of the persons in the problem. As such, when the three persons in the problem get together anything could happen, depending on personalities and on how each reacts.
8. *Paradox*: The subject gives a direct statement or question about perceived, inherently conflicting demands that are integral to the problem, not simply two solutions with different parameters. For example, the Bedroom Problem can be read in two conflicting ways. The subject notices that two different things are being said at once, both of which could change the way the problem should be solved.

Each operation was scored "absent" if there was any doubt about the response. Because of this process of elimination, it is probably safe to assume that some aspects of relativistic thought were more frequent than Table 14.6, which follows, suggests.

RESULTS

Results for only three problems, Bedrom, ABC, and Workers (#2) are reported here. The proportion of subjects passing each problem on an abstract level is displayed in Figure 14.2, by age and sex. The Bedroom problem was the most difficult. The Alphabet problem was easiest; about half the women and 86 percent of the men passed it. Age and gender were not significantly related to performance according to the Chi-square test. Nevertheless, one significant gender effect in favor of men was found on the Alphabet problem ($X^2 = 5.49$, df $= 1$, $p < .02$). Virtually all subjects passed at least one of the formal-operations problems on an abstract level.

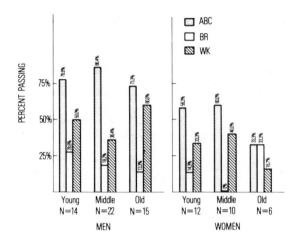

Figure 14.2. Formal Operations as a Function of Problem Content, Age, and Sex

Next, realistic formal-operational solutions were considered. The proportion of adults passing on an abstract level only, on a realistic level only, or on both levels is displayed in Figure 14.3 by problem and age. Results were collapsed across sex after gender-factors were tested and were found to be insignificant. Subjects apparently were "failing" abstract-formal operations on the Bedroom problem because they were reifying the problem. This was verified by an analysis of reasons for failure. Ironically, the one problem that could not be read in many alternative, realistic ways, the Alphabet problem, did not at all motivate adults. The average importance score given to this problem was 2.55 out of a possible 5.00. On the other hand, the problems where respondents ignored abstract demands were considered the most important. The average importance score given to these problems was 4.15. Even though demands for an abstract solution were explicitly made in the Alphabet problem itself, most adults would try out several abstract and real-life formal-operational systems on the problem. Only some of these adults passed. On any problem other than the Alphabet problem, they generally chose a nonabstract solution as being "best" after generating a number of possible logical solutions.

The younger groups passed the Bedroom problem more often than the other groups did ($X^2 = 25.49$, df $= 2$, $p < .001$). Older subjects tended to give two types of formal answers to the same problem more often than younger subjects did.

The most important finding illustrated in Figure 14.3 is that at least some members of *all* adult groups, especially older adults, could be given credit for arriving at more than one formal solution to each of various problems, even using strict criteria for passing. This means that they did shift formal systems effectively in terms of more inclusive operations, as relativistic thought would permit. In other words, ordinary adults did give at least one indication of possessing relativistic operations.

Since relativistic thinking involves more than the ability to solve a problem in two formal logical ways, evidence for other relativistic operations is presented by the problem in Table 14.6. Many respondents showed evidence of utilizing relativistic operations. There were some trends toward subgroup differences. For the Workers problem, younger men tended to give relatively few answers separating demands for "process-leading-to-solution" from demands for "one correct numerical solution" (that is, process-product shifts). More middle-aged men than middle-aged women were able to make a pragmatic commitment and choose a single solution from among several solutions. For the Bedroom problem, younger men were most likely to articulate a shift in *a prioris*. Younger persons and older men seldom mentioned the multiple causality dimension. Men, in general, more often made a pragmatic choice among several alternative solutions. Middle-aged and older men seldom noted the potentially unlimited number of solutions within the solution set. Data were collapsed across age and sex since only trends toward age/sex differences were found.

The definition of relativistic operations demands that the individual make a selection of *a priors* on which to judge the adequacy of a given logical solution. The selection is a multistep process involving the activities described above as the subjective relativistic operations, each of which provides evidence that a metatheoretical selection of

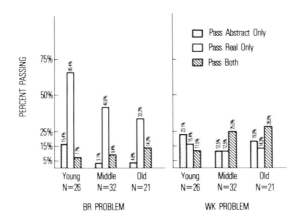

Figure 14.3. Formal Operations under Abstract and Real Constraints

Table 14.7. Activation of Relativistic Operations; Results of Their Use

Three steps might be involved in actually utilizing postformal operations once the potential for their use exists. Four steps might result from their use. The first four steps listed below were evident in the Piagetian problem solving just reported. The last three are hypothesized based on previous observations.

Activation
1. Lack of fit occurs between formal operations and reality (that is, all details cannot be accounted for; formal operation tested not supported by data). A formal-operational subject would not notice the discrepancy but would force the reality into the formal system already present. Postformal subjects would be aware of this discrepancy.
2. Search for a better fit leads to test of new systems built by shifting either a prioris, logics, parameters, transforms, metrics, and so on. Fit may then be perfect, but this is unlikely. More likely, imperfect fit with data still results, and further systems are tried.
3. Realization occurs that fit may be arbitrary, at least for the present, and that system choice must necessarily be subjective for now. Subjective choice of best-fit system occurs.

Results
1. The individual reasons that if *this* choice of formal systems is necessarily partly subjective, perhaps other choices of formal systems are, too. The individual reevaluates other formal systems already in use.
2. Several persons together judge the "best-fit" system in a case where no system completely fits a reality that involves them all and is seen somewhat differently by each. Group explorations concerning system choice lead to a consensus on the formal system to utilize in a given case. Necessary subjectivity leads to a collective cognition.
3. Shared invariants—agreed upon metrics, logics, a prioris, parameters, and so on—persist beyond an individual or a group. (Such shared referents may become a dominant philosophy or culture or belief if the necessary subjectivity or arbitrariness of the system choice is forgotten.) If the fit is still not perfect, this eventually becomes apparent. Alternative, logically competing systems are again explored.
4. The expenditure of energy involved probably precludes frequent collective postformal choices: individual searches for best-fit systems go on. Social change may result. Success, that is, construction of a formal system that fits with reality in a particular content area, would most likely lower the use of relativistic operations in that area but increase their use in other areas. But there is no limit to use of relativistic operations in understanding interpersonal relations in which one takes part, because the nature of that reality is constantly changing as a function of knowing by the participants.

competing, conflicting formal-operational solutions has been made. No one individual articulated a perfect profile of these relativistic operations, though some came close. In addition, not every problem elicited statements confirming the presence of all eight operations. As seen in Table 14.7, the very abstract problem (the Alphabet problem) was not likely to be the occasion for articulating relativistic operations. The results indicated that problem definition, parameter setting, and pragmatic metatheory choice were frequent. Explicit statements describing *a prioris* as guiding metatheory choices were given by a quarter of the respondents, on the average. Relativistic operations were most frequently voiced in response to problems with a component involving interpersonal relational understanding.

DISCUSSION

The results of this study indicate that it is possible for some adults to structure logical thinking at a stage more complex than that of formal operations. Some adults seemed to prefer this stage for solving problems involving more realistic scenarios. Interpersonal problems lent themselves to the production of relativistic operational statements. Even subjects who did not solve problems in two clearly formal-operational ways demonstrated sufficient capability for relativistic operations. This suggests that, if scoring criteria were not made so stringent, they too would be considered "relativistic operational."

It is possible that many subjects who "failed" abstract-formal operations did so because they were at a stage "beyond formal operations." They may have exercised their capacity for higher-level operations to choose a pragmatic set of *a priori* rules. Respondents seemed aware, in many cases, that choosing a formal system to employ in one problem was necessarily subjective. Of course, some adults did strongly maintain that there is one possible logical answer that is "right," responding on a formal or concrete level, but these constituted the minority in this study. In general, support was found for the hypothesis that evidence for the presence of relativistic operations can be found in the thinking of ordinary adults.

But do relativistic operations, apparent in these adults, constitute a qualitatively different stage of development? In terms of Neimark's (1975) criteria, they do. A higher level of abstraction is attained since several formal-operational systems are related in terms of a metric, such as the selection of *a prioris* and problem parameters. The elements of thought are now formal-operational systems themselves, rather than lower-level abstractions. The structure of the relations within the stage is unique since it includes necessary subjectivity and incorporation of contradiction. That is, conscious choice is required among essentially equivalent systems that are mutually contradictory and that are based on a reality partly created by the knower.

RELATIVISTIC THINKING AND OTHER
POSTFORMAL THEORIES

One striking feature apparent in the theories of postformal thought outlined in this book is the congruence among ideas developed by many thinkers working independently. This congruence is fortunate. It suggests that the general phenomenon of postformal operations exists and can be quantified and tested in diverse populations. Convergence can be found between relativistic postformal thought and the conceptualizations of Koplowitz, Labouvie-Vief, Basseches, Powell, Arlin, and others (all of whom have written chapters for this volume). As Kramer (note 35) notes, the main points of convergence are as follows:

1. the acceptance of relativism;
2. the acceptance of contradiction;
3. the integration of frames of reference;
4. pragmatism.

None of the other systems described in this book gives evidence that calls into question the existence of relativistic operations, as they have been outlined in this chapter. But several offer indirect evidence to support this theory of relativistic operations. Most of the authors in this book can be classified within the developmental framework of Piaget or Riegel. Like the author of this chapter, most posit a postformal stage that organizes several formal systems.

THE LAST WORD: SPECULATIONS ON RELATIVISTIC
OPERATIONS, SHARED COGNITIONS AND SOCIAL
BEHAVIORS, AND SOME DATA

The dilemma of choice posed by postformal operations as described in this chapter might affect the behaviors of individuals. The choice dilemma may be resolved nonadaptively when adults limit their experience to those situations where only one formal system need be considered. Or, the choice dilemma might also be resolved or exacerbated, when adults come to a consensus about meaning and choice among systems. Relativistic operations might provide an advantage over formal operations by permitting consensus understandings and maximal use of conflicting information.

Maturity probably brings acceptance of the necessary subjectivity inherent in relativistic operations carried out on reality. This acceptance would be apparent in tolerance of others' beliefs and ways of life. The struggles of the young adolescent and young adult could be interpreted as an attempt to force relativistic reality into one "correct" formal system. In this way the inconsistencies in the world and in peers fit a formal-operations template. The certainty of formal operations, supplemented by the necessary subjectivity of relativistic operations, can maximize use of conflicting information and minimize social conflict.

Individual Coping

If relativistic uncertainty is distressing, the individual might respond with various strategies to minimize personal distress, probably at the cost of adaptivity. Since the choices related to relativistic thought are often found in interpersonal cognitions, coping strategies might be seen there too. For example, consider a middle-aged adult with a family, a career, civic responsibilities. and a social life. This person is faced with endless demands to "fit" the data of this social world by choosing a viable formal-operational system for interacting with each individual at an appropriate level. If this adult makes these choices and solves these interpersonal problems, it will not happen by means of formal operations alone. Nor will the use of relativistic operations often be "perfectly" consistent with reality. But they will provide the best possible match to it. Because relativistic operations use mental energy, the adult might resort instead to the following more facile and less stressful strategies.

1. The adult might reduce stimulation by retreating cognitively and perceiving all interpersonal relations at a lower level of complexity. Instead of "receiving" the behaviors of others as they are encoded, or trying to receive them at a higher, more integrated level of complexity, the adult might interpret all of them in a simplistic way. For example, instead of trying to understand the relations that are possible with a certain individual, the adult may resort to dealing with him or her as a member of a racial group. In this case, relativistic operations are replaced by formal or concrete operations.
2. The adult might reduce stimulus overload by developing a rigid social identity that permits only certain messages to be received. If, in such a case, the adult has a self-definition capable of only certain relations, other relational stimuli are ignored.
3. The adult can reduce stimulus overload by focusing on only selected goals or interests. The effect of this tactic is similar to the effect of the second tactic. All levels of complexity are available to be used in analyzing an event, but the individual limits the types of content considered.
4. The adult might reduce overload by developing more precise understanding of all the possible structures that can underlie a perceived interaction. This is an adaptive strategy that can only come from experience and familiarity with many types of systems. If the receiver can match reception to the encoded level, conflict can be reduced. This receiver is flexible in the use of the structures. The key to this

operation would be access to a good system of transformations to relate the sets of coordinates using relativistic operations.

5. The adult might reduce stimulus overload by making a more efficient total integration. Developing the integrative skill is an adaptive solution to overload. It makes use of metatheorizing that is based on experience. No content or complexity is lost when this technique is used. The mapping surface is so large and the topography so varied that most messages fit in somewhere through use of relativistic operations.

Shared Cognition

Making a selection of *a priories,* such as metatheories, modes of logic, and parameters, in concert with other thinkers, can also ease the dilemma of choice. Such group cognition could lead to a shared set of beliefs. Adjustments in systems of interpretation can be made until a common level is reached. Alternatively, shared cognition could lead to social conflict based on lack of convergence and shared transform systems.

A preliminary test of these assumptions was made by analyzing written accounts of short-term evolution of groups that were relatively isolated from other persons. Several nonfictional accounts of this type are available, for example, Solzhenitsyn's "Gulag Archipelago" (1973) and Read's "Alive: The Story of the Andes Survivors" (1974). The latter was chosen for the preliminary analysis since that group was more thoroughly isolated for a longer period of time.

The cognitive level of a group should depend on the collective level of its participants. Levels of participants should tend to converge over time. Individual members of the group were expected to interact at several predominant levels of cognitive development. Individuals would be expected to create their own "social reality" as a group evolves.

The dialogues and interpersonal behaviors reported by Read centered on the experiences of a group of 45 Uruguyan air travelers who crashed in the peaks of the Andes in winter and were officially given up for dead. But ten weeks later two of the survivors walked out of the mountains and found help for the 14 others still alive. The analysis presented here focuses on the state of the group at the time of the crash and one month later, as expressed in the dialogues and in the reports of the interpersonal behaviors of the 19 who survived for an entire one-month period. It employs the stages or levels of interpersonal relations operations described above.

According to Sinnott's preliminary analyses (note 33), the day of the crash the survivors formed three basic types of groups. These groups were identified as family clusters, friend clusters, or isolates. Except for the few families or friends, relationships were very superficial and infrequent. In the first few moments after the crash, virtually every survivor seemed to be interpreting on level I, creating a hysterical, demanding social situation with rapidly escalating conflicts. Soon those who generally related at a level III, IV, or V were able to engage in a dialogue with others until a temporary level III milieu was reached. As a result, some degree of interpersonal calm was restored.

Those who generally related at level III/IV at the time of the crash based their understanding on role hierarchies that might well have been valid for the precrash social system but were invalid for dealing with severities on the snow-covered peaks of the Andes. Persons most frequently relating at level I generally interpreted the behaviors of everyone in the group as level I. Level III's often "talked down" to level I's, meeting them at the lower cognitive level until I's exhibited (or feigned) more complex understanding of the interpersonal event.

One month later the group appeared to have restructured its society. An ordered, logical social system appeared, one at extreme variance with the ordered, logical, highly valued social system of the group's previous experience. Individuals had had frequent and intense interactions with one another during the preceding month. One tightly clustered subgroup characterized by a flexible level V approach had appeared. Members of this group could respond on any level, depending both on the circumstances of the moment and on the level of the person with whom they were communicating. These individuals were either leaders or were extremely well liked by all, in spite of their earlier status as strangers. Many persons had reacted to intense interactions by raising their dominant social-cognitive level several steps, some achieving a level V. The most effective leaders were those who appeared to use their level V skills to coordinate the system of roles from the precrash society with the disparate system of roles in the postcrash survivor society.

A second subgroup typically responded on a level I or II, although they might temporarily feign a higher level when socially coerced. While past friendships, skills, or philosophical/ethical systems kept the first subgroup interacting with the second, the second was perceived as an infantile burden. The first group frequently interacted harmoniously within itself. Members of the second seldom did since their interactions, based on structures of social relations embedded in needs, were less mutually satisfying. Cross-group interaction took place when members of the first subgroup were flexible enough to interact at the second's lower level. However, this demanded extra effort on the part of the higher-level persons and therefore was seldom attempted. The members of the higher-level subgroup therefore experienced more stimuli for restructuring than did the members of the lower-level subgroup.

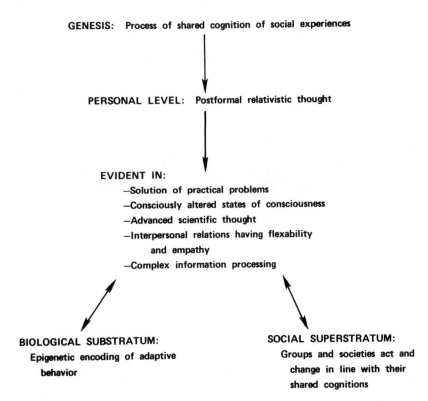

Figure 14.4. Relativistic Thought: Genesis, Effects, and Behavioral Evidence

This brief description gives some idea of the potential utility of shared cognition, motivated by resolution of the level V relativity dilemma. These topics must be more thoroughly examined before firm conclusions can be made, however.

Culture

Finally, the dilemma of choice posed by relativistic operations, if eased by group adoption of shared parameters of thought, might quite easily lead to a group behavior and belief system that persists beyond its creators. In other words, it may lead to a culture or to a social system. It would be easy to ignore the necessary subjectivity as well as the arbitrariness that was involved in the original choice or interpretive system of reality. When it becomes apparent that the shared-assumption system is not adaptive in some ways, "social change," or the exploration of alternative, competing formal systems, occurs and relativistic operations begin again. Table 14.7 and Figure 14.4 present a summary of some of the ideas described above.

The ideas in this section suggest three reasons why relativistic operations may be adaptive for mature adults and for the species. First, relativistic operations allow adults to take maximum advantage of a social world. Second, they permit not only the best choice of action but also the widest range of interpretation, in spite of imperfect information. Finally, relativistic operations permit a flexible, intelligent interpretation of complex reality to persist beyond the lifetime of a single generation.

SUMMARY

This chapter has outlined a stage of relativistic postformal operations, a stage that extends the theories of Riegel and Piaget into adult cognitive development. The operations unique to the stage have been based on an analysis of the epistemology of relativity. The genesis of relativistic operations has been described in terms of understanding interpersonal relations, a type of understanding that is relevant to adults. Data have been presented to support the existence of relativistic operations in ordinary adult thought. In addition, this chapter has speculated that relativistic thought has an impact on individual and group social behavior.

15

STAGE 4A:
CATEGORY OPERATIONS AND
INTERACTIVE EMPATHY

Philip M. Powell

This work provides a theoretical and empirical specification of postformal-operational thought. Postformal thought is examined within the contexts of advanced social role-taking and cognitive development. An extension of a sixfold role-taking typology, originally devised by Turner (1956), is used to define advanced social development. This extension has the properties of a stage. The social aspect of the postformal stage is named interactive empathy. Interactive empathy is conceived of as being partially dependent on the presence of a newly defined cognitive stage that is more advanced than formal operations. This new stage, called "category operations," is based upon category theory (MacLane, 1971). An observational study is reported that shows that the category-operational stage and its correlated social form, interactive empathy, follow Piaget's formal-operational stage.

Finally, the nature of cognitive and social development is discussed within the context of the results of the previously mentioned study. This discussion implies the existence of a new model of cognitive and social development. The model is sketched briefly, followed by a table of correspondences of several theories of cognitive and social development that places this work in perspective.

ADVANCED SOCIAL DEVELOPMENT

The advanced role-taking type of interactive empathy is based on a model of role-taking created by Turner (1956). Elsewhere, I have described this model in detail (Powell, 1980).

In essence, Turner's model is based on the concepts of role, role-playing, role-taking, role-standpoint, and reflexivity (and its converse, nonreflexivity). Role is defined not as a social position, but as a set of behaviors governed by norms and values, all of which are appropriate for a particular social position. Role-taking is observing, predicting, and anticipating the behavior of the self and of another within the context of a role that is either externally or personally assigned to a person during the course of a dyadic interaction. Role-playing is the concrete behavior based on role-taking information.

Role-standpoint is the perspective one adopts while role-taking. There are three role-standpoints. The most primitive, identification, is the result of the imitation of another's behavior. This is generally a result of an inability to separate one's own viewpoint and actions from those of a significant other. The second, the third-party role-standpoint, requires the ability to evaluate self and other from the perspective of a more or less internalized set of concrete or abstract social norms and values. These norms and values are learned from significant others. The third role-standpoint, interactive effect, requires the ability to adjust one's own behavior to accommodate it to that of another when there are no third-party norms available to guide the details of an ongoing interaction, where there are individual or shared purposes that both stimulate and maintain social interaction.

Further, reflexivity in role-taking occurs when an individual is conscious of how he or she appears to another during an interaction. For example, a person about to rob a bank might enter the bank dressed in an elegantly tailored suit, wearing a pleasant smile as he begins to interact with the bank teller. The conscious use of dress and mannerism indicates reflexive awareness. One can use reflexivity, then, to create a false impression in the minds of others, concealing one's true intentions. However, reflexivity is not necessarily used to commit unlawful or immoral acts. People may be reflexive simply by being aware of the ways in which others are experiencing them. By contrast, nonreflexivity occurs when one is unaware of such.

Reflexivity is intended as a broad concept covering everything from a simple awareness of being perceived and experienced by others, to both being aware and using the information gained from this awareness to manipulate one's own behavior. This is done to control the other's perception and experience of oneself. Anyone who has observed superior con men and poker players has an even better sense of this phenomenon.

Turner combined three role-standpoints with nonreflexivity and reflexivity, and generated six different types of role-taking. Since this volume is concerned with postformal operations in the cognitive and social realms, only the two most advanced role-taking forms devised by Turner will be described. These forms are, first, the interactive effect, nonreflexive role-taking, or type 5 for brevity, and, next, the interactive effect, reflexive role-taking, or type 6. Type 6 is the most advanced role-taking type described by Turner. Type 5 involves the ability to judge the probable effects another person would have on the achievement of an individual or on their shared purpose during an interaction. Thus, one is able to accomplish one's ends by the use of verbal argument (Powell, 1980). Turner's example of type 5 role-taking involves an effective salesperson overcoming a customer's reluctance. This may be done by questioning the customer so as to uncover and overcome negative attitudes he may have toward the product. This example is interactive because the salesperson has to deal with the customer's negative product attitudes through inter-action; for example, by asking the customer questions to unearth the reasons for his negative attitude, and then arguing against them. It is nonreflexive because the salesperson is not concerned with how he or she appears psychologically, through nonverbal behavior. The primary device of persuasion is verbal, for example, questioning and counter-argument, and not nonverbal behavior such as smiling or appearing concerned.

Type 6 role-taking involves even greater sophistication than type 5. Type 6 role-taking requires the conscious use of both verbal and nonverbal behavior to present a purposeful behavioral impression so as to achieve a desired goal. An example of type 6 role-taking is a spy who poses as a loyal, native-born citizen, to gain access to the military secrets of a foreign, enemy country. This requires a profound and subtle understanding of others, of the enemy country, and of the persona used by the spy to create the false impression of loyalty. By contrast, type 5 is based primarily on the use of verbal behavior, with little awareness of manipulating nonverbal behavior.

In the research to be described, type 5 was hypothesized to be stagelike and a developmentally less advanced form of role-taking than type 6.

The extension of Turner's role-taking typology was achieved by adding another, more advanced role-standpoint to his three role-standpoints. The fourth role-standpoint, interactive empathy, when crossed with nonreflexivity and reflexivity, led to the generation of two more role-taking types. The first is interactive empathy, non-reflexive role-taking, or type 7. It is defined as the ability to predict the verbal and nonverbal characteristics of others with accuracy. It is nonreflexive because one is unable to do this by oneself at this role-taking level. When one is functioning at a particular role-taking level, one is at that level first in respect to others, and later in respect to oneself. Specifically, we must behave first in relation to the outside world before we can discover the meaning of our actions. Then we can apply this meaning to ourselves. So, the type 7 role-taker is type 6 with respect to self-knowledge.

The next, more advanced, role-taking type is interactive empathy, reflexive role-taking, or type 8. It requires the ability to behave outwardly while being conscious of the impact of one's specific behavioral gestures. Type 8 is clearly a logical, hypothetical type, thought not to exist.

Type 7, then, represents the fourth role-standpoint of interactive empathy. Thus, it involves, most importantly, the ability to predict the characteristics of others with accuracy. It is superior to type 6 role-taking *because* of this accuracy in interpreting the behavior of others. Type 7 also includes the abilities of type 6 while the converse is not true. That is, type 6 role-takers know that their verbal and nonverbal behavior must be consistent to influence others. What they do not know is how to predict or diagnose the characteristics of another with explicit accuracy. Type 6 role-takers do not know why what they do works with a particular person. The type 7 role-taker could tell the type 6 why various verbal and nonverbal stratagems work.

These new types can be clarified by contrasting them. Briefly, type 7 role-takers can accurately anticipate others' behavior while the type 8 person, theoretically, can also influence them at will. It is important to note that the research program described here has been able to locate only type 7 role-takers.

Cognitive Prerequisites for Role-taking

In previous research, it was assumed that each Turner role-standpoint represented a qualitative level of role-taking. Then it was hypothesized that each of these levels was equivalent to a Piagetian stage. Next, it was hypothesized that the sequence of Turner's role-standpoints, from identificatory to interactive effect, was useful for determining the equivalence between Piaget's cognitive stages, after the sensori-motor stage, and the three role-standpoints. Specifically, and of critical interest, formal operations were hypothesized as being necessary but not sufficient for types 5 and 6. Also, type 5 was hypothesized to be less advanced than type 6. An earlier study supported all of these points (Powell, note 36).

Therefore, since formal operations are necessary but not sufficient for interactive effect role-taking, it is logical to hypothesize that the cognitive prerequisites for interactive empathy must transcend Piaget's last stage of formal operations. In other words, the cognitive prerequisite for interactive empathy must be a logical extension of the INRC group structure used by Inhelder and Piaget (1958) to define the cognitive processing of formal operations.

Category theory proved useful in generating this extension (MacLane, 1971). Piaget and others suggested its potential usefulness in the definition of cognitive processing (Piaget, 1972; Powell, note 37; Bart & Smith, 1974). MacLane described several different types of categories. Of these, the most relevant here is the category of groups.

This category has three defining characteristics. "First, it is composed of groups as elements. Second, every group within it is assumed to be a member of the universal class U of all groups. Third, for each pair of category objects, there exists a set of all category functions called homomorphisms which are used to map each pair of category elements into each other . . . " (Powell, 1980, p. 181). An example of a homomorphism is any set of three letters on a telephone dial with its corresponding number. More specifically, the three letters "ABC" correspond with one number, "2", to produce a many-one homomorphism. Consequently, all possible many-one mappings between two or more groups that preserve their group structure is a category of groups. So, conservation at the categorical level involves the ability to see all possible ways to map one set of things onto another while still preserving the essence of each. These category operations are introduced here as the cognitive operations for the new postformal operations stage.

Inhelder and Piaget (1958) used the group per se to describe the cognitive operations of Piaget's formal stage. Also, a category of groups operates on groups, with variations in one group related to variations in one or more other groups. Thus, category operations is at least one level of cognitive processing beyond formal operations. Commons and Richards (chapter 6, this volume) similarly argue that something operating on previous stage products is at the next stage.

A person functioning at this new level of cognitive development can see similarities where others perceive differences. Another way to observe this capacity is by contrasting the thinking of the formal-operational reasoner with that of one in category operations in the cognition of social objects, people, for example. The formal operator might approach people from different cultures as though they were essentially different from him or her. The category operator, on the other hand, might be intrigued by the way human nature could take on different forms and still generate similar feelings and experiences. In terms of the cognition of the physical world, the person in formal operations would be satisfied with analytical solutions to problems such as the billiards task discussed in Inhelder and Piaget (1958). On the other hand, the category-operations thinker would be excited by new variables and contradictions raised by the solutions to problems. For such a thinker, knowledge would be continuously incomplete because contradictions always occur due to natural or developmental limitations.

THE EXPERIMENT

An experiment was done to test some of the ideas above. It was guided by several hypotheses. These were: (1) role-taking types 5 and

6 should follow an invariant sequence as measured, with no one passing the criterion for type 6 who has not also met the criterion for type 5 role-taking; (2) the criterion for success at interactive empathy, nonreflexive role-taking should be met only by those who also met the criteria for successfully passing the measure of types 5 and 6 role-taking; (3) formal operations should be necessary but not sufficient for category operations as measured; and (4), formal and category operations should be necessary but not sufficient for interactive effect (types 5 and 6 role-taking) and interactive empathy (type 7), respectively. (This experiment is described elsewhere in greater detail, Powell, 1980.)

Method

Subjects

Subjects were 44 white participants, ages 21 to 55, all at least middle-class and with IQ's of at least 133.

Role-taking tasks. To measure types 5 and 6 role-taking, participants were asked to "sell" a dirty, defective lawnmower to the experimenter, who posed as a "customer." The purpose of this task was to determine: (1) the participant's capability to consciously shift his or her verbal arguments in order to persuade the "customer" (type 5 role-taking), and (2) the participant's capability to consciously manipulate his or her own nonverbal behavior to portray a false picture to another (type 6).

To measure interactive empathy, type 7, three sound-color films, each eight minutes in duration, were used (Cline, 1955). Each film followed the same format, which involved a film subject being interviewed on a variety of topics. After each film, research participants were asked to complete a different adjective checklist, composed of 20 adjective pairs, for each film subject. Each of these different checklists was designed on the basis of the actual lives of each of the film subjects. One adjective in each pair was designated by Cline as the correct one in describing some actual attribute of the film subject. The tasks of the participants were twofold. The first was to pick the 20 correct adjectives for each film subject. The second was to try to provide a correct reason, based on data given in each film, for the selection of each adjective. Eight minutes were allotted after each film. Participants were scored for both correct adjective choice and for correct reasons, as decided by judges provided for each chosen adjective. This was the primary measure for type 7 role-taking. Type 8 role-taking measures are not included since this type was not found.

Cognitive development. Cognitive tasks were: (1) formal operations as measured by the colored and colorless chemical task originally devised by Inhelder and Piaget (1958), and (2) category operations. Three category operations tasks were created. The first, based on Gamow's (1961) discussion of the hypercube, was a paper and pencil task that stated: "There is a concept embedded in this series (of a point, a line, a square, and a cube as drawn). Your task is to extend this series with a drawing of the next object" (Powell, note 37, p. 113). The second task stated, "Define 'objectness' or tell me the most abstract way you can characterize an object such that it is equivalent to any other object in the universe" (Powell, note 37, p. 115). The third task stated: "Given the dimensions of height, length, and depth, plus a fourth dimension of motion in space or time, define the perception of a rock in the fourth dimension" (Powell, note 2, p. 115). It should be noted that each answer required an explanation and that each participant was allotted only 30 minutes to do all category operations problems.

A description of the scoring procedures of the category operations tasks is in order, not only because these tasks are new but also because responses to these tasks provide the starting point for defining stage 4a. The scoring procedure for the first category operations task, the task involving the object beyond the cube, is as follows: (1) A score of 1 equals failure. A sample answer would "There exists no object beyond a cube." (2) A score of 2 equals transitional conserver. A sample answer might be, "an object with 16 points and 32 edges." It would be accompanied by the drawing of the object and supported by an explanation of a lower quality than those explanations rated 3. (3) A score of 3 equals conserver. A sample answer might be, "an object with 16 points, 24 surfaces, and 32 edges." An explanation would state that such an object (the hypercube) could take on many different forms in an infinite amount of time.

The next category operations task was the objectness problem. Its scoring procedure is as follows: (1) A score of 1 equals failure. A sample answer is that any object "occupies space and has weight." (2) A score of 2 equals transitional observer. A sample answer indicated that any object is composed of irreducible basic ingredients that do not change their interrelationship over time. (3) A score of 3 equals conserver. A sample answer would define an object as a set of points that change in infinite time in a concave or convex relationship among themselves. A concave relationship among points is when the points together create a curve that turns *inward*. A convex relationship is when the points together create a curve or the outer edge of an object that turns *outward*.

The last category problem is that of the rock. Its scoring is as follows; (1) A score of 1 equals failure. A sample answer would

Table 15.1. Performance on Cognitive and Social Tasks

| | | Social (Highest Stage Achieved) | | |
	Stage	Interactive Effect (Types 5 & 6)	Interactive Empathy (Type 7)	Total
Cognitive (Highest stage achieved)	Formal operations	26	0	26
	Stage 4a	9	5	14
	Category operations	0	4	4
	Total	35	9	44

indicate that over time the rock would stay the same. (2) A score of 2 equals transitional conserver. A sample answer would indicate that the person was changing his or her appearance and location but not his or her essence in relationship to the rock over infinite time. (3) A score of 3 equals conserver. A sample answer would involve the notion that over time the rock changed its appearance and location, but not its abstract essence.

Results

Briefly, the results were that all participants who were rated at the level of interactive empathy, nonreflexive role-taking (type 7), were also rated at the level of type 6 role-taking. Measures of formal operations and category operations formed an invariant sequence, as hypothesized. Formal operations and transitional responses on category operations were necessary but not sufficient for interactive effect and interactive empathy, respectively. Age was also correlated positively and significantly with role-taking behavior.

It is important to characterize likely candidates for the stage of postformal thinking. To begin, all the likely candidates that were discussed in this study were at least 30 years of age and possessed an IQ of at least 150. Other characteristics observed were a deep respect for others, openness and flexibility, and high self-esteem or transition thereto. They were also characterized by an excitement toward the unknown and a need to experience all the data, including contradictory data (Powell, note 37). Those who were at the level of interactive empathy role-taking possessed all of the above characteristics and the additional characteristic of having compensated for an earlier history of shyness (Powell, note 2).

A final word about characteristics. Only four participants out of over 500 persons tested between 1971 and 1982 use category operations. Many, if not most, of these 500 are mentally gifted. An additional 14 participants use stage 4a thinking. Table 15.1 illustrates the relationship between performance on formal and postformal cognitive tasks and performance on social role-taking tasks for the observational study mentioned above.

Discussion

Stage 4a

An analysis of the subjects' responses makes it possible to conceive of the essence of a new stage for category operations, stage 4a. To appreciate this, recall that Piaget's last substage of formal operations, stage 3b, is defined as the ability to take a problem, define its key variables, then nest these in an exhaustive matrix of possible outcomes. This is done so as to test for, keep track of, and dismiss erroneous solutions in order to arrive at a correct one.

Transitional conservers on category operations are able to do this easily but they differ from people in the lower substages of formal operations specifically in one way. That is, they take the correct solution as a starting point for generating new questions. This became more evident in a second study where participants were given several formal-operations tasks and the category operations tasks. Only a few transitional responses were obtained, but all of these were significant. A concrete context will illuminate the point. A modified version of Piaget's billiards tasks was used to test for the presence of formal operations. Like Piaget's successful subjects, many successful subjects here imagined a perpendicular line bisecting the angle of incidence and the angle of reflection so as to determine a principle that could be used for task solution. However, transitional category operations conservers did more. They were excited about the imaginary, perpendicular line. They started talking about it in an insightful way to use it to define another billiards problem in an elliptical space where it would be equivalent to a plane or a circle.

A critical difference between a stage 3b person and a precategory operations person appears to be an *openness* to the possible existence of another dimension that transcends the three dimensions. Perhaps it is this openness that triggers the start of a developmental process leading to category operations thinking. Also, this author suspects that people in transition between formal and postformal thought are beginning to generate a relativistic perspective on life. That is, they realize that the way they live is one of many possible ways life could be lived and still have both basic and self-actualization needs met. This new perspective is qualitatively different from the closed system of thought characteristic of formal operations.

It almost seems as if formal thought requires a dichotomy between subject and object. This dichotomy seems to be sublated in the fully developed category operations thinker. Consequently, the definition of the transitional postformal thinker hypothesized here accounts for the ability to treat thought as an object in such a way that one is able to generate a new psychological structure in oneself. This structure allows the emergence of a greater competence in both theoretical and psychological integration. It is also posited that this new psychological structure allows category operations thinkers to focus on certain dichotomies, such as subject-object, so intensely that critical features of these dichotomies come into awareness. Subsequently, these dichotomies cease to play a role in the thought of such thinkers.

A common argument is that one has to assume that one has powers that the object does not have in order to maintain the subject-object dichotomy. That is, one has to assume that one is not the object in any meaningful sense. However, if one observes the object carefully, one can come to experience it as an extension of one's own self in all of its potency and impotency. That is, the object is perceived and experienced only by the activity of the perceptual-cognitive systems of the self and by instrumental actions performed upon the object.

Stated differently, the object can only be known through an individual's actions as controlled by his or her central nervous system and socialization. Therefore, if persons experience any object as either less or more than themselves, then perhaps they do not know the object very well, nor do they know themselves very well.

At this juncture, it is vital to conclude this discussion with a brief presentation of a new model of cognitive and social development.

A MODEL OF COGNITIVE AND SOCIAL DEVELOPMENT

This model is based on the notion that all human beings are born with two needs, the need for knowledge and the need for recruiting others to help meet this need for knowledge. Development within the model occurs when these needs are frustrated by the inability to understand an object that cannot be escaped or denied. This partially understood object is the result of the mind not having adequate Piagetian schemes to handle it. Hence, the person must engage in further assimilational and accommodational activities to modify appropriate schemes to construct fully appropriate corresponding behaviors or schema. In other words, a partially cognizable object is so because the person lacks adequate schemes to control successful instrumental actions toward it. This inadequacy is felt as a painful state of deficiency that the person is highly motivated to attempt to alleviate. Alleviation occurs only when the object is totally understood. Then the person is able to act successfully toward the object and can control these successful actions with newly created schemes or highly modified old schemes.

The stages of development in the model are the Piagetian ones supplemented by stage 4a and category operations. Also, each Piagetian stage after sensori-motor is necessary but not sufficient for identificatory, third-party, and interactive effects. Stage 4a is the minimum prerequisite for interactive empathy, nonreflexive role-taking. Perhaps category operations may prove to be the prerequisite for type 8 role-taking, if such a role-taking type exists.

The most important result of development is the resolution of the subject-object problem. This problem is an important artifact of an inadequate central nervous system. It is the primary cause of temporal and psychological asynchronies between the development of knowledge and self-knowledge. The central nervous system is inadequate in that it is best able to cognize differences between things as opposed to similarities. This makes it extremely difficult for a person to become a categorical thinker, invested in seeing similarities among things, such as the self as subject and other(s) as objects. Indeed, persons who resolve the subject-object problem become cognitive geniuses of which there are three types (Powell, note 38). The first is the analytic genius. This type of genius is extremely capable at linear reasoning, but also has a great capacity for thinking in synthetic leaps. However, this type prefers being analytical because it feels safer. The prototype is Immanuel Kant. The second is the synthetic genius. This person is capable of analytic brilliance but prefers great leaps of thought, integrating massive amounts of data and experience. This is done so naturally that it is awe-inspiring to others who are less capable. The prototype is Albert Einstein. The last type is the true genius who can be analytic or synthetic at will. The prototype is Leonardo da Vinci.

A person who is one of these three types of genius is probably a categorical or precategorical thinker. He or she either realizes or is beginning to realize that life and externally viewed objects are nothing but oneself in disguise. This is because all things we know are the result of constraints produced both by the nature of our central nervous system and by the nature of our overt actions (Kant, 1887; Piaget, 1972). Hence, all we have experienced and all we can experience is mediated and conditioned by our own nature.

Table 15.2, which illustrates correspondence among these ideas and new stages and those of other researchers of cognitive and/or social development, is offered to clarify this chapter's contribution.

SUMMARY

A new postformal cognitive stage, "stage 4a," and a new postformal cognitive stage, "category operations," were described.

Table 15.2. Correspondences Among Cognitive and Social Theories

Categories	Piaget	Turner (1956)	Selman (1980)	Fischer (1980)	Commons and Richards (This volume)
Human Nature	Need for knowledge	Need for others	Similar to Piaget and Turner	Similar to Piaget	Similar to Piaget
Stages	Sensori-motor			Levels 1–4: Ability to form sets of concrete actions on and perceptions of things	Circular Sensory-Motor Actions and Sensor-Motor Actions
	Preoperations	Identificatory non-reflexive role-taking	Egocentric perspective taking	Level 4: Ability to form sets of concrete actions on and perceptions of things	Nominal Actions and Preoperations
	Preoperations and early concrete operations	Identificatory reflexive role-taking	Subjective perspective taking	Levels 4,5: Developing ability to represent concrete attributes of an object	Preoperations and Primary Operations
	Advanced concrete operations	Third-party non-reflexive role-taking	Reciprocal perspective taking	Levels 5,6: Developing ability to relate one representational set to another	Concrete Operations
	Early formal operations	Third-party reflexive role-taking	Mutual perspective taking	Level 7: Ability to relate two representational systems to solve simple formal operations tasks	Abstract Operations

(Continued next page)

Table 15.2 (continued)

Categories	Piaget	Turner (1956)	Selman (1980)	Fischer (1980)	Commons and Richards (This volume)
	Formal operations	Interactive effect	Societal-symbolic perspective taking	Levels 7,8: Early ability to relate one abstract concept to another	Formal Operations
New Stage	Stage 4a[a]	Interactive empathy, type 7[d]		Level 9,10: Ability to integrate within and across two or more abstract systems	Systematic or metasystematic operations
New Substages or Stages	Category operations[b]	Interactive empathy, type 8(?)[e]		Levels 11–13: Ability to integrate subject and object[g]	Metasystematic through Cross-paradigmatic Operations
End Result	Analytic or synthetic or true genius[c]	Social genius[f]	Societal-symbolic perspective taking	Integrated[h]	Integrated

[a-f] These are stages and end results invented by the author.

[g] This is this author's notion of what Fischer's levels 11–13 must be like based on category theory (MacLane, 1971).

[h] This is this author's label based on extrapolating levels 11–13 of Fischer's (1980) theory.

Two advanced types of role-taking that were thought to be theoretically correlated with stage 4a and category operations were also defined and described. These two new advanced role-taking types are: (1) interactive empathy, nonreflexive role-taking type, or type 7; and (2) interactive empathy, reflexive role-taking, or type 8. These role-taking types were derived from Turner (1956). Evidence from an observational study supported these newly formulated stages and role-taking types, except for the most advanced role-taking type, interactive empathy, reflexive role-taking.

In the results from the observational study, the characteristics of categorical and precategorical cognitive thinkers were described. Similar characteristics were described for type 7 role-takers. Next, a new model of cognitive and social development was offered. This new model led to the definition of three types of geniuses—the analytic, the synthetic, and the true. Finally, the new model was integrated with the theoretical and empirical efforts of other relevant and significant researchers of cognitive and social development.

16

POSTFORMAL EPISTEMOLOGIES AND THE GROWTH OF EMPATHY
Suzanne Benack

There are several tasks involved in the study of a stage model of cognitive development. One central task is to elaborate the formal structures of the stages. A second task is to describe the ways in which the stage structures are manifested in the concrete life of the individual during the period of the life cycle in which they typically appear. This second undertaking includes investigating such questions as: What notions of reality derive from the person's application of the stage structures to the understanding of particular concrete domains? How do different manifestations of the same structure arise and interrelate in development? Finally, how do the cognitive constructions of reality associated with a stage structure relate to the more general patterns of affective and social life characteristic of a given period of the life cycle?

Several authors in this volume have addressed the first task by proposing various models of the structure of postformal thinking. This chapter will address some aspects of the second kind of task with respect to the rise of postformal operations in late adolescence and early adulthood. First of all, it will describe the nature of "contextual relativistic" epistemological thought, a form of thinking that can be seen as an application of postformal schema to the domains of knowledge, truth, and value. Secondly, it will describe the relationship between the development of relativistic thought and the deepening capacity for empathic understanding.

RELATIVISTIC EPISTEMOLOGICAL THOUGHT AND POSTFORMAL OPERATIONS

This research takes as its starting point Perry's (1968) description of the growth of epistemological thought during the college years.

Perry interviewed students at the end of each of their four years of college, asking them "what stood out" as they looked back over their experience of the past year. Based on these interviews, Perry constructed a scheme of nine positions describing the students' changing understanding of the nature of knowledge, truth, value, and authority.

In Perry's scheme the student begins in Position 1, *dualism*. For the dualist, the world is bifurcated into right and wrong, we and they. Truth and right are absolute, objective givens, guaranteed by infallible authorities (God, parents, reason) or simply existent (Platonic forms, facts). Knowledge comes in isolated units (beliefs, propositions) whose truth is ascertained by comparing them to standards that exist apart from the knower.

This world-view becomes more complex as the student becomes aware of diversity of opinion among those taken to be representatives of the truth. At first, diversity of belief is accommodated in dualistic epistemology. Multiplicity, the realm in which all opinions possess equal validity, first appears as a special case within dualism where the final answers to some questions are not yet known. Later, it acquires a separate legitimacy of its own in some areas (humanities), but, in others (math and science), dualistic certainty remains unaltered.

The turning point in Perry's scheme occurs when the student becomes aware of the existence of a diversity of *opinions* on any given topic. He sees the existence of a diversity of *perspectives* or *contexts* from which judgments can be made on a topic. The student comes to see all knowledge as embedded in a framework of thought. "Truth," externally given, is replaced by "truths," each relative to its context of evaluation (contextual relativism). The recognition of relativism undermines thoroughly the attempt to find an absolute grounding for truth. The dualistic world-view ceases to exist, except perhaps as the special case of a particular perspective within a relativistic world.

The later positions in Perry's scheme describe the students' constructions of new grounds for making judgments in the absence of guaranteed absolute standards. Perry did not investigate the cognitive underpinnings of the move from dualistic to relativistic thought. However, the work of several authors in this volume suggests that Perry's later positions can be understood as applications of postformal reasoning to the domain of epistemology.

EPISTEMOLOGICAL AND AFFECTIVE DEVELOPMENT IN ADOLESCENCE

Several authors have considered the relationship between the development of relativistic thought and patterns of social-affective development in adolescence. Perry's (1968) and Broughton's (1978) observations suggest, and systematic studies by Gilligan and Murphy (1979) and Fowler 1981) confirm, that the sequences of epistemological development and identity formation occur in parallel. Their work indicates that a dualistic epistemology is associated with a conventional identity, and that the loss of epistemological certainty and the loss of conventional identity coincide. It also indicates that the relativistic world of multiple possible *perspectives* is paralleled by the identity confusion of multiple possible *selves*. Finally, that as the adolescent constructs the grounds for judgments of truth and validity within relativism, commitments and choices are made that define an adult identity.

The work reported in this chapter turns to another aspect of affective development in adolescence: from the adolescent's evolving sense of *self* to his or her evolving sense of the *other*. It claims that changes in this realm, too, are related to epistemological development. In particular, it attempts to demonstrate that the development of relativistic thought transforms the late adolescent's understanding of the *nature of experience*. This makes possible a more sophisticated and accurate understanding of other people's experience.

The following sections present a theoretical argument that forms of epistemological thought could be related to forms of empathic understanding. Also, the results of research that investigated the relationship between epistemological thought and the capacity for empathic understanding of a client's experience will be presented.

Several authors in this volume characterize postformal thinking in terms of the new epistemological assumptions. They describe these assumptions in ways that echo Perry's description of relativism. For example, a major feature of Koplowitz's Unitary Thought (Chapter 13, this volume) is the conscious recognition of the creative role of the subject in' constructing experience. In fact, Koplowitz cites Perry's relativistic position as an example of unitary thinking. Broughton explicitly traces the development of epistemological thinking, and his levels 5 (subjectivist) and 6 (perspectivist) correspond to Perry's relativistic positions. Arlin's eight characteristics of "optimal adult thought" include at least three that are central features of relativistic thought:

1. the ability to coordinate multiple frames of reference, a type of relativity of thought;
2. the ability to coordinate conflicting theories and systems of thought;
3. the ability to consider a rational model as one option among several in seeking solutions to problems.

All of these authors describe postformal thinking in terms compatible with relativistic epistemology. They describe the recognition of multiple interpretive frameworks for experience, the ability to compare multiple intellectual frames, and the recognition of the role of the subject in constructing knowledge and in determining truth.

In addition, the logical "moves in thought," described alternately by Basseches (Chapter 10, this volume), Fischer, Hand, and Russell (Chapter 3, this volume) and Richards and Commons (Chapter 5, this volume) are required by the tasks that relativistic thought addresses. An example is the prototypical "relativistic task," the "essay question." In this question, the student is asked to (1) compare and contrast the way that theorists from different intellectual traditions would approach a common problem and (2) evaluate the relative adequacy of the solutions that would be generated. Basseches's schemata #9 and #10 (recognizing and describing the nature of systems), and #19 and #20 (evaluative comparison of forms and coordinating systems in relation) would be necessary to accomplish the essay question task. Similarly, to compare and contrast approaches would require at least Level 8 in Fischer's scheme (abstract mappings, relating two or more abstractions). Using two perspectives to reach a solution to a problem would probably require operations at Level 9 (relating several aspects of two or more abstractions). Operations at Level 7 (forming single abstractions) would not be sufficient to accomplish any aspect of this relativistic task. Finally, in the Commons, Richards, and Kuhn (1982) system, the "compare and contrast approaches" task would seem to require a minimum of Level 2 thinking. This would allow the person to make at least single comparisons among the properties of systems.

In sum, epistemological elements of postformal thought and the analysis of the logical operations required by relativistic thought support this work. Relativistic thought can be seen as the application of postformal thinking to the domain of epistemology.

THE IMPLICATIONS OF EPISTEMOLOGICAL STAGES FOR EMPATHIC UNDERSTANDING

It has been postulated (Greenson, 1960) that empathy consists of two complementary functions. First, an affective-identifying function permits the empathizer to "let go" of his own perspective and to imaginatively take the role of the other. Secondly, a cognitive-differentiating function allows the empathizer to "step back" from this temporary identification. It allows him or her to distinguish between his or her own imaginative experience and the other's actual experience of the situation. Deficiencies in either function are seen to lead to pathologies of empathy. Inability to let go of one's own perspective or anxiety about identifying with the other results in an inhibition of empathy. Failure to differentiate between one's own and the other's perspectives results in overidentification and a distorted view of the other's experience.

This dual-process model of empathy is useful in conceptualizing the ways in which relativistic thought contributes to empathic understanding. Relativistic thought should enhance both the cognitive-differentiating and the affective-identifying aspects of empathic functioning. This claim is rooted in two features of relativistic thought. First, the nature of the *subject* is taken to be as critical as the nature of the *object* in producing knowledge. Second, the notion of truth arises with this inclusion of the subject.

The dualist understands experience as the imprinting of the nature of the object upon the passive subject. The form and character of experience is determined by the character of the objects one "takes in." The subject, in this view, is little more than a vessel, a sheet of film that records what is "really happening" outside it. The dualist recognizes that subjective factors can play a role in determining experience and that there is a distinction between "experience" and "reality." Even a ten-year-old child realizes that people may have different experiences of a common situation, depending on subjective factors (for example, eyesight, position with respect to an object). Prior to the development of relativistic thought, however, such differences in experience are understood as deviations from a common objective reality that they all approximate. Differences in perception are understood as distortions of "true" perception of an external world. Quirks in the subjects or limits in receptive capabilities (one cannot see all sides of an object simultaneously) may distort the perfect match between experience and reality. Yet, the *function* of the subject is to reproduce external reality. The veridicality of experience can be evaluated only in reference to the object. The nature of the subject is irrelevant to truth.

With the development of relativistic thought, however, the notion of objective reality, independent of the subject disappears, or at least becomes subordinate, an hypothesis, impossible to confirm and not essential to the notion of *the* truth. The nature of experience is seen as dependent upon the nature of the subject, which is now understood to contribute actively to the *creation* of knowledge. Subjective determinants of experience are viewed as the rule, not the exception. In Broughton's (1978) terms, experience overtakes reality, phenomena dominate noumena. Understanding the nature of the subjective systems that determine experience, such as intellectual paradigms, species-specific categories of thought, and cultural interpretive systems, becomes the focus of epistemological inquiry.

The move from dualism to relativism, then, fundamentally transforms one's vision of the world. The dualist sees people as living together in a common "outside" world that they all perceive similarly.

The relativist sees a world in which there is no single "given" reality. Multiple "worlds of experience" are generated by multiple epistemological subjects. Each species, each culture, each individual is seen as the center of a private world, experiencing a "reality" that may or may not overlap that of his or her fellows. In the relativist world-view, then, there is no "reality" without a simultaneous awareness of the subjective vantage point from which it is seen. There is no object without an implied subject.

This shift of emphasis is from objective factors (reality) to subjective factors (the nature of the knower). These factors are determinants of the character of experience. They have several implications for the way that the relativist views the relations among different people's experience of common situations.

The dualist sees peoples' experience as generally reflecting the nature of the external world. He or she typically perceives the experience to be identical with reality; not as "how I see things" but as "the way things are." Since people perceive the same physical and social world, the dualist assumes that their experience will be essentially identical. He or she typically does not differentiate "my experience," "others' experience" and "reality," but assimilates all of these to a general category of "the way we know things to be."

With the rise of relativism comes the ability to recognize multiple subjective perspectives on common situations. The relativist is able to differentiate not only "my experience" from "your experience," but "my perspective" from "your perspective." He or she can understand the differences in experiences as reflecting the differences in perspectives. Unlike the dualist, the relativist *expects* that people will have somewhat different interpretations of the same event. He or she sees no contradiction in multiple views of a situation, each having "validity" or "truth."

The general claim of this chapter is that the relativist's understanding of experience and of truth will enhance his or her ability to empathically understand another person's experience. This claim is examined more closely below where the particular ways in which relativistic epistemology might affect behavior are traced. The situation is that of attempting to understand another person's (call him Joe) experience of a particular situation.

ONTOLOGICAL RELATIVISM AND COGNITIVE-DIFFERENTIATING EMPATHY

Firstly, the relativist's view of experience as rooted in the nature of the subject will support the cognitive-differentiating function of empathy in several ways. To see this more clearly, the dualist will be examined. Since the dualist expects people to have similar experiences of common events, he or she will approach the task of understanding Joe's experience by attempting to understand the general nature of the situation. He or she may consult his or her own experience or knowledge of socially conventional reactions to this situation. He or she will be prone, then, to errors of over-generalization. The dualist would fail to distinguish between what he or she would feel, what "anyone" would feel, and what Joe does feel in this situation. He or she may be confused if Joe gives signs of *not* reacting the way that "everyone" does. He or she may either ignore the discrepant cues or try to convince Joe that he really does not feel that way.

The relativist, on the other hand, will have a more specific, differentiated understanding of the task. He or she not merely recognizes the *general* nature of the experience, but recognizes the *particular* nature of *Joe's* experience, as distinguished from his or her own or anyone else's. The relativist will be concerned to understand the nature of the *perspective* from which Joe views the event. The system of beliefs, values, descriptive categories, and attitudes he brings to the interpretation of this particular phenomenon are considered. The relativist takes Joe's role not by merely imagining himself or herself in Joe's situation, but by trying to imagine what it would be like to be Joe in Joe's situation. Because he or she differentiates between his or her own and Joe's perspectives on the same event, the relativist will be more likely to avoid errors of assumed similarity (projection). He or she will be more sensitive to cues that reveal the particular nature of Joe's experience. In addition, the relativist will not assume that he or she knows the character of the other's experience. He or she will advance hypotheses tentatively, flexibly modifying them on the basis of more or contradictory information.

In sum, a relativistic understanding of different subjective perspectives leads to different experiences. This understanding seems likely to support the cognitive-differentiating aspect of empathy by:

1. providing an orientation toward differentiating the other's specific experience from people's general experience of an event;
2. leading the empathizer to build a model of the other's psychic framework that can be used to imaginatively generate hypotheses about the nature of his or her experience;
3. minimizing errors of projection or assumed similarity; and
4. encouraging the relativist to be tentative in adopting an hypothesis about the nature of another's experience and to be flexible in modifying it.

These differences result in the relativists showing a more specific, differentiated, and accurate understanding of the nature of the other's experience.

MORAL RELATIVISM AND AFFECTIVE EMPATHY

The affective-regressive function of empathic understanding might also be enhanced by relativistic thought. This function permits identification and free imaginative experience of the other's world. Specifically, the relativist has a "qualified" or "complexified" moral stance toward differences in people's experience. This may enhance his or her ability to empathically experience a wider range of thoughts and feelings.

The dualist perceives truth in binary terms, if one position on a question is right, the others must be wrong. When confronted with someone whose moral position contradicts his or her own, the dualist cannot admit the legitimacy of the other's position without violating his or her dualism. Empathizing with the experience of someone who is seen as holding wrong, or immoral, beliefs and feelings presents a double-edged threat to the dualist. He or she will either experience the anxiety and discomfort associated with having an incorrect belief or an immoral feeling, or he or she will take on the other's standards and see his or her *own* beliefs and feelings as wrong.

The relativist, however, has the ability to take multiple perspectives on any question without denying the partial values and limitations of each position. Differences in opinion are not seen as negating one's own, but as the expectable result of the different subjective "lenses" through which people view reality. The relativist is less threatened by identifying with, or taking the role of, others whose values are perceived as different.

SUMMARY

A relativistic understanding of truth can facilitate both the affective-regressive and the cognitive-differentiating functions of empathic understanding. In a relativistic world-view, the differentness between people's perspectives is made prominent. The sharpness of the moral distinctions between people is softened. With the onset of relativism, one becomes both more aware of people's differences and less bothered by them. Both of these developments should lead to a greater ability to empathically understand the inner experience of others. The structure of this argument is summarized in Figure 16.1.

The hypothesis that relativistic thought is associated with higher levels of empathic functioning was tested. A research project was designed that examined the relationship between the epistemological thinking of beginning counseling students and their empathic understanding in a counseling setting. The remainder of the chapter will describe this study and its findings.

Aspect of Epistemological Thought	Implications for Understanding of Experience	Effects on Empathic Understanding
Theory of Knowledge Subjectivity: sees character of knowledge/ experience as determined by the subjective perspective of the knower	recognizes existence of different perspectives from which people view events, and the different experiences they generate; differentiates own/other's perspective; expects people's experience of common situations to differ	is *able* to monitor and manipulate own perspective; can put aside one perspective and assume another; can understand other's *perspective* as well as content of other's experience
Theory of Truth/Value knowledge-claims evaluated by multiple criteria of truth or value; multiple "truths" generated by different subjective perspectives, all having partial validity	different interpretations of an event can be seen as containing "their own truth"; validity accorded to other's experience as well as one's own	is *willing* to assume other's perspective, put aside own beliefs, values, assumptions
Theory of Knowledge Objectivity: sees character of knowledge/ experience as determined by the nature of the object of knowledge ("the known," "reality")	doesn't recognize existence of different subjective perspectives; expects people to have similar experiences of common situations	is *unable* to assume other's perspective; doesn't comprehend the task of monitoring and manipulating one's perspective on an event
Theory of Truth/Value single standard of truth or rightness; correspondence to the "real"	only one interpretation of events is correct; others must be false, distorted	is *unwilling* to assume other's perspective; feels moral opposition to adopting "false" beliefs or "wrong" feelings as though they were "true/right"

(Left margin label for first two rows: RELATIVISM; for last two rows: DUALISM)

Figure 16.1. The Implications of Epistemological Assumptions for Empathic Understanding

SUBJECTS

The subjects were 30 volunteers (18 women, 12 men) from students enrolled in a counseling course at Harvard Graduate School

Articulated Epistemology
Relativistic   Dualistic

	Relativistic	**RR**	DR
Implicit Epistemology	Dualistic	RD	**DD**

Figure 16.2. The Four Epistemology Groups. Boldface boxes correspond to Perry's positions.

of Education. All were white, most were middle-class, and they ranged in age from 21–42 years, with a median age of 28.

ASSESSMENT OF SUBJECTS' EPISTEMOLOGICAL THOUGHT

During the first weeks of the semester, all subjects were given a semi-structured interview covering a range of personal, moral, and epistemological questions. Epistemological thought was elicited in two ways. Subjects were asked to make concrete moral judgments, and their epistemological assumptions were inferred from their decision-making strategies. Subjects were also asked to explicitly articulate their epistemological theories in response to questions about the nature of knowledge and truth in several domains.

A similar follow-up interview was conducted at the end of the semester to measure any change in epistemological thinking during the study. Since only one subject showed significant movement, initial interview scores were used in data analysis.

Subjects received a score of either "D" or "R" on both their implicit and their explicit epistemological reasoning. This scoring generates four epistemological "types", summarized in Figure 16.2. The DD and RR groups correspond to Perry's dualistic and relativistic positions; these subjects showed strategies in making judgments that were consistent with their stated epistemological positions. In addition, the scoring scheme produces two additional types whose mode of making judgments is not consistent with their articulated theories, for example, the DR subjects, who take multiple perspectives into account in reaching decisions, but who articulate a dualistic theory of truth, and the RD subjects, who articulate a relativistic theory, but who, in practice, apply single external criteria of truth in decision making.

ASSESSMENT OF EMPATHIC UNDERSTANDING

As discussed earlier, subjects' empathic function was observed in their responses as counselors in role-played counseling sessions. Their task was to understand the client's experience "through his or her eyes." Twenty of the 30 subjects who had participated in the epistemology interview made their counseling tapes available for analysis. An average of five sessions was analyzed for each subject. An abridged version of each session was created by excerpting the first ten minutes of the tape plus 1, 2, or 3 additional 50-minute segments (depending on total length).

RESULTS

Fifteen of the 20 subjects whose counseling tapes were analyzed were scored as showing either completely relativistic (RR) or completely dualistic (DD) thought. The remaining five subjects were scored in one of the "mixed" categories, receiving opposite scores on explicit and implicit epistemological reasoning (RD or DR). Below, the general hypothesis that relativistic thought is related to higher levels of empathy is evaluated by looking at the empathy data for the 15 subjects who were scored as unambiguously relativistic or dualistic. Then, the counseling performance of the five mixed-epistemology subjects is assessed to determine the relative contribution of explicit and implicit relativistic thought to empathic functioning.

Comparison of the Completely Dualistic (DD) and the Completely Relativistic (RR) Subjects

Figure 16.3 gives the group means for relativists (RR) and dualists (DD) for both average-session and best-session scores on all eight numerical empathy variables. Relativists score higher than dualists in all variables. This holds for both their average and their peak performance. The relativists' superiority is particularly strong in the two overall performance indexes, overall empathy and overall non-directiveness, and on the three "quality of empathy" variables, tentativeness, internal orientation, and accuracy.

The hypothesis that relativists are more successful in assuming their client's perspective was also supported by the two groups' performance on the realm-addressed variable. Figure 16.4 shows the mean percentage of counselor statements that addressed each of four "realms" of discourse for both relativists and dualists. Relativists more often chose to address the client's experience (E2 and E3). The dualists more often addressed things outside the client's current experience (S and E1).

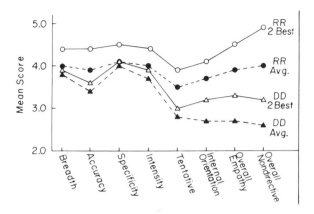

Figure 16.3. Group Means of Average and Two-Best Scores on Empathy Variables for Relativists (RR) and Dualists (DD)

The relativists showed superiority in all dimensions of empathic functioning, evident in the differences between the two groups' mean scores on both "typical" and "peak" performance as empathic counselors. On the several variables on which this superiority was most evident, the difference was virtually bimodal, as almost all relativists scored higher than almost all dualists.

The statistical significance of this finding was tested by comparing rank orderings of subjects according to epistemology and according to scores (both average and two-best) on each empathy variable using a Kendall Tau with ties (Table 16.1), corrected for continuity (Siegel, 1956). The results are summarized below.

As the tables show, a moderate and significant degree of association was found between the epistemology ranking and most of

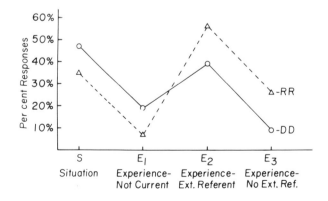

Figure 16.4. Percent Responses Addressing Each Realm of Experience: Group Means for Dualists (DD) and Relativists (RR)

Table 16.1. Kendall's Taus Indicating Strength of Association between Epistemology Group and Empathy Variables for RR and DD Subjects

	Breadth	Accuracy	Specificity	Intensity	Tentativeness	Internal Orient.	Overall Empathy	Overall Nondirect.
Averaged scores	.36	.54[a]	.16	.37	.66[c]	.65[c]	.60[b]	.58[c]
Two-best scores	.53[a]	.75[d]	.30	.61[c]	.64[c]	.55[b]	.59[b]	.63[c]

[a] p < .05
[b] p < .01
[c] p < .005
[d] p < .001

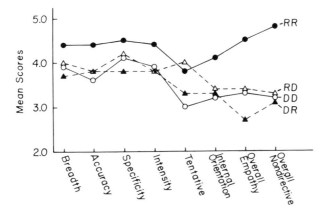

Figure 16.5. Mean Scores of Four Epistemology Groups on All Empathy Variables (Two-Best Scores)

the rankings by empathy scores. In general, there is a stronger relationship between epistemology and the *best* empathy performance than there is between epistemology and *average* empathy performance. Indeed, among the "best-performance" empathy measures, specificity is the only variable which does *not* show a significant relationship to epistemological thought.

"Mixed-Epistemology" Subjects

The above analysis of the relation between forms of epistemological thought and empathic understanding relied upon the conceptualization of epistemology as a unitary construct, as a global "position" or "stage." Our difficulties in coding a minority of subjects in terms of unitary stages of epistemology, however, led us to differentiate the two "factors" of explicit and implicit epistemological reasoning (see above). In the DD and RR groups, these two aspects of epistemological thinking co-vary. Thus, it is impossible to determine whether articulated theory, implicit reasoning alone, or a combination of the two, is responsible for the observed relationship between relativistic thought and empathic functioning.

Some preliminary speculations on this question can be developed by looking at the empathic performance of the five "mixed-epistemology" subjects. These subjects were three older women (36–42 years) who scored DR (relativistic decision making but no articulated theory), and two 28-year-olds (1 male, 1 female) who scored RD (an articulated theory of relativism, but dualistic decision making strategies).

Figure 16.5 gives the group means of average-session scores on all empathy variables for the four epistemology types (adding the two mixed groups to the DD and RR data reported previously). The RD subjects typically scored somewhat higher than the RR relativists and somewhat higher than the DD and DR groups. These two subjects performed much like the four dualists who adopted the client-centered form of response. They did not take on a predominantly empathic style until halfway through the course. The responses had much of the flat, fact-finding, often subtly directive tone that characterized the highest-scoring dualists' counseling tapes.

The DR subjects (who had no explicit relativistic theory but used relativistic reasoning in making judgments) scored below the RR and RD groups and even below the DD dualists on several empathy variables. In general, these women showed an overall level of performance similar to the lower-scoring dualists. It is interesting to note, however, the *pattern* of these womens' scores across the empathy variables in comparison to the dualists'. While the women score below the dualists on several variables, they score above the dualists on accuracy, tentativeness, and internal orientation. These are the three "quality of empathy" variables that most strongly distinguish the relativists from the dualists. It would appear that, in general, explicit epistemological theory is a better predictor of empathic functioning than is implicit epistemological reasoning since the RR and DR groups both score higher than the DR and DD groups. However, the fact that the DR women score higher than the DD dualists on exactly those variables on which the relativists perform most differently from the dualists suggests that relativistic implicit reasoning is related to an increase in empathic functioning. This increase is smaller than, but similar to, that associated with explicit epistemological theory. In addition, it appears that the variables most strongly associated with explicit or implicit relativistic thought are tentativeness and internal orientation. These are the more subtle aspects of the counselor's style that communicate a stance toward the client's experience as well as an understanding of its content.

The notion that explicit epistemology is more strongly related to level of empathic functioning than is implicit epistemology was tested. Direct comparisons were made of individuals' scores on implicit and explicit epistemology and their "two-best" performance scores on empathy variables. Recall that, originally, subjects received "relativism scores" between 0 and 3 for both implicit and explicit epistemological reasoning. Subjects were rank ordered according to three kinds of epistemology variables: (1) their explicit epistemology score, (2) their implicit epistemology score, and (3) the intersection of these two, their epistemological "type." For this third ranking, the four types were ordered as follows: RR > RD > DR > DD.

These three rankings represent, in effect, three hypotheses as to the nature of the relationship between epistemology and empathic functioning:

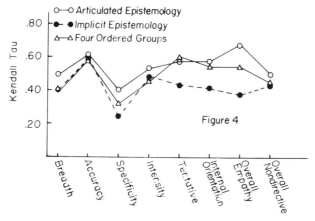

Figure 16.6. Kendall's Taus Indicating Strength of Associations between Three Epistemology Rankings and All Empathy Variables

1. Only articulated epistemological theory is related to level of empathic functioning.
2. Only decision-making strategies are related to level of empathic functioning.
3. Both aspects of epistemological thought are related to empathy, but explicit theory is the more powerful of the two.

Subjects were also rank ordered according to their two-best performances on all empathy variables. A Kendall Tau with ties, corrected for continuity, was calculated to measure the strength of the association between each of the three epistemology rankings and the eight empathy variable rankings. Figure 16.6 compares the tau values for the three epistemology rankings.

For six of the eight variables, the best "fit" between epistemology and empathy performance was found by considering articulated theory in ranking subjects. That is, the best hypothesis of the three considered here is that only explicit epistemological thought is relevant to empathic functioning. Thus, the RR relativists, who had the most fully developed relativistic theories, perform best on empathy variables. The RD subjects, who have less fully articulated theories and simple dualistic decision making processes, came next. The DR women and the DD dualists perform equally, but worse than either of the other groups.

The DR women were superior to the dualists on some empathy variables. The four groups ranking had greater power in accounting for rankings on two of the empathy variables. These findings suggest that implicit epistemology plays a role in at least some aspects of increased empathic understanding.

SUMMARY AND DISCUSSION

The results of this research strongly support the hypothesis of this work. The move from dualistic to relativistic epistemological thought is associated with a heightened capacity for more accurate and sophisticated forms of empathic understanding. However, subjects in this study were encouraged to show empathy and, indeed, were given instructions and practice in doing so. The findings do not speak to the question of whether relativists *will* typically and spontaneously display empathy. They state only that the subjects are more *able* to understand other's experience and are more responsive to training in empathy.

The research also tentatively suggests that a person's articulated epistemological theory is a better predictor of his or her level of empathic functioning than are the strategies he or she employs in making judgments and decisions. However, this finding is embedded in the most problematical aspect of the pattern of results and the one the most clearly points to the need for further study. That problem is strong sex differences in the relation of explicit and implicit epistemological thought. The fact that only women showed "implicit relativism" without "explicit relativism" suggests that other factors may be involved in addition to differences in epistemological thought.

The meaning of the more detailed findings of the study cannot yet be interpreted. A more thorough understanding is needed of the different patterns of epistemological development exhibited across sexes and in the "explicit" and "implicit" domains of thought. However, the strong relationship between forms of epistemological thought and the capacity for empathic understanding appears to hold for both men and women. At one level, this finding can be seen as supporting the theoretical model presented at the beginning of this chapter. At a more general level, it also supports the wider claim that patterns of cognitive growth are related to, and seen in, patterns of affective and social development. This points to a potentially fruitful area of inquiry: the transformations of affective life, social thought, and social relations that are made possible by the development of postformal-operational thought.

17

IDEALS OF THE GOOD LIFE AND MORAL JUDGMENT: ETHICAL REASONING ACROSS THE LIFESPAN

Cheryl Armon

This chapter presents the first analyses of data from a cross-sectional longitudinal (Baltes, Reese & Nesselroade, 1977) investigation of ethical reasoning in adulthood. It examines whether the development of reasoning about the Good and the Good Life can be described in terms of structural stages. Here the Good refers to a general system of evaluative reasoning. The Good Life represents that evaluative system as it appears in specific ideals in work, relationships, education, marriage, and so on. The chapter also examines whether such development continues into adulthood. In addition, the relationship between reasoning about the Good and Moral Judgment reasoning (Kohlberg, 1981a) is investigated.

First, the basic assumptions shaping the research approach and the analyses are presented. There follows a description of the cross-sectional/longitudinal study. The preliminary findings from the first round of analyses are then reported. Briefly, they are:

1. Theoretical analyses support the hypothesis that stages of the Good contain structural characteristics.
2. Sequentiality of stages of the Good is supported by the longitudinal analyses.
3. Postconventional stages both of the Good and of the Moral are found only in adults.
4. Structural stage development continues throughout adulthood although it decreases in rate with age.
5. Stages of the Good and Moral Judgment stages develop in a parallel fashion.

Much of the research presented here is based on numerous collaborations with and training from Albert Erdynast without which the present work would not have been possible. Part of this research has the purpose of fulfilling the partial requirement for the doctoral degree from the Harvard Graduate School of Education. Progress in this work is also indebted to Lawrence Kohlberg and Michael L. Commons.

In the discussion section, the claim that structural development in reasoning about the Good continues into adulthood is made. Criticisms of this claim from structural-developmental psychology are then presented and discussed. Then the relationship between Kohlberg's stages of Moral Judgment and the stages of the Good is discussed from both psychological and philosophical perspectives. Finally, it is demonstrated that the content of reasoning about the Good can be described and categorized in terms of traditional, formal normative ethical theories. It is further argued that not only a structural psychology of adult ethical development, but also a philosophy of adult ethical experience, is necessary for a comprehensive picture of adult ethical reasoning.

BASIC ASSUMPTIONS

The research approach uses a "circular bootstrapping" methodology (Colby, 1978). This methodology is neither purely inductive nor descriptive, but rather draws upon both theoretical and empirical considerations in order to account for development within a domain. In investigating reasoning in the domain of the Good, the approach oscillates between empirical findings and theoretical considerations from both structural-developmental psychology (for example, Piaget, 1960, 1972; Kohlberg, 1969, 1981) and formal ethics (primarily Aristotle, Epicurus, Mill, Dewey, and Rawls).

Psychologically, this approach is an application of structural-developmental theory. This theory explains much of intellectual activity in terms of culturally universal, generalizable, invariant sequences of "thought organizations." These thought organizations are represented by constructs called developmental stages. Fundamental to this paradigm is the distinction between *structures*, *elements*, and *content* (Piaget, 1969). A structure represents the whole, or organized, system of thought. The elements are the composite parts from which the whole is constructed. Transformational laws coordinate the elements within a structure. These laws regulate the activity and the development of structures by transforming elements. The structure itself is actually a system of transformational laws.

Transformations do not always lead beyond the structure. Reversible operations allow transformations to incorporate elements that belong to the system and preserve its laws, and are not developmental. In contrast, other transformations result in elements outside the system, and lead to stage development. Transformations of this sort are of a limited number in that developmental sequences end at a final stage.

Content, in contrast, consists of actual problems and tasks, including specific activities, objects, words, or materials. A structural stage, then, represents particular structures that organize the relations between elements that are embedded in content.

Kohlberg (1969, 1981) demonstrates the applicability of structural stage theory to the domain of *deontic* moral reasoning: reasoning about what is Right. He identifies six ordered stages of moral judgment. Each stage is a structural organization of socio-moral thought in a hierarchically ordered sequence. (See Kohlberg, 1981 for a description of the stages.)

Heretofore, developmental researchers have not directly investigated how individuals construct conceptions of the Good. In this chapter, it is assumed that noted moral philosophers do not have an exclusive ability to construct consistent and reliable ethical systems. On the contrary, it is posited along with Kohlberg (note 39), that all persons, young and old, are ethical philosophers in their own right. They make coherent, consistent, substantive judgments in both the areas of the Good and the Right.

Philosophically, the conception of stages of the Good is dependent on a particular conception of the person as a rational human being, capable of making and acting upon rational life choices (Rawls, 1971). In accordance with Rawls, it is assumed that persons formulate rational life plans that are organized by their conception of the Good. These conceptions are comprised of ideals and virtues whose fulfillment leads to happiness. In order to have a rational life plan based on the Good, the organization of the plan must form a structure that is generally consistent across domains of experience; that is, each individual has a consistent philosophy of what *is* good. Hence, the structure of the Good is viewed as an organization of values and ideals that generally provide individuals with both motivation and meaningfulness in life. Specifically, the structure of the Good provides a consistent set of criteria that the individual uses in making value choices.

This approach to the study of conceptions of the Good is also dependent on ethical theory for the various normative models of what the Good ought to be and for the philosophical descriptions, classifications, and analyses of judgments of the Good. Much of the traditional literature in ethics is divided into two major classes. The first contains moral theories of the Right or of obligation (represented psychologically in Kohlberg's moral judgment stages); the second contains ethical theories of the Good. The philosophic study of both judgments of the Right and and judgments of the Good have a history exceeding 2,500 years. Within the broad philosophic domain of judgments of the Good, the work presented here is specifically concerned with substantive judgments. In other words, the focus is placed on what is judged to be good and on the normative arguments or reasons given in support of such judgments.

METHODS

Subjects

At the first interview (1977), 43 individuals, ranging in age from five to 72, were interviewed (Erdynast, Armon, & Nelson, 1978). There were 11 5–13-year olds, 8 23–30-year-olds, 15 31–47-year-olds, and 9 48–72-year olds. The distribution of males and females was approximately equal both across and within age groups. Adult educational levels ranged from high school completion to doctoral degrees.

In 1981, all previous subjects were contacted. Thirty-nine out of the 43 subjects agreed to continue their participation in the longitudinal study by being interviewed every four years.

Instruments

Two interviews were given at each test time (1977, 1981): "The Good Life Interview" and Kohlberg's Standard Form Moral Judgment Interview (Form A). The Good Life Interview was designed and piloted with adult college students in 1976 and 1977. It consists of three parts. The first part contains a set of general questions concerning the Good Life and the subdomains of good work, good relationships, good education, the good of truth, knowledge, beauty, religion, sexuality, and so on. The second part contains questions concerning the individual's "real life" experiences in decision making where "goods" conflicted. The third part contains questions concerning the individual's "real life" experiences of making moral judgments as opposed to discussing hypothetical situations (as in the Kohlberg dilemmas).

The Moral Judgment Interview consists of hypothetical stories that feature deontic moral conflict. The subject is asked to make *prescriptive* responses about what should be done to resolve particular conflicts (see Colby & Kohlberg, in press, for full interview and administration procedures).

Administration

The Good Life and the Moral Judgment interviews were given in alternate order to each subject with a half-hour break between them. Each interview was conducted on an individual basis and was tape-recorded and transcribed. Total interview times ranged from one-and-a-half to three hours.

The interview method is a modified version of Piaget's clinical method. The interviewee is first asked a descriptive "what?" question and is then probed with "why?" questions. For example, in the Good Life Interview, the subject is asked, "What is good work?" and then "Why is that good?" In the Moral Judgment Interview, the question, "What should Heinz do?" is asked and then, "Why should he do that?" *Why* questions have the purpose of eliciting the underlying values and reasoning behind the choice of the *what* content.

Analyses

The structure and development of the normative conception of the Good is the primary object of analysis. Normative judgments are those that express and affirm particular ideals or rules of conduct. This should be distinguished from metaethical formulations of the nature and validity of the word or concept "good." Normative conceptions are of the form "X is good because Y."

The process of structural analysis began with the identification of consistent ways of reasoning that correspond to the theoretical specifications for a "structure of thought." A sample of reasoning was considered potentially structural if it contained thought patterns that showed evidence of a self-regulated, organized *system* of thought. Second, the identified structures were considered part of a stage hierarchy if, when compared, they could be ordered, and if, in this order, each posited "system of thought" could meet the following criteria:

1. *Qualitative difference:* Each stage is characterized by a unique pattern of thought in response to the same task.
2. *Invariant sequence:* The stages are uniquely ordered.
3. *Hierarchical integration:* The overall structures are integrative and non-interchangeable. Each results from the preceding one, integrating it as a subordinate structure. Each structure is then the basis of the subsequent one, into which it is itself integrated. If these criteria are met, each structural organization is considered a developmental stage (Piaget & Inhelder, 1969).

Prior to the analysis, it was proposed that the stages of the Good should meet these theoretical criteria and their empirical counterparts as follows:

1. *Structured whole* or "*system of thought*": Each stage of the Good should represent an organized system of reasoning if the individual responds to various content questions with consistency. If asked, "What is a good X, and why?" an individual's responses should be within half a

stage of each other, independent of the content of X, across all questions in the domain of the Good Life.

2. *Qualitative differences*: Each stage should represent a distinct and qualitatively different system of reasoning in response to the same question.

3. *Invariant sequence*: Longitudinally, subjects who change should do so progressively, from one stage to the next, without skipping stages or going backward.

4. *Hierarchical integration*: Theoretical analysis should reveal that each stage of the Good includes the one before it, not by adding new content, but by transforming the previous stage into a more highly integrated and differentiated structure.

CONVERGENT ANALYSIS

Another relatively recent approach for the general identification of structural stages is presently being developed. It is referred to as a General Model of Stage Theory (Commons & Richards, Chapters 6 and 7, this volume). The model is general enough to be applied to any sequential, cognitively based, structural stage theory. Table 17.1 describes the stages in the General Model. As can be seen in Table 17.1, postformal cognitive stages are central constructs in this model. If the proposed stages of the Good can be shown to be consistent with this model, it would lend further support to the claim that the stages are structural in nature.

RESULTS[1]

The preliminary, "clinical analysis" (Kohlberg, 1981a) of the cross-sectional and longitudinal data supported the structural nature of the Good Life stages. The ways in which the stages were proposed to meet the Piagetian criteria for a stage (described above) were borne out. Six stages of global reasoning about the Good and six stages of reasoning about Good Work resulted. Tables 17.2 and 17.3 describe the stages in the Good and in Good Work, respectively.

In addition, the stages of Good Work appear to be consistent with the General Model. Appendix A contains a demonstration of this consistency.

Stage sequentiality of the Good and Moral Judgment was supported. In both the Good and Moral Judgment, a subject's reasoning that changed stage within the four-year period did so progressively, by moving to the next ordered stage, without skipping. Figure 17.1 shows the amount, direction, and functional form of the stage change in the Good (top panel) and in Moral Judgment (bottom panel).

Table 17.1. General Model of Stage Theory

Stage No.	Name	Input	Operations	Output
3a	Primary operations	Single set of concrete particulars	Simple counting, showing comparability on basis of surface features	Single surface particulars; simple set size; multiple dual classifications
3b	Concrete operations	Mapping of surface (concrete) particulars; concrete elements such as numbers, objects	Ordering or classifying concrete particulars relative to each other	Relations of surface particulars; classes, relations, operations
4a	Abstract operations	Single set of variable values; only one operation applied to a variable	Abstractly representing elements; simple combining and permutating	Variable or single abstractions; repeated operations or relations
4b	Formal operations	Mapping (relating abstractions); iterative functions, relations, operations	Coordinating at least two operations and a relation	Two coordinated relations on variables or abstractions yielding a value; iterative operations
5a	Systematic operations	Two subdivided sets and the iterative relations or operations	Operating on operations, abstractly representing elements and all their combinations; representing the set of relations and operations within a set of systems across iterative relations and element classes in the systems produced by the operations	Systems, frameworks, paradigms

(Continued next page.)

Table 17.1 (continued)

Stage No.	Name	Input	Operations	Output
5b	Metasystematic operations	System of concretized systems	Axiomatization of relations; topological graphing; transforming systems; structural determination of morphic relations between systems	System of systems (theoretical structures) across frameworks
6a	Cross-paradigmatic	Single set (system of systems)	Metatheoretical operations; coordinating theories; examining the nature of theory	System of theoretical structures

Source: Commons & Richards, Chapter 7, this volume.

Table 17.2. Stages of the Good: Global Reasoning

I. Preconventional level
Stage 1: Radical Egoism
The Good revolves around the gratification of desires and the realization of fantasy. The Good is that which provides the individual with actual or fantasized physical experiences. *Doing* good is undifferentiated from *having* a good experience.
Stage 2: Instrumental Egoism
The Good is that which serves the individual's interests, including emotional, as well as physical, desires. There is a consistent conception of the Good that differs markedly from stage 1 in that it includes the individual's motives and intentions and the contemplation of actual consequences. There is a strong desire to be praised and liked by others and to satisfy material wants. The Good that is achieved through praising and approving can be immediate (self-other), general (stereotypical socially approved roles), or symbolic (sufficient material reward). The Good is that which results in "happiness."

II. Conventional level
Stage 3: Affective Mutuality
Good is an affective sense of happiness or fulfillment, a result of positive interpersonal experience. Good is determined by what *feels* good. There is a distinct sense that good can be determined by the absence of bad. A major component of what is good is that which helps the self and others to feel good (be happier, more successful, etc.) and promotes mutuality between self and others in the immediate social environment.
Stage 4: Individuality
Good is the expression of the individual's *self-chosen interests and values.* A central theme is "meaning." Whatever one does in life, it must be considered valuable and meaningful in a personal sense. The emphasis on individuality, however, is coupled with the awareness of the necessary adherence to moral and societal norms for the maintenance of one's good life.

III. Post-conventional level
Transitional Stage 4/5: Subjective-Relativism
The Good stands outside moral and societal norms and is a subjective-relative conception dependent on each individual's psychological reaction to particular activities, events, persons, etc. Good is that which an individual *feels or believes to be good* within the constraints of individual rights and justice.
Stage 5: Autonomy
The Good is a result of a consistent ethical philosophy that views the individual as an autonomous agent. The Good is manifested in productive, meaningful activities that not only draw upon the individual's higher level capabilities, but that are also consistent with an individual's general philosophy. There is the need to broaden the evaluation of the Good beyond the self to include a societal perspective. This is achieved through a *"balancing" of responsibility to self and responsibility to society* or humanity of which the individual sees him/herself as a part.
Stage 6: Universal Holism
The Good for the self and the Good for the society or humanity becomes integrated under a larger conception of "humanity" or "nature." The Good is universalized in that the *Good for the self is the Good for society,* because "society" is made up of many similar selves. Category conflicts between the Good and the Right are resolved because what is good must conform to universal moral principles of justice and respect for persons.

Table 17.3. Stages of Good Work

Stage 1
For children at stage 1, good work is undifferentiated from fantasized or experienced pleasurable activities or roles. There is an absence of a conception of the instrumental value of work to provide for the self's material needs.

Stage 2
At stage 2, the recognition of the reciprocal relation between working and its consequences of serving the self's needs is clear. *Doing* good work is seen not only as a source of material reward, but also as a source of satisfaction, particularly through praise from others. Same-sex, socially approved work roles are consistently mentioned. However, there is an absence of a sense of what the actual role requirements might be. *Good* work is often seen as equivalent to *hard* work.

Stage 3
At stage 3, good work is identified with socially beneficial work roles that promote mutuality between self and other in one's immediate work environment. Self-satisfaction is a result of the interactions involved in serving others–interactions that provide positive affective experience.

Stage 4
Good work at stage 4 becomes relativized to include any self-chosen activity that provides personal satisfaction or enjoyment, financial security, and something useful in terms of social utility, or that at least does not harm others.

Transitional Stage 4/5
At transitional stage 4/5, good or bad work is a subjective and a relative conception. Within the constraints of individuals' basic rights it is dependent solely on the perceived effect of the work on the worker.

Stage 5
At stage 5, good work represents meaningful, productive activities which draw on the individual's higher level capabilities. Such activities enhance intellectual and/or psychological self-development and/or creativity, and require a personal commitment. Some social commitment is also required, and one must "balance" between responsibility to self and responsibility to society.

Stage 6
At stage 6, good work is embodied in the exercising of fully realized human interests and capabilities for all persons in the context of a just society. Good work has intrinsic value and thereby results in qualitative impact on both society or humanity and the individual simultaneously.

These preliminary results support the hypothesis that stage change continues in adulthood. For the Good, 11 out of 22 adults over 30 advanced a minimum of a half stage over a four-year period, and none regressed. Similarly, for Moral Judgment, 7 out of 22 adults over 30 advanced a minimum of a half stage, and one regressed a half stage.[2]

The amount of change decreased as a linear function of the natural log of age[3] and is reported below:

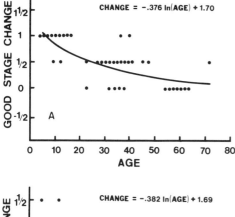

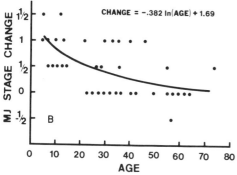

Figure 17.1. Change in Global Good Stage (top panel) and Moral Judgment Stage (bottom panel) from 1977 to 1981 as a Function of Age (1977)

Good stage change $= -0.376 \ln(age) + 1.70$, $r^2 = .524$ $F_{1,36} = 39.653$ (p = 0.000)

Moral stage change $= -0.382 \ln(age) + 1.69$, $r^2 = .338$ $F_{1,36} = 18.415$ (p = 0.000)

Although the traditional notion that the rate of stage change decreases with age is supported, the function indicates that it does not go to zero within a life time.

Postconventional stages of the Good and of Moral Judgment were only found in adults over 30 years old in the analysis of the first round of data (1977). Stage attainment in the Good and in Moral Judgment increased as a function of age. Figure 17.2 shows the level, direction, and functional form of stage attainment in the Good (top panel) and in Moral Judgment (bottom panel). As can be seen in Figure 17.2, only subjects over the age of 30 attained a post-conventional stage (4/5,5,5/6,6) of the Good, and only subjects over 26 years of age attained postconventional stages in Moral Judgment. For the Good, 8 out of 26 adults over 30 attained these stages; in Moral Judgment, 10 out of 26.

Stage attainment both in the Good and in Moral Judgment in-creased as a linear function of the natural log of age:

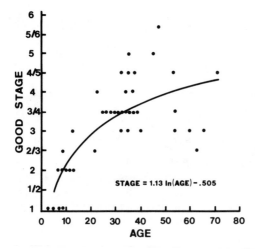

STAGE = 1.13 ln(AGE) - .505

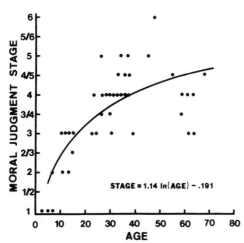

STAGE = 1.14 ln(AGE) - .191

Figure 17.2. Stage Attainment in the Good (top panel) and in Moral Judgment (bottom panel) in 1977 as a Function of Age

Good stage $= 1.132$ ln(age) $- 0.505$, $r^2 = .558$ $F_{1,36} = 45.460$ (p $= 0.000$)

Moral stage $= 1.141$ ln(age) $- 0.191$, $r^2 = .557$ $F_{1,36} = 45.422$ (p $= 0.000$)

Variation in stage attainment, however, also increased with age, a finding typically referred to in the literature as "fan spread." This variation helps explain why the issue of adult structural development is problematic.

The similarity of the results of stage attainment for the Good and for Moral Judgment suggests that they are highly correlated. The regression equation follows:

Moral stage = .946Good stage + .511, $r^2 = 0.880$ $F_{1,36} = 266.945$ (p = 0.000)

Figure 17.3 shows that this is truly a linear fit, with no curving of the points away from the best-fit regression line.

DISCUSSION

Structural change in adulthood

In the cross-sectional analysis, postconventional stages of the Good and of Moral Judgment did not occur in the present sample below the age of 26. This finding leads to the claim that post-conventional reasoning represents "adulthood stages." However, traditionally the presence of such development in adulthood has been denied in the structural-developmental literature.

Three such arguments are now critically examined. The first argument proceeds from studies of adult reasoning. It asserts that what commonly takes place in adulthood is some other, nonstructural form of development. Such development is often conceptualized as functional, task-related growth, in which stage content is enriched, rather than as a process of structural change. For example, Kohlberg (1981; see also Kohlberg & Armon, Chapter 18, this volume) advocates looking either an Eriksonian model of ego function to investigate the developmental tasks of adulthood or to Fowler's (1981) "Ethical and Religious Philosophies" for an understanding of how adults make meaning of their experience. Kohlberg and Shulik (in Kohlberg, 1981) conclude that although some older adults become quite advanced in their philosophic reflections concerning

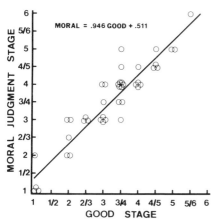

Figure 17.3. Moral Judgment Stage Scores Versus Good Life Stage Scores in 1977

such topics as the meaning of life and the coming of death, such reflections represent metaethical thinking. For these authors, the philosophical thinking that occurs in adulthood, while tremendously relevant to the understanding of adult experience, is not indicative of structural reorganization. The present author is in agreement with the view (see Kohlberg & Armon, Chapter 18, this volume) that advanced reflective thought is not necessarily evidence of structural development. Metaethical thinking centers on the nature and validity of concepts and consequently lacks the direct link to action in problem solving, a prime characteristic of structural thought.

But it is argued here that there is more to reasoning about value than metaethical thinking. A consistent ontic structure of the Good is necessary for a rational life plan and is therefore directly linked to action in problem solving and decision making. In a very concrete sense, reasoning about what is good embodies a set of criteria that the individual uses in decision making and problem resolution in the social, interpersonal, and intrapersonal domains.

It might be difficult to adhere to radical positions such as those of Socrates and Aristotle—who assert that to know the Good is to act on the Good—but it is plausible that reasoning about the Good is often directly linked to action and experience and to indirect, mediated action. Not all consistent processes of decision making, and their resultant activity, can be reduced to deontic moral reasoning and cognition. With some evidence for the structural development of reasoning about the Good in adulthood, it seems quite possible to discover and describe adult activities that provide the foundations for this development.

The second argument against the possibility of adult structural development was once advanced by Kohlberg (1969, 1971) and persists in the works of Piaget (1967). Proceeding from studies of structural development, it was concluded that the highest identified stage is already achieved by late adolescence or early adulthood. For example, Piaget believed the highest stage of cognitive development occurs in early adolescence. This argument appears to be rooted in the assumption that mental growth, like physical growth, peaks during this period.

These findings have resulted in a characterization of adult intellectual growth as horizontal décalage or reequilibration—that is, a process of applying previously attained structures to new content or activities, resulting in more competent action.

This criticism is more empirical in nature than the one previously mentioned. One cannot dispute Piaget's finding that formal operations appear in adolescence. Nevertheless, the notion that intellectual growth can only decline after the teen-age years is disconcerting. However, in Kohlberg's latest writings, he has withdrawn this claim. As a result of some scoring system revisions and the accompanying reanalysis of his longitudinal data, Kohlberg has changed his position on moral development in adulthood. Clearer discriminations between moral judgment stages 3, 4, and 5 have now led Kohlberg to claim, "there *is* a new stage in adulthood and many of our subjects continue to develop in their 20's and 30's rather than reaching a ceiling in midadolescence" (Colby, Kohlberg, Gibbs, & Lieberman, 1983). Two important findings in the present study challenge Piaget's conclusions and support Kohlberg's new findings.

First, as noted above, postconventional stages were not found in adolescence or early adulthood. Instead, they were found in subjects between the ages of 26 and 72 (as shown in Figure 17.2). Second, the adult subjects over 30 advanced both in the Good and in Moral Judgment (as shown in Figure 17.1). Such findings are evidence of adult structural development.

Gibbs' (1979) argument more radically challenges the notion of adult structural development than the two already presented. He states that structural moral development not only ends in late adolescence or early adulthood but that it does so at the conventional level. Gibbs argues that postconventional reasoning is a theorist's construct rather than an empirical, or "natural," phenomenon. He asserts that Kohlberg's stages 5 and 6 are different from stage 4 only in that they articulately formalize the moral reasoning put to use at stage 4. Gibb's position is that the ability to articulate and formalize moral principles does not meet the strict Piagetian criteria for structural development.

In response to Gibbs criticism, Kohlberg (1981b) argues that stage 5 is a culturally universal, natural stage because stage 5 reasoners base their judgments on a *universal hierarchy* of natural rights rather on the societally based rights of stage 4 reasoners. Kohlberg posits that it is this, not the use of moral theories such as social contract to justify moral judgments, that leads such reasoning to be considered a new stage.

It is argued here that postconventional reasoners cannot only formulate ethical theory, as Gibbs' claims, but they can also look upon such theories as independent "systems." Further, they can compare and contrast these systems in a way that conventional reasoners, operating in a single system, cannot. This ability distinguishes the structural features of conventional and postconventional reasoning. In addition, increasing evidence of cognitive stages beyond Piaget's stage of formal operations (Commons, Richards, & Kuhn, 1982; Richards & Commons, Chapter 15, this volume; Sinnott, Chapter 14, this volume; Powell, Chapter 15, this volume; Sternberg, Chapter 4, this volume) enhances the plausibility of structural postconventional thought.

The hypothesis that postconventional reasoning implies cognitive operations surpassing the formal-operational model described by

Piaget (1967) is corroborated by the argument presented here and the analysis presented in Appendix A. However, the investigation and identification of "postformal" operations is as yet novel and incomplete.

The relationship of Kohlberg's moral judgment stages to the stages of the Good

Philosophically, Kohlberg's Moral Judgment stages are highly related to the stages of the Good. Empirical analysis also revealed a high correlation (see results). As was seen in Figure 17.3, individuals tend to be at the same stage on both measures or at a higher stage in moral judgment. If this tendency remains consistent, it supports the notion that moral judgment stage is a necessary, but insufficient condition for the development of a parallel stage in the Good.

This form of the relationship is supported philosophically. It is traditionally accepted that a conception of justice is a precondition for a conception of the Good Life (Kant, 1887; Mill, 1861; Rawls, 1971). Ideals of the Good Life presuppose conceptions of freedom and liberty, conceptions that make possible the pursuit of the Good Life; however, ideals of the Good Life go beyond conceptions of freedom and liberty to define life values and purposes.

One perspective on the relationship between the Right and the Good concerns the "good of morality," that is, the good of right conduct. Kohlberg (1981a) claims that ethical reasoning presupposes deontic moral reasoning and it goes on "to support moral judgment and action as purposeful human activities" (p. 336). Similarly, Rawls (1971) identifies conceptions of the good as systems of motivation to follow principles of justice. An explanation of the motivation to *do* right cannot be based solely on deontic or logical considerations. As Kohlberg notes, "The 'why be moral?' question appears at the limit of moral inquiry and raises a new problem for consideration—the fundamental meaningfulness of human activity" (p. 322). It is clear that an answer to the question, "why be moral?" requires metaethical thought—thinking *outside* of logical moral inquiry and *inside* of the domain of the Good. However, such metaethical thinking does not exhaust the domain of the Good.

This is particularly true because reasoning about the Good Life involves values *outside* of the moral domain, which concerns itself primarily with judgments of right conduct. Judgments of the Good, by contrast, can be ethical judgments that concern persons, motives, intentions, traits of character, and aims, as to whether they are morally good, bad, virtuous, responsible, blameworthy, and so on. Judgments of the Good can also be nonmoral and nonethical judgments that evaluate physical properties, objects, experiences and the like. Ideals of the Good Life are contained in a broad evaluative system with metaethical, ethical, and nonethical dimensions. Therefore, while there is a strong relationship between reasoning about the Good and reasoning about the Right, it is argued here that they are separate and distinct organizations.

ADULT DEVELOPMENT AND THE CONTENT OF THE GOOD LIFE

Both Gibbs and Kohlberg correctly argue that the reflective ethical theories that tend to appear in adulthood are not in themselves sufficient evidence for the definition of structural stages (see Kohlberg & Armon, Chapter 18, this volume). In response, it was argued here that although such theories are not sufficient evidence of adult structural stages, there is structural reorganization in thinking about the Good embedded in the reflective content of adult reasoning. Certainly, for the purpose of identifying reasoning structures, the content of adult reasoning merely provides the surface-level data from which the structures are to be inferred.

However, analyses of the structures of ethical reasoning do not exhaust the examination of adult ethical thought. For adult development to be meaningfully understood, the content of ethical reasoning should not be considered trivial. While the developmental researcher is predisposed to be interested in *how* individuals reason about what is good, the normative ethical claims advanced by adults as to *what is* good are equally important. The content of ethical reasoning provides important information about both the actual activities in which individuals are involved and the aims to which they aspire.

Postconventional adults generate ethical systems, comprised of both content and structure, that are similar to those advanced by prominent moral philosophers. The two major categories of ethical theories, ethical hedonism and perfectionism, can be further broken down into subcategories as illustrated in Figure 17.4. Under the category of ethical hedonism, egoistic and social hedonism can be distinguished. In traditional ethics, egoistic hedonism tends to emphasize *pleasure* for the self while social hedonism tends to emphasize *happiness* for the self and other. Both happiness and pleasure are positive states of consciousness. However, happiness is more diffused, intellectual, and more enduring that "sensual" pleasure. Moreover, pleasure is more individualistic, no matter how distributed; happiness is more social (Smith, 1948).

Under the category of perfectionism, progressivism, rationalism, and religious orientations are distinguished. Progressivism emphasizes evolutionary change; rationalism emphasizes the specific perfection of human virtues; religious orientations emphasize the unity of persons with nature or the cosmos.

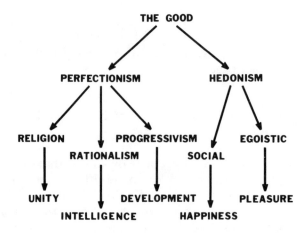

Figure 17.4. Breakdown of the Good in Traditional Ethics

These five philosophic orientations were identified in subjects' discussions of Good Work across all stages. Examples of some of these orientations, all from stage five protocols, are presented below.

Orientation: Social hedonism

Example: What is good work?

It has to be work that gives you satisfaction. Satisfaction in doing what you want to do. You Have to be happy in it. That's it, it has to bring happiness to you (case 34, age 77).

The stress on happiness or satisfaction as a good in itself follows J.S. Mill's general reasoning:

Whatever is desired otherwise than an end beyond itself and ultimately to happiness, is desired itself as part of happiness, and not desired for itself until it has become so (1861, p. 48).

Orientation: Perfectionism (progressivism)

Example: What is good work?

Good work would encompass things that add to my growth and development. Some of the components involve personal challenge (case 01, age 35).

Note the similarity with John Dewey:

Happiness is found only in success; but success means succeeding, getting forward, moving in advance. It is an active process not a passive outcome (1957, p. 112).

Orientation: Perfectionism (rationalism)

Example: What is good work?

For myself it would encompass the progression of man—meaning something that is carrying knowledge further. It's coming up with new ideas—it's carrying knowledge and ideas further from where you began with them (case 42, age 35).

The emphasis on creative ideas and the enhancement of knowledge is reminiscent of Aristotle:

A man's intellectual nature is the highest part of his being, the satisfaction that attends its activities is the highest of which he is capable (Book IV, trans. 1979).

These examples show that it is possible to classify the content of ethical reasoning by philosophical orientations, although these orientations or categories are clearly not exhaustive.

SUMMARY

This chapter has presented preliminary findings from a cross-sectional/longitudinal study of ethical reasoning that substantiate an argument for the existence of adult structural reasoning about the Good. It has been claimed that stages of ethical reasoning not only meet the criteria for a structural stage, but also that structural development both in the Good and in Moral Judgment continues in adulthood. Moreover, it has been demonstrated that higher stage adult reasoners produce ethical theories that are not dissimilar, in both content and structure, to the theories of eminent ethical philosophers. These findings suggest both psychological and philosophical validity for the idea of adulthood stages of the Good and of Moral Judgment.

It has been also demonstrated that the stages of the Good are highly related, but not reducible, to Kohlberg's stages of Moral Judgment. It was argued that reasoning about the Good often takes up where Moral Judgment leaves off to examine questions such as "why be moral?" But it was also claimed that this metaethical, reflective form of ethical reasoning does not exhaust the domain of the Good. On the contrary, it has been claimed that most "real life" evaluative judgments involve values outside of the purely moral

376 / Beyond Formal Operations

realm, that is, the realm of rules, laws, and states of justice. They are, rather, judgments that are guided by the individual's consistent system of interests, values, and purposes. Such evaluative judgments, it has been claimed, make up much of individual decision making and problem solving. Reasoning about the Good or the Good Life complements deontic reasoning about the Right, but goes beyond it to define individuals' meaningfulness in life.

Finally, the apparent existence of adulthood stages has major implications for adult psychology, generally, and for the philosophy of adult education, specifically. It has been argued that the content of adult ethical reasoning is as important as its corresponding structural skeleton. Moreover, it appears that much of this content can be classified by traditional philosophical orientation. Using this approach, researchers could proceed to not only determine *how* adults reason, but *what* they reason about—that is, the consistent goals, aims, values, and aspirations of adult ethical experience at each stage. The content of adult ethical thought provides a *philosophy* of adult ethical experience while its structure provides a developmental *psychology* of adult ethical development.

APPENDIX: DEMONSTRATION OF CORRESPONDENCE BETWEEN STAGES OF THE GOOD AND THE STAGES OF THE GENERAL MODEL OF STAGE THEORY

At stage 3, reasoning about the meaning of Good Work is restricted to a single system of the Good. Relations between self and other are identified and defined on elements within the system. This system is perceived as the self and the immediate group (such as family or office clients) with a single set of shared norms. The needs, interests, and goals of others provide the necessary elements of the system. However, there is still an absence of an external social world independent of the self—as a separate system. The absence of reference outside the self's immediate environment is illustrated in the following excerpt:

What is good work?

I think that any work that deals with people is good work. I'm sure that working with machines must be very unrewarding. Helping people ... is very worthwhile *because of the human interaction* and somewhere along the line you feel you are doing some good, and you are receiving back from it all the time. I enjoy teaching for this reason. I like to do things with them [students] that I feel will eventually be of some good and I get back so much from them too, warmth and energy.

Why it is important to be with people as part of good work?

Because I'm happier when I'm *reacting to people* (case 40, age 60).

In this example, there is consistent reference to others. However, these references are framed within the single system of direct face-to-face interaction. Such reasoning within a single system of direct-interaction is further illustrated by another subject:

What is good work?

Working with people . . . helping people . . . feeling like I'm able to do things for them or to help them feel good.

Why is that important?

I think it is important to get positive feedback and to feel some progress with the people I'm working with (case 31, age 58).

These two examples illustrate how stage 3 valuing omits the societal aspects of an ideal work concept and remains confined to social variables with which one has direct relations. These subjects recognize and identify relations between the self and other individuals, but they do not recognize and identify relations between the self and society. The Good, or value, of work is defined in terms of mutual relations within the immediate group to which the self reacts. In terms of the General Model, this "single-system" organization appears to be represented by consolidated formal operations.

The recognition of two separate systems, the self and the society, is apparent at stage 4. There is the observance that the self's system for achieving the Good can be constructed independently from the society's system of Good. Although there is the recognition of two separate systems (self and society), the individual is as yet unable to coordinate them. Moreover, although two separate systems are identified, there is an absence of the recognition that the relations between the two systems could be potentially conflictive. This can be seen in the following examples.

What is good work?

Any work is good work as long as it's productive of something useful, something that you can appreciate and that someone else can appreciate. *Something that you love doing. Something that you can construe as useful to the society* by almost any terminology you can imagine (case 41, age 35).

In this example, the notion of social utility is clear, yet it is uncoordinated with the notion of self-coordination.

> What is good work?

> In the first place it should be something useful. In the second place *it should be something you enjoy doing. It should be of some value to yourself and to society at large*, or an ideal value you are committed to. Virtually anything can be of value (case 38, age 33).

The reasoning in the above two examples goes beyond stage 3 by not only recognizing the effect of one's work on another system—the society at large—but also by acknowledging the self's needs to pursue its own satisfactions independent of the reactions of the immediate group. This stage can be identified with the "systematic" stage of the General Model because although there is differentiation of the two, self-regulating systems—self and society—there is an absence of their coordination.

At the fifth stage, however, the need for coordination between the Good for the self and the Good for the society is recognized, and there is an attempt to make complementary that which is potentially opposed. In the following example, the individual sees the need for "balance" and acknowledges potential contradiction between the self and societal systems. He or she attempts to integrate these systems within a larger framework.

> What is good work?

> First, I think that the work must have upward mobility . . . the work becomes more stimulating. But, at the same time, I feel that as you move up, *the work has to be a trade-off . . . between self-satisfaction and service.* I think the ultimate good work is when you get self-satisfaction out of service (case 17, age 34).

Here, the subject stresses the need for the self and society to mutually advance one another's interests. The systems of self and society are kept in balance through operations of abstract reciprocity. This concept is succinctly expressed in the following excerpt:

> What is good work?

> For one thing, there must be a balance. To the extent that you take from society, you must give to society. (case 207, age, 34)

There are many explicit suggestions of a broader, more exhaustive and inclusive system at stage 5, all foreshadowing development to the sixth stage. This is well illustrated in the following example.

What is good work?

I think good work allows a person to participate in something *greater than the person*. You have to be willing to take on the conflicts and the hardships in the name of something larger than yourself. And you have to be able to see that the products are indeed useful by *standards beyond your own*. I think it is really glorious when you can throw yourself into the system and participate in it and *you do not view the system as the other*. So, in my ideal world, you do what you do and it is well coordinated with everything else that is going on. (case 212, age 35).

The stage 5 ability to identify, analyze, and attempt to coordinate two distinct systems within a theory (incorporating the elements of both systems) is indicative of the metasystematic stage of the General Model.

At stage 6, the external social system and the internal social self-system are fully coordinated as subsystems of a greater system. Both can be identified as elements under a more exhaustive system such as "humankind" or "nature." The following excerpt illustrates the integration of these elements.

What is good work?

I think good work is self-producing work. That kind of activity or involvement where we are able to produce ourselves.

How does self-producing work effect others?

The self is social. We don't have a self if we don't have a society. I would think that if it is self-producing work, then you are working with a part of yourself. You would be working with what you might call the social side and if it isn't beneficial, you're hurting yourself . . . you wouldn't be self-creating (case 43, age 48).

Here, there is a conception of the person that includes both the self and the society. Whether the system is conceived as man, or nature, or something else, it maintains its equilibrium through operations that relationally affect all elements—elements that were once discrete structures or systems at stages 4 and 5. The scope of such reasoning is far-reaching, as shown in the following excerpt.

What is good work?

Good work has to take place in a context, so if we are talking about the ideal work, the context would be humanity or, rather, the entire environment. Within that context, good work would be realizing your potential, or 'self-actualization.' This is not necessarily an egoistic activity. Since you are a part of the whole, to actualize yourself is to actualize the world—for better or worse. I believe persons to be potentially good. So, if each person were to realize his or her own potential, he or she would also be realizing a better world. In terms of the specific work, this would vary. The constant would be that, whatever the work was, it would be completely consonant with the true nature of the self as that relates to the whole (case 206, age 45).

Here, at stage 6, a fully coordinated system is formed that incorporates the two previously distinct systems that were "balanced" at stage 5. This ability to form a larger, single, self-regulating organization, coordinating the elemental relations between systems within it, implies the operations of the cross-paradigmatic stage of the General Model. The table below shows the correspondences between stages of the Good and the stages of the General Model.

General Model Stage Name*	Stage Number	Good Work Stage
Formal operations	4b	3
Systematic operations	5a	3/4
Systematic operations	5a	4
Metasystematic operations	5b	4/5
Metasystematic operations	5b	5
Metasystematic operations	5b	5/6
Cross-Paradigmatic operations	6a	6

*Adapted from Commons & Richards, Chapter 7, this volume.

NOTES

1. The idea to use the natural logarithm of age was suggested by Michael Woodford. Regression analyses were performed with the help of Michael L. Commons and Richard Mattingly. The consultations of Edward DeVos and Marcus Lieberman were tremendously helpful.

2. Test-retest data are presently being collected to test for measurement effect.

3. In this, and the next three analyses, ln (age) accounted for more variance than age.

PART V

ANALYSES AND CRITIQUES
OF POST-FORMAL MODELS

18

THREE TYPES OF
STAGE MODELS USED IN THE STUDY OF
ADULT DEVELOPMENT
Lawrence Kohlberg & Cheryl Armon

Perhaps the most important issue in research regarding psycho-social change in adulthood is the question of adulthood stages. The fruitfulness of approaching personality change through adolescence using the concept of structural stages has become an agreed-upon directing premise of a large body of research. Yet, when it comes to studying adulthood personality change, there is neither clear research data nor consensus of theoretical opinion as to the plausibility of a structural stage model. It is the claim of the present authors that part of the problem hindering such consensus has been a confusion about what is actually being studied or measured. This chapter attempts to elaborate a systematic and general set of distinctions between three types of stages purported to be appropriate for the study of adult development.

The first and most notable adulthood stages are the Eriksonian functional stages (Erikson, 1963b) that trace the maturing person as that person experiences new socio-cultural spheres and roles. The second type of stages are referred to here as soft structural stages. These stages focus on the form of development, as do Piagetian stages, but they also include elements of affective or reflective characteristics that do not lend themselves to the Piagetian paradigm. Of these theories, Jane Loevinger's (1976) theory of ego development is the most completely developed and will serve as the primary example of the soft structural model. The third stage types to be distinguished in this chapter are hard structural stages, stages that have all the formal properties Piaget attributed to a stage. Kohlberg's (1969, 1981a) justice reasoning stages will be used to illustrate this approach to stage definition. Other examples would include Piaget's (1969) stages of logical reasoning and possibly Selman's (1980) stages of perspective taking.) The preliminary work of the second author

(Armon, Chapter 17, this volume) is also an attempt to define hard stages in value reasoning.

The distinctions to be made here between "hard" and "soft" structural stages have been made by other writers to whom we are indebted. However, the distinctions presented here are a little different and perhaps more elaborated. Gibbs (1979), for example, discusses the distinctions between "standard Piagetian stages" and "existential stages." For Gibbs, standard stages involve problem solving through the use of Piagetian reasoning operations while existential stages involve self-reflection upon such questions as "what is the meaning of my life or of my self?" or "what is human life all about?" Leaving aside minor differences, Gibbs' "existential" or "self-reflective" structural stages and what are referred to here as "soft" structural stages involve an ego or self, consciously making meaning for itself. In each case, the focus is on the self or ego, viewed as some form of a totality, a system of meaning that confronts the world or the "other." This is the assumption not only of Loevinger's (1976) *Ego Development,* but also of Kegan's (1982) *The Evolving Self,* Gilligan's (1982) *In a Different Voice* (contrasting a separate and a connected self), Perry's (1968) *Forms of Intellectual and Ethical Development*, and Fowler's (1981) *Stages of Faith.* For each of these authors, self-reflection and totalistic "meaning-making" are central. Furthermore, Gibbs, Loevinger, Kegan, Gilligan, Perry, and Fowler all acknowledge a moral dimension to self-reflective meaning-making. This moral dimension is referred to by Kohlberg (1981a) as an "ethical and religious philosophy." An ethical philosophy is more than a structure of moral reasoning defined by justice operations and moral conflict resolution. It also includes a conception of human nature, of society, and of the nature of ultimate reality. Classics such as Aristotles' *Ethics* or Spinoza's *Ethics* represent such total world views in which moral reasoning is embedded. Viewed in this light, the "strength" of hard stages is limited by the need to subdivide into discrete domains those world views that are in some sense a unity. What hard structural stages gain is precision in their articulation of a structural logic of stages that will survive the everchanging growth of psychological knowledge about the self, its functions and development.

The distinctions to be made between the three types of stage models will rely on the specific criteria of a hard structural stage model. In the traditional cognitive-developmental literature, the following four general criteria have been used to identify Piagetian cognitive stages:

1. Stages imply a distinction or qualitative difference in structures (modes of thinking) that still serve the same basic function (for example, intelligence) at various points in development.
2. These different structures form an invariant sequence, order, or succession in individual development. While cultural factors may

speed up, slow down, or stop development, they do not change its sequence.

3. Each of these different and sequential modes of thought forms a "structured whole." A given stage response on a task does not just represent a specific response determined by knowledge and familiarity with that task or tasks similar to it; rather, it represents an underlying thought-organization. The implication is that various aspects of stage structures should appear as a consistent cluster of responses in development.

4. Stages are hierarchical integrations. As noted, stages form an order of increasingly differentiated and integrated *structures* to fulfill a common function. Accordingly, higher stages displace (or, rather, integrate) the structures found at lower stages (Piaget, 1960).

Thus, these four Piagetian criteria will be used to distinguish the three types of stages. It will be argued that close examination of these criteria will distinguish hard Piagetian structural stages from both functional and soft structural models. If successful, it is hoped that this increased clarity will reduce some of the ambiguity present in the application of the stage construct to the investigation of adult development. The distinction between Eriksonian functional stages and hard structural stages will now be briefly discussed.[1]

The central distinctions between the Eriksonian functional stage model and the hard structural stage model can be described in terms of three of the four Piagetian stage criteria that are listed above. First, the structured whole criterion means that there is a constant form in the activity described, one that remains relatively constant across differing experiences, situations, and functions of the ego. The requirements implied by this criterion are inappropriate for a functional stage model. Functional stages are representative of differing ego functions in response to different "crises" involving particular and differing tasks. Hard structural stages, by comparison, are described in terms of different structures, or ways of thinking, in response to a single function, such as logical reasoning or moral judgment.

Second, functional stages rely on psychological rather than logical or moral philosophical accounts of the ways in which each stage brings new "strength" or "wisdom" to the individual. As a result, the functional account may be more culturally relative (though not relativistic) than the hard structural account. Hard structural stages distinguish the operative *form* of reasoning from psychological accounts of the self's concerns. In so doing, hard structural stage researchers have been able to longitudinally verify the cultural universality of the stage sequences (Nisan and Kohlberg, 1982; Colby, et al., 1983; Snarey, 1982).

Third, functional stages are not hierarchical integrations. Functional stages are "choices" or uses of new functions by an ego. Earlier functions remain in the background of a new stage. Hard structural stages on the other hand, *replace* earlier stages. Each succeeding stage transforms the previous one into a more adequate organization.

In summary, the differences between Eriksonian functional stages and hard structural stages are relatively straightforward. These differences concern not only the nature of the stages but also the focus of the theories themselves. The focus of functional stages on the self coincides with the notion of stages of an ego viewed as an executor or chooser who *uses* cognitive and other structures. In contrast, the focus of hard structural stages is upon forms of manifest reasoning rather than upon the ego's processes of choosing and defining itself.

Structural characteristics can be abstracted from Eriksonian functional stages (Snarey, Kohlberg, & Noam, 1983). Erikson himself has stated the general acceptance of the Piagetian and Kohlbergian models as "strands" of development that describe the structural basis of the individual's functional unity at each stage (1977, pp. 204–6; 1964, pp. 136–41, 171–72). Similarly, Piaget and Kohlberg have alluded to or argued for logical parallels between their theories and the Eriksonian model (Kohlberg & Gilligan, 1971; Kohlberg, 1973b; Piaget, 1973). However, Erikson's model does not have as its purpose a structural model of child and adult development.

In recent years, however, there has been the development of a number of theoretical and empirical definitions of "stages" that are considered essentially structural rather than functional. Many of these stage models do attempt to meet the four general Piagetian criteria for a structural stage. While these models attempt to meet these criteria, the degree to which they actually do meet them is uncertain. These models do have a general fit to the Piagetian criteria, but it is argued here that it is not a very close fit. For a closer fit, these general criteria must be closely examined and their theoretical and empirical requirements spelled out. It is claimed here that if these criteria are interpreted rigorously, they will distinguish hard structural stages from soft structural stages. What follows is a close examination of two Piagetian criteria: structured whole and hierarchical integration. Jane Loevinger's (1976) theory of ego development and Kohlberg's (1981a) theory of moral development will be used to illustrate this distinction.

For Loevinger, ego development is characterized by qualitative changes in complexity as the developing ego passes through an invariant hierarchical sequence of stages. The stages integrate "strands" of personality development across the dimensions of character, interpersonal style, conscious preoccupation and cognitive style. Ego development represents the development of "structures" in the cognitive-developmental sense of "an inner logic to the stages and their sequence" (1976, p. 11). The essence of ego development, states Loevinger, "is the search for coherent meaning in experience" (Loevinger & Wessler, 1970, p. 8).

To compare views of Loevinger's ego stages with what is claimed here to be a hard structural approach, an examination of shared assumptions is in order. First, the most basic shared assumption is the concept of ego. Both perspectives agree that there is a relative unity to personality—the ego—that reasons, judges, evaluates, and generally functions to make sense of the world. Second, both agree on the general requirements of Piaget's hierarchical stage model. These stages represent: (1) a structured whole that (2) develops in an invariant sequence that (3) forms hierarchical integrations. Third, both accept the idea that moral judgment and character are major aspects or dimensions of ego development, relating to a more general ego stage. A fourth area of agreement between Loevinger and the hard structural perspective concerns test construction and test scoring. Both Loevinger, who comes from a psychometric background, and hard structuralists, who have been governed by Piagetian assumptions, move away from traditional psychometric procedures and construct tests that attempt to tap underlying structures. Loevinger's approach is consistent with structuralism. She agrees that the test constructor finds developmental structures not by an inductive method but by an "abductive" method, a sort of mutual bootstrapping that involves a working back and forth between theoretical reflections and the responses subjects actually give. Fifth, although Loevinger has not claimed that her model and method have universal or cross-cultural validity, it appears that it probably does have it, in light of the support received from research in Cuaracao, Israel, Germany, French-speaking Quebec, and Japan (Kusatsu, 1978; Lasker, 1974a, 1974b, 1977; Limoges, note 40; Snarey and Blasi, 1980; Snarey, 1982; Vetter, 1978).

Leaving aside the shared general assumptions of a soft and hard structural model, the theoretical and empirical differences between them will now be discussed through a closer examination of Piagetian structural stage criteria.

The first Piagetian criterion to be closely examined is that of the structured whole. It was considered by Piaget (1960, 1972) to be the central criterion of structural stages. At the outset, there appears to be general agreement among both hard and soft structural model researchers as to the nature and conception of "structured wholeness." This general notion can be described as a conception of underlying thought organization that determines reponses to tasks that are not manifestly similar. The general empirical implication is that individuals' thinking will be at a single, dominant stage across varying content, though the presence of usage of the stage adjacent to the dominant stage may also be expected (Colby, et al., 1983).

However, a closer examination of the Piagetian construction of structured wholeness uncovers a number of marked differences between structural stage models. These differences partly revolve around a model's conception of structure itself.

For Piaget (1970), a structure is a system of transformational laws that organize and govern reasoning operations. This formalized governing system is reflected or manifested in individuals' actual *responses* to conflicts or problems (Kohlberg, 1981a). Since it is only the formal organization of reasoning operations that defines a structure, however, one is led necessarily to additional distinctions between content and structure and between competence and performance in order to maintain a methodology that can identify the structures.

In contrast, Loevinger's scheme considers structure less a form of thinking than general, stable, and consistent personality content and functions, the usage implied in the psychoanalytic concept of character structure. Structure in Loevinger's terms is a hypothetical, underlying entity of personality like the psychoanalytic ego. Because structure is an underlying hypothetical construct, it can never be directly observed. The existence of a structure can only be inferred from probabilistic signs of the hypothetical structure, rather than abstracted from observations of a phenomenon. Loevinger's actual assessment measure is based on categories of content, or mixtures of content and structure, as probabilistic signs of an underlying structure.

Since the structures themselves can never be observed, the stages that represent them are constructions of ideal types or illustrative exemplars, rather than abstracted forms or expressions of the structures themselves. An ideal type is the theoretical representation of the stage, which itself contains differing mixtures of content and structure. The glossing over of the distinction between content and structure reduces the plausibility of defining the operations that structures were intended to represent.

Similar to the distinction between content and structure, the distinction between competence and performance is also implied by the structured whole criterion since the structures themselves are manifestations of competence. The lack of a clear distinction between content and structure in soft structural stage models, however, leads to an ambiguous distinction between competence and performance.

Loevinger has attempted to address this distinction methodologically by counting higher stage responses more heavily and applying an ogive transformation to individual scores. In so doing, however, her methodological approach fails the structured whole criterion on two counts. First, her assessment procedure implies that individuals respond to an item at all stages. This means that items do not measure a subject's competence because they do not elicit a subject's highest performance. Second, and more importantly, the scoring procedure cannot directly test even the most general conception of structured wholeness since individuals are not assigned to their modal stage.

Theoretically, then, there are differences between soft and hard structural stage models concerning how to articulate the inner logic of the stages. Loevinger defines her stages partly in terms of structures, but also partly in terms of functions and motives pertaining to the whole self and its enhancement and defense (Kohlberg, 1981a). Loevinger's theory, by definition, addresses the unity of the self (Loevinger, note 41) and is dependent on the individual's reflections upon the self's psychology. Such reflections are composites of second-order or meta-modes of thinking. These reflections on the self's psychology represent one form of reflective thought but there are other examples. For instance, Fowler's (1981) stages of faith represent reflection on the self's ethics and epistemology. Broughton's (1978) stages of metaphysics represent reflections upon the meaning and nature of reality.

It is important here to note the distinction between the forms of reflection described here and Piaget's conception of "reflective abstraction." While Piaget observes that reflective abstraction accompanies movement from one stage to the next, this "reflection" is not to be interpreted such that each later stage involves a self-conscious awareness of itself or of the previous stage. On the contrary, reflective abstraction is considered to be an unconscious structural process, not the conscious formation of a theoretical perspective on one's own development.

Thus, systems of second-order or meta-modes of thinking appear to represent theories that individuals construct, not structural forms. Piagetian structures embody organized systems of operative reasoning where operations are interiorized forms of *action*. Empirically, this implies that the stages relate to action in direct ways. Soft stages do, however, appear to have qualitatively different organizations. That is, there may be an identifiable differentiation between the stages. But reflective and self-reflective forms of development do not appear to be interiorized forms of action, at least theoretically. Nor have they been shown to be directly linked to action or problem solving in the empirical arena. Loevinger and other soft structural stage researchers have not attempted to construct a methodology based on direct problem solving nor have they published studies relating reasoning in a given domain to actual behavior.

In contrast, hard structural stage models define structures in a way consistent with the Piagetian construction—as an organization of manifest thought operations. They are simply a consistent rational logic or form such as that implied by a set of logical operations identified in diverse content. This formulation, then, represents the inner logic of the stages through the identification of the specific operations that the structure is to represent.

Theoretically, hard structural stage theories rely on an abstraction from the concrete, unitary self or ego to the perspective of an epistemic self (in Piaget's logical stages) or a rational moral subject (in Kohlberg's justice stages). This distinction allows a hard structural stage model to define the stages solely in terms of cognitive or sociomoral operations, not in terms of reflections upon the self, morality, or nature.

Within Kohlberg's model, the interiorized forms of action that the operations represent are prescriptive forms of role-taking in concrete moral situations.[2] Moral stages, then, represent the different forms of reversible operations: reciprocity, equality, and universalizability. For Piaget and the present authors, justice is the structure of conflict resolution for competing claims between persons. It is the parallel in the social world to the structure of logical thought in the physical world. The justice operations of reciprocity and equality in social interaction parallel the logical and mathematical operations of reciprocity and equality in science and mathematics. In both logical and justice stages, the operations imply an equilibrative or reversible system.

Moreover, both Piagetian cognitive tasks and Kohlbergian moral judgment interviews are set up to elicit these specific, predefined operations. The tasks themselves are focused on transformational reasoning. Reciprocity, for example, is elicited by tasks that present conflicts requiring reciprocity for their resolution. In other words, in order for the methodology of the hard structural model to be consonant with its conception of structure, it must attempt an as exact as possible specification of the content and form distinction.

An illustration of this methodological procedure is available from Kohlberg's model. An original definition of moral stages and the research based on the 1958 method of assessment is summarized elsewhere (Kohlberg, 1969). There it is described how stages were assessed in terms of favored content; that is, holding together all normative content by a stage and inferring structure as an ideal type. These earlier stage assessment procedures and stage definitions partially confounded content and structure. The current assessment of moral judgment reasoning (Colby & Kohlberg, in press) differentiates the form of moral judgment from the norm favored by individuals. To explain briefly, an interview transcript is first classified by the content of the choice; second, it is classified by the content of the justification of the choice; third, it is classified by the value content appealed to in the justification. Only after classifying content according to these three content categories is an interview assessed by stage or structure. At this point, formal justice structures are identified that characterize a stage in terms of its use of the relations of reversibility, such as equality, reciprocity, and universalizability. Thus, current methods involve an explicit differentiation between content and structure.

In addition, Kohlberg's current assessment instrument and interview method taps the subject's competence rather than performance by providing probing questions that attempt to push the upper limits of the subject's thinking (Colby et al., 1983).

The second criterion to be illustrated is that of hierarchical integrations. There are differences in the interpretation of this criterion between hard and soft structural stage models. The central feature of hierarchical integrations concerns the inner logic of a stage sequence. What is required of this criterion is both theoretical and empirical support for the notion that later stages not only *replace*, but also *transform* earlier stages. Theoretically, hard structural stage models follow Piaget (1970) in asserting that to construct a model of hierarchically integrated stages is to construct a normative model of development. A normative model establishes a standard as an endpoint. It must include a philosophical as well as a psychological account of this endpoint or most equilibrated stage. Thus, each stage in the hierarchy represents an increase in correspondence with the endpoint. It must include a philosophical, as well as a psychological, Piaget and Kohlberg (1973a) relies on a conception of human rationality in that it presumes an endpoint upon which all rational agents could agree (see also Habermas, in press). Piaget's normative model has as its standard the criterion of reversibility. He formulates an endpoint of logical thought as propositional logic in terms of the INRC group.

The ambiguity of the inner logic of Loevinger's and others' soft structural stage sequences reduces the plausibility of formulating a normative model of development. However, it is claimed here that it is not possible to construct a stage sequence that conforms to the criterion of hierarchical integrations but does not specify the inner logic of the sequence in terms of its endpoint. Loevinger herself explicitly denies a normative model and makes no claim that a higher ego stage is a more adequate stage.[3]

> Who is so wise as to say which is the highest stage? Each investigator in the field has a different idea of how the highest stage should be defined (Loevinger, note 41).

From a more empirical perspective, Loevinger's stages are nontransformational. Rather than each stage representing an *integration* or *transformation* of the previous stage, new aspects are added to previous stages to define higher ones. The stages appear to be increasingly inclusive, cumulative systems. The following representation of Loevinger's I-5 and I-6 stages illustrates this point.[4]

Stage: Autonomous
Code: I-5
Impulse control/character development: *Add* coping with conflicting inner
  needs, toleration
Interpersonal style: *Add* respect for autonomy, interdependence
Conscious preoccupations: Vividly conveyed feelings, integration of
  physiological and psychological, psychological causation of behavior, role
  conception, self-fulfillment, self in social context
Cognitive style: Increased conceptual complexity, complex patterns, toleration
  for ambiguity, broad scope, objectivity

Stage: Integrated
Code: I-6
Impulse control/character development: *Add* reconciling inner conflicts
  renunciation of unattainable
Interpersonal style: *Add* cherishing of individuality
Conscious preoccupation: *Add* identity
Cognitive style: Same

Note: "Add" means in addition to the description applying to the previous level.

As stated earlier, hard structural stage models attempt to define stages in terms of discrete operations of reasoning in contrast to reflective or self-reflective metathinking. By defining the stages in terms of operations of reasoning, hard structural stage models can plausibly explicate not only the inner logic of the stages but also the inner logic of the sequence from one stage to the next. Building upon the identification of operations in reasoning, hard structural stages are amenable to formulation within a normative model.

Logic is a case of a normative model. Although different logicians and philosophers design different formulations of logic, most search for one or more formalizations upon which all rational agents could agree. The same could be said of justice structures. Rawls' (1971) theory of justice is an attempt to construct a normative model of justice, as are the works of Kant (1887), Sidgwick (1907), and Hare (1963). The main activity of normative moral philosophy is the attempt to define and justify this normative endpoint.

The focus of Piaget and Kohlberg on morality as deontological justice springs, in part, from a concern with moral and ethical universality in moral judgment. The search for moral universality implies the search for some minimal value conception(s) on which all persons could agree, regardless of differences in detailed aims or goals.

Soft stages, on the other hand, cannot be formalized in a normative model. Development to the higher soft stages is optional, not prescribed. Although such development involves increased reflectivity or complexity, it is unclear whether some of these stages are of co-equal validity. The terminus of many soft stage sequences is a mystical, transcendental, or post-rational level. Most soft stage models stem either from James Mark Baldwin's (1906) hyperlogic to some notion of totality or unity or from Klaus Riegel's (1973) hypotheses about dialectical adult thought that transcends the subjective-objective distinction. These levels move beyond the criterion of rationality, autonomy, and agreement assumed by a normative model.

A final aspect of the criterion of hierarchical integrations concerns empirical findings. To use justice stages as an example, Rest (1973) reports a Guttman Scale of cumulative sequence of comprehension. Individuals comprehended all the stages below their own but could not comprehend reasoning more than one stage above their own. He also found that individuals prefer the highest stage that they comprehend.

SUMMARY

This chapter has attempted to elaborate a set of distinctions between *functional*, *soft structural*, and *hard structural* stage models. It was argued that a rigorous application of the Piagetian criteria for a hard structural stage can distinguish these three stage models and that only hard structural stages can actually meet these criteria. Nevertheless, the reasons for the success of the Piagetian hard structural stage scheme in charting logic and justice development may be precisely the reasons that it will not be successful in charting the experience and wisdom of adulthood, including questions such as "why be moral?" or "what is the meaning of life?" The "answers" to these questions cannot be given within a rational logic of justice. Such a rational logic cannot explain the unique characteristics of adult development, with its existential, reflective theories of the human condition. The strict Piagetian stage construction may need to be abandoned in the study of adult development, but the idea of stages in adulthood should not be. There are hierarchical levels of positive development in adulthood, and this development is something other than life phases (Levinson, et al., 1978). Additionally, soft stages of the sort described here differ from Erikson's functional stages. Soft stage development depends on neither the emergence of new functions nor the performance of new tasks. Instead, soft stages depend on formal reflection. They can attempt to interpret the tasks

394 / Beyond Formal Operations

of metaphysics and religion—essentially the task of integrating the ideals of justice, love, and truth with the ultimate nature of reality. Soft stage models present a new way of doing research in adult development, a way that has *emerged from* the Piagetian paradigm.

NOTES

1. See Kohlberg (1973b) for a more complete treatment of the similarities and differences between Eriksonian stages and justice reasoning stages.

2. The moral stages have also been found to be empirically related to moral action (Kohlberg & Candee, 1981; Blasi, 1980).

3. Loevinger has been previously criticized for this omission. (See Habermas, 1975; Broughton & Zahaykevich, 1977.

4. Adapted from Table 1: Some Milestones of Ego Development, in Loevinger, 1976.

19

NOT BEYOND FORMAL OPERATIONS BUT BEYOND PIAGET

John M. Broughton

A keystone in the Piagetian theory of genesis is formal operations. In the technical terminology of logic, the formal-operational
structure comprises a lattice of Boolean functions plus a group of
transformations that operate on these functions. In more psychological terms, we could say that formal operations represents the stage
where three apical cognitive capacities are finally acquired: the total
freeing of form from content, the integration of two different forms
of reversibility, and the formation of exhaustive combinatorial
permutations. Piaget displayed relatively little empirical concern for
this stage. Nevertheless, as a description of the state of ideal
equilibrium marking the endpoint or *telos* of the stage sequence, the
formal-operations construct exerts a powerful influence. It defines
intelligence and the ultimate philosophic categories of intellectual
experience. It is the standard by which acts of reasoning are evaluated
as more or less intelligent. It also serves as the criterion by which the
different forms that intelligence takes are normatively ordered. One
could legitimately say that formal operations epitomizes the totality,
purpose, and meaning of development. This applies not only to
cognitive, but also to affective and moral development since Piaget's
most recent position on domains of development makes cognitive
structures paradigmatic for all modalities of consciousness (Piaget &
Inhelder, 1969). As the apex of development in general, formal
operations serves to characterize the adult person and provide criteria
for evaluating when someone becomes mature. Thus, although it

The author wishes to thank Eric Amsel, Michael Basseches, Paul Chevigny, and
Marta Zahaykevich for reading and commenting most helpfully on drafts of this
manuscript. Thanks also to all those friends, colleagues, and students, too numerous to
mention, who have contributed to the development of the ideas presented here. Special
thanks to Catherine Welfare and the ever-patient Teacher's College Typing Center for
help in the preparation of the manuscript.

395

stands for the end of development, the final stage is, for all intents and purposes, the true point of departure for developmental theory.

This chapter is intended as a critical assessment of those recent innovations in post-Piagetian theory that have attempted to conceptualize development "beyond formal operations." There are three sections to the argument. The first section offers a typology that classifies the different kinds of complaints leveled by different theorists against the formal-operations construct and catalogues the various revisions that they have urged. Despite important differences between the recommendations of these theorists, the majority of them turn out to have converging concerns. The second section suggests that the problems with the formal-operations construct are more fundamental than the revisionists realize. Fifteen such problems are described. The number and magnitude of these difficulties are sufficient to cast doubt on the viability of not only the formal-operations construct but also Piaget's developmental theory as a whole. In the third section, some exploratory analysis is made of the intellectual, historical, and political reasons for the emergence in Piagetian developmental psychology of a revisionist movement that fails to acknowledge the fundamental weaknesses in Piaget's theory.

"BEYOND FORMAL OPERATIONS": THREE TYPES OF REVISIONISM

Piaget's claim concerning the finality and ultimacy of formal operations in development is a clear and definite one. Nevertheless, an intrepid band of post-Piagetians has spoken out against the idea that the formal-operational structure is an adequate terminus to the developmental process. This group has been strongly influenced by the emergence of adulthood as a major social and psychological concern in the 1970s. The various theorists in the group, 40 in number, have tried to reconcile their fundamentally sympathetic attitudes toward Piaget's constructivist endeavor with their desire to locate specifically adult forms of consciousness distinct from adolescent thought.

In both pointing to inadequacies and calling for revisions in Piaget's theory, almost all of these post-Piagetian authors have exhibited what could be called a "liberal view of progress"[1] in their approach to psychological theorizing. Not surprisingly, this view toward the future fate of Piaget's theory is a rather Piagetian one. Essentially, the revisionists have argued that Piaget's theory has no fundamental problems, no basic faults; it is just young and not fully developed. From such a liberal revisionist perspective, Piaget's formal-operational construct is seen as either *erroneous, penultimate,* or *biased.*

Error

In the first type of revisionism, there is a basic acceptance of two primary assumptions: the centrality of logic to thought and the centrality of rational reconstruction[2] to development. According to this view, Piaget's theory of adolescent logic is lacking only because the particular logical model employed is incorrect. Thus Parsons (1960), Osherson (1975), and Braine (1981) have argued that Piaget described the logic of formal operations inconsistently or otherwise inadequately. A somewhat different but related position is that Piaget's account is quite reasonable and consistent in terms of formal logic but he was mistaken in thinking that this kind of logic could provide an adequate model for adolescent cognition. Ironically, the best example of this trend would be Piaget himself, who, just prior to his death, renounced formal logic as a model in favor of intentional logic, the "logic of meanings" (Piaget, 1980). Other examples are provided by Strauss and Kroy (1977) and Piéraut-Le Bonnier (1980) who called for a "modal logic" to replace Piaget's, and Apostel (1976)—one of Piaget's colleagues—who called for a "logic of action." These authors follow the example of Matalon (1962), who was perhaps the earliest to call into question the adequacy of formal logic in accounting for "natural" adolescent and adult thought.

Penultimacy

Another kind of revisionist position sees the formal-operational model as capturing an actual, penultimate phase of adolescent cognitive development, but not the final, ultimate stage of thought. From this perspective, the Piagetian theory is truncated in its upper reaches. Piaget overlooked a whole other developmental level beyond formal operations, one of mathematical logic (for example, Powell, note 42), dialectical logic (Riegel, 1973), philosophy of science (Kennedy, note 43), or metacognitive-metasystematic reasoning (van den Daele, 1975; Stevens-Long, 1979; Lefebvre-Pinard, 1980; Basseches, 1980; Fischer, 1980; Sinnott, 1981; Commons, Richards, & Kuhn 1982; Commons & Richards, Chapter 7, this volume; Sternberg and Downing, 1982; Koplowitz, note 27).[3] Pascual-Leone (Chapter 9, this volume) has gone as far as to say that Piaget overlooked five postformal stages. Whatever the specific amendments sought by these various critics, they have in common their dispute with Piaget's claim that formal-operational thought is the ideal and terminal state of cognitive equilibrium.

Bias

A third kind of revisionist position, by far the most popular, holds that Piaget's theory is biased rather than truncated or erroneous (see,

398 / Beyond Formal Operations

for example, Turner, 1973; Arlin, 1975; Gruber & Vonèche, 1976; Gilligan & Murphy, 1979). These critics often question the primacy of logic and, in some cases, call into doubt the notion that development is exclusively a process of rational reconstruction. They see the standard Piagetian account as lacking in some significant dimension. They proffer an alternative to logical thought, for example, functional or contextual reason, which is typically proposed as a counterbalance to logic and a compensation for its shortcomings.

What makes this position difficult to grasp is that its proponents are not always clear about the structural and temporal relationships that this contemporary psychic quality bears to formal logical thought. They often leave unclear the question of whether the additional cognitive quality is supposed to co-exist with logical cognition or succeed it. Edelstein and Noam (1982) are probably the only revisionists to have tackled this issue directly and clearly. The others typically fail to discuss in any depth whether the mode of consciousness that they propose is qualitatively superior to formal thought, whether it presupposes formal thought, or whether it comprises an alternative endpoint.

Despite the lack of conceptual clarity surrounding the accusations of "bias" made against the Piagetian formal-operations construct, this group of revisionists usually presents its alternative form of consciousness as a clear counterpoint to the Piagetian formal structure. There are nine basic kinds of such contrapuntal alternatives. The first variant opposes the universalism of Piaget with a *particularism*. In their critique of the postformal trend, Monnier and Wells (1980) have tried (incorrectly) to locate me in this group. A more appropriate exemplar is Gruber (1981a, b) or Gruber and Vonèche (1976). According to this unique point of view, the formal-operational stage is followed by a period in which different individuals pursue different courses toward the refinement of their own unique perspective.[4] Lefebvre-Pinard (1980) has offered a related vision in stressing the "multilinearity" of adult development.

The second variant supplements the convergent style of formal thought with a *divergent* one. It is illustrated by Arlin (1975), who proposes that the problem-solving cognitive strategies of the formal stage are succeeded by 'problem-finding' ones. In Arlin's case, this later phase is not seen as comprising a 'postformal' stage; it is considered a second formal stage. As pointed out by Winograd (1980, p. 237), this notion of "problem acquisition" is a standard concept drawn from the repertoire of management specialists such as Herbert Simon. It was introduced into developmental psychology by Robert White (1959).

The third variant opposes the Piagetian emphasis on the generalities of form with an equal but opposite stress on the specificities of *content and experience*. Proponents of this position offer, in contrast to the decontextualized thought so highly valued by Piaget, forms of cognition that appreciate and take into account *contextuality*. Fowler (1980, pp. 61–62) refers to such a structure as a "logic of conviction." Gilligan and Murphy (1979) and Labouvie-Vief (1980) have made perhaps the strongest case for this position. To some extent, the work of Perry (1968) and those influenced by him (for example, Benack Chapter 16, this volume) falls under the same rubric. A singularly interesting example of this point of view is Edelstein and Noam's (1982) argument that following the propositional structure of formal operations comes a more advanced and comprehensive structure that integrates propositional with nonpropositional contexts. They call this higher stage the "self-structure," which is concerned with reality as a whole. Gilligan and Murphy and Edelstein and Noam stress that the limits of purely logical cognition are most obvious in contexts of interpersonal communication, especially where there is an affective component. This observation leads them toward the notion that the higher and more comprehensive structure of adult thought represents the personal "ego," "self," or "identity."

In the fourth variant, closely related to the third, a *concrete* kind of cognitive structures and processes, and proposes in their wake the emergence of a normatively superior, more comprehensive, and more adequate *"recentrated"* consciousness. Arguing from an anthropological perspective, he posits that, with the development of cognitive that stresses the *functional* nature of thought viewed as a process in real time. A related position is that of Glick (1977, note 46), who argues for a functional view of rationality that takes into account the situationally sensitive deployment of formal and scientific interpretations by the subject.

A fifth variant, related to the two previous ones, but cast in a more carefully constructed theoretical matrix, is represented by Turner (1973). He argues against the definitive nature of decentrated cognitive structures and processes, and proposes in their wake the emergence of a normatively superior, more comprehensive, and more adequate *"recentrated"* consciousness. Arguing from an anthropological perspective, he posits that, with the development of cognitive recentration, the mind would interpet experience primarily in terms of its concrete mythic, ritual, and aesthetic aspects. Here, the drift of his thinking converges unwittingly with that of developmentalists like Baldwin (1915), Cassirer (1957), Kaplan (note 47), and Fowler (1980).

A sixth approach is one that argues for the superiority of *dialectical* operations over formal ones. This notion, originally put forward rather lightheartedly by Riegel (1975), has been pursued in earnest and given its best developed analysis by Buck-Morss (1979). Both Riegel and Buck-Morss stress the importance of ambivalence, ambiguity, paradox, and contradiction. They criticize the univocal, absolute, and dichotomizing nature of Piaget's formal-operations construct. Other writers of various persuasions have shown some sympathy for the "dialectical" concept, especially Arlin (1977, note 20), Sinnott and Guttmann (1978), Smith (1978), Sinnott (note 48), Basseches (1980), Pascual-Leone (Chapter 9, this volume), Edelstein and Noam (1982), Fowler (1981), and Kegan (1982).

A seventh approach, connected to the "metaphysics of relations" (Tolman, 1981) in Riegel's thinking, is proposed by Sinnott (1981). She has argued that most notions of life-span development utilize an epistemology based on outdated Newtonian approaches to the physical sciences. In place of these, she suggests a superior, *relativistic* epistemology, informed by Einsteinian and post-Einsteinian theory. Such an epistemology would permit adequate understanding of social relational realities (Sinnott, 1979). Her approach is only marginally part of the revisionist program, for two reasons. Although she does think that relativistic logic also has a cognitive-developmental basis, what she is proposing is primarily a metatheory for developmental psychology as a whole. Furthermore, she does not strictly oppose her view to Piaget's but sees Piaget as already partly relativistic in orientation, a rather debatable claim.

An eighth version emphasizes the ways in which an *existential* perspective can and must complement and enlarge the more physical version of formal cognition. In differing ways, this position has been argued strongly by Gibbs (1977) and Philibert (1981), and to a lesser extent by Guindon (1978).

Finally, a ninth variant, borrowing from both humanistic psychology and Oriental philosophy, suggests that the scientific thought advocated by Piaget naturally gives way to a broader form of *transcendental* contemplation, informed by an awareness and a creativity that override the dualism of subject and object. Gowan (1974) and Alexander (note 49) exemplify this approach.

These nine types of corrective for the "bias" in formal operations aim to ameliorate and compensate for Piaget's structuralist tendencies. The "error" and "penultimacy" critics continue to pursue the logical model, wishing only to advance it to a more consistent, coherent, and systematically inclusive level of organization. The "bias" critics, on the other hand, set themselves against the various qualities of Piaget's final stage, its cognitive, convergent, formal, logical, propositional, structural, abstract, decontextualized, general, transindividual, absolute, universalist, decentrated, dichotomizing, monological (rather than dialogical), and empirical (rather than transcendental) characteristics. As a whole, the "bias" group of critiques serves to work against Piaget's premise of a purely formal and universal epistemic subject possessing immaculate closure. The aim of the critiques appears to be an attempted modification of the terminal structure in the direction of greater flexibility and relativism, to tame it and give it a concrete and individuated personal and situational functionality.

Authors like Gilligan (1979) characterize this modification as a feminization of the traditional masculine scientific model (cf. Keller 1978; Westkott 1979; Ruddick, 1983). It could equally be called a "humanization," since it borrows many tendencies from humanistic psychology, which has traditionally been opposed to formalisms and structuralisms of any kind. It should be noted that, in such opposition, humanistically oriented psychologists typically have not understood formal or structural approaches. Thus, for example, proponents of functional and contextual approaches to cognition commonly ignore the competence-performance distinction and therefore incorrectly criticize Piaget's theory for not being an adequate performance model (Broughton, 1981b). As in American humanism and American feminism, there is quite a strong flavor of the pragmatist and functionalist traditions of the American intellectual heritage in the "postformal" movement. Needless to say, this lack of sympathy for and understanding of structuralist-developmental theory probably reflects some of the social and historical differences between the United States and Europe. The vigilant cannot help but discern across time and ocean that familiar twinkle in Piaget's eye: "Eh bien! Encore le problème américain!"

The Limits of Formal Operations

It is reasonable to consider all the theorists who have sought to transcend formal operations as "liberal revisionists" for two reasons. First, they exhibit little quarrel with the orthodoxy of Piaget's stage theory and typically do not challenge the Piagetian developmental sequence. Most support the reality and significance of formal thought. They certainly do not call into question the centrality of intelligence. Second, especially in the larger constellation just described, there is a strong relativistic tendency. The theorists typically resort to a kind of "Yalta position": Piaget's formal logic applies in his sphere, but in some other sphere an alternative form of intelligence retains control. In other words, these theorists do not seem to be engaged in a revolutionary transformation of the paradigm. They are, in fact, effectively confirming and supporting Piagetian theory. Although they call for extensions or modifications of the theory, their own contribution presupposes its general validity.

Although many authors in the last five years have discussed the possibility of cognitive levels emerging after the formal-operational stage, I apparently have the dubious merit of having coined the specific phrase "beyond formal operations" in print, and of having given it prominence in the title of my 1977 review on adolescent thinking. However, the piece so entitled was actually a *criticism* of the idea of going beyond formal operations; the phrase was encapsulated carefully in quotation marks! Unfortunately, some commentators (for example, Gruber & Vonèche, 1976; Gillieron, note 50; and Lefebvre-Pinard, 1980) have assumed since then that I was initiating and promoting a period of neo-Piagetianism in which the focus of attention would be the extension of Piaget's theory at the upper end.

Other commentators (for example, Monnier & Wells, 1980) have assumed that in my "beyond formal operations" paper (Broughton, 1977) and the subsequent "limits of formal thought" (1979a) I was advocating a kind of revisionism. They interpreted my work as acknowledging that Piaget had tied down one aspect of adolescent cognition, and as arguing that "the formal operational model... needed to be extended to cover other aspects such as the development of personality, moral development, and so on" (Monnier & Wells 1980, p. 15).

However, both my critiques were fairly explicit denunciations of formal operations. The purpose of them was to declare my apostasy; I no longer believed in formal operations *at all* as a normative model of any aspect of adolescent or adult thought. I certainly did not believe that it could be extended to cover other aspects of adolescent cognition. I was trying to demonstrate that it was already over-extended. I wished to be a fly in the ointment, not a salesperson bringing larger and better jars. What the commentators did not seem to share with me was the realization that if you try to modify the theory by changing the final stage, all the previous stages have to change too. If formal operations were to be left in the modified theory as a penultimate stage, it, too, would have to undergo serious qualitative modification. Monnier and Wells, therefore, misinterpreted my argument in a major way. As a case study in misunderstanding, then, this testifies either to a serious lack of clarity on my part or to the presence of highly developed powers of assimilation among some Piagetians!

Rather than endorsing the basic structure of Piaget's operational stage development theory by suggesting a "postformal" stage, I have been a spokesperson for a more revolutionary position, one that calls for a radical paradigm change. This position has been assumed not merely out of an excess of spleen, but rather on account of a sincere conviction that there is something fundamentally wrong with the Piagetian genetic epistemology. The problems with the formal-operations construct are only symptoms of the broader misconceptions represented in Piaget's thinking as a whole. However, they are symptoms of a particularly expressive kind, capturing in a condensed and graphic manner the contradictions and inadequacies of the whole Piagetian paradigm.

There are at least 15 major problems with the formal-operational model. These will be summarized, with references to more detailed published treatments of the difficulties where appropriate and where full replication of each argument is precluded by virtue of limitations on space. Some of these objectives are not unrelated to some of the issues raised by "revisionists." What is different is the fact that here they are each taken as refutations of Piaget's assumptions, and *tout ensemble* they are taken to comprise a critical mass that necessitates the *replacement* of Piaget's theory, not its supplementation or piecemeal alteration.

The first objection bears on Piaget's general metatheoretical framework. The objection is that the genetic epistemology within which formal operations is conceived is not adequate to the task of accounting for development. As Aristotle demonstrated long ago, biological processes, like most other fundamental ones, need to be inserted within an extra-logical framework of metaphysical concepts and principles (being, becoming, potential, and so on). It is in the Aristotelian spirit that I have called for a "genetic metaphysics" within which a genetic epistemology might regain coherent meaning (Broughton, 1980a). The fact that logic alone cannot do the job is evident from the inability of the formal-operational INRC group to account for structuralism. My remark here parallels Koyré's (1939–1940) critique of positivist history of science in which the history of physics was shown to be understandable only in terms of an underlying succession of metaphysical positions. In his youth, Piaget was decidedly metaphysical in his thinking but under the influence of early twentieth-century scientific naturalism soon lost touch with his adolescent insights (Vidal, Chapter 2, this volume; Gruber & Vonèche, 1976; Gruber, 1981).

A second problem, however, is that it is not even clear that Piaget's theory does offer a genetic epistemology. His own logicism and scientism precluded epistemology as such. He reduced the theory of knowledge to the philosophy of science. However, he was not able to ground the assumption that knowledge can be identified with its scientific branch. There is very good reason indeed to suppose that knowledge must be construed much more broadly (Habermas, 1971; Giddens, 1974; Adorno et al., 1976). Even neopositivistic philosophers like Popper no longer accept the notion that science does hold or should hold a privileged place in the domain of knowledge (Lakatos, 1970).

A series of problems with the formal operational model follows from the fact that it derives from the discredited premises of the logical empiricist or positivist philosophy of science. In particular, (the third problem) Piaget held to its antiquated notion of science (Sinnott, 1981). He emphasized the isolation of variables and the experimental determination of lawfully ordered relationships between them. His ideological commitment to the positivist tradition of objective experimentation as a method is puzzling, given that he did not exhibit allegiance to it in his own work (Broughton, 1981c). He also subscribed to the logical empiricists' image of scientific procedure as a hypothetico-deductive method. This conception, modeled upon acts of proof, has been quite thoroughly invalidated, not only for the social sciences (Larsen, in press) but also for the natural sciences (see Lakatos 1970 and the seven critiques cited in Broughton, 1977, p. 93), as indeed has the general validity of the concept of "variable" (Blumer, 1956). An example of the problems of logical empiricism in Piaget's work is, as Wozniak (1981) has pointed out, his inability to account for the processes by which hypotheses are formed and developed.

Piaget's formal-operational *telos* testifies to his adamant belief in the centrality of logic to science. However, the examination of both contemporary scientific theories and the history of scientific theorizing reveals our fourth problem. Formalized systems typically bear an accidental, not an essential, relation to scientific understanding (Feyerabend, 1975). In fact, rather than deriving from logic, science tends to thwart it (Cassirer, 1960, p. 89).

Such fundamental embarrassments are rooted in the antimetaphysical stance of logical empiricism that first gave rise to the development of narrow logical approaches to knowledge. What is of concern to formal logic is the truth or falsity of single, elementary propositions and their implicative connections, independent of any reference to the conceptual content of the propositions or their relations. In the logical empiricist tradition, a proposition has meaning only to the extent that it can be verified, and its verification entails nothing more than deciding whether or not it accords with the rules established to govern the connections of the proposition in a given logical "language." One difficulty of such a model is that it excludes from consideration as a proposition any assertion for which no truth criterion has been given. Another difficulty is that all the propositions that the logical model entertains are not of the kind that can be confronted immediately with the facts. Their truth is logical in kind, not factual.

The logical atomism of the model even renders it incapable of underwriting the scientific concept of law. To resolve the matter of scientific law requires an adequate conception of the problem of induction. But this logic is unable to articulate any such conception since it is in principle incapable of dealing with the problem of synthetic propositions. Traditionally, the latter have been relegated by logical positivism to extralogical "pragmatic" disciplines such as history and psychology. To embrace and resolve questions of fact, logic would have to engage the matter of the relationship of thought to reality, which would return it to epistemological and metaphysical questions the avoidance of which was the original motivation for its general formulation (Della Volpe, 1980).

Perhaps another way of phrasing the same objection is that provided recently by Glick (1981). Glick argues that Piaget's elevation of logic represents a subordination of experience to form. A related concern is raised in my argument (Broughton, 1981c) that Piaget subordinates the concept of "accommodation" to that of "assimilation." In the end, such theoretical strategies amount to an attempt to purchase objectivity at the expense of any capacity to discriminate factual truth from falsity (Hamlyn, 1978). One of the unfortunate sequelae of such a maneuver, the fifth problem, is the resurrection of a particularly rigid form of mind-body dualism (MacMurray, 1957).

Parallel to the third objection, the sixth problem lies in Piaget's argument that reasoning can be equated with problem-solving competence. As Strauss and Kroy (1977), Broughton (1977), Gilligan and Murphy (1979), Kitchener and Kitchener (1981), and others have noted, hypothesis testing is inadequate as a model of cognitive processes. Blasi (1983) has eloquently revealed the narrowness of this vision, which, for example, precludes the possibility of judgment as a part of intelligence. The illegitimacy of removing judgment from any account of mental processes is a tenet of all post-Kantian cognitive theory, as we were cautioned some time ago by Mansel (1851), Bradley (1883), and Bosanquet (1895), and as we have been reminded more recently by Arendt (1977; see also Bernstein (1982) and Broughton (1982a)). Related criticisms have been raised by Halbwachs (1977) and Dreyfus (1979), calling into question the possibility of representing human knowledge in formal structures.

A seventh difficulty lies in the phenomenological structure of understanding. Winograd (1980), based on his extensive experience in the computer modeling of cognition (an endeavor that was close to Piaget's heart), has concluded that formal problem-solving models are not able to do justice to the "preunderstanding" required before thought, reasoning, or interpretation can even begin to take place. This point was raised some time ago by Husserl (1978). It has been applied to cognitive science by Dreyfus (1982) and brought to bear on Piaget's theory in a critique by Merleau-Ponty (1964).

While the notion of ideal forms and cognitive competences is not to be underestimated (Broughton 1981b, d), the centrality of logic to human intelligence and reasoning processes is highly debatable. The eighth problem, pointed out by Ricoeur (1976), is that logic requires the elimination of all "surplus meaning." In positing an algebra of fixed and exact logical elements, even the most basic cognitive processes of interpretation necessary to human discourse are precluded. In short, any of the familiar forms of nonlogical symbolic consciousness are eliminated (Sullivan, 1981). Leaders in the field of "cognitive science," such as Winograd (1980), have pointed out that traditional logical systems are incapable of embodying the known properties of linguistic discourse. Piaget's own colleague, Grize (1977), concurs by pointing out that Piaget's theory cannot deal with the nature of culture because of the latter's foundation in discursive, rather than formal, realities (cf. Borel, 1978).

A ninth problem, one related to the eighth, is that the identification of thought with logic reduces the profound transformations of adult consciousness to mere changes in the content of thought (Broughton, 1979b). This is a counter-intuitive view of adult development that is also directly disconfirmed by empirical findings (for a review, see Basseches, in press). Another of Piaget's colleagues, Greco (1977), has questioned the capacity of Piaget's theoretical model to account for the role of content.

A tenth difficulty is an extension of the ninth and a consequence of the eighth. The primacy attached to logic removes any mnemonic or biographical dimension from the meaning of people's lives (Fowler, 1981). This is why Edelstein and Noam (1982) cannot be correct in their otherwise interesting assertion that the biographical dimension of the self can be accounted for by adding on one more vertical décalage at the top end of Piaget's theory. Logic *precludes* the self (Broughton, 1981e), and no amount of rational reconstruction, structural upgrading, or what Hegelians call "Aufhebung" will repair the damage. This may also explain the apparent failure of formal operations to account empirically for the development of ego-identity (Afrifah & Broughton, note 51; Broughton, 1983).

Eleventh, Piaget's austerity in narrowing mental processes to formal manipulations of logic, hypotheses, and abstract variables has effectively eliminated reflection. Inhelder and Piaget (1958) reduced reflection to logical reflexivity: the recursive action of formal thought upon concrete operations. But logical imbedding of one system in another is an insufficient condition for reflection, as both Blasi (Blasi & Hoeffel, 1974) and I (Broughton, 1974; 1977) have emphasized.

A twelfth limitation of formal operations follows from the eleventh. Piaget proposed that the logical reflexivity of formal structures is tantamount to "thinking about thinking," which, in turn, he equated with self-consciousness. Now, simply thinking about thinking no more requires self-consciousness than it does true reflection since thinking can be treated as merely a content of thought like any other content. In any case, confining cognition to logic excludes consciousness altogether (Blasi, 1983). Furthermore, Piaget's view of cognition as a categorizing process implies that thought can operate only upon objectivated external objects and their relations (Blasi, note 52). Given that the course of development is a progressive "decentration," the final stage must represent the logical limit of such a conceptual objectivation of the world. Within such a terminal structure, there is neither an empirical nor a transcendental self; such a structure is systematically incapable of comprehending subjectivity. This is more or less explicitly acknowledged by most structuralists as a logical consequence of their metatheory (cf. Caws, 1968). Therefore, formal operations is not a formalization of self-consciousness. If anything, it is close to its opposite, the formalization of the preclusion of self-consciousness (Broughton, 1981e). This certainly weakens Piaget's claim to have accounted for the self-awareness emerging in early adolescence (Broughton, 1982b). The dualistic exclusion of the subject of knowledge from the object of knowledge also reveals the extent to which Piaget's philosophy of science lags behind that of the theoretical physicists. The latter have taken the role of the observer in the observation very seriously indeed, at least since Einstein (Cassirer, 1923; Toben, 1975).

Thirteenth, the reconciliation of contradictions within the fully equilibrated logical structure appears to imply that formal-operational thought is incapable of comprehending or guiding action in relation to social structures that embody fundamental contradictions. This point has been made within philosophy (Adorno, 1973) and brought to bear on Piaget's theory by both Riegel (1973) and Buck-Morss (1979).

Formal-operational intelligence is inadequate (Lou, 1979) and, in fact, grossly inappropriate (Broughton, 1979a) as a way of understanding and of guiding action in situations of a psychological or social kind. These are inappropriately construed in terms of instrumental activity. Formal-operational intelligence cannot suffice for noninstrumental acts because nonphysical systems do not necessarily have equilibrium properties (the fourteenth problem). Furthermore, as MacMurray (1957) has shown, any approach to psychology that places the theoretic interest at the apex of mental life cannot deal with the mainstays of interpersonal life: action, sociality, intersubjectivity, and morality (cf. Broughton, 1980b; Della Volpe, 1980). In the sociopsychological world, some types of possibility have their origin in will, imagination, or creativity, rather than being already given or derived from logical permutations of givens (Blasi & Hoeffel, 1974). In general, in the sociological and psychological realms, one can isolate "variables" and carry out controlled experiments with them only to a very limited extent and primarily under artificial conditions. Consistent formal-operational behavior in these realms would amount to sociopathy. The early scheme that Piaget (1932) supplied as a developmental trajectory for moral reasoning is inappropriate as a normative system to regulate human social interaction (Broughton, note 53), as Piaget (1982) himself later admitted. Moreover, as Blasi and Hoeffel point out, possibility in human thought and conduct is not reducible to logical possibility. Such reduction effectively removes any significance from the essential mental processes of imagination (Fowler, 1981).

Finally, the fifteenth problem, it is in the very nature of the formal-operational model that it eliminates any historical dimension from cognition (Riegel, 1973; Harris, 1981; Vonèche, 1979). Both understanding and action are thereby prevented from being informed by, or bearing upon, the historical transformation of society. Formal-operational adults supposedly live in a hermetically sealed ahistorical universe where life is a matter of necessities deriving from the natural, nonmanmade laws of equilibration. Such individuals have no life histories, much as they have no memories. The elimination of the historical dimension, especially in combination with the elimination of the subjective and socio-moral qualities of development, is conducive to the kind of technological rationality that underlies the most profound problems of modernized life, including the nuclear threat (Broughton & Zahaykevich, 1982).

If, as argued at the beginning of the chapter, the formal-operations construct is the keystone of Piaget's theoretical construction, then, on the basis of the problems outlined in this section, one cannot help but fear for the whole edifice.

ROMANTICISM AND PRAGMATISM IN THE LIBERAL IDEOLOGY OF DEVELOPMENT

The inadequacies of the formal-operations construct should be viewed in the context of the broader and deeper misconceptions embodied in Piagetian psychology and genetic epistemology in general. The Piagetian framework is characterized by metatheoretical, conceptual, empirical, methodological, and practical desiderata, all of these being imbedded within systematic political and ideological distortions (Broughton, 1981, c, e, f, 1982b; Broughton et al., 1981). The whole psycho-epistemology has an apparent coherence that makes it a complex and seductive distraction from the difficult tasks still facing developmental psychology. This diversion of our attention is all the more influential in North America, alas, on account of the accommodations that Piagetian theory has made to the amalgam of pragmatism and positivism so central to the American liberal tradition (cf. Broughton, 1981a; Sullivan 1981).

Psychologists of the Piagetian persuasion have busied themselves with the reinforcement of an ideology of progress that recommends gradual, step-by-step subjection to the overbearing monarch of transcendental structural form. These psychologists are engaged in what Kuhn (1982) has called "normal science." The elaboration, extension, and fortification of the cognitive developmental paradigm is based upon a certain enlightenment optimism. In particular, it holds to the enchanting postfeudal images of bourgeois autonomy as the solution to heteronomy and independent thought as the key to freedom from oppression. Some of the reasons that these images are in fact fantasies have been recounted previously. The general drift of my reasoning was to argue that the Piagetian paradigm continues to serve an "ideological" purpose, in the pejorative sense of the word. It tends to serve primarily as a sophisticated theoretical justification of what Piagetian psychologists themselves tend to exemplify: the denial and elimination of critical social, biographical, historical, and philosophical insight.

The revisions of Piaget's theory engendered in the supposed move "beyond formal operations" are often ingenious, but do little to improve the situation. One group merely escalates the equilibration model to a higher level, leaving its fundamental problems (Broughton, 1981c) intact. In the way of improvements, the other, larger group offers only a mixture of rehashed romanticism and unabashed pragmatism. The romantics stress in opposition to rational consciousness the particular or singular, the unstructured, the imaginative, the affective, and the interpersonal. In these emphases, they adhere closely to the traditional values of their English and continental romantic forebears from the eighteenth century onward (Schenk, 1966; Hill, 1983), introduced into developmental psychology by G. Stanley Hall (see for example, 1904, p. 59). The pragmatists stress instrumental action, process, functionality, flexibility, and everyday utility. In these emphases, they merely follow the traditional values of evolutional functionalism, as it emerged in the context of liberal, corporate capitalism in the turn of the century United States (Hofstadter, 1944).

Romanticism and pragmatism are commonly conceived of as opposed and even mutually exclusive attitudes, corresponding roughly to the "female" and "male" personalities, or to Nietzsche's "Dionysian" and "Apollonian" types. In ethics, romantic intuitionism is often contrasted with pragmatic utilitarianism. However, romantics and pragmatists share the naturalist root metaphor of the organism (Pepper, 1966), the former emphasizing its extra-scientific vitality, the latter its systematic organization and successful adaptation. Both types of revisionists tend toward anti-intellectualism in their return to body and biology; both eschew judgment and reasoning. They have rewritten the enlightenment vision of autonomy respectively in terms of spontaneity and efficiency. The combination is central to modern forms of ideological liberalism.

Such liberal ideology gains a certain reputation for "humanism" by appearing to be in opposition to established ideas. In developmental psychology, the revisionists who reinterpret formal operations as erroneous, penultimate, or biased appear to be creative and innovative rebels. However, the opposition that they offer to mainstream Piagetianism is only a semblance of rebellion. Most of the revisionists adhere to the basic premises of genetic epistemology and the theory of development. They are typically quick to invoke the hostile elements of empiricism and nativism as a reason for continuing to take shelter under Piaget's umbrella. Their opposition to Piaget is not at all *radical:* it does not strike at the roots of his theory. Rather, in order to retain its novelty value, such "opposition" necessarily requires the bulk of Piaget's theory. It is a dispute *within,* not *about,* the terms of discourse set by the established position. Attempting to compensate for cognition by adding affect is to reaffirm the dichotomy of "cognition versus affect," instead of seeking some deeper conceptualization of consciousness that would obviate the need for such oppositions and the need to compensate each with the other (Broughton, 1982g). The same applies to the attempt to compensate for logical abstraction by adding a stage of concrete particularity for problem solving by adding a stage of problem finding, and so on.

It is important to realize that this pseudo-oppositional relationship is not merely an epistemic or cognitive one: it is a political relationship to established authority. There is a certain conformity and compliance concealed in the revisionist stance toward authority, since, as Hegel (1967) pointed out, it fails to dig down critically to the roots of authority and so merely subjects itself, and serves to confirm that authority in its accepted form. Revisionism even advances the established position by diminishing its apparent vulnerability. It generates the impression that the established position has been democratically subjected to manifold critiques and has responsibly undergone transformation. Consequently, the authority of the established position has not only been defended, it has been augmented and fortified. Such is the pattern of "normal science" as described by Kuhn, the business whereby a paradigmatic form of science elaborates itself and becomes further entrenched.

Regardless of the specific psycho-political meaning that can be given to the revisionist tradition, the fact remains that the postformal movement has hardly ever acknowledged any of the fifteen major inadequacies of the formal-operations construct mentioned previously. By now, the reason for this may be clear. The problems with the formal-operations construct are radical ones: they lie at the roots of the Piagetian theory. Moreover, they lead on to even bigger problems, as I have shown elsewhere (Broughton, 1981c, e). To admit their existence at the very fundaments of the theory would be to undermine both the cognitive-developmental psychology and the genetic epistemology. This in turn would subvert the whole revisionist movement. Unfortunately, such is the precariousness of a disobedient dependence that binds itself to a "parent" whose invulnerability is like that of all grandiose images, nothing more than wishful illusion.

Postformal revisions of Piaget's theory propose romantic and pragmatic endpoints to development that have traded in any possibility of true human autonomy for a humanistic version of adulthood as intuitive spontaneity or functional adaptation. Having given up freedom in theory, it is not a coincidence that they have given it up in practice as well. The act of theorizing is a form of practice, too. What is at stake is not just a choice between alternative ideas, rival concepts, or different ways of speaking. Rather, it is a question of appropriate and liberating versus inappropriate and oppressive postures in relation to the world. It is a matter of power. Until post-Piagetian developmental psychology can take a truly autonomous stance in relation to the considerable authority of Piaget's accomplishments, it will be unable to construct a theory of adolescent liberation and independent adulthood. Until such a theory is under construction, developmental psychology will exert no pressure on anyone to exercise either critical consciousness or emancipatory practice, since these will remain theoretically inconceivable. The issue is not one of the stage "beyond formal operations"; it is one of the stage "beyond Piaget."

NOTES

1. The liberal view of progress is well described and interpreted by Karier (1972) and Manning (1976). The historical roots of developmental theory in liberal progressivism are documented in Broughton (1981a).

2. "Rational reconstruction" here means any formal upgrading process, such as equilibration, whereby knowledge is given a new total structure with a higher level of reflectivity by making the latent formal presuppositions of the previous level into the explicit content of the new structure.

3. Some writers, such as Lefebvre-Pinard (1980), have implied that I am a member of their "metacognitive" group, an allegation that does not quite fit, as will become apparent below.

4. This "particularist" position can be a little confusing, since according to Gruber, *everyone* tends to form their own point of view (see Gruber & Vonèche, 1976), which therefore gives the postformal period a universal character!

BIBLIOGRAPHY

Achenbach, T. M. The children's associative responding test: A possible alternative to group IQ tests. *Journal of Educational Psychology*, 1970, *61*, 340–348.

Adelson, J. The development of ideology in adolescence. In S. E. Dragastin & G. H. Elder, Jr. (Eds.), *Adolescence in the life cycle: Psychological change and social context*. New York: John Wiley & Sons, 1975.

Adorno, T. W. *Negative dialectics*. New York: Seabury Press, 1973.

Adorno, T. W., Albert, H., Dahrendorf, R., Habermas, J., Pilot, H., and Popper, K. R. *The positivist dispute in german sociology*. New York: Harper & Row, 1976.

Allport, D. A. Attention and performance. In G. Claxton (Ed.), *Cognitive psychology: New directions*. London: Routledge & Kegan Paul, 1980.

Anderson, J. R. *Language, memory, and thought*. Hillsdale, N.J.: Lawrence Erlbaum, 1976.

Anderson, J. R. A theory of language acquisition based on general learning mechanisms. *Proceedings of the Seventh International Joint Conference on Artificial Intelligence*, 1981, 97–103.

Anderson, J. R. Acquisition of cognitive skills. *Psychological Review*, 1982, *89*(4), 369–406.

Anglin, J. M. *The growth of word meaning*. Cambridge, Massachusetts: M.I.T. Press, 1970.

Apostel, L. Logique de l'action et logique piagétienne. *Bulletin de Psychologie*, 1976, 131–138.

Arendt, H. *The life of the mind*. New York: Harcourt Brace and World, 1977.

Aristotle, *Nichomachean ethics* (translation: Ostwald). Indianapolis: Bobbs-Merrill, 1979.

Arlin, P. K. Cognitive development in adulthood: A fifth stage? *Developmental Psychology*, 1975, *11*, 602–606.

Arlin, P. K. A cognitive process model of problem finding. *Educational Horizons*, 1975–1976, *54*, 99–106.

Arlin, P. K. Toward a metatheoretical model of cognitive development. *International Journal of Human Development*, 1976, *7*, 247–253.

Arlin, P. K. Cognitive development: Model or models? In J. F. Magany, M. K. Pouben, P. J. Levinson, & P. A. Taylor (Eds.), *Proceedings of the Sixth Conference on Piagetian Theory and Its Implications for the Helping Professions.* Los Angeles: University of Southern California, 1977a.

Arlin, P. K. Piagetian operations in problem finding. *Developmental Psychology*, 1977b, *13*, 247–298.

Armon, C. *Philosophical and psychological theories of the Good: An initial synthesis.* Qualifying Paper, Harvard Graduate School of Education, 1982. 1982.

Attneave, F. Representation of physical space. In A. W. Melton & E. E. Martin (Eds.), *Coding processes in human memory.* Washington, D.C.: Winston & Sons, 1972.

de Avila, E. A., Havassy B., with Pascual-Leone, J. *Mexican-American school children: A neo-Piagetian approach.* Washington, D.C.: Georgetown University Press, 1976.

Bachelard, G. *Epistemologie.* (D Lecourt, Ed.) Paris: Presses Universitaires de France, 1971.

Baldwin, J. M. *Handbook of psychology: Feeling and will.* New York: Henry Holt, 1894.

Baldwin, J. M. *Mental development in the child and the race: Methods and processes.* New York: Augustus M. Kelley, 1968. (Originally published in 1894)

Baldwin, J. M. *Social and ethical interpretations in mental development.* New York: Macmillan, 1906.

Baldwin, J. M. *Thoughts and things or genetic logic* (3 volumes). New York: Macmillan, 1906.

Baldwin, J. M. *Genetic theory of reality.* New York: G. P. Putnam, 1915.

Baltes, P. B., & Baltes, M. M. Plasticity and variability in psychological aging: Methodological and theoretical issues. In G. E. Gurski (Ed.), *Determining the effects of aging on the central nervous system.* Berlin: Schering AG (Oraniendruck), 1980.

Baltes, P. B., Cornelius, S. W., Spiro, A., Nesselroade, J. R., & Willis, S. L. Integration versus differentiation of fluid/crystallized intelligence in old age. *Developmental Psychology*, 1980, *16*, 625–635.

Baltes, P. B., Reese, H. W., & Lipsitt, L. P. Life-span developmental psychology. *Annual Review of Psychology*, 1980, *31*, 65–110.

Baltes, P. B., Reese, H. W., & Nesselroade, J. R. *Life-span developmental psychology: Introduction to research methods.* Monterey, CA: Brooks/Cole Pub. Co., 1977.

Baltes, P. B., & Willis, S. L . The critical importance of appropriate methodology in the study of aging: The sample case of psychometric intelligence. In F. Hoffmeister & C. Müller (Eds.), *Brain function in old age.* Heidelberg: Springer, 1979.

Barlow, N., (Ed.) *Charles Darwin's diary of the voyage of H.M.S. "Beagle".* Cambridge: Cambridge University Press, 1934.

Barlow, N., (Ed.) *The autobiography of Charles Darwin.* London: Collins, 1958.

Barrett, P. H., (Ed.) *The collected papers of Charles Darwin*, 2 vols. Chicago and London: University of Chicago Press, 1977.

Bart, W. M., & Smith, M. B. An interpretative framework of cognitive structures. *Human Development*, 1974, *17*, 161–175.

Basseches, M. *Beyond closed-system problem-solving: A study of meta-systematic aspects of mature thought.* (Doctoral dissertation, Harvard University, 1978, University Microfilms International, 1979).

Basseches, M. Dialectical schemata: A framework for the empirical study of the development of dialectical thinking. *Human Development*, 1980, *23*, 400–421.

Basseches, M. *Dialectical thinking and adult development.* Norwood: Ablex, in press.

Bates, E. *Language and context.* New York: Academic Press, 1976.

Bateson, G. *Steps to an ecology of mind.* New York: Ballantine Books, 1972.

Bateson, M. *Our own metaphor.* New York: Alfred A. Knopf, 1972.

Benack, S. The coding of dimensions of epistemological thought in young men and women. *Moral Education Forum*, 7:2, 1982, 3–23.

Bender, M. B. *Disorders in perception.* Springfield, Illinois: Charles C. Thomas, 1952.

Berger, P. L., & Luckmann, T. *The social construction of reality.* Garden City: Doubleday, 1966.

Bergson, Henri. *L'Evolution créatrice.* Paris: Alcan, 1907.

Berne, E. *Beyond games and scripts.* New York: Ballantine, 1976.

Bernstein, R. Judging: The actor and the spectator. In R. Garner & R. Boyers (Eds.), *Proceedings of History, Ethics, Politics: A Conference Based on the Work of Hannah Arendt.* New York: Empire State College, 1982.

von Bertalanffy, L. *General System Theory.* New York: Braziller, 1968.

Bertenthal, B. I., & Fischer, K. W. The development of self-recognition in the infant. *Developmental Psychology*, 1978, *14*, 44–50.

Bertenthal, B. I., & Fischer, K. W. The development of representation in search: A social-cognitive analysis. *Child Development*, in press.

Beth, E. W., & Piaget, J. *Epistémologie mathématique et psychologie.* Paris: Presses universitaires de France, 1961.

Bickhard, M. On necessary and specific capabilities in evolution and development. *Human Development*, 1979, *22*, 217–224.

Biggs, J., & Collis, K. *A system for evaluating learning outcomes: The SOLO taxonomy.* New York: Academic Press, 1982.

Binet, A., & Simon, Th. The development of intelligence in children. Training School Publication No. 11, Vineland, N.J., 1916.

Birren, J. E., Kinney, D. K., Schaie, K. W., & Woodruff, D. S. *Developmental psychology: A life-span approach.* Boston: Houghton Mifflin, 1981.

Blasi, A. Bridging moral cognition and moral action: A critical review of the literature. *Psychological Bulletin*, 1980, *88*, 1–45.

Blasi, A. The self and cognition: The roles of the self in the acquisition of knowledge. In B. Lee and G. Noam (Eds.), *Developmental psychologies of the self.* New York: Plenum Pub. Co., 1983.

Blasi, A., & Hoeffel, E. C. Adolescence and formal operations. *Human Development*, 1974, *17*, 344–363.

Blos, P. *On adolescence.* Glencoe, Ill.: Free Press, 1962.

Blumer, H. Sociological analysis and the "variable." *American Sociological Review*, 1956, *21*, 633–640.

Bohm, D. *Wholeness and the implicate order.* Boston: Routledge and Kegan Paul, 1980.

Bohr, N. H. D. *Atomic theory and the description of nature.* Cambridge, England: University Press, 1962.

Borel, M. J. *Discours de la logique du discours.* Lausanne, Switzerland: Editions de L'Age d'Homme, 1978.

Bosanquet, B. *The essentials of logic.* London: MacMillan, 1895.

Boswell, D. A. Metaphoric processing in the mature years. *Human Development,* 1979, *22,* 373–384.

Boyd, D. *Rolling thunder.* New York: Dell Publishing Co., 1974.

Boyd, D. *Swami.* New York: Random House, 1976.

Bradey, F. H. *The principles of logic.* London: Macmillan, 1883.

Braine, M. Presentation at Piaget memorial conference. In J. M. Broughton, B. Leadbeater, & E. Amsel (Eds.), Reflections on Piaget, Teachers College Record, 1981, *83*(2), 151–217.

Brainerd, C. J. Learning research and Piagetian theory. In L. S. Siegel & C. J. Brainerd (Eds.) *Alternatives to Piaget, Critical Essays on the Theory.* New York: Academic Press, 1978.

Brainerd, C. J. The stage question in cognitive-developmental theory. *Behavioral and Brain Sciences,* 1978, *1,* 173–182.

Brenner, Heinrich, *Samuel Cornut.* Doctoral dissertation, University of Zürich, 1929.

Brent, S. B. Motivation, steady-state and structural development. *Motivation and Emotion,* 1978, *2,* 299–332.

Brent, S. B. *The nature and development of psychological structures.* New York: Springer, in press.

Broughton, J. M. *The development of natural epistemology in the years 10–16.* Doctoral dissertation, Harvard University, 1974.

Broughton, J. M. "Beyond formal operations:" Theoretical thought in adolescence. *Teachers College Record,* 1977, *79*(1), 87–98.

Broughton, J. M. The development of concepts of self, mind, reality, and knowledge. In W. Damon (Ed.), *New directions for child development, no. 1, Social cognition.* San Francisco: Jossey-Bass, 1978.

Broughton, J. M. The limits of formal thought. In R. A. Mosher (Ed.), *Adolescent development and education.* Berkeley: McCutchan, 1979.(a)

Broughton, J. M. Development structuralism: without self, without history. In H. K. Betz (Ed.), *Recent approaches to the social sciences.* Winnipeg: Hignell, 1979.(b)

Broughton, J. M. Genetic metaphysics: The developmental psychology of mind-body concepts. In R. Rieber (Ed.), *Body and mind.* New York: Academic Press, 1980.(a)

Broughton, J. M. Psychology and the history of the self: From substance to function. In R. W. Rieber, & K. Salzinger (Eds.), *Psychology: Theoretical-historical perspectives. New York: Academic Press, 1980b.*

Broughton, J. M. The divided self in adolescence. Human Development, 1981, *24,* 13–24.

Broughton, J. M. The genetic psychology of James Mark Baldwin. *American Psychologist,* 1981, *36*(4), 396–407a.

Broughton, J. M. Piaget's structural developmental psychology, Part I: Piaget and structuralism. *Human Development,* 1981, *24*(2), 78–109b.

Broughton, J. M. Piaget's structural developmental psychology, Part II: Logic and psychology. *Human Development,* 1981, *24*(3), 195–225c.

Broughton, J. M. Piaget's structural developmental psychology, Part III: Function and the problem of knowledge. *Human Development,* 1981, *24*(4), 257–285d.

Broughton, J. M. Piaget's structural developmental psychology, Part IV:

Knowledge without a self and without history. *Human Development*, 1981e, *24*(5), 320–346.

Broughton, J. M. Piaget's structural developmental psychology, Part V: Ideology-critique and the possibility of a critical developmental psychology. *Human Development*, 1981f *24*(6), 382–411.

Broughton, J. M. Comments in J. M. Broughton, B. Leadbeater, and E. Amsel (Eds.), Reflections on Piaget, *Teachers College Record*, 1981g, *83*(2), 151–218.

Broughton, J. M. Word and deed: Report on the conference on Hannah Arendt. *Psych Critique*, 1982, *2*, 27–31.(a)

Broughton, J. M. Review of M. Boden's 'Piaget.' *Psych Critique*, 1982, *1*, 10–11.(b)

Broughton, J. M. The cognitive-developmental theory of adolescent self and identity. In B. Lee, & G. Noam (Eds.), *Developmental psychologies of the self*. New York: Plenum, 1983.

Broughton, J. M., Leadbeater, B., & Amsel, E. (Eds.) Reflections on Piaget. *Teachers College Record*, 1981, *83*(2), 151–218.

Broughton, J. M., & Zahaykevich, M. Review of J. Loevinger's ego development: conceptions and theories. *Telos*, 1977, *32*, 246–253.

Broughton, J. M., & Zahaykevick, M. K. The peace movement threat. *Teachers College Record*, 1982, *84*(1), 152–173.

Browne, J. Darwin's botanical arithmetic and the 'principle of divergence', 1854–1858. *Journal of the History of Biology*, 1980, *13*, 53–89.

Buck-Morss, S. Socio-economic bias in Piaget's theory and its implications for cross-cultural study. *Human Development*, 1975, *18*, 35–49.

Buck-Morss, & Piaget, S. Adorno and the possibility of dialectical structures. *Stonybrook studies in philosophy*, 1979, *4*, 1–26. Reprinted in H. Silverman (Ed.), *Piaget, philosophy and the human sciences*. New York: Humanities Press, 1980; and in J. M. Broughton (Ed.) *Critical theory of development*. New York: Plenum, in press.

Bunge, M. *Method, model and matter*. Dordecht, Holland: Reidel, 1973.

Burtis, P. J. *A study of the development of short term memory in children*. Unpublished doctoral dissertation, York University, 1976.

Bynum, T. W., Thomas, J. A., & Weitz, L. J. Truth function in formal operational thinking: Inhelder and Piaget's evidence. *Developmental Psychology*, XXXX 7, no. 2.

Campbell, D. T. Evolutionary epistemology. In A. Schilpp, (Ed.), *The philosophy of Karl R. Popper*: The Library of Living Philosophers, Vol. 14, I and II. La Salle, Ill.: Open Court, 1974.

Campbell, D. T. On conflicts between biological and social evolution and between psychology and moral tradition. *American Psychological Journal*, *30*, 1975, 1103–1126.

Capra, F. *The Tao of physics*. Berkeley: Shambala, 1974.

Carey, S. *Semantics and development: State of the art*. Glutman and Wanner (Eds.), in press.

Case, R. Structures and strictures: Some functional limitations in the course of cognitive growth. *Cognitive Psychology* 6, 1974, 544–573.

Case, R. Intellectual development from birth to adulthood: A Neo-Piagetian interpretation. In R. Siegler (Ed.), *Children's thinking: What develops?* Proceedings of the Thirteenth Annual Carnegie Symposium on Cognition), 1978.

Cassirer, E. *Substance and function*. New York: Dover, 1923.

Cassirer, E. *The philosophy of symbolic forms (Vol. 3): The phenomenology of knowledge.* New Haven: Yale University Press, 1957.

Cassirer, E. *The Logic of the humanities.* New Haven: Yale University Press, 1960.

Cattell, R. B. *Abilities: Their structure, growth and action.* Boston: Houghton Mifflin, 1971.

Caws, P. What is structuralism? *Partisan Review*, 1968, *35*, 75–91.

Chi, M. T. H. Age differences in memory span. *Journal of Experimental Child Psychology*, 1977, *23*, 266–280.

Cline, V. B. Ability to judge personality assessed with a stress interview and sound film technique. *Journal of Abnormal and Social Psychology*, 1955, *50*, 183–187.

Cohen, J. A coefficient of agreement for nominal scales. *Educational and Psychological Measurement*, 1960, *20*, 37–46.

Colby, A. Evolution of a moral development theory. In W. Damon (Ed.), *New directions for child development no. 2, moral development.* San Francisco: Jossey-Bass, 1978.

Colby, A. & Kohlberg, L. (Eds), *The measurement of moral judgment: A manual and its results.* New York: Cambridge University Press, in press.

Colby, A., Kohlberg, L., Gibbs, J., & Lieberman, M. Report on a 20-year longitudinal study of moral development. *Monograph of the Society for Research in Child Development,* 1983.

Coleman, W. *Biology in the Nineteeth Century; Problems of Form, Function and Transformation.* Cambridge: Cambridge University Press, 1977.

Commons, M. L., Miller, P. M., & Kuhn, D. The relation between formal operational reasoning and academic course selection and performance among college freshmen and sophmores. *Journal of Applied Developmental Psychology,* 1982, *3*, 1–10.

Commons, M. L., Richards, F. A., & Kuhn, D. Systematic and metasystematic reasoning: A case for levels of reasoning beyond Piaget's stage of formal operations. *Child Development,* 1982, *53,* 1058–1068.

Commons, M. L., Woodford, M., Boitano, G. A., Ducheny, J. R., & Peck, J. R. The acquisition of performance during shifts between terminal links in concurrent chain schedules." In M. L. Commons, R. J. Herrnstein, & A. R. Wagner (Eds.), *Quantitative Analyses of Behavior vol. 3: Acquisition,* Cambridge, MA: Ballinger, in press.

Coombs, H. C., Dawes, R. M., & Tversky, A. *Mathematical psychology: An elementary introduction.* Englewood Cliffs, NJ: Prentice-Hall, Inc., 1970.

Coombs, C. H., & Smith, J. K. Detection of structure in attitudes and developmental process. *Psychological Review*, 1973, *80*, 337–351.

Corrigan, R. The development of representational skills. In K. W. Fischer (Ed.), *New directions for child development, No. 22, Levels in psychological development.* San Francisco: Jossey-Bass, in press.

Cowan, P. A. *Piaget with feeling: Cognitive, social, and emotional dimensions.* New York: Holt, Rinehart and Winston, 1978.

Craik, F. M. Age differences in human memory. In J. E. Birren & K. W. Schaie (Eds.), *Handbook of the psychology of aging.* New York: Van Nostrand Reinhold, 1977.

Creutzfeldt, O. Diversification and synthesis of sensory systems across the cortical link. In O. Pompeiano & C. A. Marsan (Eds.), *Brain Mechanisms of*

Perceptual Awareness and Purposeful Behavior, Vol. 8.New York: Raven Press, 1981.

Cropper, D. A., Meck, D. S., & Ash, M. J. The relation between formal operations and a possible fifth stage of cognitive develoment. *Developmental Psychology*, 1977, *13*, 517–518.

Csikszentimihalyi, M., & Getzels, J. Concern for discovery: An attitudinal component of creative production. *Journal of Personality*, 1970, *38*, 91–105.

Csikszentimihalyi, M., & Getzels, J. Discovery-oriented behavior and the originality of creative products: A study with artists. *Journal of Personality and Social Psychology*, 1971, *19*, 47–52.

Curry, H. B. *Foundations of mathematical logic.* New York: McGraw-Hill, 1963.

Cytrynbaum, S., Blum, L., Patrick, R., Stein, J., Wadner, D., & Wilk, C. Midlife development: Personality and social systems perspectives. In L. Poon (Ed.), *Aging in the 1980s.* Washington, D.C.: American Psychological Association, 1980.

Dabrowski, K. *Mental growth through positive disintegration.* London: Gryf Publishing, 1970.

Darwin, C. *The autobiography of Charles Darwin.* (N. Barlow, Ed.) London: Collins, 1958.

Darwin, C. *The collected papers of Charles Darwin,* 2 vols. (P.H. Barrett, Ed.) Chicago and London: University of Chicago Press, 1977.

Darwin, C. *Charles Darwin's diary of the voyage of H.M.S. "Beagle".* (N. Barlow, Ed.) Cambridge: Cambridge University Press, 1934.

Darwin, E. *Zoonomia; or the laws of organic life*, 2 vols. London: Johnson, vol. 1, 1794, vol. 2, 1796.

de Ribaupierre, A., & Pascual-Leone, J. Formal operations and M power: A neo-Piagetian investigation. In D. Kuhn (Ed.), *New directions for child development, No. 5, Intellectual development beyond childhood.* San Francisco: Jossey-Bass, in press.

Della Volpe, G. *Logic as a positive science.* London: New Left Books, 1980.

Delong, H. *A profile of mathematical logic.* Reading, MA: Addison-Wesley, 1970.

DeLisi, R., & Staudt, J. Individual differences in college students' performance on formal operations tasks. *Journal of Applied Developmental Psychology*, 1980, *1*, 163–174.

Dennis, I., Hampton, J. A., & Lea, S. E. G. New problems in concept formation. *Nature*, 1973, *243*, 101–102.

Dennis, W. Creative productivity between the ages 20 and 80 years. *Journal of Gerontology*, 1966, *21*, 1–8.

DeVries, R., & Kohlberg, L. Relations between Piagetian and psychometric assessments of intelligence. In L. Katz (Ed.), *Current topics in early childhood education* (Vol. 1). Norwood, N.J.: Ablex, 1977.

Dewey, J. *Reconstruction in philosophy.* Boston: Beacon Press, 1957.

Dreyfus, H. *What computers can't do: A critique of artificial reason* (2nd ed.). San Francisco: W. H. Freeman, 1979.

Dreyfus, H. *Husserl, intentionality, and cognitive science.* Cambridge, MA: M.I.T. Press, 1982.

Durkheim, E. *Selected Writings.* (A. Giddens, Ed.) Cambridge: Cambridge University Press, 1972.

Ebel, R. L., Estimation of the reliability of ratings. *Psychometrika*, 1951, *16*, 407–424.

Edelstein, W., & Noam, G. Regulatory structures of the self and "postformal" stages in adulthood. *Human Development*, 1982, *25*, 407–422.

Edwards, C. P. Societal complexity and moral development: A Kenyan study. *Ethos*, 1975, *3*, 4.

Elkind, D. Egocentrism in children and adolescents. In D. Elkind (Ed.), *Children and adolescents*, 2nd ed. New York: Oxford University Press, 1974.

Emery, F. *Systems thinking*. New York: Penguin, 1969.

Engels, F. *Dialectics of nature*. New York: International Publishers, 1940.

Epstein, H. T. Phrenoblysis: Special brain and mind growth periods. II. Human mental development. *Developmental Psychobiology*, 1974, *7*, 217–224.

Epstein, H. T. EEG developmental stages. *Developmental Psychobiology*, 1980, *13*, 629–631.

Erdynast, A. *Improving the adequacy of moral reasoning: An exploratory study with executives and philosophy students*. Unpublished doctoral dissertation, Harvard University, 1972.

Erdynast, A., Armon, C., & Nelson, J. Cognitive-developmental conceptions of the true, the good, and the beautiful. In *The Eighth Annual Proceedings of Piaget and the Helping Professions*. Los Angeles: USC Press, 1978.

Erikson, E. H. *Childhood and Society*. New York: Norton, 1963.

Erikson, E. H. *Youth: Change and Challenge*. New York City: Basic Books, Inc., 1963.

Erikson, E. H. *Childhood and Society*. New York: Norton, 1963.

Erikson, E. H. *Insight and responsibility: Lectures on the ethical implications of psychoanalytic insight*. New York: Norton, 1964.

Erikson, E. H. *Identity: Youth in crises*. New York: Norton, 1968.

Erikson, E. H. *Toys and reason: Stages in the revitalization of experience*. New York: Norton, 1977.

Fabian, V. *Language development after 5: A neo-Piagetian investigation of subordinate conjunctions*. Unpublished doctoral dissertation, University of California, Berkeley, 1982.

Fakouri, M. E. Cognitive development in adulthood: A fifth stage? A critique. *Developmental Psychology*, 1976, *12*, 472.

Feffer, M. H. A developmental analysis of interpersonal behavior. Psychological Review, 1970, *77*, 197–214.

Feffer, M. H. *The structure of Freudian thought: The problem of immutability and discontinuity in developmental theory*. New York: International Universities Press, 1982.

Feldman, D. H. *Beyond universals in cognitive development*. Norwood, N.J.: Ablex, 1980.

Feuer, L. *Einstein and the generations of science*. New York: Basic Books, 1974.

Feuerstein, R. Ontogeny of learning in man. In M. A. B. Brazier (Ed.), *Brain mechanisms in memory and learning: From the single neuron to man*. New York: Raven Press, 1979.

Feyerabend, P. *Against method*. London: New Left Books, 1970, 1975.

Fischer, K. W. A theory of cognitive development: The control and construction of hierarchies of skills. *Psychological Review*, 1980, *87*, 477–531.

Fischer, K. W. Human psychological development in the first four years. *Behavioral and Brain Sciences*, 1982, *5*, 282–283.

Fischer, K. W., & Bullock, D. Patterns of data: Sequence, synchrony, and constraint in cognitive development. In K. W. Fischer (Ed.), *New directions for child development, No. 12, Cognitive Development*. San Francisco: Jossey-Bass, 1981.

Fischer, K. W., & Corrigan, R. A skill approach to language development. In R. E. Stark (Ed.), *Language behavior in infancy and early childhood*. Amsterdam: Elsevier-North Holland, 1981.

Fischer, K. W., Hand, H. H., Watson, M. W., Van Parys, M., & Tucker, J. L. Putting the child into socialization: The development of social categories in preschool children. In L. Katz (Ed.), *Current topics in early childhood education* (Vol. 5). Norwood, N.J.: Ablex, in press.

Fischer, K. W., & Jennings, S. The emergence of representation in search: Understanding the hider as an independent agent. *Developmental Review*. 1981, *1*, 18–30.

Fischer, K. W., & Pipp, S. L. Processes of development: Optimal level and skill acquisition. In R. J. Sternberg (Ed.), *Mechanisms of cognitive development*. San Francisco: Freeman, in press.

Fischer, K. W., Pipp, S. L., & Bullock, D. Detecting discontinuities in development: Method and measurement. In R. Emde & R. Harmon (Eds.), *Continuities and discontinuities in development*. New York: Plenum, in press.

Fischer, K. W., & Roberts, R. J., Jr. *A developmental sequence of classification skills in preschool children*. Manuscript submitted for publication, 1982.

Flavell, J. H. Cognitive changes in adulthood. In L. R. Goulet, & P. B. Baltes (Eds.), *Life-span developmental psychology: Research and theory*. New York: Academic Press, 1970.

Flavell, J. H. Stage-related properties of cognitive development. *Cognitive Psychology*, 1971, *2*, 421–453.

Flavell, J. H. *Cognitive development*. Englewood Cliffs, N.J.: Prentice-Hall, 1977.

Flavell, J. H. Structures, stages, and sequences in cognitive development. In W. A. Collins (Ed.), *Minnesota Symposium on Child Psychology*. Hillsdale, NJ: Erlbaum, 1982.

Flavell, J. H., & Wohlwill, J. F. Formal and functional aspects of cognitive development. In D. Elkind & J. Flavell (Eds.), *Studies in cognitive development: Essays in honor of Jean Piaget*. New York: Oxford University Press, 1969.

Fowler, J. Faith and the structuring of meaning. In J. Fowler and A. Vergate (Eds.), *Toward moral and religious maturity*. Morristown, NJ: Silver Burdett, 1980.

Fowler, J. *Stages of faith*. New York: Harper & Row, 1981.

Freud, A. *The ego and the mechanisms of defense*. New York: International Universities Press, 1966.

Freud, S. *The standard edition of the complete psychological works of Sigmund Freud*, edited and translated by J. Strachey. London: The Hogarth Press, 1961.

Freud, S. Project for a scientific psychology (1895). In J. Strachey (Ed.), *The standard edition of the complete psychological works of Sigmund Freud*, Vol. 1. London: Hogarth Press, 1966.

Furman, I. *The development of problem-solving strategies: A Neo-Piagetian analysis of children's performance in a balance task.* Unpublished doctoral dissertation, University of California, Berkeley, 1981.

Furth, H. G., *Piaget and knowledge.* Englewood Cliffs, NJ: Prentice-Hall, 1969.

Furth, H. G. Piaget's new equilibration model. In H. G. Furth (Ed.), *Piaget and knowledge,* 2nd ed. Chicago: University of Chicago Press, 1981.

Furth, H. G., Bauer, M., and Smith, J. Children's conceptions of social institutions: A Piagetian framework. *Human Development*, 1976, *19*, 351–374.

Fuster, J. M. *The prefrontal cortex.* New York: Raven Press, 1980.

Gadamer, H. G. *Hegel's dialectic: Five hermeneutical studies* (P. C. Smith, trans.). New Haven: Yale University Press, 1976.

Gagné, R. M. Contributions of learning to human development. *Psychological Review*, 1968, *75*, 177–191.

Gagné, R. M. *The conditions of learning,* 3d ed. New York: Holt, Rinehart and Winston, 1977.

Gallagher, J. M., & Wright, R. J. Piaget and the study of analogy: structural analysis of items. In J. Magary (Ed.), *Piaget and the helping professions* (Vol. 8). Los Angeles: University of Southern California, 1979.

Gamow, G. *One, two, three . . . infinity.* New York: Viking Press, 1961.

Gardner, H. *Artful scribbles: the significance of children's drawings.* New York: Basic Books, 1980.

Gentile, J. R., Tedesco-Stratton, L., Davis, E., Lund, N. J., & Agunanne, B. A. Associative responding versus analogical reasoning by children. *Intelligence*, 1977, *1*, 369–380.

Getzels, J. W., & Csikszentimihalyi, M. *The creative vision: A longitudinal study of problem finding in art.* New York: John Wiley & Sons, 1976.

Ghiselin, M. *The triumph of the Darwinian method.* Berkeley: University of California Press, 1966.

Gibbs, J. Kohlberg's stages of moral judgment: A constructive critique. *Harvard Educational Review*, 1977, *47*, 43–61.

Gibbs, J. Kohlberg's moral stage theory: A Piagetian revision. *Human Development*, 1979, *22*, 89–112.

Giddens, A. (Ed.) *Positivism and sociology.* London: Heinemann, 1974.

Gilligan, C. Woman's place in man's life cycle. *Harvard Educational Review*, 1979, *49*(4), 431–446.

Gilligan, C. *In a different voice.* Cambridge, MA: Harvard University Press, 1982.

Gilligan, C., & Murphy, M. J. Development from adolescence to adulthood: The philosopher and the dilemma of the fact. In D. Kuhn (Ed.), *New directions for child development, No. 5, Intellectual development beyond childhood.* San Francisco: Jossey-Bass, 1979.

Glick, J. Comments in J. M. Broughton, B. Leadbeater, & E. Amsel (Eds.), Reflections on Piaget, *Teachers College Record*, 1981, *83*(2), 158–161.

Globerson, T. *Mental capacity and cognitive functioning: a developmental and a comparative study.* Paper presented at the meetings of the SRCD, Boston, 1981.

Gödel, K. Some metamathematical results on completeness and consistency; on formal undecidable propositions of *Principia Mathematica* and related systems I; On completeness and consistency. In J. Heijehoort (Ed.), *From Frege to Gödel. A Source Book in Mathematical Logic 1379–1931.* Cambridge, MA: Harvard University Press, 1977 (originally published 1930, 1931, 1931, respectively).

Goldstein, K. *The organism.* New York: American Book Co., 1939.

Gonseth, F. *Le referentiel univers oblige de mediatisation.* Lausanne, Switzerland: L'age d'homme, 1975.

Goodman, D. R. *Stage transitions and the developmental traces of constructive operators: A neo-Piagetian investigation of cognitive growth.* Unpublished doctoral dissertation, York University, 1979.

Gould, C. *Marx's social ontology.* Cambridge: MIT Press, 1978.

Gould, R. L. The phases of adult life: A study in developmental psychology. *The American Journal of Psychiatry,* 1972, *129,* 521–531.

Gould, R. L. *Transformations: Growth and change in adult life.* New York: Simon and Schuster, 1979.

Gould, S. J. *Ontogeny and phylogeny.* Cambridge: Belknap Press of Harvard University Press, 1977.

Gowan, J. C. *Development of the psychedelic individual.* Buffalo: Creative Education Foundation, 1974.

Greco, P. Statut épistemologique des concepts psychologiques chez Piaget. In B. Inhelder, R. Garcia, & J. J. Voneche (Eds.), *Epistémologie Génétique et Equilibration.* Neuchatel: Delachaux et Niestle, 1977.

Greenson, Ralph R., Empathy and its vicissitudes. *International Journal of Psychoanalysis,* 1960, *41,* 418–424.

Grize, J. B. Remarks in B. Inhelder, R. Garcia, & J. J. Vonèche (Eds.), *Epistemologie Genetique et Equilibration.* Neuchatel: Delachaux et Niestle, 1977.

Gruber, H. E. And the bush was not consumed: The evolving systems approach to creativity. In S. Modgil & C. Modgil (Eds.), *Towards a Theory of Psychological Development.* N.F.E.R., 1980.

Gruber, H. E. Courage and cognitive growth in children and scientists. In M. Schwebel, & J. Raph (Eds.), *Piaget in the classroom.* New York: Basic Books, 1973.

Gruber, Howard E. *Darwin on man: A psychological study of scientific creativity.* New York: E. P. Dutton, 1974.

Gruber, H. E. The evolving systems approach to creativity. In S. & C. Modgil (Eds.), *Toward a theory of psychological development.* Windsor: NFER Publ. Co., 1978.

Gruber, H. E. *Darwin on man.* 2nd ed. Chicago: University of Chicago Press, 1981.

Gruber, H. E. On the relation between 'Aha! Experiences' and the construction of ideas. *History of Science,* 1981a, *19,* 41–59.

Gruber, H. E. Remarks in J. M. Broughton, B. Leadbeater, & E. Amsel (Eds.), Reflections on Piaget. *Teachers College Record,* 1981, *83*(2), 204–206.(b)

Gruber, H. E., & Gruber, V. The eye of reason: Darwin's development during the *Beagle* voyage. *Isis,* 1962, *53,* 186–200.

Gruber, H. E., & Vonèche, J. J. Reflexions sur les operations formelles de la pensée. *Archives de Psychologie,* 1976, *44,* 45–55.

Guilford, J. P. Three faces of intellect. *American Psychologist*, 1959, *14*, 469–479.

Guilford, J. P. *The nature of human intelligence.* New York: McGraw-Hill, 1967.

Guindon, A. Moral development: Form, content and self. *University of Ottawa Quarterly*, 1978, *48*, 232–263.

Guyote, M. J., & Sternberg, R. J. A transitive-chain theory of syllogistic reasoning. *Cognitive Psychology*, 1981, *13*, 461–525.

Habermas, J. *Knowledge and human interests.* Boston: Beacon Press, 1971.

Habermas, J. *Theory and practice.* Boston: Beacon Press, 1973.

Habermas, J. Moral development and ego identity. (George Ellard, trans.). *Telos*, 1975, *23*, 41–55.

Habermas, J. Social science versus hermeneuticism. In N. Haan, R. Bellah, P. Rabinow, & W. Sullivan (Eds.), *Social science as moral inquiry.* New York: Columbia University Press (forthcoming).

Halbwachs, F. Remarks in B. Inhelder, G. Garcia, & J. J. Voneche (Eds.), *Epistemologie Genetique et Equilibration.* Neuchatel: Delachaux et Niestle, 1977.

Haley, J. Family therapy. In C. J. Sager and H. S. Kaplan (Eds.), *Progress in group and family therapy.* New York: Brunner/Mazel, 1972, 261–270.

Halford, G. S., & Wilson, W. H. A category theory approach to cognitive development. *Cognitive Psychology*, 1980, *12*, 356–411.

Hall, G. S. *Adolescence.* New York: Appleton, 1904.

Hamlyn, D. H. *Experience and the growth of understanding.* London: Routledge & Kegan Paul, 1978.

Hand, H. H. *The development of concepts of social interaction: Children's understanding of nice and mean.* Unpublished doctoral dissertation, University of Denver, 1981. *Dissertation Abstracts International*, in press. (a)

Hand, H. H. The relation between developmental level and spontaneous behavior: The importance of sampling contexts. In K. W. Fischer (ed.), *New directions for child development, No. 12, Cognitive Development.* San Francisco: Jossey-Bass, 1981(b).

Hanson, N. R. *Patterns of discovery: An inquiry into the conceptual foundations of science.* Cambridge, England: Cambridge University Press, 1961.

Hare, R. M. *Freedom and reason.* Oxford, England: The Clarendon Press, 1963.

Harris, A. Remarks in J. M. Broughton, B. Leadbeater, & E. Amsel (Eds.), Reflections on Piaget. *Teachers College Board*, 1981, *83*(2), 202–204.

Harter, S. Children's understanding of multiple emotions: A cognitive-developmental approach. In the *Proceedings of the Jean Piaget Society: 1979.* Hillsdale, N.J.: Erlbaum (in press a).

Harter, S. Self and self systems. In P. H. Mussen (Ed.), *Carmichael's manual of child psychology* (4th ed.). New York: Wiley (in pree b).

Hasher, L., & Zacks, R. T. Automatic and effortful processes in memory. *Journal of Experimental Psychology: General*, 1979, *103*, 356–388.

Hegel, G. W. F. *The phenomenology of mind.* New York: Harper, 1967.

Herrlich, H., & Strecker, G. E. *Category theory.* Boston: Allyn and Bacon, Inc., 1973.

Herrnstein, R. J. & Vaughan, W. Melioration and behavioral allocation. In

J. E. R. Staddon (Ed.), *Limits to action: The allocation of individual behavior.* New York: Academic Press, 1980.

Hill, M. *The schools of psychoanalysis and the concept of the ego.* New York: Columbia University Press, 1983.

Hofstadter, D. R. *Social Darwinism in American thought.* Philadelphia: University of Pennsylvania Press, 1944.

Hostadter, D. R. *Godel, Esher, Bach: An eternal golden braid.* New York: Vintage Books, 1980.

Holton, G. *Thematic origins of scientific thought: Kepler to Einstein.* Cambridge, Mass.: Harvard University Press, 1975.

Hook, S. *From Hegel to Marx.* Ann Arbor: University of Michigan Press, 1978.

Hooper, F. H., Fitzgerald, J., & Papalia, D. Piagetian theory and the aging process: Extensions and speculations. *Aging and Human Development*, 1971, 2, 3–20.

Hooper, F. H. & Sheehan, N. W. Logical concept attainment during the aging years: Issues in the neo-Piagetian research literature. In W. F. Overton, & J. M. Gallagher (Eds.), *Knowledge and development* (Vol. 1): *Advances in research and theory.* New York: Plenum Press, 1977.

Horn, J. L. Organization of data on life-span development of human abilities. In L. R. Goulet, & P. B. Baltes (Eds.), *Life-span developmental psychology: Theory and research.* New York: Academic Press, 1970.

Horn, J. L. Human ability systems. In P. B. Baltes (Ed.), *Life-span development and behavior* (Vol. 1). New York: Academic Press, 1978.

Horn, J. L. The theory of fluid and crystallized intelligence in relation to concepts of cognitive psychology and aging in adulthood. In F. I. M. Craik & S. Trehub (Eds.), *Aging and cognitive processes.* New York: Plenum Press, 1982.

Humphreys, L. & Parsons, C. Piagetian tasks measure intelligence and intelligence tests assess cognitive development: A reanalysis. *Intelligence*, 1979, 3, 369–382.

Husserl, E. *The crisis of European sciences and transcendental phenomenology.* Evanston: Northwestern University Press, 1970.

Husserl, E. *Formal and transcendental logic.* The Hague: Martinus Nijhoff, 1978 (originally published 1929).

Huttenlocher, P. R. Synaptic density in human frontal cortex—Developmental changes and effects of aging. *Brain Research*, 1979, 163, 195–205.

Ilyenkov, E. V. *Dialectical logic. Essays on its history and theory.* Moscow: Progress Pub., 1977.

Inhelder, B. Some aspects of Piaget's genetic approach to cognition. In W. Kessen & C. Kuhlman (Eds.), *Thought in the young child.* Chicago: Society for Research in Child Development, 1964.

Inhelder, B. & Piaget, J. *De la logique de l'enfant a la logique de l'adolescent: essai sur la construction des structures operatoires formelles.* Paris: Presses universitaires de France, 1955.

Inhelder, B., & Piaget, J. *The growth of logical thinking from childhood to adolescence* (A. Parsons & S. Seagrim, trans.). New York: Basic books, 1958. (originally published, 1955).

Jackson, E., Campos, J. J., & Fischer, K. W. The question of décalage between object permanence and person permanence. *Developmental Psychology*, 1978, *14*, 1–10.

Jacobson, M. *Developmental neurobiology* (2nd ed.). New York: Plenum, 1978.

Jacques, E., with Gibson, R. O., & Isaac, D. J. *Levels of abstraction in logic and human action*. London: Heinemann, 1978.

James, W. *Psychology: The Briefer course* (G. Allport, Ed.). New Hayer Tochbooks, 1961. (originally published in 1892).

Jedrzkiewicz, J. A. *Adult development and mental effort: A neo-Piagetian experimental analysis*. Unpublished M.A. thesis, York University, Toronto, 1983.

Jensen, A. R. 1972. Review of the analysis of learning potential. In A. K. Buros (Ed.), *The seventh mental measurements yearbook*. Highland Park, NJ: Gryphon Press, 1972.

Johnson, J. M. *The development of metaphor comprehension: Its mental-demand measurement and its process-analytical models*. Unpublished doctoral dissertation, York University, Toronto, 1982.

Jung, C. G. *Essais de psychologie analytique* (Y. LeLay, trans.). Paris: Librairie Stock, 1931.

Jung, C. G. *Modern man in search of a soul*. New York: Harcourt, Brace & World, 1933.

Kahneman, D. *Attention and effort*. Englewood Cliffs, NJ: Prentice-Hall, 1973.

Kant, I. [*Critique of pure reason*] (J. M. D. Meiklejohn, trans.). London: G. Bell & Sons, 1887.

Kant, I. *Foundations of the Metaphysics of Morals*. Indianapolis: Bobbs-Merrill, 1975 (originally published 1785).

Karier, C. J. Liberalism and the quest for orderly change. *History of Education Quarterly*, 1972, *12*, 35–80.

Karmiloff-Smith, A., & Inhelder, B. If you want to get ahead, get a theory. *Cognition*, 1974, *3*, 195–212.

Karplus, R., Pulos, S., & Stage, E. K. Proportional reasoning of early adolescents. In R. Lesh, & M. Landau (Eds.), *Acquisition of mathematics concepts and processes*. New York: Academic Press, 1982.

Keating, D. Adolescent thinking. In J. Adelson (Ed.). *Handbook of Adolescence*. New York: John Wiley & Sons, 1980.

Keegan, R. T., & Gruber, H. E. Love, death and continuity in Darwin's thinking. *Journal of the History of the Behavioral Sciences*, (in press).

Kegan, R. G. The evolving self: A process conception for ego psychology. *The Counseling Psychologist*, 1979, *8*, 5–39.

Kegan, R. G. *The evolving self*. Cambrdige, Mass.: Harvard University Press, 1982.

Keller, E. F. Gender and science. *Psychoanalysis and Contemporary Thought*, 1978, *1*, 409–433.

Kitchener, K. S., & King, P. M. Reflective judgment: Concepts of justification and their relation to age and education. *Journal of Applied Developmental Psychology*, 1981, *2*, 89–116.

Kitchener, K. S., & Kitchener, R. F. The development of natural rationality: Can formal operations account for it? In J. A. Meacham & N. R. Santilli (Eds.), *Social development in youth: Structure and content*. Basel: S. Karger, 1981.

Klahr, D., & Wallace, J. G. *Cognitive development: An information processing view.* Hillsdale, NJ: Lawrence Erlbaum Associates, 1976.

Koestler, A. *The sleepwalkers. A history of man's changing vision of the universe.* London: Hutchinson, 1959.

Koestler, A. *The act of creation.* New York: Macmillan Co., 1964.

Koffka, K. *The principles of Gestalt psychology.* New York: Harcourt Brace & World, 1935.

Kohlberg, L. *The development of modes of moral thinking and choice in the years 10 to 16.* Unpublished doctoral dissertation, Dept. Psychology, University of Chicago, 1958.

Kohlberg, L. The development of children's orientations toward a moral order: A sequence in the development of moral thought. *Vita Humana,* 1963, *6,* 11–33.

Kohlberg, L. Cognitive stages and pre-school education. *Human Development,* 1966, *9,* 5–17.

Kohlberg, L. Stage and sequence: The cognitive-developmental approach to socialization. In D. A. Goslin (Ed.), *Handbook of socialization theory and research.* Chicago: Rand McNally, 1969, 347–480.

Kohlberg, L. Continuities in childhood and adult moral development revisited. In P. B. Baltes & K. W. Schaie (Eds.), *Life-span developmental psychology: Personality and socialization.* New York: Academic Press, 1973b.

Kohlberg, L. The claim to moral adequacy of a highest stage of moral judgment. *Journal of Philosophy,* 1973a, *7.*

Kohlberg, L. Moral Stages and moralization: The cognitive-developmental approach. In T. Lickona (Ed.), *Moral development and behavior.* New York: Holt, Rinehart and Winston, 1976.

Kohlberg, L. *Essays on moral development, vol. I: The philosophy of moral development.* San Francisco: Harper & Row, 1981.

Kohlberg, L. The meaning and measurement of moral development. *The Heinz Werner Lecture Series, Vol XIII (1979).* Worcester, MA: Clark University Press, 1981.

Kohlberg, L. *Essays on moral development: vol. II: The psychology of moral development.* New York: Harper and Row, (forthcoming).

Kohlberg, L., and Candee, D. The relation of moral judgment to moral action. In W. Kurtines, & J. Gewirtz (Eds.) *Morality, moral behavior and moral development: Basic issues in theory and research.* New York: Wiley Interscience, (in press).

Kohlberg, L., & DeVries, R. Don't throw out the baby with the Piagetian bath: Reply to Humphreys and Parsons. *Intelligence,* 1980, *4,* 175–177.

Kohlberg, L., & Gilligan, C. The adolescent as a philosopher: The discovery of the self in a post-conventional world. *Daedalus,* 1971, *100* (4), 1051–1086.

Koplowitz, H. *The college classroom as organism: a general system theory approach to understanding and changing the college classroom.* Doctoral thesis, University of Massachusetts, Amherst, 1976.

Koppitz, E. M. *The Bender Gestalt test for young children.* New York: Grune & Stratton, 1964.

Kosok, M. *The formalization of Hegel's dialectical logic.* In A. MacIntyre, *Hegel: A collection of critical essays.* Garden City: Anchor, 1972.

Kovel, J. Rationalization and the family. *Telos*, 1978, *37*, 5–21.

Koyré, A. *Etudes Galileennes*. Paris: Herman, 1939–40.

Krajewski, W. *Correspondence principle and growth of science*. Boston: D. Reidel, 1977.

Krantz, D. H., Luce, R. D., Suppes, P., & Tversky, A. *Foundations of measurement*. New York: Academic Press, 1971.

Kuhn, D. Relation of two Piagetian stage transitions to IQ. *Developmental Psychology*, 1976, *12*, 157–161.

Kuhn, D. Mechanisms of cognitive and social development: One psychology or two? *Human Development*, 1978, *21*, 92–118.

Kuhn, D. The relevance of Piaget's stage of formal operations in the study of adulthood cognition. *Genetic Epistemologist*. 1979, *3*(1), 1–3.(b)

Kuhn, D. The significance of Piaget's formal operations stage in education. *Journal of Education,* 1979, *161,* 34–50a.

Kuhn, D., & Brannock, J. Development of the isolation of variables scheme in experimental and 'natural experiment' contexts. *Developmental Psychology*, 1977, *13*, 9–14.

Kuhn, D., Pennington, N., & Leadbeater, B. Adult thinking in developmental perspective: The sample case of juror reasoning. In P. Baltes & O. Brim (Eds.), *Life-span development and behavior*, vol. 5. New York: Academic Press, 1982.

Kuhn, D., & Phelps, E. The development of problem-solving strategies. In H. W. Reese & L. P. Lipsitt (Eds.), *Advances in child development and behavior* (Vol. 17). New York: Academic Press, 1982.

Kuhn, T. S. *The Structure of scientific revolutions* (second edition). Chicago: University of Chicago Press, 1970, 1972.

Kusatsu, O. Ego development and socio-cultural process in Japan. Journal of Economics (Asia University, Tokyo, Japan), 1978, *3,* 41–128.

Labouvie-Vief, G. Adult cognitive development: In search of alternative interpretations. *Merrill-Palmer Quarterly*, 1977, *23*, 227–263.

Labouvie-Vief, G. Beyond formal operations: Uses and limits of pure logic in life-span development. *Human Development*, 1980a, *23*, 141–161.

Labouvie-Vief, G. Models of cognitive functioning in the older adult: Research needs in educational gerontology. In R. H. Sherron, & D. B. Lumsden (Eds.), *Introduction to educational gerontology*, Washington, D.C.: Hemisphere Publishing, 1980b.

Labouvie-Vief, G. Pro-active and re-active aspects of construction: Growth and aging in life-span prospective. In R. M. Lerner & N. A. Busch (Eds.), *Individuals as producers of their development: A life span perspective*. New York: Academic Press, 1981.

Labouvie-Vief, G. Dynamic development and mature autonomy: A theoretical prologue. *Human Development,* 1982b, *25*, 161–191.

Labouvie-Vief, G. Growth and aging in life-span perspective. *Human Development*, 1982, *25*, 65–78.

Labouvie-Vief, G. & Chandler, M. J. Cognitive development and life-span develomental theory: Idealistic versus contextual perspectives. In P. B. Baltes (Ed.), *Life-span development and behavior*. New York: Academic Press, 1978.

Labouvie-Vief, G. & Schell, D. A. Learning and memory in later life: A developmental view. In B. Wolman (Ed.), *Handbook of Developmental Psychology*. Englewood Cliffs, NJ: Prentice-Hall, 1981.

Lakatos, I. Falsification and the methodology of scientific research programmes. In I. Lakatos & H. A. E. Musgrave (Eds.), *Criticism and the Growth
of Knowledge*. Cambridge, England: Cambridge University Press, 1970.

Lakatos, I. *The methodology of scientific research programmes* (J. Worrall &
G. Currie, Eds.). Cambridge, England: Cambridge University Press,
1980.

Langer, E. J. Old age: An artifact? In J. L. McGaugh, S. B. Kiesler, &
J. G. March (Eds.), *Aging—biology and behavior*. New York: Academic
Press, 1981.

Langford, P. E. The development of the concept of development. *Human
Development*, 1975, *18*, 321–332.

Lao Tsu. *Tao te ching*. New York: Random House, 1972.

Laplace, P. S. *The System of the World*. (J. Pond, trans.), London: Richard
Phillips, 1809.

Larsen, K. *Psychology and Ideology*. Norwood, NJ: Ablex Pub. Co. (in press).

Lasker, H. M. Stage-specific reactions to ego development training. In
Formative Research in Ego Stage Change: Study No. 3. Willemstad, Curacao:
Humanas Foundation, 1974.(a)

Lasker, H. M. Self-reported change manual. In *Formative Research in Ego Stage
Change: Study No. 4*. Willemstad, Curacao: HUmanas Foundation, 1974b.

Lasker, H. M. Interim Summative Evaluation Report: An Initial Assessment
of the *Shell/Humanas OD Program*. Cambridge, MA: Harvard University
Press, 1977.

Lawler, R. W. The progressive construction of mind (one child's learning
addition). *Cognitive Science*, 1981, *5*, 1–60.

Lee, L. C. The concomitant development of cognitive and moral modes of
thought: A test of selected deductions from Piaget's theory. *Genetic
Psychology Monographs*, 1971, *83*, 93–146.

Lefebvre-Pinard, M. Existe-t-il des changements cognitifs chez l'adulte? *Revue
Quebecoise de Psychologie*, 1980, *1*(2), 58–69.

Léontiev, A. N. *Le développement du psychisme. Problèmes*. Editions de l'Université
de Moscou, 1976.

Léontiev, A. N. Probleme der Entwicklung des Psychischen, 2nd edition.
Stuttgart, Germany: Fischer, 1977.

Levinson, D. J., Darrow, C., Klein, E. B., Levinson, M. H., & McKee, B. *The
seasons of a man's life*. New York: Ballantine Books, 1978.

Lewin, D. *A dynamic theory of personality*. New York: McGraw-Hill, 1935.

Linn, M. C. Scientific reasoning: Influences on task performance and
response categorization. *Science Education*, 1977, *61*, 357–363.

Linn, M. C. & Swiney, J. Individual differences in formal thought: Role of
expectations and aptitudes. *Journal of Educational Psychology*, 1981, *73*,
274–285.

Linn, M. C., Clement, C., & Pulos, S. M. Is it formal if it's not physics? The
influence of laboratory and naturalistic content on formal reasoning.
Journal of Research in Science Teaching (in press).

Loevinger, J. with Blasi, A. *Ego development: Conceptions and theories*. San
Francisco: Jossey-Bass, 1976.

Loevinger, J. & Wessler, R. *Measuring ego development. vol. I: Construction and use
of a sentence completion test*. San Francisco: Jossey-Bass, 1970.

Loevinger, J., Wessler, R., & Redmore, C. *Measuring ego development. vol. II:
Scoring manual for women and girls*. San Francisco: Jossey-Bass, 1970.

Longeot, F. *Les stades operatoires de Piaget et les facteurs de l'intelligence.* Grenoble: Presses Universitaires de Grenoble, 1978.

Lou, M. *Investigating the development of the logic involved in social/psychological reasoning.* Unpublished doctoral dissertation, University of California, Berkeley, 1979.

Lukács, G. The ontology of social being (Vol. 2): *Marx's basic ontological principles* thinking. *British Journal of Psychology,* 1961, 143–153.

Lukács, G. The ontology of social being (Vol. 2): *Marx's basic ontological principles* (D. Fernback, trans.). London: Merlin Press, 1978.

Lund, R. D. *Development and plasticity of the brain.* New York: Oxford University Press, 1978.

Lunzer, E. A. Problems of formal reasoning in test situations. In P. H. Mussen (Ed.), European research in cognitive development. *Monographs of the Society for Research in Child Development,* 1965, *30*(2, Serial No. 100), 19–46.

Luria, A. R. *The role of speech in the regulation of normal and abnormal behavior.* Bethesda; U.S. DHEW, NIH, Division of General Medical Sciences, 1960.

Luria, A. R. The frontal lobes and the regulation of behavior. In K. H. Pribram & A. R. Laria (Eds.), *Psychophysiology of the frontal lobes.* New York: Academic Press, 1973.

Lyell, C. *Principles of geology: Being an inquiry how far the former changes of the earth's surfaces are referable to causes now in operation.* 3 vols. London: John Murray, 1830–1833.

Mackworth, N. H. Originality. *American Psychologist,* 1965, *20,* 51–66.

MacLane, S. *Categories for the working mathematician.* New York: Springer, 1971.

MacMurray, J. *Self as agent.* London: Faber & Faber, 1957.

MacWhinney, B. The acquisition of morphophonology. *Monographs of the Society for Research in Child Development,* 1978, *43,* (1-2, Serial No. 174).

Manning, D. J. *Liberalism.* New York: St. Martin's Press, 1976.

Mansel, H. *Prolegomena Logica.* London: Swan Sonnenschein, 1851.

Martarano, S. C. A developmental analysis of performance on Piaget's formal operations tasks. *Developmental Psychology,* 1977, *13,* 666–672.

Marx, K. *Writings of the young Marx on philosophy and society.* Garden City: Anchor, 1967.

Marx, K., Engels, F., & Lenin, V. I. *On dialectical materialism.* Moscow: Progress Publishers, 1977.

Matalon, B. Étude génétique de l'implication. In J. Piaget (Ed.), *Études d'Épistemologie Génétique, vol. 16.* Paris, P.U.F., 1962.

Matousek, M., & Petersen, I. Frequency analysis of the EEG in normal children and adolescents. In P. Kellaway, & I. Petersen (Eds.), *Automation of clinical electroencephalography.* New York: Raven Press, 1973.

McCall, R. B., Applebaum, M. I., & Hogarty, P. S. Developmental changes in mental performance. *Monographs of the Society for Research in Child Development,* 1973, *38,* (3, Serial, No. 150).

McCall, R. B., Eichorn, D. H., & Hogarty, P. S. *Transitions in early mental development. Monographs of the Society for Research in Child Development,* 1977, *42* (3, Serial No. 171).

McCarthy, I. *The critical theory of Jüergen Habermas.* Cambridge, MA: MIT Press, 1979.

McCarthy, J., & Hayes, P. J. Some philosophical problems from the standpoint of artificial intelligence. In B. Meltzer, & D. Michie (Eds.), *Machine Intelligence 4.* New York: American Elsevier Publishing Co., 1969.

McGuinness, D., & Pribram, K. The neuropsychology of attention: Emotional and motivational controls. In M. C. Wittrock (Ed.), *The brain and psychology.* New York: Academic press, 1980.

Mead, G. H. *Mind, self, and society.* Chicago: University of Chicago Press, 1934.

Merleau-Ponty, M. Maurice Merleau-Ponty at the Sorbonne. *Bulletin de Psychologie,* 1964, *18,* 109–301.

Mill, J. S. *Three essays.* (Originally published 1861). Oxford, England: Oxford University Press, 1978.

Miller, M. S. *Executive schemes vs. mental capacity in predicting intellectual under performance among lower socio-economic status groups.* Unpublished doctoral dissertation, York University, 1980.

Minsky, M. Frame-system theory. In P. W. Johnson-Laird, & P. C. Wason (Eds.), *Thinking: Readings in cognitive science.* Cambridge, England: Cambridge University Press, 1977.

Mishler, E. G. Meaning in content: Is there any other kind? *Harvard Educational Review,* 1979, *49,* 1–19.

Monnier, C., & Wells, A. Does the formal operational stage exist? A review and critique of recent works on the subject of formal operations. *Cahiers de la Fondation Archives de Jean Piaget,* 1980, *1,* 201–242.

Montagnero, J. The various aspects of horizontal décalage. *Archives de Psychologie,* 1980, *48,* 259–282.

Moshman, D. The stage beyond. *Worm Runner's Digest,* 1979, *21*(2), 107–108.

Murphy, J. M., & Gilligan, C. Moral development in late adolescence and adulthood: A critique and reconstruction of Kohlberg's theory. *Human Development,* 1980, *23,* 77–104.

Naus, M. J., Ornstein, P. A., & Hoving, K. L. Developmental implications of multistore and depth-of-processing models of memory. In P. A. Ornstein (Ed.), *Memory development in children.* Hillsdale, NJ: Erlbaum, 1978.

Neimark, E. D. Intellectual development during adolescence. In F. D. Horowitz (Ed.), *Review of child development research Vol. 4.* Chicago: University of Chicago Press, 1975(a).

Neimark, E. D. Longitudinal development of formal operational thought. *Genetic Psychology Monographs,* 1975(b), *91,* 171–225.

Neimark, E. D. Cognitive development in adulthood: Using what you've got. In L. Troll (Ed.), *Review of human development: adult reviews.* New York: John Wiley & Sons (in press).

Neisser, U. *Cognitive psychology.* New York: Appleton-Century-Crofts, 1967.

Neugarten, B. L., Crotty, W. J., & Tobin, S. S. Personality types in an aged population. In B. L. Neugarten, (Ed.), *Personality in middle and late life.* New York: Atherton, 1964.

Newell, A. You can't play 20 questions with nature and win: Projective comments on the papers of this symposium. In W. G. Chase (Ed.), *Visual information processing*. New York: Academic Press, 1973.

Nisan, M., & Kohlberg, L. Universality and variation in moral judgment: A longitudinal and cross-cultural study in Turkey. *Child Development*, 1982, *53*, 865–876.

Nisbet, R. A. *Social change and history*. New York: Oxford University Press, 1969.

Numbers, R. L. *Creation by Law: Laplace's Nebular Hypothesis in American Thought*. Seattle: University of Washington Press, 1977.

O'Brien, D. P., & Overton, W. F. Conditional reasoning and the competence-performance issue: A developmental analysis of a training task. *Journal of Experimental Child Psychology*, 1982, *34*, 274–290.

Odom, R. O. Concept identification and utilization among children of different ages. *Journal of Experimental Child Psychology*, 1966, *4*, 309–316.

Ollman, B. *Alienation*. Cambridge, England: Cambridge University Press, 1971.

Osherson, D. N. *Logical abilities in children, vol. 3, Reasoning in adolesence: Deductive inference*. Hillsdale, NJ: Lawrence Erlbaum, 1975.

Osler, S., & Kofsky, E. Structure and strategy in concept learning. *Journal of Experimental Child Psychology*, 1966, *4*, 198–209.

Parkinson, G. M. *The limits of learning: A quantitative investigation of intelligence*. Unpublished doctoral dissertation, York University, 1975.

Parsons, C. Inhelder and Piaget's 'the growth of logical thinking': A logician's viewpoint. *British Journal of Psychology*, 1960, *51*, 75–84.

Pascual-Leone, J. *Cognitive development and cognitive style: A general psychological integration*. Unpublished doctoral dissertation, University of Geneva, 1969.

Pascual-Leone, J. A mathematical model for the transition rule in Piaget's developmental stages. *Acta Psychologica*, 1970, *32*, 301–345.

Pascual-Leone, J. On learning and development, Piagetian style: I. A reply to Lefebvre-Pinard. *Canadian Psychological Review*, 1976(a), *17* (4), 270–288.

Pascual-Leone, J. On learning and development, Piagetian style: II. A critical historical analysis of Geneva's research programme. *Canadian Psychological Review*, 1976(b), *17* 289–297.

Pascual-Leone, J. Metasubjective problems of constructive cognition: Forms of knowing and their psychological mechanism. *Canadian Psychological Review*, 1976(c), *17* (2), 110–125. (Errata: *Canadian Psychological Review*, 1976(c), *17* (4), 307.)

Pascual-Leone, J. A view of cognition from a formalist's perspective. In K. F. Riegel & J. Meacham (Eds.), *The developing individual in a changing world*. The Hague: Mouton, 1976.(d)

Pascual-Leone, J. Compounds, confounds and models in developmental information processing: A reply to Trabasso and Foellinger. *Journal of Experimental Child Psychology*, 1978, *26*, 18–40.

Pascual-Leone, J. Constructive problems for constructive theories: The current relevance of Piaget's work and a critique of information-processing simulation psychology. In R. Kluwe, & H. Spada (Eds.), *Developmental models of thinking*. New York: Academic Press, 1980, pp. 263–296.

Pascual-Leone, J. Growing into human maturity; Towards a metasubjective theory of adulthood stages. In P. B. Baltes, & O. G. Brim (Eds.), *Life-span development and behavior* (Vol. 3). New York: Academic Press (in press).

Pascual-Leone, J., & Bovet, M. C. L'apprentissage de la quantification de l'inclusion et la theorie operatoire. *Acta Psychologica*, 1966, *25*, 334–356.

Pascual-Leone, J., & Goodman, D. Intelligence and experience: A neo-Piagetian approach. *Instructional Science*, 1979, *8*, 301–367.

Pascual-Leone, J., Goodman, D., Ammon, P., & Subelman, I. Piagetian theory and neo-Piagetian analysis as psychological guides in education. In J. M. Gallagher, & J. A. Easley (Eds.), *Knowledge and development* (Vol. 2). New York: Plenum, 1978.

Pascual-Leone, J., Johnson, J., Goodman, D., Hameluck, D., & Theodor, L. *I*-interruption effects in backward pattern masking: The neglected role of fixation stimuli. In *Proceedings of the Third Annual Conference of the Cognitive Science Society*. Berkeley, California, 1981.

Pascual-Leone, J., & Smith, J. The encoding and decoding of symbols by children. *Journal of Experimental Child Psychology*, 1969, *8*, 328–355.

Pepper, S. *World hypotheses*. Berkeley: University of California Press, 1966.

Perry, W. G. *Forms of intellectual and ethical development in the college years*. New York: Holt, Rinehart & winston, 1968, 1970.

Philibert, P. The motors of morality: Religion and relation. In D. Joy (Ed.), *Moral development foundations: Theological alternatives*. Nashville: Abingdon Press, 1981.

Piaget, J. "Deux mollusques trouvés accidentellement á Neuchâtel." *Rameau de Sapin,* 1910, *44*, p. 32.

Piaget, J. "Les limnées des lacs de Neuchâtel, Bienne, Morat et des environs." *Journal de Conchyliologie,* 1911, *59,* 333–340.

Piaget, J. "Les récents dragages malacologiques de M. le Prof. Emile Yung dans le lac Léman." *Journal de Conchyliologie,* 1912, *60,* 205–232.

Piaget, J. "Premières recherches sur les Mollusques profonds du lac de Neuchâtel." *Bulletin de la Sociètè ~εℓ↑ηâteloise des Sciences Naturelles,* 1913a, *39*, 148–171.

Piaget, J. "Les mollusques sublittoraux de Léman receuillis par M. le Prof. Yung." *Zoologischer Anzeiger,* 1913b, *42,* 615–624.

Piaget, J. "Nouveaux dragages malacologiques de M. le Prof. Yung dans la faune profonde du Léman." *Zoologischer Anzeiger,* 1913c, *42,* 216–223.

Piaget, J. "Notes sur le mimétisme des Mollusques marins littoraux de Binic (Bretagne)." *Zoologischer Anzeiger,* 1913d, *43,* 127–133.

Piaget, J. "Bergson et Sabatier." *Revue Chrètienne,* 1914a, *61,* 192–200.

Piaget, J. Notes sur la biologie des Limnées abssales, *International Revue der gesamten Hydrobiologie und Hydrographie, Biologisches Supplement,* 1914b, *6*, 15.

Piaget, J. "L'espèce mendelienne a-t-elle une valeur absolue?" *Zoologischer Anzeiger,* 1914c, *44,* 328–331. (Translated in Gruber & Vonèche, 1977).

Piaget, J. *La mission de l'idée.* Lausanne: La Concorde, 1915. (Partially translated in Gruber & Vonèche, 1977).

Piaget, J. *La mission de l'idée.* Lausanne: Edition la Concorde, 1916. (Translation by H. E. Gruber and J. J. Vonèche in *The Essential Piaget.* New York: Basic Books, 1977).

Piaget, J. Letter to Romain Rolland, 1917. (Published in *Action Etudiante* (1966).

Piaget, J. *Recherche.* Lausanne: La Concorde, 1918a. (Summarized in detail in Gruber & Vonèche, 1977).

Piaget, J. "La biologie et la guerre." *Feuille centrale de la Sociètè suisse de Zofingue,* 1918b, *53,* 374–380. (Translated in Gruber & Vonèche, 1977).

Piaget, J. *Introduction àla Malacologie Valaisanne.* Sion: Aymon, 1921.

Piaget, J. *The moral judgment of the child.* London: Routledge & Kegan Paul, 1932. (Republished, New York: Free Press 1965b).

Piaget, J. *The Psychology of Intelligence.* (Piercy, M. & Berlyne, D. E., trans.) London: Routledge & Kegan Paul, 1950.

Piaget, J. Autobiography. In E. G. Boring et al. (Eds.), *A history of psychology in autobiography.* Worcester, MA: Clark University Press, 1952.

Piaget, J. *The origins of intelligence in children.* New York: Norton, 1952.

Piaget, J. *Logic and Psychology.* (W. Mays & F. Whitehead, trans.) New York: Basic Books, 1953.

Piaget, J. *The construction of reality in the child.* New York: Ballantine, 1954.

Piaget, J. Logique et équilibre dans les comportement du sujet. In L. Apostel, B. Mandelbrot, & J. Piaget (Eds.), *Logique et équilibre.* Paris: P. U. F., 1956, pp. 27–117.

Piaget, J. Logique et equilibre dans les comportements du sujet. *Etudes d'Epistemologie Genetique,* 1957, *2,* 27–118.

Piaget, J. Lettre. In an "Hommage à Arnold Reymond," *Revue de Théologie et de Philosophie,* 1959, *9,* 44–47.

Piaget, J. The general problems of the psychobiological development of the child. In J. M. Tanner and B. Inhelder (Eds.), *Discussions on child development: Proceedings of the world health organization study group on the psychobiological development of the child: 4.* New York: International Universities Press, 1960.

Piaget, J. *The origin of intelligence in children* (2nd ed.). New York: Norton, 1963.

Piaget, J. *Insights and illusions of psychology.* New York, New American Library, 1965. (a)

Piaget, J. *The moral judgment of the child.* New York: Free Press, 1965. (b)

Piaget, J. *Six psychological studies.* New York: Random House, 1967.

Piaget, J. *Biologie et connaissance.* Paris: Gallimard, 1967. (a)

Piaget, J. *Logique et connaissance scientifique.* Paris: Gallimard, 1967. (b)

Pieget, J. & Inhelder, B. Intellectual operations and their development. In P. Fraisse & J. Piaget (Eds.), *Experimental Psychology: Its Scope and Method, Vol. VII.* (T. Surridge, trans.) New York: Basic Books, 1969b.

Piaget, J. Piaget's theory. In P. H. Mussen (Ed.), *Carmichael's manual of child psychology* (Vol. 1, 3rd ed.). New York: Wiley, 1970.

Piaget, J. *Structuralism.* New York: Basic Books, 1970.

Piaget, J. *The child's conception of motion and speed,* New York: Viking Books, 1971.

Piaget, J. *Insights and illusions of philosophy.* (Trans. by W. Mays). New York: New American Library, 1971.

Piaget, J. *Biology and knowledge. An essay on the relations between organic regulations and cognitive processes.* Chicago: University of Chicago Press, 1971.(b)

Piaget, J. *Genetic epistemology.* New York: Norton, 1971.(a)

Piaget, J. Intellectual evolution from adolescence to adulthood. *Human Development,* 1972, *15,* 1–12.

Piaget, J. *The principles of genetic epistemology.* New York: Basic Books, 1972.

Piaget, J. (Ed.) *The child and reality.* New York: Grossman Publishers, 1973.

Piaget, J. Recherches sur la contradiction. *Etudes d'epistemologie genetique,* V. XXXI and XXXII. Paris: P. U. F., 1974.

Piaget, J. *Understanding causality.* New York: W. W. Norton, 1974.
Piaget, J. L'équilibration des structures cognitives (problème central du développement). *Etudes d'epistemologic génétique* (Vol. 33). Paris: P. U. F., 1975.
Piaget, J. *The psychology of intelligence.* Totowa, N.J.: Littlefield, Adams & Co., 1976.
Piaget, J. *The development of thought: Equilibration of cognitive structures.* New York: Viking, 1977.
Piaget, J. *The development of thought.* Oxford: Blackwell, 1978.
Piaget, J. The possible, the impossible, and the necessary. In F. Murray (Ed.), *The impact of Piagetian theory.* Baltimore: University Park Press, 1979.
Piaget, J. Recent studies in genetic epistemology. *Cahiers de la Fondation Archives Jean Piaget,* 1980, *1,* 3–7.
Piaget, J. *Les formes elementaires de la dialectique.* Paris: Gallimard, 1980.
Piaget, J. Reflections on Baldwin. In J. M. Broughton and D. J. Freeman-Moir (Eds.), *The cognitive-developmental psychology of James Mark Baldwin.* Norwood, N.J.: Ablex, 1982.
Piaget, J., & Inhelder, B. *The psychology of the child.* New York: Basic Books, 1958, 1969.
Piaget, J., and Kamii, C. What is psychology? *American Psychologist,* 1978, *33,* 648–652.
Piaget, J., with J. Montangero, & J. Pilleter. Les correlats. *L'Abstraction réfléchissante.* Paris: Presses Universitaires de France, 1977.
Piéraut-Le Bonniec, G. *The development of modal reasoning: Genesis of necessity and possibility notions.* New York: Academic Press, 1980.
Pitt, R. B. *Toward a comprehensive model of problem solving.* Unpublished doctoral dissertation, San Diego: The University of California, 1976.
Poincare, H. The value of science. In *The foundations of science.* (Translated by G. B. Halsted) Washington, D.C.: University Press of America, 1982.
Poincare, H. *La Valeur de la Science.* Paris: Flammarion, 1913.
Polya, G. *How to solve it.* New York: Doubleday, 1957.
Pompeiano, D., & Marsan, C. A. *Brain mechanisms of perceptual awareness and purposeful behavior.* (Vol. 8) New York: Raven Press, 1981.
Popper, C., & Eccles, J. *The self and its brain.* New York: Springer, 1978.
Powell, P. M. Advanced social role-taking and cognitive development in gifted adults. *International Journal of Aging and Human Development,* 1980, *11*(3), 177–192.
Pribram, K. H. *Languages of the brain: experimental paradoxes and principles in neuropsychology.* Englewood Cliffs, NJ: Prentice-Hall, 1971.
Pribram, K. H., & Gill, M. M. *Freud's 'project' reassessed.* New York: Basic Books, 1976.
Pulos, S. *Developmental cognitive constraints on structural learning.* Unpublished doctoral dissertation, York University, 1979.
Quine, W. V. Epistemology naturalized. In W. V. Quine (Ed.), *Ontological relativity and other essays.* New York: Columbia University Press, 1969, 69–90.
Rabbitt, P. Changes in problem solving ability in old age. In J. E. Birren, & K. W. Schaie (Eds.), *Handbook of the psychology of aging.* New York: Van Nostrand Reinhold, 1977.
Rabbitt, P. Some experiments and a model for changes in attentional

selectivity with old age. In F. Hoffmeister, & C. Muller (Eds.), *Brain function in old age, Bayer Symposium VII.* New York: Springer-Verlag, 1979.

Rabbitt, P. How do old people know what to do next? In F.I.M. Craik & S. E. Trehub (Eds.), *Aging and cognitive processes.* New York: Plenum Press, 1982.

Rama, Swami. *Freedom from the bondage of karma.* Glenview, ILL.: Himilayan International Institute of Yoga Science and Philosophy, 1977.

Ratner, N., & Bruner, J. Games, social exchange and the acquisition of language. *Journal of Child Language,* 1978, *5,* 391–401.

Rawls, J. *A theory of justice.* Cambridge, MA: Belknap Press, 1971.

Read, P. P. *Alive: The story of the Andes survivors.* New York: Lippincott, 1974.

Rest, J. R. Patterns and preference in moral judgment. *Journal of Personality,* 1973, *41,* 86–109.

Rest, J. R. New approaches in the assessment of moral judgment. In T. Lickona (Ed.), *Moral development and behavior.* New York: Holt, Rinehart, & Winston, 1976.

Reuchlin, M. L'intelligence: Conception genetique operatoire et conception factorielle. *Revue Suisse de Psychologie Pure et Appliquee,* 1964, *23,* 113–134.

Reymond, Arnold. "L'épistémologie génétique selon Jean Piaget." *Studia Philosophica,* 1950, *10,* 153–163.

de Ribaupierre, A. & Pascual-Leone, J. Formal operations and M power: A neo-Piagetian investigation. In D. Kuhn (Ed.), *New directions for child development, No. 5, Intellectual development beyond childhood.* San Francisco: Jossey-Bass, in press.

Richards, R. J. Instinct and intelligence in British natural theology: Some contributions to Darwin's theory of the evolution of behavior. *Journal of the History of Biology,* 1981, *14,* 193–230.

Ricouer, P. *Interpretation theory: Discourse and the surplus of meaning.* Fort Worth: Texas Christian University Press, 1976.

Riegel, K. F. Dialectic operations: The final period of cognitive development. *Human Development,* 1973, *16,* 346–370.

Riegel, K. F. Adult life crises: A dialectical interpretation of development. In N. Datan and L. H. Ginsberg (Eds.), *Lifespan developmental psychology: Normative life crises.* New York: Basic Books, 1975, (a).

Riegel, K. F. Toward a dialectical theory of development. *Human Development,* 1975(b), *19,* 50–64.

Riegel, K. F. The dialectics of human development. *American Psychologist,* 1976, *31,* 679–700.

Riegel, K. F. Psychology and the future. *American Psychologist,* 1978, *33,* 631–647.

Roberts, R. J., Jr. Errors and the assessment of cognitive development. In K. W. Fischer (Ed.), *New directions for child development, No. 12, Cognitive Development.* San Francisco: Jossey-Bass, 1981.

Roe, A. Psychological approaches to creativity in science. In M. A. Coler (Ed.), *Essays on creativity in the sciences.* New York: New York University Press, 1963.

Rosenberg, M. *Conceiving the self.* New York: Basic Books, 1979.

Rossi, A. S. Life-span theories and women's lives: Signs. *Journal of Women in Culture and Society,* 1980, *G,* 4–34.

Roszkowski, W. "Notes sur les Limnées de la faune profonde du lac Léman." *Zoologischer Anzeiger,* 1912, *40,* 375–381.

Roszkowski, W. "A propos des Limnées de la faune profonde du lac Léman." *Zoologischer Anzeiger,* 1913, *43,* 88–90.

Roszkowski, W. "Contribution à l'étude des Limnées du Lac Léman." *Revue Suisse de Zoologie,* 1914, *22,* 475–531.

Ruddick, S. Maternal thinking and pacifism. *Psych Critique,* 1983, *3.*

Rudwick, M. J. S. Charles Darwin in London: The integration of public and private science. *Isis,* 1982, *73,* 186–206.

Rumelhart, D. E., & Abrahamson, A. A. A model for analogical reasoning. *Cognitive Psychology,* 1973, *5,* 1–28.

Sabatier, A. *Esquisse d'une philosophie de la religion d'après la psychologie et l'histoire.* Paris: Fischbacher, 1897.

Sameroff, A. Transactional models in early social relations. *Human Development,* 1975, *18,* 65–79.

Sartre, J-P. [*Being and nothingness*] (H. E. Barnes, trans.) New York: Washington Square Press, 1966. (Originally published in 1943)

Scheidt, R., & Schaie, K. W. A taxonomy of situations for an elderly population: Generating situational criteria. *Journal of Gerontology,* 1978, *33,* 848–857.

Schenk, H. G. *The mind of the European romantics.* New York: Ungar, 1966.

Scheibel, A. B. The problem of selective attention: A possible structural substrate. In O. Pompeiano & C. A. Marsan (Eds.), *Brain mechanisms of perceptual awareness and purposeful behavior.* (Vol. 8). New York: Raven Press, 1981.

Schneider, W. & Shiffrin, R. M. Controlled and automatic human information processing: I. Detection, search, and attention. *Psychological Review,* 1977, *84,* 1–66.

Schoeneald, R. L. *Nineteenth Century Thought: The Discovery of Change.* New Jersey: Prentice-Hall, 1965.

Scholem, G. *Major trends in Jewish mysticism.* New York: Schoken Books, 1974.

Schon, D. *The displacement of concepts.* Cambridge: Tavistock Press, 1963.

Selman, R. L. The relation of role taking to the development of moral judgment in children. *Child Development,* 1971, *42,* 79–91.

Selman, R. L. Social-cognitive understanding: A guide to educational and clinical practice. In T. Lickona (Ed.), *Moral development and behavior: Theory, research, and social issues.* New York: Holt, Rinehart and Winston, 1976.

Selman, R. L. *The growth of interpersonal understanding.* New York: Academic Press, 1980.

Selman, R. L., & Byrne, D. F. A structural-developmental analysis of levels of role-taking in middle childhood. *Child Development,* 1974, *45,* 803–806.

Shaklee, H. Bounded rationality and cognitive development: Upper limits on growth? *Cognitive Psychology,* 1979, *11,* 327–345.

Shatz, M. The relationship between cognitive processes and the development of communication skills. *Nebraska Symposium on Motivation,* 1977, *25,* 1–42.

Shiffrin, R. M. & Schneider, W. Controlled and automatic human information processing: II. Perceptual learning, automatic attending, and a general theory. *Psychological Review*, 1977, *84*, 127–190.

Shock, N. W. Biological theories of aging. In J. E. Birrin & K. W. Schaie (Eds.), *Handbook of the Psychology of Aging*. New York: Van Nostrand Reinhold, 1977.

Sidgwick, H. *The method of ethics*. (7th edition). London: Macmillan, 1907.

Siegal, M. Spontaneous development of moral concepts. *Human Development*, 1975, *18*, 370–383.

Siegel, H. Piaget's conception of epistemology. *Educational Theory*, 1978, *28*, 16–22.

Siegel, H. Can psychology be relevant to epistemology? In J. R. Coombs (Ed.), *Philosophy of education 1979*.

Siegel, H. Justification, discovery and the naturalizing of epistemology. *Philosophy of Science*, 1980, *47*, (2), 297–321.

Siegel, H. On the parallel between Piagetian cognitive development and the history of science. *Philosophy of the Social Sciences*, in press.

Siegel, Sidney, *Nonparametric statistics for the behavioral sciences*. New York: McGraw-Hill Book Company, 1956.

Siegler, R. S. Three aspects of cognitive development. *Cognitive Psychology*, 1976, *4*, 481–520.

Siegler, R. S. The origins of scientific reasoning. In R. S. Siegler (Ed.), *Children's thinking: What develops?* Hillsdale, NJ: Erlbaum, 1978.

Siegler, R. S. Developmental sequences within and between concepts. *Monographs of the Society for Research in Child Development*, 1981, *46* (2, Serial No. 189).

Simon, H. A. *Models of man*. New York: Wiley, 1957.

Simon, H. A. Information-processing theory of human problem solving. In W. K. Estes (Ed.), *Handbook of learning and cognitive processes, volume 5: Human information processing*. Hillsdale, NJ: Lawrence Erlbaum Associates Publishers, 1978.

Simon, H. A. Information processing models of cognition. *Annual Review of Psychology*, 1979, *30*, 262–296.

Sinclair, H. From preoperational to concrete thinking and parallel symbolic development. In M. Schwebel and J. Raph (Eds.), *Piaget in the classroom*. New York: Basic Books, 1973.

Sinnott, J. D. Everyday thinking and Piagetian operativity in adults. *Human Development*, 1975, *18*, 430–443.

Sinnott, J. D. The theory of relativity: A metatheory for development? *Human Development*, 1981, *24* (5), 293–311.

Sinnott, J. D., & Guttmann, D. Dialectics of decision making in older adults. *Human Development*, 1978, *21*, 190–200.

Skinner, B. F. *Contingencies of reinforcement: A theoretical analysis*. New York: Appleton-Century-Crofts, 1969.

Slovic, P., Fischhoff, B., & Lichtenstein, S. Behavioral decision theory. *Annual Review of Psychology*, 1977, *28*, 1–39.

Smith, F. N. The potential in Piaget's theory for an interpretive model of adult consciousness: In R. Weismann, R. Brown, P. J. Levinson, & P. A. Taylor (Eds.), *Piagetian theory and the helping professions: Proceedings of the seventh annual conference, vol. 1*. Los Angeles: University of Southern California, 1978.

Smith, T. *Constructive ethics.* New York: Appleton-Century-Crofts, Inc., 1948.

Snarey, J. *The moral development of kibbutz founders and sabras: A cross-sectional and ten-year longitudinal study.* Doctoral dissertation, Harvard University, Graduate School of Education, 1982.

Snarey, J. & Blasi, A. *Ego development among adult kibbutzniks:* A cross-cultural application of Loevinger's theory. *Genetic Psychology Monographs,* 1980, *102,* 117–157.

Snarey, J., Kohlberg, L., & Noam, G. Ego development and education: A structural perspective. In L. Kohlberg, & R. De Vries (Eds.), *Child psychology and childhood education: A structural-developmental view.* New York: Longman Press (forthcoming).

Solzhenitsyn, A. I. *The Gulag Archipelago.* New York: Harper and Row, 1973.

Spearman, C. *The nature of 'intelligence' and the principles of cognition.* London: Macmillan, 1923.

Spearman, C. *The abilities of man.* London: Macmillan, 1927.

Spinoza, B. *Ethics.* New York: Hafner Press, 1949.

Sprague, J. M., Huges, H. C., & Berlucchi, G. Cortical mechanisms in pattern and form perception. In O. Pompeiano & C. A. Marsan (Eds.), *Brain Mechanisms of Perceptual Awareness and Purposeful Behavior,* Vol. 8. New York: Raven Press, 1981.

Steriade, M. Mechanisms underlying cortical activation: Neuronal organization and properties of the midbrain reticular core and intralaminar thalamic nuclei. In O. Pompeiano, & C. A. Marsan (Eds.), *Brain mechanisms of perceptual awareness and purposeful behavior.* (Vol. 8). New York: Raven Press 1981.

Sternberg, R. J. *Intelligence, information processing, and analogical reasoning: The componential analysis of human abilities.* Hillsdale, NJ: Erlbaum, 1977.

Sternberg, R. J. Intelligence and nonentrenchment. *Journal of Educational Psychology,* 1981, *73,* 1–16.

Sternberg, R. J., & Downing, C. J. The development of higher-order reasoning in adolescence. *Child Development,* 1982, *53,* 209–221.

Sternberg, R. J., & Gardner, M. K. A componential interpretation of the general factor in human intelligence. In H. Eysenck (Ed.), *A model for intelligence.* Munich: J. F. Bergmann-Verlag, in press.

Sternberg, R. J., & Nigro, G. Developmental patterns in the solution of verbal analogies. *Child Development,* 1980, *51,* 27–38.

Sternberg, R. J., & Rifkin, B. The development of analogical reasoning processes. *Journal of Experimental Child Psychology,* 1979, *27,* 195–232.

Stevens-Long, J. *Adult Life: Developmental processes.* Palo Alto: Mayfield, 1979.

Stone, C. A., & Day, M. C. Competence and performance models and the characterization of formal operational skills. *Human Development,* 1980, *23,* 323–353.

Strauss, S., & Kroy, M. The child as logician or methodologist? *Human Development,* 1977, *20,* 102–117.

Sullivan, E. V. Comments in J. M. Broughton, B. Leadbeater, & E. Amsel (Eds.), Reflections on Piaget. *Teachers College Record,* 1981, *83* (2), 199–202.

Sulloway, F. J. Darwin and his finches: The evolution of a legend. *Journal of the History of Biology,* 1982, *15,* 1–53.

Terman, L. M. *The measurement of intelligence*. Boston: Houghton Mifflin, 1916.

Terman, L. M. Contribution to "Intelligence and its measurement: A symposium." *Journal of Educational Psychology*, 1921, *12*, 127–133.

Terman, L. M. & Merrill, M. A. *Stanford-binet Intelligence Scale: Manual for the Third Revision*. Boston: Houghton Mifflin, 1960.

Thatcher, R. W., & John, E. R. *Foundations of cognitive processes. Functional neuroscience* (Vol. 1). Hillsdale, NJ: Erlbaum, 1977.

Thomson, G. H. *The factorial analysis of human ability*. Boston: Houghton Mifflin, 1939.

Thurstone, L. L. Primary mental abilities. *Psychometric Monographs, no. 1, 1933*. Psychometric Monographs, no. 1, 1938.

Tiguanit, Pandit R. *The philosophy of the Tripura cult: A study*. Doctoral thesis, University of Allahabad, April 1981.

Tinbergen, N. Ethology and stress diseases. *Science*, 1974, *185*, 20–26.

Toben, B. *Space-time and beyond*. New York: E. P. Dutton, 1975.

Todor, J. I. Developmental differences in motor task integration: A test of Pascual-Leone's theory of constructive operators. *Journal of Experimental Child Psychology*, 1979, *28*, 314–322.

Tolman, C. The metaphysics of relations in Klaus Riegel's 'dialectics' of human development. *Human Development*, 1981, *24*, 33–51.

Tolman, E. C. *Purposive behavior in animals and men*. New York: Century, 1932.

Tolman, E. C. Principles of purposive behavior. In S. Koch (Ed.), *Psychology: A study of a science* (Vol. 1). New York: McGraw-Hill, 1959.

Tomlinson-Keasey, C. Structures, functions, and stages: A trio of unresolved issues in formal operations. In S. Modgil & C. Modgil (Eds.), *Jean Piaget: Consensus and controversy*. New York: Holt, Rinehart, & Winston, 1982.

Toulmin, S. The concept of 'stages' in psychological development. In T. Mischel (Ed.), *Cognitive development and epistemology*. New York: Academic Press, 1971.

Toulmin, S. *Human understanding*. Princeton: Princeton University Press, 1972.

Toulmin, S. Epistemology and developmental psychology. *Nous*, 1977, *11*, 51–53.

Trabasso, T. On the estimation of parameters and the evaluation of a mathematical model: A reply to Pascual-Leone. *Journal of Experimental Child Psychology*, 1978, *26*, 41–45.

Tuchman, B. W. *A Distant Mirror: The Calamitous 14th Century*. New York: Ballantine Books, 1978.

Turner, R. H. Role-taking, role-standpoint and reference-group behavior. *American Journal of Sociology*, 1956, *61*, 316–328.

Turner, T. Piaget's structualism. *American Anthropologist*, 1973, *75*, 351–373.

Tversky, A. & Kahneman, D. Judgment under uncertainty: Heuristics and biases. *Science*, 1974, *185*, 1124–1131.

Ullmo, J. *La pensèe scientifique moderne*. Paris: Flammarion, 1958.

Vailliant, G. E. *Adaptation to life*. Boston: Little Brown, 1977.

van den Daele, L. Ego development and preferential judgment in life-span perspective. In N. Datan and H. Ginsberg (Eds.), *Life-span developmental psychology: Normative life crises*. New York, Academic Press, 1975.

Van Dijk, T. A. *Macrostructures*. Hillsdale, NJ: Erlbaum, 1980.

Vernon, P. E. The Structure of Human Abilities (2nd ed.). London: Methuen, 1961.

Vernon, P. E. *Intelligence and cultural environment.* London: Methuen, 1969.

Vetter, M. *Dimensionen des selbskonzeptes und Ich-Entwicklung.* Unpublished master's thesis. Johannes-Gutenberg Universitat, Mainz, Germany, 1978.

Vidal, F. Piaget on evolution and morality. Senior Honors Thesis, Harvard University, 1981.

Voneche, Jacques. "Utopie et psychologie de l'enfant et de l'adolescent." In P. Furter & G. Raulet (Eds.), *Stratégies de l'utopie.* Paris: Galilée, 1979.

Vuyk, R. *Overview and critique of Piaget's genetic epistemology 1965–1980* (2 Vols.). New York: Academic Press, 1981.

Vygotsky, L. *Thought and language.* (Trans. by E. Hanfmann & G. Vakar). Cambridge, MA: MIT Press, 1962.

Vygotsky, L. *Mind in society* (M. Cole, V. John-Steiner, S. Scribner, & E. Souberman, Eds.). Cambridge, MA: Harvard University Press, 1978.

Waddington, C. H. *The evolution of an evolutionist.* Ithaca, NY: Cornell University Press, 1975.

Walley, R. E., & Weiden, T. D. Lateral inhibition and cognitive masking: A neuropsychological theory of attention. *Psychological Review,* 1973, *80,* 284–302.

Watson, M. W. The development of social roles: A sequence of social-cognitive development. In K. W. Fischer (Ed.), *New Directions for Child Development, No. 12, Cognitive Development.* San Francisco: Jossey-Bass, 1981.

Watson, M. W., & Fischer, K. W. A developmental sequence of agent use in late infancy. *Child Development,* 1977, *48,* 828–836.

Watson, M. W., & Fischer, K. W. Development of social roles in elicited and spontaneous behavior during the preschool years. *Developmental Psychology,* 1980, *16,* 483–494.

Watts, A. *Psychotherapy east and west.* New York: Random House, 1961.

Watzlawick, P., Beavin, J., & Jackson, D. *The pragmatics of human communication.* New York: W. W. Norton, 1967.

Webb, R. A. Concrete and formal operations in very bright 6- to 11-year-olds. *Human Development,* 1974, *17,* 292–300.

Wechsler, D. *The Measurement of Adult Intelligence.* Baltimore: Williams and Wilkins, 1944.

Wechsler, D. *Weschler Adult Intelligence Scale Manual.* New York: The Psychological Corporation, 1955.

Wechsler, D. *The Measurement and Appraisal of Adult Intelligence* (4th ed.). Baltimore: Williams and Wilkins, 1958.

Weiskrantz, L. A comparison of hippocampal pathology in man and other animals. In Ciba Foundation Symposium, *Functions of the septo-hippo-campal system.* New York: Elsevier, 1977.

Werner, H. The concept of development from a comparative and organismic point of view. In D. B. Harris (Ed.), *The concept of development.* Minneapolis: University of Minnesota Press, 1957.

Wertheimer, M. *Productive thinking,* enlarged edition. New York: Harper and Row, 1959. (Originally published in 1945).

Westfall, R. S. *Never at rest, a biography of Isaac Newton,* Cambridge, England: Cambridge University Press, 1980.

Westkott, M. Feminist criticism of the social sciences. *Harvard Educational Review*, 1979, *49*(4), 212–219.

White, R. W. Motivation reconsidered: The concept of competence. *Psychological Review*, 1959, *66*, 297–333.

Winograd, T. What does it mean to understand language? *Cognitive Science*, 1980, *4*, 209–241.

Wohlwill, J. F. *The study of behavioral development.* New York: Academic Press, 1973.

Woodger, J. H. *Biology and language. The Tarner lectures, 1949–1950.* Cambridge: Cambridge University Press, 1952.

Woodruff, D. S. Age and experience. *Journal of the History of the Behavioral Sciences*, in press.

Woznick, R. H. Comments in J. M. Broughton, B. Leadbeater, & E. Amsil (Eds.), Reflections on Piaget, *Teacher's College Record*, 1981, *83*, 197–199.

Wundt, W. *Psychologie physiologique.* Paris: Ancienne Librairie Germer Bailliere et C., 1886.

Youniss, J. Operations and everyday thinking: A commentary on 'Dialectical operations'. *Human Development*, 1974, *17*, 386–391.

Zahaykevich, M. K. An interpretive psychology of political activism. Unpublished doctoral dissertation, Columbia University, 1983

Zajonc, R. B. Feeling and thinking: Preferences need no inferences. *American Psychologist*, 1980, *35*, 151–175.

Zukav, G. *The dancing wu li masters.* New York: Bantam, 1979.

REFERENCE NOTES

1. Vidal, F. *A guide to Jean Piaget's early biological work.* Unpublished. Archives Jean Piaget, University of Geneva, 1981b.
2. Piaget, J. "La vanité de la nomenclature." Unpublished paper, presented on September 26, 1912, at the Club des Amis de la Nature, in Neuchâtel, 1912b.; transcribed in Vidal 1981b, pp. 54–72. A critical edition is under preparation.
3. Vidal, Fernando. *Jean Piaget's conception of morality.* Paper presented at the Tenth Annual Symposium of the Jean Piaget Society, Philadelphia, 1980.
4. Fischer, K.W., & Pipp, S.L. Optimal level: A shifting upper limit in cognitive development. *Journal of Social and Biological Structures*, invited paper, in preparation.
5. Hand, H.H., & Fischer, K.W. *The development of concepts of intentionality and responsibility in adolescence.* Paper presented at the Sixth Biennial Meeting of the International Society for the Study of Behavioral Development, Toronto, Canada, August 1981.
6. Van Parys, M.M. Preschoolers in society: *Use of the social roles of sex, age, and race for self and others by black and white children.* Paper presented at the Sixth Biennial Meeting of the International Society for the Study of Behavioral Development, Toronto, Canada, August 1981.
7. Russell, S.L., & Fischer, K.W. *Optimal levels in the development of abstractions in arithmetic.* Manuscript in preparation.

8. Rest, J.R. *The impact of higher education on moral judgment development.* Paper presented at the Convention of the American Educational Research Association, Los Angeles, April 1981.

9. Russell, S.L., & Fischer, K.W. The development of arithmetic concepts: Scoring manual. Cognitive Laboratory Manual No. 6, University of Denver, 1982.

10. Sternberg, R.J., & Gardner, M.K. *Unities in inductive reasoning.* Manuscript submitted for publication, 1982.

11. Commons, M.L., and Richards, F.A. *The structural analytic stage of development: A Piagetian postformal operational stage.* Paper presented at Western Psychological Association, San Francisco, 1978.

12. Cerella, J. Personal communication, 1982.

13. Commons, M.L., Davidson, M.N., Browne, J.M.E., & Burgard, D. *The effect of repeated presentation of multiple forms of a formal-operational problem without feedback: A test of Piaget's disequilibration theory of stage transition.* Unpublished manuscript, 1981.

14. Davidson, M.N., & Commons, M.L. *How repeatedly presenting a formal-operational problem with no feedback affects the transition from concrete through abstract to formal operations: An examination of Piaget's equilibration theory of stage change.* Paper presented at Eastern Psychological Association, April 1983.

15. Armstrong-Roche, M., & Commons, M.L. Free Will Dilemma: Instrument in development at the Dare Institute, 234 Huron Avenue, Cambridge, MA 02138.

16. Blanchard-Fields, F. *Cognitive functioning in adulthood: A case for adaptive progression.* Paper presented at 1981 meeting of the SRCD, Boston, April 1981.

17. Pascual-Leone, J., Parkinson, G., & Pulos, S. *Constructive abstractions (structural learning) and concept development.* Paper presented at Canadian Psychological Association meetings, Winsdor, 1974.

18. Hooper, F.H. *Life-span analyses of Piagetian concept tasks: The search for nontrivial qualitative change* (Tech. Paper No. 46). Madison, Wisc.: The University of Wisconsin, Wisconsin Research and Development Center for Cognitive Learning, September 1973.

19. Olsen, D., Basseches, M., & Richards, F. *Dialectical thinking as a postformal-operational level of cognitive organization: The development of a comprehension and preference instrument.* Unpublished research report, in preparation.

20. Arlin, P.K. *Adolescent and adult thought: A search for structures.* Paper presented at the annual meeting of the Jean Piaget Society. Philadelphia, May 1980.

21. Smith, J. *What makes this float?* Talk given to SESAME group, University of California, Berkeley, 1980.

22. Linn, M.C., & Pulos, S.M. *Male-female differences in predicting displaced volume.* Paper presented at SRCD meeting, Boston, Mass. ARP Report #27, April 1981.

23. Linn, M.C., & Pulos, S.M. *Aptitude and experience influences on proportional reasoning during adolescence: focus on male-female differences.* Paper presented at AERA Special Interest Group, Asilomar, December 1980.

24. Apostel, L. *Construction and validation in contemporary epistemology.* Paper presented at the Archives de Jean Piaget, Geneva, June 1979.

25. Arlin, P.K. *Problem finding and problem definining from a cognitive developmental perspective.* Paper presented at the Annual Meeting of the American Psychological Association, N.Y., in September, 1979.

26. Getzels, J.W., & Csikszentmihalyi, M. *Creative thinking in art students: An exploratory study.* U.S. Office of Education Cooperative Research Report S-080. Chicago: University of Chicago, 1965.

27. Koplewitz, H. *Unitary thought: a projection beyond Piaget's formal operations stage.* Unpublished manuscript, 1978. (Available from the author at Addiction Research Foundation, 175 College Street, Toronto, Ontario, M5T 1P8, for $5.)

28. Nuernberger, P. *Consciousness, mind and brain (matter): The nonreductionist psychology of yoga.* Paper presented at American Psychological Association Annual Convention, Montreal, September 1980.

29. Koplowitz, H. *Piaget's constructionist epistemology.* Heuristic Laboratory Report, 1975. (Available from Cognitive Development Project, Physics Department, University of Massachusetts, Amherst.)

30. von Glasersfeld, E. *The concepts of adaptation and viability in a radical constructivist theory of knowledge.* Paper presented at the Theodore Mischel Symposium on Constructivism at the 7th Annual Meeting of the Jean Piaget Society, Philadelphia, May 1977. (Available from the Cognitive Development Project, Physics Department, University of Massachusetts, Amherst.)

31. Sinnott, J.D. *How adults define "intelligence in adulthood".* Paper in preparation. Psychology Dept., Towson State University, Baltimore, MD 21204.

32. Kramer, D.A. Personal communication, 1980.

33. Sinnott, J.D. *Adult intelligence as social cognitive growth: A relativistic model.* Unpublished manuscript, 1982, (Available from author at Gerontology Research Center, NIA, NIH, Baltimore City Hospitals, Baltimore, MD 21224.)

34. Sinnott, J.D. *Age-related adult strategies for solving combinatorial Piagetian problems.* Paper presented at American Psychological Association, Washington, D.C., 1982.

35. Kramer, D.A. *Postformal operational thought in adulthood? From ought to a new conception of is in adult reasoning.* Unpublished manuscript, 1981. (Available from author at Temple University, Philadelphia, PA 19131.)

36. Powell, P.M. *Cognitive and role-taking development in mental retardates and normals.* Unpublished manuscript, 1970. (Available from the author upon request.) Dept. of Educational Psychology. University of Texas, Austin, TX 78712.

37. Powell, P.M. *Higher-level cognitive and social competence stages.* Unpublished doctoral dissertation, University of Chicago, 1971. (Available from the University of Chicago Library.)

38. Powell, P.M. *Genius, under review.* Unpublished manuscript, 1980. (Available from the author, Dept. of Educational Psychology, University of Texas, Austin, TX. 78712.)

39. Kohlberg, L. *Collected papers on moral development and moral education.* Harvard University, Center for Moral Education, 1963.

40. Limoges, J. *French translation of the sentence completion test.* Unpublished

manuscript, University de Sherbrooke, Sherbtooke, Quebec, Canada, 1978.

41. Loevinger, J. *On the self and predicting behavior.* Unpublished paper presented at Washington University, 1982.
42. Powell, P.M. *Advanced social role-taking and cognitive development in gifted adults.* Unpublished manuscript, 1980, University of Texas, Austin.
43. Kennedy, J. *The stage beyond formal operations.* Paper presented at the Fifth Annual Structural Learning Conference, University of Pennsylvania, Pittsburgh, 1974.
44. Pulos, S. *Developing an interface with reality: Intellectual development beyond adolescence.* Paper presented at the Symposium on Post-Formal Operations, Harvard University, March-April 1981.
45. Labouvie-Vief, G. *Continuities and discontinuities between childhood and adulthood: Piaget revisited.* Paper presented at the Society for Research in Child Development, San Francisco, March 1979.
46. Glick, J. *Functional and structural aspects of rationality.* Paper presented at the Jean Piaget Society, Philadelphia, 1977.
47. Kaplan, B. *Lectures on developmental psychology.* Unpublished papers presented at Worcester State Hospital, 1960.
48. Sinnott, J.D. *A Piagetian dialectical approach to ecologically valid measures of adult intellectual development.* Paper presented at the Ninth Symposium of the Jean Piaget Society, Philadelphia, May 1979.
49. Alexander, C. *Theoretical and empirical implications of a stage of consciousness model for post-formal operational develoment.* Paper presented at the Symposium on Post-Formal Cognition, Harvard University, March-April 1981.
50. Gillieron, C. *Piaget's epistemic subject is not the competent subject.* Paper presented at Teachers College, Columbia University, October 1979.
51. Afrifah, A., & Broughton, J.M. *The relationship between logical and identity development.* Manuscript in preparation.
52. Blasi, A. *Role-taking and the development of social cognition.* Paper presented at the annual meeting of the American Psychological Association, Chicago, August 1975.
53. Broughton, J.M. *Is moral development good for us?* Paper presented at the Workshop on Moral Development, Loyola University, Chicago, October 1980 (c).

AUTHOR INDEX

SUBJECT INDEX

abstractions: developmental levels, studies of, 46; early, 51; emergency of, 47; high-level, 53; Level 6 representational systems, 47, 51, 63; Level 7 single, 51, 63–64, 67, 69, 70–71; and Level 8 abstract mapping, 52, 63–64, 67, 69; and Level 9 abstract systems, 52, 63–64, 70; and Level 10 general principles, 53; optimal level process, 54, 70–71; single, 51; skill acquisition process, 54–56; and skill theory, 45, 66; *See also* abstract thought

abstract thought: in adolescence, 43, 47; in adulthood, 43, 47; development of, theory of, 44–46; views of, 74–75; *see also* abstractions

accomodation, 228, 413

actions: circular sensory-motor, 132; composition of, 129–132; concatenation of two, 129; definition of, 125; and dependence on thought, 28–29; nominal, 132–133; sensory motor, 132

addition, 46, 51, 56, 67–70

adolescence: abstract thought in, 43; cognitive change in, 260; epistemological and affective development in, 241–243; and

fallback strategies, 70; formal thought in, 161–162, 176; intellectual development in, 58; and logic, application of, 166, 230; and move from intra- to inter-propositional, 159–160; *see also* adolescent thought

adolescent thought: and adult thought, differences in, 258–260; and logical relativism, 260, 262; and Piagetian model, 260–262

adolescing, versus aging, 209–212

adulthood: abstract thought in, 43; autonomy in. *see* autonomy; cognition in, 159; and content of the good life, 273–275; creative achievements in, 159; ethical reasoning in, 258; and fallback strategies, 70; intellectual development in, 409, 58, levels of. *see* intellectual development levels of; and logic, erosion of, 158; postformal cognitive operations in, 293; relativistic thought in, 312–313; reorganization during, of logic and self-regulation, 178–179; and silent operators in, decline of, 213–214; structural change in, 369; *see also* adult thought

ABOUT THE EDITORS

Michael Lamport Commons did his undergraduate work at the University of California at Berkeley, and then at Los Angeles, where in 1965 he obtained a B.A. in mathematics and in psychology. In 1967 he received his M.A. and in 1973 his Ph.D. in psychology from Columbia University. Before coming to Harvard University in 1977, where he is now a research associate, he was an assistant professor at Northern Michigan University. He coedited *Quantitative Analyses of Behavior: Volumes I, II, and III.* His research is on the perception of utility and its development in human and nonhuman organisms across the lifespan. His related research includes the perception and knowledge of causal relations and of value.

Francis A. Richards, Jr. received his B.A. in philosophy from Haverford College in 1968. Subsequently, he administered an orphanage in Addis Abba, Ethiopia. In 1974 he obtained an Ed.M. in Human Development from the Harvard Graduate School of Education. Next, he administered The Community Nursery School in Lexington, Massachusetts. In 1978, after another year at Harvard, he began doctoral studies in the Department of Human Development and Family Studies at Cornell University. His interests include cognitive, social, and personality development of adolescents and adults, the relation of work and development, and mathematical psychology.

Cheryl Armon attended the University of California at Los Angeles and Immaculate Heart College before completing her B.A. in psychology at Antioch University, Los Angeles in 1978. In 1980, she received an Ed.M. in Human Development from Harvard University, where she is presently a doctoral candidate. She teaches at Antioch University, is a research associate at the Dare Institute in Cambridge, and a research assistant at Harvard's Center for Moral Development and Education. Her current interests include the investigation of structural development in ethical reasoning, the synthesis of normative ethics and structural–developmental moral psychology, and the implications of adult ethical development for higher education.

Stage Sequences from Concrete through Postformal

Piaget	Commons & Richards[1]			Fischer, Hand, & Russell[2]			Sternberg	Kohlberg[3]	Pascual-Leone
stage name	stage name	entity be detected	levels	tier-level	proposed level sub-level	charac-teristic	stage name	stage name-characteristic	stage name
concrete II-B	3b concrete			2-IV	6-1 6-2 6-3 6-4			2-instrumental	concrete
formal III-A	4a abstract	variables or single abstractions	1.M-FA 2.H-FA 3.M-CR 4.H-CR	3-I	7-1 7-2 7-3 7-4	single set or variable values		3-mutuality	late concrete
formal III-B	4b formal	relations or double difference	1.M-FA 2.H-FA 3.M-CR 4.H-CR	3-II	8-1 8-2 8-3 8-4	mapping (relating two sets)	first-order relational reasoning	4-social system/ conscience	formal and late formal
	5a syste-matic	systems	1.M-FA 2.H-FA 3.M-CR 4.H-CR	3-III	9-1 9-2 9-3 9-4	systems (relating two sub-divided sets)		4/5-transition	pre-dialectical
	5b meta-systematic	relations between systems	1.M-FA 2.H-FA 3.M-CR 4.H-CR	3/4-IV	10-1 10-2 10-3 10-4	systems of abstract systems	second-order relational reasoning	5-prior rights/ social contract	dialectical
	6a cross-paradigmatic	systems of systems of systems	1.M-FA 2.H-FA 3.M-CR 4.H-CR			single set		6-universal ethical principles	transcendental

[1] The level name characterizes a subject's performance vis-a-vis the entities to be detected for the stage in question: M = miss; FA = false alarm: H = hit, CR = correct rejection.

[2] Sub-levels for levels supplied by editors.

[3] From Kohlberg, 1981. The editors would place Kohlberg and Armon's stage 5 at 5b.2 and 5b.3, and place stage 6 at 5b.4.

[4] Pascual-Leone, 1983.

[5] The editors would place Kohlberg and Armon's stage 5 at 5b.2 and 5b.3, and place stage 6 at 5b.4.

[6] The editors would place 4d at 5b.4.

[7] The unified theory stage not described in chapter.

[...]on[5]	Powell	Labouvie-vief	Arlin[6]	Sinnott[7]	Basseches	Koplowitz
[...]e name-[...]acteristic	stage name	level name	stage name	stage name/characteristic	phase in use of dialectical schemata	stage name
[...]strumental[...]sm	advanced concrete	symbolic	2b-high concrete	concrete	phase 1a-pre-formal early foundations	
[...]ffective[...]uality	early formal		3a-low formal (problem solving)		phase-1b formal early foundations	
[...]dividuality	formal	intra-systematic	3b-high formal	formal		formal
[...]-subjective-[...]ativism	stage 4a/ interactive empathy	inter-systematic	4-post formal a-problem-finding	relativistic/ relativised systems, meta-level rules	phase 2-intermediate d.s appear	
[...]autonomy	category operations	autonomous	b-relativism of thought c-overgeneralization d-displacement of concepts e-dialectical	unified theory/ interpenetration of contradictory levels	phase 3-2 out of 3 clusters of advanced d.s. appear phase 4-all clusters present, d.s. framework coordinated	general systems
[...]-universal[...]ategories						unitary concepts